Bertrand Russell on Modality and Logical Relevance

Second Edition

D1571049

Bertrand Russell on Modality and Logical Relevance

Second Edition

Jan Dejnožka

Ph.D. in Philosophy
J.D. in Law

Second Edition
Imprint: CreateSpace
Publisher: Jan Dejnožka
Ann Arbor, Michigan

Amazon.com and elsewhere

ISBN: 13: 978–1478292616
      10: 147829261X

Library of Congress Catalog Card Number:
2012913704

Cover Photo by Jan Dejnožka

First Edition
© 1999 Jan Dejnožka
Publisher: Ashgate
Aldershot, England
Avebury Series in Philosophy

For Chung Hwa, Julie, and Marina
with love

Praise for the First Edition

In the twenty-nine years since Russell's death, much of the major scholarship has drawn heavily on his manuscripts and unpublished correspondence. The author shows that the published Russell is capable of new interpretations; in particular, that modal notions such as possibility have a greater place in various aspects of his logical and philosophical thought than has been previously imagined.

—Ivor Grattan-Guinness, Foreword to the first edition

Dejnožka's book is the first full-length study of modality in Russell. It is useful for its very full survey of passages in which Russell makes use of or alludes to modal notions. Dejnožka's command of Russell's huge output is indeed impressive and his utilization of it thorough....

—Nicholas Griffin, *Studia Logica*

Dejnožka's book raises a very important point in the history of formal logic. Until now the major studies on this topic have drawn heavily on the development of classical logic as standardized by Gottlob Frege and Bertrand Russell. Dejnožka challenges the reader to open his mind for a new interpretation of Russell's work, in particular that modal and relevance notions have a greater place in his philosophy of logic than has been stressed before....

The best studied translation method is known as the standard translation, and it is quite compatible with Dejnožka's suggestions....

Dejnožka's book is full of material which stimulates [one] to rethink Russell's philosophy of logic and...it is greatly to the author's credit that he brings to light such a wealth of crucial issues in the history and philosophy of logic.

—Shahid Rahman, *History and Philosophy of Logic*

Table of Contents

Preface to the Second Edition

This book is the only comprehensive study of Russell on modality and logical relevance ever written. It introduces these two topics as major new areas of Russell studies. This is the second edition, revised over a period of sixteen years, and over twice as long.

Many think that Russell rejects modality and relevance. The book aims to show that: (1) he has express theories of modality and relevance; (2) his writings imply, or are at least reasonably paraphrased into, modal logics and a relevance logic; and (3) he therefore belongs to the historical and philosophical study of those fields. Thus the book is written toward reunion in logic.

Russell does not expressly state any modal logics. I argue that there are at least eight implicit modal logics in Russell, or at least that certain texts in Russell are more reasonably paraphrased into the operators of those logics than not. Shahid Rahman notes that all of my formal paraphrases are "quite compatible" with the standard translation method (Rahman 2002: 101). My paraphrases differ only in appearance from those of that method.

I distinguish Russell's implicit modal *logics* from his expressly and repeatedly stated *theory* of modality. I call his express modal theory "MDL". MDL is not a modal logic. It is not even sentential. It is a trio of definitions of propositional functions (incomplete expressions). Modal logics are sentential. That is, they prefix modal operators to statements. My names for the implicit logics always add prefixes and / or suffixes to MDL, for examples FG–MDL, FG–MDL*, and MDL–D. I formally define MDL and all the implicit modal logics in the Formalizations section at the end of the book. MDL is the main logical "building block" in all the modal logics I find implicit in Russell, and that is the basic importance of MDL in this book.

All the implicit modal logics are formalized as S5. Perhaps that is because modern classical logic in general is most like S5. All the textual research for each paraphrase is highly individualized for each implicit logic.

Russell initially *rejects* MDL, and also the possibility of a coherent modal logic, in his *unpublished* paper, "Necessity and Possibility," written ca. 1903–05 and read to an audience in 1905. But the very next year, he expressly *accepts* MDL as his *published* theory of modality (Russell 1906)—the very theory he had rejected. And he repeats that theory in published works for many years after. And other texts, scattered throughout his writings, when conjoined with his express theory, which I call MDL, imply or are at least more reasonably paraphrased than not into at least eight different implicit modal logics which Russell himself never expressly states.

MDL is the shallowest of the three levels of Russell's largely express full theory of modality. MDL is the logical level. Next deeper is the metaphysical level. The deepest level is the ontological level. Thus, concerning Russell's *theory* of modality, which the implicit logics ought to *conform* to, chapters 3–4 should receive the deepest attention from philosophers. But those who are interested only in the implicit logics, that is, only in the shallowest level of the book, will wish to focus on chapter 6.

Echoing Russell's critics in the past, some reviewers of the first edition of this book found some seeming "logical howlers" in Russell's theory of modality. I had already identified these howlers in the first edition and explained them away as being only *seeming* howlers, once Russell is understood.

Gregory Landini recently published views on Russell on modality basically consistent with mine (Landini 2007: Appendix B). He finds, as I had, that Russell anticipates Tarski and commits no howlers. He cites many of the texts I cite. I believe that once my views are understood, as I believe they have been by Landini, they will seem obvious. But as Rahman says, they need an open mind.

Russell's express adoption of Wittgenstein's theory in the *Tractatus* that entailment (or "following from") is truth-ground containment retrospectively implies that *Principia* is a relevance logic in Wittgenstein's sense. I distinguish this retrospectively implicit *Principia* relevance logic from Russell's later explicit theory of deductive inference as whole-part containment, on the grounds that the former is (1) implicit, (2) retrospective, and (3) a huge multi-volume formal logic, not a briefly stated theory.

Principia's thesis assertion operator, "⊢", is implicitly the necessity operator in each of the implicit alethic modal logics, and is implicitly the entailment operator in the implicit relevance logic. The main implicit interpretations of *Principia* are retrospective.

I argue that John Maynard Keynes' theory of probability as degree of logical relevance is the most likely origin of Russell's very similar theory of probability from *The Problems of Philosophy* on. I then argue that Keynes' theory in turn most likely originates from the concept and terminology of logical relevance in Anglo-American evidence law. Here the book includes 132 pages (368–500) on the history of evidence law. Since the evidence seems very strong for both conclusions, I further conclude that it seems very likely that Russell's theory of probability originates from evidence law indirectly through Keynes. But I have no evidence that Russell was ever aware of this indirect origin of his theory.

I can offer in this book no thorough discussion of modality and relevance in deductive logic, nor of the probability theories of Keynes or Russell, much less of the history of evidence law. I can only hope to have done enough to substantiate my interpretation of

Russell on modality and relevance in deductive logic, my interpretation of Russell's theory of probability as basically the same as, and as originating from, Keynes' theory, and my interpretation of Keynes' theory as originating in turn from evidence law.

In 2010, Ashgate wrote me that the first edition had sold out, and said they were returning all rights to me. It seems they were discontinuing their entire philosophy line. This was a blessing in disguise, since it made this second edition possible.

Reviewers of the first edition led me to explain things more clearly and fully here, though not to change my views. Their basic misunderstandings are corrected in the book, and also in the present preface. Shahid Rahman, the only logician who reviewed the first edition, was also the only reviewer who basically understood it. But then the main ideas were new to everyone, including me.

Thanks especially to several reviewers for pointing out my unfortunately casual introductory sentence (then) on page 1, "I show how Russell developed his own modal logic" (my 1996: 1; see 3). That certainly looks like I was saying that Russell states a modal logic. But we all know that he does not state any, and I never imagined that anyone would think that I thought otherwise. If those reviewers had only read the entire introduction, they would have seen that I say on page 16, "All seven of the modal logics I find implicit in Russell..." (my 1996: 16). If they had only read the first page of chapter 6, they would have seen that I say, "Then I define seven modal logics which may be implicitly attributed to Russell ...," and that I am "imputing" and "impute" the logics (my 1996: 61). It seems they never wondered why chapter 6 was in the book. For if Russell had stated a modal logic, I would have simply quoted it, instead of arguing at length in chapter 6 that various texts of his can be paraphrased into seven implicit formal modal logics. Still, the responsibility for the casual introductory sentence is mine.

The book will be understood best by those who have studied not only Russell, but also modal logic and relevance logic. Indeed, looking at Rahman's review, it may be better for readers to have studied those sorts of logic than to have studied Russell.

My first book, *The Ontology of the Analytic Tradition and Its Origins*, has been heavily re-edited too. The 2003 second reprint supersedes the original printing of 1996 with hundreds of minor corrections. There are no major changes of view.

I took the cover photo in the mountains of Greece near Delphi. The original slide is dated stamped February 1983.

Ann Arbor, Michigan
December 30, 2015

Preface to the First Edition

This book received much help from two fine logicians, Gregory Landini and Edwin Mares. I am deeply grateful to Professors Landini and Mares for their exceptional kindness in reading and commenting on this book. I am also very grateful to Layman Allen and Kenneth Blackwell for brief but important guidance. Among other things, Dr. Blackwell located Russell's unpublished manuscript, "Necessity and Possibility," for me on my pilgrimage to the Bertrand Russell Archives in 1993. Anonymous reviewers kindly provided help as well.

I owe thanks to Evan Fales, who introduced me to modal logic in his course at the University of Iowa in the 1970s, and to Richard O. Lempert and Richard D. Friedman, who respectively taught evidence and advanced evidence to me at the University of Michigan School of Law in 1995–96. Professors Lempert and Friedman both kindly commented on a draft of chapter 10 prepared for Friedman's seminar on advanced evidence. I also studied logical relevance in their textbooks on evidence law (Lempert 1983; Friedman 1991).

I thank the United States Naval Academy Research Council for research grants in 1987 and 1988. Mrs. Connie Grigor of the History Department and Mrs. Katherine Dickson of Nimitz Library were exceptionally helpful. My views do not reflect those of the United States Navy, the Department of Defense, or the Federal Government of the United States.

Material from my *Erkenntnis* paper (Dejnožka 1990) appears with the kind permission of Kluwer Academic Publishers. This book supersedes that paper by distinguishing MDL from Russell's completed modal logic. Material from my first book review in *History and Philosophy of Logic* (Dejnožka 1997) appears with the kind permission of Taylor & Francis Ltd. Material from my *Modern Logic* paper (Dejnožka 2001) appears with the kind permission of the editor of that journal.

I especially thank Willard Van Orman Quine, Nicholas Rescher, Gregory Landini, Edwin Mares, Graham Solomon, Charles Pigden, and Mark W. Dickson for permission to quote or cite their correspondence to me. Words cannot express my gratitude to my family for their love.

Ann Arbor, Michigan
February 15, 1999

1

Introduction

This book is the only exhaustive study of Russell on logical modality and logical relevance ever written. It is a book on how one can think about and interpret logic. Thus it is a book in the philosophy of logic.

The study of modality is the study of necessity, possibility, impossibility, and contingency. In our case, it is primarily the study of logical necessity, but also of causal necessity, epistemic necessity, and moral necessity.

The study of logical relevance is the study of how premises logically relate or connect to conclusions in arguments. Typically it is the study of how or in what sense premises contain or include all valid conclusions which may be deduced from them.

Many philosophers seem unaware that Russell had any views on the subject of modality at all, or think he disliked it. There are three reasons for this. First, Russell's remarks on modality are scattered throughout his works, including many works which are not primarily about logic. A full portrait of Russell on modality can be drawn only by those who have read all or nearly all of those works. And most philosophers, even many of those who write on Russell, have read very few of those works. This book will show that the time is past when logicians could write about Russell's logic in ignorance of Russell's nonlogical works. Second, while perhaps logic without metaphysics or ontology is possible, adequate scholarship on Russell's modal views without adequate scholarship on his metaphysics and ontology is not. Third, Russell's basic paper on modality, "Necessity and Possibility" (Russell 1994a / ca. 1903–05), which Russell read to the Oxford Philosophical Society on October 22, 1905 (Urquhart 1994: 507), was not published during his lifetime. It appeared in a volume of the *Collected Papers of Bertrand Russell* only in 1994. Had it been published in 1905 as the modal companion piece to "On Denoting" I believe it was, the course of modal logic—not to mention the course of Russell studies—might well have been different. This is so even though he rejects modality as too conflicted to belong to logic in that paper. For the paper states the theory of modality he accepts in published works from 1906 on.

Obviously, Russell never expressly states any modal logics. If he had, I would simply be quoting them, and there would have been no need for me to write chapter 6. Instead, it will take much work to show that various texts in Russell, scattered throughout his works, are so well paraphrased as certain modal logics, that those logics may to that extent be regarded as implicit in his writings, or at least to show that these texts are more reasonably paraphrased than not into those modal logics. This is done in chapter 6.

Russell's approach to modal notions is simple: to use notions of ordinary quantificational logic to define and analyze away modal notions. Modal notions are eliminated across the board. The individual ("existential") and universal quantifiers logically simulate and replace modal notions. These quantifiers are interpreted as functioning as if they had modal meanings-in-use. They do not in fact have modal meanings-in-use. Literally speaking, Russell has banished modality from logic; he rejects all modal entities and even modal notions. Yet functionally speaking, Russell's texts imply a modal logic (actually several) based on a rich and sophisticated eliminative analysis of modality. This is modal logic without modal metaphysics. The modern moral is that a modal logic is as a modal logic does.

It does not follow in the least from the fact that Russell eliminates modal *notions* that he cannot have an implicit modal *logic*. In fact, this is exactly like Russell's arithmetic. Russell banishes numbers from arithmetic. He rejects arithmetical entities. He finds that classes of classes logically function as, simulate, and replace numbers. And he finds that classes of classes are logical functions. This is arithmetic without numbers. An arithmetic is as an arithmetic does. Russell's famous method of logical analysis preserves the truths of arithmetic through their logical equivalence to truths about classes of classes, even while eliminating numbers as entities. Now, his logicist arithmetic is explicit, while his modal logics are implicit. But we may say that he implicitly preserves modal talk even as he implicitly eliminates modalities as entities.

There is an even closer analogy between Russell's express existential logic and his implicit modal logics. Just as he expressly eliminates existence as an entity and analyzes existence as a logical fiction—specifically, as a property of propositional functions—so he also does with the logical modalities. What is more, he analyzes logical possibility as being *the very same* property of propositional functions that he analyzes existence as being. This should be quite familiar, since he does this in several major works.

If Russell's refusal to admit modal *entities* and primitive modal *notions* were the whole story, there would be no point in writing this book. The philosophical world would be justified in saying that Russell rejected modality—end of story. But this is only half of the story. Russell found modality important enough to analyze it in at least semi-formal terms, and his analysis implies a modal logic (actually several). His approach is economical, even elegant: he eliminates and formalizes possibility in the very same way he eliminates and formalizes existence. Thus the book is an object lesson in Russell as master of dialectical thinking. It is about the sense in which he implicitly and functionally accepts modality *propositionally* even as he rejects what he regards as more primitive accounts of modality in terms of *entities* or *notions*. It is a dialectical synthesis Hegel himself might have admired.

Russell implicitly inverts Nathan U. Salmon's metaphor of pulling a rabbit out of a hat. Salmon criticizes those who pull the rabbit of modal entities out of the hat of mere considerations of language (Salmon 1981, picturing a rabbit in a hat on the dust cover). But Russell implicitly pulls the rabbit of implicit modal logics out of the hat of a world devoid of modal entities.

The only exception to this is the early Russell's admission of the modal entity of goodness in his early theory of ethics. But it is the only exception I know of, and it eventually vanishes from his philosophy. It vanishes when he replaces it with sensed happiness.

I sharply distinguish Russell's explicit *theory* of modality from his implicit modal *logics*. Russell's theory of modality is so neat and simple, one wonders why scholars have discussed his express writings on modality so little. Indeed, a few scholars have discussed it. But they have been unsympathetic, and so have helped keep it hidden under a dismissive cloud. In chapter 2, I discuss five logical howlers which Russell's express theory of modality seems to commit, including several which Alfred Jules Ayer, Nicholas Rescher, Raymond Bradley, and Timothy Sprigge have accused Russell of. I believe that these seeming howlers are all based on misunderstandings, but it will take some work to show this.

Russell's three express definitions, on which all eight of the implicit modal logics are implicitly based, are:

> $F(x)$ is necessary with respect to x =Df $F(x)$ is always true
> (true universal generalization)
> $F(x)$ is possible with respect to x =Df $F(x)$ is not always false
> (true "existential" generalization)
> $F(x)$ is impossible with respect to x =Df $F(x)$ is always false
> (true universal generalization over the negation of F)

I call this trio of definitions "MDL". MDL cannot be a modal logic, since MDL is not even sentential. That is, MDL does not prefix *statements* with modal *operators*. Instead, MDL defines modal *predicates* as being certain *quantifiers* predicated of propositional functions. That is, MDL defines its modal terms as being second-order logical predicates of logical predicates. Russell sometimes says that this is the *only* proper thing to do with modalities, since, he says, modalities *ought* not to be operators on statements or (in his logic) on propositions. It may seem that for Russell, *tertium non datur*. Yet this is not the whole story of Russell on modality. Far from it, as we shall see.

Russell's expressions "is always true," "is not always false," and "is always false" are an early version of his quantifiers. Thus we may formally paraphrase MDL as:

1. $(\Box x)Fx =$ Df $(x)Fx$
2. $(\Diamond x)Fx =$ Df $(\exists x)Fx$
3. $\neg(\Diamond x)Fx =$ Df $\neg(\exists x)Fx$

where "$(\Box x)$" means 'is necessary with respect to x', and "$(\Diamond x)$" means 'is possible with respect to x'. Of course, these are not Russell's own formalizations. I introduce them for the purpose of formalizing MDL. If nothing else, it can be seen how completely different formal MDL is from formal modal logics such as S5; see the Formalizations section in the back of this book. Looking at the formalizations there, nobody should be able to confuse MDL with S5, or for that matter, with any other modal logic. In S5 (and in any other modal logic), the modal expressions are operators on entire statements. But in MDL, the modal expressions are predicates which bind variables *within* statements. For another but essentially related point, MDL consists of *definitions*, while S5 and the other modal logics consist of *axioms*. MDL's definitions are stipulations which are neither true nor false, while axioms are true or false (and are, of course, always offered as true). I hope everyone can now tell the difference between MDL and a modal logic before proceeding any further in the book.

MDL is the basic logical building block of the 1903–05 Russell's thesis of what it is for a statement to be analytically true. (By "thesis" I mean 'axiom or theorem as opposed to a definition'.) He arrives at this thesis in three steps in "Necessity and Possibility." First, he says, "The propositional function 'x has the property φ' is *necessary* if it holds of everything" (Russell 1994a / ca. 1903–05: 518, Russell's emphasis). This is just the necessity predicate of MDL. Second, he says we can say that "a proposition of which (say) Socrates is a constituent is to be called *necessary with respect to Socrates* if there is *any* type, consisting wholly of true propositions, of which the given proposition is the instance got by substituting Socrates for the variable" (Russell 1994a / ca. 1903–05: 518–19, Russell's emphasis). He gives this example: "Socrates is identical with Socrates" is necessary with respect to Socrates because there is a propositional type, $x = x$, of which it is an instance, and all instances of that type are true (Russell 1994a / ca. 1903–05: 519). (There are two other propositional types of which it is also an instance, but most of whose instances are false: Socrates $= x$, and $x =$ Socrates.) Third, Russell states the following thesis about analytic truth. He says, "Analytic propositions have the property that they are necessary with respect to all of their constituents except such as are what I call *logical constants*" (Russell 1994a / ca. 1903–05: 519, Russell's emphasis). He gives the same example, "Socrates is identical with Socrates," since Socrates is the only nonlogical constant (Russell 1994a / ca. 1903–05: 519). We may call the third statement I quoted "G–MDL", or generalizable MDL. Note that both logical constants and nonlogical constants can occur on different type-levels. For example, in "Socrates is wise," or *Ws*, there are two nonlogical constants: *Socrates* (*s*) and *is wise* (*W*). This statement is an instance of only three types, all of which have false instances. Where *F* and *x* are variables, the three types are *Fs*, *Wx*, and *Fx*. Thus while "Socrates is identical with Socrates" is an analytic truth, "Socrates is wise" is not. Note that being analytically true, and for that matter, being necessary with respect to Socrates, are sentential operators, not predicates predicated of propositional functions.

G–MDL is a modal logic for many of us today, since many of us would allow nonlogical constant names into the vocabulary of a logic. But it is not a modal logic which I find implicit in Russell. That is because for Russell, logic is *"completely general"* (PLA 237, Russell's emphasis), while truths in G–MDL can include nonlogical constants such as Socrates. Thus Russell would not consider G–MDL even to be a logic at all, much less a modal logic.

But G–MDL is *almost* what I call FG–MDL. The only difference is that G–MDL defines necessity as *generalizable* truth and FG–MDL defines necessity as *generalized* truth. To get from G–MDL to FG–MDL, we only need to add that logical truths *are* fully ("completely") general truths, meaning that they contain *no* nonlogical constants, such as Socrates, or even wisdom (e.g. PLA 139, 240–41). Thus $(x)(x = x)$ belongs to FG–MDL, while "*s = s*" does not. Or to give another example, "$(x)(F)(Fx \lor \neg Fx)$" belongs to FG–MDL, while "$(x)(Red(x) \lor \neg Red(x))$" does not, since "Red( )" is a predicate constant. We today might wish to include the second of each of these pairs of statements as a logical truth, since it is an instance of the first statement of the pair. But for Russell, full generality is a requirement of logical truth because pure logic is completely universal; it contains only logical constants (PLA 239–41). Logicians should not be interested in empirical questions of what the real world contains. This includes particulars such as Socrates (PLA 239; IMP 198–99). It also includes those universals which can only be empirically known, such as love (PLA 239) or being earlier in time than ("before") (IMP 198–99). Russell says in 1919:

> Certain characteristics of the subject [which may be
> called indifferently either mathematics or logic] are
> clear. To begin with, we do not, in this subject, deal with
> particular things or particular properties: we deal
> formally with what can be said about *any* thing or *any*
> property. [I]n our capacity of logicians or pure
> mathematicians, we have never heard of Socrates or
> Plato....It is not open to us, as pure mathematicians or
> logicians, to mention anything at all, because, if we do
> so, we introduce something irrelevant and not formal.
> (IMP 196–97, Russell's emphasis. Compare the 1959
> Russell on Ramsey's view that logic is indifferent even
> to "the empirical fact" that we finite humans cannot
> "define an infinite class" "by enumeration;" so there is
> "no *logical* objection" to such definitions, MPD 91–92,
> Russell's emphasis; see Ramsey 1931: 41)

"Necessity and Possibility" is arguably confused on this point. For
there, as we just saw, Russell gives "Socrates = Socrates" as an
example of an analytic proposition. But he says that an analytic
proposition is one that can be deduced from the laws of logic using
laws of deduction, which are themselves laws of logic. Thus the
class of true analytic propositions is simply the class of logical
truths. Thus he implies that "Socrates" occurs in a logical truth.
Thus this example in "Necessity and Possibility" seems to imply
G–MDL. Thus the paper seems confused on whether logic is fully
general.

Let me state Landini's (1993) formalization of FG–MDL in
my own way. Where A is any *fully* or "*completely general*" (PLA
237) statement, and where the full generalization of A is $(F_1...F_m,$
$x_1...x_n)A_{F1...Fm, x1...xn}$, then:

$$\Box(A) =\text{Df } (F_1...F_m, x_1...x_n)A_{F1...Fm, x1...xn}$$

This defines perfectly what I mean by "FG–MDL". It is inspired by
Russell's statement, "Analytic propositions have the property that
they are necessary with respect to all of their constituents except
such as are what I call *logical constants*" (Russell 1994a / ca.
1903–05: 519, Russell's emphasis). But Russell's statement is a
thesis, not a definition. I would formalize it as follows. Where A is
any *statement*, and where the full generalization of A is $(F_1...F_m,$
$x_1...x_n)A_{F1...Fm, x1...xn}$, then:

$$\text{Analytically true}(A) \leftrightarrow (F_1...F_m, x_1...x_n)A_{F1...Fm, x1...xn}$$

We today are free to interpret "analytically true" as implicitly being
a necessity operator. In fact, that would be a Russellian eliminative

analysis of the necessity operator of G–MDL. But Russell would not do that in "Necessity and Possibility," since there he banishes modality as a totally confused notion. I take the liberty of using the necessary biconditional sign, which Russell would not do either. It is not even in his logical vocabulary. Russell would use the material biconditional sign and prefix the whole statement with his thesis assertion-sign. This amounts to basically the same thing. and is arguably a viable Russellian logical analysis of the necessary biconditional, though Russell does not give it. I also take a liberty in using any biconditional sign at all, since Russell's statement is a simple conditional. But I think it is clear that for Russell, all *and only* analytic truths are such that they are necessary with respect to all of their constituents. The important point is that Russell's statement is an axiom, or possibly even a theorem, but is in any case not a definition. For Russell defines "analytic" otherwise earlier in the paper. He says, "We may, then, usefully define as *analytic* those propositions which are deducible from the laws of logic" (Russell 1994a / ca. 1903–05: 516, Russell's emphasis).

I think that for Russell, both in this early paper and for some years to come, the laws of logic (which include the laws of deducibility) are just a few selected truths which are fully general. For it appears that he is not yet distinguishing fully general truth from truth in virtue of form. He says that the "laws of deduction" are "*general* propositions," and they "tell us that two propositions having certain relations of *form*...are such that one of them implies the other" (Russell 1994a / ca. 1903–05: 515, my emphasis). He says that the laws of logic are "a small number of *general* logical premises, among which are included the laws of deduction already spoken of" (Russell 1994a / ca. 1903–05: 516, my emphasis). He says, "From the laws of logic all the propositions of *formal* logic and pure mathematics will be deducible" (Russell 1994a / ca. 1903–05: 516, my emphasis). But it is not clear in "Necessity and Possibility" that logical truths are fully general, since he *also* says that "Socrates = Socrates" is an analytic proposition. Clearly, *that* statement is *not* fully general. For "Socrates" is not a logical constant. Either this paper is very sloppy, or he is not holding that all the laws of logic (including all the laws of deduction) are fully general after all. This is far worse than the existence assumption of *Principia*. There, logic assumes only that at least one thing exists. Here, logic apparently assumes that *Socrates* exists! Either that, or he is assuming a rule of universal instantiation and not mentioning it. But even tacitly assuming such a rule as part of logic completely goes against his whole conception of logic as fully general. *Within* logic, we should not even be *instantiating* the theses of logic. Nor is it easy to say that for Russell, the class of analytic truths is wider than the class of logical truths, namely, in that the former truths include instantiations of the latter. For, looking to his definitions, the class of analytic truths works out to being the class of logical truths—which are fully general. There may be no decisive solution to this puzzle of interpretation.

In short, Landini's formalization may be used to formalize G–MDL as follows. Where A is any statement, and where the full generalization of A is $(F_1...F_m, x_1...x_n)A_{F1...Fm, x1...xn}$, then:

$$\Box(A) = \text{Df} \ (F_1...F_m, x_1...x_n)A_{F1...Fm, x1...xn}$$

This defines perfectly what I mean by "G–MDL". But for Russell, this would be a thesis at best, not a definition. Nor for him would it be about necessity, but at most about analyticity, in "Necessity and Possibility." The puzzle I described about "Socrates = Socrates" is really the puzzle whether analyticity in "Necessity and Possibility" is better viewed as G–MDL or as FG–MDL. The formalization of both is the same. The only difference is that in the former, A is any *statement*, while in the latter, A is any *fully general* statement.

In *Principia* terms, fully general truths are second-order propositions (PM 163). Landini says that we must never model Russellian logical necessity in terms of Kripkean arbitrary non-empty subsets of the set of all possible worlds, with accessibility relations among the worlds in the subsets, since that would import descriptions (nonlogical constants) into the semantics for second-order logical truths, ruining Russell's treatment of modality (see Cocchiarella 1975). But I think this depends at least in part on what we count as logic as opposed to description. Strictly speaking, Frege-Russell style logicization of mathematics bases mathematics not on logic alone, but logic *plus class theory*. Is class theory then description of the world as opposed to logic? Where exactly is the boundary between description of the world and pure logic? Does not logic in some sense describe, or at least show, fully general logical classes? One might ask the same questions of Kripke's sets and subsets. And should we count possible worlds and accessibility relations as description of the world as opposed to modal logic? Or is Landini's view on Kripke's formal semantics for modal logic itself merely "semantic" in the pejorative sense? Is the key word "formal"? Or can we play semantics with that word too? If there is a "universal logic(al form)" which all logical systems are in some sense instances of, is only this universal logical form pure logical form? Or is there nothing all logics have in common as logics? Is Kripke's semantics not fully general? Is the word "pure" helpful?

Russell eventually finds that full generality is not a sufficient condition, but only a necessary condition, of analytic (and in that sense logically necessary) truth. The 1914–19 Russell therefore adds a second requirement to that of full generality, namely, that a logically true proposition be true *in virtue of* its logical form, or tautologous (KEW 51–52; PLA 237, 240–41). This implies Russell's second, mature implicit alethic logic, which I call "FG–MDL*" (pronounced FG–MDL star). In 1913, FG–MDL* is already implied simply by Russell's theory of logical form (logical structure, logical composition), where a logical form is some sort of special entity. By 1919, FG–MDL* is in effect implicitly described alternatively in terms of logical form and in terms of tautology, as if those descriptions were logically equivalent and not significantly different (IMP 199–205). This is so even though Russell finds that he can easily define "form" as what remains the same in a proposition through replacements of its constituents:

> The "form" of a proposition is that, in it, that remains unchanged when every constituent of the proposition is replaced by another. (IMP 199; see PLA 238)

but does not know how to define "tautologous" (IMP 205). He can only say that it means what used to be intended by the old term "analytic" (IMP 203–4). It seems clear that Russell would find a proposition tautologously true if and only if it is true in virtue of its form. Why then would he not to use truth in virtue of form as a technical notion to analyze the intuitive notion of tautology? This would be quite in keeping with his conception of logical analysis as eliminative. For on the face of it the two notions are coextensive, and truth in virtue of form is the clearer notion. Perhaps he finds neither notion definable. But at least he has a definition of form, and it is a small step from there to truth *in virtue of form*. And it would advance the analysis at least one step, if no further, if he were to analyze tautology as truth in virtue of form. Thus it puzzles me why he does not. Charity suggests that he would have thought of it, but that makes it only more puzzling to me why he does not. I do not have a good answer to that, so my suggestion is really now a criticism: he should have eliminatively analyzed tautology as truth in virtue of form, but did not. In the language of Russell, what does tautology add to the notion of truth in virtue of logical form? And if the concept is different, then the analysis is informative.

In any case, FG–MDL* is Russell's mature and final alethic modal logic. In both FG–MDL and FG–MDL*, there is no distinction between logical truth and logically necessary truth. That is because Russell says, "there was never any clear account of what was added to truth by the conception of necessity" (Russell 1919: 165). Note how close FG–MDL* is to being a mere generality theory, where form is defined in the block-indented quotation just above. The only new thing is the addition of truth in virtue of logical form. And one might well criticize Russell's new move by saying that on his definition of "form" as quoted above, there is "no clear account of what is added to" full generality "by the conception of" logical form. For the definition of "form" seems only to restate the requirement of full generality. Indeed, David Pears says that in his 1913 *Theory of Knowledge*, Russell simply "identifies the forms of propositions" with "entirely general facts" (Pears 1989: 177). A second criticism of Russell's new move is that the "that, in it, that" in his definition merely *postulates* forms as what completes the account of logical truth. And as Russell says in another context, postulation has all "the advantages of theft over honest toil" (Russell 1919: 71). Here Russell is like the boy who explained how cookies are made by drawing a box with dough going in one side and cookies coming out the other, and labeling the box, "In here the cookies are made." The box is logical form, and "In here logical truth is made." Nonetheless, the postulation of logical forms does make the new account different from the old one. And the new account is intrinsically or at least *prima facie* plausible to some degree. I shall discuss the reason for Russell's move from FG–MDL to FG–MDL* in more detail shortly.

MDL is the basic building block of FG–MDL* too. For it is the basic building block of FG–MDL, and FG–MDL is one of the two main logical constituents of FG–MDL*. For FG–MDL* is simply FG–MDL plus truth in virtue of logical form. This is very important to bear in mind, not only as being the implicit logical analysis of FG–MDL*, but also for an overlooked historical point. Namely, Russell first states MDL in "Necessity and Possibility," the *only* work in which he banishes modality from logic. Thus he is banishing MDL in that paper. Yet just a year later, he is expressly advocating MDL as the correct *theory* (not: logic) or core analysis of modality. And just a few years later, he is implicitly advocating FG–MDL* as the correct analysis of logical truth. And as we saw, both MDL and FG–MDL are logical constituents of FG–MDL*. We may now speak of the implicit logical truth operator of implicit FG–MDL*. On Russell's own view that the concept of necessity adds nothing to the concept of (logical) truth, that operator cannot be distinguished from a logical necessity operator. Implicitly, it is an eliminative logical analysis of the logical necessity operator, since they are logically equivalent. And such a necessity operator is implicitly the thesis assertion operator of *Principia Mathematica*. Of course, that identification is not only implicit but retrospective, since Russell advocates FG–MDL* several years after *Principia*.

Russell expressly states MDL in at least nine works over a period of at least thirty-six years (1905–40):

> ca. 1903–05 "Necessity and Possibility" (Russell 1994a / ca. 1903–05: 518)

1906 Review of MacColl's *Symbolic Logic and Its Applications* (Russell 1906: 257)

1908 "'If' and 'Imply', A Reply to Mr. MacColl" (Russell 1908: 301)

1908 "Mathematical Logic as Based on the Theory of Types" (LK 66n)

1913 "On the Notion of Cause," in *Mysticism and Logic* (ONC 176)

1918 "The Philosophy of Logical Atomism" (PLA 231, 232, 233, 240, 242, 254–55)

1919 *Introduction to Mathematical Philosophy* (IMP 165)

1927 *The Analysis of Matter* (AMA 170)

1940 *An Inquiry Into Meaning and Truth* (IMT 37)

Russell expressly uses possible worlds talk in at least nine works over a period of forty-two years (1907–48):

1907 "The Study of Mathematics," in *Mysticism and Logic* (MAL 65)

1912 *The Problems of Philosophy* (PP 78)

1914 *Our Knowledge of the External World* (KEW 145)

1918 "The Philosophy of Logical Atomism" (PLA 240)

1919 *Introduction to Mathematical Philosophy* (IMP 141, 192–93, 203–4)

1921 *The Analysis of Mind* (AMI 268)

1927 *The Analysis of Matter* (AMA 200)

1938 *The Principles of Mathematics*, (introduction to 2d ed., POM viii, "possible universes")

1948 *Human Knowledge* (HK 157)

These two periods of time overlap for some thirty-four years. In fact, there are four works which contain *both* MDL and possible worlds talk:

1918 "The Philosophy of Logical Atomism"

1918 *Mysticism and Logic*

1919 *Introduction to Mathematical Philosophy*

1927 *The Analysis of Matter*

These four works constitute a direct overlap of some ten years. The plain suggestion is that MDL is consistent with, if not also a basic part of Russell's implicit logical analysis or eliminative paraphrase of his more casual possible worlds talk, *contra* Raymond Bradley, who argues that MDL and the possible worlds talk are mutually inconsistent. Bradley seems unaware of the magnitude of the historical overlap, and correspondingly unaware of the magnitude of the inconsistency he is attributing to Russell. I shall return to this point later.

From the dates just given, it seems reasonable to infer not only that Russell holds MDL continuously from 1906 to 1940 (he rejects it only in his ca. 1903–05 paper), but that he holds MDL continuously from 1906 until he dies. It is trivial to add that since MDL basically persists unchanged throughout this period of at least thirty-five years, MDL basically persists unchanged through all the vicissitudes of Russell's logical theorizing during those years. (There are some minor casual differences in its statement.) This is not surprising. MDL is merely a definition of possibility and necessity as respectively being the very same basic notions of 'not always false' and 'always true' that Russell defines his individual and universal quantifiers as being. Russell says, "It will be out of this notion of *sometimes*, which is the same as the notion of *possible*, that we get the notion of existence" (PLA 232). It is not even a formal notation he uses in any of his logics. More precisely, MDL has and needs no special characteristic modal notation for the modalities it eliminates, precisely because it eliminates them. This is just like Russell's logicist arithmetic, which needs no special characteristic arithmetical notation for the numbers it eliminates, precisely because it eliminates them. MDL is merely an interpretive aspect of theory of descriptions. And as such, MDL has nothing to do with Russell's paradox, which is the prime mover of many of Russell's most basic changes in logic. This is much like arithmetic. Arithmetic is merely an interpretive aspect of theory of classes, even though classes have everything to do with Russell's paradox.

It would be beyond the scope of this book to describe all of Russell's logical phases in any detail—Russell claims "to have tried at least a hundred theories" to resolve his paradox by October 20, 1903 (Russell 1994: xxiii). But a brief summary of twenty main phases might be helpful:

(1) MDL is not to be found in Russell's 1903 *Principles of Mathematics*. This book was mostly written in 1900, though Appendix B, giving Russell's first theory of types, was written in late 1902. There is no hint of MDL anywhere in the book, not even in Appendix B. Instead we find a rival theory, G. E. Moore's theory of degrees of implicative necessity (POM 454 and 454n). Evidently Russell abandons Moore's theory when Russell develops MDL. There are some brief remarks about propositional form, but nothing like a theory that logical truths are true in virtue of their form.

(2) Russell may or may not have developed MDL at the time of his May 1903 no-classes logic, which uses propositional functions to eliminate classes (Russell 1994: xx–xxii; 1973a: 129–30).

(3) Russell may or may not have developed MDL at the time of Russell's 1903–04 return to a Platonic realism of classes

(Russell 1994: xxv; 1973a: 129–30), which is reflected in his 1904 paper, "The Axiom of Infinity" (Russell 1973).

(4) Russell's ca. 1903–05 "On Necessity and Possibility" is the first appearance of MDL. Logically speaking, this paper is a companion piece to Russell's 1905 "On Denoting," insofar as it defines possibility as 'not always false', since "On Denoting" defines existence as the very same 'not always false'. But Russell evidently, and in any case implicitly, rejects MDL in "Necessity and Possibility," since he banishes modality from logic altogether in that paper. But the banishment quickly ends, since he reverses course and advocates MDL as his own positive theory of modality from 1906 on.

(5) Russell almost certainly held MDL by the time of his 1905 "On Some Difficulties in the Theory of Transfinite Numbers and Order Types." This paper discusses three possible solutions of Russell's paradox: zig-zag theory, limitation of classes theory, and no-classes theory. Russell declines to choose a specific theory (Russell 1973a: 129–30). But the Feb 5, 1906 note appended to the paper shows that he soon accepts the no-classes theory (Russell 1973c: 164n; see Cocchiarella 1980: 78).

(6) Russell held MDL during the period of his May 1906 paper, "On the Substitutional Theory of Classes and Relations," which advocates a no-classes theory, this time using not propositional functions, but a propositions-constants-and-substitution method of eliminating classes, following Maxime Bôcher. This substitution method was to prove too hard to combine with theory of types (Lackey 1973a: 129–30). Note that "substitutional quantification" for the 1906 Russell is not quantification over expressions in the sense we speak of substitutional quantification today (Cocchiarella 1980: 87). For the 1906 Russell, substitution is replacement of one constant by another (Russell 1973d: 167), while determination is assigning a constant as value of a variable (Russell 1973d: 166). These two different operations lead to different results in many cases (Russell 1973d: 167–68). This is a no-classes theory. No classes, relations, or numbers are assumed (Russell 1973d: 166). But this is not merely not *assuming* classes. There really *are* no such things as classes (Russell 1973d: 166, 179). The reason why classes cannot be entities is Russell's paradox (Russell 1973d: 171).

(7) Russell held MDL during the period of his September 1906 paper, "Les Paradoxes de la Logique" ("On 'Insolubilia' and their Solution by Symbolic Logic") (Russell 1973b). Here Russell claims to prove there are infinitely many complex but single entities, namely, propositions (Landini 1993a: 373; Cocchiarella 1980: 90, 112 n.9).

(8) Russell held MDL during the period of his 1907 paper, "Mathematical Logic as Based on the Theory of Types," which states his second theory of types. The paper was published in 1908; see Russell (1973a: 132).

(9) Russell held MDL during the period of his second theory of substitutional quantification in 1908. Propositions as affirmed in 1906 remain a legitimate totality. Those propositions are now called elementary propositions (Cocchiarella 1980: 95). The terms in elementary propositions are called individuals and form the lowest logical type (Cocchiarella 1980: 95–96). As affirmed now, propositions belong to different logical types. All propositions of all types are complex but single entities.

(10) Russell held MDL while he co-authored the first volume of *Principia Mathematica* in 1910 with Alfred North Whitehead. This volume, on which Russell did most of the work, contains his third and mature theory of types. Classes are eliminated through propositional functions, which are regimented by the ramified theory of types, which is in turn mitigated by the axiom of reducibility. According to Lackey and Willard Van Orman Quine, *Principia* reduces classes to propositional functions, but then admits propositional functions as values of variables and therefore as entities (Lackey 1973: 133; Quine 1971a: 8). According to their interpretation, *Principia* inverts Russell's 1908 theory. On their view, in *Principia* it is propositions which are not entities and propositional functions which are entities (Cocchiarella 1980: 101). I have argued against the Quine-Lackey interpretation of *Principia* elsewhere (Dejnožka 2003: 167–81). But for our purposes, the important thing is that MDL, which is not mentioned in *Principia*, evidently remains unaffected in Russell's thinking.

Russell and Whitehead admit intensional propositional functions in at least three senses in *Principia*: (i) There are propositional functions that are not truth-functional, e.g., "*A* believes that *p*" (PM 8). (ii) There are propositional functions that lack extensional identities: "the same class of objects will have many determining functions" (PM 23); such functions are called formally equivalent (PM 21). (iii) There are intensional functions in the sense that their values need not be specified for them to be specified (PM 39–40). Intensional functions in sense (iii) are non-Brouwerian or are at least recursive. It would seem that all sense (i) intensional functions are sense (ii), and all sense (ii) intensional functions are sense (iii). The converses do not seem to hold, but we need not be detained by that question.

(11) Russell held MDL during the period of his 1911 lecture, "The Philosophical Implications of Logic," originally given in French, in which he says that "the validity of any valid deduction depends on its form" (Russell 1973e: 288), and during the period of

his 1912 unpublished essay, "What is Logic?," in which he defines logic as the study of forms (Russell 1912a).

(12) Russell held MDL during the period of his 1913 manuscript *Theory of Knowledge*, which advances an 'entitative' theory of logical form that proved problematic. For a fine discussion, see Griffin (1980).

(13) Russell held MDL during the period in which he wrote his 1914 *Our Knowledge of the External World*. Here Russell makes in effect the first major change in his implicit modal logic by characterizing logical truths as truth in virtue of logical form (KEW 51–52). This is the shift from implicit FG–MDL to the first version of implicit FG–MDL*. It is the only major change in his theory of logical truth since his first published acceptance of MDL in 1906.

(14) In his 1918 "The Philosophy of Logical Atomism," Russell states MDL and says that logical truths are not only true in virtue of logical form, but are tautologies as well (PLA 240–41). This is the implicit second and final version of FG–MDL*. Russell defines form as "that which is in common between any two propositions of which the one can be obtained from the other by substituting other constituents for the original ones" (PLA 238). Note again how close this is to a mere generality theory. He warns against admitting a "too substantial" sort of logical form (PLA 239). There are three reasons for thinking that logical form is now ontologically nothing. First, most of the logical connectives are now nothing (negation seems the sole exception, PLA 211, 216). Second, some of the bearers of logical form—propositions and propositional functions—are now nothing (PLA 214, 223, 230); but note that beliefs and perceivings, which are real facts, have logical forms too (PLA 224, 228). Third, forms would seem to have logically smooth identity conditions, which is typical of logical fictions. Classes and numbers have smooth identity conditions, and they are logical fictions. But again, negation is not a logical fiction.

(15) In his 1919 *Introduction to Mathematical Philosophy*, Russell states MDL and uses possible worlds talk. Logical truths are characterized in terms of truth in virtue of logical form and also in terms of tautology.

(16) In 1925, Russell sketches a major new theory of quantificational logic in the introduction to the second edition of *Principia*. This is a sketch of a difficult neo-Wittgensteinian radical extensionalist logic in which all propositional functions are truth-functional (PM xiv). There is evidently no change in MDL, which Russell reaffirms two years later.

(17) In 1927, Russell affirms MDL in *The Analysis of Matter*. Logical analysis now admits of a series of interpretations of interpretations, the final interpretation being the only one in which there are ontological commitments to entities (AMA 2–9).

Since quantification occurs on every level of interpretation, quantification as such is ontologically noncommittal. There is no commitment here to a neo-Wittgensteinian radical extensionalism. Instead, there is talk of logical structure, talk which implies intensionality in *Principia* senses (ii) and (iii).

(18) Russell held MDL during the period in which he wrote his 1938 introduction to the second edition of *Principles*. He says that "no proposition of logic can mention any particular object" (POM xi), which implies intensionality in senses (ii) and (iii). He now finds himself unable to define *either* "tautological" (POM ix) *or* "true in virtue of its form" (POM xii).

(19) In 1940, Russell affirms MDL in *An Inquiry Into Meaning and Truth*. He affirms intensionality in *Principia* sense (i), rejecting "[t]he principle of extensionality in its general form" (IMT 271; see 273). As I interpret *Inquiry*, level 0 type 0 individuals are now scattered or repeatable particular sensible qualities, instead of instances of universal sensible qualities (Dejnožka 2003: 292 n.4).

(20) In 1948, Russell affirms intensionality in *Principia* sense (i) in *Human Knowledge*. He finds sense (i) intensions demanded by inductive logic, since the classes on which probabilities are based must be intensionally defined. The reason is to explain informative theoretical identifications of classes of objects (HK 138–41, 414–15). Intensionality in *Principia* sense (ii) is also alive and well. Even though mathematical logic always tries to avoid intensions, "[t]autologies are primarily relations between properties" as opposed to their instances, and extensionally understood general sentences are rare in practice (HK 130, 138). The topic of structure sprawls across part 4, chapters 3 and 4, and part 6, chapter 6. For Russell, a structure is a complex relation which indefinitely many things can share, for example copies of a music score. This implies intensionality in senses (ii) and (iii).

This concludes my brief and perhaps cryptic survey of Russell's main logical phases. For our purposes, it is not necessary to understand these phases in any great detail. The main point is that MDL remains the same through all of them. Again, the reason is simple: MDL is merely an interpretive aspect of Russell's theory of descriptions, or more generally, of propositional functions. Its modal expressions are not even used in the formal notation, since they are eliminated. Russell has no modal notation as such.

While MDL remains the same through Russell's logical phases, there is a major change in his express thought which is, in effect, a change from implicit modal logic FG–MDL to implicit modal logic FG–MDL*. I shall now discuss the reason for this change in more detail. The general idea is, in effect, that while implicit FG–MDL may have been plausible in some of Russell's earlier logical phases, it lost its plausibility in the later phases.

There are two main reasons why fully general truth may seem a plausible account of logical truth. The first reason is more general than the first. Russell does not discuss it, but we may wish to impute it to Russell out of charity. This is simply the intrinsic or at least *prima facie* plausibility of the account. Certainly it seems plausible at least to some degree. How else can we explain the truth of fully general truth except as its being logical truth? How else could such truths be true? At least this seems plausible for fully general *universal* truths. But perhaps this is not pure charity. For when David Pears says that in his 1913 *Theory of Knowledge*, Russell "identifies the forms of propositions" with "entirely general facts" (Pears 1989: 177), this is minimal retrospective evidence that the *pre*-1913 Russell accepted the first main reason for holding that logical truth is fully general truth, namely, that the account is intrinsically plausible, since he is still tacitly appealing to it for its own sake. The second main reason for holding that logical truth is fully general truth depends on our supposing that only the actual is possible. If that is true, then fully general truth ranges not only over all that is actual, but all that is possible, and thus is logically true in virtue of being true of all possible things. The two reasons are very different, due to this very supposition. The second reason arguably applies even to fully general *existential* truths, since if only the actual is possible, then what is actual is necessary. It then follows that what is possible is necessarily possible, which is the distinctive axiom of S5. Note that one cannot object that even if the actual is *possible*, it does not follow that the actual is *necessary*. For the key word is *only*. If *only* the actual is possible, then the actual, and *only* the actual, is necessary, since it is not merely actual, but all that is even possible. To put it another way, if merely possible things as such are not actual, then only actual things can be *both* possible and actual. And Russell repeatedly says that only the actual is possible.

Concerning the second main reason, the plausibility of Russell's early account of logical truth as fully general truth depends on what his quantifiers range over in his earlier logical phases. There are two domains one might plausibly consider. (1) If the quantifiers range over all possible entities in the *Principles* manner, then FG–MDL would be a very plausible modal logic, since in *Principles*, entities include existents and nonexistents alike, so that "all entities" and "all possible entities" are co-extensive. Thus in *Principles*, being true of all entities is the same as being true of all possible entities. Now, moving from such a domain to one in which the only entities are existent entities might have been what led Russell to move implicitly from FG–MDL to FG–MDL*. But I think this is not the reason, since it is not the reason Russell states for his move to a different theory of logical truth. Also, MDL (not to mention FG–MDL or FG–MDL*) is not even offered in *Principles*. Further, as I shall argue in detail in chapter 3, there is an important sense in which Russell's post-*Principles* first-level quantifiers still *do* range over all possible entities. Namely, for the post-1905 Russell, there is a Parmenidean sense in which actual entities are the only possible entities. (2) Here is the second domain one might plausibly consider: If the first-level quantifiers range over infinitely many logically necessary entities, then *Principia*'s axiom of infinity, which says in effect that there exist infinitely many objects (PM2 *120.03), would be a logical truth in FG–MDL, as would the *Principia* assumption that there exists at least one self-identical individual. Landini focuses on domain (2), arguing that the reason for Russell's implicit move from FG–MDL to FG–MDL* concerns the axiom of infinity and the existence assumption.

Landini argues that in Russell's earlier thought, the axiom of infinity and the existence assumption counted as logical truths, since he admitted infinitely many logical entities as logically necessary beings. More specifically, Douglas Lackey says Russell claims to prove that there are infinitely many classes in his 1904 "The Axiom of Infinity" (Russell 1973a: 253). More precisely, Russell claims to prove in that paper that there are infinitely many numbers, where numbers are classes (Russell 1973: 256–59). Also see Cocchiarella (1980: 90) saying Russell claims to prove that there are infinitely many propositions in his 1906 "Les Paradoxes." FG–MDL would also have been plausible in *Principles*, in which MDL and FG–MDL are not offered, since in *Principles* all entities are individuals, and the numbers are infinitely many logical entities (see IMP 137–38 on *Principles*). But in the ramified theory of types of *Principia*, the axiom of infinity and the existence assumption are no longer logical truths, except in the trivial and question-begging sense in which they are assumptions of *Principia* logic. They logically might be false, since all individuals in the ramified theory are logically contingent. What is more, there will be infinitely many fully general truths which are not logical truths, such as that there exist at least 30,000 individuals (PLA 240). Hence Russell's move to his new theory of logical truth is crucial, since its additional requirement of truth in virtue of logical form protects him from the infinitely many counter-examples he would face if he retained his old theory that logical truth is merely fully general truth. Since the axiom of infinity and the existence assumption are no longer logical truths for Russell, Russell must move to a new theory of logical truth on which these two theses are correctly counted as *not* being logically true (Landini 1993; see PLA 237–41; IMP 131–43). In fact, Russell had already lost his ability to prove there are infinitely many propositions when he introduced orders in 1908 (Landini 1993a: 375). This concludes Landini's argument, which I have stated in my own way. As a minor technical correction, Nicholas Griffin notes that in *Principia* the axiom of infinity is not assumed but added as an antecedent to every thesis whose proof requires it (Griffin 1980: 180n). An assumed statement is a statement, not an antecedent within a statement.[1]

I accept Landini's argument. But Landini's argument reduces his own interpretation of quantification in *Principia* to absurdity. For if Landini is right that *Principia*'s individual quantifier ranges over all *entities*, universals as well as particulars (Landini 1998: 292; 1996: 293–94; 1993a: 386–87), then it ranges over infinitely many logical universals, and also over infinitely many logical forms. Then the axiom of infinity *would* be a logically necessary truth. But that is absurd. The 1911 Russell says that the axiom is "purely empirical" (Russell 1992a: 52). It is trivial that there are infinitely many logical universals and logical forms—one each for every number. And the *Principia* existence assumption follows even more trivially from the axiom of infinity. For if there are infinitely many entities, then there is at least one entity. Surely Russell and Whitehead would have seen all of this immediately.

I see no evidence of any change in the *ante rem* status of universals from Russell's 1903 *Principles* all the way to Russell's 1912 *Problems of Philosophy*. These nicely bracket 1910 *Principia* vol. 1, as well as all of Russell's work on that volume. The 1912 Russell expressly admits "abstract logical universals" (PP 109). "*All* a priori *knowledge deals exclusively with the relations of universals*" (PP 103). That includes logic. Universals are entities that "*subsist* or *have being*" (PP 100), and are timeless (RUP 124).

Landini seems unaware of the problem. He says, "Though on the present assumption universals are counted among individuals, there is no logical assumption that would ground an infinity of them" (Landini 1998: 293). Perhaps that is true for the infinitely many "relations of space and time" (Landini 1998: 292), since space and time do not belong to pure logic. Yet Landini himself characterizes the infinitely many logical forms as "objects of pure logical intuition" (Landini 1998: 294). It is also an *a priori* truth that there are infinitely many logical *universals*—on logicism, as many as there are numbers. For they are "objects of pure logical intuition" just as much as forms are. Since we are actually acquainted with many of them in thought, how can it be a mere *assumption* that the axiom of infinity is true? Would not that axiom be true *a priori*—and metaphysically necessary for logic?

In any case, Landini is wrong about *Principia* individuals. Landini claims that "universals are counted among individuals" (Landini 1998: 293). But Russell and Whitehead say, "Terms which can occur in any form of atomic proposition are called 'individuals' or 'particulars'; terms which occur as the R's occur are called 'universals'" (PM xix). Thus not only do they equate individuals with particulars, but they also say that universals are a wholly different set of terms represented by a wholly different set of expressions. Thus when they say, "We may explain an individual as something which exists on its own account" (PM 162), they do not mean "either particulars or *ante rem* universals," but only particulars. This is on pain of contradicting PM xix. Also note that "exists on its own account" is traditional terminology for particular substances.

Only particular terms can occur in "any form of atomic proposition." In fact, any atomic proposition *must* have at least one particular term. But monadic and polyadic universal terms do not and cannot occur in *every* form of atomic proposition. For example, take "*a* is red" and "*a* is larger than *b*." If the universal terms *red* and *is larger than* could occur in any form of atomic proposition, then they could replace each other so as to result in "*a* is larger than" and "*a* is red *b*." But those statements are ill-formed. Thus universals cannot be individuals. Clearly, Russell and Whitehead are explaining that individuals are their bottom-level logical subjects of predication, and that as such, they cannot be logical predicate terms themselves. But that is just to say that individuals are particulars, not universals. We must not confuse all this with the fact that for Russell, "Every complete sentence must contain at least one word which stands for a universal, since all verbs have a meaning which is universal" (PP 52). That is quite right, but no one universal can occur in every form of atomic statement, for example *red* and *is larger than*. Every atomic statement must have at least one particular term and at least one universal term. But any particular term can occur in any form of atomic statement, and no universal term can do that.

Landini rightly notes that *Principles* logic is synthetic *a priori*, if only in Kant's strict and limited sense. (Pap 1958 lists a dozen main senses of "analytic," and in some of them *Principles* is analytic.) But Landini wrongly finds this due to the "logical intuition" of logical objects (Landini 1988: 14–16, 294, citing POM 457). *Principles* eliminates intuitions from logic in every sense *but* that of acquaintance with logical entities. *That* sense is scarcely what Russell has in mind when he says he is eliminating intuitions from logic. Kant's intuitions are of space and time, not of logic. For Kant, logic is subject-contains-predicate analytic. The reason *Principles* is synthetic in Kant's sense is very different: Russell admits relational predicates. Thus Kant's subject-contains-predicate analyticity is gone. The analytic-synthetic distinction, as Russell states it in *Principles*, directly concerns the syntactical issue of subject-contains-predicate, and is totally unrelated to any intuitions (POM 4, 158, 339, 456–457, 457 n.* citing PL §11).

Nor does Landini note that just two years later, meaning from ca. 1903–05 "Necessity and Possibility" on, Russell flatly rejects Kant's two tests of analyticity and adopts a broader sense of "analytic" on which *Principles*—not to mention *Principia* and all of Russell's other deductive logics—*is* analytic. In "Necessity and Possibility," Russell rejects Kant's test of deducibility "from the law of contradiction" as "requi[ring] much modification before it can be harmonized with modern logic" (Russell 1994a / ca. 1903–05: 514; see 516). He also rejects Kant's subject-contains-predicate test, saying "With this property we need not concern ourselves" (Russell 1994a / ca. 1903–05: 516). Russell defines analytic propositions as "those propositions which are deducible from the laws of logic" (Russell 1994a / ca. 1903–05: 516). The "laws of deduction" are "general propositions," and they "tell us that two propositions having certain relations of form...are such that one of them implies the other" (Russell 1994a / ca. 1903–05: 515). The laws of logic are "a small number of general logical premisses, among which are included the laws of deduction already spoken of" (Russell 1994a / ca. 1903–05: 516). Russell says, "From the laws of logic all the propositions of formal logic and pure mathematics will be deducible" (Russell 1994a / ca. 1903–05: 516). From this point on, Russell no longer considers modern logic to be synthetic, but analytic. And the reason is that he rejects Kant's tests of analyticity as out of date and unsuitable for modern logic, regardless of how well they might have harmonized with traditional subject-contains-predicate logic. At the same time, Russell's theory of acquaintance, or as Landini calls it for Russell's logical entities, "intuition," is a basic feature of Russell's philosophy from 1905 "On Denoting" to 1918 "The Philosophy of Logical Atomism." This theory is already present in *Principles* in all but name. For Russell says in *Principles* that "indefinable entities...must form the starting-point of any mathematical reasoning," and they "must be...in some sense perceived" (POM 129). "All depends, in the end, upon immediate perception" of the "indefinable...entities" (POM 130). On Russell's own logicism, every single one of these immediately perceived indefinables in mathematics is a logical entity. And Russell's famous Principle of Acquaintance applies to logical universals and to any other logical entities, certainly in his 1912 *The Problems of Philosophy*. All this shows even more clearly that Landini's view is wrong. For it shows that for Russell, the "intuition" of (Landini's term), "immediate perception" of (Russell's *Principles* term), or "acquaintance" with (Russell's later term) logical entities continues unchanged from *Principles* to

Problems, even as Russell changes his definition of analyticity from Kant's to a more general one.

Principles is Russell's only major logical work in which he accepts Kant's tests of analyticity and deems his own formal logic synthetic according to those tests. "Necessity and Possibility" is Russell's only work in which he banishes modality from logic as being conflicted and confused, as opposed to his advocating three clear, definite, and simple eliminative definitions of modal predicates as his own positively accepted and frequently stated theory of modality.

Again, in "Necessity and Possibility," Russell equates both the laws of logic in general and the laws of deduction in particular with general truths, and also connects both with form in such a way that general truth and formal truth are not expressly distinguished as different conditions of logical truth. Thus it may be that Russell thinks, in this early (ca. 1903–05) paper, that truth in virtue of logical form is merely truth in virtue of fully general form.

In 1918 Russell argues that logical connectives such as *or* are not going about in the world. Thus he no longer admits logical universals (PLA 184, 197, 209–10) except, evidently, for negation in connection with negative facts (PLA 211–16). But that is eight years too late to help Landini. And even the 1918 Russell still seems to admit infinitely many logical forms in some sense (PLA 239). Whether Landini would count Russell's logical forms as individuals, I cannot say. But they seem to satisfy the *Principia* definition of "individual" as Landini understands it, if they are entities at all.

I discussed Landini's interpretation of *Principia* quantifiers at length in my first book, *The Ontology of the Analytic Tradition and Its Origins* (Dejnožka 2003: xxiii–xxv, 170–73). The only express textual support for his view is *Principia*'s definition of the term "individual": "We say that x is an 'individual' if x is neither a proposition nor a function (cf. p. 51)" (PM 132). This seems an odd definition because it seems to make classes individuals. But when we turn to *Principia*, we find that:

> For this purpose, we will use such letters as a, b, c, x, y, z, w, to denote objects which are neither propositions nor functions. Such objects we shall call *individuals*. Such objects will be constituents of propositions or functions, and will be *genuine* constituents, in the sense that they do not disappear on analysis, as (for example) classes do, or phrases of the form "the so-and-so." (PM 51, Russell's emphasis; note the very broad use of the word "object")

That eliminates classes. Obviously, they are not individuals. Now, all individuals are objects, and objects include particulars as well as universals. Russell says, "The universe consists of objects having various qualities and standing in various relations" (PM 43). Objects include particulars such as "the complex object 'the redness of this'" (PM 44), and universals such as red itself (PM 43; MAL 205–6). Landini wrongly converts this, claiming all *objects* are *individuals* (Landini 1998: 292 citing MAL 206). The term "object" is not logical but cognitive. Objects include all objects of acquaintance (MAL 202–4), and arguably include merely apparent entities (PM 51; compare POM 55n). In *Principia*, objects divide into all types, while individuals are only type 0 (see PM 51 as block quoted just above; 161, "The division of objects into types...;" see also PM2 203–4 on the axiom of infinity). Again, logical universals are logically necessary entities, but the axiom of infinity is logically contingent. There is no reason to believe that in *Principia* alone, Russell makes logical universals logically contingent, i.e., *in re*. Since no change is apparent in the ontological status of universals from *Principia* volume 1 to volume 2, we would even have to suppose that the 1912 volume 2 admits only logically contingent *in re* universals, despite the logically necessary *ante rem* universals—which are timeless entities in the timeless world of being—in 1912 *Problems*. This is not to mention Russell's 1911 paper "On the Relations of Universals and Particulars," where "universals do not exist in time" (RUP 124), and where Russell speaks of "the necessary universality belonging to logical categories" (RUP 123). This kind of repeated bouncing back and forth from logically necessary logical universals to logically contingent logical universals and back again, which Landini's view commits us to, seems most implausible.

Just a year earlier than *Principia* volume 2, Russell said in his 1911 paper "On the Axioms of the Infinite and Transfinite":

> *The axiom of infinity* is formulated as follows: *If* n *is any finite cardinal number, there is a set consisting of* n *individuals.* Here the word *individual* contrasts with class, function, proposition, etc., In other words, *an individual* is *a being in the actual world, as opposed to the beings in the logical world.* (Russell 1992a: 44, Russell's emphasis)

Landini and I agree that in *Principia*, classes, functions and propositions are not even "beings in the logical world." They are not beings at all. They are syncategorematic: they are mere incomplete expressions. Unlike universals, they 'disappear on analysis'. But Landini overlooks that in Russell's ontology from 1903 *Principles* to 1912 *Problems*, only particulars can be beings in the actual world. Universals are in the world of timeless being (RUP 124; PP 99–100). Thus once again, on 1910 *Principia*'s official definition, universals are not individuals. In *Principia*, when Russell says, "The universe consists of objects having various qualities and standing in various relations" (PM 43), objects include the qualities and relations themselves. But not all objects are individuals. Russell says, "We may explain an individual as something which exists on its own account" (PM 162). It is a basic doctrine of the 1903–12 Russell's ontology that only particulars *exist*; universals and forms have timeless *being* (POM 43–44, 470, 476; PP 99–100). This explains why Russell insists in "On the Axioms" that the truth or falsehood of the axiom of infinity is a "purely empirical" matter concerning the number of "physical objects" (Russell 1992a: 52). Physical objects are particulars, as both *Principles* and *Problems* abundantly confirm. In light of the purely contingent character of the axiom of infinity, this makes all the sense in the world. In contrast, for the 1903–12 Russell universals are not contingent beings. And we can think of ("conceive") and count universals regardless of whether they happen to be empirically instantiated.

Russell practically comes right out and says in three major works that *Principia* individuals are particulars. First, he says in "The Philosophy of Logical Atomism," "You can see why it is that in the logical language set forth in *Principia Mathematica* there are not any names, because there we are not interested in particular particulars, but only in general particulars, if I may be allowed such a phrase" (PLA 201). Russell is telling us in the plainest of terms that all named things, i.e. all *individuals*, are particulars. Second, in the preface to the second edition of *Principia*, in sketching his tentative new extensionalist logic, Russell says "'individuals' or 'particulars'," making the two expressions synonymous (PM xix). Third, Russell's fundamental change to his logic in the 1940 *Inquiry* is to make sensible qualities his new type 0 order 0 individuals, and he is quite clear that to make them individuals is to make them particulars (Dejnožka 2003: 292–94 n.4). Thus in three major later works, Russell equates individuals with particulars, and always with either express or implied reference back to the first edition of *Principia*.

Thus Landini misinterprets *Principia*'s official definition of individuals. I cannot repeat my entire critique of Landini here (Dejnožka 2003: xxiii–xxv, 170–73).

Russell always confines his definitions of modal operators in MDL to first-level quantification, i.e. quantification over individuals. The question arises whether his modal ideas may apply to his other levels and kinds of quantification. Insofar as there is no distinction between actual and merely possible classes, it would seem that FG–MDL would apply to any type of class quantification in *Principia*. Likewise for propositions and for propositional functions. Now in my view, *Principia* quantification over classes, propositions, and propositional functions is purely nominal or conventional, since I hold that none of these has any ontological status. But while all of these are incomplete symbols, I cannot believe they would include only the finite number of incomplete symbol-*tokens* actually written down in *Principia* notation. Thus either they are incomplete symbol-*types*, or they simply cannot be written down because they are not (complete) symbols. I incline to the former alternative because Russell is always writing them down. But either way, there seems to be no difference between actual and merely possible classes, and to that extent I think that FG–MDL would apply to them, but only in a purely nominal sense. Likewise for propositions and propositional functions.

I cheerfully follow Russell in making a casual blur. Russell sometimes speaks of existence as a property of propositional functions. That is incorrect because existence is nothing and propositional functions are nothing. Existence is itself a second-level propositional function, and nothing can be a property of nothing. Strictly speaking, Russell should speak of the existential quantifier as an incomplete symbol which has a logical universal as its determinate constituent, and which is predicated of propositional functions which are other incomplete symbols which have other universals as their determinate constituents (MAL 220–21, 220n).

What are propositional functions? For our purposes they are open sentences, i.e. logical predicates of the form "x is red." This will take a little explaining. As Landini notes, propositional functions in *Principia* are predicate variables, not predicates. In *Principia*, Russell distinguishes among predicates such as "x is hurt," predicate variables such as "$\hat{x}$ is hurt," which are his propositional functions, and propositional function variables such as "$\varphi\hat{x}$" (PM 14–15). However, Russell never discusses MDL in *Principia*. We must look instead to the works in which he discusses MDL, and see what he means by "propositional function" in those works.

Now, in the 1905 unpublished paper "Necessity and Possibility," in which Russell first introduces MDL, and in every one of the six published works in which he defines MDL and either states what a propositional function is or gives examples of propositional functions, propositional functions are always open sentences. This gives us seven works in total. They are as follows:

(1) Russell (1994a / ca. 1903–05: 518): "to propositional functions, that is, to propositions with an indeterminate subject ....For example,...'x is mortal'";

(2) Russell (1906: 257): "'x is a barrister'....is a propositional function";

(3) Russell (1908: 300, 301): "propositional functions, i.e. expressions which, so soon as we give a definite value to x (such as Mr. Smith) become propositions";

(4) LK 69 (1908): "what contains a real [or free] variable is a propositional function, not a proposition";

(5) PLA 230 (1918): "A propositional function is simply any expression containing an undetermined constituent, or several undetermined constituents, and becoming a proposition as soon as the undetermined constituents are determined." (Russell's italics removed);

(6) IMP 155–56 (1919): "A 'propositional function', in fact, is an expression containing one or more undetermined constituents, such that, when values are assigned to these constituents, the expression becomes a proposition."; and

(7) IMT 260 (1940): "A 'propositional function' is an expression containing one or more undetermined constituents x, y,..., and such that, if we settle what these are to be, the result is a proposition."

The uniformity is absolute and without exception. In every work in which Russell defines MDL and states what propositional functions are, he is clearly referring to open sentences. As to using MDL to interpret historical *Principia* in modal terms, we merely have to change our terminology and speak of predicates instead of propositional functions.

In speaking of propositional functions as open sentences, I confess to blurring any distinction between propositions and sentences which Russell may make at times. I should properly refer to propositional functions either as logical predicates or as open propositions. I simply find today's term "open sentence" more convenient. Of course, since propositional functions are nothing, open sentences are nothing.

I have been assuming a standard interpretation of the individual quantifier in *Principia* as ranging over, and as implying ontological commitment to, concrete particulars. I have flagged my skepticism about this by surrounding the so-called "existential" quantifier with double quotation marks. There are other interpretations. My own interpretation is that it can and by 1914 does range over both concrete particulars and *bene fundata* (well-founded) logical constructions which are apparent concrete particulars, and is a veridical quantifier implying no ontological commitment. "Not always false" may have begun as a sloppy way to express existential generalization in "On Denoting" in 1905, but in *Principia* it analyzes what "exists" means in veridical terms (see Dejnožka 2003: chapter 5, section 2). The difference makes no

① note the blurring of METAPHYSICAL/LOGICAL MODALITY
WITH TEMPORAL MODALITY

difference to Russell's modal theory. Whether other interpretations make a difference is beyond the scope of this book.[2]

Russell's theory of logical truth as invariance, or truth under any interpretation, anticipates Rudolf Carnap, Alfred Tarski, J. C. C. McKinsey (1945), Saul Kripke (1980), Joseph Almog (1989), and John Etchemendy (1990), and has antecedents in Bernard Bolzano and John Venn. Russell's theory resembles Bolzano's substitutional account of logical truth, which Etchemendy compares to Tarski's satisfactional account of logical truth (Etchemendy 1990: 27–33).[3] Rolf George says Bolzano "was the first to give a formal definition of the notion of consequence," and finds it "akin to that given a century later by Tarski" (George 1972: xxxiv); Russell defines "analytic consequence" in 1903–05 (Russell 1994a / ca. 1903–03: 516–17). Russell's theory of what is possible as what is sometimes the case is close to McKinsey (1945: 83) and Venn (1879: 40), with roots in Diodorus Cronus. I argue in chapter 7 that Carnap probably based his modal logic on Russell's MDL. I suggest that Russell anticipated Kripke's modal logic by over seventy years, and influenced Kripke *via* Carnap and Evert Willem Beth. I am referring, of course, not to Kripke's formal logic of subsets of possible worlds and accessibility relations, but to Kripke's ontological conception of possible worlds as mere ways of talking, and especially to Kripke's general conception of modality as essentially quantificational in nature, with necessity equating to universality and possibility equating to there being at least one thing. I also argue that Russell's logically proper names, are rigid designators in Kripke's weak sense. And I show that Russell developed a causal reference theory of naming not far from Kripke's own. All this controverts Kripke's famous critique of Russell. Russell is far closer to Kripke than Kripke thinks, or seems to say, or perhaps is willing to say—to shout as opposed to whisper. The chief whisper is about Russell's logically proper names. Kripke says that "Russell does seem to have held" that Russell's logically proper names of the same particular are "equivalent for all semantic purposes," which clearly implies that they are interchangeable *salva analycitate* in all sentential contexts (Kripke 1980: 20). But Kripke does not come out and admit that they therefore seem to be rigid designators. I omit any detailed comparison of Russell and Kripke on natural kinds as beyond the scope of this book. We may say that Russell admits natural kinds in any ultimate logical analysis that includes universals among its simple entities, and that any simples with which we are acquainted can be assigned logically proper names, such as "redness."

Russell's MDL is very congenial to Quine. Quine has very kindly written me, "Certainly I have no objection to necessity and possibility when interpreted in Russell's way" (Quine 1990b). The reason is obvious: Russell's analysis eliminates all modal entities and modal notions. One need only accept quantification theory and interpret it in a certain way. This is not to commit anyone who admits quantification to admitting a modal theory. That would be absurd. One must not only admit quantification, but also actually use it to define modal notions. But this is just what Russell does. Russell repeatedly offers a quantificational, or more precisely a veridical, definition of modal notions. That is just what I call MDL.

I find that all eight of Russell's implicit modal logics are S5 in strength. These are: FG–MDL (fully general truth as logical necessity), FG–MDL* (fully general truth plus truth in virtue of logical form as logical necessity), FG–MDL+syn (FG–MDL plus synthetic *a priori* truth as logical necessity), FG–MDL*+syn (FG–MDL* plus synthetic *a priori* truth as logical necessity), MDL–C (causal necessity), MDL–E (epistemic necessity), MDL–D (moral necessity), and MDL–D* (moral necessity) all seem to be S5. If I am right, then Russell implicitly achieves a tremendous formal simplification due to his always implicitly viewing modality in terms of his quantificational logic, which is best equated to S5 as well, as we shall see. Whether the modalities are logical, causal, epistemic, or moral is irrelevant to the question of strength. If modal logics are defined by their strength, meaning by their axioms, or more precisely, by which and how many theorems their axioms imply, with regard to form only, and not to interpretation, then what we really have here is one implicit modal logic with eight different implicit interpretations. This is logically elegant.

On February 10, 1997, I learned by electronic mail from Professor Nino Cocchiarella that some ten years earlier, in his book *Logical Studies in Early Analytic Philosophy*, he had already attributed a modal logic stronger than S5 to Russell. Chapters 6 and 7 of *Logical Studies* discuss modal interpretations of the early analysts in some detail, and it appears that without expressly saying so, Cocchiarella attributes David Kaplan's S13 to Russell. "The axioms and rules of S13 are just the axioms and rules of S5 supplemented with the following schema: if φ is a [true] modal free proposition that is not tautologous, then $\Diamond\neg\varphi$ is an axiom of S13" (Cocchiarella 1987: 238; see 11–12). Cocchiarella discusses the S-strength of modal interpretations of logical atomism in some detail.

The basis of Cocchiarella's attribution of an implicit modal logic to Russell's logical atomism is Russell's admission of negative facts, allowing possible worlds to be defined as totalities of positive and negative facts without admitting any sort of ontological status for possible worlds (Cocchiarella 1987: 247). This argument is very different from mine, and I think limited in one important respect. Cocchiarella's argument is based on the analytic-synthetic dualist nature of logical atomism. He sharply separates material properties and relations from formal properties and relations. He finds all and only the former to be external, and all and only the latter to be internal (Cocchiarella 1987: 13–14). Then he finds S13 implicit only in the "logical scaffolding of the world" (Cocchiarella 1987: 14), holding that for logical atomism, so to speak, the only modality is *logical* modality. But if we look to Russell's metaphysics, we find that when Russell rejected the theory that *all* relations (and properties) are internal, he came to hold only that *not all* material relations and properties are internal. In the 1914–18 Russell's metaphysics, a red round sensed sensibile's redness and roundness *are* internal to it, while its being sensed is external to it. A sensed sensibile, or sense-datum, logically cannot change its sensible qualities, on pain of becoming a different sense-datum. Russell says this in "The Philosophy of Logical Atomism" (PLA 203; see also RUP 119; IMT 334). A sense-datum cannot be identified in acquaintance independently of identifying its sensible qualities. Indeed, sense-data are just *instances* of sensible universals (see Dejnožka 2003: 159–60). Yet a sense-datum logically might have been merely an *unsensed* sensibile. That is, sensibilia are logically mind-independent for the 1914–18 Russell. That is not to mention that the 1914–18 logical atomist Russell still admits his own mind as a "pin-point particular" which surely has both essential (internal) and accidental (external) features. Also, that red is a color (or in modern classical terms, if anything is red then it has color), is not a formal truth; yet having color is obviously internal to being red. Therefore I expand Cocchiarella's argument to include *all* of Russell's internal properties and relations, including internal *material* properties, and not just the formal logical ones. Cocchiarella's argument better suits Wittgenstein's *Tractatus*, which is extensionalist and rejects the synthetic *a priori*. Another way to put it is that Cocchiarella is focusing strictly on Russell's logic, and not on internal relations in Russell's metaphysics. But I am happy to admit, as an expansion of my own interpretation, that Russell's third and fourth implicit alethic modal logics, FG–MDL+syn and FG–MDL*+syn, are S13 for all *formal* properties and relations, and *also* for all *internal* properties and relations. I am delighted to find such a distinguished predecessor in a colleague who has already been a helpful friend on other occasions. I highly recommend his book to anyone interested in Russell's implicit alethic modal logics.

  As to my own theory of modality, I accept Russell's MDL and supplement it with further eliminative analyses of modal notions in terms of identity, difference, and whole-part relations. I would say that if x is y in the ordinary predicative sense of "is," then y is essential to x just in case x is y in a certain special sense of "is," namely, 'y is all or part of what it is to be x'; and otherwise y

is accidental to *x*. This theory is based on and is very much like that of Panayot Butchvarov. But for *x* I use publicly available "qualified objects" in place of Butchvarov's private, nonrecurrent objects; and for *y* I use (sometimes merely probable) minimally real entities which are "out there" in place of Butchvarov's entities, which are mere conceptual constructions of his objects. These are difficult topics I cannot discuss here (see Dejnožka 2003: xxvi, 47, 61, 73, 123–35; Butchvarov 1979: 122–53, 212–38). I also hold that *x* and *y* are really distinct just in case they are wholly distinct; and if *x* and *y* are not wholly distinct, i.e., if they either overlap or coincide, then they are distinct in reason, i.e., are different things which are logically necessary to each other's existence. Further refinements of these views are possible, but this is not a book about my views. The one thing I cannot say on my view is that *x* and *y* are not wholly distinct just in case they *cannot* exist independently of each other, or just in case they *cannot* be identified independently of each, since that would bring in a modal notion of impossibility that would ruin the eliminative character of my analysis. Such whole-part ontology also goes to relevance. Talk of ontological whole, part, and overlapping invites talk of containment relevance, the main topic of chapter 9.

Even my supplementary eliminative analyses are close to Russell's views, as we shall see. For despite his great advances on traditional formal logic, Russell still offers a traditional whole-part theory of logical deduction, i.e., of logically necessary inference. Indeed, insofar as *to exist is to be identifiable*, MDL itself, by reducing existence and possibility to the same veridical notion *not always false*, reduces modal notions ultimately to notions of identity (see Dejnožka 2003: 141–42, 290). What is more, just as Butchvarov eliminatively replaces the subjunctive conditional notion of existence as identifiability indefinitely many times (i.e. we *would* single it out if we *were* there now) "with the idea that a thing exists if *there is* [indicative tense] an indefinite number of objects[,] each identical with it, whether or not we have encountered any of them" (Butchvarov 1994: 44), and just as I can do the same thing using an indefinite number of my qualified objects, so the 1914–18 Russell can do the same thing using an indefinite number of his sensed and unsensed sensibilia. And Butchvarov's singled out and unsingled out objects, my presented and unpresented qualified objects (objects of perception or thought conceived in a certain way), and Russell's sensed and unsensed sensibilia all can be directly, rigidly designated by logically proper names if apprehended. Since my qualified objects are capable of being publicly presented, they can even be rigidly designated by ordinary public names. I hold that this is possible in momentary public perceptual presentations of ordinary things in certain ways.

The prevailing view is that Russell was, if anything, even more destructive of logical relevance than he was of modal logic. I believe that Anderson and Belnap treat Russell as a chief enemy of relevance logic chiefly because they never studied his ideas with the time and care they spend on their own. They are simply not Russell scholars. I argue in chapter 9 that Russell admits three progressively stronger entailment relations very different from those of Anderson and Belnap. However, the weaker two are entailment relations only if they are truth-constrained; they are not entailment relations considered in themselves. The third relation is formal deducibility understood as truth-ground containment.

Anderson and Belnap hold that modal notions are unable to capture logical relevance. In particular, they reject the view that strict implication is logical relevance. I argue in chapter 9 that Russell implicitly analyzes modal logic and relevance logic alike in terms of his quantificational logic This is just what justifies my discussing modality and relevance together in this book. My thesis is that Russell's implicit alethic logic FG–MDL* and implicit truth-ground containment relevance logic, REL, are different implicit interpretations, or different implicit aspects, of his quantificational or, more precisely, veridical logic. For whole-part deductive inference is both containment-necessary and containment-relevant. I simply apply this general point to Russell.

In chapter 10, I suggest that John Maynard Keynes, turn-of-the-century legal scholars writing on logical relevance, early modern British legal and philosophical scholars, and ultimately Aristotle's theory of induction as intellection (not to be confused with his theory of probability as what is usually the case), are the probable origins of Russell's seemingly strange view, published only in his 1912 *The Problems of Philosophy*, that the principle of induction is a weakly self-evident *a priori* principle. I shall argue that Keynes' theory that probability is degree of logical relevance, and its undermining of the distinction between deductive and inductive (nondeductive) logic, underlie and explain the inductive epistemology of Russell's book. I also argue that Russell's theory of probability remains basically Keynesian in his 1948 *Human Knowledge* and his 1959 *My Philosophical Development*.

My own theory of logical relevance is that there is no one kind of logical relevance. I hold that in deductive logic, there are at least fifteen eclectic logically sufficient criteria of logical relevance which often give the same results. I give a chart of these fifteen criteria at the end of chapter 9. I hold that probability is degree of logical relevance. I base this not on Russell or Keynes, but on a synthetic *a priori* principle that if it objectively seems to subject *S* that proposition *P* is true, then *S* has reason to believe that *P*. This principle is based on and very much like Roderick M. Chisholm's principle, which is based in turn on the ancient skeptic Carneades (Chisholm 1966: ch. 3). For me, degree of logical relevance is degree of objective reason to believe, which is in turn degree of objectively seeming to be true. Thus my theory is not a Platonic logical theory of probability like the theories of Russell and Keynes, but is based on the phenomenological seemings presented in this world. I offer it as an improvement on Russell's mature theory in *Human Knowledge*. On my view, the principle of induction is not even weakly *a priori*, but it objectively seems to be true. I sketch my probability theory in chapter 10, note 3.

I shall conclude this chapter by discussing whether Russell would accept supervenience as Jaegwon Kim understands it. Kim's concept of supervenience is based on the ordinary intuition that if two things are physically identical, that is, have the same kinds of micro-events in the same kinds of space-time relationships, then they must be equally good. If the intuition is correct, then ethics is said to supervene on physics, regardless of whether the laws or rules of ethics can be reduced to physical laws. Likewise, physically identical paintings can only be equally beautiful (Hare 2001: 81). And if two possible worlds are physically identical in their full histories, the ordinary intuition many would have is that they must be equally good, equally beautiful, and more than that, must have exactly the same mental phenomena (if any), regardless of whether ethical life, aesthetic life, or mental life can be reduced to physical laws. The idea is that goodness, beauty, and mind must be in some basic sense dependent on and determined by, and nothing more than, physical nature, if these ordinary intuitions are correct, regardless of whether there are any lawlike reductions.

I argue in my first book that Russell is a neglected major progenitor of 'no entity without identity' ontology (Dejnožka 2003: chapters 4–5). This alone would make supervenience theory deeply congenial to the logical constructionist Russell. For example, the Frege-Russell definition of number makes arithmetic supervene on quantificational logic. Of course, it also does much more than that. It provides full definability of the laws of arithmetic in terms of the laws of logic. It even makes the supervenience mutual, since numbers are identical if and only if the corresponding classes of classes are identical. Bodies and minds supervene on sensibilia, and so on.

In the present book, I argue in effect that Russell's implicit mature modal logic, FG–MDL*, and implicit relevance logic, RSL, supervene on Russell's quantificational logic. I also argue for much more than that. I argue that the laws of these systems are definable in terms of the laws of his quantificational logic. Here again, the supervenience is mutual. For example, for Russell "It is logically necessary that P" is true if and only if "P" is fully general and true in virtue of its logical form. The supervenience is both "strong" and "global," on both Kim's original and revised understandings of those terms (Kim 1993: chapters 4, 5). On Kim's revised understanding, set of properties A strongly supervenes on set of properties B "just in case: (III) Necessarily, for any object x and any property F in A, if x has F, then there exists a property G in B such that x has G, and *necessarily* if any y has G, it has F" (Kim 1993: 80). A globally supervenes on B just in case "[a]ny two worlds indiscernible with respect to B-properties are indiscernible with respect to A-properties" (Kim 1993: 82). The supervenience is also "strengthened global." That is, "[w]orlds that are pretty much alike in B-properties are pretty much alike in A-properties" (Kim 1993: 89). These superveniences trivially follow from the supreme generality of arithmetic and logic. Arithmetic, FG–MDL*, and RSL all collapse into quantificational logic in all possible worlds. In an older terminology, all these things are distinct only in reason from each other.

2

Propositional Functions and Possible Worlds

The view generally held today is that not only did Russell not offer a modal logic (he did not), but also that he ignored modality or was against modality, and that in any case his philosophical views and his modern classical logic tended to impede the development of modal logic. We may call this view "V". Saul A. Kripke, for example, says in *Naming and Necessity* that not only did Russell have a theory "plainly incompatible with our direct intuitions of rigidity" (Kripke 1980: 14), but that one reason for this was that Russell "did not consider modal questions" (Kripke 1980: 14). Nicholas Rescher goes further in his article, "Russell and Modal Logic." There he holds that Russell, with his "massive influence" and "deliberately held negative views toward modal conceptions," was almost single-handedly responsible for "the stunted development of modal logic [for]...two generations" (Rescher 1979a: 146–48). Raymond Bradley, in *The Nature of All Being*, eagerly accepts Rescher's "fascinating, and revealing, account of Russell's 'baneful influence' on the development, and recognition, of modal logic" without any reservations (Bradley 1992: 63). And these three philosophers are only the tip of the iceberg of current opinion.

The main objective of chapters 1–8 of this book is to refute view V by presenting and explaining Russell's largely explicit three-level theory of modality, and his eight implicit modal logics.

There is much that is true and important in V. Many sorts of development in modal logic probably were impeded for many of the reasons Rescher cites. But V is not the whole truth. A more thorough study of Russell will reveal that not only is Russell deeply concerned with modal concepts, but his writings imply or can be reasonably interpreted to imply some modal logics. Let us call this opposing view "V*". I shall, of course, be arguing in favor of V*. Indeed, I shall suggest it is holders of V who have been more responsible than Russell for generations of stunted development of modal logic. And ironically, I shall suggest that this is because it is holders of V who have been responsible for generations of stunted scholarship on, and stunted development of, Russell's conceptions of modality. But I must leave that for the reader to judge.

Is Russell against modal logic? Is he against modality? Consider, for example, what he says in his 1927 *The Analysis of Matter:*

> I do not think much can be made of modality, the plausibility of which seems to have come from confusing propositions with propositional functions. (AMA 169)

But as we shall see, Russell is not rejecting modality as such, but the view that the simplest modalities are operators on propositions.

Propositional Functions

Insofar as a proposition is a true or false sentence, a propositional function would be what we call an open sentence, i.e., a sentence one or more of whose subject- or predicate-terms have been replaced with variables. Different terms are always replaced with different variables. Different occurrences of the same term, ranging from one to all occurrences, can be replaced with the same variable. Thus the original content of the proposition can be preserved to varying degrees, but never altered. The variables are said to mark argument-places, or places where arguments can be inserted. Thus where "John loves Mary" is a proposition, "x loves Mary," "x loves y," and "Lxy" are propositional functions. No ontological commitment either to propositional functions or to their properties is implied. For Russell denies that they have ontological status and calls them "nothing" (see PLA 230–31). Russell says:

> Propositional functions...are of three kinds: those which are true for all values of the argument or arguments, those which are false for all values, and those which are true for some arguments and false for others. The first may be called necessary, the second impossible, the third possible. (AMA 170)

Kripke and Rescher do not seem to be aware of this theory, which Russell also states in earlier major works such as "The Philosophy of Logical Atomism" and *Introduction to Mathematical Philosophy*. Let us call this theory of logical modality MDL. In simplest terms, MDL is a theory that the logical modalities are certain specific properties of propositional functions. For example, since the propositional function $x = x$ is always true, it is necessary. Thus the propositional function, self-identity, is necessary in MDL (compare PM 216 / *24.01; PLA 231).

To say that MDL is not a modal theory is exactly as absurd as to say that Russell has no theory of existence when he holds that existence is a property of propositional functions. In fact Russell has a sophisticated theory of existence much like Frege's. And to say that Russell would reject modal logics because he eliminates modal entities is just as absurd as to say that he rejects arithmetic because he eliminates numbers as entities. Of course he accepts arithmetic! He merely rejects its ontological interpretation in terms of arithmetical entities. Likewise, he logically *could* admit modal logics while rejecting their ontological interpretation in terms of modal entities. Of course, he does not actually admit modal logics.

Just as levels of Russellian quantification may in principle be nested any finite number of times in a single sentence, so too may predications of modality in MDL. One may nest predications of necessity over different variables of the same level, as well as over variables of different levels. One may iterate predications of analyticity, truth in virtue of form, or tautology over quoted whole sentences. All three sorts of nesting and iteration are evident in the following sentence:

> S. "'It is necessary of x that {it is necessary of F that [it is necessary of y that (if Fx, then (if Fy then Fx))]}' is tautologous" is tautologous.

S would be true for Russell. Clearly one may predicate necessity over the variables F and y even though the variable x is already modally predicated over. Russell himself did not trouble to point this out. But if this is to tinker with his notation at all, it is to tinker with it very little indeed.

Russell continues, in the passage quoted three paragraphs ago, to develop an epistemic modal theory based on MDL. Call it "MDL–E". Russell says:

> And these terms [necessity, possibility, impossibility] may be transferred to propositions when they are not known to be true on their own account, but what is known as to their truth or falsehood is deduced from knowledge of propositional functions. (AMA 170)

And here we see Russell expressly 'transferring' all modal terms "to propositions." Admittedly, they are only epistemic modal operators. But they are sentential modal operators nonetheless.

Russell had already expounded both MDL and MDL–E in his 1918 "The Philosophy of Logical Atomism," although there he had perhaps not made explicit that MDL–E applies only to whole propositions (PLA 254–55). But if MDL–E is a *de dicto* theory of epistemic modality, does that not make MDL a *de re* theory of logical modality? The answer to the question depends on the nature of Russell's propositional functions. And that in turn concerns the nature of Russell's propositions.

Now, the notion of a proposition was one of Russell's more kaleidoscopic notions, as Alan R. White has shown (White 1979: 22–23, 26); see also Candlish (1996). There are two main options. Option (1): Russell often sees propositions as linguistic in nature, as sentences, in which case propositional functions are probably also linguistic in nature. Now insofar as a propositional function is linguistic it is syncategorematic, i.e., nothing (PLA 230). On option (1) necessity is best viewed as also nothing, just as Russell should view existence on option (1). For nothing can be a property of nothing. Further, necessity is nothing because it is itself a propositional function of the second level, and all propositional functions are nothing. Option (2): Russell often holds that propositions are complex entities which sentences are about, and that we understand propositions through acquaintance with their constituents. And insofar as predicates have concepts as constituents (IMP 157–58; see POM 44), and a concept is "a universal of which we are aware" (PP 52), logical necessity for Russell is best viewed as a universal predicable *de re* of other universals, just as Russell should view existence on option (2). For universals are determinate constituents of propositional functions (see MAL 206–7, 220–21, 220n). In fact, every propositional function has at least one universal as a determinate constituent.

Four Russellian Arguments for MDL

Why would Russell offer MDL? There are four arguments he could give. We have seen that Russell treats MDL-possibility the same way he treats existence, making both the same property of propositional functions. I now suggest that two *reasons* why he makes existence second-level also apply to MDL-possibility.

The first one, best expressed in "The Philosophy of Logical Atomism," is that "There is no sort of point in a predicate which could not be conceivably false" (PLA 241). So that if existence were a property of things, then there would be no point in asserting the existence of anything. But there is a clear sense in which there is great point in saying that certain things do not exist (e.g., do not fear attack by dragons). Hence, existence is not a property of things, and neither are everything and nothing. But much the same goes for logical possibility. If logical possibility were a property of things, then there would be no point in asserting the possibility of anything. But there is much point in saying that certain things are not logically possible (e.g., do not try to square the circle). Hence, logical possibility is not a property of things, and neither are logical necessity and logical impossibility. The arguments are so close that existence and logical possibility are both construed as the very same property by Russell, the property of being not always false. Russell says in "The Philosophy of Logical Atomism":

> When you take any propositional function and assert of it that it is possible, that it is sometimes true, that gives you the fundamental meaning of 'existence'....It will be **out of** this notion of *sometimes*, which is the **same** as the notion of *possible*, that we **get** the notion of existence. To say that unicorns exist is simply to say that '(*x* is a unicorn) is possible'.
>   It is perfectly clear that when you say 'Unicorns exist' you are not saying anything that would apply to any unicorns there might happen to be because as a matter of fact there are not any....Therefore when you say 'Unicorns exist', you are not saying anything about any individual things, and the same applies when you say 'Men exist'. (PLA 232–33, Russell's italic emphasis, my boldface emphasis)

But then Russell must also hold that '(*x* is a unicorn) is possible' "could not be even significant unless there were unicorns," if it were a proposition about individual unicorns. That is by simple parity of reason. It also follows from his making possibility and existence the very same property. Even we can accept at least that what is actual is, as such, possible, if not also the converse.

The terms in boldface emphasis show that if anything, it is the notion of sometimes or possible that is primitive, and it is the notion of existence that we 'get out of it'. We may call this "derivational asymmetry." But the notions are symmetrical in the sense that they are logically equivalent, i.e., intersubstitutable *salva analycitate*. In fact, that is just why Russell can use the former notion as the logical analysis of the latter.

The second argument is that universal quantification expresses a property not of things, but of propositional functions; and existential quantification is definable in terms of universal quantification and negation. "All *S* is *P*" cannot be about all *S*'s. For we do not always know every *S*, but we do understand "All *S* is *P*" (PLA 241). But this very argument may also be given for logical necessity's being a property of propositional functions. For we can understand "It is logically necessary that (all) things be *F*" even though we do not always know every (possible) thing that is *F*. Again, the arguments are so close that Russell defines logical necessity in the same way he does the universal quantifier, i.e., as the property of being true for all values of the propositional function in question. And even we can accept at least that what is universally necessary is, as such, universally actual, if not also the converse.

Russell's two more or less explicit arguments will be our third and fourth.

Third, then, in his 1913 "On the Notion of Cause" and in his 1918 "The Philosophy of Logical Atomism," Russell argues that since a proposition is simply true or false, then if "necessary" means "what is true under all circumstances," then if it is "worth saying of something" that it is necessary, then that something must be a propositional function, $F(x)$, which "is true for all possible values of x," "for all values of its argument or arguments" (ONC 176; see PLA 231). There is a similarity to the first argument in that being "worth saying" of something is the same as being a predicate which has a "point." Also note that this third argument speaks of all *possible* values. I shall return to this point when I describe the second logical howler.

One might object to this third argument: Are there not logically necessary *propositions*? And if so, is not logical necessity plainly a property of these propositions? Does the third argument not simply beg the question whether there are logically necessary propositions? Russell's fourth argument addresses this issue. In his 1919 *Introduction to Mathematical Philosophy,* Russell says that "there was never any clear account of what [is] added to truth by the conception of necessity" (IMP 155). And since (at least for Russell) the only other option to necessary propositional truths is necessary propositional functions, necessity is a property of propositional functions. Clearly, we are adding to the concept of a propositional function when we say that a propositional function is always true, since not every propositional function is always true.

Russell suggests this fourth argument as early as 1903 in *Principles of Mathematics* (POM 454); it probably was inspired by Moore's paper, "Necessity" (Moore 1900: 296).

This concludes my presentation of the four reasons or arguments Russell has, explicitly or implicitly, for accepting MDL. The first two are implicit in his discussions of existence. The second two are explicit. I think that all four arguments beg the question. I think that there are plenty of perfectly fine predicates which apply to everything and which are nonetheless informative or "worth saying," since they express different senses. Russell himself holds that intensionally different propositional functions can be extensionally equivalent. Indeed, this defines one of the four main senses in which he uses the word "intension." And his argument that propositions cannot be necessary or possible because "Propositions are only true or false" (PLA 231) begs the question. Why, he himself allows propositions to be analytically true, true in virtue of form, and tautologous! Do these notions add nothing to the notion of logical truth, not to mention to the notion of truth? This is Russell criticism, not Russell scholarship.

I shall now critically examine the fourth argument for MDL in more detail. I see it as implying that if we are to say significantly of a true proposition that it is necessary, then the content of the concept of necessity must be clearly different from that of the concept of truth. And I think most of us would agree that logical necessity ought to be something different from truth, since some but not all truths are logically necessary. But Russell views all truths as timeless and unchanging. What sort of logical necessity could be significantly or even intelligibly different from the timelessness of the truth of any true proposition? Could any true proposition ever become false? And if not, then could any true proposition be more necessary than it already is? But surely logical truths are necessary in a way that logically contingent truths are not! The difficulty of specifying the difference may be measured by the fact that some philosophers explain logically necessary truths as those truths which are timelessly true, and others might explain them as those truths which are not only timelessly true, but which also describe timeless relations among timeless entities. There are, of course, other solutions available to Russell, and he uses them. He explains logical truth as truth in virtue of form, and also as tautology, which at least for the moment we may equate with analyticity. He does not know how to explain these notions further in turn, but either one of them would seem enough at least to distinguish logical truth from nonlogical truth, and without having to admit timeless relations among timeless entities, even though he himself does admit timeless logical universals, including timeless logical relations. And either truth in virtue of logical form or truth in virtue of logical tautology would seem to be plausible, and perhaps even reasonably and fairly clear, candidates for explaining logical necessity, even if it might not be easy to explain them further in turn.

Russell explains logical truth as truth in virtue of form, or (perhaps alternatively) as tautology (PLA 239–40). But surely Russell intends this precisely as his "account of what [is] added to truth by the conception of [logical] necessity" (IMP 155). Surely tautology and truth in virtue of form are in effect his stand-ins, explications, or even analyses, of logical necessity, even if he does not say so. Let us now ask in turn, What is added to tautology or truth in virtue of form by the conception of necessity? Naturally, the meaning of "logically necessary" can scarcely be *identified* with the meaning of either "tautological" or "true in virtue of form." Otherwise the theories that all logically necessary truths are tautological or are true in virtue of form would not be significant.

But here, it seems we cannot find what is added at all. And perhaps this is why Russell does not explain logical *necessity* in terms of tautology or truth in virtue of form, *pace* the early Wittgenstein. But by the same token, either of those notions would be an informative analysis of logical necessity. This is just the paradox of analysis. Russell's insistence that the intensional meaning of "necessary" and "true" be clearly *different* is really a requirement that analyzing logically necessary truth as logical truth be clearly *informative*. If there is "no clear account of what [is] added to truth by the conception of necessity" (IMP 155), then we do *not* have a clearly informative analysis of logically necessary truth as logical truth. But Russell's proposed analyses of logical truth, namely as "truth in virtue of form" or as "tautology," are not synonymous with "logical necessity" any more than they are with "logical truth." Thus if lack of synonymity is his argument against analyzing logical necessity as being any of those notions, then it should also be his argument against analyzing logical truth as being any of those notions. But I think we (and he) would not really want any of these notions to be synonymous with each other, on pain of precluding any informative analyses here. If I am right, then we (and he) could set up a chain of three progressively deeper informative analyses. First, we could analyze logical necessity as logical truth. Second, we could analyze logical truth in turn as tautology. And third, we could analyze tautology in turn as truth in virtue of form. This order of analysis might seem to provide the best progressively greater intellectual illumination. But surely tautology and truth in virtue of logical form are more properly, appropriately, and directly analyses of logical necessity than of logical truth. Surely they more fitly or aptly state what logical necessity is than what logical truth is. Thus when Russell says he is analyzing logical truth as truth in virtue of form or as tautology, I think he is in effect getting things backwards. Since those notions are in effect his stand-ins for logical necessity, in effect he is explaining logical truth as logical necessity, instead of the other way around. On his own views about informative analysis, I think what he should have said is that: (1) Logical tautology is best and most properly used to analyze logical necessity. (2) Logical tautology is best analyzed in turn as truth in virtue of logical form. (3) Theses (1) and (2) provide a reasonably clear account, or at any rate the clearest account we can give at this time, of what the concept of logical necessity adds to the concept of logical truth. (4) Because the concept of logical necessity does add something to the concept of logical truth, the concepts are clearly different, and we can informatively analyze logical necessity as logical truth. (5) And this is what really justifies the chain of three progressively deeper analyses proposed above. Now, if I am right that on Russell's own views, this is what he should have more properly (and more deeply) said, then his explicit analysis of logical truth as either truth in virtue of logical form or as logical tautology is his implicit though somewhat confused way of analyzing logical necessity after all.

The third argument for MDL remains justified by the fourth in that the third argument is logically consistent with attributing logical necessity to propositions in the eliminative sense I just explained. We want necessity in the mere sense of being true of all things to apply to propositional functions, but we consistently also want there to be a propositional logical necessity that applies to logical truths, and that can be logically analyzed away as being logical truth. And in effect, but without saying so, Russell achieves that when he analyzes logical truth as truth in virtue of form or as tautology. He says instead that he is dumping the concept of propositional logical necessity as not clearly adding anything to the concept of truth. But I think that is not only not his best approach, according to his own views on logical analysis, but even somewhat disingenuous. Could he really have missed that truth in virtue of form and tautology are just as viable as analyses of logical necessity as they are of logical truth, and more properly, appropriately, and directly so? Ironically, charity in interpretation seems to work to his disadvantage here. On my view, he is looking rather awkward. But this concerns only his presentation, not the substance of his views, on my interpretation of what is really going on. My charity, if that is the proper word, works to the advantage of the substance of his views. It makes his analyses deeper and more apt than he says. Thus my criticism is really an improvement.

All of Russell's other great eliminative logical analyses are informative: arithmetic as logic (basically following and crediting Frege); his neutral monism of bodies and minds as series of sensations (basically following and crediting first William James, and later on, David Hume); and space and time as relations among events (basically following and crediting Whitehead). *Principia* consists of two basic analyses: mathematics as logic, following and crediting Frege; and geometry in turn as arithmetic, following and crediting Descartes on analytic geometry. (Thus what is most original about Russell is not so much his basic analyses of things, but the way he unifies them as instances of a single comprehensive theory of logical analysis.) So what is the problem with saying he also informatively analyzes away his most basic logical modalities as properties of propositional functions in MDL, or even to saying he can informatively analyze propositional logical necessity as truth in virtue of form or as tautology? Or *is* he analyzing propositional logical necessity as those notions, but confusedly?

This concludes my critical examination of Russell's fourth argument for MDL.

Five Seeming Logical Howlers in MDL

MDL seems to commit at least five logical howlers.

The first howler of which Russell might be accused is that he has conflated logical modality with epistemic modality in his account. We can know *Fs* if we know that *s* exists and that *F*( ) is always true. But this is only epistemic necessity. But I trust that the distinction between MDL and MDL–E lays that howler to rest. Indeed, it is Russell who can and does claim to be *detecting* this confusion of logic with epistemology (PLA 254; AMA 173). I shall discuss this howler no further.

Second, Alfred Jules Ayer says that in "The Philosophy of Logical Atomism," Russell has "carelessly" conflated accidental generality with universal necessity by defining them both as the same property, being true for all values (Ayer 1971: 92). The way out of the second howler seems to be to rely on the clearer *The Analysis of Matter*. There necessity seems to be the property of being true for all *possible* values.

But what does Russell mean by "possible value"? What, indeed, does he mean by "value"? Does he mean the *argument* which a propositional function may take? For Russell, values of *propositional functions* are not arguments except, just possibly, in *Principles of Mathematics* and *An Inquiry into Meaning and Truth* (POM 20–21, 29; IMT 203). Usually propositional functions map arguments onto values for Russell. But Russell's values are not truth-values. Nor are they particulars at all. Russell's values are *propositions.* Russell makes this clear in *Principia Mathematica* (PM xx, 15, 38).[1] Thus Russell's possible values of propositional functions are possible propositions.

We are thus back to the notion of a proposition. On what I called option (1), on which propositions are spoken or written events, the second howler remains a howler unless we admit merely possible events. On option (2), on which there are arguably infinitely many actual propositions which have never been spoken or written, the howler might be silenced. For on option (2), the distinction between actual and possible propositions, that is, the distinction between actual and possible values of propositional functions, might arguably be collapsed. If all constituents of propositions are timeless, these distinctions arguably collapse on either option. But this way out would seem easier to accept on option (2), at least at first glance.

In *Principia* Russell does seem to collapse the distinction between a proposition and a possible proposition when he asserts that the totality of a function's values "comes to the same thing" as "the totality of its possible arguments [i.e. values of *variables*]" (PM 24). He also says that "all possible propositions are obtainable from matrices by the process of turning the arguments to the matrices into apparent [i.e. bound] variables" (PM 51). He speaks repeatedly of possible values (possible propositions) (PM 40, 41, 50), as well as of possible arguments (PM 39, 40, 41, 54). Possible arguments of functions are possible values of their variables. But by "possible argument" Russell means only 'actual argument which a given function logically can take'. The 1908 Russell says of the idea of a function which is always true, "A linguistically convenient expression for this idea is: 'φx is true for all *possible* values of x', a possible value being understood to be one for which φx is significant," and says, "A function is said to be significant for the argument x if it has a value (i.e. yields a true or false proposition) for this argument" (LK 72n). In *Principia*, a significant proposition is a proposition which is either true or false.

In his 1940 *Inquiry,* Russell advances a theory of syntactically possible sentences (IMT 37, 170, 182). On this theory every significant sentence has syntactic possibility, which Russell admits "is perhaps narrower than logical possibility" (IMT 170). Indeed, it may well be that some logical possibilities cannot be stated in language. This is only to say that it seems not logically necessary that every logical possibility be statable in language. (Syntactic possibility, in the sense of being syntactically well-formed, is certainly a *wider* notion than that of logical possibility, since every logical *falsehood* we can state is syntactically well-formed.) But ignoring this issue, "Jones is a unicorn" would appear to be syntactically possible just in case "Jones is a horse" and "Jones has a horn" are possible. For in general, if atomic sentences are syntactically possible, then their molecular combinations are syntactically possible (IMT 195). This takes much pressure off. But one may still ask whether, say, "Spot S is red" is syntactically possible if red is an atomic quality and nothing is red? Russell's answer seems to be that: (i) if spot S^* is, say, green, then "Spot S^* is green" is significant, i.e., syntactically possible; (ii) green and red belong to "the same category" (IMT 182), and similarly for spots S and S^*; thus (iii) substituting "red" for "green" and "S" for "S^*" results in an equally significant (syntactically possible) statement. But what if nothing has any color? What if everything is invisible? Is "S is red" then syntactically possible? For Russell, if "S is not red" is significant (syntactically possible), then so is "S is red" (IMT 172, 195). Again, in *Principia* "significant" means 'true or false'.

Now, in the 1940 *Inquiry*, propositions are beliefs that sentences express (IMT 171). So that we might explicate "possible value" as "possible proposition," where "possible proposition" is "belief expressible by a syntactically possible sentence." But Russell speaks of possible values many times in this book (IMT 82,

197, 201, 260, 264). And what he means seems to be not propositions but *arguments*, i.e., members of the class determined by a propositional function (IMT 203, 260). This seems to indicate that Russell's possible arguments are nothing more than those actual arguments which a function syntactically can take. Thus our proposed explication seems not to be faithful to this particular work. Worse, the explication does not refute or even change Russell's conception of a propositional function as *logically* possible if it is sometimes true. That is, "Jones is a unicorn" may be a *syntactically* possible sentence expressing a *syntactically* possible proposition. But since no such proposition is *true*, that is, since nothing *is* a unicorn, "*x* is a unicorn" still remains a *logically* impossible propositional function for Russell. In fact, he still offers a version of MDL in this fairly late work (IMT 37). And on the sentential level, logically impossible statements are syntactically well-formed.

The third howler is that on MDL, a propositional function is not possible unless at least one actual argument satisfies it. But consider the propositional function "*x* is a unicorn". Since nothing actually is a unicorn, "*x* is a unicorn" is an impossible function for Russell. But surely that should be a possible propositional function, since its values are logically contingent propositions. A closely related question is: Since "Jones is a unicorn" is synthetic in logical form, does this mean that impossible propositional functions can have synthetic *a posteriori* propositions as values?

Russell seems perfectly serious about necessary functions' having synthetic *a posteriori* propositions as values. He gives two examples in "On the Notion of Cause":

> For example, "if Socrates is a man, Socrates is mortal," is necessary if Socrates is chosen as argument, but not if *man* or *mortal* is chosen. Again, "if Socrates is a man, Plato is mortal" will be necessary if either Socrates or *man* is chosen as argument, but not if Plato or *mortal* is chosen.... (ONC 177)

The first example is a material implication whose consequent will be made true by any argument substituted for its logical subject which, when substituted for the logical subject of the antecedent as well, makes the antecedent true. The second example is a material implication whose true consequent is left untouched while the antecedent's subject or predicate is changed to any other argument. Russell then states this definition:

> A proposition is *necessary* with respect to a given constituent if it remains true when that constituent is

altered in any way compatible with the proposition remaining significant. (ONC 177)

This text inspired my formalization of MDL in sentence S; compare "The Philosophy of Logical Atomism" on possibility with respect to a given constituent (PLA 255). The obvious implication is that a genuinely necessary proposition is necessary with respect to *all* of its constituents (and in this 1913 article, with respect to all possible substitute constituents). But on this new definition, "Smith is a unicorn" is *still* impossible with respect to Smith. For "Smith is *not* a unicorn" is *necessary* with respect to Smith, in the absence of actual unicorns.

A fourth howler is that on MDL, which propositional functions are logically possible depends on contingent matters such as whether unicorns exist.

A fifth howler is that on MDL, the distinction between material and logical implication seems to collapse, since "(x) $(Fx \supset Gx)$" is true if and only if $Fx \supset Gx$ is necessary (R. Bradley 1992: 15; Rescher 1979a: 141–42; Sprigge 1979: 168).

The third howler seems to be the heart of the matter, so I shall discuss mainly that one. Let us consider two ways out of the third howler. The first way out would be to show that in some sense only actual things are possible things. Then if there are no unicorns, it really *is* impossible for anything to be a unicorn. This way out is challenging, but has ancient roots in Parmenides and Diodorus Cronus which we may cultivate.

The second way out is to show that in some sense only actual propositions (values) are possible propositions (values). Now things themselves may or may not be propositional constituents (or arguments). If not, then propositional constituents are either (a) names or descriptions or (b) nonlinguistic universals expressible by descriptions. These are respectively options (1) and (2) concerning propositions (see page 38); descriptions include both definite and indefinite descriptions. On (a), there is the howler that someday a new description may be spoken or written which, when substituted as an argument, makes a supposedly necessary proposition false. The escape would be to show that only actual expressions are possible expressions. But this takes us back to the first way out. On (b), if universals are timeless beings, then only actual universals are possible constituents. But even admitting the universal *unicorn* as the determinate constituent of the indefinite description "*x* is a unicorn," the description "*x* is a unicorn" is still impossible in MDL if there are no existent unicorns. Again we are driven back to the first way out.

The notion of a possible argument retains importance. For if the only arguments not to satisfy "*x* is a unicorn" are those which do not even appear to be the right sort of thing, such as apples, then there will be no interesting existence assertions at all. And the only sort of argument that can appear to satisfy "*x* is a unicorn" without succeeding would be a horse, a stuffed dummy unicorn, or some such. Russell says that "if we meet something which may be a man or may be an angel in disguise, it comes within the scope of 'all men are mortal'...." (LK 70). A phantom or hallucinated unicorn, i.e. a wild sense-datum, presented as such, would not appear to do this, for a single sense-datum as such, unaccompanied by correlated data or even by any expectations of such correlated data, is far too unlike what we call an animal. Similarly, up to some indeterminate point, for small wild groups of sense-data, i.e., "well-integrated" or even mass hallucinations.

Russell's Possible Worlds Talk

Thus MDL has its difficulties: five active howlers and a challenging way out. But Russell's intentions concerning MDL are serious. For it seems clear that he intends that MDL help analyze possible worlds talk. Seven facts support this.

First, MDL is intended at the very least to be logically compatible with possible worlds talk. Russell states MDL in at least eight published works from 1906 to 1940.[2] Russell affirms "Leibniz's multiplicity of possible worlds" or uses possible worlds talk himself in at least nine published works from 1907 to 1948.[3] Not only do these two time periods overlap, but these two classes of works have at least four members in common. The inevitable suggestion is that Russell intended MDL to be consistent with, if not also to help analyze, possible worlds talk.

The four members in common are these (the MDL cites are in chapter 1):

In *Mysticism and Logic* (1918), Russell states MDL and says, "[M]athematics takes us...into the region of absolute necessity, to which not only the actual world, but every possible world, must conform...." (MAL 55).

In "The Philosophy of Logical Atomism" (1918), Russell states MDL and says, "[A] world containing more than 30,000 things and a world containing fewer than 30,000 things are both possible...." (PLA 240).

In *Introduction to Mathematical Philosophy* (1919), Russell states MDL and says:

> Pure logic, and pure mathematics (which is the same thing), aims at being true, in Leibnizian phraseology, in

> all possible worlds, not only in this higgeldy-piggeldy job-lot of a world in which chance has imprisoned us....
>
> Viewed from this strictly logical point of view, I do not see any reason to believe that the axiom of reducibility is logically necessary, which is what would be meant by saying that it is true in all possible worlds. (IMP 192–93)

Here he regards possible worlds talk as mere "phraseology." He makes it clear elsewhere in *Introduction* that on his "robust sense of reality," there is no such thing as a merely possible object, let alone a merely possible world (IMP 168–70). Yet *in* this mere phraseology, he expressly states what we all know, that logical necessity is definable as truth in all possible worlds. Therefore, *as* a matter of mere talk, this is just how he understands logical necessity. And this is precisely a way of defining logical necessity and at the same time eliminatively analyzing modality away as mere talk.

Also in *Introduction*, he says that "Among 'possible' worlds, in the Leibnizian sense, there will be worlds having one, two, three,...individuals" (IMP 203). See also "A world in which..." (IMP 196).

In *The Analysis of Matter* (1927), Russell states MDL and says, "Given a world consisting of particulars x, y, z,....interrelated in various ways, the world which results from the obliteration of x must be logically possible."[4]

Russell upholds the conception of possible worlds in five more works, the first four of which are bracketed by publications of MDL. In *The Problems of Philosophy*, Russell says:

> Moreover, we feel some quality of *necessity* about the proposition 'two plus two are four', which is absent from even the best attested empirical generalizations. Such generalizations always remain mere facts: we feel that there might be a world in which they were false, though in the actual world they happen to be true. In any possible world, on the contrary, we feel that two and two would be four: this is not a mere fact, but a necessity to which everything actual and possible must conform. (PP 78; see 56)

In *Our Knowledge of the External World*, Russell says:

> Between philosophy and mathematics there is a certain affinity, in the fact that both are general and *a priori*. Neither of them asserts propositions which, like those of history and geography, depend on the actual concrete facts being just what they are. We may illustrate this

characteristic by means of Leibniz's conception of the
many possible worlds, of which one only is *actual*. In all
the many possible worlds, philosophy and mathematics
will be the same; the differences will be only in respect
of those particular facts which are chronicled by the
descriptive sciences. (KEW 144–45)

In *The Analysis of Mind* Russell says, "Leibniz's conception of
many possible worlds seems to accord much better [than the
coherence theory of truth] with modern logic and with the practical
empiricism which is now universal" (AMI 268). In his introduction
to the 1938 edition of *Principles of Mathematics,* Russell says:

It is easy to imagine universes in which [Zermelo's
axiom of selection] would be true, and it is impossible to
prove that there are possible universes in which it would
be false; but it is also impossible (at least, so I believe)
to prove that there are no possible universes in which it
would be false. (POM viii)

In *Human Knowledge*, Russell says, "I hold, rather, to Leibniz's
multiplicity of possible worlds" (HK 157).

Second, in *Our Knowledge of the External World,* Russell
explicitly admits possible sense-data (KEW 68) as described ideals
providing theoretical continuity for constructions (KEW 89). These
seem to be logical constructions of sense-data, which constructions
probably usually correspond to actual unsensed sensibilia. And in
his articles published in the same year, possible sense-data would
seem best glossed simply as unsensed sensibilia which you would
sense if you were in the right situation. Thus Russell admits
possible sense-data in one nonmodal sense, and might admit them
in two. This appears to collapse actual and possible sensibilia.

Third, in *The Analysis of Mind* Russell says, "We may
identify propositions in general with the contents of actual and
possible beliefs" (AMI 241). This definition succeeds in equating
actual propositions with possible ones. He admonishes us that
"logic is not interested in what people do in fact believe, but only
in the conditions which determine the truth or falsehood of possible
beliefs" (AMI 241–42). This is part and parcel of his view that
logic is fully or *"completely general"* (PLA 237, Russell's
emphasis).

Fourth, in *An Inquiry into Meaning and Truth* Russell
admits not only actual but also possible object words, and allows us
to "suppose an indefinite extension of our perceptive faculties" to
be able to admit a sufficiently large range of possible object words
(IMT 66).

Fifth, in *Human Knowledge* Russell holds that it is significant to assert that there are facts we cannot imagine, since the contradictory of that assertion is significant, and by molecular combination, the negation of every significant assertion is also significant (HK 153).

Sixth, in *Human Knowledge* Russell says we can imagine general facts where we cannot imagine particular facts which would be their instances (HK 153). Facts three through six suggest that and how Russell would find even worlds with *simple* alien objects (not: entities) not in the actual world descriptively possible.

Seventh, in *An Introduction to Mathematical Philosophy* Russell summarizes his discussion of modality not as if he rejects modality, but as if he limits its scope to propositional functions: "In all such cases, as in regard to modality in general, the propositional function is relevant" (IMP 166). Likewise in "The Philosophy of Logical Atomism," where he says, "It is important to realize that the whole doctrine of modality only applies to propositional functions, not to propositions" (PLA 231).

The seven facts just described collectively support the view that Russell intends that MDL help analyze possible worlds talk, no doubt through the basic role MDL plays in his definition of a proposition's being necessary with respect to a given constituent, and, through that, in his thesis that an analytic proposition is one that is necessary with respect to all its propositional constituents. Of course, MDL is basic to FG–MDL and FG–MDL* alike.

Raymond Bradley claims that MDL, Russell's "official" theory of modality, is incompatible with his "unofficial" uses of possible worlds talk, since the former uses a restricted domain of only actual items while the latter uses an unrestricted domain of both actual and nonactual items. Thus Bradley finds Russell guilty of "confused and inconsistent thinking," and "unable to stick with the restricted account" when it comes to distinguishing mathematics from natural science, or to explaining how it is a contingent fact how many objects exist in the actual world. For Bradley the bottom line is that the official account precludes what David Lewis calls "alien objects," i.e., objects found only in worlds other than the actual world, and thus precludes the possibility that there might have been more objects than there are (R. Bradley 1992: 16–17, 25–28, 56–60). But as we saw in the fourth, fifth, and sixth views I just described, Russell allows *descriptions* of alien *particulars* in ways easily compatible with the restricted domain of MDL. This is precisely how Russell disposes of Meinong in "On Denoting": by analyzing away definite descriptions of alien particulars. Of course, Russell does not admit alien particulars as entities.

Unfortunately, Bradley cites only a few of the papers and books in which Russell discusses modality. Thus Bradley is unable to show us the big picture. Bradley seems unaware of how often either MDL or possible worlds talk appear in Russell, of the thirty-six year period (1905–40) over which they overlap, or even of how often both occur in the very same works. Bradley says, "Oddly," Russell used possible worlds talk in 1912 (PP 78) "some six years before" converting to his official account of modality (R. Bradley 1992: 25–26). But as we saw, Russell published MDL six years *before* 1912, as well as six years after; there was no "conversion" to MDL in 1918. Bradley says that the unofficial account "is precisely the one that, in both 'The Philosophy of Logical Atomism' [1918] and *Introduction to Mathematical Philosophy* [1919], Russell repudiates in favor of his official accounts of modality and existence" (R. Bradley 1992: 25–26). But as we saw, the "unofficial account" and "official account" *both* occur in those very two works, as well as in two others (PLA 231, 240, 255; IMP 165 192, 203; see even R. Bradley 1992: 16–17). Thus there was no "repudiation" of possible worlds talk in 1918. Indeed, as we saw earlier, possible worlds talk continues to appear in 1927, 1938, and 1948. Bradley says, "Whereas Russell only rarely concedes (on what I have called 'unofficial' occasions) that there are possible worlds and possible objects that are nonactual, Wittgenstein, in both the *Notebooks* and the *Tractatus*, makes it clear that, for him" this is so (R. Bradley 1992: 60). But as we saw, Russell uses possible worlds talk (not: admits possible worlds) in nine works—over four times as many as Bradley lists for Wittgenstein.

Was Russell really so blind as to admit such blatantly incompatible views on alien objects as Bradley says he does, and to do so over a period of thirty-six years, and four times in the very same published works? Or is it Bradley who is blind due to his very limited research on Russell? Granted, I am invoking a principle of charity in Russell interpretation here. But it seems to me that I am invoking scarcely any charity at all, given the huge number of texts and the long period of time involved, not to mention Russell's logical ability.

Can the seven facts I described explain how Russell almost single-handedly stunted the development of modal logic for two generations? Are they not instead facts amplifying Russell's own modal theory? Surely Russell is not so confused as to use possible worlds talk repeatedly to clarify important views, yet advance a modal theory which, far from explaining such talk in turn, is logically inconsistent with it. It seems by far the best course to dig deeper than Russell's explicit MDL theory and delve into his ontology. For it is an ontological question whether only actual things are possible.

3

Russell's Three-Level Theory of Modality

Russell's full modal theory (not: modal logic) may be seen in his 1918 "The Philosophy of Logical Atomism." There Russell uses the expression "exists" (and its synonyms "is real," "has being," and "is actual") in three senses. First I shall explain these three senses. Then I shall show that each of these three senses is or has a corresponding dimension of modal understanding for Russell. That is, just as I shall show that Russell's ontology is rich, having a depth of three levels, I shall show that Russell's modal theory is equally rich, having a corresponding depth of three levels. I shall call this full modal theory "MDL {1,2,3}." MDL emerges as merely MDL {3}, the shallowest level in MDL {1,2,3}. MDL {1,2,3} is the full theoretical basis of Russell's implicit alethic modal logics.

Russell's three senses of "exists" are as follows:

The primary sense of "exists" is Parmenidean. It is that to be is not to be nothing. For Russell, there is no such thing as a merely possible thing. Since everything that is at all has being in this sense, it is a nonclassificatory, anti-Meinongian sense. Indeed, it is Russell's robust sense of reality (PLA 189, 216, 220, 248, 252; ONA 149; OD 55).

The secondary sense of "exists" is Berkeleyan and Humean. It is that to be real is to be correlated with other particulars (sense-data) in appropriate ways. Tables, persons, and electrons are real in this sense. Phantoms and hallucinations, or wild particulars, are not (PLA 157–58, 274–75).

The tertiary sense of "exists" is Fregean. It concerns the logical structure of existence assertions. It is that existence is a property of a propositional function, namely, the property of being sometimes satisfied (PLA 232).

These three senses are not rival views, but work together as follows: (1) The relation of the primary sense to the secondary is that particulars (sense-data) which exist in the primary sense are the fundamental building blocks for the logical constructions or fictions which exist in the secondary sense. (2) The relation of the primary sense to the tertiary sense is that conforming to the fundamental principle that all things exist in the primary sense is for Russell a logical requirement of the adequacy of any analysis of the tertiary assertoric sense (IMP 170; PLA 248, 252; ONA 153).

That is, we may *say* that certain things do not exist, but we must not construe our assertions as being *about* nonexistent things. This is just what led to Russell's theory of the elimination of definite descriptions from our assertions. (3) The relation of the secondary sense to the tertiary sense is that of truth-condition or truth-maker to truth. In the case of persons, tables, and electrons, if not also numbers, the applicability of the secondary sense of "exists" is the sufficient condition of which ordinary (pre-philosophical) things satisfy propositional functions for Russell, i.e., of which existence assertions concerning ordinary things are *true* (see PLA 271–77).

Definitions of the different kinds of logical fiction proceed by identity conditions, that is, by defining what it is to have the same thing of that kind, at least for tables, persons, and numbers (PLA 273, 277). How can logical fictions be informatively identified for Russell? The very same particulars (sense-data) found to be correlated with an initially given particular confirm both informative existence and informative identity propositions about the logical fiction in question. In contrast, we know single particulars through acquaintance, and we know them so completely that all true identity statements whose subject-terms are logically proper names of particulars are tautologous and therefore uninformative (PLA 246; OD 46).

It is crucial to understand that these three senses of "exists," or three levels of Russell's theory of existence, are not three kinds of ontological status which things may have. More precisely, the primary sense does indicate a kind of ontological status, but the other two senses do not. I shall explain this for each sense in turn.

The 1918 Russell believes things which exist in the primary sense "have the most complete and perfect and absolute reality that anything can have" (PLA 274). This is not only an ontological status, but it is his most basic, if not also his only, ontological status.

The 1918 Russell believes that what we ordinarily say exists in the secondary sense is, at least as far as we could ever know, merely a logical construction or logical fiction, i.e. literally nothing. It is crucial to realize that the secondary sense is a merely conventional, or as some say, a purely nominal sense, of the word "exists." It implies no ontological commitment to ordinary things. In fact, ontological commitment is expressly denied. This sense concerns Russell's eliminative logical analyses of what ordinary people believe and say to be real—and Russell holds that what they believe and say in this regard is (as far as we can know) mistaken (PLA 274). People believe that lions exist. Russell holds that this belief *may* be true; but as far as we can ever know from sense experience, a lion is not an entity, but a temporal series of classes of sensed and unsensed sensibilia (sensed sensibilia are sense-data). And series and classes are literally nothing. Therefore, to say that lions exist in the secondary sense is to deny ontological status to lions. However, Russell is willing to recognize it is *true* that, in a purely ordinary and conventional sense of "exists," lions, as opposed to unicorns, exist. And that is a very important dialectical consideration in Russell's ontology. Russell is not just paying lip service to a mere ordinary language use. He is accommodating our powerful common-sense belief in the existence of lions in a philosophically interesting way. That may even be an influence of Moore's common-sense realism. But a lion is at least a fiction *bene fundata*, to borrow a phrase from Leibniz. Russell analyzes lions as lawful patterns of physically real sensed and unsensed sensibilia.

Existence in the tertiary sense is not an ontological status because it is not a property of things. It is the existential quantifier. It is a propositional function predicated of propositional functions, and propositional functions are nothing (PLA 230–34). Nor does it confer ontological status on the values of the variables it binds in true statements, at least on my interpretation. I believe that by the time of *Principia*, Russell abandons the thesis that to be is to be the value of a variable. On my view, when we say, e.g., "Lions exist," the post-1910 Russell does not consider us to be ontologically committed to lions. Instead he analyzes "exists" as 'not always false', which has a veridical meaning-in-use, not an existential meaning-in-use. This complements the veridical secondary sense of "exists" as follows. Lions and unicorns alike have no ontological status and are nothing, but "Lions exist" is true and "Unicorns exist" is false in the common-sensical secondary sense of "exist." The tertiary sense of "exist" used in "Lions exist" merely reflects that fact. Even quantifying over sense-data in "Sense-data exist" does not ontologically *commit* us to sense-data, though sense-data *are* as real as anything can be. It is logically proper names which ontologically commit us to sense-data, since such names cannot name nothing. This is, I admit, a controversial view of Russell's individual quantifier. Here, I can only describe what my view is. I offer eight arguments for my view in another book (Dejnožka 2003: chapter 5, section 2). This concludes my explanation of the three senses of "exists" in "The Philosophy of Logical Atomism." For more, see Dejnožka (2003: 124–27; 1988: 156–58).

I now wish to distinguish correspondingly between: (i) a primary sense of "possible" in which all and only existents are possible; (ii) a secondary sense of "possible" in which only groups of correlated particulars are possible; and (iii) a tertiary sense of "possible" which concerns the logical structure of possibility assertions. We have already seen that for Russell, possibility in the tertiary sense is predicated of propositional functions. Just as the primary sense of "exists" is the deepest sense in Russell's theory of being, so the primary sense of "possible" is the deepest sense in Russell's theory of modality. Paradoxically, neither primary sense is significantly assertable, even though they respectively ground Russell's tertiary theories of existential and of modal assertion.

On the primary level, there are three modal features of interest. I shall discuss only particulars (sense-data), but the features would also apply to simple universals, if these exist only *in re* for the 1918 Russell. (i) The primary existence of a sense-particular is logically contingent and can be known only through empirical acquaintance (PLA 199, 202–3). What is more, sense-particulars are absolutely contingent in the sense that their existence does not logically depend on the existence of any other particular. "Each particular might happen to be the whole universe" (PLA 202). (ii) There is no such thing as a merely possible particular (PLA 259, 274). Even brief hallucinations or phantoms are "wild" particulars which are as real as anything can be. For all sense-particulars "have the most complete and perfect and absolute reality that anything can have" (PLA 274). Even what Russell calls "ideal" particulars are not Meinongian nonexistents (KEW 68, 69). They exist, or at least probably exist, as unsensed sensibilia. They are not merely possible particulars. They are probably actual particulars we could possibly sense. Descriptions of them are logical fictions, and belong to the primary level only out of logical courtesy; but they themselves belong to the primary level. Therefore to be true of all particulars is to be true of all possible particulars. (iii) The existence of a particular is transcendentally necessary with respect to thought and language. That is, it is logically necessary that a particular exist in the primary sense, in order for us to be acquainted with it or to name it. That is, an acquaintance must be an acquaintance *with* something, and a logically proper name must be a name *of* something. For Russell, the meaning of a logically proper name literally *is* the particular it names (PLA 194–95, 200–1, 243). We may call modal feature (iii) of particulars "transcendental Parmenidean" rigid designation.

To be acquainted with a particular is to single it out. And singling out is our most direct form of identification (Wiggins 1970: 315). Thus the transcendental necessity of the existence of particulars named by logically proper names implies that the problem of trans-world identity does not arise for such particulars (compare Kripke 1980: 19, 41–46). No ontological commitment to merely possible particulars or possible worlds is implied. In light of all this, we may call Russell a "transcendental haecceitist."[3]

We may say that logically proper names *both* denote and refer, and that reference is a species of denotation; but the only other sort of denotation would be the nonreferring denotation of descriptions. Thus it seems more proper simply to say that logically proper names refer. Logically speaking, definite descriptions can only be an approximation to reference in the sense of naming what we single out in acquaintance (cognitive identification).

I discuss transcendental necessity further in chapter 4.

Concerning modal feature (iii) of particulars, logically proper names of particulars are implicitly rigid designators in the Kripke's weak sense (Kripke 1980: 48–49). That is, they refer to the same particulars in all possible worlds in which those particulars exist. There are three reasons why this is so.

(a) To change the particular is to change the meaning of its name. This semantic fact logically implies that for Russell, logically proper names rigidly designate the particulars we are acquainted with in Kripke's weak sense. David Pears saw reason (a) sixteen years before I did (Pears 1972a: 37–38, 41), and speculated about reason (b) as well (Pears 1972a: 42).[1]

(b) One completely knows the meanings of the names of the particulars one is acquainted with (PLA 202–3). And it is logically impossible that one can completely know *m* if one might be mistaken about *m*'s identity. Those two epistemic facts logically imply that for Russell, logically proper names rigidly designate the particulars we are acquainted with. This is not affected by Russell's agreeing with Henri Poincaré that color indistinguishability is intransitive (KEW 112–14. For intransitivity is a relation known by description, not a sense-particular known by acquaintance (KEW 114). See also my (2003: 202–4).

(c) Russell's logically proper names do not denote; they *refer*. In terms of Keith Donnellan's distinction between referring and attributive uses of expressions, they are certainly not attributive. That is, the logically proper name "this" does not at all mean "the sense-datum now before me, whichever sense-datum it may be." It singles out this specific sense-datum as opposed to any others (see Donnellan 1972). Tyler Burge argues for (c) by appealing to (a) as follows: "Genuinely singular expressions could not fail to refer; for their 'meaning'...was their referent" (Burge 1983: 80). Indeed, "The over-arching unstated motive of Russell's approach was to produce a semantical theory purely in terms of reference, dispensing with Frege's notion of sense" (Burge 1983: 80). Even descriptions make "reference...to attributes" (Burge 1983: 80).

Thus, for at least three reasons, far from being "plainly incompatible with our direct intuitions of rigidity," as Kripke claims, Russell's theory implicitly endorses these intuitions on its deepest level.[2]

Granted, "logically proper name" in Russell's sense is not synonymous with "rigid designator." But the two expressions seem to be logically equivalent, and seem to involve much the same sort of direct reference (Recanati 1993: 10–11, 19–21; Peacocke 1975: 111; Sainsbury 1979: 63). Indeed, their non-synonomy makes my interpretation an informative analysis, and a theoretical definition.

Russell's logically proper names of sense-data are not rigid designators in Kripke's other sense, which Kripke calls strong rigid designation (Kripke 1980: 48–49). That is, they do not designate the same particulars in all possible worlds. That is because sense-data are not necessary existents. More than that, a logically proper name of a sense-datum which does not exist in world W will lack not only denotation but even meaning in W, since the sense-datum is both the meaning and the denotation of the name. However, if the 1903–12 Russell has logically proper names of *ante rem* universals, they would be strong rigid designators, since for him such universals are timeless beings in all possible worlds.[4]

On the secondary level, there are correspondingly three modal features of ordinary things (groups of correlated particulars). (i) The secondary existence of a group of correlated particulars, qua secondary existence, is not absolutely contingent, but plainly relatively contingent. That is, it logically depends on the primary existence of the sensed and unsensed sensibilia comprising the group. Absolute and relative contingency are subdivisions of logical contingency. (ii) Correspondingly, there is a clear sense of relative structural possibility of secondary existence given the primary existence of some particulars. That is, the secondary existence of an ordinary thing depends on both the possibility and the actuality of these existing particulars' being suitably correlated together. Michael Loux and William Lycan would call this a "nonmodal theory of combinatorial actualism" (Loux 1979: 48–49, 60 n.48).[5] (iii) The secondary existence of ordinary things is not transcendentally necessary. Trees are not required to exist just because we think about them, are acquainted with certain tree-like particulars, or pre-philosophically believe we name them with ordinary names. If we think we see a tree and there is no tree, then the object of our acquaintance is not a nonexistent tree, but a hallucinated or phantom, a wild *real* particular (PLA 275), or at best insufficiently many wild particulars that are insufficiently lawfully related. And for Russell, ordinary names are covert descriptions which need not be satisfied.

The possibility of secondary existence is just the possibility of informative identification. For the very particulars which, if they were suitably correlated, would constitute the secondary existence of an ordinary thing, would also be the basis of its informative identifiability. This is a form of *ens et unum convertuntur*, but only nominally so, since ordinary things are logical fictions.

On the tertiary level, there are two possible versions of MDL. On version (i), we count things as arguments of propositional functions. On version (ii), we count propositional constituents, as opposed to things, as the arguments. Here a propositional function is satisfied if and only if some propositional constituent which is an argument for it *corresponds to* some thing that exists. Russell's examples of actual arguments are always version (i). But possible *sense-data* as arguments, whether they are unsensed sensibilia or merely ideal posits, could only be version (ii). Whether they are posited theoretical ideals or actual unsensed sensibilia, they are not propositional constituents because Russell's principle of acquaintance would then require our acquaintance with them. Now, Russell does hold that we can describe things we are acquainted with (PP 53). Presumably this would include actual sense-data. I see no reason why we could not also describe possible sense-data, in either sense of "possible sense-datum." After all, Russell uses descriptions to explain away how we seem to talk about merely possible items, so why not use them to explain away how we seem to talk about unsensed sensibilia too? On version (iia) constituents are descriptions, or "incomplete symbols" (PLA 253). On version (iib) each constituent would be "composed wholly of particulars and universals with which we are acquainted" (PP 59).

The three modal features of the tertiary level are: (i) A propositional function is possible if and only if it is sometimes true. (ii) A propositional function is possible, therefore, if and only if it describes something which has secondary reality (in the case of ordinary things), or something which has primary reality (in the case of simple existents). This latter point reflects primary level modal feature (ii). (iii) A tertiary existence assertion may be said to have transcendental necessity in a derivative sense if and only if it is logically deducible by existential quantification over a logically proper name.

MDL {1,2,3} is a 'no entity without identity' theory on every level. On MDL {1}, the primary level, the existence and objectual identity of sense-data are and can only be given together in acquaintance. For sense-data are replaced by different sense-data if and only if they sensibly alter their appearance (PLA 203). MDL {2}, the secondary level, is based on a combinatorial atomism on which the very particulars (sensed and unsensed sensibilia) which constitute the correlative reality of an ordinary thing also constitute its informative identity. On MDL {3}, the tertiary level, the "fundamental idea" behind both existence and possibility is 'not always false'. Thus existence and possibility are two sides of the same coin. They are one and the same property of propositional functions, and differ only in intension. Therefore, an existence-identity connection obtains if and only if it is also a possibility-identity connection.

That is my description of MDL {1,2,3}. When we dig beneath the surface, we find that Russell has a rich and sophisticated theory of modality. Perhaps not everything is as fully or as clearly stated as we would like. Only primary level modal features (i)-(iii) and tertiary level modal feature (i) are explicitly stated. But the rest seem logically implicit in Russell's views. Thus it would seem that MDL {1,2,3} articulates Russell's full theory of modality as well as can be done.

The first way out of the third howler may now be explained. The third howler was that "*x* is a unicorn" is impossible on Russell's view, even though the existence of unicorns is logically contingent. Now, anything that exists in the secondary sense logically must also have existence in the primary sense. That is, any group of correlated particulars logically must not be nothing. For Russell, they are complex real facts (PLA 183, 192, 216). It follows that anything that has secondary existence not only has secondary level modal features (i)–(iii) relative to its secondary existence, but also has primary level modal features (i)–(iii) relative to its primary existence. In particular, unicorns, if there were any, would have primary level modal feature (ii). That is, on the primary level, the only possible unicorns are actual unicorns. And since there are no actual unicorns, unicorns *are* impossible on *that* level. And this is logically consistent with primary level modal feature (i) of absolutely contingent existence, which any actual unicorns would have. Considered as a temporal series of sensed and unsensed sense-particulars, a unicorn would have secondary existence relative to the particulars that constitute it. But considered as the sense-particulars themselves, or more precisely, as the particulars standing in the relations they do, so as to compose what Russell would call a real fact, its existence would be absolute in the sense that the unicorn could happen to be the whole existent universe.

It is perfectly consistent to assert that actual horses are absolutely contingent beings on the primary level of existence, yet are relatively contingent beings on the secondary level of existence. This concerns modal feature (i) of each of those two levels. With respect to modal feature (ii) on the secondary level of existence, unicorns are combinatorially both possible and contingent. And this is perfectly consistent with their being impossible according to modal feature (ii) on the primary level of existence. Finally, if some superior being outside space-time could be acquainted with a horse as an infinitely complex four-dimensional sense-datum and name it "H3", that being logically could assert that H3's primary existence is transcendentally necessary relative to the logically proper name "H3". But described as a horse, H3's secondary existence would not be transcendentally necessary relative to its description.

Let us now consider the third howler as it would concern the tertiary level of modal assertion. Here we simply specify the version of modal assertion and the modal level, primary or secondary, which is being asserted. For example, consider version (i) with respect to the primary level. Version (i) faithfully reflects the primary level modal features of things, since on it arguments simply *are* things. This includes primary level feature (ii). So that on version (i) with respect to primary modality, "*x* is a unicorn" is indeed impossible. For if we run through all ordinary things, we simply find no unicorns (no groups of suitably correlated particulars). So to speak, on the primary level there is nothing to *be* a unicorn.

On version (ii), the same explanation is applied *mutatis mutandis* to those things which *correspond* to the propositional constituents which are arguments for propositional functions. I conclude that Russell's reply to the third howler has been made clear by our triple distinction among modal levels.

Leila Haaparanta claims that MDL {3}, which I also more simply call MDL, is a temporal modal logic which quantifies "over time" (Haaparanta 1985: 38), "since a propositional function is called necessary, when it is always true, and possible, when it is sometimes true" (Haaparanta 1985: 46 n.26). There are three problems with Haaparanta's view.

The first problem is that MDL {3} is not a sentential modal logic in the first place, but simply a trio of definitions which eliminatively analyze certain modal predicates as certain alethic (truth-related) predicates. Thus there simply is no assignment of modal operators to sentences in MDL {3}.

The second problem is that, even ignoring that basic point and pretending Haaparanta is right that MDL {3} is a modal logic, she would still be wrong to think it could be a *temporal* modal logic. For Russell says in *Principia*, "We use 'always' as meaning 'in all cases', not 'at all times'. Similarly 'sometimes' will mean 'in some cases'" (PM 41n). Thus MDL {3} is not even a temporal modal *theory*, much less a temporal modal *logic*. Indeed, Russell expressly excludes time-variables from true general scientific laws due to his "principle of the irrelevance of the time" (ONC 198). Thus for Russell as well as Moore, it is "more accurate" to say that "truths are true at no moment" than to say "that they are always true" (Moore 1900: 297).

The third problem is, How is Haaparanta going to quantify over times themselves so as to result in modal statements for Russell—"At all times *t*, some time *x* is such that at *t*, *x* = the time

1994?" Does the particular time, the year 1994, exist at all times? Did 1994 exist in 1993 or in 1995? Or does she merely mean to say that "The Eiffel Tower is in Paris" was always true and will always be true? If so, does she take it to be a necessary truth that the Eiffel Tower is in Paris? Or that the Eiffel Tower always was in Paris and always will be? Or can she distinguish the timeless truth of truth in general from the timeless truth of necessary truth in particular? (This is part of Aristotle's problem of the sea battle.) Does she mean to saddle Russell with these views?

I see all three problems with Haaparanta's view as fatal.[6]

I would like to correct a mistake in Russell's presentation of his own views on existence. Russell says that tertiary existence is the *most* fundamental notion, while I have presented it as the *least* fundamental notion. Russell says in *Introduction*, "The notion of 'existence' has several forms...; but the fundamental form is that which is derived immediately from the notion of 'sometimes true'....Other meanings are either derived from this, or embody mere confusion of thought" (IMP 164). But he only means that it is the most fundamental notion *within logic*. For just a few pages later, he says against Meinong, "[W]e shall insist that...nothing 'unreal' is to be admitted....[T]here *is* nothing unreal" (IMP 170, Russell's emphasis). This is Russell's primary, Parmenidean sense of existence / being / reality. Yet it is clearly not derived from the form of existence which is derived from "sometimes true." Such a derivation is not even possible. Is Russell forgetting his own critique of Meinong? The derivation is the other way around. It is precisely because everything exists (is real) in ontology that in logic it is uninformative to assert that a certain something exists (is real), not to mention impossible to assert truly that a certain something does not exist, unless we make existence a property of propositional functions. I explained this in chapter 2 as the first of the four reasons why Russell would make modality a property of propositional functions (see pages 38–39).

The only other interpretation I can think of is that Russell does think his view that everything is real is strictly nonsense, but important nonsense, and is therefore, to borrow Wittgenstein's metaphor (T 6.54), in effect a ladder that must be climbed up till we get the right view in logic, and then we can discard the ladder. And while Russell rejects the sort of logical verificationism that is the basis of Wittgenstein's ladder metaphor, he does find many traditional views about existence to be categorially confused. But I reject this alternative interpretation because there is no hint of it in Russell here. Far from it, his theory that all things are real is very clear and intelligible, and so is his critique of Meinong for admitting unreal things. There is no indication whatsoever that he thinks that his own view that there is no such thing as a merely possible object is categorially confused, or is to be discarded when we get the right view in logic. There is no hint that he thinks that his own critique of Meinong is based on a "mere confusion of thought," and is to be discarded when we have transcended it and attained a true view. I also reject this alternative interpretation out of charity, since the ladder metaphor is itself unintelligible and confused. For as Otto Neurath says, if you can't say it, you can't whistle it either.

Perhaps the best interpretation is this. Russell says he does not know how to define tautology at the end of *Introduction*. In effect he ends the book at that point because he has pushed the analysis as far as he can. But the end of the book takes us back to the beginning. There he says it is equally possible that we can either arrive at ultimate simples or always be able to push the analysis one step further (IMP 4). His considered view is:

> This is a question which it is not necessary for us to decide; for our purposes it is sufficient to observe that, since human powers are finite, the definitions known to us must always begin somewhere, with terms undefined for the moment, though perhaps not permanently. (IMP 4)

The phrase "for the moment" is exactly the same as at the end of the book. And so we see that for Russell, tautology is his undefined starting point for the moment. Much the same may be said for MDL {1}, the primary, Parmenidean level of modality. That is his starting point for the analysis of modality, at least for the moment. But his primary Parmenidean beings need not be ultimate simples in the least. They only need to be the sense-data we name or think about. That implies that we are acquainted with them, but not that they are simple.

4

The Ontological Foundation

I shall now discuss the primary level of Russell's theory of modality, MDL {1}, in detail. Willard Van Orman Quine notes that Russell "stopped talking of subsistence [being as opposed to existence]...by 1914" (Quine 1971: 10). This is correct but glosses over the three major changes in Russell's theory of being from 1903 to 1914. Russell subscribed to seven Parmenidean theories of being in his career: (1) being is an entity, 1903; (2) being is the world of universals, 1912; (3) being is general timelessness, 1914; (4) primary being is transcendentally necessary for logical atoms, 1918; (5) primary being is transcendentally necessary for object words, 1940–48; (6) qualities are substantive (atoms), 1940–59. I omit *Principia*'s ontology, 1910, which I discuss at length in my (2003: 165–86).

The main trend from theory (1) to theory (6) has been from the most literally Parmenidean to the least. In theories (4) and (5), while Russell rejects being as itself an entity, he accepts what may be called "transcendental being," which is transcendentally necessary but literally nothing, at least if propositional functions are nothing. It is asserted by "$(\exists x)(x = a)$," which is always true where "a" is a logically proper name. It concerns modal feature (iii) of MDL {1}. An account of Russell's arguments for transcendental being in theories (4) and (5) is crucial to understanding Russell's motives for MDL {1}. Theory (6) is intended as a metaphysical improvement of theory (4), replacing sets of particular instances of universal sensible qualities with single repeatable sensible qualities which are "scattered" (Quine's term) sensible particulars.

Russell's Six Main Ontologies

I shall now describe these six ontologies in more detail.

First, there is the ontology of the 1903 *Principles of Mathematics*. Here Russell distinguishes being and beings (entities) from existence and existents. All entities have being, but only some entities exist, i.e., are existents. All existents are observable or causal particulars, such as sounds, smells, material points, and selves. Besides existents, entities also include: nonexistent thinkable particulars such as Pegasus; unobservable acausal particulars such as spatial and temporal points which play a role in scientific description of the actual world; logical objects; and universals. It might seem that Russell must restrict class membership to existents, so as to exclude nonexistent entities from the null class and from other classes, e.g., to exclude Pegasus from the class of horses (POM 74–76, 81). Only in this way, so one might think, would his arithmetic succeed. For *no* entities belong to the null class, and Pegasus would belong to the class of *nonexistent* horses. All entities, or terms, are so many identifiable, classifiable, "immutable and indestructible" Parmenidean beings (POM 44). If so, then there is no reason why counting and arithmetic should not apply across the board to all entities, whether they exist or not. As Frege says, following Locke and Leibniz, arithmetic is supremely general (FA 21, 31).

Being is "being *simpliciter*" (POM 449). The intension of "is" is radically different from the intension of "exists." Russell discusses being in positive terms: "Being is that which belongs to every conceivable term, to every possible object of thought..." (POM 449). Thus he uses two overlapping sorts of positive terms. First, he uses cognitive terms such as *conceivable* and *thought.* Second, he uses modal terms such as *conceivable* and *possible.* But it does not follow from these descriptions that the 1903 Russell's being is at all intrinsically conceptual or modal in character. Russell speaks in *Principles of Mathematics* of analysis, definition, characterization, and criteria (POM 27, 111–12, 137, 161, 185–86, 200, 249, 530). Now being is being *simpliciter*, so that it cannot be *analyzed* at all, much less in conceptual or modal terms. And being is presupposed by every term (POM 43, 451), so it is not definable at all, much less in conceptual or modal terms. On the face of it, Russell's discussion is a characterization which includes criteria or at least "marks" of being. One might think that there is no need for a criterion of being, since everything has being. But there is a need to tell which expressions name entities, since at least nine sorts of expressions are not names of entities in *Principles*.[1]

Thus in *Principles,* being is *intensionally* (intrinsically) nonmodal and nonconceptual. Thus Russell seems to be suggesting that being is merely *co-extensive* with being thinkable and being possible. Russell does hold that having being is co-extensive with being immutable, since he says that "every term is immutable and indestructible," term being Russell's "widest word" (POM 43–44).[2] All this seems to show that the immutability of terms qua terms is not due to any *de re* necessity of being qua being, but only to the timelessness of being. Of course terms must *have* being, but this by itself does not make them *immutable*; if Russell had admitted mutable terms, they too would have being qua terms. And of course the *entity* being could not fail to exist, and is in that sense a *de re* necessary entity, no doubt much like logical entities in general; but this is not why all terms are *immutable*. Again, the real issue is the theory of change. I see no reason to think that Russell ever changes his mind about the intrinsically nonmodal character of being.

Russell's 1903 being is Parmenidean in a thoroughly realist sense. He himself later wrote, "I had been a realist in the scholastic or Platonic sense; I had thought that cardinal integers, for instance, had a timeless being" (POM 13).

Though the 1903 Russell might have inferred the being of all terms from the timelessness of all truths, Russell did have an explanation of how an actual chair is logically contingent (POM 47–48; see Klemke 1971a: 422). Nonetheless, the difficulty of distinguishing logical necessity from timelessness may have helped lead him to adopt Moore's theory that necessity applies only to implications between propositions, specifically, that necessity is a matter of degrees of implicative necessity between propositions (POM 454). But timelessness would not apply *only* to implications between propositions. Thus timelessness cannot be *identified* with logical necessity, on Moore's theory of logical necessity. And there are no degrees of timelessness in any case.

The second Parmenidean theory of being Russell offers is in his 1912 *The Problems of Philosophy*. In *Problems*, existents and entities are mutually exclusive classes. No existents are entities, and no entities are existents. All and only particulars are existents. All and only universals are entities. Particulars come into and pass away from existence, while universals have timeless being. This is roughly Plato's two-tier world: a Heraclitean world of change, and a Parmenidean world of timeless universals in which the things of the Heraclitean world participate (PP 100). Here there is still a strong connection to Parmenidean being in the realist sense, but only for universals. "The world of universals...may also be described as the world of being. The world of being is unchangeable, rigid, exact..." (PP 100; see Quinton 1972: 103–4).

The third theory of Parmenidean being is given in the 1914 *Our Knowledge of the External World*. Russell quotes Parmenides' argument: "'It needs must be that what can be thought and spoken is; for it is possible for it to be, and it is not possible for what is nothing to be'" (KEW 130–31). Russell notes that Parmenides takes this to imply that there is a single changeless real entity, being, behind an illusory world of changing appearances, with time itself being the main illusion. Then Russell says:

> A truer image of the world, I think, is obtained by picturing things as entering into the stream of time from an eternal world outside, than from a view which regards time as the devouring tyrant of all that is. (KEW 131)

Here, the world of apparent change has timeless being, and time is like a door the static world passes through, creating the illusion that things are really changing. Thus Parmenides' argument now leads not to an entity, being, as in 1903, nor to a realm of timeless universals, as in 1912, but to the whole apparently changing world as timeless. This timeless world is more embracing than the realm of timeless universals, since it also embraces particulars. Here time is truly Plato's "moving face of eternity." This is where Russell finally ceases to oppose being to existence, as Quine notes (Quine 1971: 10).

The heart of the theory of universals is that one property can have many instances. As Butchvarov describes the theory, it is an Identity Theory of entities which remain identical across different instantiations (Butchvarov 1966: chapters 2, 4). As Butchvarov says, a universal is an important sense a potential being. That is, "a universal quality is *potentially* the quality of an individual thing" (Butchvarov 1966: 196). An *ante rem* universal carries within itself the logical possibility of being instantiated, regardless of whether it is actually instantiated or not, except for self-inconsistent complex universals such as *round and square* (Butchvarov 1966: 188–97). Talk of "potentiality" is often vague and obscure, but here it only means 'logically can be instantiated'. It is unlike talk of the causal potential of an acorn to become an oak.

Anthony Quinton omits the whole third theory from his account of Russell's views on necessity (Quinton 1972: 103–4). But the 1914 "Mysticism and Logic" essay shows Russell's great interest in it. Here Russell sees timelessness as due to Parmenides' denial of plurality: past, present, future would be a plurality. Russell claims that he does not know whether the Parmenidean One is real. But he argues against the reliability of mystical intuition of such reality. He mentions that the basis of the doctrine of Parmenidean Being is Parmenides' logical argument as to the impossibility of nonbeing. Russell then goes on to consider the unreality of time as a *separate* issue from that of unity and plurality. There the discussion is almost identical with the one in *External World* (MAL 10–20).

Transcendental Parmenideanism, feature (iii) of the primary modal level, is Russell's fourth theory. Russell holds that his theory that "one" and "being" are predicable of descriptions destroys the being of Parmenides and Plato (LK 370). Yet being remains basic to Russell's own theory, at least transcendentally on the primary level, in transcendental Parmenidean rigid designation.

By "transcendental" I mean a theory about what is, which is inferred from considerations about thought and language. For language to be thus and such, the world must be so and so. Thought and language are thus and such; therefore the world is so and so. Russell's transcendental theory is: Acquaintances and names must be *of* something at some ultimate level. We have acquaintances and names of certain sorts; thus it must be that certain things exist. "Transcendental being" is being which is inferred by means of a transcendental theory. Transcendental being is "transcendentally necessary" if the inference is logically valid. This is what I mean by transcendental necessity.

Concerning "The Philosophy of Logical Atomism," the essay in which MDL {1,2,3} is most fully present, David Pears gives well the standard account of why Russell's logical atoms 'must' exist. It is that all analysis of what complex propositions are about must come to an end with simples that exist (Pears 1972a: 28–29). That is, given that there are complexes, there must be existent simples. Though Russell himself says in that work that there need not be ultimate simples, the line of thought concerned affects that work, and the transcendental aspect is obvious. Pears clearly separates this logical issue from Russell's empiricism of identifying 'working simples' with sense-data (Pears 1972a: 37–38).[3] I disagree with Pears' view that Moore's argument against Russell's claim that simple sense-data must exist "demolished" Russell's claim (Pears 1972a: 38). Moore says you can "always say with truth of [a] sense-datum..., 'This might not have existed'" (Moore 1966: 125). Pears goes on to say that the most that can be said for Russell is that "if a particular is dubbed '*a*', it is a pragmatic contradiction to continue with the words '...does not exist'" (Pears 1972a: 39). Pears then adds that "if the dubbing is *correct,* the particular must exist" (Pears 1972a: 39). This last remark suggests what is really wrong with Moore's criticism. Moore is right but misses the mark. Russell establishes only the transcendental necessity, not the intrinsic necessity, of simples' existing. Russell says, "Each [sensible] particular might happen to be the whole universe" (PLA 202); and this makes it very clear by implication that he holds that all simple empirical particulars are logically contingent (PLA 202). Concerning modal features (i) and (iii) of the primary level of modality, Moore shows only that (i) is correct, and does not even see (iii). Pears' inference from dubbing to existing is not merely pragmatic. It is also transcendental. On transcendental argument #21 below, it is also logically valid. Note that for Russell, there is no distinction between dubbing and correct dubbing. This is implied by the nature of transcendental necessity.

In his 1945 *A History of Western Philosophy,* Russell gives a statement of what I call transcendental Parmenideanism. First, Russell quotes Parmenides' argument exactly as he did in 1914 (see page 67). Then Russell says:

> The essence of the argument is: When you think, you think *of* something; when you use a name, it must be the name *of* something. Therefore both thought and language require objects outside themselves....This is the first example in philosophy of an argument from thought and language to the world at large. It cannot of course be accepted as valid, but it is worth while to see what element of truth it contains....[The element of truth is that] it is obvious that, in most cases, we are not speaking of words, but of what the words mean. And this brings us back to the argument of Parmenides, that if a word can be used significantly it must mean *something*, not nothing, and therefore what the word means must in some sense exist.... (HWP 49)

Thus Russell finds that Parmenides was the first transcendental Parmenidean. Russell continues:

> What subsequent philosophy, down to quite modern times, accepted from Parmenides, was not the impossibility of all change, which was too violent a paradox, but the indestructibility of substance. (HWP 52)

Russell goes on to reject both substance and the related notion of essence as "a transference to metaphysics of what is only a linguistic convenience" (HWP 201). He says in the later 1948 *Human Knowledge* that "proper names, as ordinarily understood, are ghosts of substances" (HK 73; see IMT 32). But in the earlier 1918 "The Philosophy of Logical Atomism," Russell says that each particular:

> stands entirely alone and is completely self-subsistent. It has that sort of self-subsistence that used to belong to substance, except that it usually only persists through a very short time, so far as our experience goes....In that respect particulars differ from the old substances but in their logical position they do not. (PLA 204)

The 1918 work is closer to Parmenides; in it particulars, not proper names, are Russell's replacements for the substantial atoms of neo-Parmenidean ancient atomism.

Thus there are two types of transcendental Parmenideanism Russell has held: the 1918 version and the 1948 version. These are theories (4) and (5) respectively. Both theories are forms of neo-Parmenidean atomism. (4) may be called literal neo-Parmenidean atomism, and (5), nominal neo-Parmenidean atomism. This must not be confused with realism versus nominalism in the problem of universals, which is a very different problem.

I suspect that it is the transcendental character of Russell's fourth ontology that has largely kept it hidden, besides Russell's synonymous use of "has being," "is real," and "exists." Like the three earlier Parmenidean ontologies, it might have led to many nonmodal actualist theories of modality. Only such theories are ontologically eliminative of modality, as is Russell's theory MDL in terms of propositional functions and being sometimes true. Only in this sense is Russell "against" modality. But then all theories which offer significant explanations of modality are thus "against" modality. This is only our old friend, the paradox of analysis.

When Rescher says that Russell's program of logical constructions "provides yet another facet of his rejection of modality" (Rescher 1979a: 144), we see how completely Rescher has misunderstood Russell. For atomism is the whole basis of Russell's MDL {1,2,3}. It is precisely Russell's logical atoms which are named by names which must be *of* something, or are given in an acquaintance which must be *with* something, and which therefore cannot be nothing. If Russell had not admitted the Parmenidean transcendental necessity that all things have primary existence, he would never have developed his tertiary theory of existence and modality as properties of propositional functions.

Russell's Twenty-Three Arguments for Transcendental Parmenideanism

It is in the 1940–48 period that Russell embraces a fully systematic transcendental Parmenideanism. By my own count he presents, explicitly or implicitly, some twenty-three transcendental arguments that for psychology, epistemology, and language to be the way they are, there must be things out there which are something, not nothing. From language, Russell gives positive transcendental arguments concerning "primary language," and negative transcendental arguments concerning "secondary language." These are not languages in their own right; primary language is merely the set of words which are about extralinguistic existents, and secondary language consists of all other words, including words about words, as well as words not about anything, i.e., syncategorematic words, which Russell calls "incomplete." Nor must primary and secondary language be confused with the primary and secondary levels of MDL {1,2,3}. Primary or object language may be about either primary level or secondary level things. Secondary language includes tertiary level existence and modal assertions, since these predicate incomplete symbols of other incomplete symbols. The first six arguments concern matters which Russell regards not only as prelinguistic, but as prehuman (IMT 13–15; HK 94–95, 167).

Russell's twenty-three arguments are as follows.

(Psychological) Argument #1. There are no illusions of the senses, but only errors of interpretation (HK 167). Therefore sensations are as they appear to be. Therefore if sensations appear to exist, then they do exist, and are not nothing.

(Psychological) Argument #2. There is no act-theoretic distinction between a sensation and an object of sensation, or between a percept and an object of perception (IMT 114, 116, 119–20, 285, 329; HK 167–71, 205, 217–18). Therefore objects of sensation or perception are as they appear to be. And if they appear to be, then they exist and are not nothing.[4]

(Psychological) Argument #3. Perception cannot be pure interpretation, that is, interpretation that is *of* nothing. Therefore there must be something perceived which is not nothing (IMT 124–25).

(Conceptual) Argument #4. There must be a pure datum. For data cannot be conceptualization alone. Conceptualization must be *of* something (HK 167–70).

(Epistemological) Argument #5. Each datum has its own evidential weight which is not nothing. Otherwise knowledge will be impossible due to a vicious epistemic regress (IMT 124–25; see HK 157, 189–90). This weight is intrinsic, hence preconceptual.

(Classificatory) Argument #6. On pain of vicious infinite regress of classifications, there must be sensations which are preclassificatory (HK 423).

In all of the following arguments, Russell treats object words as nonexpectational, i.e., as meaning nothing beyond present perception, even though most object words, such as "cat," are in fact expectational, i.e., correlational. This concerns the secondary or correlational sense of "real" described in chapter 3.

(Primary Language) Argument #7. If there are no expectations going beyond present experience, then an object word simply, directly, and simultaneously both means and affirms the existence of some present sensation. An object word always asserts or indicates the presence of what it names (IMT 29). Therefore it has a simple affirmative nature and cannot involve denial. To deny the existence of what the object word affirms would *ipso facto* rob the object word of its very meaning, so that it would not be an object word at all.

(Primary Language) Argument #8. Since meaning in the primary language (object language) is causal, then with the right causal relation obtaining, it is tautological that there cannot be reference failure. That is, if an object word is caused to be uttered

by the object it means or names, then that object cannot be nothing, but must exist. Similarly, the truth of a judgment of perception is logically guaranteed by the causal relation it has to the fact it asserts (IMT 160). This is a causal theory of reference as rigid designation, antedating Kripke by some thirty years.

(Primary Language) Argument #9. Spontaneous language cannot lie (IMT 204–5). It is tautological that spontaneous speech expresses the speaker's state of mind (IMT 212, 215). Many object words are spontaneous. Therefore there are many sensations which are not nothing.

(Primary Language) Argument #10. In some object language assertions, the belief expressed and the fact indicated are the same state of mind. In such assertions, the possibility of falsehood "does not arise" (IMT 206). (This argument is of limited scope.)

(Primary Language) Argument #11. Language cannot be learned without an essential presupposition of correctness of meaning in teaching and learning situations. Indeed, the only possible error in primary language is social error, which is insignificant for our purposes (IMT 28; HK 116–17, 191).

(Primary Language) Argument #12. Language must begin with words that can be learned independently of other words. On pain of vicious infinite regress of verbal definitions, some words must be learned ostensively. Therefore there must be words whose meaning is external to language (IMT 25, 66, 126; HK 501–2).

(Primary Language) Argument #13. In the object language, truth is best defined as the assertion's being made about what it indicates. But then no object assertion can fail to be true, or can fail to be about something (IMT 206).

(Primary Language) Argument #14. All object words are names. And the use of expressions as names has an implication much like that intended by the ontological argument. That is, a name must be a name of something (IMT 32).

(Secondary Language) Argument #15. Lying, falsehood, and deliberate misleadingness require a consciousness of signs as signs. Therefore such linguistic acts are at most made about primary language in secondary language. Thus object words cannot be *deliberately* about nothing (IMT 62–64, 174, 204, 212). (This is a negative version of argument #9 about spontaneous language.)

(Secondary Language) Argument #16. A distinction between expressed significance (or belief) and fact indicated is needed to explain the logical possibility of falsehood. But such a distinction can only be made in secondary language, since it is about expression, and expression is language. Therefore all false existence assertions are in the secondary language, and there can be no such assertions in primary language (IMT 175–76, 183, 206).

(Secondary Language) Argument #17. All logical connectives, including negation, belong to secondary language (IMT 40–41, 64–65, 73–74, 212). Thus all denials across the board belong to secondary language. Thus all denials of existence belong to secondary language. Therefore denials of existence cannot be expressed in primary language.

(Secondary Language) Argument #18. The world can be described without employing negation (HK 500). (For) negation is not literally part of the world of observed particulars (HK 125). There is no such thing as a "not" going around which we can sense or experience. Therefore no denial of existence can be expressed in primary language.

(Secondary Language) Argument #19. Negation itself is on the most primitive level a *positive* inhibition of a *positive* response (HK 120–26). Thus there is no genuinely negative negation in the world for an object word to name. (If I may venture a criticism of Russell here, inhibition seems to remain negative even on his own analysis. For a response and its inhibition are logical contraries. For they logically cannot both be the case; and the negation in the word "cannot" is genuinely negative.)

(Secondary Language) Argument #20. Not only are logical connectives part of secondary language, but so is generalization. Existence assertions are generalizations. Thus they are secondary language (IMT 65, 88, 92–93). Denials of existence are negative existence assertions. Therefore they cannot be expressed in primary language. (This is a nice companion to argument #17.)

(Secondary Language) Argument #21. Existence assertions are tautologically implied by primary language assertions. That is because existence assertions are actually secondary language abstractions from the meaning of primary language, removing the sensational content of "*a*" and leaving only the empty syntactical form "*x*" of the expression "*a.*" Thus it is tautological that object words assertions are always about existents (IMT 142; HK 141). This is the argument that shows the deductively logical necessity of transcendental being, where transcendental being is expressed by "$(\exists x)(x = a)$", as well as that object words are rigid designators.

(Secondary Language) Argument #22. Just as the world can be described without negation or the other logical connectives, so too the world can be described without generalization, that is, without *some* and *all* (IMT 92–93; HK 501). Existence and universality are not things going about which we can sense or experience, and are not nameable in object language. Thus there is no object language "All cats" to be equivalent to a denial of the existential "Some noncats."

Secondary Language Argument #23. On the most primitive level existential and universal generalization are respectively like asserted disjunctions and conjunctions (HK 134). And *and* and *or* are not going about in the world. *And* obviously adds nothing to its conjuncts; and *or* has its prelinguistic psychological root in experienced hesitation between alternatives (IMT 83–86; HK 126, 134). Therefore there is no indefinitely long conjunction in the world that is even *like* universality for an object word to be about. Just as in argument #22, there is no object language "All cats."

This battery of arguments shows that the 1940–48 Russell is an extremely thoroughgoing transcendental Parmenidean. This is consistent with the fact that some of these arguments (#20–#23) reject existence as an entity in its own right, since transcendental Parmenideanism is not a theory about the ontological status of existence. It is important to gather these arguments in one place to show for once the full extent of Russell's commitment to the transcendental impossibility of nonbeing at the primary level of existence. For Russell himself did not do or show this. And it is too easy to be left with the impression that Russell's commitment to transcendental Parmenideanism is limited to the simple claim that a name must be the name of something. Even collecting arguments #7–#14 and #21 alone is worth while, since they are Russell's nine arguments that object words are rigid designators.

In any of the twenty-three arguments for transcendental Parmenideanism that concern existence in MDL, we may substitute "modality" for "existence." For existence assertions belong to secondary language, and existence assertions and modal assertions are intersubtitutable *salva analycitate* in MDL. That is because in MDL, Russell analyzes existence and possibility as the very same propositional function, 'is not always false' ('is sometimes true'). Note that this root notion involves truth and falsehood, which belong to secondary language. Of course, such modal assertions cannot make MDL a modal logic, since the modal expressions are predicates, not sentential operators.

Russell's sixth Parmenidean ontology is his 1940–59 modification of the substance tradition, which, we saw, he regards as Parmenidean. It is of interest to us here only as offering some new nameables, qualities, for theories (4) and (5) to concern. A quality "is a particular, not a universal," since it is an ultimate logical subject and has no instances (Russell 1989: 685). As ultimate logical subjects, qualities are "syntactically more akin to substances" than to universals, and may be rightly called "the stuff of the world" (MPD 127).

Again, this chapter is about the most fundamental level of Russell's ontology and theory of modality. Chapter 6 is on the shallowest level of his theory of modality, the logical level. Chapter 3 was on all three levels, including the intermediate level, and showed how all three levels work together as a unified theory of existence and a unified theory of modality, and as a unified theory of *both* existence and modality. The intermediate or secondary level is sufficiently covered in chapter 3.

5

Rescher's Case Against Russell

The reader will remember that V is the view that Russell ignored or was against modal logic, or at least that his views impeded the study of modality and the development of modal logic; and view V* is the denial of V. In chapters 2–4, I presented my case that Russell has a largely explicit theory of modality. I shall now examine the claims Nicholas Rescher makes on behalf of view V in his "Russell and Modal Logic," as it is only fair to consider the other side of the V–V* dispute—even though Rescher, for his part, does not consider our side at all.

First, Rescher sees Russell as "unwilling to recognize the merely possible (i.e. the *contingently* possible) as a distinct category" (Rescher 1979a: 139).—We saw in chapter 3 that Russell admits absolute contingency on the primary level of modality and relative contingency on the secondary, both being species of logical contingency. And Russell says he advocates the tertiary level of modality precisely because it makes necessity, possibility, and impossibility distinct (IMP 165).

Second, Rescher suggests that the "philosophical roots of the early Russell's discontent with mere factual truth" are found in "Spinozistic necessitarianism," adding that Russell is a "more or less classical" determinist (Rescher 1979a: 140).—In chapter 4 we saw that logical *fatalism*, i.e., the timelessness of truth, is basic to Russell's first and third theories of being, not *determinism*. As we saw in chapter 4, Russell's ontological roots concerning logical necessity are in Parmenides, not Spinoza. Russell has nothing like Spinoza's neo-scholastic, neo-Aristotelian conception of ontological essentialist causation. Russell's view of causation is thoroughly modern. He *rejects* causation, following Hume. We have not even mentioned causal determinism in describing MDL, FG–MDL, or FG–MDL*. MDL is an alethic theory, not a causal theory. It is about propositional functions such as 'always true'. FG–MDL and FG–MDL* are alethic logics, not causal logics. They are about logical necessity, not causal necessity. Our discussion of Russell on causal necessity will concern only causal logic MDL–C. In chapter 6, I find MDL–C implicit in Russell, as based on his Humean eliminative analysis of causation.

Third, Rescher says of Russell that "Like his hero, Spinoza, he was prepared to maintain that there will, in the final analysis, be a *collapse* of modality: that the actual itself is more or less necessary, so that the possible vanishes as a distinct category" (Rescher 1979a: 140).—There is an important sense in which this is true. Namely, for the post-1905 Russell the only possible objects are actual objects, in the sense that there are no merely possible objects. But this is only part of Russell's rich theory of modality. We saw in chapter 4 that the *fear* of collapse of the notions of timeless truth and of logical necessity is apparently Russell's motive for making necessity a Moorean relation of degrees of implicative necessity between propositions in *Principles* (POM 454), and for making necessity a property of propositional functions from 1905 on (IMP 165; AMA 170). Again, timelessness surely would not apply *only* to implications between propositions, so that it cannot be *identified* with logical necessity, on Moore's theory of logical necessity. And there are no degrees of timelessness in any case.

Rescher overlooks feature (i) of Russell's primary level of modality, that sense-particulars are logically contingent, and any one of them "might happen to be the whole universe" (PLA 202). From 1918 on, particulars with which we are acquainted are only *transcendentally* necessary, and only on the primary level of actuality and modality. For the 1912 Russell, only universals have timeless being; particulars are fleetingly contingent. Even the 1903 Russell, who admits necessary Parmenidean being, makes room for contingency (POM 47–48; see Klemke 1971a: 422). And the 1914 logical constructionist Russell very obviously does so as well, even though he assays being as general timelessness. It should be clear that even by 1914, Russell holds that any one sense-datum might happen to be the whole physical universe. In *Mysticism and Logic*, he says that sense-data are "extra-mental, purely physical" (MAL 123; see 118, 144, 145–47). In *External World*, he argues that "the immediate object of sense" is logically independent of our Self, since our Self is not part of the object (KEW 63; see 55, 62).

Fourth, Rescher says that "in mathematics it is altogether otiose to differentiate between the actual and the necessary, and there is no room at all for the contingently possible" (Rescher 1979a: 140). And if mathematics and logic are at bottom identical, then "a modal *logic* becomes almost a contradiction in terms" (Rescher 1979a: 141). Thus Russell's almost exclusive concern with mathematical logic is a strong reason why Russell was predisposed against modal logic (Rescher 1979a: 141).—Russell's own account of the matter is somewhat different. Russell states in the preface to *Principles of Mathematics* that mathematics is concerned not with actual objects but with "hypothetical objects" (POM xvii), and makes hypothetical assertions (POM 6).[1] Russell says:

> Thus in every proposition of pure mathematics...any
> conceivable entity may be substituted for any one of our
> variables without impairing the truth of our proposition.
> (POM 7; see KEW 148)

Thus Russell cannot even explain what mathematics *is* without introducing the very distinction between actual objects and merely possible objects which Rescher says he ignores. That Russell assays possible worlds as mere possible worlds talk does not detract from this point. Russell informally explains mathematics in terms of possible worlds as late as 1914 and 1938 (KEW 148; POM (2d ed.) viii).

Fifth, Rescher cites three points offered by Hugh MacColl which are "foundational" for modal logic:

> a. that there is a crucial difference between propositions
> that obtain merely *de facto* and those that obtain of
> necessity...
> b. that there is a crucial difference between a *material*
> implication and genuine implication...
> c. that a satisfactory logic of modality must distinguish
> between actually existing individuals and merely possi-
> ble ones.... (Rescher 1979a: 141–42)

Rescher then comments that "Russell, of course, would have none of this" (Rescher 1979a: 142). But Russell honors all three points, which I shall take up in order. In fact, he is quite close to MacColl.

(a) Rescher overlooks that Russell distinguishes between logical truths and synthetic *a priori* truths on the one hand, and logically contingent truths on the other. It is Carnap and Quine who question the analytic-synthetic distinction, not Russell. Carnap and Russell discussed the analytic-synthetic distinction. Russell never wholly abandons it, and he never abandons logical truth.

(b) Rescher overlooks Russell's threefold distinction among material implication, formal implication, and logical deducibility. I shall discuss this in detail in chapter 9, but for now the following remarks may suffice.

(b1) A material implication holds between two propositions if the antecedent is false or the consequent is true.

The relation of material implication must be distinguished from the relation of *true* material implication. The latter imposes a truth-*constraint* or truth-*filter* on material implication. In a true material implication, if the antecedent is true, then the consequent must be true as well. Russell is interested in *true* material implications because he is interested in giving not merely *valid* arguments, but *sound* arguments, which are valid arguments all of whose premises (including material implications) are *true*. In a *true* material implication, the subject-matter of the antecedent and the subject-matter of the consequent may be unrelated, but the truth-grounds of the antecedent must contain the truth-grounds of the consequent, and in that sense there is containment relevance.

(b2) A formal implication holds between classes of material implications in *Principles* and between pairs of propositional functions from 1906 on (POM 11–16, 16n; Russell 1906: 257; PM 7–9, 21; IMP 146–47, 163). In *Principia* Russell says, "A formal implication states that, for all possible values of *x*, if the hypothesis *x* is true, the conclusion *x* is true" (PM 21).[2] Thus in *Principia* a formal implication is simply a true conditional universal statement. That formal implications are necessary implications in MDL is clear in *Introduction to Mathematical Philosophy*. There Russell defines a formal implication as a propositional function of the form "φ*x* implies ψ*x*" which is always true, and then just two pages later defines a necessary propositional function as one which is always true (IMP 163, 165).

The relation of formal implication must be distinguished from the relation of *always true* formal implication. The latter imposes a truth-*constraint* or truth-*filter* on formal implication. In a true formal implication, if the antecedent is true, then the consequent must be true as well. In an *always true* formal implication, the subject-matter of the antecedent and the subject-matter of the consequent may be unrelated, but the truth-grounds of the antecedent must contain the truth-grounds of the consequent. This is truth-ground containment relevance.

On the primary Parmenidean level of Russell's theory of modality discussed in chapter 3, Russell can paraphrase subjunctive conditionals as mere *always true* formal implications. For if the formal implication is always true, then if any given instance of its antecedent *were* true, then the corresponding instance of its consequent *would* be true. Again, always true formal implications are *necessary* formal implications in MDL.

(b3) Russell distinguishes *both* material implication and formal implication from *deductively valid inference*. The former two can be known to be true if we already know that the antecedent is false or the consequent is true, while the latter must be otherwise knowable if it is not to be pointless (PM 20–21; IMP 152–53; Russell 1994a / ca. 1903–05: 515). An inference is known to be deductively valid by using laws of logic as rules of inference, and also, for the post-1922 Russell, by checking its truth-table.

All deductively valid general inferences can be rewritten as formal implications or conditional statements; the premisses simply become antecedents. But not all formal implications or conditional statements can be rewritten as deductively valid inferences. That is because formal implications include synthetic *a priori* statements, true scientific laws, and even accidental generalities.

Deductively valid inferences are not only rewritable as logically necessary conditional statements, but they also are subject to Russell's whole-part containment theory of deductive inference. Russell expressly endorses Wittgenstein's theory of whole-part truth-ground containment entailment, as we shall see in chapter 9. Russell's *Principia* thesis assertion operator emerges not only as his implicit necessity operator in FG–MDL and FG–MDL*, but also as his implicit entailment operator for conditional statements in RSL.

In *The Analysis of Matter*, Russell states his theory of deductive inference as that an existent cannot validly imply "any other existent except a part of itself," and characterizes deductive inference as C. I. Lewis's strict implication (AMA 199–200).

Further, as Andrew Ushenko observes, Russell virtually admits subjunctive conditionals as a legitimate kind of statement in the *Inquiry* (Ushenko 1989: 410–14). Besides a statement of MDL, which Ushenko quotes, the *Inquiry* includes a whole-part theory of deductive inference on which "the conclusion is part of the premisses," and which would support the use of subjunctive conditionals (IMT 37, 242).

Rescher is far from the only one to misunderstand Russell. Timothy Sprigge derides Russell's "infamous identification of material and logical implication" (Sprigge 1979: 168), and Raymond Bradley claims that MDL "precludes," and Russell "fails to draw any distinction between," material and logical implication (R. Bradley 1992: 15, 22); see Rescher 1979a: 141–42). Thus they too ignore Russell's repeatedly stated threefold distinction among material implication, formal implication, and logical deducibility. This is not to mention Russell's view that logical deducibility is strict implication. He never says that about material implication or formal implication!

I think their howler is laid to rest even by always *true* formal implication. For again, Russell has a sophisticated and complex theory on which there is a Parmenidean sense in which *always true* formal implications are necessary, based on primary level modal feature (ii), which Sprigge and Bradley overlook. But the main point is that Rescher, Sprigge, and Bradley all overlook Russell's repeatedly stated distinction between material and formal implication on the one hand and logical deducibility on the other.

(c) I come now to the last of Rescher's three points offered by MacColl. The whole point of Russell's theory of descriptions is to account for the distinction between actual and merely possible items without ontologically admitting alien objects, i.e., objects which exist only in merely possible worlds. Using descriptions,

Russell can safely speak about everything from possible sense-data (KEW 68) to possible spaces (ONA 146). Again, Russell informally explains mathematics in terms of possible worlds talk as late as 1914 and 1938 (KEW 148; POM (2d ed.) viii).

Sixth, Rescher says that "one can search Russell's pages in vain for any recognition of" C. I. Lewis, Jan Łukasiewicz, and L. E. J. Brouwer (Rescher 1979a: 143). My view is that if Russell ignored the new work of others, it was largely because he was abandoning the whole field of mathematical logic due to exhaustion (Kreisel 1972: 173–74), and due to new activities (Wang 1986: 241). In 1943, Russell wrote that he would not reply to Kurt Gödel's "Russell's Mathematical Logic" because he (Russell) had not worked on such issues in "about eighteen years," i.e., since about 1925 (Russell 1989: 741). (Russell completed the second edition of *Principia* in 1925.) This is not to mention Russell's many nonphilosophical activities after 1918.

But let us "search Russell's pages" for the three figures Rescher cites. First, as Rescher himself points out, Łukasiewicz became well-known only "after the early 1920s" (Rescher 1979a: 143). Second, Rescher singles out Lewis's 1918 *Survey of Symbolic Logic* as a book about which Russell "preserves total silence," notably in the second edition of *Principia Mathematica* (Rescher 1979a: 143.)—But Russell and Whitehead recommend Lewis's 1918 book to the public in that very edition of *Principia* (PM xlvi). Russell probably missed Lewis's book in 1918 because he was in jail half that year, working on his own final book in mathematical logic, *Introduction to Mathematical Philosophy*. And Russell does discuss Lewis in *Introduction*. He discusses two papers by Lewis and rejects strict implication for a rather technical reason (IMP 153–54). But in *The Analysis of Matter,* Russell admits Lewis's notion of strict implication and uses it to clarify the notion of a possible world:

> On grounds of logic, I hold that nothing existent can imply any other existent except a part of itself, if implication is taken in the sense of what Professor C. I. Lewis calls "strict implication," which is the relevant sense for our present discussion. If this is true, it follows that any selection of things in the world might be absent, so far as self-contradiction is concerned. Given a world consisting of particulars *x, y, z....*interrelated in various ways, the world which follows from the obliteration of *x* must be logically possible. (AMA 199–200)

Russell says "if," but it should be clear that he does accept Lewis's notion of strict implication here. In these last two works, Lewis is cited under "Lewis" in the index.

Third, Rescher says that "Russell ignores totally the development of mathematical intuitionism, especially the writings of L. E. J. Brouwer" (Rescher 1979a: 143).—But Russell mentions Brouwer in at least five major works. Russell and Whitehead recommend Brouwer's work to the public on the same page of the second edition of *Principia* on which they recommend Lewis's *Survey*. Brouwer may also be found briefly in the Introduction to the 1938 second edition of *Principles of Mathematics*, in *Human Knowledge*, and in *My Philosophical Development*. Russell's fullest discussion of Brouwer is chapters 20–21 of the *Inquiry*. One may search Rescher's essay in vain for mention of these last three works. Rescher does not even seem to have looked in the index for Brouwer in these last three; Brouwer is listed under "Brouwer." There is also a sixth mention of Brouwer in Russell's 1950 paper, "Logical Positivism" (LK 374).

Is this how Rescher searched "Russell's pages in vain for any recognition" of modality? Modality is listed under "Modality" in the indexes in *Introduction to Mathematical Philosophy* and *The Analysis of Matter*.

Seventh, Rescher says that Russell's constructionism and "dismissal of all inferred entities and processes points towards a demise of potentialities, powers, and causal efficacy that pulls the rug out from the main motivation for recognizing possibility and contingency" (Rescher 1979a: 144). Rescher thus ignores the "chief purpose" (Russell 1989: xvii) of *Human Knowledge*, which is to show that inference as opposed to construction is necessary to science (HK xiv), that scientific construction involves concealed inferences (HK 139), and that we must admit at least five postulates of nondeductive epistemic inference to have any scientific knowledge at all (HK 487). And *The Problems of Philosophy* took an *exclusively* inductive approach toward the external world! Even in the citadel of Russellian constructionism, *Our Knowledge of the External World,* the whole last Lecture is on causal inference. There Russell *defines* "causal law" in terms of inference (KEW 164). On the whole it is hard to think of anyone who has discussed more hypothetical possibilities as to the physical and spatiotemporal structure of the world than Russell has. Indeed, Russell deems his logical constructions only metaphysically conservative hypothetical possibilities, utilizing Ockham's razor (KEW 164). Can this be the Russell whom Rescher denounces as dismissing "all inferred entities"?

Eighth, Rescher says, "The logical construction of something real will, quite evidently, be a construction from elements that are themselves altogether actual (real)" (Rescher 1979a: 144). If this is offered as a reason why Russell is against modality, then Rescher has it backwards. Russell's constructionism is the very heart of his combinatorial approach to modality. Saul A. Kripke, for one, would agree with such a combinatorial approach, certainly in general terms. Russell can use Kripke's combinatorial dice-throwing analogy to possible worlds as being only ways the actual world might have been (Kripke 1980: 15–20), and can use it just as easily as Kripke. The only difference is that Russell would compare the dice to sense-particulars, and compare the ways the dice can be thrown to the ways sense-particulars can be related, using actual sense-particulars and descriptions based on properties of actual sense-particulars. Thus, if Rescher thinks that Russell has no modal theory, then Rescher must consistently hold that Kripke has no modal theory either.

Russell's logical constructionism is explicitly modeled on Leibniz's theory of monads in a way that easily leads to Russell's combinatorial assay of Leibniz's full range of possible worlds (KEW 72–73, 89, 144–145). Russell's construction of the physical world is avowedly Leibnizian; it is constructed from both actual and theoretically ideal private worlds of monadic consciousnesses, i.e., from the perspectives of both actual and theoretically possible observers (KEW 72–73, 89).

Ninth, Rescher says that "Russell was deeply caught up in the ideology of two-valued truth-functionality" (Rescher 1979a: 144). Rescher adds that since the "critical fact" about modal concepts is that they are not truth-functional, Russell was bound to reject modality as illegitimate (Rescher 1979a: 144–145).

There are four main problems with this.

The first problem is that Russell does not reject but *relocates* modality with propositional functions precisely *because* propositions are only true or false (ONC 176; AMA 170). To say that Russell rejects modality when he makes modality a property of propositional functions is just as absurd as saying that he rejects existence when he makes existence a property of propositional functions. In both cases, Russell rejects only a certain naive theory about the subject in question.

The second problem is that Rescher is making it impossible for anyone to have a modal logic where necessity equates to logical truth, and the logic is two-valued and truth-functional.

The third problem is that Rescher overlooks Russell's theory of propositional attitudes, whose sole mission is to study non-truth-functional propositional functions. Russell expressly admits and discusses such functions right in *Principia*. *Principia* volume 1, Appendix C is entirely devoted to this issue. Russell's only flirtation with extensionalist logic occurs in the preface to the *second* edition of *Principia*, when he tentatively sketches a neo-Wittgensteinian logic in which all propositional functions are truth-functional (PM xiv). The flirtation vanishes in later works. Indeed, extensionalism soon vanishes in Wittgenstein himself, when he is no longer bewitched by his Tractarian picture of an extensionalist ideal logic.

The fourth problem is that, Rescher's view that Russell accepts only two-valued logic is a half-truth at best. Russell says, "[A]ll words outside logic and mathematics are vague: there are objects to which they are definitely applicable, and objects to which they are definitely inapplicable, but there are (or at least may be) intermediate objects concerning which we are uncertain whether they are applicable or not" (HK 497; see 146–48, 424). In fact, vague statements need have no truth-value (IMT 320). "Russell used the term 'vagueness' to describe multivalence" (Kosko 1993: 19). "Charles Peirce and Bertrand Russell and other logicians had used [the term 'vague'] to describe what we now call 'fuzzy'" (Kosko 1993: 137). Thus the inventor of fuzzy sets, Lotfi Zadeh, "called 'fuzzy' what Bertrand Russell and Jan Łukasiewicz and Max Black and others had called 'vague' or 'multivalued'" (Kosko 1993: 143; see 148). The truth is that Russell finds formal three-valued logic both "possible" and exciting (Russell 1989: 681–82). Russell says, "I do not think there is anything wrong with two-valued logic, nor yet with three-valued logic. Each is appropriate for its own class of problems" (Russell 1969: 135). Nor is this just the later Russell. Russell states his main views on vagueness in his 1923 paper entitled "Vagueness" (Russell 1923).

The modal operators in all of Russell's eight implicit modal logics are non-truth-functional, as we shall see in chapter 6. Thus they count among Russell's famous propositional attitudes, none of which is truth-functional, such as belief (PM 8; Appendix C; PLA 227).

Tenth, Rescher says Russell disliked modal logic because it was "*philosophically* uncongenial" to him (Rescher 1979a: 147). My reply is the first five chapters of this book.

Interestingly, Rescher denies that Russell has a modal theory in "Russell and Modal Logic," yet claims in another article, without giving any argument, that 'Nominalism' is Russell's theory of the "ontology of hard-core possibilities" (Rescher 1979: 180). Even this view of Rescher's, that Russell's theory of *possibilia* is linguistic, is correct only for the tertiary level of MDL {1,2,3}. For the sense-data of the primary level are not only nonlinguistic but prehuman, and so are the secondarily real things of the ordinary common-sense world (IMT 13, 81; HK 94–95). But Rescher's claim does fit well with Russell's use of descriptions to speak of merely possible ("alien") objects without admitting that there are any such things. Russell can speak of anything that Meinong can, and without admitting Meinong's jungle of nonexistents.

Some nine years after Rescher wrote "Russell and Modal Logic," Rescher very kindly agreed with me that he had not read much Russell (Rescher 1988). He was very generous to me.

6

Russell's Eight Implicit
Modal Logics

I discussed Russell's largely explicit theory of modality in chapters 1–5. I shall now discuss Russell's implicit modal logics and their strength. Once again, it goes without saying that Russell never says he has a modal logic, much less states one. If he had stated one, I would simply be quoting it. Instead, I shall have much work to do to show there are at least eight implicit logics in his writings. If I am right, then it will be very hard indeed to see Russell's philosophy as being structurally against modality, or as structurally impeding the development of modal logic.

Shahid Rahman says, "The best studied translation method is known as the *standard translation*, and it is quite compatible with Dejnožka's suggestions" (Rahman 2002: 101).

After some introductory remarks, I describe my two tests for imputing an implicit modal logic to Russell. Then I distinguish Russell's largely explicit modal *theory* from his implicit modal *logics* in general. Then I define eight modal logics which may be implicitly attributed to Russell, including four alethic (logical truth) logics, a causal logic, an epistemic logic, and two deontic (ethical) logics, and assess their strength. The implicit alethic logics are implicit interpretations of *Principia*; the later or mature two are retrospectively so.

Introductory Remarks

I find that all eight implicit modal logics are at least S5 in strength. An S5 logic is a logic that has these five axioms:

1. $P \rightarrow \Diamond P$. That is, if P, then it is possible that P.
2. $\Diamond(P \ \& \ Q) \rightarrow \Diamond P$. That is, if it is possible that P and Q, then it is possible that P.
3. $(P \rightarrow Q) \rightarrow (\Diamond P \rightarrow \Diamond Q)$. That is, if P implies Q, then the possibility of P implies the possibility of Q.
4. $\Diamond\Diamond P \rightarrow \Diamond P$. That is, if it is possible that P is possible, then P is possible.
5. $\Diamond P \rightarrow \Box\Diamond P$. That is, if P is possible, then it is necessary that P is possible.[1]

The S-logics S1 through S5 are, of course, due to C. I. Lewis. Each admits its own distinguishing axiom plus the axioms distinguishing the S-logics weaker than it. For example, logic S3 is distinguished by axiom 3 and includes axioms 1 and 2, but not axioms 4 or 5. Axiom 5 is an elegant distinctive axiom for S5, since in S5 *every* modal operator applies necessarily if it applies at all. That is, in S5 what is possible is necessarily possible, what is necessary is necessarily necessary, what is impossible is necessarily impossible, and what is contingent is necessarily contingent. Thus S5 is natural and appropriate for timeless and unchanging logical, mathematical, and metaphysical systems or structures where everything is fixed. Indeed, many readers may already simply see that the 1914–18 Russell's and the Tractarian Wittgenstein's theories of logical truth as truth in virtue of timeless, immutable logical form are and can only be S5, if we analyze logical necessity as logical truth.[2]

Since I hold that all eight implicit modal logics are S5 in strength, I hold that they differ not in their strength, but only in the interpretations of their respective modal operators "□" and "◊" as logical, causal, epistemic, or deontic.

I shall paraphrase Russell's texts into each implicit modal logic one formal axiom at a time. Since there are five axioms of S5 and eight implicit logics, that ideally would be 40 formalizations altogether. But for various reasons, there are not 40 texts that correspond one-one with 40 formalizations. For example, some formalizations will be implied by structural considerations, and others by the interdefinability of the modal operators necessity and possibility. And I shall argue that while Russell implicitly accepts the distinguishing axioms of deontic S2, S4, and S5, he implicitly rejects the distinguishing axioms of deontic S1 and S3.

Our study of Russell's many writings on modality will be as thorough as we can make it, and our scholarly task is a major one. For there are many writings in Russell in many areas of philosophy to explore. And quite aside from Russell, it is commonly held to be problematic whether S5 is always the best choice for paraphrasing epistemological, causal, or ethical theories into formal modal logics. Strictly speaking, that is criticism, not scholarship; but occasional critical remarks may be helpful.

After paraphrasing Russell's writings into the eight implicit modal logics, I discuss grades of modal involvement and problems of paraphrase of ordinary *de re* modal talk, especially problems of quantification into modal contexts. Last, I discuss in what sense *Principia* is an implicit modal logic, both when it was published (implicit FG–MDL) and retrospectively (implicit FG–MDL*).

It should be obvious in advance that the modal strength of the consequence relation of modern classical logic is S5. That is simply because the logical structure of modern classical logic is such that if *P* is possible (or necessary, impossible, or contingent), then *P* is necessarily possible (or necessarily necessary, necessarily impossible, or necessarily contingent). This is or ought to be a commonplace. Arthur Prior and Kit Fine compare modern classical quantificational logic to S5 (Prior 1977: ch. 1). Kosta Došen says, "with S5 we represent in classical logic the principles of a classical deductive metalogic" (Došen 1985: 167). Graham Solomon, who kindly gave me the Došen cite, also kindly notes that the point goes back to Alfred Tarski, Kurt Gödel, and Léon Henkin (Solomon 1999).

It should also be obvious in advance, to anyone familiar with Russell's notion of logical form, that his modern classical logic ought to be, if anything, S5 all the more so. That is because for him, logical forms are timeless. It does not even matter whether they are entities (I think they are), nor whether they are propositional constituents (I think they are not), as long as they are immutable. Thus writing this chapter may seem like flying a kite to prove the existence of wind. This point applies most clearly to FG–MDL*, the alethic modal logic implicit in Russell's mature writings on logical form. It applies less clearly to FG–MDL, the alethic modal logic implicit in Russell's earlier view that logical truth is simply fully general truth. But is not full generality a sort of logical form? And for the early Russell, would it not consist of the timeless, purely logical universals of his 1903–1912 metaphysics?

Methodology and Tests of Paraphrase

This concludes my introductory remarks. I shall now describe my tests of sufficiently adequate paraphrase. They are intended as a helpful superstructure of guidance in what follows. But those who find the tests unhelpful or confusing, or even empty clanking machinery, may simply ignore them.

My own philosophy of methodology is a familiar one: A methodology can help a great deal, and may even sometimes be a practical necessity to keep things organized and uniform. But not everything can be shown by methodology, on pain of a vicious infinite regress of methodologies to show that our initial methodology is good. Therefore we must always start from something which is *not* shown by a method. Aristotle and Spinoza offer similar regress arguments. This philosophy of methodology is not universally accepted; it is foundationalist as opposed to holist. But if nothing else, it is consistent with Russell's foundationalist theories of truth, of logic, of logical analysis, and of knowledge. And I do think its use of admittedly vague but familiar and widely used legal standards of evidence may help give *some* perspective on the degree of success or plausibility of my paraphrases. Things are no better or worse in millions of legal cases around the planet.

My methodology is this. I shall find a modal logic implicit in Russell if either of two tests is met: (i) it is more reasonable than not to paraphrase Russell's thinking into the modal logic, or (ii) it is more reasonable than not to suppose that Russell would have substantially assented to the modal logic as a paraphrase of his thought. In legal terms, these are "preponderance of the evidence" tests. Preponderance is the lowest standard of evidence in law. If we go any lower, we do not even have over 50 percent odds. Of course, we cannot always "bean count" the odds. We often have to use our best judgment. See chapter 10 on this point.

I believe test (i) is Russell's own requirement for ideal or perfect paraphrase. That is because for him, paraphrase is ideally mere regimentation of informal discourse into a formal notation, so as to preserve logical equivalence for each informal statement and its formal counterpart. Thus when I use test (i), I shall be applying Russell's own ideal test to his own writings.

But in practice, Russell allows some replacement of vague thoughts by a more determinate notation. Here we cannot expect to maintain logical equivalence, since the formal counterparts are more precise than the informal statements. This sort of replacement by a more precise formal statement, which is much the same as what Irving M. Copi calls a precising definition (Copi 1978: 121–22), is emphatically not what I am doing. I shall only remark that I think it goes without saying that even in a precising formalization, Russell would require the formalization to be more reasonable than not. This may involve our judgment in balancing the letter and the spirit of the informal discourse, in assessing what the author meant or intended. It is ultimately a matter of philosophical interpretation. Russell describes this practical aim in his famous later paper, "Mr Strawson on Referring," when he speaks of the replacement of our ordinary vague thoughts with more determinate ones as all he ever really sought to do in analysis (MPD 178–79). Of course, I cannot take that much easier practical approach to formalization here, since if I did, I would not find the modal logics to be *implicit* in Russell. Also, I think he is *trying* to achieve logically equivalent paraphrases, but often fails to do so; and his recasting his paraphrases as merely precising formalizations is his way out, or his "settling for second best." But showing that in detail is beyond the scope of this book. See my (2003: 177–78) on the failure of Russell's logical analyses of minds and bodies.

Test (ii) boils down to test (i), if we suppose that Russell would always have substantially assented to formal paraphrases of his thinking which are more reasonable than not. And perhaps that supposition is fairly safe. But no one is perfectly rational all the time, and test (ii) may yield different results in the case of different thinkers. Also, it is not always the case that philosophers would assent to what is logically implicit in their writings, since it might contradict their other writings, or even be a *reductio ad absurdum* of their views. To that extent there is tension between tests (i) and (ii). But the tension is resolved by the very fact that test (i) is more basic, since it is purely rational. We simply want to know whether a certain text implies a certain statement, regardless of whether the author would agree with the implication or the implied statement. Also, test (ii) is more speculative. It calls for speculation about an author would or might have said, if asked. While this can lead to illuminating historical results, test (i) is more basic. Of course, charitable interpretation blurs the line. For texts should not be read in isolation from the context of the general views of the author, or from our evidence that the author is a generally rational person.

Again, both test (i) and test (ii) use the lowest standard of evidence, that of being more reasonable than not. This is basically the same as the "preponderance of evidence" standard in law, since that only means 'more likely than not'. But low as it is, this standard is still far stronger than a test of merely finding a modal logic to be logically *consistent* with everything or nearly everything an author says. If *P* and *Q* are logically consistent, it does not follow in the least that either logically implies the other.

Of course, we may find that the evidence meets even higher standards. It may be *clear and evident* that a certain modal axiom is implicit in Russell's thinking, or *beyond any reasonable doubt*, or even *absurd to think otherwise. Clear and evident* and *beyond a reasonable doubt* are very common legal standards. *Absurd to think otherwise* is my own term, but it is analogous to a whole collection of legal notions—face amount, face of instrument, face value, failure to state a claim, judicial knowledge, judicial notice, party admission, strict liability, summary disposition, and so on. We may also call this last and highest standard *true on the face of it*, or *res ipsa loquitur* (the thing speaks for itself).

There is no logical necessity in dragging legal standards of evidence into my philosophy of paraphrase, but I find it convenient.

Now, it is well-known that the four modal operators, necessity, possibility, impossibility, and contingency, are trivially interdefinable. Thus, in order to show that any given modal logic is implicit in Russell, we only need to find *one* of the four modal operators implicit in Russell, in order to find the other three implicit in him as well. For example, suppose we find a certain necessity operator to be implicit in Russell. Then we can simply take it as primitive and use it to define "*P* is possible" as 'It is not the case that Not-*P* is necessary'. We may then define "*P* is impossible" in turn as 'It is not the case that *P* is possible', and also define "*P* is contingent" as '*P* is possible and Not-*P* is possible'. For a second example, we may find a certain possibility operator to be implicit in Russell. Then we can use it to define impossibility and contingency as before, and also to define "*P* is necessary" as 'It is not the case that Not-*P* is possible'. I shall only give these two examples, since I shall only be finding necessity and possibility operators implicit in Russell, and we will not need to take impossibility or contingency as primitive.

Of course, we could take any author who uses ordinary language modal terms to prefix statements, and we could trivially find all kinds of implicit modal logics. But I shall confine myself to finding modal logics implicit in Russell's statements of technical *theories*. Even that might seem like running amok in Russell, since he states so many theories, but I think that really it is not. But we should *expect* to find implicit substantive modal logics in an author who states technical theories expressly using modal expressions, or technical theories that rather plainly imply modal theses.

This concludes my discussion of methodology.

Again, for purposes of brief review, I distinguish Russell's largely explicit modal *theory* from his implicit modal *logics*. Russell's full modal *theory* is MDL {1,2,3}, in which MDL appears as level MDL {3}. MDL defines a propositional function $F(x)$ as possible with respect to x just in case $F(x)$ is not always false. From the ontological point of view, MDL, or MDL {3}, is the shallowest level of Russell's theory of modality. But from the logical point of view, MDL is the basic logical building block in all eight implicit modal logics.

I proceed now to find eight implicit modal logics in Russell and to assess their strength, discussing the texts in chronological order. I omit Russell's unpublished *Theory of Knowledge*, partly to save space and partly because he abandoned it.

Russell's Implicit Alethic Logics

I do not clearly see any modal logic implicit in *Principles of Mathematics*. I do find it reasonable to *gloss* the full range of Leibniz's possible worlds as logically implicit in that work. The book would seem to make more sense that way, to be clearer and more illuminated. In fact, the 1903 Russell would take such worlds far more seriously than Leibniz does. For Leibniz, they are mere ideas in God's mind. For Russell, they would be mind-independent complex entities. Such worlds could easily be the semantic basis for a modal logic. But in *Principles*, Russell does not expressly state possible worlds theory, or even use possible worlds talk. Thus I see no implicit possible worlds modal logic in *Principles*. For the possible worlds themselves are only a helpful gloss. And I see no implication of a possible worlds *logic* in the actual texts. To be sure, if we look at the possible worlds of the best *gloss* and ask what sort of modal logic *might* be based on them, it would pretty clearly be at least S5 in strength. For the existent and nonexistent entities in *Principles* are essentially immutable. Thus they could not be other than they are. Thus what is possible (or necessary, or contingent, or impossible) could only be *necessarily* possible (or necessary, or contingent, or impossible). And that would imply the distinguishing axiom of S5. It is also worth noting that Russell's express theory of necessity in *Principles* is along very different lines. For he adopts G. E. Moore's theory of logical necessity as degrees of implication among propositions. Thus any S5 possible worlds logic we *might* find implicit in *Principles* would be a rival theory of a very different kind from the express theory, and would make *Principles* an implicitly inconsistent work, unless perhaps we were to admit two senses of "necessity" in that work, an express Moorean one and an implicit neo-Leibnizian one.

Russell's first implicit modal logic is FG–MDL ("fully generalized MDL"). It is implied by Russell's definition of analytic truth in his unpublished paper, "Necessity and Possibility." Where the laws of logic are "certain enumerate[d]" fully general truths (Russell 1994a / ca. 1903–05: 515), Russell says, "We may, then, usefully define as *analytic[ally true]* those propositions which are deducible from the laws of logic" (Russell 1994a / ca. 1903–05: 516, Russell's emphasis). It follows that all analytic truths are fully general as well. I simply use Russell's definition of analytic truth, which we today would be more likely to call a definition of logical truth, to define the logical necessity operator of FG–MDL.

Since I simply quote Russell's own definition of analytic truth to define the logical necessity operator of FG–MDL, it seems absurd to deny that this modal logic is a perfect formal paraphrase of Russell's definition.

Russell himself states the logical link of his implicit logic FG–MDL to his express modal theory MDL. He says, "Analytic propositions have the property that they are necessary with respect to all of their constituents except such as are what I call *logical constants*" (Russell 1994a / ca. 1903–05: 519, Russell's emphasis). That Russell rejects MDL and would reject FG–MDL in this paper does not detract from this point. From 1906 on, he expressly accepts MDL. And he implicitly accepts FG–MDL from 1906 until 1918, when he corrects his theory of logical truth and implicitly accepts FG–MDL*.

For Russell in this paper, analytic truths are theses. But for us, his express definition of analytic truth implicitly defines the necessity operator of implicit FG–MDL. For FG–MDL defines logically necessary truths as truths that are fully general, i.e., as truths containing only logical constants and bound individual and predicate variables. I follow Landini in proposing the following logical equivalences. Where *A* is any fully general statement, and where the full generalization of *A* is $(F_1...F_m, x_1...x_n)A_{F1...Fm, x1...xn}$, then:

$$\Box A \leftrightarrow (F_1...F_m, x_1...x_n)A_{F1...Fm, x1...xn}$$

and

$$\Diamond A \leftrightarrow (\exists F_1...\exists F_m, \exists x_1...\exists x_n)A_{F1...Fm, x1...xn} \text{ (Landini 1993)}$$

It is easy to see now how FG–MDL is logically based on MDL. For in FG–MDL, necessary truths are MDL-necessary with respect to *all* the variables they contain, and *all* the propositional functions they contain. And possible truths are MDL-possible with respect to *all* the variables they contain, and *all* the propositional functions they contain. But we must draw a distinction here. When I say that FG–MDL is logically based on MDL, I mean that MDL is *implicit* in the logical equivalences I just stated for the modal operators of FG–MDL. I did not *explicitly* use MDL in the statements, and one can *understand* the statements without understanding MDL first.

I doubt that Russell's banishing of modality in "Necessity and Possibility" includes a banishing of his definition of analytic truth as deducibility from the laws of logic. He never says he rejects that definition, nor do his arguments against modality appear to apply to his definition of analytic truth. However, he would certainly be against interpreting his notion of analytic truth as a necessity operator. I think that much is clearly implied by his banishing of modality. And this is where what the text allows *us* as a reasonable paraphrase of "analytic truth" parts ways with what *he* intends or would intend. For *we* can very reasonably view "analytic truth" as an implicit necessity operator even though *he* very clearly would not. And this is why I do not clearly see an implicit modal logic in this paper. For in the context of his banishing modality, it seems too much of a gloss going against his express intent to say that in this particular paper, to be an analytic truth is implicitly to be a necessary truth. Call it a special circumstance if you will, but here we seem to see test (ii) overriding test (i). Again, no text should be interpreted in total isolation from its context, and I find the context of his expressly intended banishment of modality overwhelming. We shall not find this special circumstance again in Russell, since he accepts MDL-modality the very next year. Thus in his later works, there is no such reason to prevent paraphrase of notions like analytic truth or logical truth into necessity operators.

The only reason there might be to prevent it would be his finding that the concept of necessity *adds nothing* to the content of those concepts. But then he is in the business of *eliminative* logical analysis, and paraphrasing such notions into necessity operators is precisely the same as providing eliminative logical analyses of necessity. And this is precisely the same as when he eliminatively analyzes numbers as classes of classes. That is just to say that the concept of number *adds nothing* to the concept of classes for him.

Russell's second and more mature implicit modal logic is FG–MDL*. FG–MDL* defines a logically necessary truth as a truth that is both (i) fully general in accordance with Landini's definitions and (ii) true in virtue of its logical form. I explained why the 1918 Russell implicitly abandons FG–MDL and implicitly adopts FG–MDL* in chapter 1.

Russell says in *External World*, in a text he apparently read to an audience in a Lowell Lecture in Boston in 1914 (KEW v n.1):

> A proposition such as "If Socrates is a man, and all men are mortal, then Socrates is mortal," is true in virtue of its *form* alone[;] thus it is equally true when we substitute other terms for *Socrates* and *man* and *mortal*. The general truth of which it is an instance is purely formal....and can be known, theoretically, without any experience of particular things or their qualities and relations. (KEW 51–52, Russell's emphasis)

This text gives us truth in virtue of form as implicitly the necessity operator of an implicit modal logic. Certainly we may formally paraphrase it as such. But it is not clear to me whether Russell is in effect distinguishing yet between what I call FG–MDL and what I call FG–MDL*. For all I can tell from this particular text, Russell is simply *equating* fully general truth with truth in virtue of logical form. That is, perhaps he thinks logical form simply *is* full logical generality, as opposed to a new additional requirement above and beyond mere full generality as such. Indeed, the two are intimately related. I think that pure logical form is *shown* in fully general statements. But an earlier text in *External World* suggests he does distinguish them:

> In every proposition and in every inference there is, besides the particular subject-matter concerned, a certain *form*, a way in which the constituents of the proposition or inference are put together....What is in common [to certain propositions] is the *form* of the proposition, not an actual constituent....[As we move from one such proposition to another, t]he form remains unchanged[,] but all the constituents are altered. Thus form is not another constituent, but is the way the constituents are

> put together. It is forms, in this sense, that are the proper
> object of philosophical logic....
>   In all inference, form alone is essential....
> (KEW 40–41, Russell's emphasis)

Here the text seems to introduce logical form as something beyond
full generality as such, or at least to imply that it is. For all fully
general propositions are equally fully general, and cannot be
distinguished from each other on that account; but they have all
sorts of different logical forms. Thus the two *External World* texts,
taken together, seem to imply the necessity operator of FG–MDL*.
But I am not completely sure that Russell is distinguishing logical
form from full generality in this book. The only thing that is clear is
that FG–MDL* is implied. For that is done by the theory of logical
form, whether logical form is the same as full generality or not.

We finally see a clear distinction between logical form and
full generality in 1918 in "The Philosophy of Logical Atomism."
This is because Russell gives an example of a proposition which is
fully general but is not *logically* true if it is true, and not *logically*
false if it is false. Thus it is fully general, but logically contingent.
Actually he gives three examples, two as certain and one as
doubtful. Russell says:

> Now I want to come to the subject of completely general
> propositions and propositional functions. By those I
> mean propositions and propositional functions that
> contain only variables and nothing else at all [except
> logical constants]. This covers the whole of logic. Every
> logical proposition consists wholly and solely of
> variables [and logical constants], though it is not true
> that every proposition consisting wholly and solely of
> variables [and logical constants] is logical....I mean by
> the form of a proposition that which you get when for
> every single one of its constituents you substitute a
> variable.... (PLA 237–38)

This already indicates that fully general truth is only a necessary
condition, and is not a sufficient condition, of logical truth. Russell
then gives his three examples:

> The proposition that there are exactly 30,000 things in
> the world can also (i.e., just like logical truths) be
> expressed in purely logical terms, and is certainly not a
> proposition of logic but an empirical proposition (true or
> false), because a world containing more than 30,000
> things and a world containing fewer than 30,000 things
> are both possible, so that if it happens that there are
> exactly 30,000 things, that is what one might call an

accident and is not a proposition of logic. There are again two propositions that one is used to in mathematical logic, namely the multiplicative axiom and the axiom of infinity. These also can be expressed in logical terms, but cannot be proved or disproved by logic. In regard to the axiom of infinity[, which states that infinitely many things exist], the impossibility of logical proof or disproof may be taken as certain, but in the case of the multiplicative axiom, it is perhaps still open to some degree of doubt. (PLA 240)

Russell then describes the missing second necessary condition of logical truth as best he can:

Everything that is a proposition of logic has got to be in some sense or other like a tautology. It has got to be something which has some peculiar quality, which I do not know how to define, that belongs to logical propositions and not to others....But what exactly that characteristic is, I am not able to tell you. Although it is a necessary characteristic of logical propositions that they should consist solely of variables,...it is not a sufficient one. (PLA 240–41)

And there it is, Russell's express statement that there are two necessary conditions which constitute the sufficient condition of logical truth. They define the necessity operator of FG–MDL*. Note that Russell does not say the second condition *is* tautology, but very cautiously says only that it is "*like* a tautology." This caution is abandoned in his later work.

Since I simply quote Russell's own analysis of logical truth to define the logical necessity operator of FG–MDL*, it seems absurd to deny that this modal logic is a perfect formal paraphrase of Russell's analysis.

One might object that Russell also says in "The Philosophy of Logical Atomism":

Much false philosophy has arisen our of confusing propositional functions and propositions....This case of *necessary, possible, impossible*, is a case in point. In all traditional philosophy there comes a heading of 'modality', which discusses *necessary, possible*, and *impossible* as properties of propositions, whereas in fact they are properties of propositional functions.
   If you take '*x* is *x*', that is a propositional function which is true whatever '*x*' may be, i.e., a necessary propositional function. If you take '*x* is a man', that is a possible one. If you take '*x* is a unicorn, that is an impossible one.

> Propositions can only be true or false, but propositional functions have these three possibilities. It is important, I think, to realize that the whole doctrine of modality applies only to propositional functions, not to propositions. (PLA 231)

But just a few pages later in the paper, Russell applies epistemic modalities to propositions. He says that when we say "It is possible that it may rain tomorrow," this may be analyzed as: "We do not know if [i.e. whether or not] it will rain tomorrow; 'It will rain tomorrow' is a value of the propositional function, 'It rains at time t'; and that propositional function is not always false" (PLA 254–55). And how can propositions "only be true or false" when he distinguishes between logical truths and nonlogical truths, between truth in virtue of form and truth not in virtue of form, and between tautology and nontautology? He even distinguishes fully general truth from truth in virtue of form!

As we saw, Russell repeats his application of epistemic modal operators to whole propositions nine years later:

> And these terms [necessity, possibility, impossibility] may be transferred to propositions when they are not known to be true on their own account, but what is known as to their truth or falsehood is deduced from knowledge of propositional functions. (AMA 170)

Here he says modal terms "may be *transferred* to propositions." Granted, these are only epistemic modal operators; but they are sentential modal operators nonetheless. This at least opens the door to sentential modal operators in general, since he clearly admits some such operators in particular.

Clearly, Russell has no intention of stating or implying a propositional modal logic in "The Philosophy of Logical Atomism." Quite the opposite, he would find such a logic to be ill-formed, a category confusion, since he says modality applies only to propositional functions. Yet in the very same paper, those of us who find that modality does apply to propositions can very easily paraphrase not only his semi-formal theory of epistemic possibility as a formal epistemic possibility operator, but also his semi-formal theory of logical truth as fully general truth that is true in virtue of logical form as a formal alethic necessity operator.

More deeply, Russell appears to misunderstand his own views, or at least their potential for further development. As early as his ca. 1903–05 paper "Necessity and Possibility," he could have used his thesis about analytic truth there to define a proposition as logically necessary if and only if every propositional function in it is MDL-necessary. This would imply FG–MDL. I think the only things preventing him are his view in that paper that the notion of modality is too conflicted to be admissible in logic, and his apparent view in that paper that (if modality is admissible in logic, then) modality applies only to propositional functions. And in 1918, he could have defined a true proposition as logically necessary if and only if every single propositional function in it is MDL-necessary *in virtue of logical form*. Why does the 1918 Russell not do this? Is it because he thinks that logical necessity adds nothing to logical truth? But then how could he forget that his whole philosophy of logical analysis consists in giving just such eliminative analyses? Or second, is it because he thinks that modality is only a property of propositional functions? But then how could he fail to see that he can easily use that very property to give formal eliminative analyses of sentential modal operators? That is a leap over the narrowest of ditches. Or third, is it because he thinks propositions can only be true or false? But then how could he give all his other sentential characterizations, such as "logical truth," "thesis," "analytic," "synthetic *a priori*," or even "causal law"? Russell's views here are conflicted, to say the least. I have just stated three conflicts. Since this is Russell criticism based on his own views, it is merely ad hominem; but it is still deep.

Russell repeats his 1918 views in 1919. In *Introduction to Mathematical Philosophy*, Russell begins as in *External World*:

> Given a [certain] proposition,...we have certain consti-
> tuents and also a certain form. But the form is not itself a
> new constituent; if it were, we should need a new form to
> embrace both it and the other constituents. We can, in
> fact, turn all the constituents of a proposition into varia-
> bles, while keeping the form unchanged....
>   And we may explain (though not formally
> define) what we mean by the "form" of a proposition as
> follows:—
>   The "form" of a proposition is that, in it, that
> remains unchanged when every constituent of the propo-
> sition is replaced by another... (IMP 198–99)

He then indicates in effect that a true fully general proposition is just one in which either MDL's "always true" or "not always false" applies to every constituent in a proposition (IMP 199). But then he says something new:

> But though all logical (or mathematical) propositions can
> be expressed wholly in terms of logical constants
> together with variables, it is not the case that, conversely,
> all propositions that can be expressed in this way are
> logical. We have found so far a necessary but not a
> sufficient criterion of mathematical propositions....

> We may take the axiom of infinity as an example of a proposition which, though it can be enunciated in logical terms, cannot be asserted by logic to be true. [For] we are left to empirical observation to determine whether there are as many as *n* individuals in the world. (IMP 202–3)

In this text, he is implicitly rejecting FG–MDL because it has only "a necessary but not a sufficient" condition of logico-mathematical truth. He then adds the missing second necessary condition, thus implicitly accepting FG–MDL*:

> It is clear that the definition of "logic" or "mathematics" must be sought be trying to give a new definition of the old notion of "analytic" propositions....They all have the characteristic...we agreed to call "tautology." This, combined with the fact that they can be expressed wholly in terms of variables and logical constants...will give the definition of logic or pure mathematics. For the moment, I do not know how to define "tautology."[1]
> 1. The importance of "tautology" for a definition of mathematics was pointed out to me by my former pupil Ludwig Wittgenstein... (IMP 204–5, 205 n.1)

And there it is a second time, Russell's statement of the two necessary conditions which constitute the sufficient condition of logical truth and which define the necessity operator of FG–MDL*. His not knowing how to define "tautology" is curious, since he has just got through explaining the obvious candidate for defining it, truth in virtue of logical form, in the immediately preceding pages. It is also Wittgenstein's obvious candidate in the *Tractatus*.

Again, the eight implicit modal logics are different interpretations of S5. That is, the modal operators must be defined differently in each of them. In FG–MDL, "□" means "true when fully generalized using only universal quantifiers." In FG–MDL*, "□" means "true when fully generalized using only universal quantifiers and also true in virtue of its form." Both interpretations are modally innocent. They contain no modal notions.

Iteration of modal operators is admissible in both FG–MDL and FG–MDL*, since we are prefixing whole statements with the operators. We can iterate operators all we want. Theory of types is not a problem, since an iterated operator is never predicated of itself, but always of a proposition.

I shall now discuss the strength of Russell's two implicit alethic modal logics. It will be convenient to begin with the later logic, FG–MDL*, since it will be clearer and easier to make my arguments in terms of the notion of logical form. Here, I shall use "→" to indicate strict implication. The symbol is C. I. Lewis's.

The distinguishing axiom of alethic S1 is that if *P*, then it is logically possible that *P*. That is, $P \rightarrow \Diamond P$. That is trivially true in FG–MDL*, due to the timeless, unchanging nature of logical form.

The distinguishing axiom of alethic S2 is that if it is logically possible that *P* and *Q*, then it is logically possible that *P*. That is, $\Diamond(P \& Q) \rightarrow \Diamond P$. That is trivially true in FG–MDL* as well, again due to the timeless, unchanging nature of logical form.

The distinguishing axiom of alethic S3 is that if *P* deductively implies *Q*, then the logical possibility of *P* deductively implies the logical possibility of *Q*. That is, $(P \rightarrow Q) \rightarrow (\Diamond P \rightarrow \Diamond Q)$. That is clearly true in FG–MDL*, again due to the nature of logical form.

I shall consider S4 and S5 next. But first, I shall make some prefatory remarks. Now, S4 and S5 use iteration of modal logics. As we saw, iteration of logical modal operators is syntactically possible in FG–MDL*, since there they operate on statements. Iterated modal operators that are entirely of the same kind are collapsible in FG–MDL*, since trivially, they will all have the same conditions of application, namely the logical form of the base statement, *P*. Thus $\Box\Box P \rightarrow \Box P$, and $\Diamond\Diamond P \rightarrow \Diamond P$. That is, the only way "It is logically necessary that it is logically necessary that *P*" could be true is if *P* is logically necessary in virtue of its logical form. And the only way "It is logically possible that it is logically possible that *P*" could be true is if *P* is logically possible in virtue of its logical form.

I proceed now to S4.

The distinguishing axiom of alethic S4 is that if it is logically possible that it is logically possible that *P*, then *P* is logically possible. That is, $\Diamond\Diamond P \rightarrow \Diamond P$. That is true in FG–MDL*, as we just saw.

The distinguishing axiom of alethic S5 is that if *P* is logically possible, then it is logically necessary that it is logically possible that *P*. That is, $\Diamond P \rightarrow \Box\Diamond P$. In FG–MDL*, if a statement is possible, then it is necessarily possible, since its possibility is in virtue of its logical form. A statement's logical form is an essential part of the statement's being the statement it is, and is timeless and unchanging, regardless of whether the logical form is itself an entity. And if a statement is necessary, then it is both necessarily possible and necessarily necessary, in virtue of its logical form. Thus FG–MDL* can only be S5. Indeed, it is absurd to think otherwise, and that is the highest evidentiary standard on our list.

As far as Russell's intentions go, FG–MDL seems best compared to S5 too. That is because it seems best to say that the 1903–1912 Russell had not yet clearly separated the two notions, (i) being a true full generalization, and (ii) being true in virtue of logical form. He would have had no need to. In fact, if asked about this, the 1903–1912 Russell might well have said that true fully generalized propositions *are* true in virtue of their form, because that simply *is* their form: full generality. In fact, the early Russell even thought he could logically prove that there are infinitely many logical entities, so that the axiom of infinity would be a logical truth. And if *that* axiom were a logical truth, then *no* true full generalizations such as "There exist at least 30,000 objects" would be counterexamples to FG–MDL. They would be logical truths just like the axiom of infinity itself, since they are logically implied by the axiom. Thus the early Russell might well have thought that full generalization simply *is* the form in virtue of which logical truths were true. Indeed, if his attempt to prove the axiom of infinity had succeeded, he would have been right, at least if we ignore the doubtful multiplicative axiom (PLA 240), and at least if we ignore any other possible counterexamples which he did not think of.

I shall offer three arguments that the 1903–1912 Russell took true full generalization to constitute logical truth. This is not the same as arguing that he took it to constitute logical form, but if the arguments succeed, it may as well be.

First, the 1903–1912 Russell draws no distinction between true full generalization and logical truth, any more than he draws a distinction between true full generalization and truth in virtue of logical form.

Second, Frege draws no such distinctions either. And as Russell and Whitehead say in *Principia*, "In all questions of logical analysis, our chief debt is to Frege" (PM viii; see POM 501). There is some literature discussing Frege's view that logical truth is fully general truth. At least, I believe I once attended a lecture attributing that view to Frege, and discussing it, by James Higginbotham at a meeting of the American Philosophical Association.

Third, when Russell finally admits in 1918 that the axiom of infinity is a logically contingent truth if it is true, and that "There exist at least 30,000 objects" is a logically contingent truth if it is true, he presents these things as valid counterexamples to all earlier theory of logical truth (PLA 237–41). He says, "I can only say...as regards the constituents of logical propositions, that it is a problem which is rather new.... I do not think any literature exists at all which deals with it in any way whatever" (PLA 239). And then he proceeds to amend the theory that logical truth is fully general truth. And what is this amendment? He adds a new condition to the condition that logical truth be fully general. Now, in addition to fully general truth, he is requiring truth in virtue of logical form as well. But in effect, that is just to state in so many words that his own earlier theory *had* been that logical truth is simply fully general truth. In effect, he is telling us what his earlier theory was, how he is correcting it now, and why he is correcting it. And I believe that is how every Russell scholar would read this text.

The first two arguments use only circumstantial evidence, and are merely negative in nature. Viewed as deductive arguments, they commit the fallacy of appeal to ignorance. Viewed as inductive arguments, I doubt the first two arguments taken together even rise to our lowest standard of evidence, preponderance of the evidence. But as inductive arguments, I think they do provide *some* support.

But the third argument uses a "smoking gun" text in which Russell evidently states what his former theory was, in the process of correcting it. I think this rises to the level of clear and convincing evidence. Thus this seems to me to be the decisive argument.

I have argued that FG–MDL and FG–MDL* are both S5. I shall now argue that in fact they are both a little stronger than S5. As before, it will be convenient to begin with FG–MDL*.

Now, Russell admits $(x)(x = x)$ as a logical truth (PM 216 / *24.01). Thus, if we are right that FG–MDL* is S5, then it is also the system Hughes and Cresswell call S5 + I (Hughes 1968: 190), where thesis I is $\Box(x)(x = x)$. Thesis I cannot be proved in S5. Thesis I is not what distinguishes S5, is not in any of the historic S-logics, and indeed is not anywhere in C. I. Lewis's books (C. Lewis 1932; 1918). Decisively, Russell holds that any true identity statement whose subject-terms are logically proper names is a tautology, i.e. a necessary truth (PLA 245–46; see 231; PM 216 / *24.01). Trivially, this includes "$a = a$" for any a. This reason why Russell's implicit FG–MDL* implicitly includes thesis I seems clear and convincing.

The argument applies to Russell's earlier implicit FG–MDL as well, since thesis I is in *Principia*, when Russell still evidently held that logical truth is just fully general truth.

However, FG–MDL* is not stronger than S5 in virtue being any of the systems S6 through S8. S1–S2–S3–S4–S5 is one series of progressively stronger systems, made stronger by the addition of a new axiom at each stage. S1–S2–S6–S7–S8 is a second such series. S6 is S2 plus the axiom $\Diamond\Diamond p$. S7 is *S3* plus the axiom $\Diamond\Diamond p$. S8 is S3 plus the axiom $\Box\Diamond\Diamond p$. The distinguishing axiom of S6 and S7 asserts that any well-formed statement is possibly possible. The distinguishing axiom of S8 asserts that any well-formed statement is necessarily possibly possible. Russell would have rejected these axioms because for him, well-formed self-contradictory statements are *not* possibly possible truths. Their logical form will not permit it. Another way to put it is that semantic model interpretations of S6 and S7 would include "non-normal" possible worlds in which self-contradictory statements are true (Hughes 1968: 279–82). Russell would never accept such worlds, not even as mere "Leibnizian phraseology" (IMP 141, 192).

Likewise for FG–MDL. Even though the pre-1905 Russell accepts merely possible entities, he rejects *impossibilia*.

Landini notes that if the five howlers were not disposed of before, they are certainly disposed of in FG–MDL* (Landini 1993). That is because Russell's deductively valid inferences can now be rewritten as formal implications which are *true in virtue of logical form*. Mere material (or even formal) implication as such is a red herring. Thus the days are gone when one could write Russell off on modality simply by finding a few seeming howlers in MDL. MDL itself, considered in isolation, is a red herring. Its importance is only as the main logical building block in FG–MDL and FG–MDL*, and in less obvious ways in all the other implicit modal logics.

FG–MDL* does not attempt to cover the whole field of what is more broadly called logically, intellectually, or conceptually necessary truth. Specifically, FG–MDL* does not attempt to capture any synthetic *a priori* truths. And we know Russell admits them as early as 1903–05. For Russell, they include "If a thing is good, it is not bad" and "If a thing is yellow, it is not red" (Russell 1994a / ca. 1903–05: 517; see PP 76, 82). Indeed, this very early admission of synthetic *a priori* truths is exactly contemporary with Russell's first presentation of his early view (in the same paper that logical ("analytic") truth is fully general truth. And as far as I can tell, he never stops admitting synthetic *a priori* truths. This gives us our third and fourth implicit alethic logics: FG–MDL+syn (FG–MDL plus synthetic *a priori* truth), and FG–MDL*+syn (FG–MDL* plus synthetic *a priori* truth). The distinction between the two is as great or as little as the distinction between FG–MDL and FG–MDL* themselves, since that is the only difference between them.

An expansion of FG–MDL* to include synthetic *a priori* truths seems easy in Russell's case. We simply apply his doctrine in *The Problems of Philosophy* that *"All* a priori *knowledge deals exclusively with the relations of universals"* (PP 103, Russell's emphasis). That includes synthetic *a priori* knowledge as well as all logic and mathematics (PP 74–77, 82, 102–3, 117). This may be regarded as an expansion of the notion of logical form into a new, more general notion of *universal* form. We may say that a truth is logically necessary in the broad sense of being *a priori* if it "deals exclusively with the relations of universals." And we may call this "truth in virtue of universal form." It remains to note that relations among universals are themselves universals for Russell, and that logical forms are in some sense clearly universal forms for Russell. After all, would he not say that two instances of modus ponens have literally the same logical form? But while synthetic *a priori* truths and logical truths would both be true in virtue of *universal* form, only the latter would be true in virtue of *logical* form; only the latter would be tautological. This gives us the fourth implicit alethic logic, FG–MDL*+syn, and by parity of reason, the third as well, FG–MDL+syn. For if FG–MDL and FG–MDL* are S5 due to the timeless, unchanging character of logical truth, or if you please, to the timeless character of logical structures of logical universals, then FG–MDL+syn and FG–MDL*+syn are S5 as well, due to the timeless, unchanging character of relations of universals in general. It remains to note that all four implicit alethic logics are S5 + I, since thesis I, $(x)(x = x)$, is true in all of them.

Russell's Implicit Causal Logic

I turn now to the causal modalities. Russell accepts a modally innocent Humean assay of causation. That is, he admits causal laws only as true empirical generalizations. His causal laws are true universal statements which are not fully generalized. They are synthetic *a posteriori*, and they include at least one descriptive (as opposed to logical) propositional function which is always true, though not due to logical form, and not *a priori*. Since this propositional function is always true, it is necessary in MDL, by definition of MDL. Thus once again, MDL is a logically necessary building block.

There is a redundance in my description: (1) that there is a descriptive propositional function in the statement, and (2) that the statement is not fully generalized, certainly not with respect to its predicates.

It might seem that there is a second and greater redundancy in that a statement is synthetic *a posteriori* if and only if it contains at least one descriptive function. But I believe that biconditional statement is false. For I believe that in Russell's logic, there are true *fully general* universal statements that are synthetic *a posteriori*, but that do not contain any descriptive functions. For example, "For any 30,000 objects, if they exist, then there exist at least 30,001 objects" is a counterexample to the biconditional. It contains no descriptive functions because it is fully general. Yet it is synthetic *a posteriori*. Since there happen to be zillions of objects, both the antecedent and the consequent happen to be true, making the whole statement true. Yet the antecedent does not logically imply the consequent. This is unlike the statement's converse, "For any 30,001 objects, if they exist, then there exist at least 30,000 objects." That one is a logical truth. But both statements lack descriptive propositional functions, and I think that is a sufficient reason why no one would accept either statement as a causal law, even though the first statement is true, universal, and synthetic *a posteriori*. This shows that not every true universal synthetic *a posteriori* statement is a causal law for Russell. Thus we also need a descriptive propositional function in the statement, if it is to be a causal law. This also allows us to refine the howler that Russell is conflating true accidental generalizations with causal laws. Namely, at least he is not conflating *fully general* true accidental generalizations, such as "For any 30,000 objects, if they exist, then there exist at least 30,001 objects," with causal laws. But the refinement is of little help. For any accidentally true universal statement that *has* a descriptive propositional function still presents the substantive howler for Russell.

We must interpret causal modal operators for Russell so as to reflect what we know of his views on both modality and causation. Our interpretation will then determine the strength of Russell's implicit causal logic, which we may call MDL–C.

Typically, for Russell, causal laws are complex relational statements, as opposed to simple "if-then" cause-effect conditional statements, so that they can describe complex systems of interacting variables (ONC 187–93). Causal laws can be conditional statements for Russell, but logically need not be, and usually are not.

I have been describing what causal laws are for Russell, but I have not yet defined them. For that, I think we need some glosses. I think that for Russell and for virtually everyone, a causal law must be true at all times, as opposed to true only for some limited time period, and must be about some regularly (universally) related set of at least two kinds of changes. Others may research Russell on this if they wish, but I think the glosses are satisfactory for us here. By "change," I mean change in the ordinary sense of the word. For Russell sometimes accepts Zeno's arguments for a static world.

Thus I think that a causal law may be defined for Russell as a true synthetic *a posteriori* statement that has at least one universal quantifier, has at least one descriptive as opposed to logical propositional function, and is as glossed. Given Russell's theory of variables, we may take it as already implied that the universal quantifier ranges over items across all space and time. This is an eliminative Humean definition that takes the modality out of causal law.

We may then define a statement as causally necessary for Russell if it is either a causal law as just defined, or is deducible from the set of all causal laws and true particular statements. This is an eliminative definition that takes the modality out of statements of causation.

We may then define a cause for Russell as anything that is describable as a cause in a causally necessary statement, as just defined. This is an eliminative definition that takes the modality out of causes in the world. It makes being a cause a function of being describable as such in a certain sort of statable true statement. The way I have put it, there can be causes for Russell even if they are never actually described in actual statements. I think this is quite correct for him.

In MDL–C, "$\Box P$" means, "P is deducible from the set of all causal laws and true particular statements," where causal laws are defined as above, that is, according to Russell's Humean analysis of cause, and where all causal laws are taken to be deducible from themselves. Thus we prefix the MDL–C causal necessity operator to a statement if and only if the statement is causally necessary for Russell, as defined two paragraphs ago.

Since I simply use Russell's own analysis of cause to define the causal necessity operator of MDL–C, it seems absurd to deny that MDL–C is a perfect formal paraphrase of Russell's analysis.

We may define P as causally possible just in case not-P is not causally necessary. Any true particular or general statement is causally possible. For no true statement can violate a causal law in the sense of contradicting it, since causal laws are true statements themselves. For no truth can contradict another truth.

The problem is whether to count any *false* statements as causally possible. This is not the same as the question whether any counterfactual statements are *true*. True counterfactuals are always causally possible because no true statement can contradict a causal law. The problem is whether it is causally possible for things to happen other than they actually do. For example, it may be counterfactually true that if I had struck the match, it would have lit. But that is logically consistent with its not having been causally possible for me to strike the match. The problem is that of determinism. If every event is causally necessary, then nothing can happen other than it does. But then the only causally possible events are causally necessary events, and no false statements are causally possible.

That no false statements are causally possible for Russell is a desirable result for the present interpretation, since it is consistent with the Parmenidean-Diodorean character of Russell's theory of modality on its deepest level. For a causal law is a true universal statement that ranges over all actual individuals. And that means it ranges over all possible individuals for Russell, in the Parmenidean sense that there are no *merely* possible individuals for Russell.

Perhaps Russell's best discussion of causal possibility is not in *External World* or "On the Notion of Cause," but in the 1910 essay "The Elements of Ethics." There Russell finds the case for (Humean) determinism "overwhelming" (PE 37, 38, 45, 59). And "if determinism is true, there is a sense in which no action is possible except the one actually performed" (PE 39, 59). This very directly gives us the distinguishing axiom of S5: If P is causally possible, then it is causally necessary that P is causally possible.

Let us now paraphrase Russell into MDL–C. I shall begin with some brief prefatory remarks on two modal truisms. Following *Principia*, we will assume that at least one thing exists.

Let P and Q be any statements. Then the modal truism, $\Box P \leftrightarrow \neg\Diamond\neg P$, is true in MDL–C. So is the modal truism, $\Box P \rightarrow \Diamond P$, due to the existence assumption and the rules of universal instantiation and existential generalization. For this truism in effect boils down to $(x)(Fx) \supset (\exists z)(Fz)$, or *Principia* thesis *9.1 (PM 131). And there we universally instantiate the antecedent to one thing that we assume exists, call it a, and then existentially generalize to the consequent.

The distinguishing axiom of causal S1 is that if P, then it is causally possible that P. That is, $P \rightarrow \Diamond P$. That is trivially true in MDL–C. For as we saw, any true statement is causally possible for Russell.

The distinguishing axiom of causal S2 is that if it is causally possible that P and Q, then it is causally possible that P. That is, $\Diamond(P \& Q) \rightarrow \Diamond P$. That is trivially true in MDL–C. For as we saw, on Russell's determinism, any causally possible statement is true. Thus $\Diamond(P \& Q) \rightarrow (P \& Q)$. Then the *Principia* simplification rule, $(P \& Q) \supset P$, gives us P. And since any true statement is causally possible, P gives us $\Diamond P$. Therefore, $\Diamond(P \& Q) \rightarrow \Diamond P$.

The distinguishing axiom of causal S3 is that if P strictly implies Q, then the causal possibility of P strictly implies the causal possibility of Q. That is, $(P \rightarrow Q) \rightarrow (\Diamond P \rightarrow \Diamond Q)$. That is clearly true in MDL–C as well. The basic reason is that all true statements are causally possible for Russell, as we saw.

Iteration of causal modal operators is syntactically possible in MDL–C, since they operate on statements. Thus we may proceed to consider S4 and S5. The question then devolves to the appropriate interpretation of iterated operators. Of course, a modal operator should always mean the same thing whether it is iterated or not. Once again, iterated modal operators entirely of *either* kind will be trivially collapsible, since they will all have the same condition of application, namely, the truth-conditions of the base statement. For here, "It is causally necessary that it is causally necessary that P" can only mean 'For the principal empirical description D in P, it is always the case that it is always the case that D'. And "It is causally possible that it is causally possible that P" can be defined by defining possibility in terms of necessity, or simply as meaning 'It is not always false that it is not always false that D'. Thus $\Box\Box P \to \Box P$, and $\Diamond\Diamond P \to \Diamond P$. And the distinguishing axiom of causal S4 is just $\Diamond\Diamond P \to \Diamond P$.

The distinguishing axiom of causal S5 is that if P is causally possible, then it is causally necessary that P is causally possible. That is, $\Diamond P \to \Box\Diamond P$. I think that will be true in MDL–C too. For P is causally possible if and only if P is causally necessary. The basic reason is Russell's causal determinism. For even Humean causal determinism gives us a causally unchanging, causally immutable world where whatever is possible is necessarily possible. To think otherwise is not to take Hume's eliminative analysis of causation seriously. And for Russell, this is true on two levels.

The first level is a trivial one. Russell holds that trivially, particular events can always be brought under uniform laws. Russell holds that infinitely many rival theories predicting future empirical observations, "all of which have exactly the same inductive evidence in their favour," are compatible with any given finite set of past observations, notably with the set of all human observations up to any given date. Most of these theories will involve artificial predictions of changes in the course of nature (HK 312–13; see AMA 232; OP 111; ONC 197–98). Thus MDL–C is trivially S5.

Second and more substantively, Russell finds the case for determinism "overwhelming" (PE 37, 38, 45, 59). And "if determinism is true, there is a sense in which no action is possible except the one actually performed" (PE 39, 59). Decisively, Russell says, "Causality belongs to the existing world" (PE 39). But a very slightly later Russell merely says that the evidence that our volitional behavior is determined in the sense of being uniform is "strong but not conclusive" (ONC 201; see KEW 163–83). And surely if the evidence that our volitional behavior is determined is strong but not conclusive, then the evidence for total determinism of the world is strong but not conclusive. For a chain is as strong as its weakest link, and here volitional behavior is the weakest link.

Of course, the howler about MDL–C is that it does not and cannot distinguish accidental universal truths from causal laws. And this in turn makes it hard to keep the two levels just described from collapsing into each other. I can only say that all Humeans on causality have this problem, and probably would do well to say that this is just how it is: there *is* no meaning to causal law we can find other than mere universality. For we are not acquainted with a relation of causation. And this is why we should take Hume's analysis of causation seriously. We might still distinguish our two levels by noting that the first level is "cooked up" universality while the second is "serious." But the bottom line for us that if this howler is successful, then it is Russell criticism, not Russell scholarship. I would have said the same thing about the five howlers raised about MDL, if they had been successful. But those howlers were misunderstandings.

If I am right, then Russell has the right strength for a causal logic. We *want* causal logic to be S5. "Iterated operators are needed in causal logic, e.g. to express...that if a certain causal law were false, such-and-such would be the case, or that it is a causal law that a certain kind of habit...arises under certain circumstances" (Føllesdal 1971: 57). Thus in general, if something is causally possible, then it should be causally necessary that the thing be causally possible, even aside from (total) determinism.

Russell uses subjunctive conditionals in discussing causal relations (PM 475–76, ONC 196). He virtually admits subjunctive conditionals as a legitimate kind of statement many years later in the *Inquiry* (Ushenko 1989: 410–14). This is perfectly consistent with my interpretation, as I explained earlier.

Again, there is nothing intrinsically modal about the causal operators in MDL–C. In keeping with Russell's Humean assay of causation in particular, and with his approach to modality in general, MDL–C is eliminative of causal modal entities and causal modal notions across the board. For there is no difference between a causal law and a true accidental generalization that conforms to the definition of causal law given in this section.

Russell's Implicit Epistemic Logic

I turn next to Russell's epistemology. I shall preface the discussion with a few brief general remarks on epistemic logic. For a more complete introduction, see Snyder (1971: 199–209).

It is not clear what the strength of epistemic logic naturally should be, and answers have been all over the map. This is partly because the word "know" is said in many ways, partly because the word may be used for a single knower ("I know"), a community ("We know," "They know"), partly because the strictness of knowing can range from Cartesian theory (where nothing is initially known except what seems to me to be the case) to ordinary language use (which can be very broad indeed), and even partly because logicians often mix epistemic logic with doxastic logic, i.e., mix epistemic operators with belief-operators. And there is an obvious whole-part connection between knowledge and belief on the traditional theory that knowledge is sufficiently justified true belief, which is also the basic framework of Russell's theory of knowledge. But all the same, we must not confuse belief, as such, with epistemic possibility. For epistemic possibility must be such that proposition *P* is epistemically possible if and only if *P* is not known to be false. And belief does not meet that requirement, since we logically need not *believe* what is not known to be false. If we believed everything not known to be false, we would be believing far more than we actually do, since there is so much we do not know; and we would be believing contrary or even contradictory claims, since we often do not know either that *P* or that not-*P*.

Vincent Hendricks and John Symons say :

> One of the important tasks of epistemic logic is to catalogue all sound and complete systems of such logics in order to allow us to pick the most 'appropriate' ones. The logics range from S4 over the intermediate systems S4.2–S4.4 to S5. By way of example, [Jaakko] Hintikka settled for S4 (1962), Kutschera argued for S4.4 (1976), Lenzen suggested S4.2 (1978), van der Hoek has proposed to strengthen knowledge according to system S4.3 (1996). [Hans] van Ditmarsch, van der Hoek and Kooi together with Fagin, Halpern, Moses and Vardi (Fagin et al. 1995) and others assume knowledge to be S5 valid. (Hendricks 2009; see also Ditmarsch 2006)

Thus if I am right that Russell's implicit epistemic logic is S5, then some would say that this is what we ought to see, and others would not. This concludes my brief general remarks on epistemic logic.

I shall formalize only Russell's already semi-formal logical analysis of our ordinary talk of epistemic possibility. Again, he says that for him, logical analysis is not (or perhaps we should say need not be) a phenomenological description of our ordinary thoughts, but is (or perhaps we should say can be) a replacement of them with clearer, more definite concepts. I added the two parenthetical disjuncts out of charity, since it is not clear to me that his logical analysis of numbers does or even could replace numbers with any clearer or more definite notions. Just look at Russell's paradox! But here my analysis aims to achieve logical equivalence with Russell's text, which is surely Russell's aim in, say, logicizing mathematics.

Thus my limited mission is to show that MDL–E is implicit in the one text I shall formalize, and is more likely than not S5 in strength. I must leave the formalization of Russell's comprehensive theories of knowledge in *Human Knowledge* and in the *Theory of Knowledge* manuscript to others.

As we saw earlier, Russell says that epistemic modal terms "may be *transferred* to propositions" (AMA 170). And we saw just how he does it in "The Philosophy of Logical Atomism." The text is this: Russell says that when we say "It is possible that it may rain tomorrow," this may be analyzed as: "We do not know if [i.e.

whether or not] it will rain tomorrow; 'It will rain tomorrow' is a value of the propositional function, 'It rains at time t'; and that propositional function is not always false" (PLA 254–55). This is clearly not a phenomenological report of our actual thoughts, since most people never think of propositional functions. Nor do we ever consciously think of the three statements Russell analyzes the given statement as being logically equivalent to, when we think of an epistemic possibility. Nor is it clear to me that Russell is replacing the ordinary statement with a clearer, more definite analysis (though it is certainly more detailed), insofar as the term "know" in the analysans is just as unclear and indefinite as the epistemic term "may" in the analysandum. Instead, it seems that on the face of it, Russell is aiming to achieve a logical equivalence between the ordinary statement he is analyzing and his analysis of it.

Now, Russell's analysis of the given ordinary statement into three more technical statements is just what I shall use to define the possibility operator of the epistemic logic I call MDL–E. It follows that MDL–E is logically implicit in Russell simply by definition. And since I simply quote Russell's own analysis of epistemic possibility to define the epistemic possibility operator of MDL–E, it seems absurd to deny that this logic is a perfect formal paraphrase of Russell's semi-formal analysis.

Russell is expressly analyzing epistemic possibility, and is thereby implicitly defining the epistemic possibility operator of the epistemic modal logic which I call MDL–E. Note that he analyzes epistemic possibility in terms of knowledge. For "We do not know" is part of his analysis. Thus he takes knowledge as primitive and analyzes epistemic possibility in terms of it. In terms of MDL–E, in effect he takes the epistemic necessity operator as primitive and defines the epistemic possibility operator in terms of it. And there is nothing wrong with that as far as it goes, since the modal operators are interdefinable, and any one of them can be taken as primitive. The only question is which one of them is most illuminatingly taken as primitive; and that would be criticism, not interpretation.

What would MDL–E be formally speaking? Where Px is the principal propositional function in proposition P, Russell is in effect defining the epistemic possibility operator "$\Diamond P$" as "$\neg \Box P$ & $\neg \Box \neg P$ & $\neg(x)\neg Px$", or even more simply, as "$\neg \Box P$ & $\neg \Box \neg P$ & $(\exists x)Px$". Note that my formal analysis of Russell's semi-formal analysis breaks things up differently, but is logically equivalent to it. I am analyzing the first statement of his analysis, "We do not know if it will rain tomorrow," as the first *two* statements of mine: "$\neg \Box P$" and "$\neg \Box \neg P$". And I am analyzing the last two statements of his analysis, "'It will rain tomorrow' is a value of the propositional function, 'It rains at time t'; and that propositional function is not always false" as the very simple *third* statement of mine: "$(\exists x)Px$".

I do not see any reason why Russell would not accept the distinguishing axioms of S1–S3 as true of the ordinary epistemic statement he is analyzing, and as true of his analysis as well, since his analysis is intended to be logically equivalent to that statement.

Axiom 1 would be, "If P is true, then P is epistemically possible." This is true on my formalization, at least in the following sense. Suppose for the sake of the argument that P is true. It is pragmatically necessary that we would not make such a supposition in the first place if we already knew either that P is true or that P is false. (Indeed, we cannot know that P is false, if P is true.) And the very truth of P would make the propositional function Px not always false. And I think that this sense is faithful to Russell's text. The formalization is $P \rightarrow \Diamond P$.

Axiom 2 would be, "If P and Q are epistemically possible, then P is epistemically possible." This is true on my formalization by the rule of simplification. If we do not know whether P and Q are true or false, and if Px is not always false and Qy is not always false, then it follows that we do not know whether P is true or false, and also that Px is not always false. The formalization is $\Diamond(P \& Q) \rightarrow \Diamond P$.

Axiom 3 would be, "If P implies Q, then the epistemic possibility of P implies the epistemic possibility of Q." That is true on my formalization, at least in the following sense. If P implies Q, and we do not know whether P is true or not, and P is not always false, then from the information just given, we do not know whether Q is true or not, but it does follow that Q is not always false. I think that this sense is faithful to the text. The formalization is $(P \rightarrow Q) \rightarrow (\Diamond P \rightarrow \Diamond Q)$.

Does MDL–E include the distinguishing axiom of S4? That is, does it include $\Diamond\Diamond P \rightarrow \Diamond P$? That is, does "It is epistemically possible that it is epistemically possible that P" imply "It is epistemically possible that P" in MDL–E? Well, in MDL–E, "$\Diamond\Diamond P$" would be "$\neg\Box(\Diamond P) \& \neg\Box\neg(\Diamond P) \& (\exists x)\Diamond Px$". If I may simplify that a bit and at the same time return to Russell's original language, it basically means only, "If we do not know if P is epistemically possible (etc.), then we do not know if P (etc.)." That should already be a self-evident truth for the ordinary sort of epistemic language Russell is analyzing. But if it helps make things clearer, we can contraposit it to "If it *is* known whether or not P (etc.), then it *is* known whether or not P is epistemically possible (etc.)." Now, contraposition goes from "If P, then Q" to "If not-Q, then not-P," or (as in the present case) vice versa, and is always a valid inference. And the contraposited statement is trivially true. If we *know* that P, then *of course* we know that P is epistemically *possible*. In simplest terms, the actuality of our knowledge implies its epistemic possibility. Likewise, if we know that not-*P*, then of course we also know that *P* is not epistemically possible. Thus if we know *whether or not P*, then we know *whether or not P* is epistemically possible. This is clear and convincing evidence, if not beyond a reasonable doubt, that MDL–E is S4.

Does MDL–E also include the distinguishing axiom of S5, $\Diamond P \rightarrow \Box \Diamond P$? I think it does. This might be most easily shown by asking another question: If I think it is epistemically possible that it will rain tomorrow, how could I not know that this is what I think? Here, too, we must not think of the analysis as phenomenological description of our mental states. We can iterate modal operators indefinitely many times in MDL–E, but clearly we do not think as many thoughts in ordinary life as we iterate operators in our logical analysis of our ordinary thoughts. I think it is also too analytic to be a phenomenological description of our thoughts if we were to say that it would be a *pragmatic* inconsistency for us to say "It is possible it may rain tomorrow, but I don't know that it is possible it may rain tomorrow." This is so even though that *is* a pragmatic consistency, on a par with "I'm awake, but I don't know it." It is even further away from phenomenology, but an even better logical analysis, to say with H. P. Grice it is a *conversational implicature* of ordinary speech that if I say it is possible it may rain tomorrow, I am conversationally implying that I know (in the ordinary sense of "know") that what I am saying is true. I think this makes it more reasonable than not, if not clear and convincing, that MDL–E is S5.

What would MDL–E's S5 axiom be formally speaking? It would be "If $\neg \Box P$ & $\neg \Box \neg P$ & $(\exists x)Px$, then $\Box[\neg \Box P$ & $\neg \Box \neg P$ & $(\exists x)Px]$". But in general, surely $\Box(A$ & B & $C)$ entails $\Box C$. And here $\Box C$ would be $\Box(\exists x)Px$. And we, not to mention Russell, would normally balk at $\Box(\exists x)Px$. How could it be necessary that it sometimes rains? But we forget that here "$\Box$" is not the logical necessity operator, but the knowledge operator. Perhaps it is *known* that it sometimes rains! And surely we (at least sometimes) *can* know if the three conjuncts of Russell's analysis of epistemic possibility apply. But the question before us is, if they *do* happen to apply, does it logically follow that it is *known* that they apply?

I think we have to refer back to the ordinary talk which Russell is analyzing. Note that his analysis of the ordinary sense of epistemic possibility is of the ordinary *empirical* sense. For we do not know whether or not every even number is the sum of two primes, and so the denial of that thesis is epistemically possible, in the sense that for all we know a proof could go either way; but it by no means follows that it is sometimes true that an even number is not the sum of two primes. Now, if I am right that Russell is analyzing *empirical* epistemic possibility, then I think the answer is to be found in a logical tie between the first two conjuncts, $\neg\Box P$ & $\neg\Box\neg P$, and the dubious third. For whatever is empirical is logically contingent. And if we do not know whether or not contingent P, then for us it is necessarily possible that contingently applicable Px is not always false, in the epistemic sense of "necessarily possible." I think that here too, it is more reasonable or not that MDL–E is S5.

Either that, or we shall have to modify Russell's analysis so that it can apply to the realms of necessary truth and falsehood, such as logic and mathematics. This can be done by changing his third clause, "it is not always false that Fx," to "it is not known that it is always false that Fx". But this is criticism, not scholarship.

A very Russellian reason why MDL–E is S5 is that there is a Parmenidean aspect of MDL–E. False statements cannot be known to be true, and propositional functions which are always false are epistemically impossible, since there are no merely possible objects. In general, what is actual is necessary, since only the actual is possible. But this applies to knowledge too. The only possible knowledge is actual knowledge. And right there we have epistemic $\Diamond P \rightarrow \Box\Diamond P$. Thus on the deepest level of Russell's theory of modality, MDL–E is S5.

This concludes my discussion of Russell's analysis of our ordinary epistemic talk. Again, I am not analyzing his philosophical theories of knowledge in this book. But if we look to his theories of knowledge in *The Problems of Philosophy*, the 1913 unpublished *Theory of Knowledge* manuscript, and elsewhere, the main thing to note in all of these works is that Russell admits universals in them. Knowledge and evidence would be relational universals for him. Thus they would be timeless and unchanging. Thus his theories of knowledge, insofar as they are *a priori*, are merely subdivisions of his general theory of *a priori* truth. Thus MDL–E is a subdivision of FG–MDL*+syn. For both are implicit in the same 1918 work, "The Philosophy of Logical Atomism." Thus MDL–E is S5 simply because FG–MDL*+syn is S5. Likewise, insofar as Russell's ethical theories (which we shall discuss next) are *a priori*, his implicit deontic logics are S5 insofar as they too are subdivisions of FG–MDL*+syn. But MDL–C is not a subdivision of FG–MDL*+syn, since causal laws are not *a priori*. And MDL–C is not even a subdivision of FG–MDL, since causal laws are never fully general (abstract). MDL–C is only a (quantified) subdivision of *always true* formal implications. For causal laws constitute the realm of synthetic *a posteriori always true* formal implications that have at least one descriptive propositional function. Recall that for Russell, there is no difference between a causal law and a true accidental generalization. But even that is enough to make MDL–C S5, on Russell's Humean theory of causal determinism. For on that theory, if nature is uniform, then MDL–C is S5. And here too there is the

Parmenidean aspect. For the only possible causes are actual causes, on Russell's primary, Parmenidean level of ontology and modality.

Russell's Implicit Deontic Logics:
Introductory Remarks

I turn now to Russell's ethics. I shall preface the discussion with a few remarks on deontic (ethical) modal logic in general.

In a deontic modal logic, necessity is moral necessity, and possibility is moral possibility. In ordinary terms, moral necessity is moral obligation, and moral possibility is moral permissibility.

My assessment of the strength of Russell's implicit deontic logics will be consistent with Don Paul Snyder's view that deontic logic in general ought to be S5, *pace* Georg Henrik von Wright, who has argued against the iterability of deontic operators (Snyder 1971: 197).[3]

Today, deontic logic is typically taken to be S5. Of course, it would have to be S5 if moral law is fixed and unchanging in a way analogous to logic or mathematics, or even to causal law. But all we need for the distinctive axiom of moral S5 is to say that if an act is morally permissible, then it is our moral duty to accept that it is morally permissible. And I for one would say that it is not only morally permissible, but also our moral duty, to accept all morality exactly as it is, including moral permissibilities.

The paradoxes of moral implication are similar to those of strict implication. "$\neg \Diamond P \supset (P \to Q)$" would mean "Doing what is forbidden commits us to doing everything" (Snyder 1971: 193). "$\Box Q \supset (P \to Q)$" would mean "What is obligatory is morally implied by everything" (Snyder 1971: 193). These, of course, require no special treatment. Indeed, one might simply accept them, much as C. I. Lewis—and I think eventually Russell—accepted the paradoxes of strict implication.①

But deontic logic sharply departs from other modal logics in the relationship of moral modalities to what is actually the case. It would be implausible to say that whatever is necessary is actual, or $\Box P \to P$. That would mean that whatever is morally obligatory actually happens, which is absurd. Likewise, it would be implausible to say that whatever is actual is possible, or $P \to \Diamond P$. That would mean that whatever actually happens is morally permissible, which is absurd. In colloquial terms, it means "Anything goes." We may call these the moral absurdities.

The standard way to avoid the moral absurdities is to avoid imputing moral characteristics to the actual world (Snyder 1971: 192–93). Historically, that is just Hume's view that no 'ought' can be derived from an 'is', or Moore's "open question fallacy" view

① Strict, or material? see pg. 116

that no fact entails a value. Russell implicitly avoids these two absurdities in this standard way, since he adopts the Hume-Moore view (PE 21–25, 58; Russell 1962: 19).

The avoidance can be technically accomplished simply by requiring that all atomic statements be prefixed by modal operators. This excludes mere atomic statements from the deontic logic. And that means that the logic cannot be used to describe the actual world, which is considered ethically neutral, but only to describe alternative ethically desirable worlds (Snyder 1971: 193 on CMn; 195). This too might be found implied in Russell by reasonable extension, though of course without ontological commitment to alternative worlds. From 1905 "On Denoting" on, Russell rejects merely possible worlds, and would rely only on descriptions of alternative ethical worlds, i.e., on mere ethical worlds talk.

Of course, we might also avoid the moral absurdities by admitting Leibniz's view that the actual world is the best of all possible worlds. On that view, it seems to follow that only the actual world is morally necessary, and even that everything in the actual world is morally necessary down to the slightest detail, since if the world is changed in the slightest, then would no longer be the same world. And since whatever is morally necessary is morally permissible, everything that actually happens would be morally permissible as well. Thus the world would be ethically non-neutral. Thus we could admit mere atomic statements after all; but all of them would be implicitly prefixed by the moral necessity operator, and also by the moral possibility operator. Perhaps this is a rash oversimplification of Leibniz, and no doubt Leibniz has more to say; but this is not a book on Leibniz. I shall merely note that this Leibnizian (or neo-Leibnizian) way out is implicitly rejected by Russell, since he rejects Leibniz's view that this is the best of possible worlds. Thus we are back to Snyder.

The axioms of deontic logic may be described as follows.

The distinguishing axiom of deontic S1 is that if P, then it is morally possible that P. That is, $P \rightarrow \Diamond P$. That is one of the two moral absurdities. Perhaps Russell could admit this axiom as a mere paradox that we can learn to live with, much as he admits the paradoxes of material implication. But I think there is a better and more appropriate Russellian answer. Namely, as we saw earlier, Russell implicitly avoids the moral absurdities because he adopts the Hume-Moore fact-value dichotomy (PE 21–25, 58; Russell 1962: 19). That is, he rejects that any "is" implies an "ought," and due to the interdefinability of the deontic operators, no "is" can imply a moral "may" for him either. Thus he implicitly requires that every statement (not just the atomic statements) in a deontic logic be prefixed by a deontic operator. Thus he implicitly rejects the distinguishing axiom of deontic S1 as ill-formed, since it contains P, and P violates the requirement. This also implicitly excludes the distinguishing axiom of deontic S3 for the same reason; but I will still discuss whether that axiom is Russellian in other respects.

The distinguishing axiom of deontic S2 is that if it is morally possible that P and Q, then it is morally possible that P. That is, $\Diamond(P \ \& \ Q) \rightarrow \Diamond P$. I think this axiom falls under Russell's rule of simplification. For otherwise the brackets would not be functioning as Russellian brackets. Thus I think that if the axiom were well-formed, it would be implicitly an instance of Russell's simplification rule. Note that even if, in some cases, the moral permissibility of P were to depend on the moral permissibility of Q, the antecedent gives us the moral permissibility of Q.

The distinguishing axiom of deontic S3 is that if P strictly implies Q, then the moral possibility of P strictly implies the moral possibility of Q. That is, $(P \rightarrow Q) \rightarrow (\Diamond P \rightarrow \Diamond Q)$. I think the best Russellian reading would be to treat the axiom as simply about two statements, P and Q, and a deontic operator must follow along with the truth-ground containment. There is certainly truth-ground containment, since the arrow means strict implication, which for Russell is deducibility. Thus I think Russell would have to accept this axiom. And for Russell, it is hard to see how something that is morally permissible could logically imply something that is not. He might accept that some major action might be permissible even if it implied some minor sub-action that was not. But the better view would be that *to the extent* that the major action implied the minor, the major action would not be permissible. Surely he is good enough at logic to be able to see that. But without further research, which I will not do here, this is just a reasonable gloss.

However, Russell rejects that any "is" implies an "ought," and due to the interdefinability of the deontic operators, no "is" can imply a moral "may" for him either. Thus he implicitly requires that every statement in a deontic logic be prefixed by a deontic operator. Thus he implicitly rejects the distinguishing axiom of deontic S3 as ill-formed, since it contains P and Q, and P and Q both violate the requirement.

The distinguishing axiom of deontic S4 is that if it is morally possible that P is morally possible, then P is morally possible. That is, $\Diamond\Diamond P \rightarrow \Diamond P$. This seems trivially correct due to the collapse of truth-grounds in iterations of the same operator.

The distinguishing axiom of deontic S5 is that if P is morally possible, then it is morally necessary that P is morally possible. That is, $\Diamond P \rightarrow \Box\Diamond P$. This seems correct insofar as ethical universals are timeless and unchanging for Russell. In fact, deontic S5 is just part of FG–MDL*+syn.

Model semantics for deontic S5 can be constructed only with a specialized set of assumptions (Snyder 1971: 192–98). Unusual assumptions need to be made about the transitivity, symmetry, and especially the reflexivity of the ethical alternativeness relationship, so as to complete the avoidance of the moral absurdities by avoiding relationships back to the actual world, which is treated as the fixed model. Also, exclusively deontic operators need to be defined, if the deontic logic is to be integrated with an alethic modal logic such as FG–MDL*. I shall not describe the details (Snyder 1971: 196–98). All this might be imputed to Russell more reasonably than not, in the name of protecting his adoption of the Hume-Moore separation of is from ought, and of facts from values. Indeed, since Russell implicitly rejects the moral absurdities as ill-formed, does this not logically imply he would accept the special reflexivity assumptions of deontic logic? After all, they are the only way to prevent the absurdities in model semantics for deontic S5. The only other option I see is to reject model semantics for deontic S5. But this option might be better than it sounds, if Russell has no model semantics.

I do not impute formal model semantics as implicit in Russell. That Russell lacks formal model semantics is criticism, not scholarship. Where Jean van Heijenoort and Jaakko Hintikka contrast model semantics with Frege-Russell universal logic, they tacitly admit that the Frege-Russell informally intended model is simply the actual world (Dummett 1995: 12, 12 n.6). I am imputing only the axioms of deontic S5 as implicit in Russell, not any formal semantics for deontic S5. But still, the actual world is Russell's (and Frege's) *implicitly* intended semantic model, since they admit no other world (compare my 2003: 279 n.12). Thus it seems we are back to Snyder again, since the actual world is his fixed model.

Russell's many popular ethical works on marriage, society, politics, and happiness have a liberal tenor that practically invites imputing to him the view that it is our duty to permit whatever is morally permissible, for the sake of human happiness. He thinks we ought to maximize individual freedom and happiness. I think that by itself makes it more reasonable than not to find deontic S5 implicit in him. But his technical works are harder to assess. I shall discuss two main phases of his ethical thinking.

Russell's Earlier Ethical Theory

I call Russell's early implicit deontic logic MDL–D. I find it implicit in Russell's major early ethical work, his neo-Moorean essay of ethical objectivism, "The Elements of Ethics," published in sections in 1910 and reproduced as a single essay in *Philosophical Essays* (PE essay 1).

Russell's philosophical writings on ethics concern what it is to be good (meta-ethics), and what things in the world are good (ethics). That is, they concern what it is to be an ethically desirable alternative world, and what things are good in such worlds. This is expressly so in "The Elements of Ethics." Just as Russell expressly adopts Leibniz's talk of logically possible worlds, he also expressly adopts talk of moral worlds, even in the course of rejecting Leibniz's optimism that the actual world is the best of all possible worlds:

> Hence the position of some optimists, that all the evil in the world is necessary to constitute **the best possible whole**, is not logically absurd, though there is, so far as I know, no evidence in its favour. Similarly the view that all the good is an unavoidable ingredient in **the worst possible whole** is not logically absurd.... (PE 56, my boldface emphasis)

Again:

> To live in a fool's paradise is commonly considered a misfortune; yet **in a world** which allows no paradise of any other kind a fool's paradise is surely the happiest habitation. (PE 57, my boldface emphasis)

Again:

> We may admit at once that **in a well-ordered world** [the doctrine that every man will best serve the general good by pursuing his own good] would be true.... (PE 49, my boldface emphasis)

Again:

> If two bitter enemies lived in different countries, and each falsely believed that the other was undergoing tortures, each might feel pleasure; yet we should not consider **such a state of things** good. We should even think it much worse than **a state in which** each derived pain from the belief that the other was in torture. (PE 57–58, my boldface emphasis)

Again:

> And when Christians affirm that **a world** created by a
> good God must be **a good world**, they do not mean that
> it must be to their taste.... (PE 21, my boldface emphasis)

Furthermore, the reason we ordinarily give for an actions's being
right is that its consequences are "likely to be...at least the **best
possible** under the circumstances" (PE 15, my boldface emphasis).

Leibniz is the source of Russell's talk of better or worse
worlds. Just ten years earlier, Russell had written a whole book on
Leibniz; the last chapter is a discussion of Leibniz's ethics (PL
chapter 16).

There is a Parmenidean aspect to MDL–D. Again, Russell
finds the case for determinism "overwhelming" (PE 37, 38, 45, 59).
And "if determinism is true, there is a sense in which no action is
possible except the one actually performed" (PE 39, 59). Thus
there is a fundamental sense in which one's actual moral act is the
only causally possible moral act. Thus the actual act, and indeed
the actual world, would be both the best possible and the worst
possible, as the *only* possible. Thus Russell is driven to admit a
second sense of "possible" in which alternative actions are
possible. The possibility of alternative actions in this sense is
compatible with determinism, and is also the sort of possibility
relevant to ethical theory. Russell calls acts which are possible in
this sense "physically possible." The basic idea is that an act is
physically possible if it "will be performed if we will to perform it"
(PE 59; see 36–45 for an extended discussion).

In "The Elements of Ethics," Russell never expressly states
that it is good that there are good things, or that it is our duty to do
our duty. In fact, someone might object that on Russell's own
views, he *cannot* find it good that things are good. Namely, he may
have thought that since goodness is an existing quality (PE 20, 21)
and since he accepts Hume's view that no value can be derived
from a fact, (PE 21–22, 58), we are not entitled to infer that it is
good (qua value from the fact) that there are existent goods, or even
that goodness is good. One reply would be that we can intuit the
fact that the universal *good* is itself good as a special relation it has
to itself. Certainly the relation would be special in violating
Russell's theory of types. But perhaps Russell's ethical universals
are commendatory as opposed to descriptive. Perhaps only
descriptive universals need conform to the theory of types. Russell
does much intuiting of goodness in other things. Why not of
goodness itself? All we need is a capacity for abstraction, a
capacity Russell admits concerning universals (PP 101). Why
would he not extend this capacity from universals that have being
(not: existence) to what could only be universal ethical qualities for
him? But the real error lies in supposing that goodness is *merely*

one entity among others. After all, it is goodness! I see no reason why Russell cannot abstract and intuit universals in values as easily as he can in things. This may seem like far too much charity on our part to waive theory of types. But then Russell does admit the Hume-Moore ought-is / fact-value dichotomy; and he does so without addressing how that dichotomy fits with his theory of types. For all we know, the entire ought-value side of it is exempt from theory of types. He simply never tells us. I think this is a legitimate and important question, to say the least.

In fact, I can hardly see how Russell could fail to intuit that the goodness of good things is itself good. Russell comes close to iteration of the same operator when he says, "I do not wish to deny that right conduct is among the things that are good on their own account" (PE 37). This amounts to saying that it is good to do acts which produce good results. And that looks for all the world like an express waiver of the theory of types for ethics. Could poor Russell have been so unaware he was violating his own theory of types in his own theory of ethics? This is beginning to look like an ordinary amount of charity in interpretation. Indeed, what is the point of his having a deep fact-value dichotomy, if his theory of types is allowed to run roughshod over the subtleties of his ethical views?

Again, intellectual intuition of the quality of goodness is merely acquaintance with a universal through the usual process of intellectual abstraction. At least, I assume the 1912 *The Problems of Philosophy* sheds definitive light on the 1910 "The Elements of Ethics" on this score. (PP 48, 51–52, 101–2). The 1912 Russell says, "Judgements of intrinsic ethical or aesthetic value are apt to have some self-evidence, but not much" (PP 117). Thus he gives value-universals no special treatment concerning their cognition. Perhaps that argues against my use of charity here; but I do not see how the argument could be conclusive. Indeed, how could Russell hold either that goodness transcends theory of types or that it does not, unless we had knowledge of it by acquaintance?

I can also hardly see how Russell could fail to agree that we have a duty to do our duty. For Russell, the objectively right act is "that one, of all the acts that are possible, which will probably produce the best results" (PE 59). It follows that "It is objectively right to do what is objectively right" means the same as "Of all the acts that are possible, it will probably produce the best results to do, out of all the acts that are possible, the act which will probably produce the best results." Or more simply, "It will probably produce the best results to do the act which will probably produce the best results." That is trivially true.

I proceed now to consider S4 and S5.

The distinguishing axiom of deontic S4 was that if it is morally possible that *P* is morally possible, then *P* is morally possible. That is, $\Diamond\Diamond P \to \Diamond P$. Where goodness and other values are intellectually intuited timeless universals, this is just like timeless logical form: if it is morally possible for P to be morally possible, then P simply *is* morally possible in virtue of its moral nature. The iteration collapses because it depends on the truth-conditions of the base statement, in this case $\Diamond P$. Thus it would be absurd to deny that MDL–D is S4. This was already noted in the brief overview at the end of the section on causality.

The distinguishing axiom of deontic S5 was that if P is morally possible, then it is morally necessary that P is morally possible. That is, $\Diamond P \to \Box\Diamond P$. Where goodness and other values are intellectually intuited timeless universals, this is just like timeless logical form: whatever is morally possible is necessarily morally possible in virtue of its ethical nature. Thus it would be absurd to deny that MDL–D is S5. Again, MDL–D is just a subdivision of FG–MDL*+syn. And once again, there is a Parmenidean aspect. The only possible duties and permissibilities are actual ones.

This concludes my discussion of whether MDL–D is S5.

Russell's Later Ethical Theory

MDL–D* is the later Russell's implicit deontic logic. His major later ethical work, the 1954 *Human Society in Ethics and Politics* (mainly written in 1946), is not a pure and simple subjectivism as some have thought (HS vii, 20, 59–72 90–96, *pace* viii on reason as the slave of the passions). I show elsewhere that from 1921 on, Russell equates degree of publicity with degree of objectivity in his ontology and metaphysics (Dejnožka 1991: 22–23, 26, 28–29, 30–34). In *Human Society*, Russell finds moral objectivity in widespread moral agreement. Nor is *Human Society* emotivist. Russell finds that ethical statements are, or can be, true or false (HS 94–96, *pace* 19, 72; see Dejnožka 1997: 53).

There is much continuity in Russell's ethical thinking from 1910 to 1954. He continues to discuss ethics in terms of alternative moral worlds:

> Borrowing a term from **Leibniz's account of possible worlds**, we may call two desires or impulses "**compossible**" when both can be satisfied, and "conflicting" when the satisfaction of the one is incompatible with that of the other....It is obvious that **a world** in which the aims of different individuals or groups are compossible is likely to be happier than one in which they are conflicting. It follows that it should be part of a wise social system to encourage **compossible**

purposes, and discourage conflicting ones.... (HS xiv–xv, my boldface emphasis)

Again:

That feelings are relevant to ethics is easily seen by considering **the hypothesis of a purely material universe**, consisting of matter without sentience. **Such a universe would be** neither good not bad, and nothing in it **would be** right or wrong. (HS 19, my boldface emphasis)

Again:

Without civic morality communities perish; without personal morality their survival has no value. Therefore civic and personal morality are **equally necessary to a good world**. (HS 22, my boldface emphasis)

Again:

In an inanimate world there would be nothing good or bad. (HS 44, my boldface emphasis)

Again:

Borrowing a term from **Leibniz**, I call a number of desires "**compossible**" when all can be satisfied by the same state of affairs; when they are not **compossible**, I call them incompatible. (HS 47, my boldface emphasis)

Again:

It may be urged that hate generates hate, and that **a world in which** hate is encouraged will be so full of strife that nobody will be able to enjoy a good life. (HS 70, my boldface emphasis)

Again:

What is meant, if anything, by saying that **a world in which** humans are happy is better than **a world in which** they are unhappy? (HS 90, my boldface emphasis; Russell "find[s] it intolerable to suppose" that something subjective is meant)

Again:

> I can make these robots do all the things that are usually praised. I can make them read the Bible. I can make them preach eloquent sermons....But if A said to B, "You ought to substitute robots for human beings, because robots do not sin," almost everybody would reply that **the robot world**, since it would be destitute of sentience, would be neither good nor bad, and would be in no way better than **a world of ordinary matter** unable to perform the robots' imitative tricks. (HS 100, my boldface emphasis)

Again:

> [Abstract considerations might make it seem that the road to universal contentment requires only] that the desires actuating the conduct of individuals should be **compossible** desires.... (HS 127, my boldface emphasis)

That is a total of nine texts in *Human Society* describing possible worlds or compossible things, and two of the texts cite Leibniz.

Another major continuity in Russell's ethical thinking from 1910 to 1954 is that the objectively right act is defined exactly the same as before, namely, as the act probably producing the best consequences (HS 95). The *only* change concerns what counts as good consequences. On the earlier theory, we wanted to maximize the production of things having an intuited quality of goodness. On the later theory, we want to maximize the general felt happiness or sense of satisfaction. Goodness, as a felt sense of happiness, remains an intrinsic quality as before, but now it is a felt quality sensed in our feelings, whereas before it was a quality intellectually intuited in things (HS 41; see 93). Thus we also have acquaintance with the quality of goodness as before, though now the acquaintance is through introspection of a feeling, or more generally of a state of mind (HS 107), rather than through intuitive intellectual abstraction (PP 48, 51–52, 101–2). Since the strength of MDL–D* depends on the definition alone, and not on the change concerning what counts as a good consequence, we may apply our analysis of the strength of implicit MDL–D to implicit MDL–D* without further ado. For both the early and the later ethical theories are equally consequentialist; and far more importantly for our purposes, both assert timeless and unchanging relations among timeless and unchanging universals. Thus both MDL–D and MDL–D* are S5 in strength, and both are equally subdivisions of FG–MDL*+syn. For both theories of ethics are synthetic *a priori*. But even if their definitions of objective rightness were analytic, and not synthetic theoretical definitions that aim to state what objective rightness is, they would still belong to FG–MDL*+syn, since they would then belong to FG–MDL*. Both theories of ethics also equally have the Parmenidean aspect that the only possible duties are actual duties, since for Russell on the deepest level, there are no merely possible items of any kind at all.

The robot world and the purely material world suggest a separation of ought from is, as before. They are worlds that contain only facts, and no values. Russell says that ethical judgments: (1) state feelings, not facts; (2) should be imperative, not indicative in mood; and (3) "clearly cannot be proved or disproved merely by amassing facts" (HS 19). Point (1) implies Russell's rejection of emotivism (HS 94–96). Point (2) seems contradicted by point (1). Should not all feelings be stated in the indicative mood? Should not all statements, as opposed to commands, be in the indicative mood? Point (3) shows that the later Russell still accepts the Hume-Moore fact-value dichotomy. Ironically, Russell's view here implies a *negative* "fact-to-value" implication that a purely robot or material or, more generally, a *non*-sentient world, *cannot* have values. One way out would be to note that the implication is from negative fact to negation of value. This is lame because the fact-value dichotomy is intended to be a general one, and not limited to denying only the validity of positive-fact-to-positive-value implications. Another way out is to contraposit the implication to the positive value-to-fact implication that if a world has value, then it has sentience. The way out is lame because contraposition is a two-way street. We can contraposit right back to the first implication, which is still from an "is" to an "absence of ought." The whole problem is that the later Russell grounds goodness, which is a value, in felt happiness, which is a fact. This contradicts the Hume-Moore position on the deepest level. And every utilitarian who grounds value in pleasure faces this problem. (Hume does not appear to be a utilitarian; see Smart 1967: 208.) But this is Russell criticism, not scholarship.

Russell's fourth "fundamental proposition," "It is right to feel approval of a right act and disapproval of a wrong act" (HS 95), suggests that he would allow iteration of moral necessity operators. Even if he is not formally iterating a formal moral operator here, he seems very close to doing so, in his rather technical language. This is a continuity with his earlier view. For the early Russell says, "I do not wish to deny that right conduct is among the things that are good on their own account" (PE 37).

The 1954 Russell thinks of moral rules as universal (HS 71), and he aims to minimize the theoretical possibility of ethical disagreement. Thus he might seem to be against defeasement, which is a way to resolve theoretically genuine ethical conflicts. But he still distinguishes objectively right acts from subjectively right acts (HS 71). Thus the later Russell still has the same logical room to allow actual duties to defease apparent ones that the earlier

Russell had. Russell also still speaks of exceptions to rules (HS 37).

The 1954 Russell also states much the same theory of free will and determinism as before, though not in the same detail (HS 79–80). Morality is consistent with determinism. Once again, there is a fundamental sense in which one's actual moral act is the only causally possible moral act. Once again, this drives Russell to find a second sense of "possible" which is consistent with determinism. This second sense is basically the same as before as well.

To sum up Russell on ethics, for our purposes there is no significant difference between the early and the later Russell on the meta-ethical level of theory of what the objectively right act is, and therefore no significant difference in strength between the early implicit MDL–D and the later implicit MDL–D*.

Since I simply quote Russell's early and later definitions of objective rightness to define the necessity operators of MDL–D and MDL–D*, it seems absurd to deny that these logics are perfect formal paraphrases of Russell's definitions.

I shall now discuss two more topics in Russellian deontics.

The Defeasibility of Moral Duties

Defeasibility is a main topic in ethics and in deontic logic. A moral duty is defeased if it is trumped by another, higher-level, moral duty in a certain situation. Both duties are taken as objective, but one is taken as more important, at least in the situation. But we can also discuss defeasibility using more complex distinctions.

Donald Nute distinguishes among *prima facie* duties, actual duties, and apparent moral duties:

> By a *prima facie* obligation, I mean something that is binding *other things being equal*....By an *actual* obligation I will mean any obligation that is binding when all relevant circumstances are considered.... [T]here may be situations in which we *cannot* know all morally relevant circumstances before deciding what we ought to do. In such a situation, we are expected to fulfill those obligations which bind us *given all we know about morally relevant circumstances*. These are what I call our *apparent obligations*. (Nute 1997: 287, my emphasis)

For Nute, one apparent obligation can defease another, if it is based on better information. That is, a new and better justified apparent obligation can defease an old apparent obligation (Nute 1997: 288). Here the situation of defeasement is the informational situation. It seems to me that an apparent obligation can also defease a *prima facie* obligation. where the new informational situation is such that the "other things" can no longer be treated as "equal." It also seems to me that an actual obligation can defease a *prima facie* one, again due to the relevance of information which the *prima facie* obligation dismissively treats as "other things." It even seems to me that a *prima facie* obligation can defease an apparent obligation, if the latter is based on dubious information which it is safer to reject under the heading, "other things being equal." Of course, an actual obligation can defease an apparent one for informational reasons. Indeed, that is the chief point of that distinction. I do not see why we could not superimpose all of these distinctions and their defeasibilities on Russell. Note that all three types of obligations are objective, even though they are all relative to the information that exists (actual), that we have (apparent), or that we are considering (*prima facie*). That is because, in a certain situation, there can really *be* all three sorts of duty, even if we might not *know* what the actual duty is.

I think enough universality can be attributed to the early Russell's moral duties that something is an actual duty for a given person in a certain type of consequential situation in the actual world if and only if it is a duty in the same type of consequential situation for all persons in all moral alternative worlds, and in fact in all logically possible worlds. That is, for Russell no actual duty can defease another actual duty, on this deepest and most universal ethical level.

But Russell does admit defeasible moral duties in a sense. He admits subjective moral duties which surely can be defeased (PE 33–36, 38, 59). For the 1910 Russell, what is objectively right is our actual obligation, and what is subjectively right is our apparent obligation. What is objectively right is what is most likely to produce the greatest amount of good, and what is subjectively right is what a moral agent would believe to be objectively right after an appropriate amount of reflection on the available information (PE 38, 59; see 27–37). Surely Russell's subjectively right duties are defeasible by his objective duties in just the manner Nute suggests. For surely new information could appear even after an appropriate amount of reflection on the available information. Indeed, Russell's subjective duties seem to be basically the same as Nute's apparent obligations. Both are defined in terms of the information available to the agent. Russell's objective duties seem similar to Nute's actual obligations, but the definitions are very different. "Considering all relevant circumstances" is intensionally very different from "most likely to maximize goodness." The definitions do not even appear to imply each other, and not even by synthetic *a priori* implication. In fact, they seem to be incommensurable desiderata for ideal or perfect duties, which Russell calls "objective," and Nute "actual."

Does Russell admit *prima facie* duties which can conflict with and be defeased by other sorts of duties, meaning either actual or subjective duties? I shall argue that he does.

Now, a simple moral rule is typically a *prima facie* rule. For it is usually simple because it dismisses considerations under the heading, "other things being equal." And Russell says, "Whenever a question is at all complicated, [it] cannot be settled by following some simple rule" (PE 28). Even the simple rules we admit are justified only as being right "in the vast majority of instances" (PE 28), and we tend to reclassify exceptional acts as not falling under the rule. For example, "Thou shalt not murder" will generally not be treated as including killing in war or in self-defense (PE 28–29). Thus a "moral code is never itself ultimate; it is based upon an estimate of probable consequences" (PE 30). "Right and wrong, since they depend upon consequences, will vary as men's circumstances vary" (PE 54). This sounds like the defeasibility of *prima facie* duties, and no doubt it often is. But the existence of an exception to a rule does not imply defeasement of the rule by another rule. It might be an unprincipled exception, at least for all we know at the time. However, our question is still answered, since it is obvious that Russell often does allow and want simple rules to be defeased in the light of fuller information. And in theory that can be by subjective duties or objective duties, or even by both. Useful rules can be simple enough to be defeased by a whole hierarchy of ascending levels of information, and Russell seems well aware of it. I assume that most if not all simple rules are *prima facie*, but that not all *prima facie* rules need be simple, e.g., in complex statutes.

We can treat Russell's definition of objective rightness as also being a supreme rule to do whatever will probably maximize goodness. In contrast, Russell's talk of moral codes is always of specific historical moral codes, and it may be that none of them is objectively right. Since all objective rules must conform to the supreme rule in order to be objective rules at all, there is no sense of conflict among objective rules.

Objective rules trump everything else for Russell, "since in fact everything either ought to exist or ought not" (PE 18). And intrinsic goodness is a property which either a thing has or it has not (PE 20). Thus in a dispute about whether a thing is good or not, one person will be right and the other wrong (PE 21). Here, things whose goodness is disputed presumably include apparent moral acts and apparent duties. Russell does all he can to explain away moral disagreements as merely apparent (PE 54–56).

That Russell speaks of the objectively right act as "that one, of all the acts that are possible, which will *probably* produce the best results" (PE 59, my emphasis) does not detract from anything I have said. By definition for Russell, the probability is simply part of what the objectively right act is. And probability universals are just as timeless and unchanging as ethical universals, or for that matter, any other universals. That it is logically possible that two or more acts can have an equal probability of producing equally best results is criticism, not scholarship. Note that this is not only a criticism of the definite description in Russell's definition, but it also raises the problem of Buridan's ass for Russellian moral decision-making. Jean Buridan, a medieval logician, posed the problem that if everything has a sufficient reason, then if we position an ass between two equidistant, equally good piles of hay, so that it has no reason to prefer eating one over the other, then it would die of starvation. Likewise for equally probable best results.

Dyadic Operators for Conditional Duties

Another main topic of deontic logic is the use of dyadic modal operators to formalize conditional moral duties (Nute 1997a: 7; Forrester 1996: 23, 48–49; Snyder 1971: 194). Russell's moral duties are conditional in that they are contingent on what happens, meaning whether they maximize production of goodness. This is the utilitarian side of Russell's ethic. Here Russell in effect requires dyadic, or better, polyadic modal operators. That is because for him, moral rightness is conditional on producing good consequences, and is thus conditional on causality, whether assayed *á la* Hume or not. Russell says, "If causality is doubted, morals collapse" (PE 38). "Right and wrong, since they depend upon consequences, will vary as men's circumstances vary" (PE 54). And since causality involves systems of interacting variables (ONC 187–93), polyadic relations are needed. Moral acts are also conditional on their physical possibility, as explained earlier (PE 39–40). The conditionality of moral duties must not be confused with their defeasibility. Also, it must be noted that in any utilitarian ethic such as Russell's, moral duties are temporally and causally postconditional (i.e. conditioned on future events), and are only logically or definitionally preconditional (i.e. conditioned on prior definition). Both points are due to the fact that he defines present rightness in terms of future consequences.

The early Russell's ethics has a basic utilitarian aspect, but this does not affect its implicit strength's being S5. That is because Russell's utilitarian definition of rightness in terms of production of goodness is an objective ethical standard based on the timeless objective nature of ethical universals. And even aside from that, any form of utilitarianism or consequentialism is meant to be objective. And while any future production of goodness involves causation, causation itself is S5 too, as we saw earlier.

It seems now that we can find deontic S5 implicit in ethical thinkers without regard for whether they are intrinsicalist or consequentialist, if only their ethics are objective and unchanging. Indeed, Snyder seems to find just that (Snyder 1971: 192–98). But that would not meet either of the two tests of my methodology. We must still discuss actual texts in Russell, if only to show that his ethics is of the objective and unchanging sort.

Review of Russell's Eight Implicit Modal Logics

Surveying all eight of Russell's implicit modal logics—FG–MDL, FG–MDL*, FG–MDL+syn, FG–MDL*+syn, MDL–C, MDL–E, MDL–D, and MDL–D*—all are S5. If I am right, then Russell has achieved a tremendous theoretical simplification due to his always interpreting modality in terms of quantification. MDL is the basic logical element of all eight. Thus whether the modalities are logical, causal, epistemic, or moral turns out to be irrelevant to the question of strength. They are merely interpretive differences.

This makes historical sense. FG–MDL+syn and FG–MDL* +syn are close to the early modern theory of necessary truths as unchanging relations of ideas, which is best seen as S5 for similar reasons. FG–MDL* has an antecedent in the Leibniz-Kant subject-contains-predicate test of analyticity, which is best seen as S5 for similar reasons. All this helps place Russell in the modern tradition of theory of necessary truth. And Russell's theory of universal natures "is largely Plato's" (PP 91). Plato's theory of timeless unchanging forms could only be S5.

The reader may object that surely causal necessity should be weaker than logical necessity or synthetic *a priori* necessity, yet here I am making all three sorts of necessity out to have the same strength, S5 (waiving S5 + I).

My reply is that the objection is a *non sequitur*. Of course, causal necessity is weaker than logical or *a priori* necessity, in the sense that we can logically conceive of a causal law as being false. But it does not follow from this that causal logic is any less S5 in strength than alethic logic. That question turns instead on which axioms are true for each logic. Here all the S5 axioms are true in all the implicit logics, and the only difference is that the necessity operator is *interpreted* differently in each implicit logic. Its various interpretations may be stated as follows:

In FG–MDL, "□*P*" means "*P* is a fully general truth."

In FG–MDL*, "□*P*" means "*P* is a fully general truth and is true in virtue of its logical form."

In FG–MDL*+syn, "□*P*" means "*P* is an *a priori* truth, where logical truth is fully general truth."

In FG–MDL*+syn, "□*P*" means "*P* is an *a priori* truth, where logical truth is fully general truth that is true in virtue of its logical form."

In MDL–C, "□*P*" means, "*P* is deducible from the set of all causal laws and true particular statements."

In MDL–E, "□*P*" means "¬◊¬*P*", where "◊*P*" means "We do not know if *P*; proposition '*P*' is a value of the propositional function *P*x; and *P*x is not always false."

In both MDL–D and MDL–D*, "□*P*" means, "It ought to be that *P*," or more precisely, "*P* probably maximizes goodness." Goodness is a conceived abstract universal in MDL–D, and is felt happiness in MDL–D*.

What difference does any of these different interpretations of the box symbol make to S-strength? None that I can see.

Using the box symbol for necessity and the diamond for possibility is always an interpretive gloss on Russell, who uses no such symbols himself. But I feel it is both shallow and uncharitable to limit the formal interpretation of any philosopher's theories to their own formal notations, if some of their theories would be better expressed in a different notation. Again, the use of the box and diamond symbols does not commit us to interpreting them as expressing modal meanings.

Referential Opacity

Another main topic in modal logic is referential opacity. That is Quine's term; Russell's term is propositional attitude. It is widely accepted that all modal operators are referentially opaque. That is, they are not truth-functional. That is, they are not truth-functional operators on any proposition *P*. That is, merely replacing true *P* with true *Q* does not logically guarantee that the operator applies to *Q* if it applies to *P*, or that it does not apply to *Q* if it does not apply to *P*.

All the modal operators in Russell's eight implicit modal logics are referentially opaque, exactly as we would expect them to be. The reason is simple. Truth-functional statement operators treat statements as mere atoms of truth or falsehood. But all the modal operators in Russell's implicit modal logics make direct or indirect reference to the form or internal structure of statements—and not all true statements have the same internal structure.

FG–MDL and FG–MDL* concern truth in virtue of logical form.

FG–MDL+syn and FG–MDL*+syn concern truth in virtue of timeless relations among timeless universals, that is, in virtue of the timelessness of the internal structure of both analytic and synthetic *a priori* truths.

MDL–C concerns the logical structure of true synthetic *a posteriori* formal implications which contain at least one descriptive propositional function.

MDL–E, MDL–D and MDL–D* are all just subdivisions of FG–MDL*+syn. MDL–D and MDL–D* may well *be* the very same subdivision, truth-wise, but would *interpret* the truths differently.

The operators of MDL–D and MDL–D* are also indirectly logically connected to the logical form of statements, since what is logically impossible logically cannot be morally necessary, and what is morally possible logically must be logically possible. They are even indirectly logically connected to the logical structure of *always true* formal implication. For an accidental universal truth is a causal law, and what is physically impossible logically cannot be a moral duty. Of course, these logical connections of deontic operators to logical form are not formal but intuitive, that is, synthetic *a priori*.

Russell, of course, can easily accommodate referential opacity with respect to modal contexts created by the use of modal operators. He already admits referential opacity with respect to doxastic contexts. That is, he admits "Smith believes that *P*" is a non-truth-functional statement. This is his theory of propositional attitudes in *Principia* (PM 8; PM Appendix C) and elsewhere.

While all the modal operators in all eight implicit modal logics are referentially opaque, none of the modal logics involves any modal entities or notions, except for MDL–D, which is based on a logically indefinable modal entity, the universal goodness. This modal entity vanishes in the later Russell's MDL–D*, and is not originally due to Russell but to Moore. Russell adopts it from Moore during Russell's early phase of neo-Moorean realism in *Principles*. The most basic or general reason for opacity in MDL–D is not the admission of this modal entity, but the indirect relationship of moral statements to the logical form of statements. Again, the operators in both implicit deontic logics are indirectly related to the logical form of statements. What is logically impossible, or even just physically impossible (i.e. universally false), cannot be a moral duty. Indeed, all the operators in all eight implicit modal logics are opaque for the general reason of logical form. However, this modal entity is certainly sufficient to do the job of creating modal opacity all by itself. Even the mere word "good" would do that, if used as a modal operator.

Quantification into Modal Contexts

Mark W. Dickson (1998) observes that Russell permits quantification into epistemic contexts as early as "On Denoting":

> [W]hen we say, 'George IV wished to know whether Scott was the author of *Waverley*', we normally mean 'George IV wished to know whether one and only one man wrote *Waverley* and Scott was that man'; but we *may* also mean: 'One and only one man wrote *Waverley* and George IV wished to know whether Scott was that man'. In the latter, 'the author of *Waverley*' has a *primary* occurrence; in the former, a *secondary*. (OD 52)

This is a scope distinction that Russell does apply to epistemic contexts and logically can apply to modal contexts. That "*wished* to know" is intentional, not epistemic, seems casual writing and insignificant. Of course, epistemic contexts *are* modal contexts, since knowledge *is* epistemic necessity.

The *Waverly* example shows that Russell can and does allow quantification into modal statements, specifically epistemic statements, just as easily as he allows it into any other statements, and even makes a primary-secondary scope distinction. The only remaining question is whether he has sufficient reason to admit *true* quantifications into modal contexts. I think we can already see that he does in fact admit them in the *Waverly* example, and has good reason to do so in that epistemic example. And I shall argue shortly that he has good reason to admit them generally.

Russell also allows quantification into intentional contexts such as belief (PM 8; PM Appendix C). Here we might treat belief as a doxastic modality.

Grades of Modal Involvement

This brings us to another main topic of modal logic, grades of modal involvement. The term is due to Quine's essay, "Three Grades of Modal Involvement." I shall now discuss the grades of modal involvement of Russell's eight implicit modal logics.

Quine's lowest grade of modal involvement occurs when "is necessary" is viewed as a semantical predicate of names. Quine argues that its seeming referential opacity is no genuine threat to extensionality, that is, to truth-functionality, since such modal contexts are not significantly different from mere quotational contexts (Quine 1976a: 161–63).

The second grade occurs when "is necessary" is viewed as a statement operator. The commitment here is to modal statement operators.

For the record, I find the distinction between the first and second grades only superficially clear. The later Frege in effect collapses it by holding that statements *are* names of truth-values. And the later Russell, and indeed Quine himself, blur it in the opposite direction by equating or assimilating words ordinarily considered names to statements. The later Russell says that "in the object-language, ...every single word is an assertion" (IMT 75). I suspect that Quine follows Russell on this. In any case, Quine's distinction vanishes if all statements are names, if all names are statements, or both. Please note that this criticism of Quine affects only our interpretation and criticism of grades of modal involvement in the later Russell.

The third grade occurs when quantification is allowed into modal contexts. This is the highest grade of modal involvement. Quine calls it a commitment to "Aristotelian essentialism." The phrase is mere picturesque advocacy against this grade. Quine merely means a general commitment to there being some things in the world that have some properties necessarily, not a commitment specifically to Aristotle's substance metaphysics of essence and accident. While in the lower two grades, the ontological *locus* of modality is only in how we talk about the world (*de dicto*), here the ontological *locus* of modality is in the world we talk about (*de re*) (Quine 1976a). According to some, a model is anti-essentialist, that is, *not* third grade, if and only if it makes all quantified *de re* formulas equivalent to *de dicto* formulas, thereby eliminating *de re* quantification (see Parsons 1971; McKay 1975). However, I find this a two-way street. If we flip this around, by definition such a model also makes all such *de dicto* quantified formulas equivalent to *de re* formulas. I offer a comparison. Curt John Ducasse says:

> [I]f the process called by Carnap translation from the material into the formal mode of speech is really translation, [then] his conclusion that sentences in the material mode really are disguised syntactical sentences, and therefore that philosophy is really syntax, would not follow. What would follow would be that either they are disguised syntactical sentences, *or* the syntactical sentences into which they are translatable are disguised sentences of the material mode, i.e., are really sentences about objects....
> It would thus be perfectly arbitrary which one of such a pair of sentences we chose to describe as a "disguise" of the other, and which one therefore to describe as what the other "really" is; and therefore it

> would be arbitrary also whether we chose to say that
> philosophy is really syntax or that syntax, or at least a
> certain part of syntax, is really philosophy. (Ducasse
> 1941: 94–95)

The same might be said of translating *de re* quantifications into *de dicto*. In fact, that seems to be an instance of Carnapian translation. And which mode of speech is a disguise of which would depend at bottom on our metaphysics, or for us, on Russell's metaphysics.

All eight of Russell's implicit modal logics are of the second grade at the very least, since all of them have statement operators.

Landini observes that in MDL, necessity with respect to *x* in *Fx* would be best viewed as a semantical predicate of names (Landini 1993: 4), since *x* would be replaced by logically proper names. I agree that this assigns to MDL the lowest grade of modal involvement. But as Landini knows, MDL is not a modal logic, since MDL is not even sentential.

De Re and De Dicto: Russell's Implicit Essentialism

I shall now argue that Russell has sufficient reason to permit quantification into modal contexts in a major subdivision of FG–MDL*+syn, the mature implicit modal logic of all *a priori* truths. At least on my interpretation, the 1905–18 Russell's theory of particulars and universals is that sensible particulars are essentially instances of sensible universals (Dejnožka 2003: 159–60). Such particulars would not be the particulars they are unless they were instances of the sensible universals of which they are instances. For them to change their sensible qualities is for them to cease to exist and be replaced by new and wholly different particulars (RUP 119; PLA 119). This is Russell's version of Aristotelian essentialism. Note that Russell speaks of sensible particulars as being substances logically speaking (PLA 201–2, 203–4). In fact, ignoring one's own mind and looking only to sensed and unsensed sensibilia, the 1914–18 Russell is best described as a superessentialist, where superessentialism is the view that every monadic property of a real particular is an essential part of its nature (modifying Blumenfeld 1982: 103). At least this is so for Russell's sensible qualities of sensible particulars, and for generic properties abstractable from the sensible qualities. Internal relations, such as that this sound is louder than that, are essential relations among Russell's sensibilia, but they do not concern superessentialism, which is only about monadic properties. At least, they do not if we do not paraphrase relational "*a* is louder than *b*" as monadic "*a* is-louder-than-*b*." Russell conversely speaks of predicates, "when convenient," as "monadic relations" in the *Inquiry* (IMT 94).

Yet it is wrong to say with Quine that now the ontological *locus* of modality is in the world we talk about. For here in the third grade of modal involvement, Russell is as eliminative of modal entities and modal notions as ever. Here the necessity operator in "$(\exists x)\Box(Fx)$" means only "It is a relationship of instantiation that," not "It is necessary that." The notion of instantiation is not intrinsically modal. It is the relation of a particular's *being* a universal, in an ontologically intimate sense almost that of identity. It is instantiational relationships which have their *locus* in the world, not any ontological necessities over and above them. This is analogous to Russell's eliminative analysis of logically necessary inference in his whole-part containment theory of deductively valid inference. There is only the whole-part containment relationship, and no necessity over and above that. For the only difference between a universal and its instances is that it is one and they are many. It is distinct from them only in reason, and in different senses they "contain" each other. "Contain," of course, is only a metaphor for each of these two *sui generis* categorial relationships.

Even if the 1903–18 Russell's particulars were bare particulars and not particular instances of sensible qualities, their individual identities would be just as essentially connected to, that is, just as essentially dependent on, the sensible qualities they exemplify. The only thing that would change is that the necessity operator in "$(\exists x)\Box(Fx)$" would mean, "It is a relationship of *exemplification* that."

Placing this sort of instantiational quantification (over sensible instances of sensible universals) into modal contexts in FG–MDL*+syn might seem to blur Gustav Bergmann's threefold distinction among three sorts of necessity: categorial necessity, analytic necessity, and synthetic *a priori* necessity. The first would be "shown not said" in an ideal language perfectly mirroring the categorial structure of the world in its syntactical structure (Bergmann 1967: 23–24). The reason for the seeming blur is this. Let *a* be a red sense-datum I now sense, and let *F* be the universal *red*. At least on my interpretation of Russell's individuals as all being particulars, the mere fact that "*a*" is a logically proper name *shows* that "*a*" means and denotes a sense-datum. For it is only by acquaintance with the sense-datum *a* that we could grasp the meaning and denotation of its name, "*a*". (For a sense-datum, both the meaning and the denotation of "*a*" are *a* itself.) And the only way we could have a *de re* necessary predication of property *F* of particular *a* would be if *F* is a sensible quality, or an abstraction from a sensible quality, of instance *a*. Thus the fact that *a* necessarily has F would be "shown not said" in an ideal language by the mere fact that "Fa" is a syntactically well-formed sentence. Thus such *de re* predication would seem to be a categorial necessity. But I classify such *de re* predication as synthetic *a priori* necessity. For the test of categorial necessity is that an attempt to express its denial in an ideal language is syntactically ill-formed. And the denial of "Fa", namely, "$\neg Fa$", is just as well-formed as "Fa" is. Likewise, when we quantify over "a", both "$(\exists x)\square(Fx)$", which says, "There exists a particular which is necessarily F", and its denial, "$\neg(\exists x)\square(Fx)$", are equally well-formed. Hence the necessity *involved in* (not: necessary *truth of*, since all of these statements are logically contingent) "Fa" and "$(\exists x)\square(Fx)$" is only synthetic *a priori*. (It could scarcely be analytic.) We can even remove the blur. In point of fact, it is *not* true that the fact that a necessarily has F would be "shown not said" in an ideal language by the mere fact that "Fa" is a syntactically well-formed sentence. That is only a necessary condition, not a sufficient one. The other necessary condition is that "Fa" be *true*. If "F" is syntactically correct for *red*, and if "a" is syntactically correct for the sense-datum I am now acquainted with, and if "Fa" is *true*, then and only then is it shown (by syntax *plus* truth) that a is necessarily F, since that is the only way "Fa" could be true at all. Again, this is where a is a sense-datum and F is a sensible quality-universal.

Perhaps the deepest inconsistency I have found in Russell is that between his essentialism and his anti-essentialism. The later (1945) Russell lambastes essentialism:

> The "essence" of a thing appears to have meant "those of its properties which it cannot change without losing its identity"....In fact, however, this is a verbal convenience. The "essence" of Socrates thus consists of those properties in the absence of which we should not use the name "Socrates." The question is purely linguistic: a *word* may have an essence, but a *thing* cannot. (HWP 200–1)

Yet the later (1940–1959) Russell also admits sensible qualities as recurrent scattered particulars, and he predicates generic universals of them which they could only have essentially. For example, a certain shade of red is a particular which essentially has the generic properties of having a color, of being visible, and of being sensible (IMT 98, 100, 227; see Dejnožka 2003: 161–62, 292–95 n.4). Thus Russell attacks traditional essentialism, but embraces his own new essentialism. As late as 1959, Russell says, "Traditionally, qualities, such as [a certain sort of] white or hard or sweet, counted as universals, but if [my 1940–1959] theory is valid, they are syntactically more akin to substances" (MPD 127). Substance and essence are revised, not rejected, in the early Russell (instances) and in the later Russell (qualities) alike. That this essentialism is not entirely shown in the formal notation does not detract from this point. At least, logically proper names always denote the post-1910 Russell's substance substitutes. They always denote individuals, that is, particulars.

Russell was much less self-conflicted in his 1918 "The Philosophy of Atomism." He compares his sense-particulars to the old substances (PLA 201–2), and presents them as instances of sensible qualities: "what I call 'particulars'—such things as little patches of colour or sounds" (PLA 179). There is no comparable lambasting of essentialism to backfire on him.

I proceed to discuss a problem of paraphrase raised by Mark Dickson. Dickson asks how Russell might translate:

> 1. "The author of *Hamlet* might not have written *Hamlet*."

Following Kripke, Dickson says that if Russell admits only *de dicto* modality, then Russell can only interpret this sentence as meaning,

> 1* "It is possible that the author of *Hamlet* did not write *Hamlet*,"

which Dickson says is a contradiction (M. Dickson 1998). This poses the problem; of course, logical possibility is meant.

I think this problem can be solved if we understand Russell's metaphysics, his logic, and his theory of paraphrase.

For Russell, paraphrase is the art of reasonably replacing unclear ordinary thoughts with canonical notation. Dickson is looking for a strong Kripkean solution in which the first occurrence of "the author of *Hamlet*" in (1) involves rigid designation, and the second occurrence is attributive. I think this type of strong solution is available to Russell, though the rigid designation will not be of the author of *Hamlet* as such, but only of a sensible aspect of him.

As to metaphysics, for the 1918 Russell a man is a temporal series of classes of sensed and unsensed sensibilia. My paraphrase would be, "The sense-datum s I now sense belongs to class c in temporal series t (where t is Russell's metaphysical analysis of William Shakespeare as he actually lived and wrote *Hamlet*), and it is logically possible that there exists at least one class $c1$ and at least one temporal series $t1$ such that s belongs to $c1$ and $c1$ belongs to $t1$ (where $t1$ is the metaphysical analysis of some possible way Shakespeare might have lived in which he did not write *Hamlet*). The fact that classes and series are logical fictions which have no ontological status, so that quantification over them is purely nominal, does not detract from the correctness of the paraphrase. It is quantification over *s* that involves quantification into the modal subcontext.

The situation is actually much more complicated than my paraphrase suggests, since there will be many ways in which what we ordinarily call the same man might have lived without writing *Hamlet.* Also, people today can no longer sense sense-data which were sensible aspects of Shakespeare, but can only use descriptions. But I think my paraphrase conveys the gist of how Russell would approach the problem.

A simpler solution would be to substitute another description for the first occurrence of "the author of *Hamlet.*" We must allow Russell charity in paraphrasing ordinary language statements into his canonical notation. No good student of the art of Russellian formal paraphrase would dream of making (1) self-contradictory by translating it as (1*). Considerations of para-phrase include not only analysis into particulars and logical fictions, but the use of plain common sense. For example, we should not translate the ordinary definite description "the charlady who ain't never done no harm to no one" as the charlady 'who in at least one moment injured the entire human race' (MPD 179). Russell's famous reply to Strawson makes it clear that Russell would find that literal translation ludicrous. Russell gives the charlady example as a parody of logicians with no common sense. The message of the charlady example is that "My theory of descriptions was never intended as an analysis of the state of mind of those who utter sentences containing descriptions....I was concerned to find a *more accurate* and analyzed thought to *replace* the somewhat confused thoughts which most people at most times have in their heads" (MPD 179, my emphasis; see PLA 179–82, 188–89 for early statements of this view of analysis in 1918).

A third solution would be to use the "On Denoting" scope distinctions directly to solve the *Hamlet* problem, by parity of reason with epistemic contexts (M. Dickson 1998). This is the solution Arthur Smullyan adopts (Smullyan 1971).

Leonard Linsky and Quine argue that Smullyan's solution is not enough (Smullyan 1971, citing *Principia*; L. Linsky 1971: 94–95; see L. Linsky 1971a: 3–4 quoting Quine). Up to a certain point we need not be detained, since in the present context, this is criticism, not scholarship. That is, if we find Smullyan's solution the only feasible one for Russell, then we would be finding Russell inadequate only if Smullyan's solution is inadequate. But I think either of our first two Russellian solutions are clearly adequate.

Quine has two arguments. First, the adoption of the scope distinction already requires the possibility of quantifying into modal contexts. Thus "the appeal to scopes of descriptions does not justify such quantification, it just begs the question" (L. Linsky 1971a: 4, quoting Quine). My response is that the adoption of scopes and of quantification are so much the same thing that begging the question is simply not an appropriate description. Except for the very simplest quantifications, they go hand in hand; we do both or do neither. This is a simply standoff of opposing logical intuitions. Neither Quine nor Smullyan has a decisive upper hand on this level of argument.

Quine's second argument is that eliminating singular terms and using only descriptions, modal features appear to shift as descriptions shift. Therefore modality appears to be a feature not of things themselves, but of how we describe them (L. Linsky 1971a: 4). Quine says:

> Mathematicians may conceivably be said to be necessarily rational and not necessarily two-legged; and cyclists necessarily two-legged and not necessarily rational. But what of an individual who counts among his eccentricities both mathematics and cycling? Just insofar as we are talking referentially of the object, with no special bias toward a background grouping of mathematicians as against cyclists or vice versa, there is no semblance of sense in rating some of his attributes as necessary and others as contingent. (Quine 1975: 199)

Quine brings out the tension latent in his second reason with a famous example which is our final problem of paraphrase:

(a) 9 is necessarily greater than 7.
(b) The number of planets is 9.
(c) Therefore the number of planets is necessarily greater than 7.

The paradox is that (a) and (b) are true, and the inference from seems valid (it relies on the principle of the indiscernibility of identicals), yet (c) seems false (FLPV 143; see L. Linsky 1971a: 2). Resolving this paradox will require us to examine Russell's logical analysis of numbers as logical fictions. In doing so, I shall revisit the three solutions to the *Hamlet* problem in order.

The first *Hamlet* solution seems hard to apply to numbers. For the 1918 Russell, numbers are logical fictions which have no sensible aspects. Yet the heart of Russell's critique of Giuseppe Peano's numbers has always been that Peano disassociates numbers from the empirical experience of counting (POM 127; IMP 9; HK 237; see my 2005–2007). In fact, Russell treats numbers much the same as bodies or minds (PLA 277). Thus rigid designation of groups of four sheep or two oranges might permit a Kripkean paraphrase *á la Hamlet*. But what about large numbers? As René Descartes observed, we cannot even distinguish a 1,000 sided figure from a 1,001 sided figure perceptually, but only intellectually. The answer is that Russell defines large numbers in terms of small numbers by mathematical induction. We could never keep Russell's complex logical analysis of a large number in our heads, but then he is in the business of replacing the simple thoughts in our heads with complex logical analyses.

The second *Hamlet* solution may seem inapplicable. The planet paradox depends directly on the description "the number of planets." To borrow a phrase from Russell, merely changing the description would have all "the advantages of theft over honest toil" (Russell 1919: 71). At least in this particular case, it seems quite ad hoc. Even worse, any reasonable paraphrase, practically by definition, would leave the logical contingency of (b) intact.

Third, there is the bare Smullyanian solution of relying directly on the scope distinctions in "On Denoting." At least Russell has this third *Hamlet* solution available. His motivation might be the bare negative one of avoiding the planet paradox. It may be a poor solution. But that is criticism, not scholarship.

Quine criticizes Smullyan's solution, which is to divide names into proper names and covert descriptions such that proper names which name the same object are always synonymous. This is certainly true of Russell's logically proper names; any identity statement flanked by logically proper names is tautologous (PLA 245, 246). It is such names which justify extending Russell's "On Denoting" scope distinction to modal contexts. Quine's criticism is that referential opacity still occurs even when "[definite] descriptions and other singular terms are eliminated altogether" (FLPV 154). He means that referential opacity occurs even when we *quantify* into modal contexts, thus placing variable expressions instead of constant expressions within modal contexts. This strikes me as an ostrich-like criticism, burying our heads in the sand when logically proper names come wandering around. It is the presence of logically proper names within modal contexts which legitimates quantification over variables within those contexts. It is not the latter which somehow avoids or invalidates the former. Worse, Quine's criticism would eliminate the very plausible application of the scope distinction to belief-contexts as well. It is hard to deny that there are things about which we have beliefs.[4]

But Quine's criticism does make a good point. Smullyan cannot live by the bare scope distinction alone, but must rely on rigid designators to make the scope distinction good. Thus the third solution (Smullyan's) depends on the first solution (mine). Thus my solution seems best, since Smullyan's solution depends on it, and the second solution seems unworkable, at least in this example.

Similarly for the query how logical fictions such as numbers can have essential properties and accidental properties. That too is criticism, not scholarship. And again I would defend Russell. The planet paradox involves not so much properties as relationships. Numbers, even as logical fictions, have definitional relationships among each other. And definitional relationships are essential relationships. This is why large numbers can be rigidly identified if small numbers are abstractly presented when we count ordinary things. (Russell admits conception, which is acquaintance with abstract entities, at least for universals, PP 52.) On the other hand, the relationship of the number 9 to the class of planets is neither definitional nor *a priori*. For Russell, the number 9 is a class of classes. It is the class of all classes having nine members. There is nothing logically necessary about the class of planets' being a member of that class of classes. Therefore it seems to me that Russell is entitled to a *de re* essentialism even for numbers as logical fictions. While numbers are not entities, they remain as objective, essentially different, and immutable as ever, so to speak.

Traditionally some descriptions reflect essences, others reflect accidents. Essences belong to metaphysics, not to language. They would not shift as descriptions shift, unless we assume they are unreal to begin with. Granted, we can *ascribe* essences to things only within our theories of things. But does it follow that every theory has a "special bias," or that things cannot *have* essences?

At the very least, Russell's understanding of epistemology, metaphysics, realism, and objectivity is so different from Quine's that we cannot say a Russellian use of Smullyan's solution is truly inadequate merely because it appears so from the perspective of Quine's philosophy. Quine has nothing like Russell's sense-data which are fully known by nonlinguistic acquaintance and which are instances of sensible universals. Russell has nothing like Quine's weak verificationism, which surely underwrites Quine's argument against essentialism. Curiously enough, Quine admits classes and, by extension, numbers as abstract objects, yet wishes to deny them essences, while Russell eliminates numbers and deems them logical fictions, yet assigns them logically smooth, logically determinate defined and essential characteristics.

At one time, Quine conceded that in a world consisting only of intensional objects, there would be no problem quantifying into modal contexts. Here an intensional object is an object x "such that *any two conditions uniquely determining x are analytically equivalent*" (FLPV 152, Quine's emphasis). That would eliminate the planet paradox. Quine gives as examples of such objects "what Frege called senses of names, and Carnap and Church called individual concepts" (FLPV 152). But Quine came to reject his earlier concession:

> For, where A is any intensional object, say an attribute, and 'p' stands for any arbitrary true sentence, clearly...
>
> (35) $A = (\iota x)[p \cdot (x = A)]$.
>
> Yet, if the true sentence represented by 'p' is not analytic, then neither is (35), and its sides are no more interchangeable in modal contexts than are 'Evening Star' and 'Morning Star', or '9' and 'the number of the planets'. (FLPV 153)

Quine goes on to observe that the same consideration shows that intensional objects are not always uniquely determined by analytically equivalent conditions, since where 'Fx' uniquely determines x, so will '$Fx \cdot p$' (FLPV 153). I note that the same consideration also shows that Quine's "lately italicized" definition of intensional objects, which I quoted from FLPV 152, is far too narrow. In fact, the consideration shows that there are no intensional objects at all, on that definition of intensional objects. I find Quine's consideration technically clever but philosophically uninteresting. I cannot think that anyone committed to intensional objects would be impressed by it. Quine has set up a straw man, a definition that is far too exclusive in the first place. That is because arbitrary, contingent p is logically irrelevant to the properties of A in any serious sense of the word "property." No wonder it kills intensional objects so easily. In contrast, I for one would think that intensional objects have indefinitely many logically contingent relationships to logically contingent things, and with no aspersion cast on their essential intensionality. For example, it is logically contingent that certain Fregean senses or Carnapian individual concepts are expressed in certain English statements.

Now, Russell's sensibilia are intensional objects just as much as senses and individual concepts are. For the meaning of a logically proper name is its denotation. And the sensible qualities of a sensibile are intensional in *Principia* sense (ii) (see page 14). Even if all and only red things were round, red and round would be two properties, not one (roundness is a "common sensible" quality which can be seen or felt). Perhaps then an intensional object is best defined as an object whose *essential* properties are intensional in *Principia* sense (ii), where properties are intensional if they map the same individuals onto the same truth-values, yet are different properties. That would explain why a logically proper name, which "is merely a means of pointing to the thing" (PLA 245), can occur with referential transparency in a modal or intentional context. If "a" is a logically proper name, and if only a is red and round, then the properties red, round, and identical to a are intensionally different. For all three map a alone onto the truth-value of truth, yet all three are different properties. And if *a* is a sense-datum—is an instance of these universals—then *a* has all three properties essentially, regardless of whether only *a* is red and round.

An interesting question I shall not pursue here is whether we should polarize the world into objects which are either totally intensional or totally extensional. Why not say that essential properties are intensional and accidental properties extensional? Ironically, that is virtually Quine's own suggestion when he says that "Aristotelian essentialism" is required for quantification into modal contexts (FLPV 155). Indeed, why not call the essential properties of even an essentially *extensional* object, defined, say, in terms of certain truth-functional mappings onto truth-values, intensional? Suppose a world of four sense-data, *a*, *b*, *c*, and *b*. Only *a* and *b* are blue. We can define a purely extensional Fregean mapping function *F* as 'the function that maps only *a* and *b* onto the True'. Then, in different senses of "essentially," *a* and *b* will be (definitionally) essentially *F* and (instantiationally) essentially blue. It will be an informative statement that a sense-datum is *F* if and only if it is blue, since *F* and blue are different properties. But then both *F* and blue are intensional properties in sense (ii), since they are two different properties had by all and only the same objects. However, *F* is not intensional in sense (iii), since we *do* have to specify which objects are *F* in order to state what *F* is (see page 14). Thus not all propositional functions intensional in sense (ii) are intensional in sense (iii) after all (see page 14).

I have been emphasizing the similarities between Russell's theory of propositional attitudes and his attendant express allowing of quantification into epistemic and intentional contexts on the one hand, and my analysis of Russell's views implying an extension of that theory and that sort of quantification into modal contexts for Russell on the other. Now let us look for any differences. In "The Philosophy of Logical Atomism," there are an apparent difference and three genuine differences which might seem to invalidate my implicit extension. My discussion will about the logical (alethic) modalities, but it will also apply to all the other sorts of modalities, since all of them are referentially opaque, which is what counts for finding that Russell's theory of propositional attitudes is applicable to them.

The apparent difference is that beliefs seem predicated of propositions, while modalities seem predicated of propositional functions. My reply is that in fact beliefs are not predicated of propositions, since beliefs are real and there are no propositions (PLA 214, 223–24). Instead, beliefs tie together the constituents which propositions only seem to. And modalities are predicated of propositional functions only in MDL. In the implicit modal logics, modalities seem to be ties much like beliefs, by parity of reason.

But whether it is merely apparent or not, the difference makes no difference to my implicit extension. For that is based on referential opacity alone.

The first genuine difference is that beliefs are real facts in the real world (PLA 214, 216–17; see 218–22), while logical truths are nothing, since they are propositions, and propositions are nothing (PLA 214, 223). But even though this difference is genuine, it does not follow that my extension of Russellian quantification into modal contexts is wrong. For the fact that beliefs are real and modalities are nothing does not preclude the latter from being propositional attitudes, or in Quine's better terminology, from being referentially opaque. Russell says, "A propositional function is nothing, but, like most of the things one wants to talk about in logic, it does not lose its importance through that fact" (PLA 230). Likewise too for modalities. Whether modalities are "propositional attitudes" in Russell's sense turns not on what they are, nor even on whether they are, but only on whether they are referentially opaque.

The second genuine difference is that true beliefs include beliefs in logically contingent propositions which describe logically contingent facts in the real world, while logically necessary truths never describe anything in the real world (compare PLA 239–41), as opposed to describing relationships among universals. Here we may as well count logical forms among universals. Granted, one might drive a wedge between the concept of a tautology and the concept of saying nothing at all about the world, not only by characterizing tautologies as describing relations among universals, but also by characterizing true universal tautologies as saying something necessarily true of all individuals. But Russell drives no such wedge. For Russell and Frege, true universal tautologies are true of *any* individuals, in the sense that they are true even if there are *no* individuals. Thus Russell and Frege reject the Aristotelian *all* with its existential import, though of course they can reconstruct it by conjoining an existential assertion with the universal assertion. But whatever the details, in the end this genuine difference makes no difference to my implicit extension either, and for the same reason as before: what counts is the presence of referential opacity, and not the ontological status of what the statements describe,

The third genuine difference is that beliefs are mental or psychological, while the logical modalities are not. In particular, since beliefs are intensional and space is extensional, a "map-in-space" cannot be made of a belief (PLA 225–26). It follows that "nothing that occurs in space is of the same form as belief" (PLA 226). By implication, beliefs are the cutting edge of Russell's mental-physical distinction. But this genuine difference makes no difference to my implicit extension either. For the logical modalities are just as intensional as beliefs, and maps-in-space cannot be made of them either. That this shows that maps-in-space cannot serve as the test of the mental-physical distinction (unless we are prepared to argue that all modalities are mental) is criticism, not scholarship. And again, what counts is the presence of referential opacity.

Of course, the *mere* presence of referential opacity implies the applicability of Russell's theory of propositional attitudes, but it does not follow from this that we can simply go ahead and quantify into the modal contexts in question. But I have provided many *de re* candidates in Russell's metaphysics to go ahead with.

Russell admits there logically can be some propositional attitudes that are not psychological. He merely says he does not know of any that are not psychological (PLA 227). This leaves room for modalities as propositional attitudes. In fact, I am surprised he did not think of them. He goes almost directly from wondering whether there are any propositional attitudes besides psychological ones (PLA 227) to defining modalities (PLA 231) in "The Philosophy of Logical Atomism," but the idea never occurs to him. I suspect that it is his very choice of the psychologistic term "attitude" that throws him off track. That is, I suspect that he did not discover that modalities are "propositional attitudes" because they are *not* attitudes in the ordinary mental sense at all. I suspect he was looking only for other psychological attitudes such as beliefs and wishes, so no wonder he could find only psychological ones. If I am right, this is only a psychological point about how his thinking was limited by his unfortunate choice of terminology. For he is quite clear that it is logically possible that not all propositional attitudes are psychological, no matter how odd that sounds in his terminology. This shows that he has the right concept in mind, namely referential opacity. But he is still thrown off by his own psychologistic terminology for that concept, when he actually goes looking for further examples. At least, that is how it seems to me.

Dagfinn Føllesdal shows there is a strictly parallel problem with quantification into causal contexts:

> (a*) It is causally necessary that the man who drank from that well got poisoned.
> (b*) The man who drank from that well is the man born at place p at time t.
> _____
> (c*) Therefore it is causally necessary that the man born at p at t got poisoned. (Føllesdal 1971: 53)

The conclusion does not follow because the two descriptions of the man are not causally equivalent (Føllesdal 1971: 54).

Føllesdal presents the paradox in terms of our ordinary pre-philosophical understanding of causation. But the paradox persists on Russell's Humean analysis of causation as nothing but natural uniformity. To that extent the Humean analysis is a worthy analysis of our pre-philosophical understanding, since it preserves the paradox. Indeed, we may apply Humean analysis to Føllesdal's own example. For even if drinking water from a certain well causes death only in the Humean sense that everyone who drinks it dies, the paradox remains, since there is no Humean necessity that the man born at p at t be poisoned. Thus MDL–C faces the paradox. I shall now suggest how Russell (and Hume) can resolve it.

Føllesdal's solution is to restrict definite descriptions to those that describe the same events in all physically possible worlds (Føllesdal 1971: 60). That solution is available to Russell for MDL–C. Of course, we must remember that merely possible worlds have no ontological status for Russell, and that Russell's physically possible worlds are merely worlds having the same uniformities as the actual world. But Russell has a stronger solution. The 1914–18 Russell analyzes both natural uniformities and lawfully behaving ordinary physical things in terms of temporal series of classes of sensed and unsensed sensibilia. And we can name any sensibile we sense with a logically rigid logically proper name, which is far more than we would need for causally rigid designation, if there could be any causally rigid designation.

Føllesdal's example is of physical causation. The paradox arises equally well for mental causation. Gustav Bergmann once gave this example in seminar: thinking of the death of a friend causes me to feel sad.[5] Where the thought of my friend's death is also the thought I have now, it is not causally necessary that the thought I have now cause me to feel sad.

This leads to a paradox concerning Russell's attempt to use propositional attitudes to divide the mental from the physical. For if there can be no map-in-space of *any* propositional attitude, then maps-in-space of physical causation and mental causation are equally impossible. This beards the Russellian test in its own den. Even more interestingly, one would think there could at least be maps-in-space of mere natural uniformities. But not so. For Humean causation is nothing but natural uniformities, and Human causation is a propositional attitude, and thus can have no map-in-space. We also see once again how awkward the term "propositional attitude" can be. The reason for these paradoxes is easily explained. Space is both spatially extended and truth-functionally extensional in the sense of mereological sets. But any type of causation is intensional in that it concerns something more than this. Even a Humean causal law is a causal law in virtue not only of what it describes in the world, but also in virtue of the internal structure of the law itself, that is, in virtue of what it is to be that sort of causal law. This is shown by Føllesdal's example of the man who drank from the well. Even if we give causation a merely Humean interpretation, the example is still paradoxical. For the paradox is purely due to the shift in intensional description of the man, from a description under which the poisoning is necessary *á la* Hume (because everyone who drinks from the well is poisoned) to a description under which it is not (because not everyone born when and where the man was born is poisoned). Perhaps Kant's famous Humean observation might also help: We see the sun and feel the warm stone, but we do not perceive the sun *causing* the stone to warm. And if we did perceive it, then the causing would just be another extensional event, and we could draw a map-in-space of causation after all. Indeed, on Kant's theory of causation, causation is an unconscious mental attitude, in that we unconsciously impose causation on reality. Of course, even perception is intensional. Perception itself is referentially opaque. I may not perceive that the hooded man is my brother, even though he is. But even if we could perceive the sun causing the stone to warm, I would be referring to the perceived event, not to our perception of it. It is not the referential opacity of the (*per impossibile*) perception of causation that Føllesdal's paradox is due to, but the referential opacity of causation itself, even under Hume's interpretation of causation.

The Hooded Man is a paradox due to Eubulides. There are parallels in Aristotle. Where Frege has differences in sense, and Russell has differences in description, Aristotle has differences in formula. We may know Coriscus in the Agora, but not Coriscus in the Lyceum (*Physics* 219*b*), or recognize the road from Athens to Thebes, but not the road from Thebes to Athens (*Physics* 202*b*). What, then, about cause in Aristotle?

Føllesdal's paradox arises for all four kinds of traditional Aristotelian cause. Føllesdal's example concerns efficient physical cause, which I have expanded *á la* Bergmann to include efficient mental cause. That leaves formal, material, and final cause.

As to formal cause, the form of Socrates is humanity. Where the human Socrates is the thing in the forum, it is formally causally necessary that the human Socrates eat and breathe. But it is not formally causally necessary that the thing in the forum eat and breathe.

As to material cause, the material of the Eiffel Tower is iron. Where the iron Eiffel Tower is the tallest structure in Paris, it is materially causally necessary that the iron Eiffel Tower have a certain atomic structure and be heavier than water. But it is not materially causally necessary that the tallest structure in Paris have that atomic structure or be heavier than water.

As to final (teleological) cause, the final form of an acorn is oak treehood. Where this acorn is the thing I just picked up off the ground, it is teleologically necessary that this acorn tend to grow into an oak tree. But it is not teleologically necessary that the thing I just picked up off the ground tend to grow into an oak tree.

The paradox also arises for action by an agent, where an action is due to the agent's deliberation and choice. In fact, this is a redundant point. Deliberate choice is merely an instance of the paradox for intentional contexts in general. Føllesdal says:

> [While Quine's paradox] is directed against the logical modalities, it can be paralleled for any type of nonextensional construction. In fact it would show that any attempt to build up adequate theories of causation, counterfactuals, probability, preference, knowledge, belief, action, duty, responsibility, rightness, goodness etc. must be given up, since, presumably, any such theory would require quantification into nonextensional contexts. (Føllesdal 1987: 101)

Føllesdal is right about theories of such things only if adequate theories of them must be extensional. I would think the opposite: theories that adequately state what intensional things are can only do so intensionally. (Regardless of whether it is adequate, even Hume's theory of cause is intensional.) But Føllesdal does show perfectly that all forms of causation and action, and many other things, are intensional. And an even more general point might be made on the ontological level of Quinean or other theories of 'no entity without identity'.

Referential opacity always essentially involves informative identity. All the examples show this. And it is trivial that any informative identity statement—which for Russell always involves at least one description (PLA 245–47)—logically can give rise to a paradox of referential opacity. In this sense, all descriptions (or Fregean senses, or Aristotelian formulae) are intensional. And this suggests a deeper level of analysis.

So far, we have followed Russell in treating informative objectual identities as facts to be discovered and to be described by informative identity statements. (I use the word "fact" loosely, so as not to imply commitment specifically to Russell's metaphysical category of facts.) This is a Russellian presupposition of the Quine-Smullyan-Føllesdal discussion. But for Panayot Butchvarov, the concept of identity is something we find ourselves *imposing* on the objects of our perception or thought, so as to organize and classify them into entities (Butchvarov 1994: 46–47; 1979: 44–45). And when we impose the concept of identity, so as to identify the objects as being the same entity, we simply *enforce* indiscernibility in some way (Butchvarov 1979: 66). That is, we adjudicate which, if any, properties of the various objects we attribute to the entity which we judge the objects 'are'. More precisely, we do this to the extent that we can. We might sometimes reserve adjudication until we have more information.

For example, the Evening Star necessarily appears in the evening, since it is descriptively so named, and the Morning Star necessarily appears in the morning. But when I astronomically identify the Evening Star with the Morning Star, and judge that both objects of perception are the planet Venus, then I can enforce the view that Venus appears both in the morning and in the evening. Or where the object of perception I singled out yesterday was red and the object of perception I single out today is white, and where I judge that both objects are appearances of the same unchanging flower, that my object of perception yesterday was red only because the flower was bathed in a red light, and that the flower is bathed in white light today, thus revealing its true color, then I can attribute whiteness to the flower both as it was yesterday and as it is today.

We might use Butchvarov's analysis to go back through all the examples with various results, depending on how we enforce indiscernibility in any particular case. For example, consider the consciousness-brain process identity thesis of John J. C. Smart and Ullin T. Place. If a yellowish-orange after-image really *is* a brain process, then perhaps there is a sense in which some brain processes *are* yellowish-orange (compare and contrast Place 1970; Smart 1970). Or if beliefs *are* brain processes, then perhaps there is a sense in which there *are* maps-in-space of beliefs after all, since there can be extensional maps-in-space of brain processes. In fact, if we leave causality out of it, brain processes simply *are* in space.

The 1914 Russell would be congenial to this result in his own way. For he holds that sense-data are physically real. He logically constructs the brain as a temporal series of indefinitely many sensed and unsensed sensibilia, one of which is the yellowish-orange sense-datum in question. There might be no physical brain at all hiding behind the cognitively impenetrable barrier of sense-data. Yet the yellowish-orange sense-datum is as mind-independently real as anything can be for the 1914 Russell, and is a logical part of his logical construction of the brain, which is physically real in virtue of that, at least in Russell's secondary or correlational sense of "real." Thus for the 1914 Russell, something physical—part of my brain, a part which is *also* a sense-datum of mine—*is* yellowish-orange.

In like manner, if the number of planets really *is* nine, then perhaps there is a sense in which the number of planets *is* necessarily greater than seven after all (Butchvarov 1979: 127–28).

But there is also a sense for Butchvarov in which the number of planets is *not* nine, insofar as these are different objects of thought (Butchvarov 1979: 127). This revives the second *Hamlet* solution, not indeed by substituting a new description, but by substituting a different rigidly designatable Butchvarovian object of perception or thought.

Butchvarov's essences are not Aristotelian in the sense of being *de re* simply speaking. For Butchvarov finds the distinction between *de dicto* and *de re* confused (Butchvarov 1979: 124–26). For Butchvarov, the essence of an object is the entity or the kind of entity we classify it as being. And while things never force us to classify them in a certain way, and classification is a conceptual as opposed to factual activity, classifications are factually based on objective similarities in the world, and some classifications are objectively more reasonable than others (Butchvarov 1979: chapter 5; 1970: 6–11). In fact, it is theoretically possible that there is a single most reasonable classification. We cannot dismiss *a priori* the possibility of a true classification of things in this sense. In contrast, Quine polarizes the essence question into a simplistic yes-no, realist-relativist dilemma. I profess surprise because Quine has plenty of dialectically accommodating approaches of his own on other subjects. Indeed, waiving the difference between Quine's neural stimulus patterns and Butchvarov's phenomenology of objects we single out in thought, perception, or memory, Quine's theories of naturalism and of the immanence of truth would seem quite congenial to Butchvarov's sort of theory of essence.

All this is a measure of the depth of Butchvarov's theory of identity. However, this book is not the place to discuss his theory in detail. I shall merely mention that I myself find room both for our impositions of the concept of identity and also for there being objectual identities in the world independently of our impositions.

Another Russellian presupposition of the Quine-Smullyan discussion is that descriptions are always used attributively and never referentially. Keith Donnellan identifies and questions this presupposition in his landmark paper, "Reference and Definite Descriptions" (Donnellan 1972). Of course, this only postpones the discussion to the level of referential uses and attributive uses of descriptions. But the referential use of descriptions does explain how the number of planets can be said to be necessarily greater than seven. Namely, we logically can use "the number of planets" referentially, so as to refer to and rigidly designate the number nine. This is another theory I cannot discuss in detail in this book. But I do not understand why Quine never mentions Donnellan. For Quine is not one to avoid problems or fail to enrich the discussion.

The weight of everything we have discussed carries over to deontic logic. The reason for quantifying into moral contexts is to assert that people have *de re* moral obligations (Forrester 1996: 91–92). James W. Forrester raises the referential opacity problem for moral contexts:

> (a**) Smith ought to kill Brown.
> (b**) Brown is the finest man in town.
> (c**) Therefore Smith ought to kill the finest man in town. (Forrester 1996: 78)

And as we saw earlier, Føllesdal does so for "duty, responsibility, rightness, [and] goodness" (Føllesdal 1987: 101). Russell can use the first *Hamlet* solution. The 1910 Russell of "The Elements of Ethics" is not a logical fictionalist. But there will still be rigid designation of a sense-datum causally connected with Brown, while "the finest man in town" is purely a description. There will also be rigid designation of the intrinsic quality of goodness, since we are acquainted with it through intellectual abstraction. The distinction between acquaintance and description goes back at least to 1905 "On Denoting" (OD 41, 56).

Similarly for the 1954 Russell of *Human Society*, who is not a logical fictionalist either. There is rigid designation of sensed events causally connected with the probably existing Brown, and rigid designation of happy states of mind through introspection. In general, all the goods of this world will be causally connected with sensed events which can be rigidly designated, as well as with felt states of happiness which can be rigidly designated too.

Forrester argues for resolution of the deontic paradox with a semantics of morally possible worlds. He notes that such worlds need not have any ontological status (Forrester 1996: 90). In light of Russell's repeated use of possible worlds talk in his two greatest ethical works, Russell would seem highly sympathetic. Forrester discusses alternative moral worlds similar to the actual world, so as to pursue moral casuistry. Russell does that, but he also discusses worlds very different from the actual world, so as to make deep theoretical points. For Russell, even a robot world can at least negatively illuminate our understanding of ethics.

This concludes my discussion of Russell's grades of modal involvement. Everything is at least second grade. There are at least two things for Russell which are third grade: quantifications over (1) instances in *de re* instantiations of sensible qualities, and (2) rigidly designatable sensed particulars in logical analyses of ordinary things into sensed and unsensed sensibilia. Among the latter, I would also include Russell's sensed countings of ordinary things, as being or including rigidly designatable sensed aspects of numbers. Russell would probably never admit such aspects, even though empirical countings are essential to his criticism of Peano's theory of number (see my 2005–2007). I see no reason why numbers cannot have empirical aspects for Russell, in the sense of being describable as being included in empirical descriptions of the number of sheep we count in various pastures. They need not occur in pure arithmetic, nor can they.

Besides sense-particulars, which can be rigidly designated if we sense them, the only other categories the 1918 Russell admits are universals (including relations) and minds. Surely universals and minds have essential features and relations. Surely red is essentially a color, and color is essentially a universal. And surely a mind is, at the very least, essentially able to be acquainted with things. Not only that, but we are acquainted with universals and with our own mind. Consider Russell's principle of acquaintance as applied to "I conceive the universal *red*." Thus these too can be rigidly designated. Thus it appears that *everything* is third grade for the 1918 Russell. We see again that without studying Russell's metaphysics and ontology in depth, we cannot hope to understand his views on modality.

Interpreting *Principia* as an Implicit Modal Logic

My final topic is whether *Principia* is implicitly a modal logic, and if so, which one, FG–MDL or FG–MDL*. My answer is that it was implicitly FG–MDL at the tine it was written, but it can also be retrospectively interpreted as implicitly FG–MDL*, which is surely the deeper and more illuminating way to understand it.

I would like to make five main points.

First, denying that *Principia* is an implicit modal logic because it does not admit any primitive, irreducible modal entities or notions is exactly as absurd as denying that *Principia* is an existential logic because it does not admit any primitive, irreducible property of existence. Indeed, Russell defines *both* "is possible" and "exists" as the very same notion, "sometimes true," which Russell takes as "the fundamental logical idea, the primitive idea" in "The Philosophy of Logical Atomism." This 'sometimes true' is what Charles H. Kahn would call a "*veridical* 'is'," and is neither a modal notion nor an existential notion as such (Kahn 1986: 3–4, 8–9, 12–13, 16–17, 20–22, 26–27).

Second, when *Principia* was written, Russell's implicit alethic logic was still his earlier one, FG–MDL. For him, logical truth was just fully general truth. Thus the implicit logical necessity operator of FG–MDL can only be interpreted as implicitly being the thesis assertion operator "⊢" of historical *Principia*. For that is the operator that indicates logical truth in *Principia*. If you accept the argument of the present chapter, then it is absurd to think otherwise.

Third, in 1918 Russell adopts his mature theory of logical truth as fully general truth plus truth in virtue of logical form, and his implicit alethic logic changes accordingly from FG–MDL to FG–MDL*. Therefore, retrospectively, from 1918 on, the implicit logical necessity operator of FG–MDL* can only be interpreted as implicitly being the thesis assertion operator "⊢" of *Principia*. And if we accept the argument of this chapter, then it is absurd to think otherwise. This is a deeper and more illuminating understanding of *Principia* because FG–MDL* is a deeper and more illuminating understanding of logical necessity than FG–MDL.

Fourth, that *Principia,* as implicitly being either FG–MDL or FG–MDL*, is closest to an S5 logic was surely unintentional on Russell's part. Even by 1919, he seems to have known only two papers by C. I. Lewis, and he rejected them as unhelpful (IMP 153). But Russell's much later statement in *The Analysis of Matter* (1927) that deductively valid inference is strict implication in Lewis's sense is explicit and very much intentional (AMA 199). Retrospectively, then, from 1927 on, Russell implicitly takes the *Principia* thesis operator as implicitly indicating strict implication for all *conditional* (if-then) theses of *Principia*, as well as still implicitly indicating FG–MDL* logical necessity for *all* theses of *Principia*.

But fifth, I think it was more likely than not intentional that Russell wanted *Principia* to be understood as interpretable in terms of the shallowest level of his modal *theory*, namely, in terms of MDL. For it is obvious that *Principia* is systematically rewritable using MDL's modal predicates "is necessary" and "is possible" to replace all occurrences respectively of "always true" and "not always false", or even (*mutatis mutandis*) of the universal and individual quantifiers. And surely Russell must have known this. For he expressly and repeatedly *defines* "is necessary," as the predicate of propositional functions, "always true," and expressly, repeatedly *defines* "is possible," as the predicate of propositional functions, "not always false." What would one expect the poor man to do, sit down and literally rewrite the whole of *Principia* when he could explain how to rewrite *Principia* modally using a brief trio of definitions? This is just what Russell does in famous works such as "The Philosophy of Logical Atomism," *Introduction to Mathematical Philosophy,* and *The Analysis of Matter.* Surely it must have occurred to this great logician that in writing those three brief definitions, he was showing us how to paraphrase *Principia* into MDL (though not into a modal logic). Granted, the best of us sometimes cannot add one and one, or see what is staring us in the face. But could Russell have missed *that*?—Could he have missed it *eight times*? There is at least one good argument for the affirm-ative: almost everybody *else* missed it eight times.

Russell published MDL after *Principia* vol. 1, in 1913, 1918, 1919, 1927, and 1940. He also published MDL twice in 1908 *during* the writing of *Principia* vol. 1, and once in 1906 *before* starting to write *Principia*. (Russell and Whitehead wrote *Principia* vol. 1 from 1907 to 1910.) Thus Russell published MDL eight times: before, during, and after the writing of the first volume of *Principia*. How could interpreting *Principia* modally by means of MDL have failed to occur to him? How could it have failed to occur to any Russell scholar? Russell handed us MDL on a silver platter eight published times.

Those who still hold that the *Principia* Russell dislikes or avoids modality might wish to explain why Russell and Whitehead use the following expressions in the first sixty pages of *Principia*:

—"possible determination(s) (of...variable(s))": 4 times, p. 5
—"every possible determination to x": 1 time, p. 15
—"all possible values [of x, x and y, $\varnothing$]": 6 times, pp. 21, 41, 49, 50, 51 (twice), 52
—"whatever possible value $\propto$ may have": 1 time, p. 25
—"there are necessarily possible arguments with which we are unacquainted": 1 time, p. 40 (perhaps Russell is committed to alethic iteration after all!)
—"every possible value of x": 1 time, p. 40
—"possible values of x": 1 time, p. 40
—"all *possible* arguments": 1 time, p. 41
—"possible values of $\varnothing\hat{z}$": 1 time, p. 49
—"some (undetermined) possible values": 1 time, p. 49
—"all possible propositions and functions": 1 time, p. 51
—"all possible functions": 1 time, p. 53
—"the totality of its possible arguments": 1 time, p. 54
—"the possible arguments": 1 time, p. 54

Are these the expressions of authors who dislike modality? Those who are bewitched by the standard picture of *Principia* may refuse to see it, but these expressions should now appear in a different light. Obviously, Russell uses "possible" to mean 'of the correct logical type'. And most readers of *Principia* will assume that type-possibility is all that Russell has in mind. But recall Parmenidean primary level modal feature (ii), that there are no merely possible entities. Thus for Russell, actual entities of the proper logical type are the only possible entities of that type. Primary level modal feature (ii) dates back to his 1905 "On Denoting" (OD 45), which is two years before he started to work on *Principia*. And from 1905 on, he never abandons his view that on the deepest ontological level, the only possible things are actual things.

However, it seems clear that he was, or at least ought to have been, well aware that the *Principia* universal and individual quantifiers can be interpreted or rewritten respectively as the modal predicates "is necessary" and "is possible" of his own repeatedly stated modal *theory*, meaning MDL. It seems far more reasonable than not, and it takes very little charity to suppose, that he intended, and expected others to figure out, that *Principia* can be rewritten using the modal predicates of MDL to replace the quantifiers, or at least the expressions "always true" and "not always false". It would have been pretty hard for him to miss that!

Even if I am right, *Principia* remains a modally innocent work on the ontological level. For as I have been explaining over and over, MDL is an eliminative analysis of modality that analyzes modal entities and notions away. And in this respect, MDL is vintage Russell. It is his *typical* kind of eliminative logical analysis. It is also part and parcel of his theory of propositional functions, which is the general version of his theory of descriptions, which he uses to eliminate definite descriptions and their apparent reference to merely possible entities.

The argument of this chapter is not intended to bear any weight of proof at all that Russell intended that *Principia* be interpretable as a modal *logic*. To the contrary, it seems clear that he did not. For he never offers an express modal logic, and never expressly offers *Principia* as interpretable as a modal logic. I have argued only that based on Russell's other writings, it seems beyond doubt that *Principia* was *implicitly* FG–MDL at the time it was written, and *implicitly* became FG–MDL* retrospectively when he corrected his theory of logical truth in 1918.

7

Russell's Implicit Possible Worlds Semantics

Russell never says he has a modal logic, much less that he has a semantics for a modal logic. Nor does he admit any merely possible worlds. He rejects ontological commitment to any merely possible entities. But he does use possible worlds talk many times. Clearly he finds some pedagogical or explanatory value in doing so. And far from being incompatible with his possible worlds talk, Russell's main implicit alethic modal logic, FG–MDL*, logically can be used as an eliminative analysis to explain away truth in all possible worlds as truth in virtue of logical form. Conversely, Russell's possible worlds talk logically can be used to explain, and serve as the semantics of, his implicit FG–MDL* logic. That is, truth in virtue of logical form can be explained as truth in all possible worlds, *or* vice versa. This is not to claim very much. In fact, I think this meets the evidentiary standard of beyond a reasonable doubt, if not absurd to think otherwise. But I think I am claiming more than has ever been claimed before, if only due to the lack of earlier comprehensive studies of Russell on modality. So far, I have only been discussing what is *implicit* in Russell, and not what he may have *intended*, or might have *agreed* with if asked.

The main question explored in this chapter is whether it is implicit in Russell's writings that a statement is a *Principia* thesis in the sense of being a logical truth if and only if it is, in Russell's possible worlds talk, true in all possible worlds. The qualification "in the sense of being a logical truth" is intended to exclude any statements whose status as a logical truth has been questioned or denied by Russell himself, notably the statement that there exist infinitely many things (the axiom of infinity), the statement that there exists at least one thing (the existence assumption), and the multiplicative axiom. I think the answer to the main question is trivially yes. The secondary question is whether Russell himself would have agreed, if asked. Based on his own many uses of possible worlds talk over the years, I think it is clear that he would have. The tertiary question is whether he would have agreed, if asked, that his own possible worlds talk could serve as *semantics* for *Principia*. Simply based on his open mind, and on our answers so far, I think he would find it both interesting and possible, much as he finds three-valued logic (Russell 1989: 681–82). But even if we accept all that, there is still much to discuss.

Russell's Use of Possible Worlds Talk

As we saw in chapter 1, Russell uses possible worlds talk in at least nine works over a period of forty-two years (1907–48):

> 1907 "The Study of Mathematics," in *Mysticism and Logic* (MAL 65)
> 1912 *The Problems of Philosophy* (PP 78)
> 1914 *Our Knowledge of the External World* (KEW 145)
> 1918 "The Philosophy of Logical Atomism" (PLA 240)
> 1919 *Introduction to Mathematical Philosophy* (IMP 141, 192–93, 203–4)
> 1921 *The Analysis of Mind* (AMI 268)
> 1927 *The Analysis of Matter* (AMA 200)
> 1938 *The Principles of Mathematics*, (introduction to 2d ed., POM viii, "possible universes")
> 1948 *Human Knowledge* (HK 157)

But why does Russell use possible worlds talk so often when he ontologically rejects merely possible worlds? What is his motive?

Kripke's excellent distinction of two very different motives one might have for using talk of possible worlds should make clear what I have in mind in my interpretation of Russell. Kripke says:

> I do not think of 'possible worlds' as providing a *reductive* analysis in any philosophically significant sense, that is, as uncovering the ultimate nature, from either an epistemological or a metaphysical point of view, of modal operators, propositions, etc., or as 'explicating' them....The main and the original motivation for the 'possible worlds analysis'—and the way it clarified modal logic—was that it enabled [set theoretic extensional formalization]. It is also useful in making certain concepts clear. (Kripke 1980: 19 n.18, Kripke's emphasis)

Kripke is distinguishing two motives: reduction, and clarification. Kripke is right that epistemological or metaphysical reduction can be distinguished from clarification, especially formal clarificaiton. *Cognitive* or phenomenological reduction, which Kripke does not mention, can be distinguished as a third motive a philosopher might sometimes have for analysis. Cognitive reduction is analysis of the meaning of a statement in terms of how we think of things. However, when we think of a statement as necessary or possible, we ordinarily never think of it in terms of how many possible worlds it would be true in. In point of empirical fact, we do not, and cannot, determine if a statement is necessary "by running through all the possible worlds in our heads" (Kripke 1980: 38).

(This must not be confused by the fact that this empirical fact is no *logical* objection to defining necessary truth as truth in all possible worlds; see MPD 91–92; Ramsey 1931: 41.) Thus we do not, and cannot, *cognitively* reduce the ordinary meaning of our ordinary talk of modality to thoughts about possible worlds. Thus I think no one has cognitive reduction in mind as a motive for offering a semantic analysis of necessary truth in terms of possible worlds. Indeed, that is quite the opposite of what Russell does as analysis, insofar as he seeks to replace our ordinary thoughts with clearer and more definite ones. But when we paraphrase our ordinary talk of statements as necessary or possible in terms of possible worlds, it is formally helpful as clarification. Thus we can distinguish even cognitive reduction from clarification. Thus the general distinction between reduction (either metaphysical or phenomenological) and clarification seems quite sound.

There is, of course, a trivial sense in which metaphysical reduction is metaphysical clarification, epistemological reduction is epistemological clarification, and so on. That is just clarification of the metaphysical *order* of things, the epistemological *order* of things, and so on. And that is very different from *pedagogical* clarification. For in order to clarify some order of things, we have to get the order of things right. To clarify it *is* to get it right. But in pedagogical clarification, anything goes, even misdescription *á la* Donnellan. And in formal clarification, anything formal goes, even formal misdescription *á la* Quine, who will use any artifice.

Kripke says that clarification, as opposed to reduction, is his own only motive in using possible worlds talk. Clarification is Russell's only motive too. Obviously, Russell can reductively, or more precisely in his case, *eliminatively* analyze modality in terms of possible worlds, since he denies there that are any merely possible worlds. I am merely saying that implicitly, Russell *could* use his talk of possible worlds not only for informal clarification of various modal concepts, as he actually does, but also to formalize his own theories of logical truth. It is clear that he does not actually use possible worlds talk to formalize anything—not even the most obvious candidate, truth in virtue of logical form. My point is that his mature analysis of logical truth as fully general truth that is truth in virtue of form, i.e., as fully general truth that remains true in virtue of its form no matter what (nonlogical) terms we could possibly substitute for the variables in a statement (IMP 199), is logically equivalent to defining logical truth as formal truth that is true in all possible worlds. In fact, "no matter what terms we could possibly substitute" is just a different version of "no matter what possible world we consider." Thus Russell's mature theory of logical truth implies that Russell logically can use either of his two concepts—truth no matter what possible terms are substituted, and truth in all logically possible worlds—to analyze away the other eliminatively. I imagine that he uses the first of these two concepts because he admits logical forms, but rejects merely possible worlds. Certainly it would *seem* awkward to reject merely possible worlds and them use them to analyze logical truth, even if possible worlds were a mere form of talk. But more seriously, to analyze logical truth in terms of possible worlds would be, in effect, to analyze *logical forms* away eliminatively. Even worse, it would be to analyze *entities* (logical forms) in terms of *non*-entities (possible world). And he certainly would not want to do *that*. But by going in the opposite direction, i.e., analyzing possible worlds in terms of logical form, he is analyzing *possible worlds* away eliminatively. And that is a good result for him, since he rejects them anyway, using his theory of descriptions. But look at what we have just said. Namely, the reason he analyzes logical truth in terms of formal intersubstitutability of terms, instead of possible worlds, is not a *formal* reason at all. It is an *ontological* reason. For he is already using theory of descriptions to eliminate merely possible entities in his ontological battle with Meinong. Formally, either analysis would be just as good, since they are logically equivalent. And my only point here is the formal one that formally speaking, he could have used possible worlds semantics just as well. Also, formally speaking, he could deepen the analysis he gives by further analyzing intersubstitutability of any possible terms in terms of possible worlds talk. However, it is unclear to me that this could be done for the motive of further clarifying the nature of logical truth, except in the merely pedagogical sense of using more, so to speak, picturesque language. Talk of possible worlds is more exciting and fun than talk of nonlogical terms.

　　I am not saying that any logic in which false sentences can be written is implicitly a possible worlds logic. I am saying Russell expressly uses possible worlds talk, expressly says that logic and mathematics are true in all possible worlds, and expressly analyzes logical and by extension mathematical truth as truth in virtue of logical form. And I am saying it would be absurd to think that his talk and his analysis are not logically equivalent for him, or that he is unaware of that. And I am saying that using express texts from his own writings, formally speaking he could have used possible worlds talk as his semantic analysis of logical truth, either directly, or indirectly as an analysis of truth in virtue of form. Recall that the latter is merely a formal version of fully general truth.

　　To make the same point another way, there is a trivial sense in which anyone can use possible worlds talk to formalize modal logic, namely, in the sense that possible worlds talk actually has been and therefore logically can be so used. The actuality implies the possibility. But that would not be Russell scholarship.

The scholarship is to note that Russell actually uses possible worlds talk to clarify logically necessary truth on an informal level, and actually offers the theory that logically necessary truth is truth in virtue of logical form. Thus I am saying that it is structurally possible for Russell to have had a possible worlds semantics for logical truth based on materials that exist in his texts.

I shall now discuss the details for the two major implicit alethic modal logics for logical or analytic truth. Please note again that Russell's only implicit motive for a possible worlds semantics would be clarification, not reduction of any kind, and that he does not in fact offer such a semantics.

I argued in the last chapter that retrospectively, *Principia* is implicitly FG–MDL*. And I showed that Russell uses possible worlds talk often in his writings, and uses the word "possible" and its variants often in *Principia*. Thus we might start by looking at least briefly at the general logical structure of *Principia*, to see to what extent it might be structurally glossed as a possible worlds logic. Russell says, "The universe consists of objects having various qualities and standing in various relations" (PM 43). Thus the universe can be described by a complex propositional function, or even propositionally described by a long conjunctive general sentence generated from a matrix, if the universe is finite (PM xxix, intro. to 2d ed.; 161–62):

> A "matrix" is a function of any number of variables...
> which has elementary propositions as its values[; and it]
> is used for the purpose of generalization. A "general
> proposition" is one derived from a matrix by generaliz-
> ation. (PM xxii–xxiii, introduction to 2d. ed.; see 162)

Since every possible world is different from every other in some definite way, in principle we only need to use different definite descriptions in each possible world matrix. Thus it is easy to see how Russell and Whitehead can (in principle) *falsely* assert the existence of any finite *merely* possible world. (For them, only the *actual* world can be *truly* asserted to exist.) For any such world there will be a matrix which generates a unique description of that world. Matrices generate "any possible function other than a matrix (PM 162)," and all possible general sentences. And each simple existent can be distinguished from every other simple existent by definite descriptions, thanks to *Principia* *13.01. Thus for any finite possible world, there is a matrix which generates a long conjunctive quantified sentence asserting the existence of that world. And any orderly infinite possible worlds can be described by a finite matrix including mathematical induction. The infinitely many natural numbers can be so described, and they can be used in turn to describe, for example, Hilbert's Grand Hotel, which has infinitely many finite rooms in a row. More generally, we may say that perhaps *per impossibile*, any infinite possible world can be so described if we had, perhaps *per impossibile*, an infinitely long matrix for it. It is not clear from Russell's express definition of a matrix whether it must be "a function of any" *finite* "number of variables," or whether the number of variables can be infinite. But for Russell, it seems clear that all true or false statements must be finitely long, so as to have determinate truth-conditions. And that would seem to include "[a]'general proposition'...derived from a matrix by generalization." Hence the *per impossibile*.

It may seem shocking to call *Principia* an implicit possible worlds logic on that basis, but the point is in fact trivial. That is because the generation of statements that fully describe merely possible worlds from matrices amounts only to completing propositional functions by binding their variables with quantifiers. The only difference is the difference between real (free) variables and apparent (bound) variables, a distinction Russell eventually finds "no need" for (PM xiii). Again, Russell admits no merely possible facts described by false statements, which is what all such generated statements would be except for the one describing the actual world. That high water mark of Russell interpretation confines the gloss.

Logic concerns not just logical truth, but logical inference. Russell distinguishes deducibility from both material implication and formal implication (PM 20–21). Implicitly, Russell logically can formalize logical deducibility as inference which is true in all possible worlds, or as inference such that in no possible world is an instance of the antecedent true and the corresponding instance of the consequent false. This point, too, is trivial.

That structurally speaking, Russell could have easily used possible worlds semantics for logical truth helps illuminate how Russell's MDL anticipates Carnap's state-descriptions, or classes of statements in a language S which contain every atomic statement of S or its negation. State-descriptions are the basis of Carnap's semantic approach to modal logic (Carnap, 1967a: 9). For Rescher, modal logic began with MacColl and C. I. Lewis, but "[i]t was Carnap who first successfully elaborated the possible-world semantics which those who followed in his wake were to build up into the grandiose structure we know today" (Rescher 1979a: 146).

There is a gross inconsistency in holding that Carnap had a possible worlds logic, but that Russell structurally could not. For Carnap, in his *Meaning and Necessity,* makes modalities into properties of propositional functions in exactly the way MDL does, and rejects the nonactual possibles of Lewis in exactly the way Russell rejects those of Meinong and MacColl (Carnap 1967a:

65–67).[1] We know that Carnap studied Russell's works extensively in the early 1920s. *Meaning and Necessity* was published in 1947, over forty years after Russell's review of MacColl in *Mind*, and almost thirty years after "The Philosophy of Logical Atomism." Thus Carnap's modal theory seems based on, if not simply copied from, Russell's MDL in these respects.

Carnap's logic and Russell's implicit FG–MDL* are both S5 as well. But the *reason* why they are both S5 is very different in each case. In his "Intellectual Autobiography," Carnap says he prefers S5 because it decides more modal questions than the other S-logics do (Carnap 1963). In contrast, Russell's implicit FG–MDL* is S5 not by intent at all, since Russell is totally unaware that his later writings on logical truth logically imply FG–MDL*. Instead, FG–MDL* is S5 because Russellian logical form is timeless and unchanging. Of course, this is arguably implicitly why Carnap's logic is S5 as well, but there is a major caveat here. Namely, for Carnap, analytic truth is relative to one's logical system or language, and a statement that is analytic in one system may be synthetic in another. In contrast, Russell flatly says that if a statement is logically true, then that is the end of the matter, and there is something wrong with any logical system in which that statement is not counted as logically true (POM xii, introduction to 2d ed., criticizing Carnap).

That structurally speaking, Russell could have easily used possible worlds semantics for logical truth also helps illuminate how Russell anticipates Kripke's modal logic. Loux says Kripke's "work suggests...that...the modal operators function as something like quantifiers...." (Loux 1979: 27). Thus my claim that Russell indirectly influenced Kripke through Carnap and Beth should be no surprise. Don Paul Snyder says, "Both Hintikka and Kripke owe a debt to Beth's notion of 'semantic tableaux', and Beth, in turn, to Carnap's 'state descriptions'" (Snyder 1971: 99n). The Kripke of *Meaning and Necessity* also looks much like Russell. Both are nonmodal combinatorial actualists. Both reject merely possible entities. Both hold that unicorns are not possible because there are no actual unicorns. Both base possible worlds talk on truth-functional combinations of atomic statements whose constituent names rigidly designate actual entities. Granted, there are also deep differences on: (1) what rigid names refer to—ordinary things for Kripke and sense-data for Russell; (2) the precise linguistic *locus* of modality—individual propositions for Kripke, propositional functions for Russell; and (3) semantics—models, world subsets, and accessibility relations for Kripke, the actual world for Russell. See page 8 on Russell's not using Kripkean world subsets and accessibility relations, and see page 119 on the actual world as Russell's implicitly intended semantic model.

Those who deny that Russell has an implicit modal logic because it eliminates any ontological commitment to modal entities and any use of modal notions are placed in the unhappy position of having to deny that Carnap and Kripke have express modal logics. For Carnap's and Kripke's express modal logics do the same thing.

Wittgenstein might be a link between Carnap and Russell. Carnap says his state-description method has origins in the *Tractatus* (Carnap 1967a: 9). But Kripke's dice-throwing analogy of ways the world might have been to ways some dice might have been thrown could easily have been offered by Russell (Kripke 1980: 16–20). Interestingly enough, in light of Kripke's gambling analogy, all four—Russell, the early Wittgenstein, Carnap, and Kripke—connect possibility with probability. But of course, many philosophers have done that.

The Tractarian Wittgenstein says that "if a thing *can* occur in a state of affairs, the possibility of that state of affairs must be written into the thing itself" (T 2.011). "If I know an object I also know all its possible occurrences in states of affairs. (Every one of these possibilities must be part of the nature of the object.) A new possibility cannot be discovered later" (T 2.0123). Thus he eliminates modalities in the sense that all possibilities are contained in actual objects. Again, there are no alien objects in the *Tractatus*, since all Tractarian objects are in all possible worlds.

Not only is Russell a nonmodal combinatorial actualist, but he accepts a form of logical fatalism. Just as the past cannot be other than it was, the present cannot be other than it is, and the future cannot be other than it will be. Otherwise they violate the law of noncontradiction (MAL 195–96). Nothing can be altered. This neo-Parmenidean existence-identity connection is eliminative of modality, since the law of noncontradiction involves no modal notions. Such a logical fatalism does not preclude possible worlds in the sense of mere ways of talking. In fact, our talk of possible worlds is just one of the things that cannot be other than they are. And another thing that cannot be other than it is for Russell is the logical contingency of the empirical world.

For Russell and Kripke alike, merely possible worlds are not literally described, since there is nothing there to describe. For both of them, possible worlds are only stipulated or specified. Russell says that "where we are concerned not merely with what does exist but with whatever might or could exist, no reference to actual particulars is involved" (PP 56). I think that here Russell is not only talking about merely possible particulars, but also about merely possible worlds. His point is simply that for him, merely possible particulars cannot be named, but can only be described, since they are not there for us to be acquainted with. (Merely possible particulars must not be confused with wild particulars, which are real particulars with which we are acquainted, but which count as hallucinations on the secondary level of reality due to their lack of sufficient lawful correlation with other sense-data.) But I can see no reason why Russell would be against talk of merely possible worlds in which some but not all of the particulars are actual particulars, or in which all of the particulars are actual particulars, but related in relationships other than their actual ones.

Now, Russell's theory of descriptions is essentially related to his theory of universals. For Russell, every description must have a universal as its determinate constituent. This is required by his principle of acquaintance: "Every proposition which we can understand must be composed wholly of constituents with which we are acquainted" (PP 58, Russell's emphasis deleted). And for Russell, "Every complete sentence must contain at least one word which stands for a universal, since all verbs have a meaning which is universal" (PP 52). But then which descriptions are possible essentially depends on which universals are possible. Can there be alien universals? Can they be described using actual universals?

The first thing to note is that for Russell, alien universals could only be alien *instantiated* universals. For his universals are *ante rem*. They are timeless entities in the timeless world of being. Thus the only possible universals for him are actual universals. But there can be there can be alien universals for him in the sense that they are instantiated in at least one merely possible world and are not instantiated in the actual world. He does not discuss this, but the structural possibility of such universals for him is quite clear.

Thus alien universals are instantiated universals. They are universals that are instantiated, not instantiations of universals. By definition, their instantiations are in at least one merely possible world and not in the actual world. They are just as real as non-alien universals. For all universals are equally real in the world of being, regardless of whether they are instantiated or not, much less with regard to which worlds they are instantiated in. Merely possible worlds that contain alien universals would not have any more or less ontological status than merely possible worlds that contain only instantiations of non-alien universals, i.e., universals which are instantiated in the actual world. For all merely possible worlds are equally nothing.

Due to the principle of acquaintance we can only describe merely possible worlds via actual universals that we are actually acquainted with (Russell calls this "conception" (PP 52). But I think this certainly can include generic descriptions containing generic universals to say intelligibly by existential quantification *that there might have been some* specific universals, such as certain specific colors or sounds, other than the ones there actually are. Recall that in *Human Knowledge*, Russell says that we can imagine general facts where we cannot imagine particular facts which would be their instances (HK 153). Even on the logicization of mathematics, including geometry, *empirical* shapes presented in acquaintance are not an exception to this, since *they* are not logical fictions. Only logically abstract shapes are logical fictions of pure geometry. Thus we can describe specific empirical alien shape-universals as well, though not with ontological commitment.

Where possible worlds are worlds of possible *existents*, no universal as such can be an alien universal. For universals belong to the world of *being*, not to the world of *existence*. There can be alien instantiations of universals, but not alien universals. This is perhaps most clearly seen in the 1912 *Problems of Philosophy*.

Nonexistent Facts and Negative Facts

Russell rejects merely possible or nonexistent facts. He says, "There are no false facts" described by false statements (PLA 209). But he does admit negative facts, such as the fact that the Empire State Building is not wooden (PLA 211–16; Russell 1971c: 287). As Herbert Hochberg says, "'Negative' entities are one thing; nonexistents are another" (Hochberg 1978: 294).

Negative facts are the facts described by true negative statements, such as "The Empire State Building is not wooden." As Hochberg notes, positive and negative facts differ not in constituents but in positive or negative "quality" (Hochberg 1978: 220). Russell says that a quality is not a constituent of a fact, but a "characteristic of a form" (Russell 1971c: 287). He means that if we take a statement and its denial, they have the same constituents. For the only difference is that the denial contains a "not," and this "not" does not indicate a constituent, but instead belongs to the logical form of the denial (Russell 1971c: 287). The later Russell says that negation is not literally part of the world of observed particulars (HK 125). There is no such thing as a "not" going around which we can sense or experience. Russell says nothing further about the qualities of facts. He says the difference between positive and negative facts is "ultimate and irreducible" (Russell 1971c: 287; see PLA 216; compare Plato, *Sophist* 263*a*). I think he is wrong. Surely negative facts reduce to negated positive facts.

If Russell's positive and negative qualities are what Frege would call "forces," such as Frege's forces of assertion, question, or command, then Russell has two assertoric forces, one positive and one negative, where Frege has only one positive assertoric force. If so, then Russell is liable to Frege's persuasive arguments in his paper "Negation" that there should only be one positive assertoric force governing the assertion of sentences, and that the proper *locus* of negation is within asserted sentences (TW 117–35). Charity therefore suggests that assertoric force is not what Russell has in mind for his qualities. But perhaps charity is not needed, since Frege's assertoric force, which is indicated by his judgment-stroke, is far closer in function to what is indicated by Russell and Whitehead's thesis assertion-sign in *Principia* than to Russell's positive and negative qualities. This *Principia* sign is positive and applies to any provable thesis regardless of whether the thesis describes a positive or a negative fact.

Qualities are characteristics of logical forms. Logical forms and their characteristics are not assertoric forces, but belong instead (along with propositional constituents) to what is asserted. Nonetheless, Russell's qualities still seem uncomfortably close to Frege's forces. In effect, Russell seems to be blurring Frege's distinction between assertoric force and what is asserted. Perhaps we should simply find the Russell texts (PLA 211–16; Russell 1971c: 287) inconclusive. But the decisive point for me is that Russell's sole purpose in positing qualities is to ground the difference between positive and negative facts. And that has nothing to do with asserting them, nor with which ones we assert. I conclude that Russell's qualities are not Fregean or neo-Fregean assertoric forces.

Regardless of what negative facts are, and granting that they are just as real for Russell as any other facts, they seem closer to merely possible facts than one might think. For to think of any merely possible fact, we can simply think of a negative fact as having a positive quality, or think of a positive fact as having a negative quality. In fact, the corresponding thoughts would be logically equivalent. I wholly grant that all facts are real for Russell, and that they cannot be real without having their proper qualities. For Russell, there are no merely possible facts. I suggest only that we can *attend to* a real fact and *think* or *conceive* of it as having the quality other than the one it has. (This is not the same as being acquainted with negative facts, which are always real facts.) For the principle of acquaintance only requires that for us to understand a proposition, we must be acquainted with its constituents, not with the fact it describes (PP 58). We must not be confused here by the fact that Russell calls acquaintance with universals "conception" (PP 52). Facts are not universals, and conceiving merely possible facts is not conceiving real universals.

Hochberg says, "Russell held it to be obvious that we are not acquainted with negative facts," (Hochberg 1978: 296; see Russell 1971c: 317; IMT 81–83, 92–93, 162–64; HK 121–26, 132–37). I agree, if perceptual acquaintance is meant. For example, if I see that spot *a* is red, I can infer that *a* is not green, *a* is not blue, and so on. But I am only acquainted with the fact that *a* is red, and not with indefinitely many negative facts about all the colors that *a* is not as well. And again, Russell's principle of acquaintance does not require us to be acquainted with *any* facts. We understand true or false propositions by being acquainted with their constituents. And false propositions do not describe facts at all; if they did, they would be true propositions. But surely Russell holds that we can *think* of negative facts and can identify their constituents and their qualities in thought and discourse. How else could he give examples or describe, much less assert, his own theory? How else could he uphold his principle of acquaintance for either negative propositions or false propositions?

Now, for Russell the two statements, "The Eiffel Tower is iron" and "The Eiffel Tower is not iron," have the very same constituents and logical form, except that the first has a positive quality characterizing its logical form and the second a negative quality. They differ only by a "not." If we understand "not," then they are equally thinkable, though only one is true. Thus it is thinkable that the Eiffel Tower is not iron. (I think no one would seriously say that Russell would deny this.) Now, one major way to think of a merely possible world is simply to think of a set of compossible statements at least one of which denies an actual fact. (The modal term "compossible" may be eliminatively analyzed away using the nonmodal term "logically consistent." The other major way is to describe possible alien facts in general terms; and here every general statement has its denial from which it differs only by a "not." Thus Russell can use possible world semantics by description of merely possible facts just as easily as he can use negative facts as the semantic basis of negative truths. There is no difference except for shifting around constituents and qualities. The principle of acquaintance is satisfied throughout because we are always acquainted with the constituents of the statements. Russell does not say whether we are acquainted with qualities. But due to his principle of acquaintance, I do not see how he could say we could understand any statements about them if we were not acquainted with them. For qualities are "ultimate and irreducible" (Russell 1971c: 287). We may as well say they are simple. Could we know these simple qualities only by description?

Russell does not say so, but his two qualities of positive and negative would be universals. For they are common to many. For each of them characterizes indefinitely many logical forms. Thus we would be acquainted with them by conception, just as we would with logical universals, or for that matter any universals (PP 52). The only other alternative would be knowledge by description. Also note that qualities belong to logical form, and logical forms are universals, since they are common to many.

Russell ontologically rejects merely possible facts. They cannot even be existent facts with their qualities thought of as reversed. For Russell, there is no such thing as a false fact. As for merely possible facts, so for merely possible worlds. That shows the high water mark of Russell interpretation again. That must never be forgotten in interpreting Russell.

In the previous chapter, I argued that *Principia* is implicitly FG–MDL, and retrospectively is implicitly FG–MDL*. I have now suggested two main ways that work together with this, two main ways that Russell structurally can use his own possible worlds talk as a semantics for *Principia* considered as an implicit modal logic. The first way is based on the *Principia* concept of a matrix. The second is based on Russell's concept of a negative fact. Both ways are structurally possible in terms of Russell's own views in logic (matrices) and metaphysics (negative facts). Thus they illuminate the place of *Principia* on the conceptual map of Russell's own philosophy. But as scholarship, they can never commit Russell to merely possible facts. Russell says, "It may be laid down generally that *possibility* always marks insufficient analysis: when analysis is completed, only the *actual* can be relevant, for the simple reason that there is only the actual, and that the merely possible is nothing" (ONA 153). On the related topic of potentiality, or possibility to become, he says, "The concept of potentiality is convenient in some connections, provided it is so used that we can translate our statements into a form in which the concept is absent....But when potentiality is used as a fundamental and irreducible concept, it always conceals confusion of thought" (HWP 167).

Possible worlds need not have ontological status in model semantics (Forrester 1996: 90). The post-1905 Russell's possible worlds have no ontological status. They are nothing. I gloss them as a special kind of logical fiction. Where Russell deems a vector of motion "doubly a fiction" because motions are fictions and vectors of motion are not even motions but mere creatures of analysis (POM 474), a merely possible vector of motion in a merely possible world would be triply a fiction, lacking ontological status on three counts. To Russell, possible worlds are "Leibnizian phraseology" (IMP 141, 192). We speak of merely possible worlds either as ways the actual world might have been, or by description of alien objects.

Rigid Designators and Trans-World Identity

As we saw, Russell's logically proper names are his rigid designators. There is no problem of trans-world identity for them.

Words that indicate universals are rigid designators for him too. But universals are in the world of timeless being, not in the world of changing existents. In that sense, they are in no possible world of existents, not even the actual world of existents. In the world of timeless being, there is properly speaking no distinction between actual and merely possible universals, since all of them are equally entities. Therefore there is no problem of trans-world identity for universals either. There are two reasons. First, their names (as opposed to descriptions of them) are rigid designators. And second, they are not in any possible worlds of existents to begin with. Those two points might seem to contradict each other, insofar as rigid designation is precisely across possible worlds, and they are not in any possible worlds. The resolution is that their instantiations are; and insofar as we are naming instantiated universals across possible worlds, our names for them are rigid. Of course, "trans-world identity" is mere Leibnizian phraseology for Russell, since he rejects merely possible worlds. I am using only possible worlds talk here.

But the problem of trans-world identity might be thought to arise for ordinary individuals such as minds and bodies, since they are logical constructions, at least for the 1914–21 Russell. I think that in the deepest sense it does not arise. Logical constructions are logical fictions. They are strictly nothing. Thus there are literally no minds or bodies even in the actual world. Thus the question whether a certain actual body might be the same body as a certain merely possible body in a certain merely possible world is strictly ill-stated, since it is based on the false assumption that there is a body there at all. Nonetheless, Russell does wish to preserve ordinary ways of ordinary ways of talking and thinking in his logical analyses of ordinary minds and of ordinary bodies, even though strictly speaking his analyses are intended as replacements of our ordinary thoughts with different and more precise thoughts. We may also recall that while bodies and minds are logical fictions, he does admit real physical and (I think) mental facts. Thus I think we should try to say what can be said about the apparent problem of trans-world identity for minds and bodies, even though strictly speaking they are unreal, and it is his sense-particulars that are real entities with rigid trans-world identities.

Determining the extent to which Russell's constructions of minds and bodies can maintain, or can be known to maintain, identity across possible worlds would be a matter of how strictly the constructions are defined across worlds in terms of their constituent actual particulars. For only the actual particulars with which we are acquainted have semantico-epistemic rigid trans-world identities. Russell does not address this question. But as we saw, Russell repeatedly upholds Leibniz's possible worlds as a logically viable or intelligible, not to mention helpful and clarificatory, way of talking. And looking especially at *External World*, whose main point is to construct ordinary things as classes of sensible particulars which conform to the laws of physics, and which maintain their identities across the perspectives of both actual and hypothetical observers, it is obvious that Russell is telling us that his analytic constructions of ordinary things extend to ordinary counterfactual situations, such as different ways certain billiard balls might have struck each other. But his only test of the trans-world identity of ordinary things such as billiard balls would be, in effect, sufficient lawful correlation, since for him there are no logically proper names, and thus no rigid designations, of such ordinary things.

Internal Relations and Essential Properties

It is time to revisit *de re* and *de dicto* more deeply.

If Russell's logically proper names are rigid designators and if their denotations therefore have stipulated, unproblematic trans-world identities, then do their denotations have any essential or necessary, i.e., *de re* properties? Raymond Bradley speaks of Russell's "wholesale attack" on the notion of a nature as part of Russell's rejection of internal relations, and says that "Russell gave [*de re* modal notions] no role whatever in his actuality-oriented account of logic" (R. Bradley 1992: 22, 25). Bradley then says:

> Russell does not, so far as I know, expressly claim that properties and relations are *never* internal to...the objects that have them. But that seems to be his official position. In short, it seems as though he is committed to...the rejection of de re modal [notions].... (R. Bradley 1992: 24)

Where Bradley is cautious, John G. Slater proclaims:

> Since asymmetrical relations cannot be analysed away, and therefore must be accorded a place in logic, Russell saw no reason to exclude any relational statement. Thus, in his work on logic, he adopted the position that all relations are to be treated as external to their subjects. (J. Slater 1997: vii)

This is simply false. Russell admits both internal relations and external relations. Only asymmetrical relations are external relations. And since not all relations are asymmetrical, not all relations are external. Slater's interpretation would be correct if and only if the only relations Russell admits are asymmetrical, and that is far from being the case, as Slater well knows. Nor does Slater cite any text in which Russell says that all relations are external; nor can he, since that is not Russell's view. Slater does give a good summary of Russell's argument that all asymmetrical relations must be external (J. Slater 1997: vii). But Slater never shows that or how Russell's argument would apply to symmetrical relations; nor can he, since that argument does not apply to symmetrical relations.

Russell does admit external relations. Indeed, he is famous for it. His admission may be found in major works ranging over a period of 59 years, most notably *The Philosophy of Leibniz*, *Philosophical Essays*, *Our Knowledge of the External World*, and *My Philosophical Development*. It is the foundation of what Russell calls the "one major division in my philosophical work," his one "revolution" (MPD 9). This is, of course, Russell's abandonment of Kant and Hegel for a Moorean realism, or more precisely, Russell's abandonment of monistic idealism for a pluralistic realism. In this "so great a revolution" (MPD 9), Russell says:

> I was more concerned than [Moore] was with certain purely logical matters. The most important of these and the one which has dominated all my subsequent philosophy, was what I called 'the doctrine of external relations....Just after developing this view in my book on *The Philosophy of Leibniz....* (MPD 9–10)

I shall not discuss Russell's argument for external relations and his consequent rejection of monism and acceptance of pluralism in detail here; see (PE essay 6; POM ch. 26; KEW 44–46, 119–20; MPD 9–10, ch. 5). My concern is only with whether Russell admits *only* external relations, or whether he *also* admits, or at least leaves philosophical room for, internal relations.

I would like to make four main points.

First, Russell never argues that there are no internal relations, but only that not all relations are internal. He rejects only the "axiom of internal relations" that "'*Every* relation is grounded in the natures of the related terms'" (PE 139, my emphasis). Thus he only argues that not every relation is internal.

Second, Russell's argument for external relations is that there are asymmetrical relations whose relata must be different. But he distinguishes asymmetrical relations from both *nonsymmetrical* as well as *symmetrical* relations. He says, "All relations that are not symmetrical are called *nonsymmetrical*....A relation is called *asymmetrical* when, if it holds between A and B, it *never* holds between B and A" (KEW 44). Thus, out of three kinds of relations,

Russell's chief positive argument for external relations concludes that only *one* of these three kinds cannot be grounded in the natures of the related terms. In fact, he says in *Principles* that terms that "are symmetrical and transitive—such as equality and simultaneity—*are* capable of reduction to what has been vaguely called identity of content" (POM 226, Russell's emphasis). He immediately goes on to say that "this in turn must be analyzed into sameness of relation to some other term" (POM 226), since all "the so-called properties of a term are, in fact, only other terms to which it stands in some relation" (POM 226). This amounts to denying that there *are* any properties as opposed to relations. But this further reduction does not invalidate his point that symmetrical transitive relations can be reduced to properties. If such properties can be further reduced to relations, that is simply irrelevant to whether the initial relations, such as equality and simultaneity, satisfy the definition of an internal relation as a relation that is reducible to properties of the relata.

Supporting this is a text Bradley and Slater overlook. Russell says in *External World*:

> Let us now [ask] whether all relations can be reduced to predications.
> In the case of symmetrical relations...some kind of plausibility can be given to this doctrine. A symmetrical relation which is transitive, such as equality, can be regarded as expressing possession of some common property, while one which is not transitive, such as inequality, can be regarded as expressing possession of different properties. But when we come to asymmetrical relations,...the attempt to reduce them to properties becomes obviously impossible. (KEW 45)

Russell is telling us that out of three kinds of relations, it is 'plausible' to 'regard' two kinds as internal relations; and only one kind is "obviously" not. I think we may simply say it appears that for Russell, two kinds are internal, and one kind is not. Even the example of equality is the same.

Third, Russell's arguments for external relations basically concern only relations among *particulars*, notably among whole things and their parts, and most notably between the monistic whole and all things in the world as its parts. All of his *properties* and *relations*, that is, all of his *universals*, would be natures of things and also have natures of their own. That is, they would have essential properties of their own and stand in essential relations to each other. These truths, such as that red is a color, are synthetic *a priori* as opposed to categorial, since their denials are well-formed, and they are *a priori* but not analytically true for Russell.

Fourth, Russell's argument that asymmetrical relations are external does not even appear to apply to symmetrical relations. According to Slater, the gist of the argument is that if we reduce, say 'greater than' in "This thing is greater in magnitude than that" to the properties of magnitude of the relata, then these properties must be such that one is greater than the other, so that the relation of 'greater than' is not eliminated at all (J. Slater 1997: vii). But as Russell points out, in the last text I quoted from *External World* (KEW 45), the relation of 'equal to' *does* appear to be eliminated if the relationship is equality of magnitude and the magnitudes are equal. For then we do not have two magnitudes standing in an uneliminated relation of equality. We have one and the same property of magnitude, which each relatum has (KEW 45). That is, the extension of the argument to symmetrical properties is inconsistent with Russell's theory of universals. Now, one might insist on the extension and say that any inconsistency with theory of universals is Russell's problem. One might even say that the relation of identity is uneliminated, since the magnitudes are after all identical. But this is working uphill. It is not mere charity to suppose that Russell would have been aware of the inconsistency, when he himself points out that the argument does not appear to extend to symmetrical relations (KEW 45). And it is hard to think of a less likely candidate for external relation than the relation of self-identity. For not only is that relation symmetrical, but all resemblances—which are symmetrical relations—can be analyzed as identities of generic properties; see Butchvarov (1979: 205).

Those are the four main points I wish to make. I conclude that Russell admits one kind of external relations, and two kinds of internal relations. I proceed to the closely related topic of essential properties, including essential relations arguendo.

For Russell, that a particular red sense-datum is essentially red would be implied by the *truth* of "*R(a)*," where "*a*" is a logically proper name. For (1) the meaning of a logically proper name is the sensed particular it denotes, and (2) a sensed particular is an *instance* of a quality-universal. I argue elsewhere that for the 1912–27 Russell, sensed particulars are instances of quality-universals (Dejnožka 2003: chapter 5, section 2). Russell says, in his 1911 paper, "On the Relations of Universals to Particulars":

> According to the...view, which admits particulars, what exists here is...an instance of whiteness, a particular of which whiteness is the only predicate except shape and brightness and whatever else is *necessarily* connected with whiteness. (RUP 111, my emphasis)

He says, concerning "white patches," that his argument "forces us to admit that it is particulars, i.e., *instances* of universals, that exist in places" (RUP 112–13, Russell's emphasis). Where an instance of a specific shade of whiteness is concerned, the "whatever else" presumably includes hue, saturation, and brightness as "necessarily connected with whiteness" in the white patch, as well as generic universals such as color, visible quality, and property. Indeed, any actual color patch is *given* as an instance of both specific qualities and generic universals (PP 101). Thus "particulars, i.e., *instances*" have many *de re* properties.

Russell says in his 1912 *The Problems of Philosophy*:

> Let us give the name of "sense-data" to the things that are immediately known in sensation: such things as colours, sounds, smells, hardnesses, roughnesses, and so on. (PP 12)

Bare particulars are not on the list. Bare particulars are not colors, sounds, smells, hardnesses, or roughnesses. Nor is there any doubt that Russell admits such sense-data into his ontology of entities. He says, "A particular patch of colour which I see...simply exists" (PP 113). It is not a logical construction or, in his later, more accurate terminology for the same thing, a logical fiction. It is therefore not logically analyzed by Russell into a bare particular's exemplifying a universal. It is only analyzed into a color and a shape. He says we have "a single sense-datum which has both colour and shape: the colour is red and the shape is round" (PP 114). He then says that after we analyze "the datum into colour and shape," our judgment then recombinatively states "that the red colour is round in shape" (PP 114). It may sound odd to say that colors have shapes. But he is talking about a particular color datum, not a color universal. And he does make it very clear that it is not a bare, featureless particular that exemplifies the shape, but a particular datum of color that has it. One may wonder why he could not just as well put things the other way around and say the shape is red in color. The only answer that I find plausible is perhaps charitable: intuitively, it just seems more natural that a particular color datum should be delimited by a shape, a mere limit or terminus to the expanse of color, than that the shape should be filled out by the color, as if the shape were a sort of bucket with sides. This is a weak answer. It is not as if the color were a sort of stuff that can be cut into a shape either. What if our entire visual field were a single red sense-datum? Would it have a shape? Would it be a sort of rough, fuzzy oval in the case of binocular vision? Would it be surrounded by the sort of fuzzy darker reddish brown that always subliminally surrounds what we see, and which we can attend to if we look for it at the edges? If so, then the single red sense-datum would not occupy our entire visual field after all. All the same, a particular color seems more substantive, so to speak, than a particular shape, and even more so if a color can shapelessly occupy our entire visual field. For going in the other direction, we are not going to see any colorless shapes in our visual field. Even a so-called colorless glass of colorless water is not a colorless gap or void in our visual field.

A bare particular is an instance only of bareness and of particularity. A bare particular is not an instance of a color or of a sound. If it were, it would not be bare. If there are bare particulars, their relation to universals would have to be something very different from the relation of being an instance. Bergmann uses the term "exemplification." That may seem not very different from "instantiation." But these are subtle distinctions, and he has to use *some* term. Since he is very clear about the meanings he assigns to his terms, there is really no terminological problem here.

In his 1918 "The Philosophy of Logical Atomism," Russell gives as examples of his sense-particulars "such things as patches of colour or sounds" (PLA 179). Patches and sounds are not bare particulars. They are instances of quality-universals. Nor is there any evidence that Russell analyzes his sense-particulars into bare particulars, as if he somehow thought his sense-particulars were two particulars rolled into one, the sense-particular itself and a bare particular which is its ontological constituent. Where is there any such analysis in Russell? Nor does he analyze the *atomic fact* that this sense-particular, say, this color patch, is red, as having two particulars as constituents of the atomic fact, the patch itself, which he expressly admits is the sense-datum, plus a bare particular which he secretly admits as its constituent. Needless to say, the fact would scarcely be atomic if he did. It would be complex. For it would include two atomic facts: the fact that the sense-datum is an instance of a quality-universal, plus the fact that the bare particular exemplifies the same universal. There simply is nothing like this in Russell. He always treats the sense-datum as being the only particular, and as being an instance of a universal.

Also, Russell holds the traditional view that we learn universals by a process of abstraction from particulars (PP 101). But we cannot abstract universals from bare particulars, except for bareness and particularity. I am not saying that a bare particular theorist cannot give an account of the process of abstraction. I am only saying that it would be impossible to interpret Russell's theory of abstraction in terms of a bare particulars theory. For his theory is that universals are abstracted from particulars. But if his particulars were bare, he would be unable to abstract any universals from particulars at all, except for bareness and particularity. Of course, we could always argue that his particulars are bare and he fails to see the problem this causes for his theory of abstraction. But how likely is that?

It might be objected to my interpretation that the later Russell argues repeatedly against admitting instances of sensible qualities on the ground that they would be (or be like) unknowable substrata or substances that differ only numerically. And what could they be but bare particulars? I have three replies to this.

First, this misdescribes what the later Russell's arguments are about. He is not rejecting instances, but substances. It is substance that he calls "a kernel of pure 'thinghood'" (HWP 468). It is substances that would make "it possible that this and that should have exactly the same predicates," and therefore indiscernible, so that "Counting will be impossible" (IMT 129–30; see 97 and MPD 119–20). Yet in the very same works that the later Russell rejects substances or even the need for proper names, he admits instances as constants, i.e., as values of variables (HK 73–74; see MPD 124). Indeed, it is precisely the thesis that instances are substances that he rejects, because such a particular "cannot be defined or recognized or known" (HK 293; see 294). Instead, the later Russell says that "an 'instance' of a quality [is] a complex of compresent qualities of which the quality in question is one" (HK 298; see MPD 121–22). In other words, they are "such things as little patches of colour or sounds" (PLA 179), just like the old sense-particulars of 1918, but with a different analysis based on a different theory of particulars and universals.

Second, we cannot simply assume, on the basis of these texts in the later Russell, that the early Russell conceived of his sense-particulars as bare substrata or substances. For the 1914–18 Russell was basically against substances too (PLA 203–4); by 1918 the only one he admits is his own self (metaphorically) as a "pin-point particular" (MPD 120). We cannot even assume that Russell is discussing his own earlier theory of instances. For as we saw, the early Russell always describes his instances as patches of color, sounds, and so on, and never as bare particulars.

Third, bare particulars are not substrata or substances to begin with. Bergmann rejects traditional substances and admits bare particulars as a very different alternative. He holds that far from being unknowable substrata, we are acquainted with bare particulars in the sense that we are acquainted with the numerical difference of, e.g., phenomenal spots having exactly the same color, size, and shape. Therefore it would be a *non sequitur* to infer that Russell is rejecting bare particulars when he rejects unknowable substances or substrata. Granted, Russell's views are not Bergmann's. Both accept the principle of acquaintance: "Every proposition which we can understand must be composed wholly of constituents with which we are acquainted" (PP 58, Russell's emphasis deleted). And for both, this includes particulars. But for Bergmann, we are acquainted with bare particulars in the merely numerical sense just indicated. And when Russell says, "In order to understand a proposition in which the name of a particular occurs, you must already be acquainted with that particular" (PLA 204), he means "what I call 'particulars'—such things as little patches of colour or sounds" (PLA 179).

Even if I were wrong and the 1911–18 Russell admits bare particulars like Bergmann's or Edwin B. Allaire's, such particulars would not be *identifiable* independently of the qualities they exemplify (see Bergmann 1971a; Allaire 1970; 1970a), and in that sense they would be essentially related to those qualities in spite of all their bareness. And obviously, bare particulars are essentially bare, essentially particular, and essentially exemplificative, much as instances are essentially instantiative and essentially particular.[2] And for the 1912 Russell every verb, common noun, and adjective represents a universal (PP 94–95; LK 156). That would include "bare," "particular," "instance," and "exemplification" alike. Thus ironically, even a bare particular is an instance of some universals, namely bareness, particularity, and exemplificationhood. This may seem to show that the very concept of a bare particular that exemplifies and does not instantiate properties is self-defeating. But I see nothing logically inconsistent in a bare particular that exemplifies its specific universals and instantiates its categorial universals. In fact, I think we should expect that. There is also a second way out. José Benardete once said in metaphysics class that certain descriptions, such as "bare," seem to function not to ascribe a property, but to deny that a thing has any properties. If so, then a particular could be essentially bare, yet not instantiate a property of bareness, since there would be no such property for it to instantiate. Compare "This glass is empty." Surely we are saying that there is nothing in the glass, not that it is full of something called emptiness.

Crucially, the slightest presented change in a sense-datum results *ipso facto* in a new sense-datum (RUP 114, 199; PLA 203). Can we seriously think that for Russell, this green patch might have been a sound, or a generic universal? Can we even think that for Russell, it might have been blue? No, there is essence aplenty here. We can also see that and how, *mutatis mutandis*, a bare particular is, for all its bareness, essentially identifiable only in terms of the properties it exemplifies. For the slightest presented change also results in a new bare particular, on the bare particular theory. At any rate, I agree with Bergmann on that.

All this is arguably compatible with Russell's whole-part containment eliminative approach to modality. That an instance of red is essentially red, or that a bare particular is essentially bare, cannot literally be analyzed in terms of wholes and parts, but it is at least analogous to whole-part analysis. For an instance of red is wholly red, and a bare particular is wholly bare. More than that, an instance's being an instance of red "consists entirely in its being" red, and a bare particular's being bare "consists entirely in its being" bare, to borrow a phrase from Butchvarov (1989: 67, 71). Thus we may assimilate Russell's theory of particulars, on either the bare or the instance interpretation, to his modally eliminative whole-part theory of deductive inference, which I shall discuss in chapter 9.

Note that on either analysis, the instance analysis or the bare particular analysis, the relation of being equally red is a symmetrical and transitive relation, and is therefore an internal relation for Russell. Indeed, there would be something wrong with any ontological analysis of being red on which the relation of being equally red were not symmetrical and transitive, not to say internal.

Alien Objects Revisited

I return to alien objects, which were briefly discussed in chapters 2, 5, and earlier in the present chapter, but now under the heading of possible worlds semantics. Again, an alien object is an object that exists only in some possible world or worlds other than the actual world. Again, Bradley argues that there is a great actualist-nonactualist difference between Russell and the early Wittgenstein, in that the early Wittgenstein admits alien objects while Russell rejects them (R. Bradley 1992: 38–40). Again, this is incorrect. Both thinkers reject alien objects, but for fundamentally different reasons.

Russell rejects alien objects because for him there is no such thing as a merely possible object (and therefore no such thing as a merely possible world). There can be "alien objects talk" in the same way there can be possible worlds talk, namely, by description without any ontological commitment. But while alien objects (and the possible worlds they are in) can be described, they cannot be known by description, since they are not there to be known. They can be described in either of two ways. First, they can be described in the process of describing ways the actual world might have been. And I have abundantly shown the ways in which Russell can extend talk of the ways the actual world might have been, so as to allow talk of alien objects without according alien objects any ontological status. Second, of course, alien objects can be described *simpliciter*.

For the early Wittgenstein, there can be no alien objects because every object is in every possible world, including the actual world. "If all objects are given, then at the same time all *possible* states of affairs are also given" (T 2.0124). "Objects contain the possibility of all situations" (T 2.014). "It is obvious that an imagined world, however different it may be from the real one, must have *something*—a form—in common with it. Objects are just what constitute this unalterable form" (T 2.022, T 2.023). Thus objects constitute not only the "substance" (T 2.021) but also the "form" (T 2.023) of the world, and indeed of all possible worlds (see M. Black 1970: 9, 58–61). Thus objects subsist, i.e., have necessary existence (T 2.024). And since they have necessary existence, they exist in all possible worlds, including the actual world. This connection between truth in virtue of logical form and truth in all possible worlds is intimate indeed. For objects contain all possible worlds and also constitute logical form.

For Wittgenstein, a world is defined by what is *not* the case in it as much as by what is (T 1.11, T 1.12, T 2.0121, T 2.04, T 2.05, T 2.06, T 2.063.) "The existence and non-existence of states of affairs is reality" (T 2.06). "The sum-total of reality is the world" (T 2.063). Granted, the totality of existing states of affairs determines the totality of nonexisting states of affairs (T 2.05). But the converse is true as well. The two mentioned totalities determine each other. And that includes determining all the objects they contain.[3]

Compare Russell on positive and negative facts. For him, every positive statement and its denial differ only by a negation. Ignoring vagueness (PLA 179–80), only one statement in each such pair of statements is true, and only one is false. If the positive statement is true, it describes a positive fact, and its denial describes no fact. If the negative statement is true, it describes a negative fact, and the positive statement describes no fact. Now, the totality of positive statements and their denials determine each other. And the totality of positive facts and negative facts determines the actual world, and also determines all the objects the actual world contains. See "The Philosophy of Logical Atomism" (PLA 182–88).

For both Russell and the early Wittgenstein, the world is not fully described by a mere list of the objects, properties, and relations it contains. We also need to know which objects have which properties, and which entities (objects, properties, and relations) stand in which relations. To know this is to know the facts that compose the world. Likewise for any merely possible worlds, regardless of whether they have being, have objects that are beyond being and nonbeing *á la* Meinong, or are mere talk *á la* Russell.

Wittgenstein's transcendental Parmenideanism is stronger than Russell's. In Kripkean terms, a Russellian logically proper name is a rigid designator in the weak sense that it has the same denotation in every possible world in which the denoted particular occurs. For its meaning is its denotation; to change its denotation is to change its meaning. Since the existence of a Russellian sense-particular is logically contingent, no such particular can occur in every possible world. Each of Russell's particulars "might happen to be the whole universe" (PLA 202)—or not. But Wittgenstein's object-names are rigid designators in the strong sense that they name the same object in every possible world. That is because (1) every object is in every possible world for Wittgenstein, unlike for Russell, and (2) the meaning of an object-name is its denotation for Wittgenstein, just as it is for Russell (Pitcher 1964: 49; T 3.203). Thus for both Russell and the early Wittgenstein, to change the denotation of an object-name is to change the very meaning of the name. However, if Russell's *ante rem* universals could be named by logically proper names, they would be rigidly designated in Kripke's strong sense. For to be in the world of universals is *in effect* the same as to be in all possible worlds for Russell. This is so even though for Russell, universals are not in the actual world of existents, but only in their own world of being, and even though there are no merely possible worlds, but only possible worlds talk. Of course, the same cannot be said of *instances* of universals. Instances are not in all possible worlds. Not every possible world has an instance of red.

Russell and the early Wittgenstein follow Leibniz and ultimately Parmenides in holding that *ens et unum convertuntur*. Both hold that composite things are not real beings (Dejnožka 2003: chapter 5, section 2; M. Black 1970: 58–61). But they have very different interpretations of *ens et unum convertuntur*. For the early Wittgenstein requires that an object be a logically necessary being while Russell forbids it, at any rate for sense-particulars. Thus Wittgenstein's simples are necessary beings, while Russell's are logically contingent, at any rate if they either are or are logical parts of sense-particulars. In this respect, Wittgenstein's view seems far closer to that of Parmenides than Russell's does. One qualification of the foregoing is that Russell holds that *facts* are both real and composite. In that sense, he does admit logically composite entities. But he denies that "the ordinary objects of daily life" are "complex entities" (PLA 190). And he holds that sense-particulars "have the most complete and perfect and absolute reality that anything can have" (PLA 274). And that includes any simples with which we *may* be acquainted in sense-experience (PLA 202).

These considerations outweigh Bradley's arguments, which I shall not address.

I shall conclude this chapter by repeating part of chapter 2, but with new emphases.

In *Introduction to Mathematical Philosophy*, Russell states MDL (IMP 165) and says,

> *Pure logic*, and pure mathematics (which is the same thing), *aims at being true, in Leibnizian phraseology, in all possible worlds*, not only in this higgeldy-piggeldy job-lot of a world in which chance has imprisoned us....
>
> Viewed from this strictly logical point of view, I do not see any reason to believe that the axiom of reducibility is *logically necessary, which is what would be meant by saying that it is true in all possible worlds.*
> (IMP 192–93, my emphasis)

In this dramatic passage, he regards possible worlds talk as mere "phraseology." He makes it clear elsewhere in *Introduction* that on his "robust sense of reality," there is no such thing as a merely possible object, let alone a merely possible world (IMP 168–70; see PLA 216). Yet *within* this mere phraseology, he expressly equates three things: logical truth, logically necessary truth, and truth in all possible worlds. What is more, he states in this passage that logical necessity is what is *meant* by "truth in all possible worlds." Therefore, *as* a matter of mere talk, this is just how he *would* understand logical necessity, and a fortiori, logical truth. And this is precisely a way of defining logical necessity while at the same time eliminatively analyzing it away as mere talk. Does not the last sentence of the passage not almost expressly permit a possible worlds semantics for logical necessity, which for Russell is just logical truth?

Of course, a full statement of possible worlds semantics would not only interpret logical necessity as truth in all possible worlds, but would also interpret logical impossibility as truth in no possible world, interpret logical possibility as truth in at least one possible world, and interpret logical contingency as truth in at least one possible world plus falsehood in at least one possible world. But since the four modal operators are interdefinable, we need only one of them to be so interpreted. And we have that in the block-indented quotation of Russell on this page. He inverts the point and says that when we say a proposition is true in all possible worlds, we mean that it is logically necessary. But the two expressions are synonymous for him in any case, and this implies that he has an implicit possible worlds semantics.

8

The Motives and Origins of Russell's Theory of Modality

I return now to Russell's three-level theory of modality, which I described in chapter 3. I shall offer five possible motives, or sets of motives, for why Russell might have held this more or less express theory. The fifth set will include a summary of Russell's ca. 1903–05 paper, "Necessity and Possibility." Then I shall discuss speculations as to the theory's possible historical origins. Next, I offer some criticisms of Russell's theory of modality. Then I briefly summarize the results of the first eight chapters. Last, I suggest that MDL, the third level of the three-level theory of modality, is the most natural theory of modality for the modern classical logic tradition of Frege, Russell, Wittgenstein, and Quine.

Possible Motives for Russell's Theory of Modality

I begin, then, with Russell's possible motives for holding his three-level theory of modality.

First, there is the eliminative motive we just saw Russell so eloquently emphasize in the previous chapter. Carnap and Kripke share it. Russell's main reason is ontological: his belief that only the actual exists. Another reason is epistemic and methodological: his acceptance of Ockham's razor.

Second, there is the intuition that possibility and existence are equatable notions. Others have shared this intuition. Leibniz explicitly equates existence with possibility in statements of the form "(Socrates homo) est," which is Leibniz's analysis of "Socrates est homo" (Burkhardt 1988: 187). John Venn says, "[T]o say that anything is possible...is equivalent to saying that...it is occasionally actual" (Venn 1879: 40). John Passmore says of Hilary Putnam, "'There exists a set of mathematical integers satisfying a mathematical condition' is not, [Putnam] says, significantly different from 'it is *possible* to select integers so as to satisfy this condition'" (Passmore 1985: 93). Arthur N. Prior and Kit Fine say, "It has been...evident that there are close structural analogies between modal logic and quantification theory....It is much less usual to turn the parallels...in the opposite direction, and present quantification theory...as...a disguised theory of modal logic. Such a move, all the same, is in principle possible, and there is more to be said for it than one might at first imagine" (Prior 1977: 9–10). Prior says of Georg Henrik von Wright's 'existential modalities', "'*X*'s are universally *Y*'s'...has a similar ring to '*X*'s are necessarily *Y*'s' and similarly implies...'*X*'s are sometimes *Y*'s'. Again, the one-way implication 'If something necessarily *F*'s then necessarily something *F*'s' is like the implication 'If something *F*'s everything then everything has something that *F*'s it', with a second-order quantification in place of the modality" (Prior 1967a: 11; see Wright 1957: 58, 66, 69, 74). Charles Sanders Peirce says, "The simplest account of necessity is the scholastic, according to which the necessary...proposition is a sort of universal proposition; the possible...proposition, a sort of particular proposition" (Peirce 1960: 89). Michael J. Loux notes that Saul A. Kripke's modal operators are like quantifiers (Loux 1979: 27). The only difference between MDL and all these equations of possibility with existence, and of necessity with universality, is the difference between real (free) variables and apparent (bound) variables, a distinction Russell eventually finds "no need" for (PM xiii). And Willard Van Orman Quine has written to me about MDL, "Certainly I have no objection to necessity and possibility when interpreted in Russell's way" (Quine 1990; compare FLPV 4; PQ 114, 292).[1]

Third, MDL {1,2,3} is Russell's comprehensive three-level theory of modality with ontological and metaphysical motivations: Parmenidean on level (1), Berkeley-Humean on level (2), Fregean on level (3). Russell's motivation is to make all three of these levels work together in an overall theory connecting his quantificational logic with his theory of logically proper names as referring to sense-data and with his theory of ordinary things as only correlatively real—not to mention with his theory of modality. Basic to this family of motives is Russell's 'no entity without identity' theory of secondary correlative identities based on rigidly designatable primary "given" identities of sense-data, where to be informatively identified is to be secondarily real. Again, MDL is MDL {3}, and thus plays a major role in the comprehensive theory.

Fourth, there are at least four other motivations Russell might well have had for MDL.

(4a) David Pears suggests that MDL is an attempt to generalize Hume's definition of cause in terms of constant conjunction. MDL generalizes a "parsimonious theory of physical necessity" of lawlike universal conditionals to all universal sentences derived from propositional functions that are always true by binding their variables with universal quantifiers. Of course, Pears is aware that this has difficult consequences. I might mention one myself: "$(x)(x = x)$" does not state a *physical* necessity. But while Pears does not say so, this suggestion is very plausible in Russell's "On the Notion of a Cause." For there Russell analyzes the very first definition of causal necessity he considers directly in terms of MDL. Here Pears anticipates my discovery of Russell's implicit causal modal logic, MDL–C.

(4b) Pears recalls that there is an ordinary sense in which we say that a sentence must be true if it is instantiated from a true universal sentence. This fine suggestion seems supported by the relevant passages in "The Philosophy of Logical Atomism," and elsewhere (Pears 1967: 249–259), and seems to fit MDL perfectly. But as we shall soon see, Russell rejects (4b).

(4c) Russell himself seems to suggest in "The Philosophy of Logical Atomism" that the motive of MDL is to analyze propositional epistemic possibility. Russell says that when we say "It is possible that it may rain tomorrow," using the word "possible" in an ordinary sense, this may be analyzed as: "We do not know if it will rain tomorrow; 'It will rain tomorrow' is a value of the propositional function, 'It rains at time t'; and that propositional function is not always false" (PLA 254–55). Thus MDL is basic to Russell's analysis of epistemic possibility. Indeed, this Russell quotation defines the possibility operator of implicit MDL–E.

(4d) MDL, as a modification of Hugh MacColl's theory of *certainty*, is a theory of necessity as the probability of 1 (MacColl 1906: 6–7). In his 1919 *Introduction*, Russell says:

> If "Φx" is an undetermined value of a certain propositional function, it will be necessary if the function is always true, possible if it is sometimes true, and impossible if it is never true. This sort of situation arises in regard to probability, for example. Suppose a ball x is drawn from a bag which contains a number of balls: if all the balls are white, "x is white" is necessary; if some are white, it is possible; if none, it is impossible. (IMP 165, Russell's emphasis)

Thus motive (4d) seems quite express. This is a frequency theory of probability.

I have two comments about this fourth set of possible motivations. First, except for Russell's rejection of (4b), all of them are compatible with the present interpretation and greatly enrich it. Second, it might seem that when Russell first published MDL in 1906, his only express motive was (4d). His suggested epistemic motive in 1918 may seem Johnny come lately in particular. But MacColl's notion of certainty is, after all, epistemic. And Russell says, "Where it is worth our while to say that a *proposition* is possible, the fact rests upon our ignorance. With more knowledge we should know [the proposition's truth]. Possibility in this sense thus becomes assimilated to probability" (AMA 170). Here motive

(4c) is logically a further amplification or elaboration of motive (4d), adding to it our lack of knowledge.

Russell's "Necessity and Possibility" Paper

Fifth, the richest and most complex set of motives for MDL is in Russell's unpublished paper, "Necessity and Possibility" (Russell 1994a / ca. 1903–05). This is not only his longest and most complete discussion of modality, but it also contains his first statement of MDL. It is his only unpublished writing on MDL. It is also his only writing on MDL in which he rejects MDL. The inevitable suggestion is that he did not publish it because he felt uncomfortable about rejecting MDL. In every later, and what is the same, every published writing in which he states MDL, he accepts MDL.

I summarize "Necessity and Possibility" as follows.

Russell begins the paper by saying that traditional modal distinctions are mainly erroneous and confused, that the modalities "must be primarily predicates of propositions," and that necessary propositions themselves "may happen also to be necessary" (Russell 1994a / ca. 1903–05: 508). Thus, at least for any *viable* modal theory, he clearly states that the modalities are primarily propositional and that the necessity operator is iterable, and he clearly implies that the necessity operator is iterable indefinitely many times. He also agrees with tradition's minimal requirements "that a necessary proposition must be true, and that a possible proposition is one [whose] contradictory is not necessary" (Russell 1994a / ca. 1903–05: 508). He makes it clear that he is discussing logical modalities such as the necessary and the contingent, and not epistemic notions such as the *a priori* or the empirically known (Russell 1994a / ca. 1903–05: 511).

Russell presents MDL as preserving the virtues while avoiding the difficulties of a series of earlier theories of necessity, including those of Immanuel Kant, F. H. Bradley, Bernard Bosanquet, G. E. Moore, and MacColl. Kant errs in making the copula the *locus* of necessity instead of the whole proposition. Bradley, by making a proposition necessary if it is implied by another proposition, makes all propositions necessary. Bosanquet, by making the logical connectives of implication and alternation, or if you please, consequents and alternatives, the *loci* of necessity, overlooks that many hypothetical and disjunctive propositions are true but not necessarily true. Moore, by making one proposition more necessary than another if it is implied by more propositions than the other, assigns all true propositions the same degree of necessity, since every true proposition is implied by any proposition. The pre-Kantian view that necessary propositions are analytic may be updated by defining analytic propositions as those propositions which are entailed by the laws of logic. But even then there will be indefinitely many necessary propositions which are not analytic, namely, the synthetic *a priori* propositions. Russell cites a synthetic *a priori* proposition about a color incompatibility (red-yellow) and another about an ethical incompatibility (good-bad). Russell then in effect approves of Pears' second suggested motive: propositions may be called necessary if they are members of classes of true propositions which differ only by substitutions for the same constituent. Here Russell approves of MacColl's theory, except for MacColl's failing to distinguish propositions from propositional functions, which are the proper logical subjects of modal predicates. (Russell's own criticism of Kant needs the same modification.)

Russell finds that the definition of a necessary proposition as one whose denial is self-contradictory cannot be "harmonized with modern logic" (Russell 1994a / ca. 1903–05: 514). He wishes to preserve "[t]he old identification of the necessary with the analytic" (Russell 1994a / ca. 1903–05: 514), but finds that better definitions of analyticity and of deducibility are needed. He proposes to define deducibility first, and then define analyticity in terms of deducibility.

Russell begins by distinguishing material implication from deducibility. He says:

> [I]f we regard q as deducible from p whenever p [materially] implies q, all true propositions are deducible from the law of [non]contradiction. But in the practice of inference, it is plain that something more than [material] implication must be concerned. The reason that proofs are used at all is that we can sometimes perceive that q follows from p, when we should not otherwise know that q is true; while in other cases, "p [materially] implies q" is only to be inferred either from the falsehood of p or from the truth of q. In these other cases, the proposition "p [materially] implies q" serves no practical purpose; it is only when this proposition is used as a means of discovering the truth of q that it is useful. Given a true proposition p, there will be some propositions q such that the truth of "p [materially] implies q" is evident, and thence the truth of q is inferred; while in the case of other true propositions [q], their truth must be independently known before we can know that p [materially] implies them. What we require is a *logical* distinction between these two cases. (Russell 1994a / ca. 1903–05: 515, Russell's emphasis; see 517 repeating that implications which can be known only by knowing

that the antecedent is true or that the conclusion is false
"have no practical utility")

Russell then says that the only way he has thought of to make this logical distinction is to admit there are laws of deduction which:

> tell us that two propositions having *certain relations of form*...are such that one of them [materially] implies the other. Thus q is deducible from p if p and q either have one of the relations contemplated by the laws of deduction, or are connected by any (finite) number of intermediaries each having one of these relations to its successor. (Russell 1994a / ca. 1903–05: 515, my emphasis)

He finds that this definition is "purely logical" and covers "exactly the cases" we consider to be cases of logical deduction "without assuming either that p is false or that q is true" (Russell 1994a / ca. 1903–05: 515). Russell never deviates from this basic understanding of the distinction between material implication and logical deducibility in any later work. The preceding quotation contains is a very early reference to logical form, but no clear distinction between fully general implication and implication in virtue of logical form. He is not saying in this early paper that logical form is a second condition, in addition to that of full generality. I take this to be obvious on its face. But if an argument is needed, it would be that otherwise Russell would never have needed to correct his early understanding of logical truth as fully general truth, since he would already have understood logical truth as truth in virtue of logical form as early as ca. 1903–05.

Russell says, "We may, then, usefully define as *analytic* those propositions which are deducible from the laws of logic" (Russell 1994a / ca. 1903–05: 516, Russell's emphasis). Here he is "adopting a suggestion of [Louis] Couturat" (Russell 1994a / ca. 1903–05: 516). He says that "the class of analytic propositions is an important one" (Russell 1994a / ca. 1903–05: 516).

Russell then defines q as an analytic consequence of p if and only if "p [materially] implies q" is analytic (Russell 1994a / ca. 1903–05: 516–17). He then notes that on his definitions, "q is an analytic consequence of p when and only when q is deducible from p" (Russell 1994a / ca. 1903–05: 517).

Russell says that we may now say, if we wish, "that a necessary proposition is an analytic proposition," and this would be a "precise meaning" (Russell 1994a / ca. 1903–05: 517). "But the *feeling* of necessity does not answer to this definition; many propositions are felt to be necessary which are not analytic" (Russell 1994a / ca. 1903–05: 517, Russell's emphasis). Thus he rejects the identification of necessary propositions with analytic propositions, that is, the explanation of logical necessity as analyticity, not because he finds anything wrong with analyticity, but only because he finds our intuitions of logical necessity to be wider in scope than the class of analytic propositions. Perhaps that is because of his admission of synthetic *a priori* truths, taking logical necessity in its broadest and most inclusive sense. But he could simply restrict logical necessity to formal deductive logic. It is precisely there that logical necessity would be plausibly equated with analytic truth. And within that limited and appropriate logical *locus*, it never occurs to him that if there is no logical equivalence, the very situation cries out for applying his own philosophy of analysis as the replacement of our vague intuitions (e.g. logical necessity) with more definite concepts (e.g. analytic truth). Perhaps this is because he has not yet developed that alternative conception of logical analysis, and still thinks of logical analysis as always a matter of finding a logically equivalent statement.

Russell then explores what it might mean to be a necessary proposition. First, he considers taking a necessary proposition to be a proposition which is an instance of some class of true propositions (Russell 1994a / ca. 1903–05: 517). This is motive (4b) as described earlier. He then rejects (4b). For on (4b), we should correlatively define a proposition as possible "if there is something which can be substituted for [the subject] so as to make the proposition true" (Russell 1994a / ca. 1903–05: 517). And that definition is "more or less paradoxical," "for example,...Socrates might be a triangle, because there are triangles" (Russell 1994a / ca. 1903–05: 517). But Socrates cannot be a triangle because he is a man, and men cannot be triangles. Russell notes that "'Socrates is a man *and* a triangle' is impossible according to the definition" (Russell 1994a / ca. 1903–05: 517, my emphasis). But then in order to tell whether a proposition about Socrates is possible, "there is no ground for stopping short of *all* his properties; and then true propositions in which he occurs are possible, and false propositions in which he occurs are impossible" (Russell 1994a / ca. 1903–05: 518, Russell's emphasis). And that is absurd. But Russell feels that this approach does cover many ordinary cases which we say are possible. If I think that a cab's number might have had four figures instead of five, he says that really the subject is "felt as a variable: it is not felt as fully determinate, but as an indeterminate member of some class;" thus "it is natural" to consider the modalities as properties of propositional functions, as opposed to being operators on propositions (Russell 1994a / ca. 1903–05: 518). He then offers these definitions:

> "The propositional function '*x* has the property *Φ*' is
> *necessary* if it holds of everything; it is *necessary*
> *throughout the class u* if it holds of every member of *u*."
> "The propositional function '*x* has the property *Φ*' is
> *possible* if it holds of something; it is *possible within the*
> *class u* if it holds of some member of *u*." (Russell 1994a
> / ca. 1903–05: 518, Russell's emphasis)

Now, "*x* is a triangle" is duly impossible with respect to the *class*
of humans, since no human is a triangle (see Russell 1994a / ca.
1903–05: 517–18). Russell says he thinks that these two definitions
are substantially Hugh MacColl's, but criticizes MacColl for not
distinguishing propositions from propositional functions" (Russell
1994a / ca. 1903–05: 518). He finds "no particular objection to
these definitions, except that they do not make necessity and
possibility a property of propositional functions" (Russell 1994a /
ca. 1903–05: 518). He then warns us, "Some care is required in
giving precision to the suggestion with which we started, that the
definitions are to be applied to propositions by regarding the
subject of the proposition as variable" (Russell 1994a / ca.
1903–05: 518). Namely, where there is more than one occurrence
of the subject-term, say "Socrates", we must eliminate scope
ambiguity by specifying which occurrences of "Socrates" are to be
considered when deciding whether a proposition is "*necessary with*
respect to Socrates" (Russell 1994a / ca. 1903–05: 518, Russell's
emphasis). To eliminate scope ambiguity, Russell decides to define
a proposition as necessary with respect to Socrates if *any* of the
propositional functions resulting from treating *any* combination of
occurrences of "Socrates" as occurrences of the same variable is
always true, that is, always results in a true proposition no matter
what we substitute for "Socrates" in those occurrences (Russell
1994a / ca. 1903–05: 518–19). This approach is the widest or most
inclusive one possible.

One advantage of this approach is that it turns out that, as
Russell says, "Analytic propositions have the property that they are
necessary with respect to all of their constituents except such as are
what I call *logical constants*" (Russell 1994a / ca. 1903–05: 519,
Russell's emphasis). Here, of course, as we saw earlier, analytic
propositions are just fully general truths. Russell does define them
as deducible from the laws of logic, but does not yet distinguish
that from fully general truth as such, despite that remark about
"certain relations of form" (Russell 1994a / ca. 1903–05: 515).
Years later, Russell finds that analytic propositions must also be
true in virtue of their logical form, where logical form is something
more than just being fully general. A second advantage of this
approach is that it explains our feeling that necessary propositions
are timelessly true, since time-bound truths are generally true at

some times but not at other times (Russell 1994a / ca. 1903–05: 519).

Russell then finds a counterexample to his analysis in its application to propositions involving time. Namely, we feel that "For any *x*, if *x* is a moment in time then *x* occurs after the death of Cromwell or before the Restoration" is most certainly true, but not a *necessary* truth, since it is a merely contingent fact that Cromwell died before the Restoration. Russell's reply is that we feel with equal right that it *is* impossible for any event to occur before the death of Cromwell but after the Restoration, since Cromwell *did* in fact die before the Restoration. Here Russell is already setting the stage for banishing modality from logic for the reason that our feelings of modality are conflicted.

Russell argues that probability is not the same as degree of possibility, since assignments of probability are "often, if not always, more or less arbitrary" (Russell 1994a / ca. 1903–05: 519–20). This argument is puzzling. What are "degrees of possibility"? And why are they not exactly as arbitrary as the ostensibly corresponding "assignments of probability"? But the argument need not detain us.

Russell admits that it may be possible to develop a better analysis of modality than the one he has just given. But now he gives an argument "[t]hat the feeling of necessity is...complex and muddled" (Russell 1994a / ca. 1903–05: 520), and concludes that "modality ought to be banished from logic" (Russell 1994a / ca. 1903–05: 520). The argument is a sort of proof by cases, with at least four main cases to consider. He says, "The feeling of necessity...is...compounded of such elements as the following" (Russell 1994a / ca. 1903–05: 520):

(1) the feeling that a proposition can be known [independently of experience, i.e., *a priori*]; Epistemic modal.
(2) the feeling that a proposition can be *proved*; Alethic modality? Logical modality =
(3) The feeling that a proposition can be deduced from ? the laws of logic[, i.e., is analytically true in Russell's sense];
(4) The feeling that a proposition holds not only of its Extensional / actual subject, but of all subjects more or less resembling Quant. modality its actual subject, or, as an extreme case, of all subjects absolutely. (Russell 1994a / ca. 1903–05: 520)

He then criticizes these four elements of the feeling of necessity as follows.

He says element (1) concerns epistemology, not logic.

He says element (2) "makes the necessary coextensive with the true" (Russell 1994a / ca. 1903–05: 520). I find this criticism ① bizarre. Even Russell holds elsewhere that not every truth can be

Because 'necessity' is a category within various types of modalities – alethic, epistemic, doxastic, etc.

proved, on pain of vicious infinite regress of proofs. Perhaps he means that every necessary truth can be proved in some system of proofs, if not every one in the same system. But that is a dubious view. And it is not his view. His view is that if propositions are formally true, then "every logic must include them," and if not, then "every logic must exclude them" (POM xii).

He says element (3) better describes "the class of *analytic* propositions" (Russell 1903–05: 520, Russell's emphasis).

He says element (4) more properly applies "to *propositional functions* than to propositions" (Russell 1994a / ca. 1903–05: 520, Russell's emphasis).

Russell then concludes with two premises of a modus ponens, leaving the reader to draw the obvious conclusion:

> I conclude that, so far as appears, there is no one fundamental logical notion of *necessity*....If this conclusion is valid, the subject of modality should be banished from logic, since propositions are simply true or false, and there is no such comparative and superlative of truth as is implied by the notion[of] necessity. (Russell 1994a / ca. 1903–05: 520, Russell's emphasis)

Thus he implicitly rejects his thesis that analytic truths are MDL-necessary with respect to every propositional function they contain, since he rejects MDL.

Of course, Russell's argument to banish modality from logic because our modal intuitions conflict is obviously bad. For *all* our interesting logical intuitions conflict. Thus, on *that* argument, we ought to banish *logic* altogether. And perhaps perceiving the obvious badness of this argument might be a main reason why Russell comes to accept MDL as his "fundamental notion" of modality the very next year.

It might be suggested that Russell is really finding modality *too* conflicted, for any modal logic to be possible, unlike the *lesser* conflicts of our intuitions in other areas of logic. But this is a slippery slope. How much conflict in our intuitions is too much conflict for a logic to be possible? Can we not simply base different logics on different intuitions? Indeed, intuitions change. Russell himself accepts MDL the very next year. And by what yardstick are we measuring degrees of conflict of intuitions across all the areas of logic? How can we be sure that the modal conflicts are greater or less than all the other conflicts, such as relevance conflicts? Thus, even though this objection is a very natural one, I remain persuaded that Russell's argument to banish modality is obviously bad.

A second main reason why he accepts MDL the next year is surely this. Even in "Necessity and Possibility" itself, he says he has "no particular objection to these definitions, except that they do not make necessity and possibility a property of propositional functions" (Russell 1994a / ca. 1903–05: 518). Thus in effect he finds MDL, which *does* make the modalities properties of propositional functions, technically acceptable even in this very paper. And surely this is also why the whole business about how our feelings of necessity are "confused and muddled" simply drops out of the picture from 1906 on. For the reason behind this main reason, so to speak, is that his whole philosophy of analysis is precisely to "replace" our ordinary "somewhat confused thoughts" (MPD 179) with new thoughts which are "not really....the same" thoughts, but which are "much more analytic and precise" (PLA 188–89; see 179–81). Therefore, on his own philosophy of analysis, he has nothing to complain about. And perhaps this is also why he never had "Necessity and Possibility" published. Namely, in effect he found MDL technically acceptable in that very paper, and this is basically all his philosophy of analysis requires. That is, perhaps he soon noticed that his final argument and conclusion in that paper were basically inconsistent with his own philosophy of analysis. But perhaps his conception of logical analysis had not yet developed to that later level of clear articulation.

A third main reason is the most obvious one: MDL simply works out so nicely for Russell's quantificational logic. For MDL is basically quantificational itself. And Russell already *has* it almost all worked out in "Necessity and Possibility." Namely, a statement is logically necessary just in case it is MDL-necessary with respect to every propositional function it contains (and also, as he adds much later, true in virtue of its form). And a statement is logically necessary if and only if it is analytically true, as those terms are defined in "Necessity and Possibility."

This concludes my review of "Necessity and Possibility."

From 1906 on, concerning necessity, element (4) is basic. But element (4) merges into element (3) because an analytic statement is trivially necessary with respect to every variable. Element (1) comes in because every analytic truth is *a priori*. Even element (2) applies, if we allow proof of every logical truth by truth-table.

Of course, even from 1906 on, Russell still eliminates modal notions in the sense of providing an eliminative logical analysis of them. That is precisely what MDL is: a logical analysis that replaces three modal notions with three veridical notions. This has seemed to some to show that Russell has no modal logic, but only an existential logic, since he never says he eliminates existence from logic. But this is confused. I have already described the eliminative aspect of Russell's general theory of logical analysis several times in this book. There is no "asymmetry" between existence and modality here. Russell banishes any entity or notion of existence from logic in exactly the same way. For Russell, *neither* existence nor possibility is a fundamental notion. He reduces them both to the very same "fundamental...idea," 'not always false' (PLA 254). This 'not always false' is neither an existential nor a modal notion, but a semantic, more precisely a veridical, notion. (Besides truth, the other main semantic notion is reference.) And 'not always false', as an incomplete propositional function, is strictly nothing. Thus existence and possibility are equally nothing. Indeed, they are the very same nothing, namely 'not always false'. Thus those who deny that *Principia* is implicitly a modal logic because possibility is nothing for Russell are placed in the position of having to deny that *Principia* is an existential logic. For existence is equally nothing for Russell. It would be folly to argue that Russell has an existential logic but no modal logic because Russell "banishes" modality yet somehow "admits" existence. For Russell, the idea that existence is a property of things "is rubbish" (PLA 252). Existence is not "going about" (PLA 223) in the world any more than possibility is (PLA 230–58). Even Russell's motives are essentially the same in both cases. As we saw in chapter 2, the 1918 Russell says, "There is no sort of point in a predicate which could not be conceivably false" (PLA 241). Russell is arguing that if existence were a property of things, then everything would exist, and it would be pointless to assert the existence of anything. Thus, existence is a useless notion unless it is applied to propositional functions, since not all propositional functions are 'not always false'. And in his 1912 "On the Notion of Cause," Russell argues in basically the same way that since a proposition is (timelessly) true or false then if 'necessary' means "what is true under all circumstances," then if it is "worth saying of something" that it is necessary, then that something must be a propositional function, since not all propositional functions are 'always true' (ONC 176). The symmetry between these arguments is that being something worth saying is the same as being a predicate which has a point. The symmetry is perfect. Existence and possibility are equally nothing, yet play an equally meaningful role in Russell's post-1905 logic, because both are reduced to the same nondenoting expression, which expression has a useful "meaning in use." That Russell says that "Lions exist" and "Lions are possible" are asymmetrical (PLA 255) does not detract from this point. Russell is merely saying that he would analyze "Lions are possible" as meaning "that a *sort* of animal may be the *sort* we call 'lions'," and that in this sense, we may also say that "Unicorns are possible" is true (PLA 255, Russell's emphasis). I would say that this quotation defines the possibility operator of a second implicit epistemic logic, MDL–E*, which would bring the total of

Russell's implicit modal logics up to nine. But I see this as a mere application of MDL–E. All it does is substitute "sort of animal" for "lion." Echoing Quine's term "semantic ascent," this may be called classificatory ascent; the MDL–E analysis remains the same. And echoing Ockham's razor, I do not wish to multiply Russell's implicit modal logics beyond necessity.

Principia as Implicitly Modal Logic FG–MDL

For Russell, a modal logic is as a modal logic does, and an existential logic is as an existential logic does. *Principia* functions as, i.e. reformulates, i.e. simulates, both an existential logic and a modal logic. But *Principia* is, literally speaking, neither. Literally speaking, it is a veridical logic. I have offered elsewhere eight arguments that the *Principia* individual quantifier *implies* no ontological commitment, though of course first-level propositional functions *can* be satisfied by genuine individuals (Dejnožka 2003: chapter 5, section 2).

Landini raises what is surely the chief objection in every reader's mind. Namely, *Principia*'s logic cannot be a modal logic because it does not even appear to be a modal logic. It appears to be an existential logic (Landini 1993). Landini is observing that considered entirely by itself, *Principia* is not, does not appear to be, and was not intended to be a modal logic. My reply is that this is totally irrelevant to my argument. Surely *Principia* does not have to appear to be a modal logic, in order to be implicitly interpretable as a modal logic! I am not sure it even has to appear to be a *logic*, as opposed to a menu or a music score. This is perhaps the only good point made by the formalists—indefinitely many strings of marks on paper can be *used* or *interpreted* as a logic—or a modal logic. For example, even the *actual* meaning of "Roast beef $12.99" can be reasonably interpreted to mean or imply, "It is legally necessary that if you eat the roast beef, then you pay $12.99." Even the *actual* meaning of a crescendo mark can be reasonably interpreted to mean, "It is aesthetically necessary that if you play this measure, you increase the volume." And this is not to mention completely changing the meaning to something else that merely has the same formal structure. Compare the later Wittgenstein on language-games. And if a menu or music score (or a map of the Moon) can be used as a modal logic, surely *Principia* can.

Principia as Implicitly Modal Theory MDL

I turn now from interpreting *Principia* as a modal *logic* (FG–MDL, or retrospectively as FG–MDL*) to interpreting it as a modal *theory* (MDL). Let us compare *Principia* to a hammer and modal theories to doorstops. The hammer is not, does not even appear to be, and was not intended to be a doorstop. If you look at the hammer alone, probably it would never occur to you that it might be used as a doorstop. But suppose the manufacturer writes three brief lines, showing how some basic features of the hammer allow it to function also as a doorstop, and publishes those three lines in eight books and papers appearing before, during, and after he manufactures the hammer, and all aimed at the general hammer-buying public. Though the three lines of print are not packaged and sold with the hammer itself, since after all the hammer is intended to be a hammer and is sold only as a hammer, would you not say that the manufacturer also consciously intended to provide his public a key to using the hammer as a doorstop, should they desire to use it that way, and to make his public aware of the fact that the hammer could be so used? Well, that is just my argument that Russell probably intended that his readers could figure out that the universal and individual quantifiers of *Principia* can be interpreted respectively as "It is necessary with respect to *x* that" and "It is possible with respect to *x* that." For he states MDL in at least eight published works from 1906 to 1940. For the cites, see chapter 1.

I am told the analogy is crude. My reply is that it is crude but effective. For it is intended only to make a crude point, namely, that we can show other people how things that appear to be and are intended for one purpose can work in fact just as well for other purposes. That very limited point is the only point of the analogy. And if that point is successful, then so is the analogy.

Where my hammer-doorstop analogy breaks down is not with the doorstop, but with the hammer. For *Principia*, at least on my view, is not an existential logic *either*. It is a veridical logic which can simulate *both* an existential and a modal logic. Russell explains the first simulation in *Principia*, but explains the second only in the eight publications of MDL I listed. A more complete analogy, though equally crude, is that *Principia* is like an axe that can be used as either a hammer or a doorstop.

Landini's objection emerges as merely Ptolemaic. Granted, *Principia* does not appear to be an implicit modal logic or implicit modal theory. But then the Earth does not appear to revolve about the Sun.

The Dating of "Necessity and Possibility"

When was "Necessity and Possibility" written?

Alasdair Urquhart says, "Russell uses an example in his paper which suggests it was written on Tuesday 17 October 1905" (Urquhart 1994: 507). But this calendar calculation example dates only one sentence of the paper (Russell 1994: 511; see 654). Urquhart admits that the paper must be partly composed of material from an earlier draft, since some manuscript leaves are renumbered. Urquhart finds that "some version of the paper may have existed in May 1905, to judge by the entry in Russell's engagement diary" (Urquhart 1994: 507).

Kenneth Blackwell argues in his preface to the typewritten archived Ms. that "Necessity and Possibility" could not have been written before July 1900, since it cites Moore's "Necessity" in the July 1900 *Mind*. But this argument, too, directly dates only a tiny portion of the paper.

Francisco Rodríguez-Consuegra suggests the paper was written c. 1902 (Rodríguez-Consuegra 1991: 224). He observes that Russell probably had already accepted MacColl's theory of strict implication as a fundamental relation, and also MacColl's contextualist theory of the priority of propositions over their constituents, before 1900 (Rodríguez-Consuegra 1991: 12). In *Principles*, of course, Russell attributes both theories to MacColl (POM 12). But this argument is a *non sequitur*. It does not follow that just because Russell probably accepted those two views of MacColl's before 1900, that Russell started writing his paper "Necessity and Possibility" two years later. That does do not even appear to follow. This is a probability argument at best, and a rather uncertain one at that.

I myself can date "Necessity and Possibility" only as after *Principles*, which accepts Moore's theory of logical necessity, so that Russell has not yet banished modality from logic, and has not yet rejected Moore's theory in particular; and as before his review of MacColl's *Symbolic Logic and Its Applications* (Russell 1906: 257), where he first accepts MDL, thus ending his banishment of modality. More precisely, we know that Russell wrote the paper before October 22, 1905, since he read it on that day to the Oxford Philosophical Society (Urquhart 1994: 507).

That MDL is logically compatible with the admission of mere *possibilia* in *Principles*, and is also compatible with the rejection of mere *possibilia* in "On Denoting," does not detract from the points I just made. Yes, MDL is valid either if it ranges over all possible objects, or if it ranges over all actual objects, where the only possible objects are actual objects. In fact, the second alternative is a special case of the first. Thus MDL is *compatible* with the *Principles* ontology, which admits nonexistent entities. Thus Russell could have developed MDL before he abandoned that *ontology*. Indeed, he probably knew MacColl's theory of modality in 1897, since both contributed papers to the 1897 *Mind*, and MacColl's paper states the theory. But while MDL is compatible with the mere *possibilia* of *Principles*, MDL is not compatible with the *theory of necessity* in *Principles*. What is more, Russell is well aware of that. *Principles* endorses Moore's theory of necessity as degrees of implication, and "Necessity and Possibility" specifically rejects that theory (Russell 1994a / ca. 1903–05: 513–14). And MDL is clearly inconsistent with Moore's theory considered as a complete theory of necessity. For Moorean degrees of necessity concern implications among propositions. There is no place for Moorean degrees of necessity in MDL, nor can Moorean degrees of necessity be properties of propositional functions. That brackets the paper between *Principles* and October 22, 1905, when Russell read the paper to the Oxford Philosophical Society (Urquhart 1994: 507). Unlike Urquhart's calendar example and Blackwell's Moore citation, MDL is basic to Russell's paper. The whole point of the paper is to crown a survey of theories with the best theory, namely his own theory, which includes MDL as the basic building block—and then reject even his own theory because he finds that no logic can resolve all the conflicts among our modal intuitions. And even more basic to "Necessity and Possibility" is its banishing modality from logic in general, which includes rejecting Moore's theory in particular. Still, Russell might have drafted most of his "Necessity and Possibility" survey of earlier theories of modality before he wrote *Principles*. That might even help explain why he settled on Moore's theory in *Principles*: namely, he found all theories earlier than Moore's to be defective. Thus his "Necessity and Possibility" survey of theories, at least of the theories earlier than Moore's, may well antedate *Principles*.

This concludes my survey of motives of MDL. I proceed to discuss the possible historical origins of MDL in Frege, Peirce, Bolzano, MacColl, Leibniz, Venn, and Aristotle.

Possible Origins of Russell's Theory of Modality

Haaparanta sees MDL as possibly originating from Frege's equating necessity with generality in *Begriffsschrift* sect. 4 (Haaparanta 1985: 38–40, 46 n.26). The citation is correct, but there are three uses of "necessary" in section 4, and only the third is like MDL. These uses are: (a) Frege equates "necessary" or, more accurately, "apodictic" (absolutely demonstrable or certain) propositions with propositions derivable from true analytic general axioms. The derived proposition need not be general; it can be an instance of a general one. Frege is saying that formally marking a proposition as apodictic adds nothing to showing it can be derived from such axioms. His point is very much like Russell's point that calling a proposition logically necessary adds nothing to saying it is logically true. Frege then says that to call a proposition possible is either (b) to say it is not known to be demonstrably false (this anticipates MDL–E) or (c) to say that the universalization of its negation is false (this anticipates MDL). On (c), it is possible that this crow is white, if not all crows are nonwhite. This implies that it is necessary that this crow is white, if all crows are white. But Haaparanta overlooks the deepest text. In *Grundgesetze der Arithmetik*, Frege holds in effect that there is no such thing as a merely possible object (TW 222). Thus the only possible objects are actual objects. This implies that true universal propositions are true of all possible objects, simply by virtue of being true of all actual objects, and are therefore necessary in the Parmenidean sense. Thus with respect to modal feature (ii) of the primary modal level, a Fregean influence on Russell is not only possible but likely. Both are committed to ontological Parmenideanism, though Frege might not have known very much about Parmenides.

Simo Knuuttila compares MDL to Peirce's 1901 *Baldwin's Dictionary* entry "Modality" (Knuuttila 1981: ix–x). There Peirce says, "The simplest account of necessity is the scholastic, according to which the necessary...proposition is a sort of universal proposition; the possible...proposition, a sort of particular proposition" (Peirce 1960: 89). A Peircean influence is theoretically possible. Frege is, of course, more likely than Peirce to have influenced Russell. Russell and Whitehead say, "In all questions of logical analysis, our chief debt is to Frege" (PM viii). Still, Haaparanta and Knuuttila show that the idea was already available when Russell wrote: Frege and Peirce had just published versions of it. Russell cites Peirce several times in *Principles* and might have read Peirce's entry in *Baldwin's Dictionary* as early as 1901. But Russell knew very little about Peirce, and probably did not even know about Peirce's logic diagrams (Dejnožka 2012: 29–30).

Bernard Bolzano is another possible influence. Russell's early theory of logical truth as fully generalized truth resembles Bolzano's substitutional theory of logical truth (Bolzano 1972 / 1837: 193–99), which John Etchemendy compares to Alfred Tarski's satisfactional theory of logical truth (Etchemendy 1990: 27–33). Rolf George says Bolzano "was the first to give a formal definition of the notion of consequence," and finds it "akin to that given a century later by Tarski" (George 1972: xxxiv); Russell defines "analytic consequence" in ca. 1903–05 (Russell 1994a / ca. 1903–03: 516–17). Russell cites Bolzano's *Paradoxes of the Infin-*

ite four times in *Principles*. Bolzano anticipates Frege-Russell logicism by suggesting in 1810 that "a discussion of mathematical method is basically nothing but logic" (George 1972: xxvi). Donald A. Steele says Bolzano says $7 + 5 = 12$, Kant's example of a synthetic *a priori* truth (Kant 1950 / 1783: 16), is analytic in his own "[carefully formulated] senses...and, in particular, free from intuitions'" (Steele 1950: 19). Steele says Bolzano gives an "all but logistic definition of 'to determine' and 'similar to'" (Steele 1950: 20). Bolzano was the major transitional figure in logic between Leibniz and Frege (Kluge 1980: 231–80) and arguably influenced Frege's sense-reference distinction (Grossmann 1968). Bolzano counts some logical truths as synthetic (Berg 1962: 102); Russell deems logic synthetic in Kant's sense in *Principles* (POM 457). But Bolzano's theory of logical truth is not in *Paradoxes* (Bolzano 1950). Kenneth Blackwell finds no evidence in the Bertrand Russell Archives that Russell ever read *Theory of Science*, the book containing Bolzano's theory of logical truth.

As the reader may have suspected for some time, my view is that MDL is a modification of MacColl's theory of a "certainty," an "impossibility," and a "variable." The chief reason is that Russell expressly says so:

> Mr. MacColl speaks of 'propositions' as divided into the three classes of certain, variable, and impossible. We may accept this division as applying to propositional functions. A function which can be asserted is certain, one which can be denied is impossible, and all others are (in Mr. MacColl's sense) variable. (LK 66)

Russell's earliest published statements of MDL are generally replies to MacColl, and generally use 'certain' in place of 'necessary' for a propositional function's being always true, following MacColl. See Ivor Grattan-Guinness (1985–86: 118–19). Russell's innovation is to predicate modalities of propositional functions instead of propositions as MacColl does. In this connection it is worth noting that, as Douglas Lackey and Storrs McCall observe, Hugh MacColl anticipates strict implication (Russell 1973: 307; McCall 1967: 546; see also Rodríguez-Consuegra 1991: 12). C. I. Lewis says that "MacColl's book....is a highly complex system, the fundamental ideas and procedures of which suggest somewhat the system of Strict Implication" (C. Lewis 1918: 108). Lewis says that "material implication is the basis of every calculus of propositions except MacColl's and Strict Implication" (C. Lewis 1918: 327). Thus, much like everyone else, Lewis overlooks Russell's deducibility (analytic consequence) relation, not to mention Russell's whole-part containment theory of deductive inference.

It takes the 1905 Russell's genius to see that one can eliminate MacColl's "unreals," yet retain MacColl's notion of strict implication and his general conception of modality in the "On Denoting" logic. Russell is not just moving beyond MacColl's unreals. Russell sees that he can reject his own nonexistent beings from his 1903 *Principles*, yet retain MacCollian strict implication in the form of a propositional function's being necessary if it is always true, just in case the only possible objects are actual objects. Regarding logically necessary truths as true in all possible worlds, including deductive implications, Russell does not expressly speak in *Principles* of possible worlds as entities which enjoy a literal and timeless being, but he might as well have. Such worlds would be identifiable in terms of their constituent entities, including properties and relations (Dejnožka 2003: 158). The post-"On Denoting" Russell speaks of possible worlds repeatedly, but without ontological commitment, and only through *false* description.[2]

From 1880 to 1905, MacColl published a series of seven papers in *Mind* explaining his logic. MacColl hints at his theory of modality, and already explains implication, in 1880 (MacColl 1880: 54–55). MacColl states his theory of modality in several works (MacColl 1897: 496; 1900: 79; 1902: 356; 1903: 356), and employs it in two papers in 1905 (MacColl 1905a: 79; MacColl 1905b: 391). In *Principles*, which was mainly written in 1900, Russell cites two of MacColl's papers, those published in 1880 and 1900, and cites MacColl's earlier papers in *Proceedings of the London Mathematical Society* (POM 12n, 22n).

The 1905 *Mind* is a MacColl-Russell show. It includes the sixth and seventh papers in MacColl's series, and Russell's "On Denoting," which cites two of MacColl's *Mind* papers. It also includes a discussion note by Russell on MacColl, and MacColl's reply. Some say that Russell savages MacColl as outdated in his 1906 *Mind* review of MacColl's *Symbolic Logic*. The truth is that aside from disagreeing on whether to admit mere *possibilia* and on whether to predicate modalities of sentences or of propositional functions, both courteously agree that they have more in common than not. The first sentence of the review implies that Russell is familiar with *all* of "Mr. MacColl's papers in *Mind* and elsewhere" (Russell 1906: 255). MacColl also gave a series of seven papers "On the Calculus of Equivalent Statements" in *Proceedings of the London Mathematical Society* beginning in 1877–78, and gave papers on his system in the *Educational Times* in 1871 and 1877. Russell does find MacColl a little idiosyncratic, but brightly says this helps "prevent the subject from getting into a groove" (Russell 1906: 260 n.65).

Russell's criticism of MacColl implicitly vanishes when Russell abolishes his own distinction between real (free) variables and apparent (bound) variables, and in effect finds that "'*Fx*' is always true" is logically equivalent to and rewritable as "$(x)(Fx)$" (PM xiii, 1927 2d ed. of *Principia*). Russell seems oblivious to the implications of this abolition for his main criticism of MacColl. Indeed, it might seem that Russell's own theory is now liable to the very criticism Russell makes of MacColl. For, to repeat part of my earlier quotation of Ducasse in another context, it is:

> perfectly arbitrary which one of such a pair of sentences we chose to describe as a "disguise" of the other, and which one therefore to describe as what the other "really" is.... (Ducasse 1941: 94–95)

Thus it seems that Russell and MacColl sink or swim together. Of course, of two mutually rewritable statements, one might better explain or illuminate the other than the other way around. More deeply, one statement might be closer to the truth, or if you please, to reality, than the other. That could be key to the subtle dialectics of Carnap versus Quine on realism (see my 2006). So let us look into that.

Those who hold with Frege, MacColl, Quine, and arguably the later Russell that in some sense meaning is holist or contextual, meaning that in some sense statements are prior to their constituent terms, might argue MacColl's propositional approach to modality is in that sense deeper and more illuminating than Russell's approach. But a meaning foundationalist might point out in return that Russell is using propositional function modalities as "building blocks" out of which whole modal statements are logically constructed, and that in that sense, Russell's approach is deeper and more illuminating. For example, a proposition is FG–MDL-necessary =Df every propositional function in it is MDL-necessary. Thus this is a standoff, at least at the level of which theory of meaning is correct. A meaning holist might complete the formal symmetry of the standoff by noting that propositional function modality *á la* Russell can be defined in terms of propositional modality. For example, a propositional function is MDL-necessary =Df it is a propositional function in some statement that is FG–MDL-necessary. Thus on the formal level, we are looking at Tweedledum and Tweedledee.

Still on the formal level, one might suggest that Russell's criticism of MacColl remains unchanged by his abolition of the distinction between real and apparent variables. For Russell is still free to argue that the modalities are better defined as quantifiers within quantified sentences than as operators on sentences. To borrow a phrase Russell uses elsewhere, we may say that Russell's criticism is merely one of *"formal* defect" in MacColl's theory (HK 380, Russell's emphasis). In support of this, we might cite Russell's argument that just as we want predications of existence to be significant even though we already know that everything exists, so we want modal predicates to be significant even though we already know that everything in the actual world is possible. We might then urge, following Russell, that the best or only way to honor that argument in our formal notation is to make (existence and) the modalities properties of propositional functions, as opposed to properties of all or some things. My reply is that Russell's "'*Fx*' is necessary (always true)" is rewritable in my own notation for MDL-necessity as "$(\Box x)(Fx)$". And that in turn is logically equivalent to, not to say identical to, "$\Box(x)(Fx)$" in FG–MDL.

Still on the formal level, one might suggest that if there is any formal defect, it is Russell's. For his 'always true' is merely a primitive version of his later universal quantifier. It is primitive in not allowing multiple quantification. My notation for Russell's MDL removes this defect. For the defect vanishes as soon as we formalize MDL using bound variables. Ironically, to that extent my notation fails as a rewrite of Russell's MDL, since it fails to preserve the formal defect in MDL. But I can appeal to Russell's own conception of logical analysis as replacing vague notions with more determinate ones. For we may say MDL is vague (not to say hopeless) on the subject of multiple quantification. Certainly my notation provides a determinate approach to multiple quantification while MDL does not. In plain terms, "is always true" and "is not always false" simply will not do. We need "is always true with respect to *x*" and "is not always false with respect to *y*" so that we can distinguish different variables for different quantifiers.

Thus to use Ducasse's words it seems "perfectly arbitrary" on the formal level whether to side with Russell or MacColl on whether modalities are (fundamentally) predicates of propositional functions or are operators on statements. The issue then devolves to one's theory of meaning. Perhaps one might expect a standoff there as well. But the question what is the true theory of meaning, and its implications for the modalities, are beyond the scope of this book.

Russell says he adopts Peano's distinction between real (free) variables in propositional functions, and apparent (bound) variables in quantified statements, in his 1903 *Principles* (POM 13). Frege had already made the distinction, but Russell says he had basically finished writing *Principles* before he started to read Frege with any serious understanding. Thus it is only in 1908 that Russell says, "The distinction...was, I believe, first emphasized by Frege" (Russell 1971a: 66), though he attributes the terminology to

Peano (POM 13). Russell has a section on apparent variables, a section on real variables, and a third section on their connection in *Principia* (PM 16–20). He still admits apparent variables, and by implication the distinction between apparent variables and real variables, as late as his 1919 *Introduction* (IMP 161). He abolishes the distinction no later than his introduction to the 1927 second edition of *Principia*. There he says:

> Another point about which there can be no doubt is that there is no need of the distinction between real and apparent variables, nor of the primitive idea "assertion of a propositional function. (PM xiii)

No doubt Russell calls the free variables in propositional functions "real" partly because of the historical and conceptual origin of this sort of variable in mathematics. Indeed, the reason Russell gives is that if the variables are bound, then "we have now a genuine proposition,..: the variable is absorbed in the same kind of way as the x under the integral sign in a definite integral, so that the result is no longer a function of x" (POM 13). Likewise for Frege.

Russell and Leibniz

While MacColl was the main influence on the form of MDL, Leibniz may have been the main influence on Russell's full theory of modality, MDL {1,2,3}. Russell wrote a book on Leibniz published in 1900, some three to five years before Russell first developed MDL. This book about Leibniz does not contain MDL or any of Russell's own implicit modal logics (Russell 1937 / 1900). It is not even a book about Russell. But Russell does find that Leibniz is committed to holding that only the actual is possible. Russell says of Leibniz, "If every proposition ascribes a predicate to some existent, then we cannot maintain, as an ultimate truth, that the non-existent is possible....Thus Leibniz falls...into a Spinozistic necessity: only the actual is possible, the non-existent is impossible, and the ground for contingency has disappeared" (PL 183). And this view is basic to the primary, Parmenidean level of Russell's theory of modality. However, Russell finds room for contingency, as I explain in chapter 3.

I shall now discuss five similarities between Russell and Leibniz.

First. Hans Burkhardt notes that Leibniz explicitly equates existence with possibility in statements of the form "(Socrates homo) est," which is Leibniz's analysis of "Socrates est homo" (Burkhardt 1988: 187).

Second, Burkhardt says, citing Wolfgang Lenzen (Lenzen 1984):

> Thus, even though he develops no modal syllogistic, Leibniz has, with his intensional interpretation of the four categorial sentence-forms and of the syllogism, provided at the same time what is in effect a modal interpretation. And Leibniz can therefore also interpret his calculus of *'entia'* in the *'General Investigations'* not only as a concept calculus but also as a modal statement calculus. The basic calculus of this work is a concept calculus with strict implication, equivalent to the [C. I.] Lewis System S2. (Burkhardt 1988: 188–89)

Here we see a perfect parallel of Russell to Leibniz with respect to providing a modal interpretation of nonmodal logic. We may even use Burkhardt's words and say that when Russell published MDL, he "provided at the same time what is in effect a modal interpretation" of *Principia*. "And" Russell "can therefore also interpret his" *Principia* "not only as" an existential (or veridical) logic, "but also as a modal" theory. Burkhardt even mentions Russell's book on Leibniz in passing.

Third, Robert Merrihew Adams attributes S5 to Leibniz (Adams 1982: 243). This would make both Leibniz and Russell S5, at least on my interpretation of Russell. However, Burkhardt attributes only S2 to Leibniz (Burkhardt 1988: 189, 193). If Burkhardt is right, that would be a major dissimilarity between Leibniz and Russell. Neither Burkhardt nor Adams gives an argument. I shall give two. My first argument is that for Leibniz, if *p* is possible, then *p* is necessarily possible in virtue of what may be called the logically static definitional nature of Leibniz's possible worlds. Much like Russell's sense-data, if we change the slightest thing, we have a different possible world. My second argument is that for Leibniz, God sees that all truths are analytic and therefore necessary. And this would include true possibility-statements.

Third, both Leibniz and Russell basically deny that merely possible worlds have any ontological status. For Leibniz, they have "no reality outside God's mind....Thus none of them *really* exists (i.e. exists...extramentally) until God decides to make one of them actual" (Blumenfeld 1982: 111). Thus neither Leibniz nor Russell can accept David Lewis's counterpart theory with ontological seriousness (Blumenfeld 1982: 110–11). David Lewis's counterpart theory can be used to interpret Leibniz only in an ontologically attenuated sense (Blumenfeld 1982: 111–12). Here Leibniz emerges as the ancestor of Russell and Kripke alike, since Kripke too denies ontological status to merely possible worlds. Of course, Russell has no problem of identifying counterparts across possible worlds anyway, any more than Kripke does, not only because for him there is no such thing as a merely possible world, but also because in possible worlds talk, Russell's logically proper names are rigid designators, as I argued earlier.

Fifth, Leibniz's theory of logically necessary truth as truth in all possible worlds is not only the source of Russell's possible worlds talk, but it may have inspired the full generalization theories of logical necessity of Bolzano, Frege, and the early Russell alike. That all three knew Leibniz's theory is beyond question.

Russell and Aristotle

We can go much earlier than Leibniz for anticipations of, or possible indirect influences on, Russell. I proceed to describe four parallels between Russell and Aristotle.

First, Niiniluoto helpfully suggests that Russell belongs to a more general trend in modern logic toward understanding modality in terms of probability, of which John "Venn was the main British advocate" (Niiniluoto 1988: 280). Russell was aware of Venn. MacColl was well aware of Venn and might have been an intermediary between Venn and Russell. Venn says in his 1879 paper in *Mind*, "According to well known results of the Theory of Probability, to say that anything is possible...is equivalent to saying that...it is occasionally actual" (Venn 1879: 40). Venn was the leading nineteenth century advocate of Aristotle's frequency theory of probability, on which what is probable is what is usually the case. For Russell, a mathematical probability is "the ratio of the numbers of two finite classes," i.e., a frequency relation between two propositional functions, while an epistemic probability concerns individual propositions, i.e., the objective or rational credibility of a proposition in light of "all relevant evidence" (HK 381; see 384–91). The former relates to MDL, and the latter to MDL–E. For MDL concerns propositional functions, and MDL–E concerns individual propositions. The mathematical probability of 0 is just impossibility in MDL. And the epistemic probability of 0 is just impossibility in MDL–E. And physical coincidences (physical possibilities) as well as regularities (causal necessities) seem subsumable under Russell's purely mathematical probability theory. This confirms that Pears' motive (4a) from the fourth group of motives is on target. John Maynard Keynes says:

> Necessity and Impossibility, in the senses in which these terms are used in the theory of Modality, seem to correspond to the relations of Certainty and Impossibility in the theory of probability....Almost up to the end

of the seventeenth century the traditional treatment of modals is, in fact, a primitive attempt to bring the relations of probability within the scope of formal logic. (Keynes 1962 / 1921: 16n)

Keynes goes on to criticize Venn's attempt to banish modality from logic and relegate it to theory of probability (Keynes 1962 / 1921: 98). We may recall from chapter 7 that Russell, Wittgenstein, Carnap, and Kripke all connect modality with probability. We now see they also belong to a long tradition of connecting modality with probability theory, based on Aristotle's frequency theory of probability.

A second parallel between Russell and Aristotle is this. In light of Diodorus Cronus and Aristotle as precursors of MDL, it is interesting that Nino Cocchiarella assesses Diodorus's modal theory as at least S4 and Aristotle's as S5. (Cocchiarella 1991: 249–52; 1984: 346–52). Thus Aristotle's theory is virtually the same strength as FG–MDL and FG–MDL*. However, Cocchiarella is assessing Aristotle's and Diodorus's theories of temporal necessity, while MDL is not a temporal modal theory, as we saw at the end of chapter 3. FG–MDL and FG–MDL*, of course, are not temporal modal logics.[3]

There is a third parallel between Aristotle and Russell. Niiniluoto notes that Antoine Cournot could accept physical chance despite his determinism, since intersections of different causal chains or series "cannot be predicted from knowledge about the series" (Niiniluoto 1988: 296; see Engel 1988: 226–27). Russell accepts independent causal lines in *Human Knowledge*, and could easily accept physical chance in Cournot's Aristotelian sense of coincidence, perhaps as a matter of degree, since the independence of causal lines is never complete (HK 459, 490).

These first three parallels between Russell and Aristotle on modality are a welcome addition to my efforts to assimilate Russell's 'no entity without identity' ontology to Aristotle's ontology of real identity and rational identity, or in more familiar though slightly less fundamental terms, of real distinction and distinction in reason (Dejnožka 2003: 215–31, 233–36, 244–47, 269–72; see 14). And in fact, this suggests a fourth ontologico-modal parallel. Just as both Russell and Aristotle espouse whole-part containment theories of logically necessary inference, so they both admit necessary containments of distinctions of reason within real things. In Aristotle's case, this means the distinctions of matter and form, and of genus and species, within a substance. In Russell's case, a color patch is a real and indivisible thing which necessarily has both the shape and the color it does. Recall that color patches and other sense-data occupy the logical position of substances for Russell (PLA 201–2).

Returning now to the origins of MDL's equation of necessity with universality and of existence (or 'not always false') with possibility, it might seem that the safest answer to the question of historical origins is simply that the idea was in the air for many centuries, and perhaps especially in the nineteenth century. But that general truth is trumped by the "smoking gun" text in which Russell specifically cites MacColl as the origin. Whether MacColl was influenced in turn by Venn, Bolzano, Leibniz, or Aristotle, I must leave to others to investigate.

While I have been liberal in speculating about Russell's motivations, there is one motivation Russell does not have. Ilkka Niiniluoto says, "If a propositional function contains a time variable (e.g., 'It is raining in London at time t'), then Russell's definition amounts to the statistical theory of modality, which entails the Principle of Plenitude" (Niiniluoto 1988: 291). This principle is that "no genuine possibility remains unrealized." (Knuuttila 1988: vii). Arthur O. Lovejoy found it in Plato (Lovejoy 1974: 52–53); Richard Sorabji and Jaakko Hintikka have debated whether it is also in Aristotle (Sorabji 1980: 128–35). Insofar as the principle describes the potentiality of a thing to actualize itself, Russell would reject it, since Russell rejects potentialities. He says, "The concept of potentiality is convenient in some connections, provided it is so used that we can translate our statements into a form in which the concept is absent....But when potentiality is used as a fundamental and irreducible concept, it always conceals confusion of thought" (HWP 167). Again, MDL is not a temporal modal theory (*or* logic), *pace* Haaparanta (see pages 61–62).

Summary of Russell on Modality

To summarize this book so far, I have argued for two main conclusions. First, scattered throughout his writings, Russell has both a largely express modal theory that has three levels that work together in a unified theory. Second, also scattered throughout his writings, there are at least eight implicit modal logics in Russell's philosophical theories on various topics.

Rescher holds that by reading Russell, two generations of logicians were kept from developing modal logic. But I find that it was, if anything, by *not* reading Russell that this occurred. Russell gives so many statements of all three levels of his modal theory, and uses possible worlds talk so many times in so many major works, that *overlooking* them is incredible. Russell cannot be blamed for four generations of stunted scholarship by logicians who read only his purely logical works, and did not read all of his writings across the board. Indeed, one of his major *logical* works contains both MDL and possible worlds talk, as well as his theory that logical truth is fully general truth that is true in virtue of its logical form: *Introduction to Mathematical Philosophy*.

Ten Criticisms of Russell on Modality

So far in this book, I have been defending Russell against his critics, largely by showing that they do not know Russell very well. Now that we have comprehensively examined Russell on modality, I would like to offer ten criticisms of my own.

First, Russell gives some half a dozen nonequivalent casual formulations of MDL–E in "The Philosophy of Logical Atomism" (PLA 254–55). I will not try to sort them out here. We may say the differences in statement only add to the richness of his suggestions.

Second, Russell says that in ordinary language "Lions exist" does not mean 'Lions are possible' because the former asserts that "*x* is a lion" is sometimes true, while the latter means that "*x* is a sort of animal" is sometimes true, where lions are a sort of animal (PLA 255). But such "classificatory ascent" is well-formed if and only if there is a higher sort. For it cannot even be formulated for a highest classification or summum genus. For example, suppose that *animal* is a summum genus. Then on Russell's analysis, we cannot say "Animals are possible," since there is no higher classification that animals are a sort of. Compounding the absurdity, we can say that lions are possible, even though lions are a sort of animal, and we cannot say that animals are possible. The situation is even more absurd for kind-monists. For if kind-monism were true, i.e., if there were only one kind of thing, hence only one summum genus, say bodies, then even though lions are possible, and lions are a sort of body, *nothing at all* could be said to be a possible body. Yet surely lions, animals, and bodies are all logically contingent.

Third, the only way out of the second problem is to deny that there are any summa genera, or highest classifications. For if there is always a higher sort, then anything can be said to be possible in a well-formed statement. But I shall now argue that any such infinite series of sorts would be a vicious infinite regress. For on Russell's classificatory ascent, lions and unicorns are not possible unless, say, animals are. But animals are not possible unless, say, living things are. And so on. Therefore there must be a highest sort whose possibility stops the regress. But per my second criticism, no such highest sort is possible, which is absurd.

Fourth, since Russell does not see the second and third problems, neither does he see the most natural solution. Namely, we can use classificatory ascent for all sorts *except* ultimate sorts; and we can simply use ultimate sorts themselves to say that the ultimate sorts are possible. Thus ultimate sorts would be used to analyze possibility both for themselves and for penultimate sorts, but in different ways. This solution is ad hoc, but it would easily handle the second and third problems. For there would no longer be the problem analyzing possibility-statements for ultimate sorts described in my second criticism, and the ultimate sorts would end the vicious regress of sorts described in my third criticism. The only price we pay is that we cannot say that an ultimate sort is possible unless something exists that falls under that ultimate sort. In our example, we can say that lions are possible even if no lions exist, but we cannot say that bodies are possible unless at least one body exists. But it seems to me that there is something at least somewhat intuitively satisfying about saying that an ultimate category is not possible if nothing falls under it, and also something intuitively satisfying about being able to say that lions are possible even if no lion exists. Thus perhaps my solution is not ad hoc after all. But I grant that intuitively, we should be able to say that bodies are possible even if bodies are an ultimate category and no bodies exist. That is because bodies are logically contingent. Thus I think there is a conflict in our intuitions about what we can legitimately say about the possibility of ultimate categories. We may say that if bodies are an ultimate category and there are no bodies, then we feel that bodies are not possible in a Parmenidean sense, but we feel that they are possible in the sense that they are logically contingent.

The next three criticisms parallel the preceding three.

Fifth, classificatory ascent is basic to Russell's distinction between syntactical possibility and logical possibility, since he explains the former in terms of classificatory ascent. Recall how "Spot S is red" is syntactically possible if red and green belong to the same higher classification, such as color, and some things are green (see IMT 182). Russell wants to keep the distinction because he thinks syntactical possibility and logical possibility differ in scope of application. For every statement of a logical contradiction is syntactically well-formed, and therefore logical contradictions are logically impossible but syntactically possible. But if, say, body and mind are ultimate categories, then he cannot say that "This is a body" is syntactically possible because bodies and minds belong to the same category and some things are minds, since there *is* no higher category that they both belong to. Thus a summum genus is not syntactically possible because there is no higher sort.

Sixth, this leads to a vicious infinite regress of syntactic possibilities. The argument is basically the same as the argument for my third criticism.

Seventh, since Russell does not see the preceding two problems, he does not see their most natural solution. I think the solution is to admit any *summum genus* as a special, merely syntactical (in the sense of logical grammar) higher category. Note that my fourth and seventh criticisms recommend the same special status for ultimate sorts, i.e., *summa genera*. My way out prevents the same two problems for Russell's theory of syntactic possibility that it does for Russell's theory of the MDL-possibility of lions. Namely, on Russell's theory, (1) a *summum genus* is not syntactically possible because there is no higher sort; and (2) this leads to a vicious regress of syntactic possibilities. In both cases, my way out is a limited ad hoc repair to Russell's theories so that he can keep his theories. Of course, MDL-possibility is not at all the same as syntactic possibility. What is syntactically impossible is ill-formed. But what is MDL-impossible is well-formed. In fact, on Russell's view, "Lions are impossible" is syntactically possible if and only if "Lions are possible" is syntactically possible, since the only difference is a negation. The two statements are respectively "'x is a lion' is always false" and "'x is a lion' is not always false." Both statements are clearly well-formed for Russell in MDL.

Eighth, that propositional functions are nothing because they are incomplete is a *non sequitur*. Incomplete books and buildings are not nothing. And if propositional functions were nothing, then there would *be* none for us to talk about; or if there were different ones, then at most one of them could be nothing. Also recall that each propositional function has a determinate constituent (a universal) and an "undetermined constituent" (a variable) (MAL 220–21, 220n). Only the undetermined constituent is nothing. The theory of definite descriptions cannot come to the rescue, insofar as that theory only explains away how we appear to single out *complete* entities in language, such as the present King of France. For a logically incomplete description of any kind would make any statement in which it occurs logically incomplete, hence ill-formed and without a determinate truth-value. Granted, we can *say* "The propositional function *horse* is incomplete" in ordinary language. But if we do, we run into the problem Frege calls the problem of the concept *horse* in his paper "On Concept and Object." Frege says:

> It must indeed be recognized that here we are confronted
> by an awkwardness of language, which I admit cannot be
> avoided, if we say that the concept *horse* is not a

> concept, whereas, e.g., the city of Berlin is a city, and the
> volcano Vesuvius is a volcano....A concept is the
> reference of a predicate; an object is something that can
> never be the whole reference of a predicate, but can be
> the reference of a subject. (TW 46–48, cite omitted)

The definite description "the concept *horse*" is seen to be logically incomplete when it is written in a clear formal notation with an undetermined constituent marking the argument-place "( )" for purposes of quantification. Shifting to Russell's logic, the definite description is then "The propositional function *horse*( )", and the statement is, "The propositional function *horse*( ) is incomplete." Of course, this criticism assumes that Frege is right on the essentially predicative nature of properties, and that formal notation ought to reflect that. But even aside from Frege's metaphysical views on concepts (Frege's term for properties) and objects, Frege's view that variables must be bound by quantifiers if statements are to be logically well-formed and have determinate truth-values is persuasive for modern classical. See my (2003: 275–77) for my critique of Russell's critique of Frege on this issue.

Ninth, when Russell abolishes the distinction between real and apparent variables, his criticism of MacColl on modality also vanishes. See pages 204–5.

Tenth, I return full circle to the howlers Russell has been accused of. In deductive inference and in Russell's implicit modal logics, the howlers are defeated by Russell's theory of deducibility, especially as supported by his whole-part containment theory of deducibility as truth-ground containment. (On the latter, see the next chapter.) As to MDL, the howlers are defeated by Russell's Parmenidean view that only the actual is possible. For on it, if "x is a horse" is always true, then "x is a horse" is necessary. In both cases, Russell's critics did not study Russell enough. They fail to see that Russell has these ways out. Thus I go well beyond the critics when I criticize one of these two ways out.

I believe that the howler-critics are defeated by Russell's theory of deducibility as truth-ground containment. Insofar as they criticize Russell's theory of deductive inference, their focus on material implication instead of deducibility is simply inexcusable. See the next chapter for the full story.

But I believe Russell's Parmenidean theory of modality, as it applies to MDL, is mistaken for two reasons. First, it involves an ambiguity. Second, it is on an inappropriate level of depth. (So this criticism is really two criticisms.)

The ambiguity may be seen in statements like, "If every marble in the urn is red, then any marble I draw out will be red." The statement is tautological. The consequent is deducible from the antecedent. If we restate it in MDL as a conditional ("if-then") propositional function, the propositional function is always true out of logical necessity. But this cannot be said for the antecedent and the consequent considered by themselves, even if they too are always true. Supposing that all three propositional functions are always true, meaning the conditional propositional function, its antecedent, and its consequent, all three are *MDL*-necessary. Yet only the conditional propositional function is *logically* necessary. It follows that MDL-necessity is not logical necessity. Instead, it is ontological, specifically Parmenidean, necessity. And that suffices to defeat the howler-critics of MDL.

This in itself is not a problem for logic. I mean that there is nothing wrong with MDL being the basic logical building block for alethic logics like FG–MDL and FG–MDL*, and with MDL-necessity being ontological while their sort of necessity is logical. To think otherwise is to commit the fallacies of composition and division.

But it is a problem for appropriateness of level in Russell's full three-level theory of modality. MDL belongs to the third and shallowest level, the level of logic. Parmenidean necessity belongs to the primary and deepest level, the level of ontology. The issue then devolves to how these levels work together for Russell, or how they most appropriately work together, in his complex but unified theory of modality.

Surely the most appropriate application of Parmenidean necessity is to Russell's theory of transcendental Parmenideanism. And that theory applies most appropriately to Russell's theory of logically proper names as rigid designators of entities that must be there to be denoted. And that has nothing to do with MDL as such. For MDL concerns propositional functions, not logically proper names. The inevitable suggestion is that if Russell's Parmenidean necessity is to apply appropriately to MDL, then the scope of MDL's variables must be restricted to things that are or at least can be named by logically proper names. And this calls for adding an antecedent, "if x can be named by a logically proper name," to all propositional functions in MDL. And the very awkwardness of this is a measure of the inappropriateness of thinking of MDL-necessity as Parmenidean. Thus the howlers apply to MDL as Russell states it after all. But they can still be defeated by my proposed filter or constraint of requiring the variables to range over only the entities that Russell *does* consider to be possible if and only if they are actual. That rules out marbles, which are logical fictions for him. But it includes sense-particulars. See chapters 3 and 4. No doubt we wish *Principia*'s individual variables to range over marbles too. But that concerns *Principia* considered as a veridical logic, not as ranging only over transcendentally necessary entities.

This concludes my ten criticisms of Russell on modality. Whether the criticisms ultimately have merit or not, at least they are based on a comprehensive study of Russell on modality, and thus should not be easily refuted simply by pointing out over-looked texts, as the purported howlers of MDL were. I confined myself to "in-house" criticisms that illuminate Russell, because this is a scholarly work.

I shall defend Russell against an eleventh criticism. Raymond Bradley says MDL is incompatible with the possibility that there are 30,000 objects in the world because on MDL, "x is a world and x contains 30,000 objects" is possible if and only if it is sometimes true—which would be the case only if the *actual* world has 30,000 objects (R. Bradley 1992: 16; see PLA 240).

Now, there are at least three ways to defend Russell against Bradley simply by pointing out texts Bradley overlooks.

First, Bradley's argument ignores Russell's philosophy of paraphrase as replacing our vague ordinary thoughts with more precise and unproblematic language. In fact, Russell would not paraphrase "It is possible that there are just 30,000 objects" as "'x has 30,000 objects' is sometimes true," but as "Being 30,000 in number is a *sort* of numerosity, and 'x has a *sort* of numerosity' is sometimes true." For as we saw earlier, Russell would paraphrase "Lions are possible" not as "'x is a lion' is sometimes true," but as "Lions are a *sort* of animal, and 'x is a *sort* of animal' is sometimes true" (PLA 255). Here I omit my criticisms of classificatory ascent, since this is merely a matter of Russell scholarship.

Second and ironically, the logical contingency of "x is a world with 30,000 objects" is Russell's own example of why logical truth is not just fully general truth, but is fully general truth plus truth in virtue of logical form (PLA 240). And the truth of that statement, as Russell says, is an empirical matter (PLA 240). Thus Russell solves the problem not by using MDL, but by improving his theory of logical truth. In my interpretation, this is just where and why Russell implicitly moves from implicit FG–MDL to implicit FG–MDL*. MDL by itself was never intended to solve this sort of problem. It is not a modal logic of logically possible statements. It is merely a trio of definitions of propositional functions. The best I can say on behalf of Bradley is that MDL is closer to FG–MDL than it is to FG–MDL*. But the problem is solved by FG–MDL*. If it helps, we may say that the problem is also solved correspondingly in terms of implicit MDL*, where a propositional function is always true in MDL* if and only if it is (1) always true in MDL, and (2) always true in MDL in virtue of its logical form. Clearly, "'x has 30,000 objects' is sometimes true" is not true in virtue of its logical form.

Third, Russell can appeal to primary level modal feature (ii) of his theory of modality. That is, he can appeal to the fact that intuitively, there *is* a sense in which only the actual is possible. Here I omit my criticisms of MDL-Parmenideanism, since this is merely a matter of Russell scholarship.

This concludes my threefold reply to Bradley. The replies also kill the howlers described in chapter 2. Thus Russell expressly states *three* ways to kill the howlers: (1) classificatory ascent; (2) his requirement that logical truth be true in virtue of logical form, which is his implicit move from implicit FG–MDL to implicit FG–MDL*; and (3) his neo-Parmenidean ontology, on which only the actual is possible.

MDL's Conceptual Place in the Analytic Tradition

MDL would seem to be the most natural theory of modality for analytic philosophers in general to use. The three basic elements are simply (a) an acceptance of propositional functions, (b) a rejection of merely possible, i.e., nonexistent, things, and (c) an interpretation of modal notions in terms of the semantic (veridical) notions of 'always true' and so on. But whether MDL really merits the title, "most natural modal theory for the analytic tradition," is best seen by comparing the four great analysts on MDL: Frege, Russell, Wittgenstein, and Quine.

As to element (a), all four analysts use quantification over variables. Even the later Wittgenstein makes existence a second-level predicate (RFM 186 / V #135).

As to element (b), all four analysts are neo-Parmenideans. None of the great analysts admits nonexistent objects. All of them analyze "nothing" away as 'not anything'. Again, even the later Wittgenstein makes existence a second-level predicate (RFM 186 / V #135).

Frege requires that every true or false statement have a denoting logical subject (TW 62–63). This is his version of the traditional principle that a proposition must say something about something. In *Grundgesetze der Arithmetik*, Frege holds in effect that there is no such thing as a merely possible object (TW 222).

From "On Denoting" on, Russell rejects merely possible objects.

The early Wittgenstein admits a neo-Parmenidean logical atomism in the *Tractatus*. As noted earlier, Tractarian objects are in all possible worlds; therefore all of them are in the actual world; therefore none is a merely possible object. Wittgenstein says that his Tractarian objects and Russell's individuals were Plato's primary elements (PI #46; see *Theaetetus* 201–2). And Plato's primary elements were a direct response to Parmenides.

I suggest that even the later Wittgenstein has a theory about ordinary language and phenomena such that genuine reference, by expressions associated with paradigmatic criteria of identity, is not to nothing. Fiction is a language-game that is played, but it is a derivative game, parasitic on talk about the world. Surely the later Wittgenstein would regard admitting nonexistent entities in any literal, ontological sense as a bewitchment of grammar.

Quine's thesis that to be is to be the value of a variable smacks of the Parmenidean. Following Russell, he rejects merely possible objects. No doubt he would also find them unscientific, i.e., unnecessary to his naturalism.

As to element (c), insofar as all four analysts accept quantificational logic and reject merely possible objects, all four already implicitly equate existence with possibility and universality with necessity. Frege, Russell, and Quine obviously accept this sort of quantification. They also expressly reject merely possible objects (TW 222; OD 54–55; FLPV 4–5). Quine has even kindly written me, "Certainly I have no objection to necessity and possibility when interpreted in Russell's way" (Quine 1990). Thus elements (a) and (b) are the core elements of MDL. For together, they imply element (c). (Thus the term "element" is strictly a misnomer in the case of (c).)

The two core elements of MDL both seem present in the later Wittgenstein: (a) the core of quantificational logic, that numbers are properties of concepts (RFM 186 / V *35), and, as the most natural gloss on *Investigations*, (b) an implied rejection of merely possible entities as a bewitchment of grammar. The later Wittgenstein's conventionalist theory of necessity is as irrelevant to MDL as is Quine's naturalistic thesis that no statement is immune from revision.

Granted, insofar as FG–MDL* is based on a notion of logical form, tautology, or analyticity, the Quine of "Two Dogmas of Empiricism" would reject FG–MDL* (Quine 1971a). And no doubt the later Wittgenstein would do likewise. But I am not trying to show that *FG–MDL** is the most natural modal *logic* for the analytic tradition. I am only trying to show that *MDL* is the most natural modal *theory* for that tradition.

I concede that the early Wittgenstein expressly rejects MDL:

> It is incorrect to render the proposition '∃x· Fx' in the words, '*Fx* is *possible*', as Russell does.
>   The certainty, possibility, or impossibility of a situation is not expressed by a proposition[al function],

but by an expression's being a tautology, a proposition with sense, or a contradiction. (T 5.525; see M. Black 1970: 286; Anscombe 1971: 158)

Wittgenstein's reason is that a modality "must reside in the symbol itself" (T 5.525). Thus he places modalities among the things he thinks should not be "said" but "shown," while Russell "says" that certain functions are possible. In effect, Wittgenstein is jumping directly from rejecting MDL to accepting FG–MDL*, bypassing FG–MDL altogether. For he *starts* from a theory of logical truth as truth in virtue of form (truth-tables show molecular form). Thus he simply misunderstands Russell. For Russell never intended that MDL be a theory of logical truth. MDL is merely a trio of definitions of propositional functions. If the early Wittgenstein had wanted to impress, he should have criticized Russell's theory of logical truth as truth in virtue of form instead. But he cannot, since that is basically his own theory as well, and may well be due to Russell in the first place, though the details differ greatly.

Another reason why Wittgenstein rejects MDL might be that MDL makes all true generalities necessary M. (Black 1970: 286). But Wittgenstein's "improvement" of MDL largely maintains the structure of MDL. In fact, except for the new notion of tautology, his "improvement" is basically the same as the 1918 Russell's theory of logical truth (implicit FG–MDL*). The very words "certainty, possibility, or impossibility" recall Russell and even MacColl. Thus Wittgenstein never sees that what he considers his improvement on Russell's MDL is Russell's own requirement that logical truth be true in virtue of form in his mature 1918 theory of logical truth, which still implicitly uses MDL as a logical building block. This use of MDL is easy to see if we first go through the intermediate stage of implicit FG–MDL, since FG–MDL is just the application of MDL to every propositional function within a statement. The mature theory merely adds the requirement of truth in virtue of form. MDL, which Russell expressly states in this 1918 work, remains a logical building block within the original, still-kept requirement of fully general truth.

In fairness, Wittgenstein might well have had no access to Russell's 1918 "The Philosophy of Atomism" before the *Tractatus* was first published in 1921 in German as *Logisch-Philosophische Abhandlung*. Wittgenstein was a prisoner of war, and Russell did not know if Wittgenstein was even alive (PLA 177). The gist was in 1914 *External World*, but it was a very brief gist. Of course, Wittgenstein was well aware of Russell's 1913 *Theory of Knowledge* manuscript, which Wittgenstein criticized. This is not to mention Russell's 1912 *Problems*, which clearly anticipates the theory of logical truth as truth in virtue of logical form, and which Wittgenstein called the "Penny Dreadful."

Again, MDL is the shallowest of Russell's three levels of modality. Wittgenstein is very close to Russell on the deeper levels. Most importantly, on the deepest or Parmenidean level, there are no Tractarian alien objects. Not only do all objects exist, but their existence is a transcendental necessity (M. Black 1970: 46–48, 57; M. Hintikka 1986: 111; Pitcher 1964: 42–43). Wittgenstein traces his own transcendental Parmenideanism, as well as Russell's earlier transcendental Parmenideanism, to a common origin in Plato. Wittgenstein says that his objects and Russell's individuals were Plato's primary elements (PI #46; see *Theaetetus* 201–2; Pitcher 1964: 43). And Plato's elements are neo-Parmenidean.

Thus, waiving the saying-showing distinction (why pick on MDL when the whole *Tractatus* condemns itself for trying to say the unsayable?), Wittgenstein seems committed to MDL whether he admits it or not. Just like MDL {1,2}, the *Tractatus* is nonmodal combinatorial actualist. Objects are primary level and facts are secondary level. The transcendental necessity of object-names is shown in T 3.203, T 3.221. The primary level modal features of objects are amplified in T 2.0122, T 2.0123, T 2.0124, T 2.014, T 2.0141. Secondary level modal feature (ii) of facts is given in T 2.03–T 2.063. Max Black is right that Wittgenstein's semantic argument, that we could never know the sense of a statement unless there were extralinguistic 'terminal' objects, is not the traditional argument that complex beings are not real beings and must be composed of simple objects because "it is impossible that all existence should be conditional" (M. Black 1970: 58–61). But in truth-conditional semantics conjoined with logical analysis of things into simple objects, the arguments coalesce, as Russell well knew (PLA 178–204; HWP 48–52). Here the conditionality would be that of identities of the defined things' definitionally depending on the identities of the defining things.

Thus MDL seems to be the most natural modal theory for the analytic tradition. But due to lack of any intent to interpret modal notions in terms of quantificational notions in MDL's way, MDL is not actually held by any great analyst other than Russell himself. In fact, the early Wittgenstein expressly rejects MDL. But in my opinion this is only because he mistakenly treats an essential cogwheel (MDL) as if it ought to be, and was intended by Russell to be, the completed watch (FG–MDL*).

Of course, Russell briefly rejected MDL too, but that was only in 1905, and for very different reasons. From 1906 on, Russell accepts MDL.

Russell has been criticized for misunderstanding the early Wittgenstein. Here we might also wonder how fully Wittgenstein understood Russell. Happily, the present book is more concerned with their similarities.

This concludes my discussion of Russell on modality. I have omitted some of his most suggestive ideas on modality. There is his refutation of Leibniz's theory of necessary propositions as analytic in *The Philosophy of Leibniz*. There is his refutation of Kant's transcendental theory of necessity in *Principles of Mathematics*. There are his hints that our feeling of causal necessity comes from the ancient belief in fate in *A History of Western Philosophy*. There is his location of natural kinds not among sense-data, but among the most remote constructions of physics in *Human Knowledge* (HK 318, 344). Crowning all, there is his celebration in *External World* of the liberating influence of the new logic, which allows so many metaphysical possibilities that Ockham's razor must be wielded right and left. "We may sum up...by saying that *philosophy is the science of the possible*" (MAL 106–7, Russell's emphasis).

9

Russell's Implicit Relevance Logic

So far in this book, I have argued that Russell is functionally a modal logician having a largely explicit theory of modality and at least eight implicit modal logics. That may seem revolutionary enough. Now I shall attempt to show that Russell is functionally a relevance logician as well, having both a largely explicit theory of relevance and an implicit relevance logic. And that may seem to fly altogether in the face of contemporary wisdom.

Russell never says he has a relevance logic and never offers one. If he had offered one, I would simply be quoting it, and there would have been no need for me to write the present chapter. Instead, it will take much work to show that various texts in Russell, scattered throughout his works, are so well understood as implying a certain relevance logic, that the logic may to that extent be regarded as implicit in his writings, or at least to show that these texts are more reasonably understood than not as implying that relevance logic. More specifically, I shall argue that Russell's later writings retrospectively imply that Russell's *Principia* logic has a deep relevantist aspect, confirming my interpretation of his earlier texts, including texts in *Principia* itself. If I am right, then it will be very hard indeed to see Russell's philosophy as being structurally against relevance, or as structurally impeding the development of relevance logic.

I am not arguing that Russell has an implicit relevance logic *distinct from* his *Principia* logic. Instead, I am arguing for an implicit *interpretation* of that logic as relevantist, and a retrospective one at that, since it is based on his later theory that "following from" is truth-ground containment. This is much the same as what I did in chapter 6 when I argued that FG–MDL* is a retrospective implicit interpretation of *Principia* as a modal logic, in that case based on Russell's later theory of logical truth. We may call Russell's implicit relevance logic "RSL". My thesis, then, is that *Principia* is implicitly RSL. The standard of proof is only that this is more reasonable than not. But I think the fit is perfect.

Even if the grand ballroom of *Principia* is modern classical logic, there are many rooms in the mansion of Russell's logical thinking. One of these rooms, I shall argue, is an implicit relevance logic. Or to use a more apt metaphor, I shall show that Russell's implicit (from 1918 on) modal logic FG–MDL* and his implicit (from 1922 on) relevance logic RSL are, both retrospectively, two sides of the veridical coin of his *Principia* logic. I shall argue that it is at least more reasonable than not to interpret *Principia* at least retrospectively as implicitly being RSL, based on the later Russell's explicit relevance theory, first published in 1922, and stated in published works over a period of over thirty-seven years.

RSL is stronger than the standard relevantist logics such as E, T, and R, since more can be proved in it. That is because modus ponens, disjunctive syllogism (modus tollendo ponens), and other modern classical argument forms are provable in it. Indeed, the very concept of relevance in Russell is deeper and more general than anything on offer in the relevantists. For Russell's concept of relevance is that of whole-part truth-ground containment entailment.

Nothing in Alan Ross Anderson's and Nuel D. Belnap's great two-volume work, *Entailment: The Logic of Relevance and Necessity,* suggests its authors think that Russell was an implicit relevantist. Quite the opposite, they identify Russell as a major architect of a logical tradition, often called modern classical logic, which they believe finds the notion of logical relevance irrelevant to logic:

> As is well-known, [the] notion of relevance was central to logic from the time of Aristotle until, beginning in the nineteenth century, logic fell increasingly into the hands of those with mathematical inclinations. The modern classical tradition, however, stemming from Frege and Whitehead-Russell, gave no consideration whatever to the classical notion of relevance, and in spite of complaints from certain quarters that relevance of antecedent to consequent was important, this tradition rolled on like a juggernaut..., without seeming to require the traditional notion of relevance at all. (Anderson 1975: xxi)

Similarly for the Dunn-Gupta anthology, *Truth or Consequences: Essays in Honor of Nuel Belnap* (Dunn 1990a).

But just what *is* the ancient classical concept of relevance? The core idea is that a conclusion must *follow from* its premises, that is, be *connected* to or *related* to its premises in some way. This core idea is over two thousand years old (Anderson 1975: 17). The question is really *how* it is related. The traditional answer is that the premises must *contain* the conclusion in some way. The problem is then to specify the *way* it is contained. Anderson and Belnap claim to solve this problem with their theory of "variable sharing," where the variables range over atomic statements. The basic idea is that an argument is relevant if and only if the atomic statements in it literally occur in both its conclusion and premises in a pattern they find acceptable. Thus for them, the containment is of atomic statements (or variables). In my view, this is a very limited conception of relevance. There is variable sharing in Aristotle's syllogistic logic (very different from Anderson-Belnap variable sharing), and it plays an essential role in defining the syllogistic format. But that role is only in the service of something deeper and more essential to logic for Aristotle: class member-ships, containments, and exclusions. And implicitly the deepest thing in classical Aristotelian relevance is containment of truth-grounds, i.e., the truth-possibilities that make a statement true.

I think it is intuitively obvious that implicitly, containment of truth-grounds is the deepest and most general concept of relevance in traditional logic. Class containment is clearly a narrower concept, and so are any *specifically* accepted patterns of variable sharing. Compare Russell on the limited duality of class inclusion with propositional implication, finding that propositions are more fundamental than classes (POM 11–13). Truth-ground containment is the sine qua non. For no form of class or variable containment can possibly be acceptable if the truth-grounds of the conclusion are not contained in the truth-grounds of the premises. But if the truth-grounds *are* contained, then the class or variable containments are automatically correct for that reason, and for that reason alone. The right patterns of class or variable containment are definable as just those patterns which ensure truth-ground containment, whatever patterns they may be. Thus the deepest and most general concept of relevance is semantic as opposed to formal. For truth-grounds essentially concern truth. And truth is one of the two basic semantic notions. The second basic semantic notion is reference. And insofar as class and variable containments are referential, then truth is prior to reference, at least as far as the relevance of premises to conclusions in deductive arguments is concerned. This is consistent with the (also traditional) primacy of reference over truth in forming true or false statements from referring terms in the first place.

I suspect that many logicians will already see the writing on the wall at this point. For truth-ground containment is just what the early Wittgenstein's concept of "following from" or "contains," that is, his concept of relevance, is all about. And Russell expressly endorses Wittgenstein's concept of "following from" or "contains," that is, Wittgenstein's concept of relevance, first in his 1922 introduction to Wittgenstein's *Tractatus*, and then in several later major works. And that is the deepest and most general concept of deductive logical relevance that there is or can be. Anderson and Belnap do not mention any of this.

Most logicians restrict logical relevance to deductive logic, and in this chapter I do so as well. In chapter 10, I shall consider an extension of the concept of logical relevance to inductive logic. On that extension it will be inappropriate to speak of *following* from, but we may still speak of the relation of premiss to conclusion as a *weaker* logical relationship of *partial* truth-ground containment. This purely logical interpretation of probability is in Wittgenstein's *Tractatus* too, but I shall mainly discuss Russell and John Maynard Keynes in chapter 10.

The 1919 G. E. Moore is said to be the first to use the word "entailment" as a term of art to refer to logical relevance (Moore 1951: 291; Prior 1967a: 6). Entailment is simply the converse of following from. *P* entails *Q* if and only if *Q* follows from *P*.

Anderson and Belnap

Anderson and Belnap tell a story on which Russell's logic fails to include an adequate notion of logical relevance. I shall tell their story in eight stages. I shall discuss only the propositional calculus; there will be no need for us to discuss the extension of Anderson-Belnap tautological entailment to quantificational logic.

Stage 1. The irrelevance of material implication. The story begins with Russell's notion of material implication. By definition, statement *a* materially implies statement *b* if and only if *a* is false or *b* is true, or both. Thus material implication is defined as failing to obtain if and only if *a* is true and *b* is false. Therefore material implication is by definition the logically minimal relationship for preserving truth in moving from *a* to *b*.

The paradoxes of material implication are that a false statement materially implies every statement, and a true statement is materially implied by every statement. In effect, in the former case, a material implication statement, $P \supset Q$, is true solely because its antecedent, *P*, is false. Thus the truth or falsehood of its consequent, *Q*, is irrelevant to whether it is true. In effect, in the latter case, a material implication statement, $P \supset Q$, is true solely because its consequent, *Q*, is true. Thus the truth or falsehood of its antecedent, *P*, is irrelevant to whether it is true.

Thus Anderson and Belnap would find Russell's formal implications irrelevant as well, since a formal implication is in effect just a class of material implications.

Stage 2. The irrelevance of strict implication. The second stage of the story concerns C. I. Lewis's attempt to improve on material implication by explaining entailment as strict implication. The paradoxes of strict implication, which Lewis discovered himself, are that an impossible statement strictly implies every statement, and a necessary statement is strictly implied by every statement. In the former case the strict implication obtains solely because of the impossibility of the antecedent statement. In the latter case it obtains solely because of the necessity of the consequent. Thus strict implication does not appear to be a relation of entailment any more than material implication did (Anderson 1975: 163–67, 462–71; see Wright 1957: 172–81; E. Nelson 1930: 445). Anderson and Belnap infer that relevance logic is not reducible to modal logic (Anderson 1975: 462–71). Wright agrees. Wright says that "if *p* entails *q*, then *p* also strictly implies *q*," but that the converse is not true (Wright 1957: 177).

Stage 3. The irrelevance of formal deducibility. Moore understood entailment to be the converse of formal deducibility (Moore 1951: 291). The standard positive definition of entailment, pioneered by Wright, formally developed by Wilhelm Ackermann, and further refined by Anderson and Belnap, is that an inference is an entailment if and only if it is deductively valid independently of whether the premiss is false or conclusion true (Snyder 1971: 215–16). But Anderson and Belnap argue that deducibility alone is not enough for entailment. They note that on, say, the Montague-Henkin definition of formal deducibility, any necessarily false conjecture would imply that Fermat's last theorem is true (Anderson 1975: 17–18). In fact, we might speak of paradoxes of deducibility which are identical or virtually identical with the paradoxes of strict implication. Therefore they impose a constraint of nontriviality on deducibility to eliminate such paradoxes (Snyder 1971: 216).

Stage 4. Vague initial conceptions of entailment. We come now to certain expressions of the nature of entailment which go in the right direction, but which are too vague to be formally decidable. The basic idea was first expressed by Everett J. Nelson, who "argued that entailment in this sense must express an inner connection between the propositions it relates, and cannot hold merely on account of some property (falsehood or truth *or* impossibility or necessity) that one of the propositions may possess on its own" (Prior 1967a: 6). Nelson held that entailment is a relation between the meanings of antecedent and consequent; it is an intensional relation (E. Nelson 1930: 443, 445).

Anderson and Belnap agree that entailment is an intensional relation (Anderson 1975: xxi–xxii). They go on to quote Wright and Peter T. Geach with approval. Wright says:

> *p* entails *q*, if and only if, by means of logic, it is possible to come to know the truth of *p* → *q* without coming to know the falsehood of *p* or the truth of *q*. (Wright 1957: 181)

Geach says:

> I maintain that p entails q if and only if there is an *a priori* way of getting to know that $p \supset q$ which is not a way of getting to know either whether $[\neg]p$, or whether q. (Geach 1972: 179–80; my $p \supset q$ replaces Cpq)

Anderson and Belnap say, "These proposals seem to us to be on the right track, but they need improvement" (Anderson 1975: 152, 215–16). The chief problem they find is informality. Of course, they have already rejected material implication, strict implication, and deducibility as formalizations.

Stage 5: Primitive entailment defined. As the first step in defining entailment, Anderson and Belnap offer an initial definition of primitive entailment as a formally decidable containment relation. After rejecting a formalization proposed by T. J. Smiley, they propose this formalization:

> We shall say that a primitive entailment $A \rightarrow B$ is *explicitly tautological* if some (conjoined) atom of A is identical with some (disjoined) atom of B. Such entailments may be thought of as satisfying the classical dogma that for A to entail B, B must be "*contained*" in A. (Anderson 1975: 155, their emphasis)

Stage 6: Primitive entailment generalized. Anderson and Belnap generalize their definition so as to handle more complex arguments as follows:

> We...call an entailment $A_1 \vee ... \vee A_m \rightarrow B_1 \& ... \& B_n$ in normal form *explicitly tautological* (extending the previous definition) iff for every A_i and B_j, $A_i \rightarrow B_j$ is explicitly tautological (sharing); and we take such entailments to be valid iff explicitly tautological. (Anderson 1975: 156, their emphasis)

In effect this yields a branching tree of primitive entailments such that the tree covers every possible assignment of truth-values to the atomic statements in the argument (Anderson 1975: 156).

Stage 7: Tautological entailment defined. As the third step in defining entailment, Anderson and Belnap say that by definition, an inference is a tautologous entailment if and only if the premiss and conclusion are truth-functional and if the inference is validated by some normal form generalization of primitive entailment:

> We call an entailment $A \rightarrow B$ where A and B are purely truth functional, a *tautological entailment*, if $A \rightarrow B$ has a normal form $A_1 \vee ... \vee A_m \rightarrow B_1 \& ... \& B_n$ which is explicitly tautological. (Anderson 1975: 157, their emphasis)

In effect, tautological entailment has two conditions: (1) the whole inference is valid in the sense of modern classical truth-functional validity, i.e., truth preservation; and (2) the inference satisfies the variable sharing requirement that, where an atom is an atomic statement or its negation, there is *some* way to rewrite the conjoined premisses in disjunctive normal form (a disjunction of conjunctions of atoms), and *some* way to rewrite the conclusion in conjunctive normal form (a conjunction of disjunctions of atoms), so that *each* disjunct of the premisses' normal form contains *some* conjoined atom that is (identical with) *some* disjoined atom in *each* conjunct of the conclusion's normal form. This may be called their *atomic (or variable sharing) requirement*. The disjunctive normal form for the premisses is basically a way to represent the truth-table, with each disjunct of *A* representing a row on which all the premisses are true. However, a statement can have more than one conjunctive normal form and one disjunctive normal form. Other normal forms can be derived by using logical equivalence rules approved by Anderson and Belnap as preserving relevance. Sometimes an entailment can be shown by only one of several normal forms. This does not mean that showing an entailment is a non-mechanical art, since the normal forms are finite in number.

Anderson and Belnap cite Kant's theory of subject-contains-predicate analyticity as a precursor, and state that their formal criterion of entailment honors the ideas of Wright, Geach, and Smiley (Anderson 1975: 155). That every atom in the premiss must literally reappear as a disjunct within every conjoined disjunction of the conclusion might be called literal relevance. I ask the reader to take special note that here Anderson and Belnap expressly characterize their formal theory of entailment as a containment theory. Literal relevance is literal containment of premiss-atoms as conclusion-atoms. Note also that this sort of normal form inference is diagrammatic, specifically, tree-like. It diagrams truth-possibilities of rows of truth-tables, and certain restricted ways truth flows from premiss to conclusion. Despite the great technical differences, the comparison of their normal form inference to Kant on containment is apt.[1]

Anderson and Belnap admit that any truth-functionally deducible inference "entails a (very weak) tautology, consisting of a disjunction of various special cases of $A \lor \neg A$. But [that] is a far cry from admitting that a contradiction entails any old thing, or that any old thing entails an excluded middle" (Anderson 1975: 163).

Anderson and Belnap note that to prove *B*, we need not use *A* even if *A* is relevant to *B*. For there might be other relevant ways to prove *B*. Also, "for *A* to be relevant to *B*...it need not be *necessary* to use *A* itself in the deduction of *B* from *A*", since *A* might be "found to be unnecessarily strong" (Anderson 1975: 31, their emphasis). This concerns what may be called use-relevance.

Stage 8: Critique of Russell. Anderson and Belnap now apply their account to Russell. They find that some of Russell's theses are tautological entailments and others not (Anderson 1975: 154; 1992: 488). Their atomic requirement excludes hypothetical syllogism from being a tautological entailment:

> As an example, we show that $(p \supset q) \mathbin{\&} (q \supset r) \to p \supset r$ is invalid. By the definition of "$\supset$," we have $(\neg p \lor q) \mathbin{\&} (\neg q \lor r) \to \neg p \lor r$ which has a normal form, $(\neg p \mathbin{\&} \neg q) \lor (\neg p \mathbin{\&} r) \lor (q \mathbin{\&} \neg q) \lor (q \mathbin{\&} r) \to \neg p \lor r$. But $q \mathbin{\&} \neg q \to \neg p \lor r$ is not an explicitly tautological entailment; hence the candidate fails. (Anderson 1975: 157, my negation sign)

On their own view, they should add, "and this is the only normal form for hypothetical syllogism there is," but we may let that pass. They argue that in their own logic, "if $A \to B$ and $B \to C$ are tautological entailments, so also is $A \to C$" (Anderson 1975: 160). But their dismissal of modern classical hypothetical syllogism will make the logic of their hero, Aristotle, in particular the Barbara syllogism, a stumbling block for them, as we shall see.

The atomic requirement also excludes modus ponens and disjunctive syllogism (Anderson 1975: 165). The proof is simple in each case. The modus ponens premisses go from $P \mathbin{\&} (P \supset Q)$ to the logically equivalent P $\mathbin{\&}$ $(\neg P \lor Q)$, then to normal form $(P \mathbin{\&} \neg P) \lor (P \mathbin{\&} Q)$ using distribution, one of the rules Anderson and Belnap allow for converting the conjoined premisses to disjunctive normal form (Anderson 1975: 156). Clearly the first disjunct, $(P \mathbin{\&} \neg P)$, fails to contain the sole atom of the conclusion, Q. Disjunctive syllogism is even easier. The conjunction of its premisses goes directly into the very same normal form by distribution, with the same result. Or as they would more simply say, modus ponens is the inference of Q from $(P \supset Q)$ and P, where Q is any old statement and need not have any intensional relationship to P; and disjunctive syllogism is the inference of Q from $(P \lor Q)$ and $\neg P$, where Q is any old statement and need not have any intensional relationship to P.

Anderson and Belnap soften their rejection of disjunctive syllogism by finding it not very apt for interpreting ordinary language disjunctive arguments in the first place. They recount the ancient and medieval stories about the relevantist Dog who, with his "proclivity for intensional senses of 'or'" and "astounding logical acumen" is able to infer, by smelling all roads on which the Man did not pass, on which road the Man did pass (Anderson 1975: 165–66; Meyer 1975: 296–300). The Dog is somehow using an intensional disjunction, or a truth-functional disjunction "in a *very* special case" (Meyer 1975: 297). What Anderson and Belnap have in mind is that the Dog's use of "or" implies subjunctive conditional statements such as, "If the Man were not to pass by on this road, then he would pass by on some other road." They take the modern classical truth-functional "or" to have no such implications (Anderson 1975: 176).

The key to Anderson and Belnap is their requirement of formal purity for logical relevance. Their strong formal definition of tautological entailment leads them to their system E of tautological entailment, which is weaker than, i.e., proves less than, the modern classical logic of Russell. This is due to the very strength of their requirement that deductive inferences be tautological entailments. The sole substitution of logical operator is that of tautological entailment for material implication. All other logical operators remain the same, and truth-functionality is retained.

This concludes the Anderson-Belnap critique of Russell as irrelevant. I shall now tell a somewhat different story of my own, including a critique of Anderson and Belnap.

Considerations on Russell and Relevance

In his review of Anderson (1975), Geach protests that any logical system which rejects disjunctive syllogism as an entailment must be crazy, since disjunctive syllogism is a paradigm of valid argument (Geach 1977: 495; see Read 1988: 136–37). We must be clear on what Geach has in mind. While Anderson and Belnap reject disjunctive syllogism as an entailment, they never reject it as truth-functionally valid on the modern classical truth-table approach to validity. Of course it is valid on *that* approach. What they are really rejecting is the truth-table approach to validity as a reliable approach to *entailment*, because it validates disjunctive syllogism, which they do not count as an entailment. The problem Geach sees is therefore, Which logical inferences are reliable? That is, which rules of inference preserve logical relevance, i.e. genuine following from?

The real problem is philosophical: Just what is logical relevance? What is the best concept of it? Anderson and Belnap are challenging Geach's assumption that because disjunctive syllogism is a paradigm of truth-functional validity, it is a form of entailment (following from). Of course, they criticize Russell for admitting disjunctive syllogism and material implication. But for them the real problem is that they can find *no* formal connective in Russell which they would consider to be relevant implication. That is, they can find no form of implication in Russell which validates what they consider entailments, and which invalidates what they consider non-entailments.

The basic theme of my story is that there are many reasonable conceptions of relevance which do accommodate the Frege-Russell inferences, and no one conception corners the market. I am contending only that the modern classical concept of relevance as truth-ground containment entailment should be part of any *full* account of relevance, since it is the *deepest and most general* concept of relevance. In seeking to state what logical relevance is, we will find that there is no one thing which it is. Not even modern classical truth-ground containment can corner the market. Surely no amount of formal sophistication can provide a single, definitive formalization of relevance. What would such an account be like?

Now, we have ordinary intuitions of logical relevance, and we develop theories to articulate and explain those intuitions. We can and must appeal to our intuitions in assessing our theory of relevance. This is our only way to ensure that we are explaining relevance, or "saving the appearances" of relevance, as best we can. And, to borrow a phrase from Russell in another context, we wish to accumulate a stockpile of puzzles about relevance for our theory to explain (OD 47). Our stockpile includes the paradoxes of material implication, strict implication, and deducibility.

Just as the ca. 1903–05 Russell found that our feelings of logical necessity conflict and cannot all be captured in a single theory or conception of necessity (Russell 1994a / ca. 1903–05: 519), so too it may be for our feelings of logical relevance. In particular, many seem to have the intuition that Russellian deducibility *is* entailment. That notably includes Geach. It seems that Anderson and Belnap have the opposite intuition. That seems a simple standoff. But as I see it, the Russellian-Geachian intuition is strong enough and widely held enough that there is a rebuttable presumption that deducibility is a kind of entailment. That is, if deducibility does not square with the Anderson-Belnap conception of relevance, then the burden is on Anderson and Belnap to rebut the presumption that deducibility is a kind of entailment.

I proceed to describe some basic categories of logical relevance. I shall draw three initial general distinctions. The first is between broad and narrow senses of relevance. The second is between full and partial (or degree) senses of relevance. The third, which is the most important one for discussing Russell versus the anti-Russellian relevantists, is between extensional and intensional senses of relevance.

First, there are relevance logicians in a broad sense and relevance logicians in a narrow sense. That is, I accept the basic idea of the Belnap-Dunn distinction between *relevance logicians in the wide sense*, "who believe that it is worth paying attention to the concept of a relevant connection between statements and worth using formal techniques in an effort to get clear on the idea of relevance," and the narrow *relevantist*, who "rejects classical [two-valued] logic and instead adopts tautological entailment as the proper standard of correct inference" as opposed to the "*classicalist*, who subscribed to two-valued logic as *the* organon of inference" (Anderson 1992: 489). Indeed, it may already strike many readers as intuitively odd that logically relevant deductive inference should *forbid* or *preclude* the use of exactly two truth-values, truth and falsehood. That would strike down most of the logical tradition as irrelevantist. It would even strike down Anderson and Belnap's own system E, which is two-valued, and many other relevantist logics.

The broad Nelson-Wright-Geach conception of entailment as an intensional inner connection cannot be replaced by any one narrow formalization, such as the definition of tautological entailment offered by Anderson and Belnap. To think it can be is to misunderstand the Procrustean nature of bright line definitions. As Aristotle says, to expect more precision than a subject-matter allows is a mark of lack of education. And ironically, Aristotle's remark applies to logic itself. Wright agrees:

> It may be objected that [my, meaning Wright's] definition is *vague*, since we have not explained what 'means of logic' are. I believe that this vagueness is, so to say, of the nature of the case. I do not think that one can lay down hard and fast criteria for what is to count as *logical means* (any more than one can lay down hard and fast criteria for what are inductive grounds). But I do not think that *this* vagueness impairs a definition of entailment. (Wright 1957: 181)

To borrow a phrase from Russell, there is "no backward road" (OD 50) from any formal definition of relevance to our broad initial conception of it. And there may be no one best forward road either, except in the sense that truth-ground containment entailment is the deepest and most general concept of relevance.

I shall argue later that Russell is an implicit relevance logician in both the broad sense and in a narrow sense which is opposed to that of Anderson and Belnap. I mean that Russell's basically express admission of a theory of relevance is precisely for modern classical logic. But first I wish to recall my argument from chapter 5 that Russell is not strictly a modern classicalist. That is, Russell holds that two-valued logic is not the sole possible, or even sole desirable, organon of inference.

Once again, we must look to Russell's many writings on vagueness from 1914 to 1948. Endorsing vagueness is one of the few constants persisting through Russell's many changes in philosophy. Russell has a rich and sophisticated theory of vagueness with three levels. First, on the metaphysical level, vagueness is as real as anything can be. For sense-data or percepts are vague, and they are as real as anything can be. Second, on the epistemological level, all data are vague (MAL 111; the notion of a datum is epistemic). All three bases of knowledge are vague: "(1) faint perception, (2) uncertain memory, (3) dim awareness of logical connection" (HK 393–94; (3) recalls Nelson's emphasis on inner connection). Russell holds that understanding vagueness is basic to understanding inductive logic (Russell 1993 / 1913: 174–76; HK 335–44, 380–98). Third, on the logical level, Russell says, "All ostensive definitions, and therefore all definitions, are somewhat vague" (HK 424).

Bart Kosko hails Russell as a major precursor of fuzzy logic. I entirely agree with Kosko's portrait of Russell's views on vagueness as double-aspected. That fuzzy logic is an applied logic and not a formal logic fits nicely into Kosko's double-aspected portrait. Russell's black-and-white formal logic tries to eliminate fuzziness from the world (Kosko 1993: 288). But as to the real world and our knowledge of it, Russell insists, "Everything is vague" (PLA 180; quoted by Kosko 1993: 121). Russell says "all words outside logic and mathematics are vague: there are objects to which they are definitely applicable, and objects to which they are definitely inapplicable, but there are (or at least may be) intermediate objects concerning which we are uncertain whether they are applicable or not" (HK 497; see 146–48, 424). In fact, vague statements need have no truth-value (IMT 320). "Russell used the term 'vagueness' to describe multivalence" (Kosko 1993: 19). "Charles Peirce and Bertrand Russell and other logicians had used [the term "vague"] to describe what we now call 'fuzzy'" (Kosko 1993: 137). Thus the inventor of fuzzy set theory, Lotfi Zadeh, "called 'fuzzy' what Bertrand Russell and Jan Łukasiewicz and Max Black and others had called 'vague' or 'multivalued'" (Kosko 1993: 143; see 148). Nor is this just the later Russell. Russell states his main views on vagueness in his 1923 paper entitled "Vagueness" (Russell 1923).

Russell says that three-valued logic is both "possible" and extremely interesting (Russell 1989a: 681–82). He says, "I do not think there is anything wrong with two-valued logic, nor yet with three-valued logic. Each is appropriate for its own class of problems" (Russell 1969: 135). He may have always been so open.

To sum up, Russell accepts modern classical two-valued logic—but only "as appropriate for its own class of problems" (Russell 1969: 135). Thus the Belnap-Dunn distinction between relevantists and modern classicalists is too simplistic and polarized to categorize Russell adequately.

The second general distinction among relevance logicians I wish to make is the one between deductive (full) and inductive (partial or degreed) conceptions of logical relevance. If this second distinction is acceptable, then we have a four-part matrix of kinds of relevance: broad and deductive, broad and inductive, narrow deductive, and narrow inductive. C. D. Broad says, "[Deductive i]mplication may perhaps be regarded as the strongest probability relation, or better as a limit of all possible [inductive] probability relations." (Broad 1922: 73; 1968: 54). Thus we may also speak of broad inductive relevance as broad weak deductive relevance, and speak of narrow inductive relevance as narrow weak deductive relevance.

There are at least four possible kinds of partial relevance to explore: (1) partial normal form tautological entailment; (2) a rethinking of the paradoxes of material implication and strict implication; (3) synthetic *a priori* entailment; and (4) Wittgenstein's Tractarian theory of purely extensional probability as the number (or percentage) of rows of a truth-table on which the statement in question is true. On this last kind, implication is expressly the limit of probability. I shall consider these four kinds in order.

(1) We have already seen the first kind of partial relevance in the Anderson-Belnap critique of disjunctive syllogism. Where $((p \ \& \ \neg p) \lor (q \ \& \ \neg p))$ is the single disjunctive normal form premiss of disjunctive syllogism, Anderson and Belnap say that conclusion q would not relevantly follow from the first disjunct, $(p \ \& \ \neg p)$, since p and q are or can be totally unrelated to each other. But they admit that if the second disjunct, $(q \ \& \ \neg p)$, is true, the conclusion q relevantly follows from that disjunct. This might reasonably be called a situation of partial entailment. To be sure, in a tree-branching approach to relevance (or to deductive validity, for that matter), all the branches of the tree must check out. Otherwise a proof could be like a room with many doors, one of which is left unlocked. But there is more than one way to fasten a door. In particular, since the first disjunct is self-contradictory, the premiss would be true if and only if its second disjunct were true. (Note that the previous sentence is a subjunctive conditional, a criterion of relevance for Anderson and Belnap.) On this picture, the relevance flow goes not directly or simply from the first disjunct to the conclusion, but first goes from the first disjunct to the second disjunct, in virtue of their being the only disjuncts of the statement, and only then from the second disjunct to the conclusion. Thus the relevance flow is mediated in the sense of having two stages. It moves first horizontally within the disjunctive premiss, and only then vertically to the conclusion. In terms of the door analogy, the

disjunctive premiss is a room containing two alternative doors. If one of the two doors is self-fastened by being self-contradictory, that would seem highly relevant (to say the least) to the question whether we should try *the other door*. Thus the relevance flows from one door to the next. Only then does it move to the task of escaping from *the room*. And here the second, open door would seem highly relevant (to say the least) to the task of escaping from the room. Compare the relevantist Dog looking for which road its master took. If you please, there is a tacit closure condition, "and these are all the disjuncts (doors, roads) there are." This is an example of what I later call the "thread" test of entailment, and also falls under what I later call the truth constraint and the soundness constraint.

(2) Let us look again at the paradoxes of material implication. Suppose that both paradoxes are found in a single statement. That is, suppose a material implication statement in which the antecedent is false *and* the consequent is true. Now, if Anderson and Belnap are to prevail, the two irrelevancies should add up to a total of zero relevancy (compare Anderson 1975: 3–5, 215–16). For example, consider the statement, "That the Moon is made of cheese materially implies that the Eiffel Tower is in Paris." This material implication instantiates both paradoxes of material implication. Its false antecedent and true consequent are totally unrelated to each other in content. According to Anderson and Belnap, the falsehood of the antecedent makes the consequent irrelevant, but at the same time the truth of the consequent makes the antecedent irrelevant. Thus, on their account, *both* the antecedent and the consequent are irrelevant to the truth of the statement. So *everything* contentual is irrelevant. How then do they explain the truth of the statement? Given the meaning of material implication, there is no doubt the statement is true. Call this Double Irrelevance Dilemma #1.

Of course, Anderson and Belnap would dispel the dilemma by noting that a *true* material implication is true in virtue of its definition, and that my example simply satisfies the definition trivially twice over. But while this is quite correct as far as it goes, I think that a deeper, subtler, more illuminating analysis is available. This is the modern classical analysis involving truth-ground relevant containment and the truth constraint of using only *true* material implications.

The same point applies to the paradoxes of strict implication. Consider the statement, "That the Moon is round and not round strictly implies that one plus one equals two." This strict implication is an instance of both paradoxes of strict implication. Its impossible antecedent and its necessary consequent are totally unrelated to each other in content. According to Anderson and

Belnap, the impossibility of the antecedent makes the consequent irrelevant, while at the same time the necessity of the consequent makes the antecedent irrelevant. Thus on their account, both the antecedent and the consequent are irrelevant to the truth of the statement. So everything contentual is irrelevant. How then do they explain the truth of the statement? Given the meaning of strict implication, there is no doubt this statement is true as well. Call this Double Irrelevance Dilemma #2.

Of course, Anderson and Belnap would simply reply that the statement trivially satisfies the definition of strict implication twice over. But is this the whole story?

I think the answer lies in regarding material implication and strict implication as partial entailments in a very special sense. What is needed to complete them as entailments is what logicians call a constraint or filter. I think their constraint is truth. That is, I think that *true* material implication and *true* strict implication are deductive entailments. The constraint also collapses the distinction between the second and fourth kinds of partial entailment. (I have yet to discuss the fourth kind.) For if we apply the constraint, in effect we are considering only the rows in the truth-table on which the implication statement is true. But on those rows, the consequent is always true if the antecedent is true. Thus on this constraint, if the antecedent is true, then the consequent is reliably, truth-ground containment relevantly true.

We can now explain the two dilemmas more correctly and therefore more illuminatingly. If we look to the truth-table, we see that on every row on which a material implication statement is true, its truth *does* depend on the truth-values of *both* its antecedent and its consequent. It depends on *both*, and depends on both *equally*. This is the basic concept of relevance as truth-ground containment at work. This is the deeper, subtler, more illuminating explanation we were looking for. Similarly for strict implication. We can see that simply by noting that a strict implication statement cannot be true if its antecedent is true and its consequent is false. It emerges that where Anderson and Belnap find double irrelevance in the two dilemmas, the truth is that on the deepest, most general level of truth-ground containment entailment, we have double, or total, relevance.

Philo of Megara more or less gave the first definition of material implication. His teacher, Diodorus Cronus, rejected Philo's definition, in effect for giving rise to the paradoxes of material implication. Diodorus then offered his own definition of entailment more or less as strict implication. Prior observes that Diodorus faced much the same paradoxes of strict implication which C. I. Lewis does (Prior 1955: 193–94). Now, this is the same Diodorus who collapsed the actual with the possible. In terms of the present interpretation of Russell, there is less to the clash between Diodorus and his famous pupil than there has appeared to be from ancient times to the present day. In fact, Russell seems to reconcile them completely. For Russell accepts both Philonian material implication and Diodorean strict implication. They play different but complementary roles in his logic. Indeed, the latter presupposes the former. Recall again the truth constraint.

(3) The third kind of partial relevance concerns the synthetic *a priori*. Russell accepts synthetic *a priori* inferences as valid which are not deductively provable. He sometimes calls them "derivable" as opposed to "deducible." He accepts them as early as "Necessity and Possibility" (ca. 1903–05). There they include "If a thing is good, it is not bad" and "If a thing is yellow, it is not red" (Russell 1994a / ca. 1903–05: 517); see PP 76, 82). All such inferences fail R. W. Binkley's criterion of entailment that the inference be formally provable under certain conditions (Snyder 1971: 216). But they are "'classical' examples of entailment" (Geach 1972: 181).[2] They make Russell an implicit relevance logician in the broad positive sense. Nelson's inner connection criterion is negatively fulfilled by the *intrinsic* mutual exclusions of pairs of universals such as good and bad, yellow and red. Recall that Russell never rejects internal relations. He merely rejects the view that *all* relations are internal, and admits some relations that are external (PE 139–46; MPD 42). For positive intrinsic connections among universals, we need only consider the *a priori* truth "Red is a color," which was never conclusively shown to be an analytic truth in the great debate on that matter, except perhaps in some extremely broad and vague sense of "analytic," such as 'true in virtue of meaning'. Color only partially determines what it is to be red, and red is only one of many colors, and in that sense only partially determines the essential scope of color; but that is enough for them to be internally related or connected. Russell says, "*All* a priori *knowledge deals exclusively with the relations of universals*" (PP 103). There could scarcely be a stronger statement of, or implication that, the *a priori* nature of synthetic *a priori* truth is grounded in the essential relatedness, the intrinsic connect-edness—or negatively, the equally essential and intrinsic mutual exclusion—of certain universals. Geach says, "whatever is red is colored" is one of the "'classical' examples of entailment" (Geach 1972: 181).

I classify synthetic *a priori* entailment as a kind of partial entailment not because it is less than fully (intuitively) deductive, but because in cases like "If a thing is red, then it has a color," we cannot logically analyze the conclusion as contained in the premiss. More precisely, we may agree that part of what it is to be red is to have a color. But then what is the *rest* of what it is to be red? What is the "other part" of red? The only answer there can be is, just red. But red cannot be a proper sub-part of itself. Thus the whole apparatus of literal whole-part containment simply does not apply. We have only something resembling that. But we do have at least that resemblance, if part of what it is to be red is to have a color. That is, evidently we have some sort of *sui generis* relation between red and color which is *like* the relationship of whole-part containment. This problem will be familiar to students of the theory of universals. The popular terminology is that red is a "determinate" of the "determinable" color, and a specific shade of red is in turn a determinate of the determinable red. See "Determinables and Determinates" (Searle 1967). This terminology is intuitively suggestive. But it only states the problem which a theory of universals needs to explain. For the genus-species relation is a determinable-determinate relation too; but there we can state the differences that differentiate one species from another within the genus. The problem of the red-color case is precisely that we cannot specify a difference that differentiates red from the other colors other than red itself. Butchvarov has several fine theoretical discussions of the problem within his own theory of universals, and more generally within his theory of objects and entities (Butchvarov: 1989: 66–72; 1979: 163–64; 1966: ch. 4; see 151–52). Butchvarov discusses Aristotle, Thomas Aquinas, John Cook Wilson, H. W. B. Joseph, and Brand Blanshard. I have not found any mention of the problem in Russell, not even in his later works, in which specific qualities instantiate generic universals (IMT; HK; MPD), nor in Moore. For the later Russell, a specific quality "is a particular, not a universal" (Russell 1989: 685).

(4) The fourth and last kind of partial entailment I shall discuss is degrees of probability in the purely logical theory of probability. In his 1912 *Problems of Philosophy*, Russell admits degrees of strength of *a priori* inference. He speaks of degrees of self-evidence which give a "greater or less presumption" of truth (PP 118; see 60, 68, 70–81, 82; see POM 17).[3] Russell's chief example is the principle of induction, which he holds is not itself inductively justifiable because, following Hume, experience cannot make it in the slightest degree probable (PP 68, 70, 76). But while Hume rejects the principle and embraces skepticism, Russell impales himself on the other horn of the dilemma of induction by accepting the principle as rationally self-evident to some degree less than that of intuitive deductive validity. The 1912 Russell is committed to the view that the principle of induction is a weak synthetic *a priori* truth, which collapses the third and fourth kinds of partial entailment. Whether we agree with him or not, Russell is committed to there being some sort of inner connection between universals concerning regularities in the past and universals

concerning events in the future. That seems enough to make the 1912 Russell an implicit relevance logician in the broad positive sense.[4]

Russell's Three Implicit Entailment Relations

The three most important relations concerning logical relevance in Russell are *true* material implication, *always true* formal implication, and deducibility. In *Principles* Russell uses "implies" to denote material implication, (POM 16n), "if-then" to denote formal implication (POM 16n), and "therefore" to denote deduction (POM 35). I shall discuss these three relations in order.

1. The relevance of true material implication. Material implication is a relation between two propositions. In *Principles of Mathematics*, it is basic. It is indefinable because any attempted definition would involve implications (POM 14). However, it is explained as behaving according to a logical rule: "If p [materially] implies q, both are false or both true, or p is false and q true; it is impossible to have q false and p true, and it is necessary to have q true or p false" (POM 15). The modal terms "impossible" and "necessary" here may seem confusing. Russell merely means that given the definition of material implication, the features he describes are accordingly impossible or necessary. He immediately goes on to describe the paradoxes of material implication, "that false propositions imply all propositions, and true propositions are implied by all propositions" (POM 15).

Like Frege, Russell never uses material implication in the way Anderson and Belnap deride. That is, in a proof, he never establishes the truth of a material implication by showing that its antecedent is false or by showing that its consequent is true. Quite the opposite, he seeks to derive truths from truths, in this case to deduce the truth of the consequent from the truth of the antecedent. In fact, all of Frege's and Russell's logics are *axiom systems* in which all deductive inferences are from axioms assumed to be true to theorems whose truth needs to be rigorously proved. Frege vehemently and repeatedly denies that inference can ever be from anything but true premises, and he also says all inferences involve "logical relations" between premiss and conclusion, i.e., relations which could only be internal (Frege 1980: 16, 79, 182; 1979: 204–5; see Dummett 1981: 432–33). Notably, this include modus ponens, whose major premise is a material implication. That all of the premises of a proof must be true is the *truth contraint* (or *truth filter*) on deductive inference. This is simply to say that we will not accept an inference unless all the premises are true. This constraint is part and parcel of modern classical relevant inference.

And it explains why modern classical logicians are not so "stupid" as to accept the paradoxes of material implication and strict implication *simpliciter*, or so "dishonest" as to avoid ever actually offering absurd "proofs" of statements based on paradoxes they supposedly "officially" accept as permitting valid inferences, as Anderson and Belnap seem to think (Anderson 1975: 5, 17–18, 328–30). Do they not know that for Wittgenstein, the purely logical probability of a *mere* material implication (not: a *true* material implication)'s being true is only 75%? For it is true on only three of the four rows of its truth-table (T 4.464, 5.15–5.156). But the probability of a *true* material implication's being true per truth-table is trivially 100%. And more to the point, if a material implication and its antecedent are both true, then the probability of its consequent's being true per truth-table is 100%.

Russell emphasizes the importance of *true* implication in his 1911 "The Philosophical Implications of Mathematical Logic":

> It is necessary that the hypothesis *truly* implies the thesis. If we make the hypothesis that the hypothesis implies the thesis, we can only make deductions in the case when this new hypothesis truly implies the new thesis. Implication is a logical constant and cannot be dispensed with. Consequently we need *true* propositions about implication....This necessity for *true* premises emphasizes a distinction of the first importance, that is to say the distinction between a premise and a hypothesis. (Russell 1973e: 290, Russell's emphasis)

It is the last sentence quoted that is truly important for us.

True material implication is a relevance relation because it is a whole-part containment relation, though of a very different sort from Anderson-Belnap tautological entailment. (This makes *always true* formal implication a containment relation as well, since a formal implication is in effect a class of material implications.) What is contained is not some actual atomic statement in the manner of Anderson-Belnap, but something far more subtle and abstract: truth-grounds, that is, those distributions of atomic truth-possibilities that make a statement true. In a *true* material implication, all the truth-grounds of the consequent are truth-grounds of the antecedent. And that sort of truth-ground containment of the conclusion is formal and tautological.

Truth-tables make truth-ground containment intellectually visible for disjunctive syllogism, modus ponens, and hypothetical syllogism. We can also diagram such truth-ground containments using Venn diagrams. When we diagram the premisses of a valid argument, we will find that we have already diagrammed the conclusion (Copi 1978: 207–8; Gardner 1968: 49–50; Prior 1955:

171–72). Containment of the conclusion could scarcely be clearer or intellectually more visible.

I briefly note that a proof is sound if it is deductively valid *and* all of its premisses are true. That a proof must be sound is the *soundness constraint* or *soundness filter* on deductive inference. This is simply to say that we will not accept an inference unless not only are all the premisses true, but the inference is valid as well. The soundness constraint logically includes the truth constraint. It should be obvious that modern classical logicians really impose the soundness constraint, and not merely the truth constraint, on their logical proofs.

2. The relevance of always true formal implication. Formal implication is the relation between propositional functions "which holds when the one...implies the other for all values of the variable" (POM 14). That is, a formal implication is simply a conditional propositional function. Russell also calls formal implication a relation between "assertions" (POM 5). Either way, he means to distinguish the *inference* of one asserted statement by another asserted statement, i.e. of a conclusion by a premiss, from the *implication* of a consequent by an antecedent within a single asserted conditional statement (Wright 1957: 166–67). Either way, a "formal implication asserts a class of [material] implications" (POM 38, 41). "Russellian 'formal' implication is simply universal material implication" (Prior 1955: 197).

Russell finds material implication and formal implication "to be essential to every kind of deduction" (POM 33).

If we go into the logical substructure of its antecedent, every material implication is rewritable as a formal implication. For example, in "$P \supset Q$", let P be "Socrates is wise." "Socrates is wise $\supset Q$" is true if and only if "(x is wise and x = Socrates) $\supset Q$" is always true.

Russell already suggests some sort of inner connection in formal implication when he says that the variability it involves "seems to show that formal implication seems to involve something over and above the relation of [material] implication, and that some additional relation must hold where a term can be varied" (POM 39). But the suggested additional relation is merely class inclusion, and moreover the suggestion does not occur in every case (POM 39, 41). My own suggestion is that we have the inner connection of truth-ground containment only for *always true* formal implications.

Since an *always true* formal implication is in effect a class of *true* material implications, an *always true* formal implication is a relevance relation in the same way a *true* material implication is.

In 1910 *Principia* vol. 1, Russell explains the importance of using formal implications which are known to be always true:

> There is also a **practical ground** for the neglect of such [material] implications, for, speaking generally, they can only be *known* when it is already known either that their hypothesis is false or that their conclusion is true; and in neither of these cases do they serve to make us know the conclusion, since in the first case the conclusion need not be true, and in the second it is known already. Thus such implications do not serve the purpose for which implications are chiefly **useful**, namely that of making us know, by deduction, conclusions of which we were previously ignorant. *Formal* implications, on the contrary, do serve this purpose, owing to the psychological fact that we often know "$(x):\varphi x. \supset . \psi x$" and φy, in cases where ψy (which follows from these premisses) cannot easily be known directly. (PM 21, Russell's italic emphasis, my boldface emphasis)

Edwin Mares compares this practical ground to Grice (Grice 1989: chapter 4, see especially 61), and calls this pragmatic relevance as opposed to logical relevance (Mares 1997). I think that Mares is confusing the logical relevance (the truth-ground containment entailment) of *always true* formal implication, as I just explained it, with its practical importance. Thus he misses that this is not a different sort of relevance, which we might call pragmatic or practical relevance, but a pragmatic or practical *constraint* on logical inference. More deeply, looking to the language of the indented quotation just given, which makes it clear that the real issue is our *knowledge* of what is true, it is an *epistemic* constraint, as Shahid Rahman has noted (Rahman 2002). More generally and most obviously, *always true* is by definition a truth constraint.

    3. *The relevance of deductive inference.* For Russell, deductive implications are strict implications (AMA 199–200), and are also truth-ground containment relevant entailments (see PLA 240–41; IMP 203–5). This is just how modal logic and relevance logic are implicitly two sides of the coin of Russell's deductive logic.

Russell on Relevance: A Chronological Review

    I proceed to give a chronological review of Russell on deductive relevance, including his conception of truth-ground containment tautological entailments, from 1903 *Principles* to 1959 *My Philosophical Development*. We will see that Russell is deeply interested in relevance throughout his main philosophical career, a period of 56 years, and that his views are on relevance are plausible throughout, even though they are modern classical views.

Relevance in *Principles*

Russell states his main views on the nature of logic in his 1903 *Principles*, and except for his view on how Platonically real or how merely linguistic logic may be, they change little over the years. How many axioms and primitive terms may be needed is, of course, a mere matter of elegance, and similarly, I think, for his later dropping the distinction between real and apparent variables.

In *Principles*, Russell already distinguishes among material implication, formal implication, and deductive validity. He endorses material implication as the minimal truth-preserving implication relation for proof purposes, and develops formal implication from material implication to suit the completely general nature of logical and mathematical inference. But deductive inference or deducibility is what Russell's conception of proof is all about.

On Russell's logicist program of rewriting mathematics as logic plus class theory, mathematical proof is deductive logical proof as well. He says, "It seems plain that mathematics consists of deductions" (POM 4). He says, "By the help of ten principles of deduction, and ten other premises of a general logical nature..., all mathematics can be formally deduced" (POM 4). He adds, "The general doctrine that all mathematics is deduction by logical principles from logical principles was strongly advocated by Leibniz" (POM 5).

For Russell, deduction essentially involves the relation of formal implication, due to the completely general nature of logic (POM 14; see POM 5), and therefore also essentially involves the relation of material implication, since a formal implication logically equates to a class of material implications (POM 13). Logic studies implication, which holds among propositions, while formal implications hold among propositional functions (POM 14). But even ignoring that merely formal difference, a deductive inference is far more than just a formal implication. The substantive difference is this. All a formal implication does is satisfy the requirement of complete generality. The second requirement, truth in virtue of logical form, is not satisfied by formal implication alone. That is, a deduction must not only be a formal implication, but it must also be valid in virtue of its form. Not only that, but its premises must be true. Here I am slurring over the technical difference between an inference from one statement to another and a single conditional statement, not to mention a formal implication of one propositional function by another. This is harmless here, since all are mutually rewritable.

"Symbolic or formal logic...is the study of the various general types of deduction" (POM 10), and "is essentially concerned with inference in general" (POM 11). "[T]he formal properties of a relation [or of any proposition] may be defined as those that can be expressed in terms of logical constants" (POM 11).

Russell implicitly imposes a truth constraint on deduction, at least in mathematics, when he says that "all mathematics is deduction by logical principles from logical principles" (POM 5). For surely he would not call a proposition a logical principle unless it were true.

Russell says that propositional (material) implication is indefinable, since the only way to define it, i.e., in terms of truth and falsehood, involves implications (POM 14). Thus, even though inference must meet the minimal condition of preserving truth, i.e., "it is impossible to have q false and p true, and it is necessary to have q true or p false" (POM 15), "this still leaves implication fundamental, and not definable in terms of disjunction" (POM 15) and negation. Note that Russell's use of the terms "impossible" and "necessary" reveals a modal aspect of material implication. But the aspect is innocent. He merely means impossible or necessary per the definition of material implication.

Relevance in "Necessity and Possibility"

In his ca. 1903–05 paper "Necessity and Possibility," Russell expressly identifies necessary connection in a hypothetical proposition with logical deducibility of its consequent from its antecedent (Russell 1994a / ca. 1903–05: 513). This is already enough to meet Nelson's and Wright's tests of entailment, respectively, that some inner connection is needed, and that this connection is deducibility. Russell then gives his post-Kantian explanations of deducibility and analyticity. He reiterates the paradox of material implication that a true proposition is implied by every proposition (Russell 1994a / ca. 1903–05: 514). He then gives what I call his Deducibility Argument, which I quoted in chapter 8. His aim is to distinguish material implication from deducibility. He says:

> [I]f we regard q as deducible from p whenever p [materially] implies q, all true propositions are deducible from the law of [non]contradiction. But in the practice of inference, it is plain that something more than [material] implication must be concerned. The reason that proofs are used at all is that we can sometimes perceive that q follows from p, when we should not otherwise know that q is true; while in other cases, "p [materially] implies q" is only to be inferred either from the falsehood of p or

from the truth of q. In these other cases, the proposition
"p [materially] implies q" serves no practical purpose; it
is only when this proposition is used as a means of
discovering the truth of q that it is useful. Given a true
proposition p, there will be some propositions q such
that the truth of "p [materially] implies q" is evident, and
thence the truth of q is inferred; while in the case of
other true propositions [q], their truth must be
independently known before we can know that p
[materially] implies them. What we require is a *logical*
distinction between these two cases. (Russell 1994a / ca.
1903–05: 515, Russell's emphasis; see 517 repeating
that implications which can be known only by knowing
that the antecedent is true or that the conclusion is false
"have no practical utility")

Russell then says that the only way he has thought of to make this
logical distinction is to admit there are laws of deduction which:

tell us that two propositions having *certain relations of
form*...are such that one of them [materially] implies the
other. Thus q is deducible from p if p and q either have
one of the relations contemplated by the laws of
deduction, or are connected by any (finite) number of
intermediaries each having one of these relations to its
successor. (Russell 1994a / ca. 1903–05: 515, my emphasis)

He finds that this definition of deducibility is "purely logical" and
covers "exactly the cases" we consider to be cases of logical
deduction "without assuming either that p is false or that q is true"
(Russell 1994a / ca. 1903–05: 515). Russell never deviates from
this basic understanding of the distinction between material
implication and logical deducibility in any later work. Note again
the very early reference to logical form, and that there is no clear
distinction between fully general implication and implication in
virtue of logical form. He is not saying in this early paper that
logical form is a second condition in addition to that of full
generality. Again, I take this to be obvious on its face; but if an
argument is needed, it would be that otherwise Russell would never
have needed to correct his early understanding of logical truth as
fully general truth, since he would have already understood logical
truth as truth in virtue of form as early as ca. 1903–05.

Referring to the ten principles of deduction in *Principles*,
Russell says, "We may then say that q is *deducible* from p if it can
be shown *by means of the above principles* that p [materially]
implies q" (Russell 1994a / ca. 1903–05: 515, Russell's emphasis).
Russell goes on to argue that *deducible from* cannot replace

materially implied by, since the former presupposes the latter in its definition (Russell 1994a / ca. 1903–05: 515).

Russell briefly repeats the Deducibility Argument just two pages later, stating it a little differently, but not substantially so:

> Implications which are not analytic can only be practically discovered if it is independently known that the premiss is false or that the conclusion is true, or if the implication can be made analytic by adding to the premiss a proposition whose truth is independently known. But in such cases (except sometimes in the third case), implications have no practical utility. (Russell 1994a / ca. 1903–05: 517)

The Deducibility Argument meets the Nelson-Wright-Geach tests of inner connection, deductively provable connection, and *a priori* connection. In fact, Wright's deducibility criterion is expressly satisfied. Russell is not only expressly claiming but is very carefully arguing that logical inference requires a relationship of following from, and that this relationship is deducibility.

Also in "Necessity and Possibility," Russell defines "'*p* materially implies *q*' is analytic," or what is the same, "*q* is an *analytic consequence* of *p*," as meaning the same as "*q* is deducible from *p*" (Russell 1994a / ca. 1903–05: 516–17). Russell goes on to argue that the class of analytic propositions is narrower than the class of necessary propositions, since not every necessary proposition is deducible. This is where he gives examples of synthetic *a priori* statements: "If a thing is good, it is not bad" and "If a thing is yellow, it is not red" (Russell 1994a / ca. 1903–05: 517). For more on "Necessity and Possibility," see my summary of that paper in chapter 8.

Relevance in *Principia*

In 1910 *Principia* vol. 1, Russell distinguishes material implication from formal implication virtually as before (PM 20). He then argues as before that a third relation, that of deducibility, is needed. One must not be confused here. He says his main relation of implication among propositions is material implication, but he only calls it that when he needs to distinguish it from formal implication (PM 7). He defines *p* materially implies *q*, or the "Implicative Function," as "the proposition that either not-*p* or *q* is true" (PM 7). (Perhaps it is this definition that throws relevantists off the track.) He basically equates modus ponens with disjunctive syllogism at this point, though without using those names (PM 7).

But he says "the process of inference" must not be confused with (material) implication (PM 7).

Russell says, "The sign "⊢," called the 'assertion-sign', means that what follows is asserted" (PM 8). He means, of course, that a statement the sign prefixes is asserted *to be true*. He says:

> *Inference.* The process of inference is as follows: a proposition "*p*" is asserted, and a proposition "*p* [materially] implies *q*" is asserted, and then as a sequel the proposition "*q*" is asserted. The trust in inference is the belief that if the two former assertions are not in error, the final assertion is not in error. (PM 8–9, Russell's emphasis)

Whether he equates being true with being "not in error" (PM 8–9) in the manner of the Tractarian vanishing double negation, or is stating his conception of truth preservation very cautiously here, I do not know. (Compare IMT 276 on how double negation fails if the law of excluded middle in its semantic form fails. Russell's view that most things in the world are vague implies that the law of excluded middle does not apply well to our talk of things in the world; but he does hold that the law applies in the logically "smooth" realm of logic and mathematics.) In any case, it is clear that an inference is not at all the same as a material implication. For a material implication is a single conditional statement, while an inference is an argument with two premises and a conclusion, specifically a modus ponens, both of whose premises are asserted to be true. That mere logical deducibility is not enough for proof, and that it must also be the case that all the premises in the deduction are true, is the soundness constraint. The essential relation between inference and material implication is, then, that an *inference* has, by definition, a material implication as its major *premiss*. Just as in *Principles*, logic in *Principia* is the study of *inference*, and is *not* the study of material implication. It follows that logic for Russell is essentially the study of modus ponens. Here he is very close to Frege, who relies on modus ponens as almost his only rule of inference in logic (Dejnožka 2012: 83).

As we saw earlier in this chapter, Russell says:

> [Material] implications which are not particular cases of formal implications have not been regarded as implications at all. There is also a practical ground for the neglect of such implications, for, speaking generally, they can only be *known* when it is already known that either their hypothesis [i.e. antecedent] is false or that their conclusion [i.e. consequent] is true; and in neither of these cases do they serve to make us know the

conclusion, since in the first case the conclusion need not be true, and in the second it is known already. Thus such implications do not serve the purpose for which implications are chiefly useful, namely that of making us know, **by deduction**, conclusions of which we were previously ignorant. (PM 20–21, Russell's italic emphasis, my boldface emphasis)

This is the *Principia* Deducibility Argument. Russell is warning us that deductive inferences are useless if they are based on our knowing either that the premiss is false or that the conclusion is true. He is constraining useful deductive inference to cases where (1) the premisses are *true* and (2) we show that the conclusion is true on the *basis* of the truth of the premisses. This is the most basic form of use-relevance, if I am right that truth-ground containment is the most basic form of relevance. We may say Russell is saying that an implication is useful if and only if the premiss is used, or if you please, must be used, to arrive at the conclusion using this particular argument in our particular epistemic situation. For it is obvious that such usefulness is relative to what we already know.

Russell immediately continues:

> *Formal* implications, on the contrary, do serve this purpose, owing to the psychological fact that we often know "$(x)(\varphi x \supset \psi x)$" and φy, in cases where ψy (which follows from these premisses) cannot easily be known directly. (PM 21, Russell's emphasis, my scope brackets in the major premiss)

Of course, the last quoted sentence only postpones the question to, How do we know "$(x){:}\varphi x. \supset .\psi x$" is true? The situation cries out for deducibility as the way we *know or show* that φx formally implies ψx. The key term is really "by deduction" in the quotation before. This term shows that Russell thinks of deducibility as the relation of deductive inference in *Principia*, just as in *Principles* and in "Necessity and Possibility." Also in the previous quotation, Russell in effect presents modus ponens not as consisting of three propositions, but as consisting of one proposition as major premiss and of two propositional functions, one as minor premiss and the other as conclusion. This throws light on the essential role formal implication plays in formal or deductive inference. (There is also a minor slide from mention to use, since only the major premiss is in double quotes; Russell is noted for being casual on use-mention.)

There are three main things to note. First, Russell has the very same problem with material implication that the relevantists do. Second, in order to solve it, he is introducing two constraints within his own logic: (a) he is restricting inferences to cases where *all the premisses are true* (or at least not in error); and (b) he is requiring inferences to have a *formal relationship* between premisses and conclusion. The third main thing to note is that the text is subtle evidence that Russell is tacitly equating completely general truth with truth in virtue of form, and a fortiori, deductive inference with fully general inference. That is because the only thing he actually requires for inference in virtue of logical form here is formal implication—which is nothing more than fully general implication, since logic for Russell is fully general. But at the same time, he does want inferences to be deductively valid, that is, to follow from logical principles by logical principles. And that means that he is tacitly equating fully general truth with truth in virtue of form, and fully general inference with deductive inference. That is in fact a very plausible equation; but as we saw in chapter 1, Russell eventually finds counterexamples.

Just as in *Principles*, deduction in *Principia* presupposes and cannot be material implication (PM 90). In *Principia*, the sole modification to the *Principles* deducibility relation is that Russell narrows his list of principles of deduction down to five (PM xiii). Years later he accepts Jean Nicod's narrowing the list down to one principle of deduction using a single undefined logical constant, the Sheffer stroke (PM xiii; IMP 149; IMP 148 adds two non-formal principles to the one formal principle of deduction).

That Russell *regards* deducibility as a relevance relation should be clear from the fact that he thinks its value lies in the relatedness or connectedness of premiss to conclusion. The whole contrast of deducibility to a mere (that is, nondeducible) material implication lies precisely in the *un*relatedness of the truth-value of the antecedent to the truth-value of the conclusion in a mere material implication. A conclusion is deducible if and only if the premiss's truth logically necessitates the conclusion's truth.

Russell says, "When...*q* **follows from**...*p*, so that if *p* is true, *q* must also be true, we say that *p implies q*" (PM 94, Russell's italic emphasis, my boldface emphasis). He says:

> Now in order that one proposition may be **inferred from** another, it is necessary that the two should have that relation which makes the one a **consequence** of the other. When a proposition *q* is a **consequence** of the proposition *p*, we say that *p implies q*. Thus **deduction** depends upon the relation of *implication*.... (PM 90, Russell's italic emphasis, my boldface emphasis)

The key to understanding this is the Deducibility Argument. *Pace* Anderson and Belnap, Russell would not infer *q* from *p* solely due to the truth of *q*, or solely due to the falsehood of *p*, any more than they would. The constraint imposed by the Deducibility Argument is precisely on the validity of the inference, that is, on what counts as following from.

Relevance in *External World*

In his 1914 *Our Knowledge of the External World* , Russell repeats his Deducibility Argument for the need for some relation beyond that of material implication for logical inference (KEW 49–50). He says that premiss and conclusion in logical inference must be *connected*; the conclusion must *follow from* the premisses (KEW 49–50). He says:

> There can be no inference except where propositions are *connected* in some such way, so that from the truth or falsehood of the one something *follows* as to the truth or falsehood of the other....The practical utility of inference rests upon this fact. (KEW 50, my emphasis)

Practical utility was his argument for constraining formal inference to relevant inference in *Principia* as well.

Specifically, deducibility is a *whole-part relation* (KEW 63). He says, "The only way, so far as I know, in which one thing can be *logically* dependent upon another is when the other is *part* of the one," e.g., "without...pages[,] no book" (KEW 63, Russell's emphasis). Here he is in basic agreement with Nelson and Wright. Also in *External World*, Russell explains logical truth as true in virtue of logical form, and understands deductively valid inference as validity in virtue of logical form (KEW 41, 42, 49, 51).

Relevance in "The Philosophy of Logical Atomism"

In his 1918 "The Philosophy of Logical Atomism," Russell says that mathematics is logic because it can not only be rewritten as logic, but "can also be deduced from the premises of logic" (PLA 240). He then says:

> Everything that is a proposition of logic has got to be in some sense or other a tautology. It has got to be something that has some peculiar quality, which I do not know how to define, that belongs to logical propositions and not to others....They have a certain peculiar quality which marks them out from other propositions and enables us to know them a priori. But what exactly that characteristic is, I am not able to tell you. [I can only say

> that while] logical propositions...should consist only of
> variables,...that is [only] a necessary characteristic,...not
> a sufficient one. (PLA 240–41)

This discussion of tautology is completely in line with his earlier discussions of deducibility. For only logical deductions, as opposed to material implications and to formal implications, can and must be tautologies. Both logical truths and valid inferences are tautologous. Indeed, valid inferences are rewritable as if-then logical truths.

Relevance in *Introduction*

In his 1919 *Introduction to Mathematical Philosophy*, it may appear that Russell is no relevantist. He starts well by saying that in logic and in all mathematics, we need formal deduction, notably as opposed to Kantian intuition in geometry (IMP 144–45). He says that "we may regard deduction as a process by which we pass from knowledge of...the premiss, to knowledge of...the conclusion" (IMP 145). He says that logical deduction must be "*correct*" (IMP, his emphasis), meaning that premiss and conclusion must be so related "that we have a right to believe the conclusion if we know the premiss[es] to be true" (IMP 145–46). He says that valid inference requires two things: (1) that the premiss(es) be true, and (2) that the premiss(es) and conclusion stand in the relation of implication (IMP 146). He admits other forms of valid inference, but says "it seems natural to take 'implication' as the primitive fundamental relation, since this is the relation which must hold between *p* and *q* if we are to be able to infer the *truth* of *q* from the *truth* of *p*" (IMP 146, Russell's emphasis). So far, everything he says is exactly what relevantists would want him to say. So far, his heart seems in the right place as far as relevance is concerned. But then he appears to veer off on what appears to be a very different tack. He says, "But for technical reasons this is not the best primitive idea to choose" (IMP 146). He wants to take implication "in the widest sense that will allow us to infer the truth of *q* if we know the truth of *p*" (IMP 147). He then famously takes "'*p* implies *q*'...to mean "not-*p* or *q*" (IMP 147).

However, the just-quoted "if we know the truth of *p*" (IMP 147 shows that he retains his truth constraint, i.e., his requirement that the premiss(es) be true. That is, he has in mind by "implication" not mere material implication as such, but *true* material implication. Also, that text and the others just quoted indicate that he retains his epistemic constraint as well. But there is far more going on in *Introduction* than just those things.

In *Introduction*, Russell repeats his Deducibility Argument for the need to admit logical deducibility three times, each time in more detail than the last, and every time in connection with deducibility as opposed to formal implication (IMP 145–46, 149, 152–53). Russell calls this relation "formal deducibility" (IMP 153). He distinguishes it from C. I. Lewis's strict implication only for the reason that the latter is not truth-functional (IMP 154). Possibly Russell has in mind synthetic *a priori* strict implications such as "'Everything is red' strictly implies 'Everything has color'." It does not seem to occur to Russell that his formal deducibility is at least a *species* of strict implication; he does not expressly address that classificatory question.

Most importantly, Russell says:

> There is, if I am not mistaken, a certain confusion in the minds of some authors as to the relation. between propositions, in virtue of which an **inference** is **valid**. In order that it may be **valid** to infer *q* from *p*, it is only necessary that p should be true and that the proposition "not-*p* or *q*" be true. Whenever this is the case, it is clear that *q* must be true. But **inference** will only in fact take place when the proposition "not-*p* or *q*" is **known** otherwise than through knowledge of not-*p* or knowledge of *q*. Whenever *p* is false, "not-*p* or *q*" is true, but is **useless** for **inference**, which requires that *p* should be true. Whenever *q* is already known to be true, "not-*p* or *q*" is of course also known to be true, but is again **useless** for **inference**, since *q* is **already known**, and therefore does not need to be inferred. In fact, **inference** only arises when "not-*p* or *q*" can be **known without our knowing already** which of the two alternatives it is that makes the disjunction true. Now, the circumstances under which this occurs are those in which certain **relations of form** exist between *p* and *q*. For example, we know that if *r* implies the negation of *s*, then *s* implies the negation of *r*. Between "*r* implies not-*s*" and "*s* implies not-*r*" there is **a formal relation** which enables us to know that the first implies the second, without having first to know that the first is false or that the second is true. It is under such circumstances that the relation of **implication** is **practically useful** for drawing **inferences**. (IMP 153, Russell's italic emphasis, my boldface emphasis)

In this remarkable passage, Russell ties it all together. He sharply distinguishes validity from inference. It is inference, not validity, that he really considers to be his relevance relation. All inferences are valid implications, but not all valid implications are inferences. For an implication to be an inference, the implication must not only be valid, but its validity must be due to a relationship of logical form. And that is because an implication is useful if and only if it goes from the premiss to the conclusion, that is, if we can come to know the conclusion on the basis of our knowledge of the premiss, and not because we either know that the premiss is false or already know that the conclusion is true. Thus for Russell, an inference's logical form is what makes it use-relevant, and use-relevance is defined in terms of the epistemic situation.

At this point I think there is no question but that Russell intends to have, and believes he has, a relevance theory in the narrow positive sense. He has given his Deducibility Argument at least seven times in four works, three of which are published. We found two occurrences of the Deducibility Argument in "Necessity and Possibility," one in *Principia*, one in *External World,* and three in *Introduction*. Even in *Principles*, Russell distinguishes among material implication, formal implication, and deduction (POM 4–5, 12–16). He does not give his Deducibility Argument there, but does give an argument somewhat like it (POM 522). His implicit characterization of deducibility as tautological accords with our present-day understanding of entailment as tautological, as witness Anderson's and Belnap's terminology of "tautological entailment." For their part, Anderson and Belnap overlook the Deducibility Argument altogether, the pragmatic and epistemic constraints, and even the truth and soundness constraints, and along with the latter two constraints, the distinction between validity and inference.

Late in *Introduction*, it might seem that Russell is casting doubt on a key notion of his theory of deducibility. He says that "the characteristic of logical propositions that we are in search of....we may call *tautology*" (IMP 203), and then he admits he does "not know how to define 'tautology'" (IMP 205). However, a more careful reading of the text indicates that he is not casting any doubt on the *existence* of tautology, but only on whether we can *define* it. The text reads:

> *For the moment,* I do not know how to define "tautology"....in spite of *feeling thoroughly familiar with the characteristic* of which a definition is wanted. At this point, therefore, *for the moment,* we reach the frontier of knowledge [of] the logical foundations of mathematics. (IMP 205, my emphasis)

These words at the end of the book take us back to its beginning. Russell says that the natural numbers, "though familiar,...are not understood," and "are by no means easy" to define (IMP 3). Then he says:

[H]uman knowledge must always be content to accept some terms as intelligible without definition, in order to have a starting-point for its definitions. It is not clear that there must be terms which are *incapable* of definition: it is always possible that [we] *might* go further still. On the other hand, it is also possible that, when analysis has been pushed far enough, we can reach terms that really are simple....This is a question which it is not necessary for us to decide;...it is sufficient to observe that, since human powers are finite, [our definitions] must always begin somewhere, with terms undefined **for the moment**, though perhaps not permanently. (IMP 3–4, Russell's italic emphasis, my boldface emphasis)

That "it is perfectly possible to suppose that" analysis might go on forever, "and that you never reach the simple," though he himself does not "think it is true" (PLA 202), is one of Russell's major themes, which he later discusses at length using the terminology of "logical structure" and "minimum vocabulary" (AMA 1–9; HK part 4, ch. 1–4). We see that far from arguing for a total skepticism in the foundations of logic, Russell is merely taking tautology, a familiar characteristic, as our current starting point. Tautology may even *be* simple, i.e., indefinable. Russell believes there are many sorts of simples (PLA 270). But our job as analysts is to push the analysis as far as we can; and if we think we might push it further but do not presently see how, then we let it go "for the moment." This is the spirit in which Russell's later discussions should be understood.

Though it might not have occurred to Russell, I think the most natural suggestion would be to analyze tautological truth as truth in virtue of logical form (see IMP 199, 203–5). He gives an excellent reason for thinking so: He says, "It is obvious that a proposition which is a tautology is so in virtue of its form" (AMA 172). And the notion of truth in virtue of logical form would seem clearer and more illuminating than the notion of tautology.

As if in answer to my suggestion, in 1938 Russell raises the same question about truth in virtue of form which he had raised about tautology: Can it be analyzed (POM vii)? Is truth in virtue of form indefinable, or is it merely undefined "for the moment"? The important point is that for Russell, his being unable to answer this question is no reason for skepticism about the foundations of logic. In fact, it is not even "a question which it is...necessary for us to decide" (IMP 4).

Russell puts the matter even more plainly a few pages later in *Introduction*:

> We already have some knowledge (though not
> sufficiently articulate or analytic) of what we mean by
> "1" and "2" and so on, and our use of numbers in
> arithmetic must conform to this knowledge....[A]ll that
> we can do, if we adopt [Peano's] method, is to say "we
> know what we mean by '0' and 'number' and
> 'successor', though we cannot explain what we mean in
> terms of other simpler concepts." It is quite legitimate to
> say this when we must, and at some point we all must;
> but it is the object of mathematical philosophy to put off
> saying it as long as possible. By the logical theory of
> arithmetic we are able to put it off for a very long time.
> (IMP 8)

As Russell explains two years later in 1921,

> It is not necessary, in order that a man should "under-
> stand" a word, that he should "know what it means," in
> the sense of being able to say "this word means so-and-
> so." Understanding words does not consist in knowing
> their...definitions.... (AMI 197)

Thus tautology can be a familiar characteristic, and we can even
understand the word "tautology," without knowing how to define
tautology in terms of simpler concepts.

Russell still holds that analysis logically can be endless in
1948 in *Human Knowledge* (HK). He says:

> The ultimate units so far reached may at any moment
> turn out to be capable of analysis. Whether there must be
> units incapable of analysis because they are destitute of
> parts, is a question which there seems no way of
> deciding. (HK 252; see 259)

Russell holds that analysis might be endless as late as 1959 in *My
Philosophical Development*. He says, "As regards simples, I can
see no reason either to assert or to deny that they may be reached
by analysis" (MPD 164). This might seem ambiguous. Does he
mean that there are simples but we might never reach them, or that
there might be no simples? Russell resolves this ambiguity by
quoting his own earlier statement in "The Philosophy of Logical
Atomism": "[I]t might be that analysis could go on forever" (MPD
164 quoting PLA 202). He also quotes his earlier statement in
Human Knowledge that "there seems no way of deciding" whether
"there must be" simples (MPD 165 quoting HK 252).

Excursus: Can Logical Analysis be Endless?

That analysis might be endless was not always Russell's view. We have seen that he did not "think it is true" that analysis is endless, even though he thought it was possible, in 1918 (PA 202). But he definitely believed in 1903 that there are simple entities. In *Principles*, he says that in mathematics, "the indefinables are obtained primarily as the necessary residue in a process of analysis" (POM xv). Part One is entitled, "The Indefinables of Mathematics." Russell gives us a laundry list in chapter 16, which is entitled "Whole and Part": "Simple terms, such as points, instants, colours, [and] the fundamental concepts of logic" (POM 137). He says that "redness and colour...appear to be equally simple" (POM 138).

Also, Russell's 1924 paper "Logical Atomism" does not fit the general pattern. There he says, "I confess it seems obvious to me (as it did to Leibniz) that what is complex must be composed of simples" (LK 337). This could be a very brief change of view, soon recanted, a mental slip, or simply casual writing in a popular survey paper. Of course, *Principles* and "Logical Atomism" support each other. But as we have seen, the general trend is for Russell to hold a neutral view. And even in "Logical Atomism," Russell says, "A logical language will not lead to error if its simple symbols" do not stand for simple objects (LK 337). He says, "The only drawback to such a language" is that it cannot discuss anything simpler (LK 337; see also 340 saying it is "in the highest degree probable that [the structure of reality] is more fine-grained" than we have found so far). He then confesses that nonetheless, it "seems obvious to me that what is complex must be composed of simples" (LK 337). He gives no argument for this, perhaps because it seems obvious to him, but perhaps also because he can think of no argument to give.

I would now like to discuss the concept of endless logical analysis as an instance of infinite regress. What does Russell think of infinite regresses in general? He agrees with Ramsey that our human inability to traverse an infinite series in logic is not a point of logic as such, but a mere practical limitation on our part (MPD 91). That said, he thinks that some regresses are benign and others are vicious. He argues against Aquinas' vicious regress arguments for God's existence by pointing out that the negative integers are benignly endless (HWP 462). Later in the same work he argues specifically against Aquinas' first cause argument that "the series of proper fractions has no first term" (HWP 587). These are arguments by analogy. He is expressly comparing Aquinas' regress arguments for God, and is implicitly comparing his own view that there logically can be an endless regress of logical analyses of things, to what he is holding forth as examples, not say paradigms, of benign regresses in mathematics. This, of course, is not good enough by itself. For it is generally held that all analogies limp (*omnis analogia claudicat*). But I myself do not hold that *all* analogies limp. Elsewhere, I note that a certain shade's analogy to our paradigms of, say, red, may be so great as to be (intuitively, not formally) logically sufficient for the shade's being a shade of red (my 2003: 235). It logically could even be a *purer* shade that, so to speak, is *encircled* by our existing paradigms (say, by brick, scarlet, and crimson), and thus could be even *more* red than our existing paradigms are. Alternatively, it could be on a *par* with them—different, but *equally* red. That might be compared to being another point on the encircling circle of existing paradigms. My other example is of substance theories: "surely the substances of Descartes, Spinoza, and Locke so closely resemble Aristotelian substances that they cannot fail to be substances too" (my 2003: 235). But regardless of whether I am right, we need to investigate further. For the analogies Russell is concerned with do not even appear to be encircling ones, or to be much like my color or substance theory analogies at all. And in philosophy, surely many or perhaps most analogical arguments limp at least somewhat. Whether such arguments succeed might ultimately be a judgment call in some difficult cases. We might even arrive at a judgment that we ought to *refrain* from judging either to accept or to reject some analogical argument as intuitively valid, because it is not clear how close the analogy is to my two paradigmatic examples of an intuitively valid analogical argument. That is, it might not be clear whether the analogical argument in question is encircled by paradigmatic intuitively valid analogical arguments like mine, or even whether it is on a par with them. Our logical intuitions are often weak and imperfect, and often conflict. But there is nothing wrong with talk of analogies among analogies, or of relevant analogies between analogical arguments with respect to their validity.

Let us provisionally assume, as I think many philosophers would, that there can be both good (benign) or bad (vicious) infinite regresses. The negative integers and fractions regresses seem quite benign. Almost everyone would admit that these series not only *do* have no end, but for mathematical reasons *cannot* have an end. But it is not so clear in the case of a causal series' needing a first cause, or a series of ontological dependencies' needing a first being whose existence depends on the existence of no other being in turn. And Russell himself admits at least three regress arguments as genuinely vicious. First, in *Human Knowledge* and in *My Philosophical Development*, Russell follows Keynes in holding that probable knowledge must start somewhere (HK 368–69; MPD 149). In effect, this is a version of Aristotle's vicious regress argument that not all knowledge can be proved by argument, since we must start arguing from some premiss. Second, in *A History of Western Philosophy*, Russell adduces a vicious regress of false appearances argument for the view that there must be some appearances that really are as they appear to be (HWP 129). Third, Russell admits the existence of universals based on a vicious regress of resemblances argument (RUP 111–12). Now, is Russell's view that logical analysis can be endless more analogous to the two benign regresses of numbers he admits? Or is it more analogous to the three vicious regress arguments he admits? He provides no test to distinguish benign regresses from vicious ones. More precisely, he provides no test to distinguish the vicious regress arguments he accepts as valid (concerning knowledge, cognitive appearances, and universals), from the ones he rejects as invalid (concerning first cause and necessary being) due to their sufficient analogy (in his view) to benign arithmetical regresses. Thus we are on our own, in figuring out how Russell might best answer these questions based on his own views.

I can think of two reasons why Russell might find a regress of logical analyses benign. ("B" is for benign.)

(B1) The obvious analogy would be of logical analysis to numerical divisibility, insofar as logical analysis is a kind of logical division. Here the regress most like that of logical analysis would seem to be the divisibility of fractions regress. For logical analysis is a logical division of things into simpler logical components.

(B2) For Russell, mathematics is itself logically analyzed into logic plus class or set theory. Thus for him, the negative integers and the fractions of his benign series are literal examples of logical analysis.

But I can also think of six reasons why Russell ought to find that a logical analysis regress would be more like his own vicious regresses. ("V" is for vicious.)

(V1) The numbers regresses are obviously benign while the logical analysis regress is not obviously so.

(V2) The numbers regresses are obviously benign because they are *provably* endless, while it is not clear what would count as a proof that the logical analysis regress is endless (or not).

(V3) That Russell logically analyzes negative integers and fractions is a red herring. He does analyze them. But the series of negative integers is not an endless series of logical analyses, but of numbers. Each member of the series is not a logical analysis of the member that precedes it. Similarly for the series of fractions. Russell's logical analyses of these sorts of numbers are finite and even brief, since the analyses are in effect of all of the numbers of each sort at once using mathematical induction.

(V4) Russell has got at least one of his supposedly benign mathematical regresses backwards. The series of proper fractions, i.e., of fractions whose numerator is less than their denominator, consists of all fractions between one and zero. It has no first *or* last member. The larger proper fractions approach the number one as an asymptote, and the smaller proper fractions approach zero as an asymptote. But the series of negative numbers is very different in that regard. That series has no last member. But if you flip the series around, you *must* start the series of negative integers with negative one. Likewise, you *must* start the series of fractions that are regularly diminishing halves (½, ¼, ⅛,....) with one half. (This series is not Russell's example.) In that sense, the series of negative numbers and the series of diminishing halves *are* vicious regresses, since they logically must start with a first member of the series. To think otherwise is to look through the wrong end of the telescope, that is, at the wrong end of the series. And it really is the wrong end, since what would correspond to the first cause or necessary being, the thing that *starts* the series, would be negative one or one half.

Now, reasons (1)–(4) only show (negative) dissimilarities between a logical analysis regress and Russell's two officially admitted benign numbers regresses. We not yet even offered a case for (positive) similarities between a logical analysis regress and Russell's three officially admitted vicious regresses. I shall do so now.

(V5) All of Russell's genuinely vicious regress arguments aim to settle genuine philosophical controversies by showing the need to admit metaphysically problematic entities in order to stop the regresses. And Russell treats, correctly, I think, the possibility of a logical analysis regress as just such a genuine philosophical controversy. For simple entities are metaphysically problematic in general. Again, unlike his provably endless benign numbers series, it is not as if he can prove that logical analysis *must* be endless. And that would be the only way to prove that it *is* endless. Ironically, then, his own view that analysis *may* be endless makes the argument for the opposite view, that analysis must end with simple entities, far more like his own vicious regress arguments —and precisely because he accepts them as genuinely vicious, i.e., as substantive. We may call this the substantive similarity.

(V6) There is a formal similarity as well. The conclusion of a vicious regress argument is always that at some stage, the regress must stop. This is not at all the same as saying that the argument must be substantive or metaphysically problematic. And the only kind of *argument* there could be about a series of logical analyses is that the regress must stop somewhere. Otherwise we have no argument, but just an endless series of analyses.

My conclusion, based on weighing (B1)–(B4) against (V1)–(V6), is that the regress argument that there must be simples if there are complexes would be of the genuinely vicious *sort* for Russell. This is not to say that the argument is *sound* for him; in fact, his mature view is that it is not. But I can think of at least seven caveats which should be discussed. ("C" is for caveat.)

(C1) My arguments are ad hominem. For I have based them on the regress arguments *Russell* accepts or rejects as benign or vicious. Someone else might accept or reject the opposite of what Russell does. This caveat is not very serious; it concerns mere rephrasing. All of my points would seem to remain valid on a general level. But more to the point, I was only discussing what Russell would think.

(C2) Making analogies between a logical analysis regress and *substantive* regress arguments is not the same as making analogies to regress arguments, substantive or not, that are *known* to be vicious. For as far as we can tell in advance of our investigation, a substantive regress *issue* might well be solved by finding the regress benign after all. That is, a regress might be benign, but not *obviously* so. But I was only discussing what Russell knows (or takes) to be a vicious regress.

(C3) More generally, we must not confuse the metaphysical question whether there are, must, or can be simple entities with the epistemological question whether anything "can be *known* to be simple," nor yet with the methodological question whether we should simply "abstain from asserting that the thing we are considering is simple," in which case Russell says, "It follows that the whole question whether there are simples to be reached by analysis is unnecessary"(MPD 123, Russell's emphasis). And when he says that analysis "*may*" be endless, he might mean only that it logically can be endless as far as we actually know, or could know. But I have only discussed Russell on these options, and he seems clear on the differences. And here too, everything he says is quite consistent with its being a substantive issue whether analysis is or can be endless. In fact, he seems to be saying that we should abstain from asserting that there are simples, and find the question whether there are simples unnecessary, on methodological grounds precisely because we cannot prove whether analysis can be endless, or at least cannot prove it at this time, and because this does not invalidate the limited progress in analysis that we have made so far.

(C4) Whether logical analysis *in general* can be endless must stand or fall with whether all *instances of* logical analysis can be endless. As far as we can tell in advance, there logically might be general arguments for the general thesis, or we might have to resort to arguing about each instance, such as logical analysis of bodies, logical analysis of minds, logical analysis of space-time, logical analysis of numbers, and so on. For example, the logical analysis of bodies might end with sense-data, while the logical analysis of minds might be endless.

(C5) It is not clear how many of the regresses we have discussed, such as of negative integers, fractions, first cause, necessary being, false appearances, nondemonstrative knowledge, and universals, count as logical analyses in the first place. What would we be analyzing? The causal or ontological foundation of the world? The definitional foundation of negative integers? The logical basis of any of the series? No, when we argue that on pain of vicious regress, there must be a first member of some series, we are not analyzing *what* that first member is. We are only arguing *that* it must exist. Nor are we necessarily defining or analyzing the series, or the rest of the members of the series, in terms of the first member. This is very clear in Russellian mathematics. Russell does not define the negative integers in terms of -1, nor does he define the series of proper fractions that starts with ½ and progressively diminishes by half in terms of ½. Instead, he defines all negative integers across the board, and all fractions across the board, in terms of the cardinal numbers (IMP 64). And what can we call analysis in the other regresses? Suppose we start from the causes we find around us now and successfully argue back to a first cause, an uncaused cause. Of course we have not analyzed the first cause itself. We have only argued that it must exist, given the causes we find around us. But what then have we analyzed—the causes we find around us? What have we learned about their nature, other than that they require a first cause? Or have we analyzed the causal series from them back to the first cause, or perhaps the general nature of a causal series? But in giving his vicious regress of resemblances argument, Russell *is* giving a logical analysis of statements about ordinary properties in terms of universals as opposed to resemblances. And in giving his vicious regress of appearances argument, he *is* analyzing the nature of appearances qua appearances, at least as genuine as opposed to false. And when he asks whether analysis may be endless, this does concern the nature of logical analysis.

(C6) Similarity (V6) arguably begs the question. If Russell says that analysis may be endless, then he is not making but rejecting the vicious regress argument that there must be simples.

(C7) I have been skipping about Russell's whole lifetime of philosophy here. There is no one work in which he holds all of the views I attribute to him in this section. But nonetheless, I think that my temporally composite picture of his views may be fairly helpful.

I have been considering reasons for and against whether Russell should have said that analysis may be endless, based on his own views. I now give my own argument that analysis may be endless, in the zetetic sense of as far as we could ever know.

My argument is an analogical one. I compare the question whether there must be simples if there are complexes to the question whether the decimal expansion of pi contains three 7's in succession, granting the expansion is endless. Wittgenstein made this question famous in analytic philosophy (PI #352 using 7777, at least in Anscombe's edition), and uses it as the basis of a criticism of Russell's view that it is theoretically possible to show that "777" exists somewhere in the expansion without being able to specify where, i.e., without being able to produce an actual example (RFM 185 / V #34 using 777). Wittgenstein does not cite the origin of the 777 example in either of these works, nor does he mention that the example can be used to support both sides of the question of realism, and more generally of objective truth, in mathematics. (On Russell's logical fictionalism, mathematics is still objectively true). The result is that whole books have been written on Wittgenstein, and specifically on his philosophy of mathematics, which do not mention these things either. Thus Wittgenstein and at least some of his scholars create the impression that the example is Wittgenstein's and that it definitely supports Wittgenstein's philosophy of mathematics.

Russell says in at least two works that the question whether the decimal expansion of pi contains "777" is a "stock example" of Brouwer's school of mathematical intuitionism, which uses it to try to show that the law of excluded middle, in its semantic version that every "syntactically significant" statement is true or false, is false (HK 142; MPD 82). George Pitcher says, "In March 1928, Wittgenstein heard...Brouwer...lecture on the foundations of mathematics" (Pitcher 1964: 8). Herbert Feigl, who was there, said this was what inspired Wittgenstein to return to philosophy (Pitcher 1964: 8 n.8), though not everyone in the literature agrees. Whether Wittgenstein learned about pi examples from Brouwer or someone else at the lecture, or already knew about them years ago, I leave to the reader to inquire. Brouwer used pi-type examples as early as 1923 (Brouwer / 1923: 337, "0123456789") and 1908 (Brouwer 1975 / 1908: 110, two different sorts of examples involving the expansion of pi). But Dirk van Dalen says, "The use Wittgenstein makes of the decimal expansion of π is closer to Borel's examples" (Dalen 2013: 519).

The "777" example is no longer a good one. Robert Clark says that "'777'...certainly does occur in the decimal expansion of PI—quite early, in fact" (Clark 1998). I am not sure what counts as "early" in an infinite expansion (isn't it everything?), but it seems the question is closed. If so, we may use "777777" or any number of other examples instead. No particular importance attaches to decimal expansions of pi. Goldbach's conjecture, or any other open question in mathematics about the occurrence or non-occurrence of something in an infinite series, would do just as well. I myself will simply pretend the "777" example is still good for the sake of the argument.

The issue is this. We know "777" occurs in the expansion of pi if we actually find it; but if we do not in fact find it, we may not be able to show whether or not it occurs, since we limited humans cannot carry out an endless expansion.

The analogy is of 777 to simples. By analogy, then, we can show that simple entities exist if we actually arrive at them in our logical analysis; but if we do not in fact find them, then we may not be able to show whether or not there are any, since we cannot carry out an endless analysis. Of course, this assumes there is a test of (or argument for) the simplicity of a thing independently of *our* being unable to define that thing. But I think an independent test is required anyway, so as to resolve the main issue of whether complexes must ultimately be composed of simples, unless we are simply to *assume* that there must be simples if there are complexes. The assumption is very plausible. Many have found it intuitively correct *simpliciter*. But we would like to prove it if we can. Should we then take it as an unproved and perhaps unprovable *axiom*? The issue is, of course, an instance of the more general question of how to tell whether an infinite regress is benign or vicious. For we could show that there must be simples if there are complexes only if we could show that an infinite regress of analyses, or perhaps better, an infinite regress of *more complex* things' being composed of *less complex* things, is vicious.—But if we cannot show that, should we take it as an axiom that complexes entail simples? I would suggest that calling something an axiom, i.e., a logically primitive necessary truth, does not make it so.

The conclusion of my argument is that just as 777 may or may not occur in the decimal expansion of pi, so there may or may not be simples. The "may" is zetetic, i.e., as far as we can know.

I will consider one objection to my argument. I have argued that for Russell, the argument that there are complexes, therefore there are simples is best classified as of the genuinely vicious sort; but that while he initially accepted it as sound, he came to reject it as unsound, so that he no longer held that its conclusion is known to be true. (He found no other way to know that.) But no one is arguing that 777 is or must be a first member of the pi series that stops a regress. For the decimal expansion of pi is a benign infinite series. There need not be a last number. In fact, it appears that there is and can be no last number. And while flipping the series would give it a necessary first member, namely the 1 in 3.14159..., my analogy was to the unflipped series. My reply is that this is a genuine difference, but not a difference relevant to my argument. Why would it be relevant? I was only concerned with whether we might ever know whether 777 appeared *in* the series. I waive the reply that even a vicious finite number series might be so long that we could never tell within human history whether 777 occurs in it, since that reply fails to concern the principle of the thing. The relevant comparison is simply that just as 777 may or may not occur, so simples may or may not occur.

I shall now offer an argument that analysis might *not* be endless. The argument is perhaps too easy, but it might succeed. All the benign regresses, i.e., all the regresses that are provably endless, are essentially defined or definable by mathematical induction. But no vicious, and not even any problematic regress, is so defined or definable, for otherwise it would be benign. They are not defined by performing some specific, definitive operation over and over again, first on some initial member, and then on each successor, so as to specify and define exactly what each successor is and must be. Instead, they merely require that there be *some* further stage, *whatever* it might be. For example, the benign regress of negative numbers logically requires that the series logically must go -1, -2, -3, and so on. There is no other way the series can go, no other way it can be, since it is defined by its defining mathematical induction. But the problematic regress of the first cause argument for God merely requires that every event have *some* cause, whatever it may be. We might playfully describe the difference *á la* Donnellan by calling benign regresses "referential" and problematic or vicious regresses "attributive." Now, the thesis that analysis may be endless is not defined by mathematical induction, and cannot be. For if it were, it would be definably, provably benign. More deeply and more to the point, each further level of analysis would be a defined successor, and we could prove in advance not only that it exists, but *exactly what it is*, just as we can prove that not only that a successor to -1 exists in the series of negative numbers, but that it is specifically, and can only be, -2. But in logical analysis, we cannot simply stipulate every next level of analysis in advance by referring back to some initial principle of mathematical induction that defines the whole series of analyses. There is no royal road to philosophy, and no royal road to logical analysis. At least, I can see no magical pill of mathematical induction here. The best we could hope for is to discover some common principle after all the logical analyses have been given. Anything else would beg the question as to what the right principle is. Therefore the analysis regress is not provably benign. Therefore it may have an end.

The argument is perhaps too easy, because it simply assumes that all benign regresses are mathematically inductive. If "benign" simply means good, safe, or (what is the same here) endless, this assumption would be a synthetic *a priori* truth at best, and might not be a truth at all. I am not sure what a proof of the assumption would even be like. But this point might be moot. I was only arguing that the analysis regress is not *provably* benign. It may still *be* benign. The question then devolves to whether there is some *other* way that the analysis regress is provably benign. And I see no other way.

It is, in a certain sense, hard to prove that there are *not* any simple entities. I myself would generalize a very perceptive remark by Kripke in another context, parenthetically rewriting it to say the following:

> Perhaps we may try to [argue] that [a certain ostensible simple entity] is even more *sui generis* than we have argued before. Perhaps it is simply a primitive [entity], not to be assimilated to [any other entities], but a[n entity] of a unique kind of its own.
> Such a move may be in a sense irrefutable, and if it is taken in an appropriate way [one] may even accept it. But it seems desperate: it leaves the nature of this postulated primitive [entity] completely mysterious. (Kripke 1982: 51, Kripke's italics)

I take this to apply to every area of philosophy across the board. In this sense, I find it hard to show that there are *not* any simple logical entities, ethical entities, aesthetic entities, mental entities, physical entities, and so on. But it may be hard to say *which* entities they are even if we have a list to choose from, such as the logical operators, which are multiply interdefinable, and are all definable in terms of truth-values. So, is it truth-values? Or are *they* definable? But even if we cannot prove there are no simples, analysis logically can still be endless. For to infer that there are simples from the fact that we cannot prove there are none is to commit the fallacy of ignorance.

If arguments and analogies fail to determine the benignity or viciousness of a controversial regress, the question devolves to our *sui generis* simple direct logical intuition of whether the regress is benign or vicious. And our logical intuitions can differ. Without an independent check, we cannot even confirm the plain difference between "It is impossible for me to see that *P*" and "I see that it is impossible that *P*." For more on infinite divisibility, see my brief discussion of infinitesimals in the next chapter, and my (1989).

This concludes my discussion of whether there logically must be simple entities, or whether logical analysis logically can be endless, and of how Russell ought to handle this question based on his own views on regresses. Again, our interest in this general topic lies specifically in whether notions such as deducibility, truth in virtue of logical form, and tautology must be accepted, if at all, as primitive, inexplicable notions, or whether they can be logically analyzed. Russell's final answer is that "the whole question...is unnecessary" (MPD 123).

Wittgenstein's Impact on Russell on Relevance: Relevance in Russell's Introduction to the *Tractatus*

Russell's most famous express endorsement of deductive inference as following from and as truth-ground containment is, of course, in his introduction to Wittgenstein's *Tractatus*. He says:

> [W]e arrive at an amazing simplification of the theory of inference....Wittgenstein is enabled to assert that...if p **follows from** *q* the meaning of *p* is **contained in** the meaning of *q,* from which of course it results that nothing can be **deduced from** an atomic proposition [except itself]. All the propositions of logic, he maintains, are tautologies, such as '*p* or not-*p*'. (T: xvi, my boldface emphasis)

Russell is clearly aware that truth-tables are diagrams that logically analyze *following from* as tautological truth-ground containment. See T 5.101, 5.12, 5.121. 5.122. 5.132. All that is missing is our *word* for this today, "relevance."

For Wittgenstein, truth-functional deducibility is both a containment and a relevance relation. Wittgenstein says:

> T 5.101....I will give the name *truth-grounds* of a proposition to those truth-possibilities of its truth-arguments that make it true.
> T 5.11 If all the truth-grounds that are common to a number of propositions are at the same time truth-grounds of a certain proposition, then we say that the truth of that proposition **follows from** the truth of the others.
> T 5.12 In particular, the truth of a proposition '*p*' **follows from** the truth of another proposition '*q*' if all the truth-grounds of the latter are truth-grounds of the former.
> T 5.121 The truth-grounds of the one are **contained in** those of the other: *p* **follows from** *q*.
> T 5.122 If *p* **follows from** *q*, the sense of '*p*' is **contained in** the sense of '*q*'.
> T 5.132 If *p* **follows from** *q*, I can make an inference **from** *q* to *p*, **deduce** *p* **from** *q*.

T 5.133 All **deductions** are made *a priori*. (Wittgenstein's italic emphasis, my boldface emphasis)

All this is a revealing gloss on Russell as well, since this is just the view he is endorsing in his Introduction to the *Tractatus*.

The chief question of interpretation is whether Wittgenstein is saying there is truth-ground containment and following from if and only if (1) *all* truth-grounds of the premiss are contained in the truth-grounds of the conclusion in the Aristotelian sense of "all," in which there is at least one truth-ground of the premiss (this is called the existent import of the Aristotelian "all"); or else (2) *if* there are *any* truth-grounds of the premiss, then they are contained in the truth-grounds of the conclusion (this is called the modern classical "any," which lacks existential import); or else (3), where there is more than one premiss, there is at least one row of the truth-table on which all the premisses are true, and on any such rows, all the truth-grounds are contained in the truth-grounds of the conclusion; or else (4) where there is more than one premiss, if there are any such rows, then their truth-grounds are contained in the truth-grounds of the conclusion.

On interpretation (1), the sole premiss is logically possible, since it is true on at least one row of the truth-table.

On interpretation (2), the sole premiss can be logically impossible, since it can be false on all rows.

On interpretation (3), the premisses are compossible, since there is at least one row on which they are all true.

On interpretation (4), the premisses can be incompossible, since there need not be a row on which they are all true.

Interpretations (1) and (3) go hand in hand. Interpretations (2) and (4) go hand in hand. In fact, (3) and (4) are redundant, since we can rewrite any finite number of premisses as a single premiss which conjoins them. So let us discuss just (1) and (2).

The chief importance of distinguishing interpretations (1) and (2) is that (1) imposes a possibility constraint on the proof. That is, in order for a conclusion to follow, it must be logically possible that the premiss be true. However, the premiss can be actually false; and the truth-table for material implication guarantees that any conclusion follows from a false premiss. This is called ex falso quodlibet sequitur, or from a false premiss everything follows. In modern terms, this is one of the paradoxes of material implication. But (2) does not impose a possibility constraint. For (2) allows conclusions to follow from a logically impossible premiss. This is ex impossibile quodlibet sequitur, or from an impossible premiss everything follows. But the way truth-tables are set up, it is more precisely ex contradictione quodlibet, or from a contradiction everything follows. In any case, in modern terms, this is one of the paradoxes of strict implication.

We cannot tell from the texts we have quoted so far which interpretation, (1) or (2), is best. But other texts make it clear that Wittgenstein accepts ex contradictione, and this implies that (2) is correct, at least on a principle of charity in interpretation, meaning that we charitably assume that the *Tractatus* is self-consistent. That said, Wittgenstein never actually argues from false or impossible premisses, and to that extent we may say that his concept of truth-ground containment as following from merely concerns validity, or more precisely what Russell would call deducibility due to logical form, where the logical form is shown by the truth-table. And to the same extent we may also say that in practice, Wittgenstein imposes the truth and the soundness constraints on his actual proofs. The one caveat to this might be that he seems to consider the whole book as an argument from nonsensical sentences to a mystical point of view that cannot be stated in language. This is where his famous "ladder" metaphor comes in. We climb the ladder of his book up to the new point of view; but the new point of view cannot be said, and this includes discarding the ladder as part of what cannot be said. I see this as a different kind of issue altogether. For Wittgenstein is not at all saying that from a nonsensical sentence, everything (that makes sense) follows. He is saying at most that from nonsense, nonsense follows. And he is not even saying that. For nonsensical statements cannot be assigned truth-tables, since they have no truth-values. And he cannot speak of truth-ground containment or following from except in terms of truth-tables. Therefore there is no ex absurdum (or ex nugarum) quodlibet for him.

Wittgenstein's treatment of deducibility suggests a way to embrace the paradoxes of strict implication. Namely, in terms of truth-functional containment, impossible antecedents may be said to contain everything and necessary consequents contain nothing. As Irving M. Copi says, "So the correct answer to the question, 'What happens when an irresistible force meets an immovable object?' is 'Everything!'" (Copi 1978: 335).[4] Prior adds:

> E. J. Nelson argues that 'entailment', i.e. the converse of 'following from', must consist in a definite inner connexion between antecedent and consequent, and cannot be present through some peculiarity (necessity, impossibility, truth, falsehood) attaching to either proposition alone. (For some reason he does not consider the possibility that what Lewis's paradoxes show is precisely that necessary and impossible propositions as such *have* a definite inner connexion with all propositions whatever.) (Prior 1955: 196)

Wittgenstein argues that the "definite inner connexion" described by Prior actually exists:

> T 5.142 A tautology **follows from** all propositions: it says nothing.
> T 5.143 Contradiction is that **common factor** of propositions which *no* proposition has in common with another. Tautology is the **common factor** of all propositions that have nothing in common with one another.
>   Contradiction, one might say, vanishes **outside** all propositions: tautology vanishes **inside** them.
>   Contradiction is the **outer limit** of propositions: tautology is the unsubstantial point at their **centre**.
> (Wittgenstein's italic emphasis, my boldface emphasis)

The inner connection in either case is just the common factor. It is common knowledge that a tautology says nothing about the world. We do not need to look out the window to see whether "Either it is raining or it is not" is true. And a person willing to affirm a contradiction would seem willing to affirm anything and everything.

Thus I agree with Richard M. McDonough that Wittgenstein "anticipates" the relevantists even while remaining a modern classical logician (McDonough 1986: 89; 264–65 n.5). McDonough speaks of ex falso (McDonough 1986: 264 n.5), but his argument is really about ex contradictione quodlibet:

> Wittgenstein is making a point about the nature, not challenging the existence, of the "proof."....[H]e is only saying that this "proof" must be conceived differently from the proof of a genuine proposition by means of logic.
>   Strictly speaking, nothing is proved in the "proof" that anything follows from a contradiction ....One has only, in a mechanical manipulation of signs, shown that '(P & not-P) ⊃ Q' is a tautology. (McDonough 1986: 93)

Thus there are two levels to interpreting Wittgenstein here. On the shallower level, Wittgenstein would agree that P & $\neg P$, therefore Q, is valid for any old Q, and in this sense would admit that a contradiction entails *everything*. But on the deeper level, he would say that a contradiction entails *nothing*, since $(P$ & $\neg P) \supset Q$ is a mere play of symbols, an empty tautology that says nothing about the world. That is, in tautologies and contradictions alike, the logical symbols are not playing the role they play in logically contingent statements. They are not functioning to help formulate contingent statements about the world, but are emptily interacting only with each other. Thus on the deeper level, ex contradictione nihil sequitur (nothing follows from a contradiction) precisely because a contradiction is nothing, and de nihilo nihil fit (nothing follows from nothing). McDonough has an excellent and extensive scholarly argument which I cannot describe here (McDonough 1986: ch. 2–4; see especially ch. 3; compare Ramsey 1931: 12).

Gregory Landini beautifully adds:

> Wittgenstein writes that "tautologies and contradictions show that they say nothing"; they "lack sense" but are "part of the symbolism" (TLP 4.461). Venn's propositional diagrams nicely illustrate Wittgenstein's ideas. In a logically perfect language the status of an expression as tautologous, contradictory, or contingent is built into (shown by) the syntactic conditions for the representation of genuine assertions. A propositional tautology shades nothing, and contingencies shade some but not all areas. In Venn diagrams, tautologies and propositions are not genuine statements. A genuine statement is made by shading some, but not all, areas of the diagram. All tautologies have nothing shaded; they are just the overlapping circles—the scaffolding. [And all contradictions shade everything. "P & $\neg P$" shades the P-area and also all not-P areas.] Indeed, in Venn's propositional diagrams, [all] formulas that are logically equivalent have exactly one and the same representation. (Landini 2007: 123; see ch. 4 generally)

This ties modern classical logic in general, and the early Wittgenstein in particular, with traditional geometrical diagrams. Landini shows that and how everything follows from a contradiction, and that and how a tautology follows from everything, with visible representation of the truth-ground containments in Venn diagrams.

In slightly different language, we use Venn diagrams to represent a necessary statement by *not* marking any circles in any way. Thus, in diagramming any statement, all necessary statements are, in effect, already diagrammed in advance, even before we diagram the statement in question. It is in this sense that any statement visibly contains all tautologies, since the "scaffolding," i.e., the Venn circles themselves, are just as visible as any shadings of them. We represent a self-contradictory statement by shading all areas of all circles. In this way, where "P and not-P" is the contradiction, we shade both the "P" area and all not-P areas. And where shading is saying, this is just how to say a contradiction is, in effect, already to say everything. To sum up, on the whole-part theory of deduction it is plausible to say that for Russell and

Wittgenstein alike, impossible propositions contain the content of all propositions, and necessary propositions have no content. Wittgenstein and Russell may be wrong, but their view is far from rash or ill-considered, and Anderson and Belnap are wrong to ignore it.[5]

Anderson and Belnap miss that Wittgenstein's analysis is all about logical relevance in a purely extensional sense of containment. Truth-grounds are just those assignments of truth-possibilities that make a statement true. The various logics of the relevantists merely add various intensional constraints to the extensional genus of modern classical tautological relevance which Wittgenstein reveals.

Truth-tables are just another sort of diagram in which to diagram the premises is already to diagram the conclusion of a valid argument. And we could just as easily use shading and non-shading in place of the letters "T" and "F". Again, Venn diagrams can be and have been used to rewrite truth-tables as expressly geometrical diagrams, so as to show containment of the conclusion (Copi 1978: 207–8; Gardner 1968: 49–50; Prior 1955: 171–72).

Relevance in *Outline*

In 1927, Russell expands his conception of deducibility in an important way. He says in *An Outline of Philosophy*:

> I think we may lay it down that, in mathematics, the conclusion always asserts merely the whole or part of the premises, though usually in new language....We may sum up this discussion by saying that mathematical inference consists in attaching the same reactions to two different groups of signs..., whereas induction consists... in taking something as a sign of something else. (OP 87)

He adds:

> Thus the usual cases of induction and deduction are distinguished by the fact that, in the former, the inference consists in taking one sign as a sign of two different things, while in the latter the inference consists in taking two different signs as signs of the same thing. (OP 90)

Relevance in *The Analysis of Matter*

In the same year, Russell elaborates on this new conception in *The Analysis of Matter*:

> [A]n analytic proposition [is] one whose truth could be known by means of logic alone....We must ask ourselves, therefore: What is the common quality of the propositions which can be deduced from the premisses of logic?
>
> The answer to this question given by Wittgenstein in the *Tractatus Logico-Philosophicus* seems to me the right one. Propositions which form part of logic, or can be proved by logic, are all *tautologies*—i.e. they show that certain different sets of symbols are different ways of saying the same thing, or that one set says part of what the other says....
>
> I accept the view, therefore, that some propositions are tautologies and some are not, and I regard this as the distinction underlying the old distinction of analytic and synthetic propositions. It is obvious that a proposition which is a tautology is so in virtue of its form, and that any constants which it may contain can be turned into variables without impairing its tautological quality. (AMA 171–72; see 199)

This breath-taking passage equates five things: formal deducibility, analytic consequence, tautological inference, inference in virtue of logical form, and a whole-part containment theory of deductive inference on which the conclusion of a valid argument says all or part of what the premises say, but in different language. The whole logicist theory that logic and mathematics are identical (POM v, vi), that mathematics can be deduced from logic, is clarified by this quintuple equation. For now the idea is simply that mathematics says all or part of what logic says, though in different language.

My only quibble is that on this view, $A \supset A$ is not a tautology, since it fails to say the same thing in different ways, and since A does not say part of what A says, but all of what A says. I think this is simply an oversight on Russell's part. I think saying a thing is part of itself, though not a proper sub-part, would be too cheap a gloss. But there is a dispute about $A \supset A$ in the literature. Some hold that $A \supset A$ is not a genuine inference and *should* be ruled out. Strawson says that repetition is not reasoning (Strawson 1985: 15). But Anderson and Belnap find $A \supset A$ trivially correct, and would be in big trouble with their own definition of tautological entailment if they did not; they also discuss Strawson (Anderson 1975: 7–8). But the quibble here is only that $A \supset A$ is a tautology in the *Tractatus*, and therefore is or ought to be for the later Russell. In what follows, when I speak of whole-part truth-ground containment, this is to be understood as including $A \supset A$ as well.

Later in *The Analysis of Matter*, Russell says, "On grounds of logic, I hold that nothing existent can imply any other existent except a part of itself, if implication is taken in the sense of what Professor C. I. Lewis calls 'strict implication', which is the relevant sense for our present discussion" (AMA 199–200). Here Russell is not only admitting that deducibility is strict implication in Lewis's sense, but is also implying that strict implication is a whole-part containment relation. There should be no doubt that Russell is talking about deducibility when he speaks of logic.

Relevance in the Second Edition of *Principles*

In 1938, in his introduction to the second edition of *Principles*, Russell says:

> In order that a proposition may belong to mathematics it must have a further property: according to some it must be "tautological," and according to Carnap it must be "analytic." It is by no means easy to get an exact definition of this characteristic... (POM ix)

As we saw a few pages ago when we discussed *Introduction*, this is not a problem that Russell thinks we need to be concerned with. The natural suggestion, again, is to define tautology or analytic truth as truth in virtue of logical form. However, Russell indicates in effect that this would only postpone the problem to defining truth in virtue of logical form. For he says a few pages later:

> The fundamental characteristic of logic, obviously, is that which is indicated when we say that logical propositions are true in virtue of their form....It seems to me that [any candidates for axiom status, such as the multiplicative axiom or the axiom of infinity,] either do, or do not, have the characteristic of formal truth which characterizes logic, and that in the former event every logic must include them, while in the latter every logic must exclude them. I confess, however, that I am unable to give any clear account of what is meant by saying that a proposition is "true in virtue of its form." But this phrase, inadequate as it is, points, I think, to the problem which must be solved if an adequate definition of logic is to be found. (POM xii)

This is also in effect Russell's take on the contemporary problem of universal logic. For the problem of what is universal to all logics worthy of the name boils down to the problem of defining what a logic is. And it is very reasonable to think that Russell's phrase "'true in virtue of its form'....points" not only to the problem, but to its solution. Indeed, if truth in virtue of logical form is indefinable, then Russell (or Wittgenstein) has already *found* the solution, at least as far as a solution can be found.

Landini says, "Interestingly, Russell does not endorse Wittgenstein's notion of tautologyhood in the introduction to the second edition of *The Principles of Mathematics* (1937)" (Landini 2007: 111). (The second edition appeared in 1938, not 1937.) I think this is triply confused.

First, Landini says that Russell's notion of tautology and Wittgenstein's are not exactly the same: "the agreement is more appearance than substance" (Landini 2007: 112). Thus Russell might be discussing his *own* notion of tautology, wherever he does not mention Wittgenstein.

Second, Russell *is* endorsing that there is a *property* of logical truths, a property which some *call* tautology and others analyticity. Once again, but adding italics to show the point, Russell says in this 1938 introduction, "In order that a proposition may belong to mathematics it *must* have a further *property*: according to some it must be 'tautological', and according to Carnap it must be 'analytic'.\" It is by no means easy to get an exact definition of *this characteristic*" (POM ix, my italics. Thus if it seems that Russell is *not* endorsing tautology, then the seeming is "more appearance than substance," where the appearance is the *description* of the property as tautology and the substance is the *property* itself. I have already discussed such texts at length earlier in this book.

Third, if what I have said is right so far, then there is a third confusion. For when Russell says, "according to some it must be 'tautological'" (POM ix), to whom is he referring by "some," if not to Wittgenstein? This it appears he is endorsing Wittgenstein after all. I mean that he is endorsing the substance (the property Wittgenstein is after), if not the appearance (Wittgenstein's description of this property).

And surely Landini does not mean to say that Russell stops endorsing *tautology* in 1938 (1937 per Landini): Russell endorses tautology in *Inquiry* (1940), *Human Knowledge* (1948), and *My Philosophical Development* (1959).

Relevance in *Inquiry, Human Knowledge,* and *My Philosophical Development*

In his 1940 *Inquiry*, Russell holds a whole-part "theory of analytic inference. An inference is defined as analytic when the conclusion is part of the premisses" (IMT 242). In effect, Russell explains this theory "in terms of the principle that it is never possible to deduce the existence of something from the existence of something else" (AMA 286; see 286–87). Thus he still holds that deducibility is a whole-part containment relation.

In his 1948 *Human Knowledge*, Russell says, "Nothing but tautologies can be known independently of experience" (HK 345). He says, "Tautologies are primarily relations between properties, not between the things that have the properties" (HK 138). Tautology plays brief but important roles in the book (HK 138–39, 375) and is listed in the index.

In his 1959 *My Philosophical Development*, Russell says:

> Wittgenstein maintains that logic consists wholly of tautologies. I think he is right in this, though I did not think so until I had read what he had to say on the subject. (MPD 88)

While Landini (2007: 112) might still argue that Russell did not *understand* "what [Wittgenstein] had to say on the subject" (MPD 88), it is clear that the 1959 Russell is giving a ringing endorsement not only of the theory that logical truth is *tautology*, but also of what he *thinks* is Wittgenstein's view of tautology. And who knows on what level of generality Russell's endorsement of Wittgenstein on tautology might be?

Russell says more fully:

> Wittgenstein maintains that logic consists wholly of tautologies. I think he is right in this....There is another point connected with this which is very important, and that is that all atomic propositions are mutually independent. It used to be thought that one fact could be logically dependent upon another. This can only be the case if one of the facts is really two facts put together. From 'A and B are men' it follows logically that A is a man, but that is because 'A and B are men' is really two propositions put together. (MPD 88–89)

Thus the 1959 Russell finds tautology "connected with" the whole-part containment theory of deduction. Exactly as he did in the 1927 *Analysis of Matter*, he ties truth-ground containment entailment to truth-functional tautology—exactly as he should. For entailment is just tautology in the case of arguments and conditional statements.

The emerging picture is that Russell connects tautology with truth-ground containment deductive inference in eight major published works from 1922 to 1959. As just reviewed, they include his Introduction to the *Tractatus* (1922), *An Introduction to Philosophy* (1927), *The Analysis of Matter* (1927), Introduction to the second edition of *Principia* (1927), the *Inquiry* (1940, *Human Knowledge* (1948), and *My Philosophical Development* (1959).

This concludes my chronological review of Russell on deductive relevance. It appears that Anderson and Belnap have not read a single major work of Russell's on deductive inference as truth-ground containment tautological entailment. Or if they have, they have not offered a single discussion of Russell on the subject. Nor do they discuss *true* material implication or *always true* formal implication. All they discuss is unfiltered, unconstrained material implication, as if Russell thought material implication were the same thing as deducibility. Again, they seem unaware that for Wittgenstein, a mere material implication as such (not: *true* material implication), far from equating to a deductively valid inference, has only a 75% purely logical probability of being true, since it is true on only three of the four rows of its truth-table (T 4.464, 5.15–5.156). They overlook not only the truth constraint, but the soundness, epistemic, and pragmatic constraints as well, all of which are hiding in plain sight in Russell's logical writings.

The Concept of Relevance as Containment

The traditional intuitive conception of relevance behind Russell's theory and relevantist theories alike is that the content of the conclusion of a deductively valid argument is "contained" in the contents of its premises. And what could be more of an *inner connection* of logical relevance than Wittgenstein's and Russell's whole-part truth-ground containment relation? Is not the truth-ground part (the conclusion) *within* the truth-ground whole (the premisses)? What could be a greater endorsement of *following from* than to say that the presence of a part follows from the presence of a whole of which it is part? How could Nelson, Wright, and Geach be any more satisfied that Russell is an implicit relevance logician? And if Anderson and Belnap cite Kant's whole-part containment theory of analyticity as their precursor (Anderson 1975: 155), then they should cite Wittgenstein and Russell on truth-grounds as well.

Clearly, premisses' containment of the truth-grounds of the conclusion is an internal relation. And as we saw, Russell does not reject internal relations, but admits external relations in addition to internal relations. He rejects only the view that *all* relations are internal (PE 139–46; see MPD 42).

Even Moore, Russell's friend and colleague, completely misunderstands Russell's deducibility relation. Moore says:

> Mr. Russell, in the *Principles of Mathematics* (p. 34), treats the phrase "*q* can be deduced from *p*" as if it

> meant exactly the same thing as...."*p* materially implies
> *q*"; and has repeated the same error elsewhere, e.g., in
> *Philosophical Essays* (p. 166)....But I imagine that Mr.
> Russell himself would now admit that [this] is simply an
> enormous "howler"; and I do not think that I need spend
> any time in showing that it is so. (Moore 1951: 303–4)

Moore wrote that in 1919. Russell had already given his Deducibility Argument three times, and gave it three times more in 1919.

The containment theory of logical deduction is subject to a famous traditional objection, which is a demand to specify exactly where the content of the conclusion is located in the content of the premises. One stock example is the story that before an expected guest speaker arrives, the priest tells the congregation that the first penitent whose confession he heard as a young priest had confessed to murder. Then the speaker arrives and introduces himself by saying that he was the priest's first penitent. The inference that the guest speaker is a murderer is clear. But where is the content of that conclusion among the contents of the premises? It is not in what the priest said, since then the conclusion could have been inferred from what the priest said alone. Nor is it in what the guest speaker said, for the same reason. But how could it be located in both?

Russell would not have been impressed by this objection any more than Frege would have been (Frege 1974: 100–1), since both allow novelty of description of the content of the premises in the conclusion. Indeed, Frege poses this question himself, and more generally than just for syllogisms. Frege says:

> New propositions must be derived from [the laws of
> number, or any plurality of logically true premises]
> which are not contained in any one of them by itself. *No
> doubt these propositions are in a way contained covertly*
> in the whole set taken together, but this does not absolve
> us from the labour of actually extracting them and setting
> them out in their own right. (FA 23)
>   The truths of arithmetic would then be related
> to those of logic in much the same way as the theorems
> of geometry to the axioms. *Each one would contain
> concentrated within it* a whole series of deductions...
> (FA 24, my emphasis)

Here Frege says twice that he is a containment theorist of logical deduction. But where is the conclusion located in the premises?

The objection is misplaced. The error lies in asking where the *conclusion* is located in the premises. The real issue is where its *truth-grounds* are located. And the truth-table shows exactly where they are located. Their location can also be shown by Venn diagrams. Both propositional logic and quantificational logic can be diagrammed using Venn diagrams. In writing the premisses of any valid argument, we will find that we have already written the conclusion (Copi 1978: 207–8; Gardner 1968: 49–50; Prior 1955: 171–72). We can even see how the conclusion is written, step by step. Whether different premisses are *asserted* by different people is irrelevant.

The relevantists are just as subject to the same objection, and so is any logician. No matter what the logic, if there is more than one premiss to an argument, and if all the premisses are necessary to show validity, then only a person who knows that all the premisses are true can know by means of that argument that the conclusion is true. The point is quite trivial, and it scarcely applies to modern classical logic alone.

Nicholas Griffin objects that "the term 'relevant logic' [now has] a specific meaning" which excludes modern classical logic (Griffin 2001: 293). My reply is that insisting on mere established meanings to settle philosophical issues has all "the advantages of theft over honest toil" (Russell 1919: 71). It begs the question, sweeps the issues under a definitional rug, and closes the mind. Griffin is simply refusing to permit any new advances in the study of relevance. Many other obsolete meanings were once thought to be well settled too, for example, that physical matter is corpuscular in Newton's sense. This ironically puts Griffin on the wrong side of his own Newton comparison (2001: 293). It is Anderson and Belnap's atomic statements that equate to Newton's corpuscles. People like Griffin once refused to reclassify whales as mammals because it was well settled that the term "whale" meant 'big fish (with whale differentiae)', which excludes mammals. Closer to home, Griffin has placed himself in the position of traditionalists who believed logic was final and complete in Aristotle. For Griffin is implying that the concept of relevance has been made final and complete by some recent relevantists. But like all formal sciences, and science in general, relevance moves on.

What really matters is not which definition is given earlier or later in time, but which definition is best. We can stipulate how we use the word "relevant"or "physical" as a verbal convention, but we cannot stipulate the best answer to a philosophical or scientific question. Nor should we judge a term incorrectly used merely because it becomes broader or narrower in scope than what is now the convention.

Griffin rejects my view merely because it makes modern classical logic a relevance logic (2001: 293). The truth is that if our concepts improve, then our classifications improve, and our terms change in meaning and scope. Indeed, as our definitions change, synthetic sentences can even become analytic and vice versa (Russell 1976: 139, 247). Is not what we count as belonging to a species relative to our concept of that species? Would we really wish to insist that a whale is a fish merely because "fish" has a conventional meaning, 'finned animal that lives and swims in water'? Yet just as whales can be and have been reclassified as mammals on a deeper conception of what a mammal is and what a fish is, so too modern classical logic can be reclassified as relevant on a deeper conception of what relevance is.[6]

In contrast to Griffin, Igor Sedlár says, in his review of my book, *The Concept of Relevance and the Logic Diagram Tradition*: "Yes, classical validity can be seen as invoking a...notion of containment—containment of truth-grounds. Yes, this notion can be found in the writings of outstanding modern classical logicians such as Wittgenstein or Russell. Yes, the relevantist's notion of relevance...can be seen as a species of a broader genus[, namely, truth-ground containment]...I do not think that relevance logicians will find much to argue against" (Sedlár 2014: 130).

Relevance and the History of Logic Diagrams

I have suggested that truth-ground containment is relevant containment. I have also noted that this can be shown by diagrams. Venn-style diagrams can be and have been used to diagram modern classical logic. And truth-tables are themselves diagrams.

My basic argument that modern classical logic is relevant is this. 1. If the premisses of an argument contain its conclusion, then the argument is relevantly valid. 2. If in the very act of diagramming all the premisses of an argument we also diagram its conclusion, then the premisses contain the conclusion. 3. Modus ponens, disjunctive syllogism, and many other arguments that violate Anderson-Belnap variable sharing can be and have been so diagrammed; and likewise for modern classical logic in general. 4. Therefore such arguments are relevantly valid; and likewise for modern classical logic in general.

This argument may seem decisive; see my (2012) for an extended discussion devoting a chapter to discussing each premiss. But the history of logic diagrams may help illuminate things further.

The diagram test of entailment has a long history behind it, ironically very much in keeping with Anderson's and Belnap's own view that the "notion of relevance was central to logic from the time of Aristotle" (Anderson 1975: xxi).

John Venn's famous circular diagrams have antecedents in the circular diagrams of Leonhard Euler (1707–83), G. W. Leibniz (1646–1716), J. C. Sturm (1661), and Alstedius (1614). Hundreds of geometrical diagrams of other sorts—squares, circles, triangles, parallelograms, angles, lines—have been used to depict the deductive validity of arguments by W. S. Jevons (1835–82), Augustus De Morgan (1806–71), Johann Heinrich Lambert (1728–77), Immanuel Kant (1724–1804), Gottfried Plouquet (1759), Joachim Lange (1712), R. Sanderson (1680), Petrus Tartaretus (1581), Ludovicus (Juan Luis) Vives (1555), and Alexander of Aphrodisias (Alexander Aphrodisiensus, fl. 200 A.D.); this is not to mention allied geometrical usages such as the *Ars Magna* of Ramon Llull, the Tree of Porphyry, and Aristotle's Square of Opposition (Venn 1971: 504–27; Prior 1955: 108–9, 127–31, 156; Bocheński 1961: 259–62, 272).[7] Leibniz and Kant both have subject-contains-predicate containment tests of analytic truth. Kant's second test, that the denial of the proposition leads to contradiction, arguably was meant to come to the same thing *via* an eliminable double negation after the subject is analyzed, with the first test being the basis or explanation of the second. I find that intrinsically plausible because surely Kant did not intend his two tests to have different results. Yet I recall no Kant scholar who even suggests the idea. Contemporary literature on necessary truth assigns the second test a life of its own (Sumner 1969: 7; Pap 1958: Glossary), no doubt due to the Frege-Russell expansion of logic.

Charles Sanders Peirce is a prolific diagrammer who considers his "logical graphs" to be his "greatest contribution to logic" (Peirce 1886: v; see 293–470). He considers logical diagrams or their "equivalent" necessary to human reasoning:

> Every addition or improvement to our knowledge, of whatsoever kind, comes from an exercize [sic] of our powers of perception. In necessary inference my observation is directed to a creation of my own imagination, a sort of diagram or image on which are portrayed the facts given in the premises; and the observation consists in recognizing relations between the parts of this diagram which were not noticed in constructing it. Different persons no doubt construct their logical diagrams in different ways; many probably very oddly; but every person must construct some kind of diagram or its equivalent, or he could not perform necessary reasoning, at all. It is a part of the business of logic to teach useful ways of constructing such diagrams. (Peirce 1886: 331)

Peirce also believes that any logical reasoning can be diagrammed. He says, "Come on, my Reader, and let us construct a diagram to illustrate the general course of thought; I mean a System of diagrammatization by means of which any course of thought can be represented with exactitude" (Peirce 1933: 411). I find the thesis that diagrams are necessary to reasoning not confirmed by my own introspection, and in fact phenomenologically false. And I find that the thesis that all reasoning can be diagrammed remains to be established in detail. Perhaps it can never be established in detail, since a new form of reasoning might always be just around the corner. In fact, it may sometimes be misleading, constraining, or even dangerous to represent reasoning by a diagram (Shimojima 1996: 527–40, enlarging on Jon Barwise and John Etchemendy). The whole preface to the second edition of Kant's *Critique of Pure Reason* is a warning against the use of concrete illustrations to guide our abstract reasoning (Kant 1965 / 1787: 17–37). But I presume this does not include logic diagrams, since Kant himself uses them to represent logical inference forms (Kant 1988 / 1800), and since logic diagrams that illustrate logical arguments are not exactly empirical objects that illustrate metaphysical theories. My own thesis here is only that valid diagrammability is a logically sufficient condition of logical relevance. However, I find it plausible to suppose that "ugly diagrams" are a criterion of inference failure (Lucas 1990). And while diagramming has been distinguished from visualizing on the ground that diagrams are always determinate while visualizing is often vague on details (Giaquinto 1993), I have seen many diagrams that are expressly designed to omit details; and arguably that is one of their main functions.

Since geometry is synthetic and logic is analytic for Kant, is a geometrical logic diagram of a logical argument a problem for him? No, this oversimplifies Kant on geometry. Kant says in the *Critique of Pure Reason*, "Some few fundamental propositions, presupposed by the geometrician, are, indeed, really analytic, and rest on the principle of contradiction....; for instance,... the whole is equal to itself; or...the whole is greater than its part" (Kant 1965 / 1787: B16–17). Kant repeats the point in the *Prolegomena to Any Future Metaphysics*: "Some other principles, assumed by geometers, are indeed actually analytical...for example...the whole is greater than the part" (Kant 1950 / 1783: 17). This clearly implies that whole-part containments in literally geometrical diagrams of valid logic arguments represent analytic inferences for Kant.

Peirce succeeds in diagramming logically possible worlds:

> The whole range of logical possibility may be represented by an imaginary sheet of paper occupying the whole field of vision. Every point on this sheet is to represent some conceivable state of things, of which the real state of things is one, undistinguished from the rest. Everything learned cuts off and removes from this sheet some part and leaves a range of possibility less than the whole range of logical possibility, but still containing the

unknown point which represents the actual state of things. (Peirce 1886: 331–32)

Peirce also represents each possible world as a separate sheet of paper:

> But in the gamma part of [existential graphs] all the old kinds of signs take new forms....Thus in place of a sheet of assertion, we have a book of separate sheets, tacked together at points, if not otherwise connected. For our alpha sheet, as a whole, represents simply a universe of existent individuals, and the different parts of the sheet represent facts or true assertions made concerning that universe. At the cuts we pass into other areas, areas of conceived propositions which are not realized. In these areas there may be cuts where we pass into worlds which, in the imaginary worlds of the outer cuts, are themselves represented to be imaginary and false, but which may, for all that, be true.... (Peirce 1933: 399; see 400–1)

Thus "Peirce was, in effect, setting up" Evert Willem Beth's semantic tableaux and was anticipating Kripke's semantics for modal logics (Prior 1967b: 548). See chapter 7 for more.

Don D. Roberts's book on Peirce's graphs discusses Peirce on material implication, formal implication, deduction, strict implication, necessity, possibility, modal logic, tautology, truth-functional conditionals, and many other topics (Roberts 1973). Peirce can diagram statements such as $(\neg\Diamond p \to \neg p)$ (Roberts 1973: 83, 108). He has a way to diagram all the sentential modal operators and their iteration (Roberts 1973: 80–86). There are also at least two proofs that "Peirce's system of existential graphs is sound and complete," including a proof by translation into first-order logic by Roberts and a game-theoretic proof by John Sowa (Shin 1994: 186). B. H. Slater amends the graphs and extends the first-order logic proof (B. Slater 1998).

Peirce also discusses the history of diagramming, including Euler, Lambert, Alstedius, Vives, Friedrich Albert Lange, and Venn (Peirce 1933: 294–99). Peirce attributes the word "graph" to his friends W. K. Clifford and J. J. Sylvester (Peirce 1933: 421). Following Lange, Peirce holds that the reason for diagramming arguments is not to establish their validity "—as if anything could be more evident than a syllogism—" but to explain *why* they are valid or not (Peirce 1933: 300). I gloss that as showing by diagrams whether their conclusions are containment-relevant or not. Since this is not a book about Peirce, I will simply say that Peirce seems to have been the most prolific diagrammer of all.

Venn sums up his own history of logic diagrams by saying, "Indeed to anyone accustomed to visualizing geometrical figures it seems likely that Aristotle's [logic] would naturally present itself in the form of closed figures of some kind successively including each other" (Venn 1971: 507). Martin Gardner adds,

> Aristotle's way of classifying syllogisms was to divide them into three "figures" depending on the "width" or "extension" of the middle term (i.e. whether it concerned all or part of its class) as compared with the width of the other terms. Later logicians, classifying syllogisms by the *position* of the middle term, added a fourth figure. (Gardner 1968: 32–33, Gardner's emphasis)

Thus it seems Aristotle represents logical extension and position by geometrical extension and position. The great Aristotle scholar W. D. Ross confirms this:

> [M]uch of Aristotle's terminology in [the doctrine of the syllogism] has a mathematical air—["figure," "distance," used of the proposition,] "boundary," used of the term. It is not unlikely that he represented each figure of the syllogism by a different geometrical figure, in which the lines stood for propositions and the points for terms. (Ross 1960: 36–37)

Ross identifies the specific terminological source as theory of proportion (Ross 1960: 37). Ross notes that Aristotle's only model of a developed science was geometry (Ross 1960: 47). George Englebretsen goes even further:

> We know that Aristotle himself used some kind of diagram system in teaching his syllogistic. This is evident from his vocabulary, if nothing else. He made essential use of (Greek versions of) such terms as "middle," "extreme," "figure," and "term[inus]" (= "end point"). (Englebretsen 1998: 7–8)

Mark Greaves says, "Aristotle himself appears to have employed diagrams, now lost" (Greaves 2002: 116), and cites two "smoking gun" texts from Aristotle in which Aristotle evidently refers to diagrams and to places in diagrams. I shall quote the first text more fully than Greaves does, and I shall also add editor J. L. Ackrill's note 3:

> When three terms have the following mutual relation: the last is wholly within the middle, and the middle is either wholly within or not wholly within the first, there must

> be a perfect syllogism relating the extremes. I call the
> Middle Term the one that is within another and has
> another within it; in the lay-out[3] it has the middle place.
> 3. Clearly a reference to a diagram, now lost. (*Prior
> Analytics* 25*b*36ff. as translated and edited in Aristotle
> 1987: 27; compare Greaves 2002: 116)

I shall quote the second text just as Greaves does, but I shall add
editor Ackrill's note 5:

> [W]hat is predicated of both I call the Middle Term;
> what this is predicated of, the Extremes; the extreme
> lying nearer the middle, the Major Term; the one lying
> further from the middle, the Minor Term. The middle is
> placed outside the terms and first in position.[5]
> 5. This reference is not to logical relations of terms, but
> to their places in some diagram. (*Prior Analytics*
> 26*b*36ff. as translated and edited in Aristotle 1987: 29;
> compare Greaves 2002: 116)

Thus it appears that Aristotle himself uses literally geometrical
diagrams to show visible containment of the conclusion for all of
his syllogisms—including Barbara, which is in effect hypothetical
syllogism, and which Anderson and Belnap must therefore reject.
Greaves offers a reconstruction of Aristotle's diagrams for the first
three figures (Greaves 2002: 117) and cites Kneale (1984 / 1962:
71–72) for further discussion.
    Some say "Aristotle never intended" the syllogism to be
"an instrument of discovery," but "a purely expository and didactic
device which provided an explanation of a conclusion which was
known in advance" (Gaukroger 1989: 31; see 20 citing Barnes
1975: 65–87). This makes sense to me. But I would like to add a
second and deeper reason which is also very Aristotelian. I think
that like Peirce, Aristotle did not use diagrams to prove what is
often already obvious, but to show the "why," that is, to show why
the conclusion follows by showing how it is contained in the
premisses. Of course, both possible motives are mutually consistent
and, in Aristotle, are deeply related. That is because for Aristotle,
the true reason for a thing is the most general reason for that thing;
and this is indicated in a universal major premiss of a syllogism.
    Anderson and Belnap are the ones who insist that logic
from Aristotle to the nineteenth century is relevance logic. But it is
precisely the Aristotelian relevance tradition which represents the
relevance of its entailments by means of diagrams, starting with
Aristotle himself. Thus Anderson and Belnap are in no position to
complain about my diagram test of entailment. It is used by the
very tradition they commend, and by their great hero.

Frege and Russell would accept all of Aristotle's valid syllogisms as a limited part of modern classical logic, and can easily paraphrase the existential import of Aristotle's universal quantifier by using the modern classical universal quantifier together with the existential one.

The theory that the premisses of all deductively valid syllogisms implicitly contain their conclusions was evidently known to Aristotle (Ross 1960: 41, 216), and arguably goes back to Plato's *Meno* (Whately 1851: 269). I imagine that Whately has in mind Plato's theory that *a priori* truths are somehow contained in our soul even if we often do not consciously know a certain *a priori* truth until it is somehow elicited from us, much as we often do not consciously know a certain conclusion even if we already know the premisses; and in that sense the premisses are contained in our soul, even if they are not always contained *a priori* in the *Meno* manner. I imagine that in both cases, what our soul, or what the premisses, contain is much the same: the truth-grounds of the *a priori* truth in *Meno* situations, and the truth-grounds of the *a priori* validity of the conclusion in cases of deductive inference. My compliments to Whately on a very pretty comparison. But I am not sure the comparison is close enough to call the *Meno* the origin of the view that conclusions of valid arguments are in some sense contained in their premisses. For truth is not the same as validity. The premisses of a valid argument need not be true *a priori*, or for that matter, even true at all; and not every truth is conditional (if-then) in form.

John Locke's famous criticism that valid syllogisms contain their conclusions is as follows:

> This way of reasoning discovers no new proofs, but is the art of marshalling and ranging the old ones we have already....Syllogism is, at best, the art of fencing with the little knowledge we have, without making any addition to it. And if a man should employ his reason all this way, he will not do much otherwise than he who, having got some iron out of the bowels of the earth, should have it beaten up all into swords, and put it into his servants' hands to fence with and bang one another. (Locke 1959 / 1690: vol. 2, 401–2)

Since Aristotle evidently did know that the premisses of deductively valid syllogisms implicitly contain their conclusions, this criticism would not have impressed Aristotle in the least. Ironically, Locke's own criticism includes Aristotle's real reason for giving syllogistic. Namely, in battles of the intellect, swords are more useful than iron that is still in the bowels of the earth. And Aristotle's swords are all organized into a classificatory hierarchy for maximum usefulness. This is but a small part of the large case that can be made for the early modern philosophers' simply not understanding the ancient and medieval philosophers very well.

Largely due to Locke, valid syllogisms came to seem so uselessly circular, due to assuming the conclusion in the premises, that in the early nineteenth century Richard Whately is able to speak of implication as *virtual assertion* (Whately 1851: 17, 266). Whately is moved to point out a sense in which syllogisms can be informative in situations like the priest-confessee situation I just described. Whately's own example is that of laborers who dig up a horned fossil skull, where a naturalist "who is not on the spot" knows that "all horned animals are ruminant" (Whately 1851: 266). Neither the laborers nor the naturalist is in a position to infer that this skull is that of a ruminant animal. The conclusion would be a new truth or discovery for all of them. But Whately distinguishes between two senses of "new truth" and "discovery." *Information* concerns new matters of fact not *implied* by anything we knew before, while *instruction* concerns consequences of previous knowledge which never "*struck*" us before (Whately 1851: 268–72). The conclusion would be only instruction, not information, to the laborers and the naturalist considered as a group. Whately gives his own geometric account of the distinction:

> Reasoning has been aptly compared to the piling together blocks of stone; on each of which, as on a pedestal, a man can raise himself a small, and but a small height above the plain; but which, when skilfully built up, will form a flight of steps, which will raise him to a great elevation. Now (to pursue this analogy) when the materials are all ready to the builder's hand, the blocks ready dug and brought, his work resembles...*instruction*: but if his materials are to be entirely, or in part, provided by himself—if he himself is forced to dig fresh blocks from the quarry—this corresponds to the other kind of Discovery. (Whately 1851: 272)

As for Locke's swords and Whately's blocks of stone, so for Venn's diagrams, and for logic diagrams in general. All reveal deductively valid arguments as whole-part containment relations.

Cicero, Sextus Empiricus, Descartes, Locke, Arnauld, Leibniz, Kant, and John Stuart Mill all find that conclusions of valid syllogisms are contained in the premises (my 2012: 123–24, 130–31). Leibniz and Kant find that logical truths, including if-then logical truths, are analytic.

Coming up to Russell's time, William Stanley Jevons uses Eulerian diagrams in his 1870 *Elementary Lessons in Logic* (Jevons 1965 / 1870: 129–33; see 142). Jevons accepts Barbara (Jevons

1965 / 1870: 137, 140, 145), and modus ponens and hypothetical syllogism (Jevons 1965 / 1870: 161–62), and says that inclusive disjunctive syllogism "is always of necessity cogent" (Jevons 1965 / 1870: 166). He also uses line-like long narrow darkened isosceles triangles ("a line thickened towards the subject") (Jevons 1965 / 1870: 188–89). See also his slightly later major logical and scientific work, *The Principles of Science* , where he again accepts Barbara and inclusive disjunctive syllogism (Jevons 1958 / 1877: 55; 77).

In his 1887 *Studies and Exercises in Formal Logic*, John Neville Keynes says, "[I]n the conclusion of every syllogism, 'we repeat less than we are entitled to say', or, if we dare to put it so, 'drop from a complex statement some portion not desired at the moment'" (N. Keynes 1887: 190 twice quoting Alexander Bain as already quoted on his previous page, 189 citing Bain, *Logic, Deduction*). Neville Keynes diagrams propositions first, following Hamilton, Jevons, Venn, and Euler (N. Keynes 1887: 119), and then diagrams syllogisms (N. Keynes 1887: pt. 3, chs.1, 5). Neville Keynes then admits disjunctive syllogism for inclusive disjunctions (N. Keynes 1887: 278–79, and recognizes that it is equivalent to modus ponens (N. Keynes 1887: 280). He accepts modus ponens and finds it analogous to"the categorical syllogism *Barbara*" (N. Keynes 1887: 268, N. Keynes' emphasis). Needless to say, he accepts Barbara and hypothetical syllogism (N. Keynes 1887: 214–15; 265). He diagrams inclusive "*A or B*" using two overlapping and fully shaded circles (N. Keynes 1887 336 n.1). Phyllis Deane says, "The *Formal Logic* proofs were read in full by John Venn....The first signed review was by Venn....Venn's review seemed both authoritative and laudatory" (Deane 2001: 116–17).

Ramsey sums things up nicely:

> In the case of logically conclusive arguments I can accept the account of their validity which has been given by many authorities, and can be found substantially the same in Kant, De Morgan, Peirce and Wittgenstein. All these authors agree that the conclusion of a formally valid argument is contained in its premises; that to deny the conclusion while accepting the premises would be self-contradictory; that a formal deduction does not increase our knowledge, but only brings out clearly what we already know in another form; and that we are bound to accept its validity on pain of being inconsistent with ourselves." (Ramsey 1931: 185)

More could be said about the history, but I think this is enough for our purposes. In effect, Ramsey beautifully supports my view that: (1) Kant's two tests of analyticity (that the subject contains the predicate, and that the denial of the statement leads to self-contradiction) are logically equivalent; (2) the first test is the reason why the second test works; and (3) the tests are also tests of the validity of inferences, where the premiss equates to the subject of an analytic statement, and the conclusion equates to the contained predicate. For obviously, subject *S* contains predicate *P* if and only if "*S* is not *P*" implies the contradiction "*S* is *P* and *S* is not *P*."

In diagramming entailments geometrically, I am not suggesting a geometric semantics, model, or interpretation for logical relevance. Indeed, for my purposes here, it would be enough to make a mere comparison by analogy to diagrams to illuminate the containment aspect of entailments.

Volume 2 of *Entailment* contains a discussion by Alasdair Urquhart of projective geometric models of logic (Anderson 1992: § 65 / Urquhart 1992: 348–75). Urquhart sums up:

> [O]ne of the main aims of this section is to make logicians aware of the rich possibilities offered by the techniques of classical synthetic geometry in the field of relevance logics....
> The connection between projective geometry and relevance logics is both simple and natural, and it makes sense to ask why it was not investigated earlier.
> (Urquhart 1992: 357)

This overlooks the forest for a tree. Per Kant, geometrical diagrams have been used for centuries to show *analytic* whole-part relevant containment. And if Anderson and Belnap are right that their hero Aristotle is relevantist, then "the connection between...geometry and relevance logics" *was* "investigated earlier" by thousands of logicians. It was investigated by every traditional logician who ever used a diagram. This includes the whole crowd of logicians and mathematicians from Peirce and Venn through Euler and Leibniz, all the way back to Alexander of Aphrodisias and Aristotle himself.

Urquhart also overlooks that Frege compares the very objectivity of logic to the duality thesis of projective geometry in *The Foundations of Arithmetic*, where statements split up or carve the objective contents of propositions as easily as maps split up the Atlantic Ocean and the North Sea. For Frege, logically equivalent statements simply split up propositional contents in different ways (TW 46 n.*; see 46–50). Thus for Frege, the contents of premises always contain the contents of valid conclusions; they simply split up the contents differently. And this containment of propositional content is just what makes Frege a relevantist, *pace* Urquhart.

Urquhart also misunderstands classical geometry. Classical geometry is not at all synthetic when it comes to the crucial point for our purposes, whole-part containment. There, classical geometry is analytic, at least according to Kant. As I noted a few pages ago, Kant says in the *Critique of Pure Reason*, "Some few fundamental propositions, presupposed by the geometrician, are, indeed, really analytic, and rest on the principle of contradiction....; for instance,...the whole is equal to itself; or...the whole is greater than its part" (Kant 1965 / 1787: B16–17). He repeats this in the *Prolegomena to Any Future Metaphysics*: "Some other principles, assumed by geometers, are indeed actually analytical...for example ...the whole is greater than the part" (Kant 1950 / 1783: 17). The whole equates to the subject of an analytic statement, and the part to the contained predicate. Frege misunderstands geometry on this crucial point for geometrical interpretations of logic and thereby of arithmetic. On geometry, Kant was more analytic than Frege!

We may say that such principles are intuitively analytical, but geometrical wholes can be formally defined in terms of their parts and their relationships. See Shin (1994) on diagram logics.

My claim is only that whether or not all entailments can be geometrically represented, the diagram test of entailment is a good one. My claim is only that *if* an inference *is* represented as valid by a geometrical diagram, then the containment of the conclusion in the premises is shown, and the inference is an entailment.

In light of René Descartes' algebraicization of geometry, which obviously applies to Venn diagrams and all other geometric logic diagrams, I might add that volume 2 of *Entailment* also surveys the fortunes of algebraic models of relevance logics (Anderson 1992: 87–117; see Anderson 1975: 180–90). Urquhart contrasts the algebraic approach with the set-theoretic approach of Richard Routley's and Robert K. Meyer's relational semantics, which Mares says "refutes" the containment theory of relevance (Anderson 1992: 155; Mares 1997; Routley 1973). I think "refutes" is too strong a word, and not only because proofs can be diagrammed with diagrams. The issue also concerns what we mean by containment. The notion of containment need not be specifically geometrical. I suggest that much like Saul Kripke, Routley-Meyer have their own notion of containment in terms of set-theoretic membership and inclusion.

Urquhart cites J. C. C. McKinsey and Alfred Tarski as pioneers of neo-Boolean algebraic interpretations of modal and intuitionistic logic (Anderson 1992: 155). On the algebraicization of modal logic, McKinsey acknowledges debts to Tarski, Morris Kline, and the work of Stanisław Jaśkowski as reported by Tarski, but awards the palm of originality to a 1938 paper by Tsao-Chen Tang (Tang 1938; McKinsey 1941: 128 n.11, 129, 129 n.12, 129 n.13). Tang offers a proof that "every provable sentence of the Lewis calculus corresponds to a true equation of topology, although no proof is given for the fact that every true equation of the given topological system corresponds to a provable sentence of the Lewis calculus" (McKinsey 1941: 129 n.13). Tang uses modified Venn diagrams to explain his view (Tang 1938: 739). Thus in effect using the diagram test of entailment, Tang confirms that the Lewis calculus is a relevance logic. See also Edward V. Huntingdon's 1935 paper, "The Mathematical Structure of Lewis's Theory of Strict Implication" (Huntingdon 1935).[8]

Russell is closer to all this than one might think. If we look at the big picture, does not *Principia* basically consist of two main stages: first, logicizing arithmetic following Frege, and second, alegbraicizing geometry following Descartes? Thus *Principia* is like one big Barbara syllogism: If all arithmetic, including algebra, is logic; and if all geometry is algebra, then all geometry, and by extension all mathematics, is logic. It is really no secret. Russell duly cites both Frege and Descartes as early as *Principles* (POM xviii, 157). Thus in basic conception, *Principia* is far less original than one might think. Granted, a great deal is going on in *Principia* that is not in Frege or Descartes. Indeed, every single sentence is different. But then as Hegel says, the detail is always changing. And much of the new detail in *Principia* can be eliminated.

Disjunctive syllogism can be represented by a Venn-style diagram. Let one of two just-touching circles represent p and the other q. To assert that p or q, mark the place where the circles touch with an "x". Then to assert that not-p, shade in the circle depicting p. This bumps the x over to the interior of the circle depicting q, and that asserts the conclusion that q (on placing and bumping x-marks, compare Copi 1978: 211).[9]

Modus ponens can be represented in much the same way. Let one of two just-touching circles represent $\neg p$ and the other q. Rewrite $(p \supset q)$ as $(\neg p \lor q)$ and proceed as before. For Peirce's propositional calculus graphs, which take a different approach, see Roberts (1973: 132, Appendix 2, Table of Logical Notations; see 45, 139 on representing modus ponens).

Venn-style diagrams also show against intuitionistic logic that the law of excluded middle can be constructed after all. It can be constructed by mental diagram as easily as anything else in modern classical logic, and the mental diagram would be a simple mental picture. It might be objected that this argument has all the simplicity and all the preposterousness of Moore's famous proof that there is an external world because he knows his hand exists. My reply is that it has the same simplicity (and subtlety), but the subject matter is different. For we can see that excluded middle is a tautology as easily as we can see any other fairly simple tautology by using Venn diagrams. And Brouwer has it backwards if he thinks (I do not think he does) that examples of open questions about the decimal expansion of pi, considered simply as such, cast any doubt on excluded middle. It is the other way around. If excluded middle is true, then such open questions are genuine questions. Brouwer is simply assuming that excluded middle is false, or at least that its proper interpretation is epistemological. And the assumption that it is epistemological is self-defeating in much the same way the verificationist and pragmatic theories of truth have been shown to be self-defeating. Just as the verificationist theory of truth is itself empirically unverifiable, and just as the pragmatic theory of truth is itself without practical utility, so the epistemological or constructive theory of logical and mathematical truth in general, and of the law of excluded middle in particular, cannot itself be constructed. For Brouwer's theory could only be synthetic *a priori*, and formal constructions can only be analytic. Even worse, in effect we construct the denial of intuitionism when we construct excluded middle. I say in effect because the denial of intuitionism is just as synthetic as the theory of intuitionism. This also sheds light on the conflict between Brouwer's intuitionism and Kurt Gödel's famous undecidability proofs. For Gödel's proofs are constructions, and are underwritten by the far simpler construction of excluded middle. Dalen says, "Gödel was quick to understand Brouwer....Gödel's subsequent research beautifully illustrates how to use the tools of logic to obtain conceptually significant results" (Dalen 2013: 520). And in simplest terms, Gödel is proving that there always *are* open questions in the systems he discusses. He is constructing the existence of unconstructable truths. Therefore, as we know, Gödel is no intuitionist, but a mathematical realist. My conclusion is that per Gödel, indefinitely many mathematical statements have no constructions and might possibly never be constructed; but also per Gödel, the denial of intuitionism as a general theory of truth has in effect been constructed, because the truth of excluded middle has been constructed. Intuitionism is shown false on its own grounds. It is self-defeating, just as verificationism and pragmatism are. Of course, it can still be important and useful in certain limited areas, just as they can. We expect scientific theories to be verifiable. We expect social action theories to be useful. We even expect mathematical theorems (not: mathematical statements in general) to be proved (constructed). Here we may take a theorem as a one-statement theory, and a theory as an opinion as to what is the case. As a general rule, we expect appropriate justification for our claims to know or have evidence for something. But we make no claims like that for all the statements we can state.

Brouwer, by the way, says that Barbara "is nothing more than a tautology" (Brouwer 1975 / 1908: 109).

It might be objected that the diagram test of entailment is a test that Frege and Russell cannot use without circularity. After all, their project is to deduce mathematics from logic, and the diagram test of entailment goes in the opposite direction. It uses geometry to tell which inferences are genuine entailments. Surely this is why Frege and Russell almost never use diagrams.

The objection may be elaborated. Frege was misunderstood by logicians like Venn and Ernst Schröder because they thought he was representing or modeling logic as a kind of algebra much as George Boole did, and could not see how Frege was any improvement on Boole. Frege's revolution was to invert the Venn-Schröder methodology and represent algebra as a kind of logic. That is the whole difference between Fregean *lingua characterica* and Leibnizian *calculus ratiocinator*.

Logic diagrams not only seem to take Frege and Russell in the wrong direction, but they seem to bring in geometric intuition, which Frege and Russell wish to avoid. For them it would be a retrograde step back to Kant.

Frege also assails diagrams as limited in scope of proof because they are limited to proving uninformative conclusions (Heijenoort 1977: 1–2; Frege 1979: 31–35; 1972: 17–19).[10]

Thus the use of the diagram test to validate entailments for Frege and Russell seems to undermine their whole logicization of mathematics.

I would like to make seven points in reply to this objection.

First, the test can still provide analogical illumination of the containment aspects of deduction, truth-tables, and so on, from a point of view external to the logicist project. Thus we might go beyond Frege and Russell and allow the mathematical illumination of logic. As I said earlier, this would be enough to show that modern classical logic has its own deep concept of relevance.

Second and better, logicization has one purpose and the test has another. Logicization is a project of defining and explaining what mathematics really is, namely, logic. In contrast, the diagram test aims only to distinguish entailments from non-entailments.

Third and along the same lines, diagramming logic is not the same as providing a geometrical semantics for logic; but even such semantics need not try to explain what logic is. The Polish and allied logicians who used mathematical interpretations of logic in their metalogical proofs of theorems about logic were not interested in explaining the nature of logic. They wanted to prove things *about* logical systems—to prove things about what can or cannot be proved *in* them. There is no circularity, no begging of the question on what logic is, by these logicians' proofs. And the same thing applies to the diagram test of entailment. It is really proving something *about* modern classical logic, namely, that its proofs are truth-ground containment entailments.

Fourth and elegantly, to the extent that Russell successfully logicizes geometry, he logicizes all literally geometrical logic diagrams, and thereby logicizes the diagram test of entailment. Thus he implicitly validates the test's use as a purely logical device, and eliminates any reliance on mathematical intuition. I already said or implied as much when I suggested that basically, *Principia* is just Frege's logicism extended to Descartes' analytic geometry.

Fifth and similarly, Sun-Joo Shin's formalization of diagram logic eliminates all mathematical intuitions from the diagrams (Shin 1994).

Sixth, some logic diagrams are not literally geometrical to begin with. Notably, truth-tables and truth-trees are not literally geometrical, yet they are clearly logic diagrams.

Seventh, Frege and Russell overlook that in the crucial respect of whole-part containment, geometry *is* analytic, per Kant in the *Critique* and the *Prolegomena* as quoted twice before.

This concludes my reply to the objection of circularity and to its elaboration.

While Frege almost never uses geometrical illustrations of logic (TW 159 is a cautious exception), there is a sense in which Frege's entire notation is visibly diagrammatic. Eric Hammer and Shin call it his "two dimensional concept-script" (Hammer 1998: 1). I cannot recall Russell's ever using geometry to illustrate logic, and his notation, most of which was invented by Whitehead and Peano (Russell 1994: xxxix), is not diagrammatic in appearance. However, his logic is diagrammatic in the sense that it is meant to be an ideal language mirroring the structure of the world.

Russell says, "[I]n a logically correct symbolism there will always be a certain fundamental identity of structure between a fact and the symbol for it;...the complexity of the symbol corresponds very closely with the complexity of the facts symbolized by it" (PLA 197). He says that the language of *Principia* was intended to be "completely analytic [in that it] will show at a glance the logical structure of the facts asserted or denied" (PLA 198). This is more true of atomic facts than of molecular facts (PLA 211).

Russell is very close to the early Wittgenstein on ideal language analysis, a fact which some have allowed the differences to obscure. There is something expressly diagrammatic about Wittgenstein's picture theory of meaning in the *Tractatus*. Robert Howell inverts this in his essay, "The Logical Structure of Pictorial Representation," which discusses the logical form of statements about pictures (Howell 1974). We may speak of Russell as having a picture theory of meaning too, if not exactly the same as Wittgenstein's.

Russell drew several unpublished maps of the logical form of propositions (see Candlish 1996; Dejnožka 1997: 50–51). There is a map of the logical structure of belief in "The Philosophy of Logical Atomism" (PLA 225). Russell says, "This question of making a map is not so strange as you might suppose because it is part of the whole theory of symbolism" (PLA 225).

Russell's Whole-Part Containment Theory of Inference

As we saw, Russell holds a whole-part containment theory of deductive inference in eight major published works from 1922 to 1959, from his Introduction to the *Tractatus* to *My Philosophical Development*. Since there seems no question that this is true, the remaining questions are interpretive. Bill Everdell says:

> In his third draft of *The Principles of Mathematics*, written in 1899–1900, Russell said of Whole and Part that it was an indefinable relation "so important that almost all our philosophy depends upon the theory we adopt in regard to it" (*Collected Papers*, 3:119). By October he had abandoned the draft, writing in the margin "*Note*. I have been wrong in regarding the Logical Calculus as having especially to do with whole and part. *Whole* is distinct from *Class*, and occurs nowhere in the Logical Calculus, which depends on these notions: 1) implication, 2)...and 3) negation....(in *Collected Papers*, 3: xxviii). (Everdell 1997: 393 n.35)

But in the published *Principles*, Russell makes the class-member relation one of the three main *kinds* of whole-part relation (POM 139) . Thus "whole is distinct from class" only as a genus is distinct from one of its species.

In *Principles*, chapter 6, "Whole and Part," Russell comes very close to admitting a whole-part theory of deductive inference. He rejects the theory because he finds two objections to it. His first objection is that "it seems necessary to regard" the whole-part relation as simple, but the relationship of logical priority is complex, since for A to be logically prior to B not only must B imply A, but A must not imply B (POM 138). This is unfortunate because it would seem that where B implies A and A does not imply B, A is simpler than B (POM 137–38). It would seem that A and B are of "equal complexity" if and only if they logically imply each other (POM 138). Russell finds that this is implied by "the theory that intension and extension vary inversely" (POM 238). This objection vanishes, as far as I know, in Russell's later writings. One might be tempted to say that when Russell moves, almost twenty years later, to Wittgenstein's whole-part *truth-ground* containment theory deductive inference, this objection must vanish because the containment is obvious as a matter of truth-ground inclusion. In fact it would be a special instance of Russell's *second* major kind of whole-part relation in *Principles*, the kind where one aggregate contains "some but not all the terms of" another aggregate" (POM 139). Russell says that this relation, though different from the class (or aggregate)-member relation, is "also one which would be commonly called a relation of part to whole" (POM 139). His example, "the relation of the Greek nation to the human race" (POM 139), shows he really means cases where all the members of one aggregate are also members of the other, but the other has some members which are not members of the first. He contrasts that with the relation "of Socrates to the human race," and says, "This most vital distinction is due to Peano" (POM 139). Russell deems *both* of these two different kinds of whole-part relations to be apparently simple (POM 138). And there is no need to bring logical priority into our definition of deductive inference as the aggregate of the truth-grounds of the premises' containing all the truth-grounds that the aggregate of the truth-grounds of the conclusion contains. Yet this is splitting a fine hair. For if *B* deductively implies *A* and *A* does not deductively imply *B*, is not then *A* logically prior to and, in the Greek nation-human race membership containment sense, logically simpler than *B*? I think the real answer is that whole-part containment in this second sense is just as logically complex as the logical priority relation is, and for basically the same reason. For two things are required in each case. Just as *B* must imply *A* and *A* not imply *B*, so every Greek must be human and (it must be at least logically possible that) not every human is Greek. If we now substitute truth-grounds of *A* for Greeks and truth-grounds of *B* for humans, we have the logical equivalence of logical priority with one-way aggregative truth-ground containment. And on the theory of inverse variation of intension and equivalence, we have identity of content of logical priority of *A* to *B* with one-way truth-ground containment of *A* in *B*. Thus Russell is mistaken in thinking that his second kind of whole-part relation is simple. In fact all three of his major kinds of whole-part relations are complex, since he holds that the whole must contain the part and the part not contain the whole, which is yet another conjunction of two statements. Thus my view is that this first objection is confused because *Principles* itself is confused. On the one hand, Russell insists on his intuition that the whole-part relation must be simple. On the other, he holds that when we spell it out, this relation amounts to two things: the whole contains the part, and the part does not contain the whole.

Russell omits discussing $A \supset A$. That is not a case of logical priority, but it is a case of logical implication, specifically of mutual implication; and he should have discussed it here.

The second objection is that he holds that being red implies having color, and he finds red and color to be equally simple, so that color cannot be a part of red. One might reply that we might very reasonably hold that being red includes having color even if there is no second part to red. That is, one might hold that not all inclusion relations are like that of species to genus, where the species always contains both a genus and a difference. One might hold instead that the red-color inclusion relation is simply one of determinable to determinate (W. Johnson 1921: ch. 11). Secondly, one might reply that color relationships are synthetic *a priori*, and that whole-part deductive inference is analytic *a priori*. The whole-part theory of deductive inference applies only to logically formal analytic inferences, and not to synthetic *a priori* relationships. But the best reply is that Russell has forgotten his own theory of logic as fully general truth. "If anything is red, then it has color" is not fully generalized. A fully generalized statement contains only variables and logical constants, and "red" and "color" are neither. Thus Russell's example is not an example of a logical statement on his own theory of logic. Nor is there any doubt that he holds this theory of logic in *Principles* (POM 7). Since mathematics is logic, its "variables have an absolutely unrestricted field," and its "constants...are to be restricted to logical constants" (POM 7). That is, he implicitly holds FG–MDL in *Principles*. And when Russell implicitly moves to FG–MDL*, the objection vanishes on *two* counts. First, as before, "If anything is red, then it has color" is not fully general. Second, it is not true in virtue of logical form.

Ironically, this very sort of color example emerges years later as a stumbling block to the *Tractatus* on truth-ground containment as the explanation of all *a priori* truth. Did Russell forget his own color objection in *Principles* when he endorsed truth-ground containment theory in his introduction to Wittgenstein's *Tractatus*?—Could Wittgenstein, who admired *Principles* but might not have read very much of it, have forgotten it?

Russell says in *Principles* that had he not found those two objections, "it would be tempting to" define the whole-part relation in terms of logical priority (POM 138).

Of the three basic kinds of whole-part relation Russell admits in *Principles*, class membership, aggregate containment, and propositional containment (POM 138–39), it is really the third that would be the best and most natural one for whole-part deductive inference. For inference is of statements from statements, not of members from classes or of aggregates from aggregates.

Members, classes, and aggregates are not even true or false. But this does not detract from anything I have said.

How then are we to take Russell's talk of deductive inferences as whole-part relations? Is it literal, or merely analogical and representational? The problem with taking it in the most literal metaphysical sense in the case of disjunctive syllogism, for example, is that Russell comes to reject disjunctive facts (PLA 211; IMT 83–88). Thus facts will not always appropriately contain facts. But his talk might still be literal. In the *Inquiry* it seems to be beliefs that deductively contain beliefs (IMT 242). This is an unhappy idea; people are notorious for believing premises but not the conclusions the premises deductively imply. We might then gloss Russell as holding that insofar as propositions are distinct from the facts they describe (compare PLA 182–88), propositions deductively contain propositions. This avoids the problem with beliefs. But then a new problem arises: propositions are literally nothing, at least in *Principia*. Containment would not seem very literal. Since *Principia* propositions are incomplete symbols with meanings in use, perhaps we could allow that meanings in use deductively contain meanings in use. But the best solution is, as Russell says, "A propositional function is nothing, but, like most of the things one wants to talk about in logic, it does not lose its importance through that fact" (PLA 230). Alternatively, perhaps judgments deductively contain judgments, where judgments are neither propositions nor beliefs. But much as with belief, people often judge that the premises of an argument are true but not its conclusion. So "judgment" would have to mean something other than the actual judgments people make. It would have to mean something more like a statement or proposition, or better, as in Russell's thesis assertion-sign or in its origin, Frege's judgment-stroke (PM 92 n.*), a judgment that a proposition is true. The best gloss on the later Russell might be that containment is of propositions understood as *possible* beliefs. For Russell, there literally are no merely possible beliefs. But he seems to cash out that notion in terms of dispositions (see IMT 182–94). Of course, the gloss would need scholarly and critical clarification. We might also consider whether containment might be of possible judgments by other possible judgments, but I shall not pursue the matter further. For all the problems vanish when we hold that what is deductively contained for Russell is truth-grounds.

The Thread Test of Logical Entailment

I shall now describe a second test or logically sufficient condition of logical entailment which I call the logical thread test.

When we use argument patterns as rules of inference to prove the validity of stages of more complex arguments, the sort of relatedness involved is quite clear and quite different from that provided by Anderson-Belnap tautological entailment. We do not always find that some atomic statement or its negation in the conjunctive normal form of the antecedent literally recurs in the disjunctive normal form of the consequent. In fact, the rules approach does not even guarantee that we will discover whether the argument is valid. The only guarantee is that *if* a logical thread is found, then the argument is valid. And if the argument *is* valid, we usually do find at least one logical thread which leads from premiss to premiss, and eventually to the conclusion. If the argument is fairly simple, this is usually quite easy. We look not for literal recurrences of atomic statements as such, but instead for a series of linked argument-patterns. In effect, we are telling a detective story of how the consequent follows from the antecedent. If we use rules of inference, this is how we find the proof. This is how the proof makes sense to us. Typically we look first for one fairly simple argument pattern involving certain atomic statements, then for another fairly simple argument pattern involving at least one of the same atomic statements or its negation, such that we can relate the two patterns together into a sorites or chain of arguments. Then we try to build the chain far enough that we arrive at the conclusion. Two logicians may find two different proofs of the validity of the same argument, and one proof may be shorter and more elegant than the other. Often there is no one atomic statement whose presence must be continued throughout the chain; one atomic statement may drop out and others take its place. Thus a formal logical thread is much like Wittgenstein's famous thread of ordinary use, no single fiber of which need last the whole length of the thread (PI #67), at least in this one respect; of course, a formal thread is formal, and each term in it is univocal.

Not only can disjunctive syllogism and modus ponens be used as rules of inference to find a thread through a more complex argument, but the thread test can be used to validate them as well.

Disjunctive syllogism, i.e., inferring q from $(p \lor q)$ and $\neg p$, is a very short thread with two fibers. The first fiber, $\neg p$, knocks out the first disjunct in the disjunction by negating it, and then drops out of the thread, having done its job. The other fiber, which is the second disjunct, q, then takes over and establishes the conclusion through literal identity with it.

Modus ponens, i.e., inferring q from $(p \supset q)$ and p, is another very short thread. Fiber p establishes the antecedent of the conditional through literal identity with it. The other fiber, which is the consequent, q, is then seen to be true by *true* material implication, since we assume that the conditional, as a premiss, is true. Then q establishes the conclusion through literal identity with it.

Russell's proofs are always threads. Anderson and Belnap would find such threads irrelevant. But any first-year logic student would appreciate the relatedness or connectedness involved (see Copi 1978: 322–23).

A logical thread is a diagram of truth-ground flow. The modern classical logic thread test preserves and is thereby validated by truth-ground containment. Thus the truth-table test is basic and the thread test is derivative. It is merely a way of making a truth-ground flow intuitively visible. Both tests are diagram tests. The trade-off is intuitive visibility of truth-ground flow at the price of losing mechanical visibility of proof success.

The thread conception of relevance and the truth-table conception of relevance coalesce in the intuitive but mechanical truth-tree method of deductive inference as popularized by Richard C. Jeffrey (Jeffrey 1967). Here the logical thread is the flow of assumed truth down the branches of the tree. Jeffrey's trees actually assume the negation of the conclusion and try to block the flow; and if this fails, they thereby show the flow to the conclusion, which is the real intent. Thus they are a form of indirect argument. They aim to prove that the denial of the conclusion we wish to prove is false.

Since the tree method is a kind of logical thread, it gives us a second validation of disjunctive syllogism and modus ponens by the thread test. Modern classical trees are validated by the concept of relevance as truth-ground containment. And as diagrams, they are a form of the diagram test of entailment. There is no need to construct special "relevantist" trees to show entailment, as Jeffrey later did, though of course one can do so if one wishes, for special and more limited relevantist logics.

Besides Russell's rules-of-inference threads and Jeffrey's mechanical trees, there is a third way to try to find a thread through disjunctive syllogism. Namely, we can use a more perspicuous symbolism. At least, Wittgenstein thinks we can:

> T 5.1311 When we infer q from $p \lor q$ and $\neg p$, the **relation** between the propositional forms of '$p \lor q$' and '$\neg p$' is masked, in this case, by our mode of signifying. But if instead of '$p \lor q$' we [use the Sheffer stroke to] write, for example, '$p|q.|.p|q$', and instead of '$\neg p$', '$p|p$', ($p|q$ = neither p nor q), then the **inner connexion** becomes obvious. (my boldface emphasis)

Thus Wittgenstein not only sees the problem which disjunctive syllogism poses for logical relevance long before Anderson and Belnap do, but he also offers a solution. Surely Russell, who came to admit the Sheffer stroke as replacing his own whole set of logical operators, can and should make use of Wittgenstein's solution.[11]

There is something geometrical about the logical thread test of entailment. A logical thread can be represented by a zig-zag line so as to diagram the pattern of a proof by rules of inference. It is common for teachers of first-year logic to circle the components of the premisses and conclusions in an argument and draw connecting lines which in effect show the truth-flow of the proof being constructed. Each zig or zag represents the use of some rule of inference, and the whole line shows a logical order of use of the rules. Each premiss which plays a role in the proof is in effect a horizontal segment of the line; the conclusion will always be a segment of a valid proof. The line is a selective, inverted sort of tree diagram. (Actually, it is Jeffrey's method which inverts things by assuming the denial of the conclusion.) To be relevant to the proof is to be connected in the line. Premisses or premiss components which are not part of the "line of proof" are irrelevant, i.e., unrelated to the proof. Of course, a premiss might be irrelevant in one line of proof, but relevant in another. In a valid line of proof, the conclusion as a whole is the final part of the line or thread.

It appears to be little known that Quine uses truth-trees in 1959 in *Methods of Logic*, some eight years before Jeffrey. Perhaps that is because Quine discusses them very briefly, presents them as only one technique among many, and introduces them under another and far less catchy name, "truth-value analyses." Quine says:

> This is called a *truth-value analysis*. The general method may be summed up as follows. We make a grand dichotomy of cases....Then [we keep going down the branches] until we end up with [truth, falsehood], or some schema. If a schema results, we then proceed to develop, under that schema, a new bipartite analysis. We continue thus until all end results are [truth or falsehood]. (Quine 1959: 26–27, Quine's emphasis; see 22–31)

In this book, Quine admits several techniques: truth-trees, rules of inference (logical threads), truth-tables, and Venn diagrams. He dislikes truth-tables due to their "cumbersomeness when many letters are involved" (Quine 27n.).

Jeffrey says his "truth trees (one-sided semantic tableaux)" method has its origins in Herbrand via "Beth's method of semantic tableaux" and in Smullyan "(from whom I borrowed the idea of one-sidedness which reduces tableaux to trees)" (Jeffrey 1967: vii–ix). The origin is actually more complex, and is best described as a community effort (Anellis 1990). Lewis Carroll's falsifiability tree method for syllogisms was written in 1894, lost around 1900, and then rediscovered. See Bartley (1972); Carroll (1977 / 1896: Book 7); Anellis (1990); Abeles (1990).

Intensional and Extensional Relevance

The third major distinction among kinds of relevance is the one between intensional and extensional relevance. Truth-ground containment is extensional relevance. As we saw, the relevantists insist the conception of relevance is and can only be intensional.

Anderson and Belnap find sharing of "meaning content" or "intensional meaning" to be the intuitively correct concept of logical relevance, and to need only adequate formalizing as variable sharing (Anderson 1975: 32–33; 152–55; compare 176–77). They say their view opposes that of "the extensional community" (Anderson 1975: 36), and sails against "the prevailing Extensional Winds" of modern classical logic (Anderson 1975: 256).

The intensional-extensional distinction is ancient, going back at least to Porphyry, if not to Aristotle; and the traditional concept of a geometric figure is intensional (Bocheński 1961: 258–59). This makes logic diagrams intensional, in keeping with Nelson's view that entailment is an intensional relation. This intensional character, together with the whole-part containment character of logic diagrams, justifies the diagram test of entailment: an argument is an entailment if its validity can be represented by a diagram such that in diagramming the premises, we also diagram the conclusion. This is consistent with Kant's view that geometrical whole-part containments are really analytic, insofar as analyticity is understood to be truth in virtue of intensional meaning. It also raises a nice question of how extensional modern classical logic really is, since analyticity is often deeply associated with that logic. I proceed, then, to ask if Russellian deducibility, in the sense of Russellian truth-ground containment, is extensional or intensional.

As we saw in chapter 1, there are at least three senses of the word "intension" stated in *Principia*. (i) There are propositional functions that are not truth-functional, e.g., "A believes that p" (PM 8). (ii) There are propositional functions that lack extensional identities—"the same class of objects will have many determining functions" (PM 23); such functions are called formally equivalent (PM 21). (iii) There are intensional functions in the sense that their values need not be specified for them to be specified (PM 39–40).

Now, a certain deductive argument might be validated by one diagram test of validity but not by another. For example, one test might be designed only for propositional logic and the other for both propositional logic and quantificational logic. Or one test might be more limited in its scope of applicability than the other in some other way. Such tests would not be intersubstitutable *salva veritate*. In effect, this makes diagram tests, and more generally all tests of validity, intensional in *Principia* sense (i).

At the same time indefinitely many diagram tests (literally geometrical, truth-table, truth-tree, and so on) can validate exactly the same class of deductive arguments. In effect, this makes diagram tests, and more generally all tests of validity, intensional in *Principia* sense (ii).

Finally, tests of validity can be known to work even if we cannot specify all their instances in advance. In effect, this makes all tests of validity intensional in *Principia* sense (iii).

To sum up, all tests of truth-ground containment are intensional in all three *Principia* senses of "intension." This might seem hairsplitting with respect to sense (i), since normally we would want all such tests to be quite general and also to yield the same results. But I think I have shown that all such tests are intensional in senses (ii) and (iii) fair and square. And my point about sense (i) is fair enough as far as actual practice and historical development go. It is not as if every test of validity ever developed has given exactly the same results as every other test.

But the basic tests of validity in modern classical logic basically all give the same results. That is to say, they are basically extensionally identical in results. This is in contrast to relevantist logic, where new tests are offered and provide different results all the time.

We must not confuse modern classical truth-ground validity with its tests. It is extensional, insofar as truth-tables are; but its tests are not. And its tests belong to modern classical logic just as much as it does. This is not just some hairsplitting distinction to save modern classical logic from the intensionalist relevantists. Testing validity is basic to logic. More generally, tests are means of modes of determining something. They are more like Fregean senses than like Fregean references.

We have now set the stage for discussing Russell on the famous intensional "or," which is the key to the relevantist attack on disjunctive syllogism. I shall argue that Russell's "or" is just as intensional as any relevantist "or," even using the relevantists' own test that disjunctions must imply subjunctive conditionals.

The argument is easy. We can simply go through Russell's three senses of "intensional" in *Principia*, and ask if the term "or" is or can be intensional in any or all three of these senses, either in a formal notation or in ordinary language.

Again, sense (i) is the non-truth-functional sense. Sense (ii) is the sense in which different functions map the same arguments on the same values. Sense (iii) is the sense in which a property can be specified without knowing (and without even being able to know) all of its instances in advance. The question then devolves to our actual use or uses of "or,"and to Russell's formal paraphrase(s) of them.

Now, how do these three senses apply to "or" for Russell? The "or" Russell defines in his formal logic is truth-functional and is thus extensional in sense (i). But it is intensional in senses (ii) and (iii). As to sense (ii), "instead of '$p \lor q$' we [can use the Sheffer stroke to] write...'$p|q.|.p|q$'" (T 5.1311). These two propositional functions are formally equivalent. Thus "or" is clearly intensional in sense (ii). And as to sense (iii), we can define how to apply "or" in terms of its truth-table without knowing (and without even being able to know) every statement in which it can be used in advance. Thus "or" is clearly intensional in sense (iii).

Thus Russell's "or" is just as intensional as Anderson and Belnap's, since their logic is truth-functional too, and so their "or" is not intensional in *Principia* sense (i) any more than Russell's is.

I have four comments.

First, it may surprise the relevantists, but Russell holds that intensional definition is more fundamental than extensional definition. For we can always replace the latter with the former, but cannot always replace the former with the latter (IMP 12–14). This is implied by the "no backward road" thesis of "On Denoting" (OD 50), which says that since intensions are related many-one to extensions, we can go forward from a single intension (qua mode of presentation) to a single determinate extension, but not back from the extension to a single intension. Thus for Russell, an intensional definition of "or" is not only possible, but would be more basic than an extensional definition of "or."

Second, Russell is best viewed as defining his formal "or" both intensionally and extensionally, and more fundamentally intensionally. For he defines inclusive disjunction as the *function* or *property* having a certain truth-table. And this truth-table logically can be described in indefinitely many ways, so that these ways are all intensional in sense (ii).

Third, if there were no intensional "or" in a formal notation, then the question of that notation's adequacy for formalizing the ordinary "or" would devolve to the question of reasonable paraphrase. In the case of the relevantist Dog, who is inferring that the Man must have gone down this road because the Man did not go down that one (Anderson 1975: 165–66; Meyer 1975: 296–300), the paraphrase is easy. We only need to add a closure clause asserting that these are all the roads the Man could have taken. Russell can simply bury the modal aspect of the inference (i.e. bury the word "could") within the propositional function "*x* is a road the Man could have taken" without affecting the extensionality (truth-functionality) of the inference. And no doubt any closure clause will contain a propositional function which is intensional in senses (ii) and (iii). Even the relevantist Dog will flub his inference if his argument lacks closure on the roads the Man could have taken, i.e., closure on the logically possible combinations of truth-values of the disjunctive statement about all the roads in question.

Fourth, Anderson and Belnap's test of the intensionality of "or" is its implication of subjunctive conditional statements such as "If the Man went down this road, then I would have smelled his scent on that road." Russell's "or" passes this test with flying colors, since it implies subjunctive conditional statements. For it is defined in terms of *truth-possibilities*. Every row in the truth-table defining it shows one of the four *logically possible* combinations of truth-values of the disjuncts. And this logical modality leaves the door wide open for subjunctive conditionals, just as much as causal or epistemic modalities do. This is not even to mention the closure clause that these are all the roads the Man could *truth-possibly* have gone down.

Allow me to elaborate. Here is the truth-table for Russell's truth-functional "or":

$p \lor q$
T T T
T T F
F T T
F F F

The four possible combinations of truth-values of *p* and *q* are given in the first and third columns. The truth-value "*p* ∨ *q*" is defined as having, for each of these four possible combinations, is given in the middle column. Now, does not the bottom row, for example, logically entail by definition that if "*p*" and "*q*" *were* both false, then "*p* ∨ *q*" *would* be false? Where is there any difference between modern classical "or" and relevantist "or" on implying subjunctive conditional statements?

At the same time, of course, talk of truth-possibilities is for Russell just that—mere talk. They are not entities. They have no ontological status. Yet even mere talk of truth-possibilities permits and requires indefinitely many subjunctive conditional statements to assert indefinitely many hypothetical possibilities concerning disjunctive statements. In fact, the astute reader will have already noted that this is nothing special about the modern classical "or".

Obviously, *all* of the modern classical logical operators are defined by truth-tables, and therefore by truth-possibilities. Therefore all of them both permit and require subjunctive conditional statements to describe the full meaning of their use.

Anderson and Belnap have invented a mirage. There is no intensional "or" above and beyond the extensional "or." There are not two kinds of disjunction, one intensional and the other extensional, that we can set down side by side and compare. Instead, there are three *senses* in which any single one ordinary use or formal use of the word "or" is, or is not, intensional. The truth-table for Russell's "or" is truth-functional and therefore makes it extensional, but only in sense (i). Russell's "or" is intensional in sense (ii), since there are functions formally equivalent to $p \lor q$, for example $p|q.|.p|q$. Russell's "or" is also intensional in sense (iii), since its application to disjunctive statements is completely general and is defined without knowing all such statements in advance. How is any of this different in any truth-functional relevantist logic?

As Andrew Ushenko observes, Russell basically admits subjunctive conditionals in the *Inquiry* (Ushenko 1989: 410–14). The *Inquiry* includes a statement of MDL, which Ushenko quotes, and a statement of the theory of analytic inference: "the conclusion is part of the premisses" (IMT 37, 242). Russell is entitled to infer logical subjunctive conditionals informally from deductively valid arguments, and to paraphrase subjunctive conditionals formally as deductive implications. Indeed, in *The Analysis of Matter*, Russell equates his deducibility with C. I. Lewis' strict implication (AMA 199–200); and strict implications imply subjunctive conditionals. Similarly, causal laws imply causal subjunctive conditionals, even when Russell ontologically analyzes and formally paraphrases causal laws as formal implications. I discussed these matters in chapter 5.

Summary of the Chapter So Far

To sum up this chapter so far, when truth-functional logic and logical relevance are both properly understood, Russell is seen to have an implicit relevance logic. He is a relevantist in a broad deductive sense, and I think arguably in a narrowly defined truth-table sense as well. Russell does not use the current jargon of "relevance," but he does accept and use Wittgenstein's terminology of "contains" and "follows from." Of course, we must look beyond mere terminology to what the terminology is used to mean.

Russell admits three progressively narrower and stronger forms of implicit entailment: *true* material implication, *always true* formal implication, and deducibility, which he equates to strict implication in 1927. Anderson and Belnap would deny that any of these are forms of entailment; but I have shown that all three forms involve visibly diagrammable truth-ground containment.[12]

True material implication is the most primitive and broad relevance relation Russell has. By definition, material implication does not obtain if the move from antecedent to consequent fails to preserve truth. Thus the *truth* of a material implication statement logically implies that if the antecedent is true, then the consequent is true. True material implication is truth functional and is therefore extensional in sense (i). But the true material implication function is formally equivalent to other formal functions, for example, one using the Sheffer stroke. Therefore true material implication is intensional in sense (ii). And its defining truth-table is understood without having to understand all material implication statements in advance. Thus true material implication is intensional in sense (iii). Thus true material implication satisfies four criteria of entailment: Nelson's intensionality and inner connection criteria, Wittgenstein's whole-part truth-ground containment test, and the diagram test.

An *always true* formal implication is in effect just a class of true material implications, so basically the same comments apply.

Deducibility satisfies seven criteria of entailment: Nelson's intensionality and inner connection criteria, Wittgenstein's whole-part containment test, Geach's *a priori* criterion, Binkley's criterion that the inference be provable under certain conditions, Wright's deducibility criterion, and the diagram test. As a general rule, the thread test will apply too.

Russell's disjunctive syllogism, hypothetical syllogism, and modus ponens, considered both as validated by the truth-table and truth-tree methods, and as rules of inference themselves, satisfy the same seven criteria of entailment that modern classical deducibility in general does.

Anderson and Belnap uphold traditional logic's concern for relevance against Russell. Yet it is traditional logic which upholds a whole-part theory of deductive inference and uses a diagram test to diagram containment of the conclusion in the premises, so as to show it follows from them. Russell adopts a whole-part theory of deductive inference, and this naturally invites using the diagram test for his logic as well.

Traditional logic sees formal validity as logical relevance, and views formal deducibility as *following from*. It views fallacies of relevance as committed by arguments purporting, but only purporting, to be deductively valid (Copi 1978: 87–88). Fallacies of relevance "bear directly on validity" (Sylvan 2000: 40). This last point makes sense only if successful deductively valid arguments *are* relevant.

Anderson and Belnap find it ironic that modern classical logic textbooks often have a chapter on informal relevance fallacies, yet use strict implication or even material implication in their formal chapters, since they hold that such relations of implication are not forms of relevant entailment in the first place (Anderson 1975: xxi, 17). But as I see it, the real irony is that these formal chapters generally use truth-tables and even Venn diagrams to show that to diagram the premises is already to diagram all valid conclusions. That is, the irony is that these chapters generally *do* show whole-part relevant truth-ground containment, and show it visibly for all to see. Russell's student Copi (1978) and Quine (1959) are stock examples of this. Anderson and Belnap do not even seem to know that these things are logic diagrams, much less that they visibly show truth-ground containment entailment. Even more ironically, Anderson and Belnap's gibe applies just as well (or poorly) to their hero, Aristotle. For Aristotle discusses informal relevance fallacies, yet his Barbara syllogism is equatable with hypothetical syllogism. And Aristotle evidently uses literally geometrical diagrams to show the whole-part containment validity of all of his valid syllogisms, including Barbara.

The truth is that fallacies concern irrelevance in purported deductively valid arguments in modern classical logic just as much as in relevantivist logic (see Copi 1978: 88). Fallacies of relevance, such as appeal to authority, appeal to popular belief, or argument against the person giving the argument, as opposed to merits of the argument itself, can ruin a modern classical argument just as easily as they can ruin a relevantist argument—and vice versa.

The problem with Anderson and Belnap is their limited conception of relevance. This leads them to insist they have a definition of entailment as opposed to a mere sufficient condition. They think they prove that disjunctive syllogism is *not* a form of entailment, by definition of "entailment." But all they really show is that *their* criterion fails to show that disjunctive syllogism is a form of entailment. Their insistence on defining entailment as their own limited notion of tautological entailment blinds them to the fact that some *other* sufficient test of entailment might show that disjunctive syllogism is an entailment after all. In effect, they are committing the fallacy of appeal to ignorance, and are hiding that behind the cloak of their narrow definition of entailment.

Truth-ground containment is the summum genus, and thus the sine qua non, of entailment. It is as simple as that. For with it, we have entailment, and without it, we do not. It is the reason why Anderson and Belnap's tautological entailment succeeds. It is also the reason why disjunctive syllogism and modus ponens succeed.

Only truth-ground containment corners the market on relevance. Thus Wittgenstein and Russell, not Anderson and Belnap, corner the market.

Still, Anderson's and Belnap's definition of tautological entailment is a major achievement. It may be taken to define a special sort of relevance, which we may call literal atomic relevance. Thus it enriches our concept of relevance in the way only imaginative and insightful formalizations can. I am happy to hail it as a major new species of entailment. I wish only to show how much they have in common with Russell as fellow relevantists. In this chapter, I am mainly writing toward reunion in logic.

I think Russell himself might admire the Anderson-Belnap definition of tautological entailment, but would observe, as I have, that it is far from being the only kind of whole-part entailment. I think he would note that his own logic has deeper, more general truth-ground containment entailment relations which Anderson and Belnap fail even to recognize as such. And as we saw, Russell admits three kinds of whole-part relations in logic as early as *Principles* (POM ch. 16), any one of which could serve as the basis for its own kind of whole-part entailment.

I suspect that Anderson and Belnap never really read their supposed chief opponent, not even his purely logical works. For example, they unquestioningly accept Nicholas Rescher's report that "the enormous authority of Lord Russell was responsible for the fact that the voice of MacColl and others interested on modal logic went unheard" (Anderson 1975: 256). If they had reviewed the Russell literature before the second volume of *Entailment* appeared (Anderson 1992), they should have at least found my early critique of Rescher's claims (Dejnožka 1990). Their cites to Russell himself are almost nonexistent.

An Objection Considered

One might object that even if Anderson and Belnap did know all these things about Russell, they still would not be impressed. My reply is that there is indeed a deeper explanation of why Anderson and Belnap reject modern classical logic. They may not be Russell scholars, but as Layman Allen observes, they are among the best logicians in the world. They have devised a very strict definition of tautological entailment because they are very conservative about what to admit as logically following from what. Further, they want the definition to depend purely on the logical form of the argument. Although their various logics have semantic interpretations, they do not want the presence of entailment to depend on a semantic requirement that all the premises of the argument be true, or even be assumed to be true for the sake of testing for entailment. It is their formal purity, their great caution concerning what is reliable inference, and their very great sense of logical responsibility, which lead to their definition of tautological entailment.

There are at least six possible replies to this objection.

First, one might reply that Russell is just as formal as they are, since he has no semantics. Jean van Heijenoort says, "Semantic relations are unknown" in Frege and Russell (Heijenoort 1977: 326). And many might at least agree with Douglas Lackey that "*Principia* lacks any explicit formal semantics" (Russell 1973a: 253). The problem with this reply is that it is false. Russell does have semantics. They are informal semantics. In fact, it is hard to think of what exercises Russell more in logic than the two basic semantic relations, reference and truth. And as I noted earlier, his implicit intended semantic model is the actual world, since for him there is no other world (see pages 119, 165).

Second, one might simply chalk up the modern classical vs. relevantist conflict to different logical intuitions on relevance. We may just have different logical intuitions. If so, then I suspect that Anderson and Belnap are outvoted. But this is not a matter for voting, and the reply leaves us with a mere standoff as opposed to a theoretical resolution.

Third, *true* material implication and *always true* formal implication *are* formally determinate. They are formally determined by the *true* rows of the truth-table. All the rows of a truth-table are formally determined by matrix; and the requirement that material implications be true and that formal implications be always true is a row-constraint on the matrix. Deducibility, when defined in terms of truth-tables, is formally determinate as well. This shows the formal rigor of all three of Russell's implicit forms of entailment.

Fourth, semantic criteria of relevance can be just as rigorous as purely formal notational criteria. For semantics can be formalized too. In fact, since truth is one of the two basic semantic notions (the other one is reference), *truth*-tables are semantic formalizations by their very nature. I think that this is already a sufficient reply to the objection, but there is a deeper reply as well.

Fifth, by insisting that relevance is purely formal, Anderson and Belnap are wrong on the deepest and most general level. For that level is truth-ground containment, and is therefore essentially semantic, since it essentially involves truth, one of the two basic semantic notions. Truth-ground containment is the genus and Anderson-Belnap tautological entailment is a species. All

Anderson-Belnap entailments are truth-ground entailments, but not all truth-ground entailments are Anderson-Belnap entailments.

Sixth, I thought Anderson and Belnap were intensionalists! They complain loudly about how modern classical logic sails on "the prevailing Extensional Winds" (Anderson 1975: 256), and hold up the intensional "or" as the key to what is wrong with disjunctive syllogism. But when they give their own definition of tautological entailment, they jettison all intensions in favor of a purely formal extensional (truth-functional) approach. This reply is more than a mere ad hominem. It points out an internal tension in their views. But even though the conflict is not a formal contradiction but a mere tension, it is a huge tension between two of their most basic views.

Let us proceed to the heart of the Anderson-Belnap critique. They find one and the same problem in modus ponens, disjunctive syllogism, and hypothetical syllogism alike. Namely, there is a disjunct of the form "*P* and not-*P*, therefore *Q*" in the normal form analysis of each of them. This is the only disjunct they complain about, and the only problem they find. Thus their critique of all of these forms really boils down to a rejection of ex contradictione.

There are at least three ways to look at this.

First, there is the way Anderson and Belnap look at it. They reject ex contradictione as a *non sequitur* on its face, since it fails to meet their variable sharing requirement, and therefore they reject any argument form whose normal form contains it as a disjunct. For them, the irrelevance of any such forms directly follows from the irrelevance of ex contradictione itself. They view it as a hole in the proof through which truth ought not to flow. It is the only problem they find. They mention nothing else. Therefore it is their diagnosis. Their prognosis or solution is to use intensional "or." But as we saw earlier, Russell's "or" is just as intensional as theirs. Therefore their solution is just as available to him.

Second, we may view ex contradictione as not a hole but a patch that *stops* the leaking of truth. All things do follow from a contradiction, or would, if a contradiction, *per impossibile*, could be true. But since it cannot be true, the self-contradictory disjunct in the normal form simply and really blocks the flow of truth through that disjunct. This is the most elegant answer.

Third, we can also look at this in terms of constraints. In modern classical logic, we can use any one or more of several constraints to banish ex contradictione. We may require that our arguments have true premises, or at least compossible premises. We may require that our arguments be sound, which implies that all their premises are true. We may even require that premises and conclusion be related in some way that excludes ex contradictione.

But such constraints cannot be *directly* applied to modus ponens, disjunctive syllogism, or hypothetical syllogism, so as to exclude ex contradictione. For none of these argument forms, as such, includes or requires a self-contradictory statement as a *premiss*. Some *instances* of these forms have self-contradictory premisses, but that is irrelevant here. What we would apply the constraints to would be any self-contradictory *disjuncts* in the *normal forms* of arguments.

Accordingly, I propose we can broaden all these constraints so as to apply to disjuncts of normal forms of argument. If we do, then the three argument forms in question will be purged of the self-contradictory disjuncts in their normal forms, and their validity will then be determined by their remaining disjuncts. And as we saw, even Anderson and Belnap do not criticize the relevance of the remaining disjuncts.

My second and third replies are logically equivalent. They function in exactly the same way. They differ only in conception. On my second reply, contradictions are viewed as patches that block the flow of truth through disjuncts, simply because they cannot be true. On my third reply the disjuncts vanish. They are viewed as banished from the argument by my extension of the constraints to such disjuncts. Thus while my second reply is more elegant in avoiding constraints, it is not the only sufficient reply.

Historically, thousands of logicians have found modus ponens, disjunctive syllogism, and hypothetical syllogism to be valid argument forms, and even intuitive paradigms of validity, for thousands of years. But we might venture that this is not how they all viewed ex contradictione. This might be so even though ex contradictione quodlibet sequitur is enshrined in Latin. Surely many found it harder or more puzzling to accept than, say, modus ponens. Why is that? Is there any single reason? Is it simply because normal forms were not yet available, so that traditional logicians could not see that ex contradictione is a disjunct in the normal form of modus ponens? This might be the answer that Anderson and Belnap would give. My answer is different. By its very nature, ex contradictione is valid per Wittgenstein and Landini. But by its very definition, it cannot be sound, since its premiss cannot be true. (Here I ignore paraconsistent logic.) In fact, by its very nature, it is constrained on every level except mere deducibility or validity as such. It cannot be sound. Its premiss cannot be true, nor even possibly true. But none of these constraints applies to these argument forms as such: modus ponens, disjunctive syllogism, and hypothetical syllogism. These constraints only apply to some *instances* of those argument forms.

Modus ponens does not live by ex contradictione alone. Ex contradictione is not all there is to modus ponens. It is only one logical part (one disjunct out of two) of the normal form analysis of modus ponens. Above all, we do not *look* at modus ponens the way we look at ex contradictione. When a first-year logic student looks at modus ponens, s/he more or less normally and immediately sees a perfectly unobjectionable argument form. But the same student normally and immediately feels that there is something wrong with ex contradictione. Why is that? Is it due to ignorance of the normal form analysis? Or is it because the premiss cannot be true?

At this point, I think we have at the very least a standoff at the level of ordinary logical intuitions. For who is to say whether we should reject modus ponens because we reject ex contradictione as clearly wrong, or classify ex contradictione as a constrained disjunct because we accept modus ponens as clearly right? It may be almost witty to say here that one philosopher's modus ponens is another philosopher's modus tollens. It is far more important to note that we are not just trying to save the appearance that modus ponens is all right, to explain why it is all right. Ex contradictione has got to go anyway. Considered simply by itself, it can never be used to prove anything because though valid, it cannot be sound. I know that Anderson and Belnap are attacking its relevant validity, not its soundness. But they are operating in an extremely restrictive species of relevance, while I am operating in the summum genus.

Is it possible that the Anderson-Belnap critique is based on a fallacy of composition? Is it possible that, considered by itself, ex contradictione is just as irrelevant as they say it is, but considered as a logical part of modus ponens, it plays a valid function of blocking the flow of truth? Again, there is more to modus ponens than just ex contradictione, and our intuitions about the two argument forms are very different too, even if (or perhaps because) one is a disjunct of the normal form of the other.

Just how *does* ex contradictione function within modus ponens? How, indeed, do *any* disjuncts function within a disjunctive normal form? How do they function in any disjunction? From the very fact that they are disjuncts, it sounds like they essentially function just like the disjunctive branches of a tree diagram. Now, truth flows along the branches of a deductive tree diagram unless it is stopped by a formal contradiction. Metaphorically speaking, that is how logic trees work. In the negative sort of tree, we write down all the premises and the negation of the conclusion, and then draw out the tree. If every branch is blocked by a contradiction, then if all the premises are true, then the negation of the conclusion cannot be true; hence the conclusion must be true. Now, it seems to me that this is exactly how ex contradictione functions as a disjunct in the normal form of modus ponens. Namely, the disjunct is a branch, and the contradiction blocks it off. For the contradiction cannot be true.

And therefore we cannot use this path, but must look to the other disjunct to settle things, which of course it does. Even Anderson and Belnap have no problem with the other disjunct. And this shows that Anderson and Belnap indeed commit a fallacy of composition. For if they were right, then ex contradictione would have to be a *conjunct*, not a disjunct, in the normal form of modus ponens. For modus ponens would be logically committed to ex contradictione as a *valid* or *viable* avenue to the conclusion only if the latter were a *conjunc*t of the former. For the truth of "A and B" is committed to the truth of "B", but the truth of "A or B" is not committed to the truth of "B" at all. But the self-contradictory disjunct in the normal form of modus ponens functions in exactly the opposite way. Far from purporting to be a *valid* avenue, it functions to *block* the way.

The seven criteria of entailment which I oppose to the Anderson-Belnap definition largely run together as a pack. Insofar as an *a priori* true statement is a statement whose truth is knowable in virtue of its meaning alone, the *a priori* and intensional criteria collapse into each other. Insofar as all *a priori* statements are analytic, where an analytic statement is a statement reducible to a logical truth by replacing terms with synonyms or definitions, the *a priori* and deducibility criteria collapse into each other. Insofar as a deduction is whole-part if and only if it can be diagrammed, the whole-part and diagram criteria collapse into each other. Insofar as an inference is valid (or a conditional statement is true) in virtue of its meaning alone if and only if the premisses (or antecedent) contains the conclusion (or consequent), the intensional and whole-part criteria collapse into each other. Insofar as the whole-part theory of logical deduction is true, the deducibility and whole-part criteria collapse into each other.

There is an arcane literature suggesting that such collap-sings have limits. See Benardete (1958), Casullo (1996), and Kripke (1980: 14–15, 35–38, 54–57, 75–76, 78–79, 80–91, 96n, 135–38, 158–60) on exotica such as the analytic *a posteriori*, the fallible *a priori*, the contingent *a priori*, and the necessary *a posteriori*. Chapter 10 of this book belongs to that arcane literature. It discusses the concept of the "weak" *a priori* and the theory that empirical probability is really degree of logical relevance. The present chapter concerns only deductive modern classical logic and its relevantist critics.

At the least, Russell is an implicit relevance logician in the broad deductive sense. Over a period of at least thirty-seven years, he admits a relation of deducibility which he comes to equate with analytic consequence, consequence in virtue of logical form, and tautological consequence. He accepts a whole-part theory of logical deduction. His formal deductions are schematic, and a schema is essentially a diagram. And a truth-table is visibly a diagram.

Russell also admits synthetic *a priori* entailments, such as that what is red has color. Geach says, "whatever is red is colored" is one of the "'classical' examples of entailment" (Geach 1972: 181). That what is red has color is not a whole-part relation, but at least it is an internal relation (POM 138; compare Dunn 1990: 77, 80–81, 83 on relevance as an internal relation). This is intuitive deductive entailment as opposed to formal deductive entailment. Of course, such statements are not fully general and thus do not belong to logic as Russell understands it.

The 1912 Russell is also an implicit relevance logician in the broad inductive (weak deductive) sense. He admits degrees of self-evidence among his *a priori* deductive principles, and admits at least one weak deductive principle, the principle of induction, for whose internal relation he gives no positive description. Nor can he, since it is synthetic *a priori*, and weak synthetic *a priori* at that.[13]

This chapter is just one more testament to the richness, depth, and variety of Russell's logical thought. Of course, the room of relevance in Russell's mansion of logic must not be confused with the mansion itself. Granted, the grand ballroom is modern classical logic. But the grand ballroom must not be mistaken for the room of relevance. For the grand ballroom is explicit and the room of relevance is implicit. But while they are different rooms, they are distinct only in reason.

Russell on Relevance and Modality

Anderson, Belnap, and Meyer argue that "[r]elevance is not reducible to modality" (Meyer 1975: 462–71, boldface emphasis deleted). Wright says that entailment "is not a purely modal idea" (Wright 1951: 9). Meyer says:

> The mistake is to think that one needs some *modal* intuitions to formalize entailment. [R]*equiring* such modal intuitions is overkill. If one has a decent →, the *theoremhood*, as a matter of logic, of A → B is what is needed that A should entail B. [C. I.] Lewis introduced (in effect) the □ of modern modal logics because he did *not* have a decent →; he only had ⊃. So he tried to cook up a decent → (again, in effect) by *defining* A → B as □(A ⊃ B). But, if one *already* has a decent →, it is at best redundant to *characterize* A → B as □(A ⊃ B). It may be *worse* than redundant; why should a decent → have a □

built into it in this way? (Meyer 1985: 620, Meyer's emphasis; see 618–30)

Meyer is not proving that we can never define relevance in terms of modality, but merely saying that we should not if we can avoid it. This is like Aristotle's rule for definition by genus and difference: "A definition should not be negative where it can be affirmative," where it is admitted that "many terms...are essentially negative and...*require* negative definitions" (Copi 1978: 157, Copi's emphasis). Likewise, we might then argue, extensional relevance is essentially containment of truth-possibilities, and so *requires* modal definition. But this is not what the Tractarian Wittgenstein and Russell are saying. They are neither explaining relevance in terms of modality, nor modality in terms of relevance. They explain *both* truth-possibilities and following from, i.e., containment of truth-grounds, in terms of *truth-tables*, and therefore ultimately in terms of *logical form*. And if they have a decent diagram for truth-tables, we would *expect* their concept of extensional following from to follow from that. In fact, proving an entailment by diagramming its truth-ground containment is precisely the modern classical proof of theoremhood that Meyer overlooks.

  Also, if the sort of definition Meyer is criticizing is based on a logical equivalence, then it is not "redundant" but informative analysis. It would be quite the opposite of redundant. It would be eliminative, or at most constructional. This is all the more so because C. I. Lewis proposes to eliminate the single concept of entailment with not just *one* other concept, but with *two*: necessity and material implication. If Lewis has a logical equivalence, then we would certainly not wish the definition to go in the other direction. And as it happens, though the concepts of extensional containment relevance and of necessary validity are very different, they *are* logically equivalent in modern classical logic. The general concepts of a truth-table and of logical form are neither modal nor relevant but timeless, or understood in abstraction from time. They are not relevant because relevance (and for that matter validity) apply only to inferences and to conditional statements, while truth-tables are far more general in their scope of applicability. Thus, although it took Russell until 1927 to see it, he was right to equate his own concept of deducibility with Lewisian strict implication.

  Meyer could only be implicitly objecting to Wittgenstein's and Russell's supposed view that truth-possibilities define truth-ground containment, and thus define relevance in terms of modality. But that is not actually their view. Indeed, truth-grounds *are* truth-possibilities. But truth-possibilities are defined as combinations of truth-values, i.e., as rows on truth-tables, i.e., ultimately as part of logical form. Thus the so-called "truth-possibilities" are modally innocent. They are eliminatively analyzed away in terms of the two truth-values, truth and falsehood, as is relevance. Meyer, of course, is not discussing Wittgenstein or Russell here, but C. I. Lewis. But he might have written his very fine paper differently if he had understood Wittgenstein and Russell and addressed their views.

Meyer says that if we have a good entailment relation, there should be no need to bring modality into it. If he were right, then the converse might be equally well argued. Namely, if we have a good modal operator, then there should be no need to bring relevance, specifically entailment, into it. Yet logicians have been trying to explain modality in terms of relevance for some time now; see José Luis Berbeira Gardón (1998) for a survey. My own view is that if we have a good *truth-table*, then there should be no need to bring *either* relevance *or* modality into it. Instead, we should use truth-tables to analyze *both* modality and relevance away.

I do not see this as a matter of "which logic we are working in." I tend to agree with Russell that logical statements are either logically true or logically false, and that every logical system should contain all the logically true ones and none of the logically false ones (POM xii). Thus I think logical systems ought to differ only in other ways. For example, relevantist logics can be species of modern classical logic. Or proof procedures can vary, and so on. Of course, even what might be called "unserious" logics, such as paraconsistent logics, can be of logical interest in some sense even if they admit logical falsehoods as truths.

Broadly distinguishing intensionality from extensionality, I hold that relevance and modality are intensionally different, even though they are logically equivalent for conditional statements. I mean that $P \supset Q$ is a truth-ground containment relevant entailment if and only if it is logically necessary, and that this equivalence is conceptually informative. Again, the reason for the equivalence is that both are definable in terms of a third notion, that of truth-tables, and basically in the same way.

Even on an ordinary, broad notion of intensionality, and quite aside from Wittgenstein's technical analysis, we may find reason to believe that relevance and modality are conceptually connected. We may find that there is something relevant about modality, and something modal about relevance. Specifically, if an entailment obtains, then it obtains necessarily. And conversely, if a conditional statement is necessarily true, then it must be a relevant entailment. Certainly this is so for Anderson and Belnap. That is their entire general requirement for logical proof. This must not be confused with their specific definition of tautological entailment.

All this reminds me of Grice and Strawson's "family circle" of intensional terms in their defense against Quine's critique of intensionality (Grice 1956). Indeed, relevance and modality would seem to belong to that very same circle of intensional terms, since analyticity is a paradigmatic member of the circle; and surely relevance and modality are intimately related to analyticity. For if a conditional statement is analytically true, then it is both necessarily true and a relevant entailment, simply on the face of it.

Implicitly speaking, Russell subtly and elegantly collapses *both* modality and relevance into his *Principia* logic. He admits no modal entities or notions. Nor does he admit logical relevance as a primitive relation or notion. His veridical logic implicitly functions as a modal logic and *also* as a relevance logic—and also as an existential logic. All three of the forms of entailment he admits are truth-functional and occur in FG–MDL and FG–MDL* alike. Deducibility essentially involves MDL as the basic building block. Russell says that "the immense majority" of deductions in *Principia* involve assertions of propositional functions (PM 95). I take it that he has *always true* formal implications in mind.

As the two retrospectively implicit sides of the coin of *Principia*, RSL and FG–MDL* are extensionally one and the same logic. Therefore the modal strength of RSL is identical to that of FG–MDL*. Therefore RSL is S5, which is stronger than E.

It is worth comparing Russell with Frege on connecting modality and relevance. It may be recalled that Russell says, "We may, then, usefully define as *analytic* those propositions which are deducible from the laws of logic" (Russell 1994a / ca. 1903–05: 516, Russell's emphasis). Frege says in his 1879 *Begriffsschrift*:

> The apodictic judgment differs from the assertory in that it suggests the existence of universal judgments from which the proposition can be inferred, while in the case of the assertory one such a suggestion is lacking. By saying that a proposition is necessary I give a hint about the grounds for my judgment. *But, since this does not affect the conceptual content of the judgment, the form of the apodictic judgment has no significance for us.*
> If a proposition is advanced as possible, either the speaker is suspending judgment by suggesting that he knows no laws from which the negation of the proposition would follow or he says that the generalization of this negation is false. In the latter case we have what is usually called a *particular affirmative judgment* (see §12). "It is possible that the earth will at some time collide with another heavenly body" is an instance of the first kind, and "A cold can result in death" of the second. (Frege 1977 / 1879: 13, Frege's emphasis)

According to the *Oxford English Dictionary*, the term "apodictic," or "apodeictic," which is notably used by Kant, means 'absolutely demonstrable, absolutely certain, necessary'.

Heijenoort interprets the Frege text as follows:

> Frege dismisses modal considerations from his logic with the remark that they concern the grounds for accepting a judgment, not the content of the judgment itself. (Heijenoort 1977: 2)

But Frege's remark on apodictic judgment is, at best, correct only in the immediate context of his discussion of conceptual content in sects. §§2–3. In the larger context of *Begriffsschrift* as a whole, it is quite false. For *Begriffsschrift* is full of demonstrations of theorems which Frege clearly regards both as certain and necessary. Indeed, he begins the work by discussing the importance of reliable proof. Frege says:

> [W]e can inquire, on the one hand, how we have gradually arrived at a given proposition and, on the other, how we can finally provide it with the most secure foundation. [T]he answer to [the second question] is connected with the inner nature of the proposition concerned. The most reliable way of carrying out a proof, obviously, is to follow pure logic....My initial step was to attempt to reduce the concept of ordering [a proof] in a sequence to that of *logical* consequence....To prevent anything intuitive from penetrating here unnoticed, I had to bend every effort to keep the chain of inferences free of gaps. [This] led me to the idea of the present ideography. Its first purpose, therefore, is to provide us with the most reliable test of the validity of a chain of inferences....That is why I decided to forgo expressing anything that is without significance for the *inferential sequence*. In §3 I called what alone mattered to me the *conceptual content*. (Frege 1977 / 1879: 5–6, Frege's emphasis)

Frege is telling us in effect that the "first purpose" of the work is to make all proofs apodictic. For the only secure foundation in logic is one which ensures logical truth, that is, logical necessity. Note also Frege's two uses of the word "reliable." Reliability of proof is the main reason why relevantists want to show entailment. Here we see that Frege has the same concern.

Second, as no doubt the reader has noticed, Frege is telling us that conceptual content alone matters to him precisely *because* it is what alone matters to apodictic proof. The idea of importance to us is that two statements have the same content if and only if they have the same consequence classes. Karl Popper says that his own notion of verisimilitude:

> combin[es] two notions, both originally introduced by Tarski: (a) the notion of *truth*, and (b), the notion of the (logical) *content* of a statement; that is, the class of all statements logically entailed by it (its "consequence class," as Tarski usually calls it).... (Popper 1979 / 1972: 47, citing Tarski 1956 (1st ed.): essay 7; see Popper 2007 / 1963: 315–20, 527–35; Tarski 1983 (2d ed.): essays 3, 5, 7)

In effect, this equates content containment with following from. I cannot discuss Popper or Tarski here. But I wish to note that this equation, and Tarski's notion (b), were "originally introduced" by Frege. This has been raised as the question whether, for Frege, logically equivalent statements express the same thought (sense). Dummett and I agree that they do not (Dejnožka 2007: 68–69); the notorious texts are Frege (1970: 46 n.*, 80). But it is the early Frege, who has an undifferentiated notion of propositional content not yet split into sense and reference, who clearly states Tarski's notion (b). Frege says in *Begriffsschrift*:

> A distinction between *subject* and *predicate* does *not occur* in my way of representing a judgment....[T]he contents of two judgments may differ in two ways: either the consequences derivable from the first, when it is combined with certain other judgments, always follow also from the second, [and conversely,] or this is not the case. The two propositions, "The Greeks defeated the Persians at Plataea" and "The Persians were defeated by the Greeks at Plataea" differ in the first way. Now I call that part of the content that is the same in both the *conceptual content*. Since *it alone* is of significance for our ideography, we need not introduce any [ordinary grammatical subject-predicate] distinction between propositions having the same conceptual content. [I]n a judgment I consider only that which influences its *possible* consequences. (Frege 1977 / 1879: 12, Frege's emphasis; compare 1970: 46 n.*)

This, I submit, is the first statement of extensionalist relevant containment in the analytic tradition. Frege is expressly defining "conceptual content" as being "that part of the content that is the same in both;" and what is the same in both is precisely having the same *consequences*. He is not describing the nature of conceptual content (is not offering a theoretical definition), much less arguing for it, but is merely offering a stipulative definition of conceptual content, in accordance with his sole interest in inference.

Thus Heijenoort is doubly wrong. First, he overlooks that *Begriffsschrift*'s primary purpose is to provide apodictic proofs, that is, to prove that his theorems really *are* necessary; and he overlooks that the work mainly consists of what Frege considers to be just such proofs. And he overlooks that this is precisely because Frege equates being necessary with having apodictic grounds. Thus, far from dismissing modality, Frege's primary purpose is to prove that his theorems are necessary truths. Second and more subtly, Frege is not distinguishing apodictic grounds from conceptual content in the first place, much less dismissing the former from his logic. Quite the opposite. The two notions not only work together, but they do so because Frege definitionally links them together. For he defines having the same conceptual content precisely as having the same logical consequences. This is a sort of identity definition much like his implicit definition of the number of *F*'s and the number of *G*'s as the same if and only if the concepts *F* and *G* are equal, meaning there is a one-one correspondence of *F*'s and *G*'s (see my 2003: ch. 3, sect. 1).

Frege goes on to say that apodictic truth is truth inferable from universal judgments (Frege 1977 / 1879: 13). This suggests that he understands necessity as what is, or what is inferable from, what is always true. And that seems to imply that he would accept FG–MDL, the theory that logical truth is fully general truth. For it takes little charity to assume he would not regard true causal laws as belonging to logic at all, much less as being apodictic.

Thus just like Russell, Frege implicitly links modality and relevance together through the notion of deduction as containment, or in Frege's terminology, deduction as logical transformation of conceptual content. For Frege, a theorem is necessary just in case it is apodictic, that is, is absolutely deducible. And it is deducible just in case it is nothing but a transformation of the conceptual content of its grounds. That is, it is deducible just in case its conceptual content is contained in the conceptual content of its grounds. This may be called conceptual content containment entailment.

I would like to make four more points about Frege.

First, Frege is not an eliminativist like Russell, but a reductionist. When Frege defines numbers as logical objects, he is not eliminating numbers as logical fictions as Russell does, but is instead reducing them to, i.e., reclassifying them as, existent logical objects. Thus when Frege defines necessity as apodicity, he is not eliminating necessity as a logical fiction, but is instead reducing it to, i.e., reclassifying it as, apodicity.

Second, charity suggests that Frege intends his axioms to be their own grounds (or in at least some cases to have definitional grounds), hence to be apodictic too, hence to be necessary too. This is on pain of a vicious infinite regress of apodictic grounds of apodictic grounds. For otherwise his necessary theorems would be grounded on axioms which are *not* necessary, which seems odd if not absurd. Whether Frege's synthetic *a priori* axioms in geometry are also apodictic in his sense is, I think, a question of semantics. Here we may admit a distinction between analytic and synthetic *a priori* proof. Would we wish to say that Frege denies there is proof in geometry?

Third, charity suggests that necessity and possibility are interdefinable for Frege, even though Frege distinguishes two senses of "possible" but states only one sense of "necessary" in the *Begriffsschrift* text with which I started this discussion of Frege. It is a commonplace that necessity and possibility are interdefinable. Hence we may say that each of Frege's two senses of "possible" implies a corresponding sense of "necessary." And if neither of these is identical with Frege's expressly stated sense of "necessary," then we may say that he has three senses of "necessary," one of which is express and the other two implicit. As it happens, Frege's first express sense of "possible" would seem to imply a corresponding sense of "necessary" which is somewhat similar to, though not at all the same as, his express sense of "necessary." This is the sense of "possible" in which "the speaker is suspending judgment by suggesting that he knows no laws from which the negation of the proposition would follow" (Frege 1977 / 1879: 13). The reason I find this only similar to, and not at all the same as, "possible" in the sense that its denial not known to be apodictic is Frege's example of the former: "It is possible that the earth will at some time collide with another heavenly body" (Frege 1977 / 1879: 13). For no astronomical law is logically demonstrable, much less apodictic. I conclude that Frege has six modal notions in *Begriffsschrift*, three express and three implicit. For he expressly states one sense of "necessary" and two of "possible," and these imply three corresponding implicit senses, respectively one of "possible" and two of "necessary." This is not a criticism of Frege for failing to note that his express notions of necessity and of possibility are not interdefinable. Rather, I praise him for his positive contribution of his express notions. And he never claims they are interdefinable.

Fourth, Frege's view that necessity concerns the grounds for a judgment does not tell us whether he holds that logical truth is just fully general truth, or holds that it is fully general truth plus truth in virtue of form. For that would concern the nature of the grounds themselves, and he does not tell us what their nature is with respect to that issue. Likewise for Russell's view in "Necessity and Possibility" that "We may, then, usefully define as *analytic* those propositions which are deducible from the laws of logic" (Russell 1994a / ca. 1903–05: 516, Russell's emphasis), since the question whether analytic truth is just fully general truth, or is fully general truth plus truth in virtue of form, then devolves to the nature of the laws of logic themselves, and he does not tell us what their nature is with respect to that issue. My suggestion is that at this early time (1879 for Frege, ca. 1903–05 for Russell), it seems on the face of it that Frege and Russell did not even make such a distinction. And until Russell discovered his counter-examples to the theory that logical truth is fully general truth, he (or they) had no *reason* to make it. If so, then we might as well say that for Frege, fully general truth just *is* truth in virtue of form. This supports my earlier textual interpretation of *Begriffsschrift* as basically saying or implying as much for universal judgments taken as the ground of apodicity. For it takes little charity to suppose that Frege would not take less than fully general truths, for example astronomical laws, as logical truths at all, much less as apodictic, and still less as grounds of apodicity. But while Frege's term "universal judgments" easily suggests that he has fully general true judgements in mind, it conveys no hint of a separate and additional requirement of truth in virtue of form.

Fifteen Criteria of Entailment

The eclectic yet often overlapping, rebuttably presumptive, logically sufficient criteria of entailment we have discussed in this chapter are listed below, along with some main logicians who I believe employ them:

1. Formal deducibility: Frege, Russell, Nelson, Wright, Ackermann
2. Deducibility using rules of inference: Frege, Russell, Quine
3. Intuitive validity (synthetic *a priori* "derivability"): Russell
4. *A priori* connection: Russell, Wright, Geach
5. Intensional connection: Russell, Nelson
6. Containment: Aristotle, Kant, Wittgenstein, Russell, Quine)
7. Diagram test: Aristotle, Kant, Venn, Peirce, Quine
8. Truth-table test: Wittgenstein, Russell, Quine
9. Truth-tree test: Carroll, Quine, Jeffrey
10. Thread test: Frege, Russell, Quine
11. *True* material implication: Philo of Megara, Frege, Russell
12. *Always true* formal implication: Frege, Russell
13. Strict implication: Diodorus Cronus, MacColl, Lewis, Russell
14. Primitive entailment: Anderson-Belnap
15. Tautological entailment: Anderson-Belnap

No doubt there are many other sufficient criteria as well. The point of the list is to show that even in deductive logic, the expression "logically relevant" is multiply—indeed, extremely—ambiguous, and there may well be no one thing that entailment is. Thus the field is a very rich one for study. But truth-ground containment is the summum genus and sine qua non of entailment.

The list seems safe from reflexive problems. That is, the list purports to be of logically sufficient criteria of entailment, and intuitively, all the criteria on the list seem to be themselves logically relevant to questions of entailment.

Five Constraints on Proofs in Modern Classical Logic

There are at least five constraints on modern classical logic proofs which I think any reasonable modern classical logician would accept, for the proof to be sound and for the conclusion to be proved from the premisses in a useful, significant manner:

1. It must be possible for all the premisses to be conjointly true.
2. All the premisses must be true.
3. The proof must be truth-functionally valid.
4. The proof must be directional.
5. The proof must be indexable.

Constraint (1) rules out ex contradictione. (2) rules out ex falso. (3) is truth-ground containment entailment. (2) and (3) conjoined may be called the soundness constraint. (4) means that the proof must actually go from premiss to conclusion, or in indirect proof, from conclusion to premiss, and not be solely based on either the falsehood of the premiss or the truth of the conclusion. (5) means in simplest terms that we must be able to state when each premiss and each rule is used. This is a mechanical accounting rule to ensure the proof is determinate. If the premisses are true, modus ponens and disjunctive syllogism easily satisfy all five constraints. Recall that Anderson and Belnap's *only* objection to these two argument forms is that when they are analyzed in normal form, each has a disjunct which is an ex contradictione. And any of constraints (1), (2), and (4), if applied to such disjuncts, as I think we can and must, would block them from being counted as valid conduits of truth flow. Therefore, when we assess the validity of these argument forms, we must consider only the *other* disjuncts. And of course there is nothing wrong with *them*. For a more detailed discussion of the constraints, see my (2012: ch. 7); I simplify and present them a little differently here.

Contextual and Cognitive Aspects of Relevance

I proceed to some remarks on the contextual and cognitive aspects of relevance in Russell.

Analyzing the contextual or situational aspects of relevant inference has been a natural consequence of ordinary language philosophy (Restall 1996; Sperber 1986). Russell understands and accommodates ordinary language relevant inferences. Understanding them is the first step in the process of paraphrasing them into his canonical notation. The problems of paraphrase include vagueness, pragmatics, and plain common sense—which last is ignored if we translate the ordinary definite description "the charlady who ain't never done no harm to no one" as 'the charlady who in at least one moment injured the entire human race'. Russell's famous reply to Strawson makes it clear that Russell would find that literal translation ludicrous. Indeed, Russell gives the charlady example precisely as a parody of logicians with no common sense. The message of the charlady example is that "My theory of descriptions was never intended as an analysis of the state of mind of those who utter sentences containing descriptions....I was concerned to find a more accurate and analyzed thought to replace the somewhat confused thoughts which most people at most times have in their heads" (MPD 179; see PLA 179–82, 188–89 for early statements of this view of analysis in 1918). To do that well, Russell obviously needs to know what these confused ordinary thoughts are. This general point naturally includes ordinary relevant inferences. For example, as noted earlier, Russell can easily paraphrase the Dog's inference with a closure clause on the roads "and these are all the roads the Man could have taken," thus simply burying the modal term "could" in the propositional function "x is a road the Man could have taken" without affecting the validity of the inference. Russell can even further paraphrase the "could" by replacing it with "a more accurate and analyzed" nonmodal term that is reasonably appropriate, that is, reasonably truth-preserving, in the particular situation at hand. That should not be too hard, since what road the Man "could" have taken is already vague. How far away do the roads have to be, and what condition do they and the Man have to be in, before the Man "could" not have taken them? Does the Man's knowledge of or beliefs about the roads help determine what roads he "could" have taken? (Compare a prison where the prisoner does not know a very simple way out.) When does a path become a road? Here Anderson and Belnap are playing Strawson to Russell's truth-ground containment relevant Dog.

Russell is well aware of the existence of ordinary language speech acts. He antedates J. L. Austin in distinguishing locutionary from illocutionary acts. Russell makes the distinction in *Human Knowledge*: "A man may express sorrow...by saying 'Alas!' or 'Woe is me!' He may communicate...by saying, 'Look.' Expression and communication are not necessarily separated; if you say, 'Look' because you see a ghost, you may say it in a tone that expresses horror" (HK 59). This too concerns the paraphrase of ordinary inference (see Dejnožka 2003: 210–13).

As to the cognitive aspect of communication and relevant inference, which Dan Sperber and Deirdre Wilson, following H. P. Grice, emphasize (Sperber 1986), the 1914–48 Russell admits egocentric particulars with which we may be acquainted, and which are nameable as "this" and "that," as the ontological basis of his analysis of indexical cognition in pragmatics. This may not be the Grice-Sperber-Wilson approach, but at least Russell cannot be accused of ignoring the issue of cognition. Indeed, as opposed to behaviorism, which he rejects, Russell is a veritable champion of cognition.

Conclusion

I conclude this chapter by agreeing with Ramsey that:

> In the case of logically conclusive arguments I can accept the account of their validity which has been given by many authorities, and can be found substantially the same in Kant, De Morgan, Peirce and Wittgenstein. All these authors agree that the conclusion of a formally valid argument is contained in its premises; that to deny the conclusion while accepting the premises would be self-contradictory; that a formal deduction does not increase our knowledge, but only brings out clearly what we already know in another form; and that we are bound to accept its validity on pain of being inconsistent with ourselves. (Ramsey 1931: 185)

The only ones who do not seem to see that all this applies to modern classical logicians are the relevantists.

In terms of the standards of evidence used in chapter 6, it seems beyond a reasonable doubt that truth-ground containment is a form of relevant containment, hence of entailment. For we can simply see the containment in truth-tables. Indeed, it seems absurd to deny it. But in view of the opposition of the relevantists, it may be best to say that at least historically speaking, the jury is still out.

If asked where Russell's implicit relevance logic is located in his writings, we may answer that it is located in *Principia*, right along with his implicit modal logic. The implicit necessity operator for all logical truths, and the implicit relevance operator for all logically true conditional statements, is simply the *Principia* thesis assertion-sign.

For further reading, please see *The Concept of Relevance and the Logic Diagram Tradition* (my 2012). I am happy to note that two years after he received a copy, Jon Michael Dunn asks

> whether the concept of relevance is relevant to the study of what Anderson and Belnap call "relevance logic." The answer should be "Of course!" (Dunn 2015: 1)

I agree completely. To think otherwise is to commit an Alice in Wonderland "Let's change the subject" fallacy. Compare the fallacy of four terms in three-term syllogistic logic, where the fourth term changes the subject.

10

Probability as Degree of
Logical Relevance

In his 1912 *The Problems of Philosophy*, Russell holds that the principle of induction can be neither proved nor disproved, nor even rendered probable or improbable in the slightest, by experience. He infers that if it is to be accepted at all, then it must be accepted on the basis of its "intrinsic evidence" (PP 68, 70, 76). Such evidence must be *a priori*, and therefore must be exclusively based on relations among universals (PP 101–10, 149). Since the principle is not formally demonstrable, its self-evidence must be intuitive. And since the principle is not certain, its degree of self-evidence must be less than that of full certainty (PP 114–18).

This view is not only astonishing in itself, but it appears to imply something even more fantastic: that logical relevance has degrees which are degrees of probability. That would collapse the distinction between deductive and inductive logic as different kinds of logic. There would only be a distinction of degree.

It would seem that ever since Aristotle invented formal logic over two thousand years ago, logicians have understood logical relevance as being a conclusion's *following from* premises with logical necessity. Thus it would seem that logical relevance has always belonged to deductive logic. The one thing logicians seem to agree on without exception is that logical relevance obtains only within deductive logic, and never for probabilistic arguments. For the premises of a probabilistic argument are not and logically cannot be logically relevant to its conclusion. For if they were, then the conclusion would follow from the premises with logical necessity, not merely with some degree of probability.

Thus the 1912 Russell appears not only confused as to the epistemology of induction, but even as to its logic. He is not only conflating the inductive with the *a priori*, but he is even conflating deductive logic with inductive logic. How is this possible?

Theory of Probability in *Problems*

It may be well to describe the 1912 Russell's theory briefly at the outset. It will be useful to discuss both induction and the causal relation, since they are arguably closely related, and since Russell treats them in the same way.

Russell states four closely related versions of the inductive principle (PP 66–67). We may ignore the differences for present purposes. He argues that since the inductive principle cannot be either proved or disproved by experience without begging the question by assuming the principle, "we must either accept the inductive principle on the ground of its intrinsic evidence, or forgo all justification of our expectations about the future" (PP 68). He says "the inductive principle itself cannot be proved by induction" (PP 84). He agrees with Hume that the connection of cause and effect is not *formally* deductive, but finds it a *non sequitur* to infer that there is nothing *a priori* about the connection (PP 83). He agrees with Kant that the connection of cause and effect is synthetic as opposed to analytic (PP 83–84). All our empirical generalizations are ultimately based on the inductive principle, since they are "derived from instances, and not an *a priori* connexion of universals" (PP 107). But he holds that the inductive principle itself is *a priori*. He speaks of "some wholly *a priori* principle, such as the principle of induction" (PP 149, Russell's emphasis). As such, it is wholly a matter of relations of universals. For "*All* a priori *knowledge deals exclusively with the relations of universals*" (PP 103, Russell's emphasis). But while it is purely and wholly *a priori* (PP 149), it is by no means as certain as our *a priori* knowledge in logic and mathematics. Russell says, "The inductive principle has less self-evidence than some of the other principles of logic" (PP 117). The term "some of the *other* principles of logic" is confusing, since surely he holds that, like the causal principle, the inductive principle does not belong to formal deductive logic at all. Russell never tells us just how self-evident the inductive principle is. And perhaps its degree of self-evidence is logically indeterminate. In fact, it would seem absurd to assign it a determinate degree of intrinsic probability. Could it be 93% probable? But since it would have the sort of self-evidence that belongs to judgments as opposed to acquaintance with a fact, its degree of self-evidence, determinate or not, might be anywhere on the scale "from the very highest degree down to a bare inclination in favour of the belief" (PP 138). I think that for Russell its likelihood of being true, as opposed to its degree of self-evidence, increases with time, since likelihood is largely a matter of coherence with all our probable views (PP 140), and we are discovering new uniformities all the time. In his review of John Maynard Keynes' *A Treatise on Probability*, Russell quotes Keynes as making this last point (Russell 1922: 157).

In *Problems*, Russell appears to treat causation in the same way he treats induction. He says that "the principle that sense-data are signs of physical objects is itself a connexion of universals" (PP 148–49), and that whenever we go beyond immediate experience, which always requires knowledge by description, "we need some connexion of universals" (PP 148). But then, assuming that due to (1) the sheer universality of causal laws and (2) our own finite limitations, it follows that causal laws always range over things we are not directly acquainted with. And from this it follows further that the causal principle that all events are governed by causal laws must be known *a priori* too, if they are known at all. Thus Russell agrees with Kant that causation is synthetic *a priori*. But he rejects Kant's view that causation is synthetic *a priori* specifically because it is innate to us and is unconsciously imposed by our minds on our experience (PP 73–74, 86–90; see 159). Instead, for Russell, the principle of causation seems to be synthetic *a priori* simpliciter, though weakly so, like the principle of induction. This raises the question whether either principle might be more strongly self-evident than the other. I see no reason why either would be. And on the face of it, they seem so linked that they would stand or fall together to the same indeterminate degree.

Keynes as Origin of Russell's Theory

I hold that the 1912 Russell's theory of probability is best interpreted as basically being an adoption of, and also as basically being the same as, the probability theory of John Maynard Keynes. Keynes developed a theory of probability which interprets degrees of probability as degrees of logical relevance, and published it in 1921 in his *A Treatise on Probability*. In chapter 1, "The Meaning of Probability," Keynes says on the first page, "The terms *certain* and *probable* describe the various degrees of rational belief about a proposition which different amounts of knowledge authorize us to entertain" (Keynes 1962 / 1921: 3, Keynes' emphasis). Keynes says "describe," not "define." Yet surely his description is intended to be of the essence of probability, of what it is to be probable. Surely Keynes would not think that probability could be anything different in even one possible world other than the actual world. Thus I take Keynes to be really saying that probability essentially *is* degree of rational belief. And degree of rational belief is just what he means by degree of logical relevance. It is not just a theoretical definition. It is a logicist definition intended to belong to logic.

Keynes discussed probability with Russell on and off from 1904, when Keynes read a paper on probability to the Apostles, until 1913. Thus Keynes easily could have inspired Russell to admit degrees of logical relevance. Not only is the historical timing right, but Keynes is famous for pioneering the view. That is how I explain Russell's admission of the principle of induction as a weak logical principle in 1912. Keynes' theory that probability is degree of logical relevance, and its undermining of the distinction between deductive and inductive logic, underlie and explain the epistemology and logic of Russell's book.

My interpretation is strongly supported by a "smoking gun" text in the preface to *The Problems of Philosophy*: Russell says:

> I have derived valuable assistance from unpublished writings of G. E. Moore and J. M. Keynes: from the former, as regards the relations of sense-data to physical objects, and from the latter as regards probability and induction. (PP vi)

Richard B. Braithwaite notes that Russell thanks Keynes—and *only* Keynes—for "valuable assistance" on "probability and induction" (Braithwaite 1975: 237). And if Russell is not referring to Keynes on degrees of logical relevance, it is hard to see what else he could be referring to. The "unpublished writings" surely include Keynes' *Treatise* manuscript as the main writing.

Robert Skidelsky, the Keynes biographer, agrees:

> Keynes' view of induction as a logical principle influenced Russell, who acknowledged his debt to Keynes in his *Problems of Philosophy* (1912). (Skidelsky 2005: 286)

João Paulo Monteiro speaks not of influence, but of adoption:

> Russell's own despair with what he was able to see in Hume's philosophy led him, as is well known, to adopt Keynes's theory of induction, and to remain faithful to this theory at least from 1912, in *The Problems of Philosophy*, to 1948 in his *Human Knowledge*. (Monteiro 2001: 66)

Thus the view that Russell adopted Keynes' theory of induction and accepted it throughout his philosophical career is not only "well known," but even seems uncontroversial. I agree with Braithwaite, Skidelsky, and Monteiro in everything they say on this, including Monteiro's statement that Russell accepts Keynes' theory of induction from 1912 to 1948.

In his *Treatise*, Keynes says that probability is a relation of *partially* following from:

> Inasmuch as it is always assumed that we can sometimes judge directly that a conclusion *follows from* a premiss, it is no great extension of this assumption to suppose that we can sometimes recognise that a conclusion *partially*

follows from, or stands in a relation of probability to, a premiss. (Keynes 1962 / 1921: 52, Keynes' emphasis)

This sounds as if Keynes views entailment, or following from, as deductive validity, and views probability as partial entailment, or partial following from, in indefinitely many degrees. Per his other views, not all of these degrees would be numerically measurable. Further, it sounds as if he views deductive entailment as a limit to which probability approaches indefinitely closely, on a scale that covers all logical relevance, with deductive relevance at one end and zero relevance at the other.

Donald Gillies concludes from the just-quoted text:

> So a probability is the degree of a partial entailment. Keynes further makes the assumption that if *e* partially entails *h* to degree *p*, then, given *e*, it is rational to believe *h* to degree *p*. (Gillies 2003: 115)

I agree with Gillies's first sentence completely. But because I do, I find that what Gillies calls Keynes' further assumption is not an assumption at all, but part of a threefold theoretical identification of degree of probability with partial entailment, and also with degree of rational belief. This threefold identification implies *six* assumptions. For in general, any triple identification, $A = B = C$, implies if *A* then *B*, if *B* then *A*, if *A* then *C*, if *C* then *A*, if *B* then *C*, and if *C* then *B*. I leave it to the reader to work out the six assumptions from the second sentence of the Gillies quote.

Here Russell and Keynes belong to a major early modern tradition of understanding probability as purely logical and *a priori*. This is the tradition of Leibniz, Bernoulli, Laplace, Lambert, Bolzano, De Morgan, Boole, Peirce, and MacColl (Hailperin 1988). Keynes attributes the origin of the "subject matter" of his book to Leibniz (Keynes 1962 / 1921: xiii). Leibniz says, "I have said more than once that we need a new kind of logic, concerned with degrees of probability..." (Leibniz 1966 / 1765 / 1704: 466). This should remove the impression that the 1912 Russell has a historically isolated, oddball theory of probability. Russell does not discuss Leibniz on probability in his Leibniz book (PL), or anywhere else I know of. It is Keynes' influence that brings Russell into this Leibnizian tradition. But the 1912 Russell qualifies for membership in any case.

Keynes' general idea that a probable inference is a partial logical entailment is also found in Russell's greatest student, Ludwig Wittgenstein (T 5.15). Max Black says:

> Wittgenstein's theory of probability is of the type commonly called 'logical', of which other well-known

instances are the theories of Laplace, Keynes, and Carnap. Such theories characteristically construe probability as a logical relation depending solely on the meanings of the propositions involved. (M. Black 1970: 247)

I am merely adding Russell to the list.

Georg Henrik von Wright says, "Aristotle says in the *Rhetoric* that the probable is that which usually happens" (Wright 1960: 167). The great Aristotelian tradition of frequency theory of probability makes probability theory empirical in that the naturally occurring frequencies we start from in natural science must be empirically observed. However, the theory is logical insofar as the notions of "many" or "few" members of a class are logical notions. This makes *reasoning* about probabilities *a priori*. And induction, or reasoning from particular instances to universal conclusions, is a purely intellectual activity for Aristotle (Ross 1960: 43) as well. Keynes and the 1912 Russell are not frequency theorists, but their theories appear less unusual in this perspective as well.

To classify probability as part of logic, with probability being purely logical and approaching logical truth as an asymptote, as Leibniz and Keynes do, is a plausible view that, as we have just seen, belongs to a main tradition of probability theory. However, I wonder if it might be more illuminating to speak of probabilistic relevance and logical modality here, than to speak of probability and logical truth. I shall offer three arguments for this.

First, probabilistic relevance approaches logical necessity as its asymptote; therefore it is best classified as belonging to logic. This argument is, of course, inconclusive. We might as well say that yellow and orange approach red as an asymptote; therefore yellow and orange are best classified as belonging to red. It might be that our only possible reply is that we have a simple intuition that logic and color differ in this respect. Of course, different people have different intuitions. Thus our argument could neither be strictly proved nor strictly refuted. For our own intuition might be either the correct one or the incorrect one. But we might also reply that the premiss is really that logical necessity is the *only* asymptote that (increases in) probabilistic relevance logically can approach. (This is why I said "*its* asymptote.") But yellow can and does approach *any* other color as an asymptote. For example, yellow approaches green through degrees of yellowish green, and so on. Therefore color asymptotes are very unlike the asymptote of logical necessity. And the respect of nonresemblance could scarcely be more relevant. All the same, if my argument is ultimately based only on a simple classificatory intuition, then its strength is only the strength of this intuition. My rejoinder is that this is only to be expected, since there is a very ordinary sense in which deductive logic is ultimately based on our logical intuitions. But my rejoinder is somewhat lame, since there are many different deductive logics based on many different logical intuitions.

Things are often clearer in philosophy of mathematics. Consider the series of proper fractions that are regularly diminishing halves: ½, ¼, ⅛,.... The series approaches zero as an asymptote. Zero cannot be a member of the series. The fractions may serve to represent regularly diminishing positive probabilities, and zero may serve to represent zero probability in the sense of deductive logical impossibility. (The number one would represent logical necessity.) Thus such proper probabilities cannot belong to deductive logic. Yet all the fractions in the series and zero are equally numbers; and at least on the logicist program, all equally belong to logic. Therefore the study of probability, or at least of such proper fractional probabilities, belongs to logic. One might object that the term "proper" is ambiguous. A proper fraction is a fraction whose numerator is smaller than its denominator, while a proper probability is a probability lying between logical necessity and logical impossibility. My reply is that in this example, all proper fractions represent proper probabilities, but zero cannot.

Second, it seems necessary that relevance in general shift multivocally across topics exactly as modalities do. I mean that just as we speak of logical, scientific, political, social, aesthetic, ethical, and epistemic necessities and possibilities, so we speak of logical, scientific, political, social, aesthetic, ethical, and epistemic relevancies which are more than merely possible but less than necessary. (Readers of chapter 6 will recall that an ethical necessity is the same as a duty, and being epistemically necessary is the same as being known.) Therefore, in the topic of deductive logic, just as in any other topic, there is a type of relevance that is more than mere logical possibility but less than logical necessity. I rate this second argument as illuminating and plausible. The problem with it is, of course, that logic might be an exception to the general rule that relevance and necessity shift multivocally across topics. For all the other topics concern both *a priori* and contingent matters, and so have conceptual room for a concept of relevance which is more than mere possibility but less than necessity. But deductive logic is only *a priori*, and there seems to be conceptual room only for the deductive sort of logical relevance we discussed in the last chapter, and for Wittgensteinian truth-table probability. My reply is that we commonly *do* speak of probability in the other deductive sciences. In particular, we often use "rough mathematics" involving rounded numbers, other approximations, "short cut" calculations, and even educated guesses based on our mathematical experience. We often estimate, for example, that the number we seek is probably greater than a certain round number, or probably within 100 integers of that number. The problem with my reply is, of course, that this would only equate to our educated guesses that some deductive argument is probably valid, based on, say, an experienced but quick look at its structure. We could accept *that* use of "probable" in deductive logic and still reject the assimilation of *epistemic* probability to logical necessity as an asymptote. My rejoinder would be that that use is a form of epistemic probability itself, and it is specifically intended to approach to the correct mathematical answer as an asymptote. My rejoinder does not logically remove the problem, but at least it reveals a strong tension, going beyond the mere ad hominem, in the objector's position. For it is something of an internal conflict to admit the ordinary use of rough arithmetic as giving approximations to the *mathematical* truth, approximations which have increasing degrees of epistemic probability depending on how rough they are, and at the same time to reject the view that epistemic probabilities increasingly approximate to *logical* truths depending on how rough the approximations are. Indeed, for Russell mathematics is but a species of logic.

My third argument is for the premiss that probabilistic relevance approaches logical necessity as an asymptote. It is ultimately intuitive, but relies on the common understanding of deductive logical relevance as some sort of connectedness or relatedness of the premises to the conclusion. Let us grant that probabilistic relevance is some sort of rational objective relatedness, and that so is deductive relevance. But that gives us right away a higher genus of which both of these sorts of relevance are species, namely, rational objective relatedness of premises to conclusion in general. But logic is just primarily the study of rational objective inference. Thus both sorts of relevance belong to logic. I think the objection here would be that this argument begs the question. For the whole question is whether probabilistic relevance is the sort of relevance that belongs to logic in the first place. Also, intuitions can differ.

My three arguments that probability belongs to logic are all inconclusive. Still, they may help illuminate what is conceptually at stake. Indeed, there are those who find it obvious that "the epistemic notion of probability...is nothing but the notion of rational belief" (Butchvarov 1970: 316). And reason is just what logic in the broad sense is.

Russell's Influence on Keynes' Theory

I hold that Keynes developed the theory of probability as degree of logical relevance, and Russell adopted it and modified it slightly over the years. But I shall argue that Keynes' theory is based in turn partly on Russell's 1903 *Principles of Mathematics*.

It seems clear that Keynes was making a brilliant new extension of ideas he found in Russell's *Principles*. That Russell's 1903 *Principles* should thus be an indirect source of his own 1912 *Problems* theory of induction should not be surprising, since both works belong to Russell's early phase of Platonic realism of "abstract logical universals" (PP 109). That *Principles* accepts a jungle realism of nonexistent beings, and *Problems* does not, is simply irrelevant.

Russell published *Problems* in 1912, and Keynes published his *Treatise* in 1921. But they were friends at least as early as 1904, the year after *Principles* was published (Russell 1987: 68). Russell says:

> I first knew Keynes through his father....
>   I had no contact with him in his economic and political work, but I was considerably concerned in his *Treatise on Probability*, many parts of which I discussed with him in detail. It was nearly finished in 1914, but had to be put aside for the duration [of the war]. (Russell 1987: 68)

Both Russell and his student, C. D. Broad, wrote reviews of the *Treatise* the year after it was published (Russell 1922; Broad 1922). Their reviews remain excellent discussions of the *Treatise* today, and perhaps there are no better brief introductions to the work. Russell and Broad praise the work highly; and while they offer criticisms, they give the impression that they agree with most of it. Broad "well remembers going over the proofs of the earlier parts of it in the long vacation of 1914 with Mr. Keynes and Mr. Russell," and says he is "substantially in agreement with" Keynes (Broad 1922: 72). Indeed, Broad joined Keynes and Russell in taking the logicist approach to solving the problem of induction, and took it at the same time they did (Wallenmaier 1967). Russell says, "The book as a whole is one which it is impossible to praise too highly" (Russell 1922: 159).

That Keynes was "much influenced by Bertrand Russell" is clear (Keynes 1962 / 1921: xiii). Skidelsky says:

> Moore, Russell and Keynes were all philosophic realists: they insisted on the *reality* of the intuitive knowledge

which was the foundation of all knowledge. They believed that to *perceive* qualities or logical relations was to perceive *something*; that the indefinable objects of thought had a 'real' existence, and that this reality was ...necessary to guarantee the truth of the intuition ....Russell confessed that when he wrote *The Principles of Mathematics* he shared with Frege a belief in the Platonic reality of numbers, which people a timeless realm 'of Being'. Keynes, too, wrote that probability is a 'real objective relation' which we 'cognise'. (Skidelsky 1994: 68, Skidelsky's emphasis)

Skidelsky continues:

Keynes worked on his thesis on probability in 1906 "under the joint influence of Moore's *Principia Ethica* and Russell's *Principia Mathematica*" [quoting Keynes] What he got equally from Moore and Russell (but perhaps also from his father) was the idea that logic was the foundation of philosophy, and that the foundational truths of ethics, mathematics and science were self-evident logical propositions, incapable of proof or disproof. A crucial debt was to Russell's extension of logic from its traditional subject-predicate form, exemplified by the syllogism, to include 'real' or 'external' relations....The recognition of such relations was fundamental to any principle of ordering or ranking. Equally important was Russell's distinction between magnitude and quantity....It makes sense to call A happier than B, not to say he is 50 per cent more happy. Russell's emphasis on the relational aspect of logic was fundamental to Keynes' theory of probability, though Keynes extended the scope of logical relations to include non-demonstrative inference. (Skidelsky 1994: 74; see Keynes 1962 / 1921: 6, 8, 90 on probability as a relation)

Skidelsky is right about all of this. And Skidelsky corrects Keynes for citing *Principia* as an influence in 1906 (Skidelsky 1994: 658 n.56). In 1906 Keynes could not have been influenced even by the unpublished manuscript of *Principia*, since Russell and Whitehead wrote it from "1907 to 1910" (Russell 1987: 155). Surely this was a slip on Keynes' part, and Keynes meant to say *Principles*. Instead it is Keynes' final *Treatise on Probability* that discusses *Principia* and not *Principles*, as Piero V. Mini observes (Mini 1994: 41; Keynes 1962 / 1921: 19n, 115).

One key element of the *Treatise*, the thesis that it is false that "two magnitudes of the same kind must be numerically comparable," and specifically, the observation that "thirty per cent.

healthier or happier," is "destitute of meaning," is in *Principles* (POM 176). The distinction between quantity and magnitude is there as well (POM 157–83). The admission of relations (POM 95–100), and their use to define ordered series (POM 199–226), are in *Principles* too. And so is the foundational logicist approach. And Keynes was surely aware of *Principles* as early as 1904, the year he presented his first paper on probability. This was, after all, the year he first met Russell. They must have become good friends quickly, since it was also the year of Keynes' famous attempt to escape from his admirers by staying with Bertrand and Alys Russell in their cottage—a secret visit interrupted by twenty-six unexpected guests (Skidelsky 1986: 124, 152–53, 183–84; Russell 1987: 68).

    Annabella Carabelli adds:

> In his discussion of the measurement of probability in the first version of the *Principles of Probability* (1907), Keynes considered the contemporary status of the philosophy of measurement and, in particular, of the measurement of relations. His main interest is in the 'philosophy of magnitude', not in the mathematics of magnitude....He devotes particular attention to Russell's *Principles of Mathematics* (1903). (Carabelli 1992: 6; see 5–10)

    Later on, *Principia* was a major influence on Keynes too. R. F. Harrod cites *Principia* as the source of Keynes' views that probabilities are features of propositions as opposed to events in the world, and that the task of a science of probability is to derive theorems from as few axioms as possible (Harrod 1951: 653–54). Harrod notes that this would make Keynes as indebted to Whitehead as to Russell (Harrod 1951: 653–54, 654n); both Whitehead and Russell praised the *Treatise* (Harrod 1951: 135).

    However, Skidelsky, Harrod, and Carabelli find nothing in Russell to explain Keynes' specific theory that probability is degree of logical relevance. That is not in either *Principles* or *Principia*. Russell does briefly discuss what he calls empirical "induction" in *Principles* (POM 441–42), but he is really sketching an analysis of abduction, which we now call "inference to the best explanation." Russell's only purpose in writing about "induction" there is to sketch what is logically needed to tell which kind of geometry applies to the actual world, given our empirical observations. Granted, Keynes might have simply applied Russell's *general* view in *Principles* that logic is the foundation of mathematics to mathematical probability theory in particular. But that only gets us a logicization of mathematical probability theory, not a theory that epistemic probability is degree of logical relevance.

Russell, of course, does not use the terms "relevance" or "logical relevance" in *Problems* to describe his probability theory or his theory of induction. But this is only to say that my thesis is not handed to us on the platter of express terminology.

Other Influences on Keynes

It is easy to place Keynes on the Russellian conceptual map of logical relevance as discussed in chapter 9, and of modality as discussed in chapter 6. For Keynes says in his *Treatise*,

> We have still, however, to make precise what we mean by...one proposition *following from* or being *logically involved in* the truth of another. We seem to intend by these expressions some kind of transition by means of a *logical principle*. A logical principle cannot be better defined, I think, than in terms of what in Mr. Russell's *Logic of Implication* is termed a formal implication. (Keynes 1962 / 1921: 124, Keynes' emphasis)

We may charitably say this puts Keynes on the level of *always true* formal implication in Russell's theory of logical relevance, and squarely on the level of implicit FG–MDL in Russell's views on modality. It appears, then, that Keynes never made the jump with Russell to implicit FG–MDL*, and is thus relying on a theory of logical truth which Russell rejected three years before Keynes' *Treatise* was published.

Nor is there in Keynes any concept of modality as based on truth-tables, of relevance as truth-ground containment, or of purely logical probability as based on truth-tables in the *Tractatus*. For Tractarian probability admits of limited degrees indeed. Every probability is a proper fraction whose numerator is the number of rows on which a statement is true and whose denominator is the total number of rows in its truth-table. A or $\neg A$ is 100% probable, $A \lor B$ is 75%, A is 50%, $A \& B$ is 25%, $A \& B \& C$ is 12.5%, and so on. Nothing can be 76% or 49% probable. In the *Tractatus*, nothing can fail to have a numerically determinate probability. Among logical theories of probability, it is hard to conceive of anything more deeply inimical to Keynes, even though Keynes speaks of *"partial"* following from, and even though both Wittgenstein and Keynes make logical necessity the asymptote of logical probability.

There were many influences on Keynes' *Treatise*. The young Keynes often heard his father, John Neville Keynes, and his father's closest friend, William Ernest Johnson, discuss logic; both made well-known contributions to logic (Skidelsky 1986: 69; Harrod 1951: 6–8).[1] The impact of Moore on the 1904 Keynes was tremendous (Skidelsky 1996: 36–37; 1994: 68, 74; 1986: 133–34; Bateman 1991: 56–59; Davis 1991: 89–92; Fitzgibbons 1991: 127–30; Braithwaite 1975: 242–45). Keynes' view that probability is indefinable seems inspired by Moore's view that goodness is indefinable (Harrod 1951: 652). Keynes' first paper on probability, read at the January 23, 1904 meeting of the Apostles (Cambridge Conversazione Society), and entitled "Ethics in Relation to Conduct," was a critical discussion of Moore's *Principia Ethica* (see Skidelsky 1986: 152–53). For Keynes, Moore's open question test, "This has property F, but is it good?" arguably applies to probability too: "This stands in relation R to body of evidence e, but is it probable?"

In his *Treatise*, Keynes cites Johnson, Moore, and Russell as chief influences (Keynes 1962 / 1921: xiii). Broad is very good at describing Johnson's contributions (Broad 1922), but does not mention degrees of logical relevance as one of them. And surely Moore did not develop a theory of inductive degrees of logical relevance, but had only the theory of deductive "degrees" of implicative logical necessity which Russell adopted in *Principles* (POM 454n). In fact, Keynes says that Moore's ethical theory of the future consequences of our acts "must be derived from the empirical or *frequency* theory" (Keynes 1962 / 1921: 310, my emphasis). This implies that Keynes believes that Moore has a theory of probability incompatible with his own, and does not believe that Moore is the source of his own.

Keynes completed the first draft of the *Treatise* on September 29, 1910 (Skidelsky 1986: 255). In 1914 his father Neville Keynes, Johnson, Russell, Moore, and Broad read the proofs and presumably offered suggestions (Skidelsky 1986: 285). However, it seems unlikely that any of those proofreaders is the origin of the theory that probability is degree of logical relevance. At any rate, I found nothing in their works to suggest that.

Mini notes that Keynes distances himself from his father's traditional logic (Mini 1994: 33). And Carabelli argues that Keynes tries to distance himself from Moore and Russell (Carabelli 1991: 120n). Keynes' 1904 paper criticizes Moore. And if Keynes is really the source of Russell's theory of induction as a weakly self-evident *a priori* principle, as Russell appears to say in *Problems*, then the reverse would not be true. Broad says he follows Keynes on probability, so the reverse would not be true.

Finally, there is the extensive list of works Keynes cites in his bibliography (Keynes 1962 / 1921: 431–58). Keynes confesses he did not read them all (Keynes 1962 / 1921: 432), but he did read a great deal. Harrod speaks of Keynes' "immense erudition" on probability and says, "It may well be that Keynes had a wider knowledge of the literature of probability than he ever acquired in his chosen subject of economics" (Harrod 1951: 136). Thus there are hundreds of potential sources of the theory of degrees of logical relevance.

Keynes was primarily an economist; but no economist seems to be the origin of his theory that probability is degree of logical relevance. I shall discuss the economists Keynes knew best, Francis Ysidro Edgeworth and Alfred Marshall, later in this chapter. I found nothing on logical relevance in *German Social Democracy*, Russell's 1896 book on economics and political science, either.

Keynes already spoke of "irrelevancy" in his 1904 paper (quoted in Skidelsky 1986: 184), and that seems to eliminate any origins of the theory later than 1904.

Thus from everything that has been said so far, it seems that we should be looking for a pre-1904 source which is outside of Keynes' readings in logic, philosophy, and economics.

The main object of this chapter is to argue it is more likely than not that the origin of Keynes' theory of logical relevance is not to be found in logic, philosophy, or economics, but in evidence law. I have, of course, already given my negative case that it is not likely to be found in any logician or philosopher. Perhaps I should restrict that claim to logicians and philosophers Keynes would have been likely to read. For as we shall see, many lawyers studied logic and philosophy in the centuries before Keynes, and studied them on theory of evidence. Thus logicians and philosophers might still have influenced Keynes indirectly, through their influence on the history of evidence law.

I shall begin with a brief review of probability theory because that our main topic, but also because knowing what the main probability theories are will help us tell whether and when Anglo-American evidence law is concerned with these theories. But since we are concerned with origins of any kind, we will be looking for anything *like* Keynes' theory in evidence law, regardless of whether the old evidence law treatise writers took it from a theory of probability, or even considered it to be a theory of probability.

Probability Theory: Introduction

Probability theory divides into (i) mathematical statistics, also known as the probability calculus, dating to the seventeenth century, and (ii) its several interpretations. The calculus itself is as unobjectionable as arithmetic or algebra. But people have never agreed on how to interpret its key undefined notion, the notion of probability, or if you like, h/e, the probability of hypothesis h given evidence e. Arguably, there is no single best interpretation.

The previous chapter was all about diagramming logical relevance in deductive logic. And whether or not we logicize mathematics, we all know that mathematics can be diagrammed. Thus, insofar as the probability calculus is part of mathematics, it should come as no surprise that it too can be diagrammed, and that there can be diagrammable containments of probabilities within probabilities in probability arguments.

If probabilities can be assigned numbers at all, then they can be graphed. John Neville Keynes says, "In the use of statistics, considerable assistance may often be derived from the employment of diagrams" (N. Keynes 1986 / 1917: 339). More fully, Neville Keynes says:

> In the use of statistics, considerable assistance may often be derived from the employment of diagrams. The graphic method is not only useful for the popular exposition of statistics...; but it also has a genuine scientific value. Thus by means of graphic representation we may employ the special method of quantitative induction called by Whewell the method of curves. (N. Keynes 1986 / 1917: 339–40)

And just as there can be logics of "many" and "few," there can be diagrams of relations of merely greater or lesser probabilities. Such diagrams can be made numerical too, but they would use ordinal numbers instead of cardinal numbers. Just as the hardness scale for minerals allows a Venn diagram of the hypothetical syllogism, "Diamond is harder than carborundum, carborundum is harder than shale, therefore diamond is harder than shale," so too we can diagram the hypothetical syllogism, "It is more likely that the sun will rise tomorrow than that there will be a solar eclipse, it is more likely that there will be a solar eclipse tomorrow than that the sun will cease to exist, therefore it is more likely that the sun will rise tomorrow than that it will cease to exist."

Besides cardinal probabilities and ordinal probabilities, Maynard Keynes admits incommensurable probabilities. These are the only probabilities that cannot be diagrammed, since they cannot even be ranked or classified ordinally.

The great legal scholar John Henry Wigmore is famous for his argument charts. These directly concern the stages of a legal argument, but their purpose is to help assess the likelihood of the argument's success. "Wigmore's...Chart Method of analysing mixed masses of evidence...., Bayes' Theorem and other axioms of probability, are extraordinarily flexible and powerful tools which, if used with sensitive awareness of their nature, make clear the operation of 'subjective' values, biases, and choices at almost every stage of complex intellectual procedures" (Twining 1994: 6–7). Thus Wigmore admits diagrams of probability arguments.

There are three main rival interpretations of the probability calculus: frequency theory (Aristotle); logical theory (Keynes); and subjectivist theory (Ramsey).

Aristotle's Frequency Theory of Probability

The frequency interpretation of probability starts with Aristotle, who defines probability as what is usually the case: "A probability is a thing that usually happens" (*Rhetoric* 1357*b*35 / Aristotle 1968c: 1332). John Venn was its champion in the nineteenth century; Richard von Mises and Hans Reichenbach were its main champions in the twentieth. Again, the frequency theory is a logical interpretation of probability, insofar as the notions of "many" or "few" members of a class are logical notions. But actual frequencies are empirical, so we need empirical interpretations of this logical interpretation of probability. There is nothing wrong with having interpretations of interpretations. For example, Russell interprets ordinary things in terms of molecules, molecules in terms of atoms, and atoms in terms of quantum events (see AMA 2–9). Indeed, empirical interpretations of frequency theory are just *applications* of frequency theory.

The frequency theory is naturally popular with scientists, statisticians, and epidemiologists. In fact, it is basic for anyone who works with huge populations of repetitive items. But it is hard to apply to unusual or nonrecurrent events. It is also hard to apply if the events in question belong to two equally huge opposing classes of events, and occur more frequently in the less relevant class.

Keynes' Logical Theory of Probability

Keynes developed his theory of probability as logical relevance to replace frequency theory, at least as Keynes found it in Moore. Keynes gives a purely logical interpretation of probability as degree of logical relevance, where relevance is a logically intuited relationship among propositions. Besides Russell and perhaps Russell's student Broad, Keynes is the only major thinker in 1912 who interprets probability as degree of logical relevance.

Keynes says of "the term *probability*": "In its most fundamental sense, I think, it refers to the logical relation between two sets of propositions" (Keynes 1962 / 1921: 11, Keynes' emphasis). The first set describes the body of evidence, and the second the "object of...rational belief" (Keynes 1962 / 1921: 12). Keynes also allows two derivative senses. (1) The term can mean the degree of rational belief which we are entitled to have based on our evidence; and (2) it can even be elliptically used to mean the probability of the statement believed (Keynes 1962 / 1921: 11–12). Derivative sense (1) is the sense with which we are most directly concerned. Derivative sense (2) is casual and strictly incorrect, since the probability of the statement believed is essentially related to, and therefore must be tacitly understood as related to, the body of evidence the probability is based on.

Keynes finds that being probable is just as *"relational"* as being equal to, being greater than, or being three miles distant from (Keynes 1962 / 1921: 6–7), Keynes' emphasis. This does not mean that probability is relative. Keynes' example illustrates this well. The fact that I was three miles from home yesterday remains objectively true even if I am home today. Likewise, the fact that a view was improbable based on the evidence I had yesterday remains objectively true even if the view is probable based on the evidence I have today. We may say Keynes' view is that probability statements are logically indeterminate (logically incomplete) unless they have two logical subject-terms, one about a body of evidence, and the other about the object which the evidence is ostensibly evidence for. That is, probability statements essentially assert that a relation of probability obtains between those two relata. Keynes cites Ludovicus Martinus Kahle, Boole, and Laplace as his predecessors in holding "[t]hat "probability is a *relation*" (Keynes 1962 / 1921: 90–91, Keynes' emphasis).

Keynes means by "degree of logical relevance," degree of objective rational credibility. This concept is not at all the same as the concept of degree of probability or likelihood, and that makes Keynes' definition significantly informative, and *prima facie*, synthetic *a priori*. I plan to show later that this is Russell's view as well.

Keynes says:

[I]n the sense important to logic, probability is not subjective. It is not, that is to say, subject to human caprice. A proposition is not probable because we think it so. When once the facts are given which determine our knowledge, what is probable or improbable in these circumstances has been fixed objectively, and is independent of our opinion. The Theory of Probability is logical, therefore, because it is concerned with the degree of belief which it is *rational* to entertain in given conditions, and not merely with the actual beliefs of particular individuals, which may or may not be rational. (Keynes 1962 / 1921: 4, his emphasis)

He repeats this view: "[I]f our grounds are reasonable, are they not in an important sense logical?" (Keynes 1962 / 1921: 98). Besides its *a priori* character, this is all he means by calling his theory a logical theory. And here I would like to make a major classificatory point. Merely to be *a priori* is not yet to be analytic *a priori*, or logical in the formal sense. For there is also the synthetic *a priori*. But there is also a second, broader sense of "logical" in which even the synthetic *a priori* is logical. And that is precisely Keynes' sense of being rational and objective. For if Kant and Frege are right that geometry is synthetic *a priori*, for all that it would still be just as rational and objective as logic or arithmetic. And in point of fact, I think Keynes' intuitions of degrees of relevance are synthetic *a priori*. My tests are simply Russell's: the statements describing relevance relations between bodies of evidence and our hypotheses are not fully generalized, nor are they truth-preservingly fully generalizable. Still less are they true in virtue of their logical form. Therefore, if such statements are true *a priori*, then they can only be synthetic *a priori* truths. Even if we speak generally of bodies of evidence 1, 2,...*n*, and similarly of hypotheses 1, 2,...*n*, as well as of relations 1, 2,...*n* between bodies of evidence and hypotheses, this is still not full generality. For terms like "hypothesis" and "body of evidence" are descriptive terms, not logical terms. Nor are they variables. If they were, we should be able to substitute "apple" and "cat" for them, or any other terms we like, and preserve the truth of our original statements of relevance relations. The truth is quite the opposite. Judgments of degree of relevance for Keynes are nothing without their particularity; and the only fully general theory here is the uninterpreted probability calculus.

Keynes says that "probability is, in the strict sense, indefinable" (Skidelsky 1986: 183; 2003: 109 quoting Keynes 1908). Skidelsky is right to note Keynes' qualification, "in the strict sense." Many simply hold that probability is indefinable for Keynes, such as Harrod (1951: 652) and even Russell (OP 286; HK 373; MPD 142). But Russell says more cautiously in his review of Keynes only that "Mr Keynes holds that a *formal* definition of probability is impossible" (Russell 1922: 152, my emphasis). Keynes actually says:

> A *definition* of probability is not possible, **unless** it contents us to **define** degrees of the probability-relation by reference to degrees of rational belief. We cannot analyze the probability-relation in terms of **simpler** ideas. (Keynes 1962 / 1921: 8, Keynes' italic emphasis, my boldface emphasis)

Keynes is saying that we cannot define probability in the sense of analyzing it into simpler ideas. He is saying that we cannot give a *compositional* definition of probability. Now, if we define degree of probability as degree of rational belief, the term "degree of" occurs on both sides of the definition, and that term is therefore not a logical part of what is actually being defined. Clearly, in "degree of probability =Df degree of rational belief, we are really defining "probability" as 'rational belief'. If we treat 'rational belief' as a simple term that does not break down into two simpler ideas, 'rational' and 'belief', then we are defining probability without analyzing it into simpler ideas. Instead, we are defining probability as being something equally simple, namely, rational belief. This is a *theoretical definition*. To give a theoretical definition of a thing is to state what the thing is, typically in terms of a scientific or other theory (Copi 1978: 140–41). From Aristotle on, this has been widely regarded as the most important kind of definition. And Keynes' theory is a theoretical definition. For whether he calls it a definition or not, he is saying that this is *what* probability *is*: degree of rational belief. The definition is not only theoretical, but is also an *informative identification*, since the terms "probable" and rational belief' express very different intensional senses.

A second view, better than the first, is that defining degree of probability as degree of rational belief is compositional because "rational" and "belief" are two different concepts. In fact, this looks for all the world like a definition by genus and difference, with belief as the genus and rational as the difference. Even if we held that all belief is intrinsically rational—which is decidedly not Keynes' view, since he says "the actual beliefs of particular individuals...may or may not be rational" (Keynes 1962 / 1921: 4)—the concepts of rationality and of belief would be different, though distinct only in reason, so that the definition of probability as rational belief would still be logically compositional.

A holder of the first view might reply that the definition is really of degree of probability as degree of *rationality* of belief. For that is what counts, and not the degree of *strength* of belief, i.e., degree of *psychological* certainty or conviction, to which it is chiefly opposed. And I am sure that is what Keynes has in mind. For he says it is "the degree of belief which it is *rational* to entertain" Keynes 1962 / 1921: 4, Keynes' emphasis).

But a holder of the second view the objector might rejoin, "But rationality *of* what? Of a theory? Of a course of action? Here for Keynes it must be rationality *of belief*, and so belief must be a logical element in the definition after all."

A subtle holder of the first view might reply that if every belief were essentially minimally rational, then rationality and belief would be not *wholly* distinct, and thus not *really* distinct, but only *formally* distinct *á la* Scotus, or distinct only in reason.

A subtle holder of the second view might reply, "Yes, but rationality and belief are still not the same. Even on the view that all beliefs are minimally rational, belief and rationality are different *because* they are formally distinct, or distinct in reason." And it is in this sense that I think Keynes' definition of (degree of) probability as (degree of) rational belief logically must be compositional after all. And we might arguably even consider it a definition by genus and difference. However, if all beliefs were essentially minimally rational, then belief could not be the genus, since rationality could not function as a difference. Instead, rationality would have to be the genus, and the differences would be things like theory, course of action, or belief. But if we take that approach, we must be sure that "reason" is said univocally, and not ambiguously, nor *pros hen* in Aristotle's sense of *pros hen*, in which living bodies are primarily or literally healthy, and climates and foods are said to be healthy in a derivative sense if they tend to produce healthy living bodies, and urine is said to be healthy in another derivative sense if it is the sort of urine produced by healthy living bodies. But for present purposes, we need not reach such questions. It is enough to note that belief and rationality are distinct in reason, and are therefore different, and that therefore the one definition of probability which Keynes says he *would* accept *is* logically compositional, *pace* Keynes—and that therefore probability is not indefinable for Keynes after all. Of course, he may still *take* it as a primitive term in his theory, even though I think we must say it *is* not in fact genuinely primitive. Since I agree with Keynes that beliefs logically need not be rational, I can take the definition as defining probability by the genus belief and the difference rational. Thus I criticize Keynes for not noticing that if "it contents us to define degrees of the probability-relation by reference to degrees of rational belief," then we *do* in fact "analyze the probability-relation in terms of simpler ideas" (Keynes 1962 / 1921: 8), namely, the two simpler ideas of belief and rationality. Obviously he distinguishes these two ideas, since he says "beliefs may or may not be rational."

I proceed to compare Keynes' theory of probability with the definition of relevance in the American *Federal Rules of Evidence* (*FRE*) Rule 401, and also with Bayes' Theorem.

Keynes offers an initial simple definition of "irrelevance" as follows: if $h/e1,e2 = h/e1$, then $e2$ is irrelevant to $h/e1$ (Keynes 1962 / 1921: 54–56; I alter his notation). This means that if the probability of hypothesis h given bodies of evidence $e1$ and $e2$ is the same as the probability of h given $e1$ alone, then $e2$ is irrelevant to establishing h. This conception of irrelevance is basic to discussions of logical relevance in today's evidence law casebooks, such as the one by Richard O. Lempert and Stephen A. Saltzburg (Lempert 2011: ch. 3).[2]

Keynes' initial simple definition of irrelevance seems to be a negative version of the definition of relevance in *FRE* Rule 401:

> **Rule 401. Definition of "Relevant Evidence"**
>   "Relevant evidence" means evidence having any tendency to make the existence of any fact that is of any consequence to the determination of the [judicial] action more probable or less probable than it would be without the evidence (West Publishing Company 1995: 24).[3]

Unless Keynes allows *e1* to be nothing, Rule 401 improves on him by not requiring a prior body of evidence *e1*. Thus Rule 401 avoids the vicious infinite regress of prior bodies of evidence which Keynes faces. (This is an old criticism of Keynes; I am merely noting that Rule 401 avoids it.) But Rule 401 appears to be worse than Keynes in that it does not admit of degrees of relevance. Lempert says of Rule 401:

> There are no degrees of relevance; evidence is either relevant or it is not. Strictly speaking, it is a mistake to say that one item of evidence is *"more relevant"* than another. What differentiates items of different evidentiary weight is *probative value*, i.e. their power to persuade a reasonable person about a fact in issue Admissible evidence varies widely in probative value.
> (Lempert 2011: 213, Lempert's emphasis)

Lempert is correctly reporting current legal usage, but this seems to be a mere difference in terminology. The nineteenth century legal scholars often write as if having relevance and having probative value are the same. Indeed, one might define relevance as having any degree of probative value greater than zero. Of course, "any" is a logical term, but "zero" is not, unless we are logicists. To make the definition more purely logical, we may say that to be relevant is to have *some* probative value. In any case, if we define relevance as having at least *some* minimal (or non-zero) probative value, then we reject degrees of relevance, and admit only degrees of probative value. That may make relevance a useful threshold requirement for the admissibility of evidence in a courtroom. But it is just as silly as saying that to be probable is to have at least minimal (or non-zero) logical relevance, and on that basis denying that there are any degrees of probability, and admitting only degrees of logical relevance.

If we are to admit a definition here at all, I think the only one that makes any theoretical sense, as opposed to practical or courtroom sense, is to define degree of probability as degree of logical relevance. This is what Keynes has in mind. And we would not wish to reverse the definition, since probability is the more obscure term, and is the term we wish to illuminate. Lempert does not discuss Keynes here (Lempert 2011: 213). But surely Lempert would agree that any conflict between Rule 401 and Keynes is merely verbal. In *court*, Rule 401 is useful, since there we wish to have a threshold requirement for the admissibility of evidence. But in *theory of probability*, we wish to state what probability is. And here, we wish to preserve and illuminate its essential feature of having various sorts of degrees, which intuitively include cardinal, ordinal, and incommensurable degrees. Degrees of logical relevance seem to do this perfectly.

Bayes' Theorem is used as "a method for using assumed probabilities to derive other probabilities" (Friedman 1991: 66n.) It is an equation for multiplying or dividing probabilities. Ephraim Nissan says:

> **Bayes' theorem** When dealing with a hypothesis H, and some evidence E, Bayes' Theorem states:
>
> $$P(H\backslash E) = P(E\backslash H)P(H)/P(E)$$
>
> this can be read as follows: The *posterior probability* $P(H\backslash E)$, i.e. the probability that H is true given E, is equal to the product of the likelihood $P(E\backslash H)$, i.e., the probability that E given the truth of H, and the *prior probability* $P(H)$ of H, divided by the *prior probability* $P(E)$ of E. (Nissan 2012: 1029–30, Nissan's emphasis)

Nissan's "this can be read" is already an interpretation of the theorem, in terms of probability, evidence, and hypothesis. It is the *further* interpretation of the term "probability," in terms of a theory of probability, such as Aristotle's, Keynes', or Ramsey's, that would concern us here. Nissan's prior probabilities are Friedman's assumed probabilities. Bayes' Theorem itself, of course, belongs to the uninterpreted probability calculus.

Keynes calls Bayes' Theorem the "first...appearance" of "the Principle of Inverse Probability, a theorem of great importance in the history of the subject" of probability (Keynes 1962 / 1921: 174). Keynes discusses the principle's history, proof, and formulation (Keynes 1962 / 1921: 174–81, 379–80), and discusses "various arguments which have been based upon it...in Chapter XXX" (Keynes 1962 / 1921: 174). Keynes, of course, has no real choice about accepting Bayes' Theorem, since it is part of the probability calculus, and his theory must interpret that calculus, if his theory is to be considered an adequate theory of probability.

Bayes' Theorem is not the same as Keynes' definitions of irrelevance. Keynes says:

> The simplest definition of Irrelevance is as follows: h_1 is irrelevant to [conclusion] x on evidence h, if the probability of x on evidence hh_1 is the same as its probability on evidence h.[1] But for a reason which will appear in Chapter VI., a stricter and more complicated definition, as follows, is theoretically preferable: h_1 is irrelevant to x on evidence h, if there is no such proposition, inferrible from h_1h but not from h, such that its addition to evidence h affects the probability of x.[2] Any proposition which is irrelevant in the strict sense is, of course, also irrelevant in the simpler sense; but if we were to adopt the simpler definition, it would sometimes occur that a part of evidence would be relevant, which taken as a whole was irrelevant. The more elaborate definition by avoiding this proves in the sequel more convenient. If the condition $x/h_1h = h/h$ alone is satisfied, we may say that the evidence h_1 is 'irrelevant as a whole'.[3]
>   It will be convenient to define also two other phrases. h_1 and h_2 are independent and complementary part of the evidence, if between them they make up h and neither can be inferred from the other. **If x is the conclusion, and h_1 and h_2 are independent and complementary parts of the evidence, then h_1 is relevant if the addition of it to h_2 affects the probability of x.**[4]
> 1. That is to say, h_1 is irrelevant to x/h if $x/h_1h = x/h$.
> 2. That is to say, h_1 is irrelevant to x/h, if there is no proposition $h'_1/h_1h = 1$, $h'_1/h \neq 1$, and $x/h'_1/h \neq x/h$.
> 3. Where no misunderstanding can arise, the qualification 'as a whole' will be sometimes omitted.
> 4. I.e[.] (in symbolism) h_1 and h_2 are independent and complementary parts of h if $h_1h_2 = h$, $h_1/h_2 \neq 1$, and $h_2/h_1 \neq 1$. **Also, h_1 is relevant if $x/h \neq x/h_2$.** (Keynes 1962: 55, Keynes' italic emphasis, my boldface emphasis)

It should be clear that Keynes' two definitions of irrelevance are negative versions of Rule 401, and are logically more precise than Rule 401, the second even more so than the first. It should also be clear that the two boldfaced sentences are positive versions of Rule 401, and are logically more precise than Rule 401, the second even more so than the first. The two boldfaced sentences appear to be statements, not definitions; but they could be considered as definitions, or as helping further logically clarify the two negative definitions Keynes gives. Except for the greater degree(s) of precision, and except for the fact that the two boldfaced sentences appear to be statements of a principle, and not definitions, all of four of these appear to be logically equivalent to Rule 401. Certainly they all discuss relevance in terms of probability, just as Rule 401 does.

But this is true only on the surface of Keynes' theory. At bottom, Keynes reverses Rule 401. For at bottom, he understands probability as degree of logical relevance.

Four closely related comments follow.

First, Rule 401 defines relevance in terms of probability, and that is what Keynes does in his various versions of the Principle of Inverse Probability. But for Keynes, the whole question is what probability is in the first place. The fundamental task of probability theory is to answer that question. Aristotle, Venn, Keynes, Ramsey, Mises, and Reichenbach all agree that probability is the obscure and basic notion needing explanation.

It may seem that all this makes Keynes' theory circular. For Keynes holds that probability is degree of logical relevance, and then defines irrelevance (twice) in terms of probability. This might also seem to mean that Keynes has two notions of relevance, one which he takes to be primitive and to define probability, and one which he takes to be defined in terms of probability. But this is not so. His use of the word "relevance" is univocal. His definition of probability as degree of logical relevance (or rational belief) is fundamental. It is his metaphysical theory of the nature of probability as timeless, intuited logical relevance. The definition of irrelevance in terms of probability is his formalization. It is his formally defined *test* of when irrelevance occurs, and conversely, of when relevance occurs. The test succeeds precisely because probability *is* degree of logical relevance. For essential identity implies logical equivalence.

Second, to distinguish Bayes' Theorem from Rule 401 and from Keynes' definition of probability as degree of logical relevance, we need only note that they are definitions, while Bayes' Theorem is an uninterpreted theorem of the probability calculus. As such, Bayes' Theorem ought to be adequately interpretable by any serious theory of probability, including Aristotle's frequency theory, Keynes' logical theory, and Ramsey's subjectivist theory. Clearly, neither Rule 401 nor Keynes' definition of probability as degree of logical relevance is an uninterpreted theorem of the probability calculus. They are not theorems at all, but definitions. Far from being uninterpreted, they are definitional interpretations. Granted, definitions do imply axioms. In general, definition $F =$Df G implies the axiom that F is logically equivalent to G. However, they interpret the axioms they imply, as well as any theorems the axioms imply.

Third, Rule 401 does not even attempt to interpret the probability calculus. For it defines relevance in terms of probability, and leaves probability undefined. Rule 401 does not tell us how to understand probabilty in turn. Is probability a matter of frequency? Is it a matter of logical intuition? Is it a matter of willingness to bet? As far as Rule 401 is concerned, probability could be any of these things. Ramsey criticizes Keynes for making this mistake. Ramsey says "it is as if everyone knew the laws of geometry but no one could tell whether any given object were round or square" (Ramsey 1931: 162; compare Frege 1974: 35–36; Russell 1956 / 1897: 40, 72–74, 80, 93, 101, 104–5). Ramsey is wrong about Keynes, since Keynes does tell us what he thinks probability is. But Ramsey's point does apply to Rule 401.

Fourth, if Rule 401 is an endorsement of Keynes, then it is a rejection of all of Keynes' rivals. And the chief rival to Keynes, the frequency theory, is the one used by scientists dealing with mass repetitive phenomena, as in mass toxic injury cases. We would be treated to the spectacle of Rule 401's using Keynes' interpretation of probability to evaluate scientific theories which are based on the chief rival to Keynes, or for that matter, to evaluate the frequency theory itself, as well as all other rivals to Keynes' theory. Those who favor Keynes might not find that a bad idea, and it certainly is an interesting one. But it would make Rule 401 beg the question of what probability is by simply assuming that Keynes' theory is correct, since Rule 401 certainly does not argue for that.

I discuss Rule 401 further in the section "Anglo-American Relevance Law Today." For more on Bayes' Theorem, see Bayes (1963) and Swinburne (2002), both of which contain Bayes' paper. There are large literatures on Bayes in both philosophy and law.

I shall now discuss Locke, Leibniz, and Jakob (also called James) Bernoulli as major antecedents of Keynes.

In his *An Essay Concerning Human Understanding*, book 4, chapter 16, "Of the Degrees of Assent," Locke discusses witnesses and testimony in an ordinary general sense. For Locke, degrees of assent are or correspond to degrees of probability. He says, "The grounds of probability...as they are the foundations on which are *assent* is built, so are they also the measure whereby its several degrees are, or ought to be regulated" (Locke 1959 / 1690: vol. 2, 368, Locke's emphasis). Like Keynes, Locke makes probability relative to a body of evidence. Locke says:

> Probability is likeliness to be true, the very notation of
> the word signifying such a proposition, for which there

be arguments or proofs to make it pass, or be received for true. The entertainment the mind gives this sort of propositions is called *belief, assent,* or *opinion,* which is the admitting or receiving any proposition for true, upon arguments or proofs that are found to persuade us to receive it as true, without certain knowledge that it is so. (Locke 1959 / 1690: vol. 2, 365, Locke's emphasis)

The context makes it clear that such "arguments or proofs" are less than logically certain. His general distinction is between uncertain probability and certain demonstration. This is basically the same as Keynes on probability as relational, if we replace Locke's term "arguments or proofs" with Keynes' term "body of evidence."

Leibniz was an encyclopedic thinker one of whose many fields of study was jurisprudence. His *New Essays,* book 4, chapter 16, "Of the Degrees of Assent," corresponds to and comments on Locke's *Essay,* book 4, chapter 16, "Of the Degrees of Assent," which I discussed in the previous paragraph. (*New Essays* is a dialogue: Theophilus represents Leibniz, and Philalethes represents Locke.) In his book, Leibniz finds examples of Lockean degrees of assent in the law, including evidence law. He says, "When jurists discuss proofs, presumptions, conjectures, and evidence, they have a great many good things to say on the subject and go into considerable detail....The entire form of judicial procedures is, in fact, nothing but a kind of logic, applied to legal questions" (Leibniz 1966 / 1765 / 1704: 464). He also cites physicians as recognizing "many differences of degree among their signs and symptoms," and adds, "Mathematicians have begun, in our own day, to calculate the chances in games" (Leibniz 1966 / 1765 / 1704: 465).

Leibniz says, "I have said more than once [on pages 206, 373] that we need a new kind of logic, concerned with degrees of probability, since Aristotle in his *Topics* could not have been further from it: he was content to set out certain familiar rules..." (Leibniz 1966 / 1765 / 1704: 466, editor's bracketed page cites).

Russell wrote his first philosophy book on Leibniz. Probability is not a topic, but empirical knowledge is. Russell discusses *New Essays* on the thesis that all necessary truth, including mathematical truth, is analytic. At least by implication, that would include the probability calculus. See Russell (1937 / 1900: ch. 14).

I turn now to Bernoulli. In his book, *History of Probability and Statistics and Their Applications before 1750,* Anders Hald distinguishes "[o]bjective, statistical, or aleatory probabilities" and "[s]ubjective, personal, or epistemic probabilities" (Hald 2003: 28, Hald's emphasis deleted). Hald says of the latter:

Such probabilities refer to our imperfect knowledge and thus only indirectly to the things or events about which a statement is made. Some philosophers consider epistemic probability, which they call logical probability[,] as a measure of the strength of a logical relation between two propositions, i.e., a weaker relation than that of logical consequence. (Hald 2003: 28)

Hald's notion of indirect reference ("refer...indirectly") in this text is an instance of Russell's notion of propositional attitude, and of Quine's notion of referential opacity. Hald says, "A clear distinction between the two kinds of probability is due to James Bernoulli (1713)" (Hald 2003: 28). Hald says, "According to Hacking (1971), similar ideas had been previously expressed by Leibniz; however, Bernoulli gave the first systematic exposition of these fundamental concepts, and his formulations and viewpoints have been influential ever since" (Hald 2003: 247, cites omitted; see 247–54). Hald says that for Bernoulli, "probability is a degree of certainty and as such a measure of our imperfect knowledge; probability is personal in the sense that it varies from person to person according to his knowledge, and for the same person it may vary with time as his knowledge changes" (Hald 2003: 249). This is basically the same as Keynes on the variability of probability across persons and times, if we replace Bernoulli's term "knowledge" with Keynes' term "body of evidence." Hald adds, "The distinction between objective and subjective probability was [also] formulated clearly by Cournot (1843...)" (Hald 2003: 246).

Finally, I shall make a distinction between the mathematics and the philosophy of Keynes' theory of probability, only to set it aside. Vincent Barnett says, "...Keynes' book was soon made almost completely obsolete as a mathematical theory of probability by the publication of A. N. Kolmogorov's groundbreaking *Foundations of the Theory of Probability* in 1933, which pioneered a comprehensive set-theoretic approach to the subject" (Barnett 2013: 121). Barnett concludes that "it would not be too far from the truth to suggest that" Keynes' *Treatise* is now "mainly valuable for" what it has to offer "outside of mathematics" (Barnett 2013: 121, Barnett's emphasis). This is a mathematical criticism and does not concern Keynes' philosophical theory. In fact, even Barnett finds the philosophical theory "valuable" (Barnett 2013: 121).

Ramsey's Subjectivist Theory of Probability

Keynes' theory was criticized in turn by the brilliant young Cambridge mathematician Frank Plumpton Ramsey, whom Keynes and Russell knew well (Harrod 1951: 320–21). Ramsey champions the subjectivist theory of probability, which may be found in his *The Foundations of Mathematics*, posthumously edited and published in 1931 (see Skidelsky 1994: 67–73). Ramsey criticizes Keynes for relying on logical intuitions which nobody could intuit. Ramsey cannot discover such intuitions in himself, and finds that other people's supposed logical intuitions conflict with each other (Ramsey 1931: 161–63). Ramsey abandons objectivism concerning the probabilities of specific events' occurring, and cashes out the rationality of our probabilistic beliefs about specific events in terms of their pragmatic success (Ramsey 1931: 171ff). Specifically, he cashes out subjective belief in terms of observable willingness to make bets (Ramsey 1931: 172, 183).

Ramsey admits two basic requirements: (i) not allowing Dutch book, that is, not allowing betting against your own bet; and (ii) general overall "consistency" in the learning process of making successful bets (Ramsey 1931: 176–83; see Skidelsky 1994: 70–71; Bateman 1991: 59–61; Davis 1991: 99–100; Braithwaite 1975: 240–41). As to requirement (ii), Ramsey holds that in the long run, such a program would *approximate* objective probabilities (Ramsey 1931: 182–83).

Subjectivism dates back at least to Venn, if not also to Augustus De Morgan (Venn 1964; Mares 1997). I think that Jeremy Bentham, whom Ramsey cites, anticipates subjectivism by construing probability in terms of tendencies of facts to produce convictions in the mind, and by construing probability ultimately in terms of its utility (see e.g. Bentham 1827: 1, *pace* Ramsey 1931: 173). As a utilitarian, Bentham's basic approach "is the utilitarian one of allowing all rationally helpful evidence to be considered by the tribunal of fact, subject to guidance as to its weight," notably in his major work *Rationale of Judicial Evidence* (Murphy 2008: 8). This too is subjective in the sense that utilitarianism cashes out values in terms of pleasures and pains. I shall not attempt to determine the ultimate origins of subjectivist probability here; the first utilitarians in any case were the ancient Epicureans.

Ramsey's theory avoids some major difficulties with the other theories. As long as people are willing to bet, it does not matter whether the events are uniform or unique, nor whether they are more frequent in less relevant classes and less frequent in more relevant classes. Those were the main difficulties with the frequency theory. And Ramsey obviously does away with logical intuitions, the mysterious and often conflicting relations basic to Keynes' theory.

I shall offer five criticisms of Ramsey.

First, there cannot be a learning process for unique events. This kills Ramsey's second basic requirement.

Second, on his own admission, Ramsey's program is only a theory of mathematical *approximations* to probability. But how could we know whether his program approximates objective probabilities in the long run, unless we already know what the objective probabilities *are*? And if we already know them, then why should we be satisfied with mere approximations, when we already have the thing itself? It would be like returning to the shadows in Plato's cave after being out in the sunlight. Like the imitative poets Plato criticizes, Ramsey is a mere imitator of, or approximator to, the real thing.

Third, if my first criticism is correct, then the question is, What *is* the true theory of probability? That is, which theory of probability best describes the objective probabilities to which Ramsey's subjective probabilities merely approximate? It cannot be, of course, Ramsey's own theory, since we need an objective theory, not a subjective approximation. Even worse, we do not want Ramsey to be approximating to himself. Curiously enough, Ramsey himself appears to answer this question. He says, "And the answer is that it will in general be best for his degree of belief that a yellow toadstool is unwholesome to be equal to the proportion of yellow toadstools which are in fact unwholesome" (Ramsey 1931: 195). Thus Ramsey appears to admit the frequency theory as the true theory of objective probabilities, to which his subjectivist theory approximates. But even if that is not the case, my criticism remains.

Fourth, Ramsey is right that our ostensibly logical intuitions about probabilities often conflict, and that this casts doubt on their reliability. But it is a *non sequitur* to infer from this that such logical intuitions do not *exist*. Evidence is often conflicting and doubtful no matter what our theory of probability is. In particular, I see no reason why our probability intuitions would be either more or less conflicting or doubtful than our sense-perceptions. Eyewitnesses are notoriously conflicting and unreliable. Does it follow that sense-perceptions do not exist? Does it follow that there are no sense-perceptible objects such as trees? Ramsey's criticism even applies to his own theory. Our bets are often conflicting and doubtful, and at least as much as our logical intuitions. This includes bets across persons, bets across time for the same person, and cases where one person at one time is internally conflicted on how to bet. In fact, if we all always bet the same way, there would be no games of chance, and far less conflict in human affairs. Life would be very different from what it is. Thus Ramsey's theory is no better than the others in this regard. Namely, on his own criticism, we *ought* to conclude that bets do not exist any more than logical intuitions do. That bets obviously *do* exist is intended by Ramsey to avoid the problems he raises with logical intuitions. But ironically, it is a counterexample to his criticism that what is conflicting and doubtful does not exist. is This may be called Ramsey's gambling problem. Of course, it is not a counterexample to his criticism that he is unable to apprehend any such logical intuitions; my next criticism will address that issue.

Fifth, it has been long noted that we cannot apprehend *any* relations as if they were objects, but only as they occur in relational situations. Whether the relations are specifically logical intuitions or other relations of apprehension does not matter in the least to the general problem. On this general level of our being unable to apprehend any relations at all, Ramsey's criticism of Keynes is not on the appropriate level of depth. For on this level, his criticism would apply not just to Keynes' theory in particular, but to all theories across the board which admit relations, including any other probability theories. Indeed, Ramsey's criticism applies to his own admission of deductive logical relations. It seems that on his own view, he can apprehend deductive logical relations such as modus ponens, but cannot apprehend inductive logical relations such as probability relations. Of course, he can consistently admit the intuition (what else could it be?) of deductive logical relations which are abstract entities, and reject both the intuition of and thereby the abstract entityhood of nondeductive logical relations, since the two sets of relations are mutually exclusive. But that is very awkward. indeed. For all logical relations belong to the same metaphysical and cognitive category. I do not see how he is entitled to admit that we can intuit deductive logical relations, but not nondeductive logical relations.

That deductive logical intuitions are often exact and agreed upon, while nondeductive logical intuitions are often inexact and conflicting, is a fig leaf. The leaf is the word "often." Nondeductive logical intuitions are often neither inexact nor conflicting. And there are plenty of deductive logical intuitions which are both conflicting and doubtful. Just look at any subtle logic paper. Why, chapter 9 of the present book is all about the conflict between two entire families of logical intuitions about which deductive logics to count as reliable logics at all! On his own arguments, is Ramsey going to reject deductive logical intuitions and approximate to deductive logical relations by betting on them in a learning process?

All the criticisms given so far have nothing to do with the question whether probabilities are logical, or are to be assimilated to deductive logic, or approach to logical necessity as an asymptote. For even if we reject the view that probability relations belong to the specific category of logical relations, all the problems would remain. For all these relations are intellectual and abstract in general, and that is enough for my criticisms to succeed.

Sixth, making Dutch book logically can be and often is just as objective and rational as making non-Dutch book. Some Dutch oddsmakers can be and often are rationally better than others. For example, suppose five horses are in a race, and ten oddsmakers, who are the only oddsmakers available, all offer different odds. Each horse is favored to win by exactly two of the oddsmakers. Smith makes Dutch book by placing bets on each horse to win with the first set of five oddsmakers, each of whom has picked a different horse to win; and Jones does likewise with the second set. Clearly Smith could consistently make a better profit, or at least avoid a greater loss, over time than Jones. If it aids the imagination, we may suppose that Smith places bets with amateur oddsmakers who are just starting on their own learning curve, and Jones with seasoned experts. That is to say, if we flip around from Ramsey's negative requirement *not* to allow Dutch book to be made *against* yourself, to cases where you *must* allow Dutch book to be made against you by *someone*, it would be objectively far better to be a Smith betting against inept oddsmakers than a Jones betting against good ones, because you would probably make more money, or at least lose less.

I have been describing an example which applies directly and reflexively to the Dutch book aspect of Dutch book bets. But it is easy to see that how good the horses are is the other main factor.

So, why does Ramsey insist on his requirement (i)? That is, why is he so against Dutch book? Why does he think it would not have just the same sort of objective learning curve as non-Dutch book? Why would he not think a theory of probability ought to apply to Dutch probabilities just as much as to non-Dutch ones?

I suggest that it is just as basic to objective probability theory to explain how to minimize your guaranteed losses, as it is to explain how to maximize your non-guaranteed gains. That is to say, Dutch and non-Dutch bookmakers alike ought to have the objective rationality of their bets grounded in the same general theory of objective probability. And while such a general theory logically could be a "mixed" theory, using, say, frequency theory to explain Dutch objective probabilities and using Keynes to explain non-Dutch objective probabilities, that would be very odd if all the bets were on the same thing, say, if they were all on the very same horse race. It is easy to see why we might consistently use Keynes for *horse races* and frequency theory for *roulette*, since these are mutually exclusive categories, and since racing odds (not: bets) are typically conflicting and doubtful, while roulette odds are typically uniform and clear. But if all the betting is on horse races, then there simply *is* no difference between Dutch and non-Dutch objective probabilities, except for the mere fact that the Dutch ones are Dutch and the non-Dutch ones are not. Of course, it could sometimes be that some particular horse race is very predictable and some roulette wheel is not. But the whole idea of a mixed theory of probability is to use appropriate theories for appropriate situations, typically frequency theory for uniform events and some other theory for anomalous or unique events. For unique events, Keynes seems best. By definition, unique events are not what is usually the case. That all events might be unique does not detract from this point. And per my first criticism, there is no learning curve for unique events. That all events might be unique does not detract from this point either.

Of course, there can be a huge area between strictly unique events and strictly uniform events. Perhaps we could have a three level theory with frequency theory for uniform events, Ramsey's theory for fairly anomalous events for which there is a learning curve, and Keynes' theory for unique events, or at any rate for events sufficiently anomalous that there can be no learning curve. Intuitively, that seems rather satisfying. For it appeals to all of the reasonable, ordinary intuitions that each of the three theories appeals to, and always in the situations appropriate to each theory. But if Keynes is good enough for unique events, why not also for anomalous events, or even for all events?

It emerges that there are at least three senses of objectively "coherent" or "consistent" betting on a learning curve over time. First, there is Ramsey's sense, in which making Dutch book is prohibited. Second, there is the opposite sense. in which making Dutch book is the only type of bet available. Here the learning curve can involve not only the odds of a horse winning, but the odds of the oddsmakers' competency. But that could also be a factor where Dutch book is prohibited. Third, there is the most general and in that sense deepest sense, in which it is coherent or consistent to pick a strategy that maximizes profit and minimizes loss for all bets in general, regardless of whether they are Dutch.

More deeply, this means that there are three different senses or kinds of objective, rational betting probabilities. Ramsey's is one of the two shallow and limited ones, and the third is the deepest and most general one, since it is the genus of which the first two kinds are species. And surely we ought to pursue the deepest and most general theory. This leaves out Ramsey practically by definition. But Keynes' theory should apply to Dutch book just as well as to non-Dutch book, and so should frequency theory. And perhaps that is why those two theories make no prohibitions against Dutch book. In any case, those two theories' not making Dutch book a factor makes them in that sense more general than Ramsey's, and in that sense deeper. Here we seem to have an argument for a general level mixed theory consisting of Keynes' theory and frequency theory. Theoretically we could add

Ramsey at the lower level of non-Dutch book bets; but why should we?

We can see now that by prohibiting Dutch book, Ramsey is picking one conception of consistency or coherence, and one conception of objective rationality, over others, and is picking an essentially limited conception: it is limited by that very prohibition.

Perhaps the most general level can be Ramseyan, even if it cannot be Ramsey's theory. That is, perhaps we can make Ramsey's theory fully general by (a) dropping the Dutch book requirement, (b) keeping only the general consistency requirement, and (c) interpreting that requirement in terms of the third and most general sense of consistent rational betting strategy. On such a fully general Ramseyan theory, making Dutch book on yellow toadstools would approximate exactly as well to the actual frequency of healthy toadstools in the long run as making non-Dutch book. If it aids the imagination, we may suppose that our Dutch bookmaker gradually moves in a Ramseyan rational learning process from novice to veteran in choosing which sets of toadstool oddsmakers to place bets with. But even this fully general Ramseyan theory would still face my first four objections. (This sense of "fully general" probability theory must not be confused with Russell's sense of "fully general" statement, which means that the statement consists only of variables and logical constants.)

Economic theory is largely based on probability, as Keynes and Ramsey well know. And people face win-win and lose-lose life choices perhaps at least as much as win-lose. I am tempted to suggest that most of the people in this world face more choices of the least among evils than brilliant young academicians protected from the world in their Cambridge ivory tower, and that perhaps this is why it never occurred to Ramsey that exactly the same probability theory can and must apply to the choices of the masses, as to the choices of the more fortunate few who can often actually *win* or lose, or even choose the best among good outcomes. There might even be some truth in that, but I decline to make such a judgment, because we are all human and we all have problems, even those who are in the so-called ivory tower. Ramsey in particular died young, and I am sure there were some lose-lose choices there. Not only that, but he was sympathetic to the unfortunate. My suggestion is simply that the general sort of probability theory that covers *all* of our life choices, be they win-lose, win-win, or lose-lose, is best. Please note that of these three sorts of choices, two are of the Dutch book *sort*; we might call win-win "*converse* Dutch book." Of course, there are also "break even" choices where all the odds are even; but we cannot have a rational theory of them precisely because there is no reason to prefer one choice over another. This is the problem of Buridan's ass, who is equidistant from two equally good piles of hay, and who dies of starvation because it has no reason to prefer one pile to the other. This is Buridan's counterexample to the principle of sufficient reason, which says that everything has a reason. Hegel goes so far as to say that where a rational parliament cannot find a reason to prefer one policy over another, meaning a reason good enough to prevail by rational vote, it is perfectly fine to have a constitutional monarch whose sole function is break tie votes, even by arbitrary whim, precisely because it does not rationally matter. Of course, Hegel is one of the most ironic of thinkers. I am sure he is well aware that one might just as well flip a "monarch coin."

Another way to put my sixth criticism is this. Just like the probability calculus, a probability theory must apply in all possible worlds. For probability theories interpret the probability calculus, which is a branch of mathematics; and mathematics is true in all possible worlds. Now, in some possible worlds there are only lose-lose choices, in others only win-win, in still others, only win-lose, and in still others, some mix of these choices; and the rest have no probability choices at all. We may respectively call these five sorts of worlds: Dutch book worlds, converse Dutch book worlds, non-Dutch book worlds, mixed worlds, and non-probability worlds in which all events are either known to be determined or known to be capricious. Ramsey's theory fails the possible worlds test because it fails to apply to the first two of these five sorts of possible worlds. But it can be fully generalized so as to pass the test, simply by doing away with any reference to Dutch book. At least, it will then pass the test with respect to my sixth criticism; but I also offered five other criticisms. Please note that a mixed probability theory must apply in all possible worlds, but its disjuncts need not do so. Within a mixed theory, worlds of uniform events would be best for frequency theory, and Keynes' theory would be best for worlds of unique events.

My criticisms of Ramsey are not intended to be conclusive. I think they are right as far as they go; but there is more to Ramsey that is beyond the scope of this book. See Zabell (2005: 126–34).

Much like Keynes', Ramsey's mathematics is out of date (Zabell 2005: 131–34 discussing Bruno de Finetti). And just as with Keynes, Ramsey's philosophical interest is unaffected by this.

This concludes my survey of the main probability theories. There are many different technical probability theories, and as far as I can see, there logically can be indefinitely many.[4]

The Ontological Locus of Probability

Each of the three main probability theories just discussed assigns probability to a radically different ontological *locus*. This in itself is food for thought.

Aristotle's frequency theory locates natural or empirical probabilities in the natural world, or in classes of natural things.

Keynes' logical theory places all probabilities in a timeless Platonic realm. They are timeless relations among what can only be timeless propositions.

Ramsey's subjectivist theory locates probabilities within ourselves. They are our dispositions (our willingness) to bet, as modified over time into a learning curve based on our rewards (bets won) and punishments (bets lost). This is classic psychology of reinforcement theory with positive and negative reinforcements.

We may add that Hume's skepticism locates probability as being nowhere. But Hume's theory of causation assigns a mixed location to causation, partly in nature (constant conjunction) and partly in ourselves (habitual expectations). Perhaps then Hume could have assigned probability the same mixed location, partly in nature (frequent conjunction) and partly in ourselves (less habitual expectations).

The main food for thought on this level is this. Shakespeare may be right that our faults lie "not in the stars, but in ourselves." But can we seriously think that the likelihood that the sun will rise tomorrow lies in ourselves, and not in the star and its planet?

Modern Evidence Law on Logical Relevance

I shall argue that Keynes' theory that probability is degree of logical relevance most likely originates from evidence law, and that therefore Russell's theory most likely does too, indirectly through Keynes.

The main argument of the present chapter may be stated as a syllogism. (1) From 1912 *Problems of Philosophy* on, Russell's theory of probability originates from Keynes and is fundamentally that of Keynes. This is both accepted in the literature (Skidelsky 2005: 286; Monteiro 2001: 66) and fairly obvious from a "smoking gun" acknowledgment by Russell in the book's preface (PP vi), not to mention from the nature and timing of Russell's theory. (2) The circumstantial case is overwhelming that Keynes' theory of probability originates in turn from Anglo-American evidence law and is fundamentally that of Anglo-American evidence law. It will take 132 pages (368–500) to show this. This is except for Keynes' Platonic realism, which originates from and is basically the same as that in Russell's *Principles*. (3) Therefore, the circumstantial case is overwhelming that except for its Platonic realism, Russell's theory of probability indirectly originates from Anglo-American evidence law through Keynes, and is fundamentally that of Anglo-American evidence law. Premiss (2) and conclusion (3) are new to the study of Russell on probability, and bring it to a new level of depth and understanding.

Keynes admired English evidence law. He praised judges for understanding that probabilities can rarely be assigned exact numerical values. He clearly wished to conform his theory of probability to the law in this regard (Keynes 1962 / 1921: 24–27). Perhaps then Keynes developed his theory of logical relevance from evidence law as well. But how? And from what sources?

Leading scholars on the legal origins of probability, such as Barbara Shapiro and Ian Hacking, have nothing to say about the legal origins of logical relevance. Shapiro's *Probability and Certainty in Seventeenth-Century England: A Study of the Relationships between Natural Science, Religion, History, Law, and Literature* has nothing on point (Shapiro 1983). Shapiro's second book, *"Beyond Reasonable Doubt" and "Probable Cause": Historical Perspectives on the Anglo-American Law of Evidence*, and Hacking's book, *The Emergence of Probability: A Philosophical Study of Early Ideas about Probability, Induction and Statistical Inference* trace the legal origins of probability theory back to Roman law and canon law (Shapiro 1991: 235–55; Hacking 1978: 85–91). But these excellent books do not even attempt to trace the origins of Keynes' theory of probability as degree of logical relevance, or to trace the origins of logical relevance as it is understood in *Federal Rules of Evidence* Rule 401 and similar rules today. To his credit, Peter Murphy, in *Murphy on Evidence*, sect. 1.4.1, "Nature of probability in judicial reasoning," says, "Among the more important older contributions [is] J. M. Keynes, *A Treatise on Probability*" (Murphy 2008: 6 n.17). But even Murphy mentions Keynes only on probability, not on logical relevance.

Perhaps the leading scholars have nothing to say because there simply *is* no theory of probability in the old legal treatises, except for some remarks about the "common course of events" which suggest the frequency theory offered by Aristotle and Venn. The frequency theory is the chief historical rival to Keynes' theory, as Keynes was well aware (Keynes 1962 / 1921: 92ff.). In contrast, Keynes interprets degrees of probability as degrees of intuited logical relevance—as Platonically real logical relations among propositions describing evidence and propositions describing what the evidence is evidence for. I very much doubt that in general, Anglo-American evidence law can be saddled with an extreme metaphysical realism of this sort. Only evidence law's superficial, syllogistic deductive format for probability arguments might appear to be Platonically real, and even then only for any metaphysical realists in the crowd. But in any case, since the leading scholars do have nothing to say on our topic, we are left to investigate on our own.

My primary aim is to document the extent, substantially and in detail, but not comprehensively or exhaustively, of the Anglo-American evidence law literature on probabilistic logical relevance before Keynes wrote on the topic. To this end, it is more important what was published when, and how available it was to Keynes, than who wrote it. Thus I shall not care whether a text is a plagiarism, or written "with" someone, or even posthumously published, so long as Keynes could have read it before he developed his theory.

I shall focus mainly on law treatise writers in the modern period. For our purposes, this period starts with John Locke, since Descartes is not an origin of logical relevance in evidence law. I shall only briefly mention or discuss ancient and medieval legal sources, so as to give a minimal sense of historical perspective.

I mainly want to show the development of the concept of probabilistic relevance in the evidence law, so as to show that historically speaking, this is probably where Keynes got the idea. I also want to give something of the flavor of the concerns the law had with relevance, so as to see *why* relevance developed as a major topic in the law, and eventually as the most fundamental concept of evidence in law today. But for the most part, I shall omit explaining minor technical points in the texts to follow, and let the legal literature speak for itself on the main points in which we will be interested. I hope the few comments I do make will help philosophers identify and understand the main legal issues. I hope at least that they will learn more about the modern history of evidence law than they knew before. But they will not learn as much as they would from legal scholars who devote their careers to that subject.

Two legal scholars, J. L. Montrose and William Twining, give fine introductions to evidence law in this period (Montrose 1992 / 1954; Twining 1994: ch. 3; and much more briefly, Twining 1985: ch. 1). Their introductions basically agree on the main points. In fact, Montrose's 1954 paper is reprinted in Twining's and Alex Stein's 1992 anthology, *Evidence and Proof.* In what follows, I follow Montrose and Twining closely. I disagree only with their interpretation of Geoffrey Gilbert and William Best. For I find that Gilbert and Best have a relevant evidence rule, and they deny that.

I also recommend a fine introduction to modern evidence law that was written at the end of the period itself by an active participant. This is Courtenay Peregrine Ilbert's article on evidence law in the 1902 *Encyclopedia Britannica* (Ilbert 1902). And perhaps the best introduction specifically to logical relevance in evidence law is still George F. James, "Relevancy, Probability and the Law" (James 1941). This too is reprinted in Twining and Stein, eds. (1992). James wrote well after the period I discuss, but his championship of logical relevance was instrumental in America's adopting that concept as fundamental in *Federal Rules of Evidence* Rule 401.

My aim is not to provide a full history of modern evidence law, nor even of the topic of logical relevance within modern evidence law. My aim is only to provide sufficient evidence for my claim that it is more probable than not that Keynes' concept and terminology of logical relevance came from the legal tradition. To this end, I will err on the side of abundance. Certainly, I would not like to understate my case! But my task is only to prepare a review of this area good enough for its purpose, which is to show how much more likely it is that Keynes acquired his conception of probability as relevance from the legal community than from anywhere else, including from his own inventive mind. This last alternative is the main account accepted today, and the main rival to my own. Its chief proponent is Robert Skidelsky, who is in my opinion the world's best Keynes historian.

Moore is the point of departure proposed by this main rival account. It appears to be Skidelsky's view that Keynes read Moore's book *Principia Ethica*, was horrified by Moore's account of probability, though praising and accepting almost everything else, and basically went on to develop his own theory of probability all by himself. Thus Skidelsky's view is not at all that Moore was the origin of Keynes' theory, in the positive sense that Moore held that probability is degree of relevance, and Keynes came to agree with him. Skidelsky's view is that Moore is the origin only in the negative sense that Keynes felt that Moore's work was inadequate, and that this inspired Keynes to work out his own original theory.

Skidelsky is well aware of the many sources Keynes cites in his *Treatise* for many of his views about probability. But Skidelsky has nothing to say about the origin of Keynes' theory that probability is degree of logical relevance, except that it sprang out of Keynes himself, like Athena from the head of Zeus. In contrast, my view is that the origin is like the actor's phony deus ex machina on the stage, where it merely looks like a god is rising up onto the stage all by himself, and the real work is done by someone else hidden under the stage, whose machine is lifting the actor up.

Skidelsky is a wonderful scholar, and the learning has been almost entirely on my side. I greatly appreciate all his books on Keynes. However, I disagree with Skidelsky on this one point of origin. For I think that the legal literature is the probable origin of Keynes' theory that probability is degree of relevance. Naturally, most people outside the legal profession would not know anything about this. And this includes most, if not all, Keynes and Russell scholars. And such a legal origin is far from clear from Keynes' *Treatise* itself, even if you know where to look. So, much research will be involved. The case for my view will take time to present.

There is a sharp divide in professional training on "logical relevance" between philosophers and attorneys. The studies appear to be completely different, and the term appears to have completely different meanings. Philosophers study deductive logical relevance as it was discussed in chapter 9. They study systems of formal logic, and try to paraphrase the inferences found in ordinary talk, science, or elsewhere, into those formal systems. But lawyers study logical relevance as the most basic concept of probabilistic evidence. Evidence law would be the first thing even a mere law student would think of as a possible origin of Keynes' term "logical relevance." For Keynes is concerned with probabilistic evidence, and the evidence law concept is basically the same as Keynes'. Keynes, of course, reconciles the two studies by making deductive relevance the asymptote of probabilistic relevance. And I further reconcile them by noting that both are mere species of the genus of objective rational relation or connection. But the argument needs developing. How could it be likely, or even possible, that Keynes knew anything about evidence law? He is famous for philosophy and economics, and not in the least for law. Where is the connection between Keynes and evidence law?

I shall discuss only the general concepts of probabilistic relevance and of evidence admissibility. I shall not discuss more limited and specific concepts of relevance, such as doubtful relevance or conditional relevance, or more limited and specific concepts of admissibility, such as limited admissibility or weight of the evidence as a factor in determining admissibility. See Murphy (2008: 31–33) for a description of those more limited concepts.

I shall present my sources basically in a historical time line of authors by date of publication. The time line is accurate for the sources I use. I omit many works, and many editions of the works I discuss. I believe further research is not needed, and would only strengthen my case. Just as with fossils, so any earlier finds would only push my time line further back in time, and any other finds would only show the widespread flourishing of logical relevance in evidence law even more.

For these reasons, I would be the first to admit that my presentation of the modern history of evidence law is incomplete. I am only pointing out that a complete presentation is not my aim.

I shall start with the earliest works we will consider. Since they are the most remote from our own time, they can be the most difficult and obscure. I hope they may at least become clearer in retrospect when we come to the nineteenth century materials.

I shall discuss all or nearly all the great names of modern evidence law: Edward Coke, Geoffrey Gilbert, William Blackstone, John Morgan, Samuel March Phillipps, Thomas Starkie, William Mawdesley Best, Jeremy Bentham, Simon Greenleaf, John Pitt Taylor, James Fitzjames Stephen, James Bradley Thayer, and John Henry Wigmore, plus a few more to round out the picture.

I shall often specify which bar an author belongs to. This may help to give some geographic sense of the spread of the talk of relevance across the Anglo-American world. But that is not my main reason for doing so. In fact, far from giving a good sense of the spread, the bars are mostly just English or American. And I am really interested only in the four English bars, or as I may as well say, the four London bars: The Inner Temple, The Middle Temple, Gray's Inn, and Lincoln's Inn. I am interested most of all in the Inner Temple. For Keynes was a member of the Inner Temple, dined there a few times, and presumably had access to the law library. And many of the law treatise writers I discuss were also members of the Inner Temple. I think this significantly increases the likelihood that Keynes acquired the concept of logical relevance from evidence law. Indeed, he may well have learned of it directly from fellow members of the Inner Temple. If he even mentioned at lunch that he was interested in probability, by way of introducing himself and his chief interests to the lawyers dining with him, surely it would have been the first thing they told him. Certainly it would have been the most relevant.

The History of Logical Relevance in Evidence Law

I turn now to the history of evidence law, and mainly to modern Anglo-American evidence law, on the topic of relevance. I shall present an extremely brief sketch of this history. Even this single topic is a huge area that would take several books to cover. I shall mainly concentrate on the nineteenth century, that is, on the legal literature that was flourishing just before Keynes came along. Twining says:

> The study of...[the logical aspects of] evidence and proof in forensic contexts....can be traced back all the way to classical rhetoric,.....from Corax of Syracuse in the 5th century BC. [The intellectual history of] inductive logic [is] inextricably bound up with the long and complex

story of rhetoric as an academic subject[, and] part of the
trivium of logic, grammar and rhetoric. (Twining 1994:
4)

Douglas Walton says:

> The notion of relevance in argumentation has ancient
> roots, both in the classical *stasis* theory of Greek
> rhetoric, and in the Aristotelian theory of fallacies (Wal-
> ton 2005: 116, Walton's emphasis, cites omitted)

Socratic dialectics or eristic might be called higher forensics.
Indeed, law schools today often pride themselves on using what
they call the Socratic method.

    I turn now to England. For the most part, I shall omit the
influence of ancient Roman or medieval canon (church) law on
English law. Historically, one would expect canon law in England
to flourish in the Middle Ages, and Roman law to be studied in
England in the Renaissance as part of the general influx of Greek
and Roman texts.

    Frederick Pollock and Frederic William Maitland say of
the old Anglo-Saxon law, "Trial of questions of fact, in anything
like the modern sense, was unknown. Archaic rules of evidence
make no attempt to apply any measure of probability to unknown
cases" (Pollock 2010 / 1898: 43 citing Brunner 1887). "Oath was
the primary method of proof, an oath not going to the truth of
specific fact, but to the justice of the claim or defense as a whole"
(Pollock 2010 / 1898: 43).

    The first English evidence law treatise, in effect, was by a
highly respected medieval judge, Lord Justice Henry (or Henrici)
de Bracton (originally Bratton or Bretton) (c. 1210–c. 1268). I say
"in effect" because it was not a separate work, but part of his
master work, *De Legibus et Consuetudinibus Anglaie* (*On the Laws
and Customs of England*). Bracton wrote *De Legibus* no later than
1256, less than two centuries after the Norman Conquest. The
evidence law part of it shows no signs of using probable or relevant
evidence. Bracton was satisfied if twelve lords swore an oath on
the justice of a claim or defense. I read once that this was probably
a more reasonable approach for the times than one might think,
since if you could get twelve lords to agree on anything, it was
probably true. In any case, Bracton was reporting how things were.
Bracton was an ecclesiastic, and was also influenced by Roman
law. Thus he belongs in both the canon law and medieval Roman
law traditions. He is generally regarded as the best English legal
scholar of the Middle Ages. *De Legibus*, or the four volumes he
was able to finish, is regarded as by far the best contemporary
account of medieval English law.

There were other early authors besides Bracton. Thomas Blount (1618–1679) posthumously says, in the third edition of his *Law-Dictionary and Glossary*:

> He who peruseth all the *Saxon, Danish,* and *Norman* laws published by *Brompton, Lambard,* and others; and all the antient Books treating of the Common-Law, as *Bracton, Fleta, Glanvill,* &c. will find them very difficult to be understood without the help of this *Dictionary*; for the *Jus Anglorum* of the *Saxons,* the *Danelaga* of the *Danes,* and our *Common Law,* which from thence was collected by the *Normans,* are all delivered in very abstruse and uncommon Words....; and where the *Latin* is plain, the Sense is obscure.... (Blount 1717, To the Reader, Blount's emphasis)

The first two authors Blount lists are John Brompton and William Lambard. "Fleta" is not actually the name of a person, but came to be the nom de plume of the anonymous English author who wrote a law treatise in Fleet Prison (Gaola / gaol / jail de Fleta / Fleet Jail) ca. 1290. It is thought that Fleta was one of several judges imprisoned by King Edward I. Lord Chief Justice Ranulf de Glanvill (c. 1112–1190) is also called Ralph Glanville.

We now come to early modern times. I will not take much time with Locke and the other philosophers. (I already discussed Locke and Leibniz.) Suffice it to say that they studied evidence, and the evidence law writers studied them. Locke in particular was admired by the early evidence law writers. All this is still a little remote for our purposes, and is more in the nature of setting the stage for the legal talk of relevance to come.

Edward Coke

I begin with Sir Edward Coke (1552–1634). I shall discuss him somewhat indirectly. Blount says in his *Law-Dictionary*:

> EVIDENCE (*Evidentia*) is used generally for any proof, be it Testimony of Men, Records or Writings....**It is called *Evidence*, because thereby the point in Issue is to be made *Evident*** to the Jury; *Probationes debent esse Evidentes, i.e. perspicuæ & faciles.* See *Coke on Litt., fol.* 283. Blount 1717: pdf file pages 134–35, Blount's italic emphasis, my boldface emphasis)

Coke upon Littleton dates to 1628 (Macnair 1999: 21), or 276 years before Keynes read Moore's book. Blount is not citing Thomas Littleton himself (ca. 1415–1481), but Coke's work on Littleton.

Coke's work is not really about Thomas Littleton (ca. 1415–1481) very much; it is really about the laws of England. I take the last sentence to say, "See Sir Edward Coke on Sir Thomas Littleton, folio 283" of *Institutes of the Laws of England.* Per the Inner Temple online site, both Coke and Littleton were members of the Inner Temple. Coke was also a student at Trinity College, Cambridge University, just like Russell; Keynes went to King's College, also at Cambridge University.

Blount's definition may seem little more than a circular definition of evidence as that which makes something evident to someone. But I think that more than this going on here. First, there is a complex relation. Item *A* is evidence just in case there exists an item *B* and a person (or jury) *C* such that *A* makes *B* evident to *C*. The "thereby" indicates that evidence is that *by which* something is shown or made evident to someone. Second and more important for our purposes, evidence is positively characterized as being relevant. It is evidence for the point in issue, as opposed to some extraneous or irrelevant point. Third and also very important to us, the phrase "It is called *Evidence*, because" implies that this is a definition of evidence. It is a statement of what evidence is. It states that to be evidence is to be relevant, that is, to make the pont in issue evident (to someone). This definition is a positive characterization. But I think that an exclusionary aspect is implied by the fact that the characterization is definitional. Namely, it is implied that if evidence is not relevant, then it is not evidence.

Even if the definition is circular, that is the least important thing to note. Dictionary definitions are often circular, yet that does not prevent their being useful and illuminating in various ways. The only important thing for us is that the definition defines evidence in terms of relevance, thereby making evidence essentially relevant.

The "Probationes" maxim appears to be relevantist as well. For it appears to be offered as the ground of, or at least as a comment on, the thesis that the word "evidence" means 'that which makes the point in issue evident'.

Per Seymour S. Peloubet (1844–1914), the full and correct maxim is *Probationes debent esse Evidentes, id est perspicuæ et faciles intelligi,* and may be translated, "Proofs ought to be evident, that is, clear and easily understood" (Peloubet 1880: 231 citing "COKE, LITT. 283.a"). As before, "Litt." is Littleton. This maxim might be considered to state the *mode*, or *ideal mode*, of relevance. That is, "Proofs ought to be so related to, or connected to, or so probative of, the point in issue that the relationship, connection, or relevance is evident, that is, clear and easily understood." I take it that clarity and ease of being understood are two very different but related things. For a long and complex proof may be very clear step by step, but still hard to understand because it is complicated. Of course, both clarity and ease of being understood are mere modes of relevance, and not relevance itself, which is a third thing. However, there is a negative limit. If evidence is totally unclear, or impossible to understand, then it is not relevant.

Many things are both clear and easily understood without being relevant. The main relationships of the Eiffel Tower to the pen on my desk are obvious: the Tower is far larger, far heavier, at a certain distance from my pen, and so on. But it is not evidence for anything about my pen. Conversely, a gun thrown into a river after a murder may be very relevant indeed. It may be the murder weapon. But if it is found by chance by a swimmer years later, its relevance might not be clear or easy to understand at all. The swimmer might not even have heard of the murder.

Thus perspicuity ("perspicuous" is sometimes used to translate *perspicuae* in the maxim) and relevance are very different relations. But just as someone who is not swimming well enough is not swimming at all, evidence which is not clear enough is not evidence at all, just as an unintelligible proof is no proof. Thus some minimal clarity, or better, intelligibility. is essential to being evidence. Perhaps that is what Coke, whom Peloubet was citing, has in mind when Coke says posthumously in 1823:

> Evidence, *evidentia.* This word in legall understanding doth not only containe matters of record,...which are called evidences, *instrumenta,* but in a larger sense it containeth also *testimonia,* the testimony of witnesses, and other proofes to be produced and given to a jury, for the finding of any issue joined betweene the parties. And **it is called evidence, because thereby the point in issue is to be made evident** to the jury. *Probationes debent esse evidentes (id est) perspicuæ et faciles intelligi.* But let us now returne to *Littleton.* (Coke 1823: folio page 283a, sect. 485, Coke's italic emphasis, my boldface emphasis)

Again, that seems both relevantist ("thereby the point in issue is to be made evident") and definitional ("it is called evidence, because"). And for Coke, the "Probationes" maxim appears to be relevantist. For he appears to be offering the maxim as the ground of, or at least as a comment on, his view that the word "evidence" means 'that which makes the point in issue evident'. We may now see that the "thereby" also appears to indicate that the mode, or ideal mode, of evidence is evidentness, or obviousness. If I am right, then at least for Coke, that mode, or at least its being the ideal mode, would seem essential to the nature of evidence as well.

One might question whether someone encountering this maxim, and no more, might be led to think of the concept of relevant evidence. I am not sure that is so. First, the term "relevant" is not used. Second, the ordinary understanding of evidentness and evidence, or if you please, obviousness and relevance, are different concepts. I think that very few people, other than those familiar with the history of evidence law, would see any relationship between evidentness and relevant evidence. You would have to know that 'evidence for the point in issue' is legalese for relevant evidence, and you would have to notice that the *probationes* maxim is being cited in support of the legalese. The size and weight of the Eiffel Tower are evident and obvious, without the Tower's evidently or obviously being evidence for the existence of my pen. But that only shows the difference between a mode as it applies to a thing (the Eiffel Tower) considered in itself, and the same mode as it applies to any evidentiary relation between that thing and another thing (my pen).

I briefly return to Blount, our point of departure for the *probationes* maxim. There is no entry for "relevancy" in Blount's *Law-Dictionary*. Nor would I expect there to be, since the main use of that term comes later in the legal literature. But here we must distinguish between a term and what it means. This is just like deductive relevance in Wittgenstein's *Tractatus*. Wittgenstein does not use the current term "relevant," but surely he is talking about we now call deductive relevance when he speaks of truth-ground *containment* and of *following from*. See chapter 9.

The title page says that Blount is "of the *Inner-Temple*."

William Nelson, Samson Eure, and Giles Duncombe

Michael Richard Trench Macnair says:

> The first free-standing book on evidence is William Nelson's *The Law of Evidence*, published 1717.[27] Slightly earlier is Sir Jeffrey Gilbert's "Treatise" on *Evidence*[, which] was published [posthumously] as a free-standing book in 1754. There are earlier instances of the general usage. The trial lawyers' manual *Tryalls per Pais*, first published in 1665, had a short chapter on *Evidence* in this sense, elaborated in subsequent edit-ions[29];....
>
> The law of evidence stated in Gilbert and Nelson, and in earlier treatments, and which appears in the cases (which I will call for convenience the 'old law of evidence') had two fundamental elements,
>
> The first, though usually treated second in the sources, is a body of rules about **what evidence will**

maintain an issue; that is, the substantive relevance of evidence....To give a couple of examples from the first edition of *Tryalls per Pais*:

> But if a feoffment be pleaded in fee, upon issue non feoffavit modo et forma, a feoffment upon condition **is no evidence, because it does not answer the issue; and wheresoever Evidence is contrary to the issue, and does not maintain it, the evidence is not good**. 11 Hen 3 Feoffments 41....[34]

27. The book is anonymous, and the *National Union Catalogue* offers an attribution to Gilbert. The traditional attribution in England is to Nelson, and the style is most unlike Gilbert's style.
29. The first edition is by S. E. of the Inner Temple; chapter 11 on evidence occupies 18 pages. The second edition by G. D. of the Inner Temple is attributed to Giles Duncombe.....
34. Page 141. (Macnair 1999: 20–23, cites omitted, Macnair's italic emphasis, my boldface emphasis)

Thus Macnair finds a relevance rule in 1665 *Tryalls / Tryals / Trials per Pais / Country / Countrymen / jurymen of one's own country*. That is because Macnair rightly finds it obvious that to "answer" or "maintain" the point in issue is just to be relevant evidence. This is the typical terminology for relevance during the modern period of English law. We saw it in Coke, we see it here in 1665 *Tryalls*, and we will see it repeatedly in the sections to come.

Macnair says the 1665 first edition of *Tryalls* is by "S. E.," or posthumous Samson Eure (d. 1659). Montrose and Twining omit Eure. Macnair attributes the second edition to Giles Duncombe. Thus I think it safe to say that Macnair would find a relevance rule in both editions, since basically the same text Macnair quotes is in both. Macnair says he also finds a relevance rule in Nelson and in Gilbert. I shall not discuss Nelson, but I discuss Gilbert's relevance rule in the sections on Gilbert and Burke.

It seems that for Eure, just as it was for Coke, relevance is necessary to, not to say essential to, or definitional of, evidence. That seems evident from the phrase Macnair quotes from Eure: "is no evidence, because it does not answer the issue." That is, if proposed evidence does not "answer the issue," then it is by that very fact not evidence at all. No doubt "is contrary to the issue," which sounds confusing to modern ears, simply means "does not answer the issue," or as we might say today, "does not concern the issue."

The 1665 *Tryalls* was published 239 years before 1904, the year Keynes read Moore's book and read his first paper on probability to the Apostles. No doubt the fief (land or property) case that Nelson cites is earlier than that, looking to the cite, 11 Hen 3 Feoffments 41.

There is also a 1666 version called *Tryals*. I do not say the 1666 version is a second edition, since the 1666 version does not say it is a second edition. Yet it is not a mere reprint, since the wording is not exactly the same, as the reader will see.

In 1666, the posthumous Eure says in *Tryals per Pais*, Cap. 11, "Evidence," citing Coke:

> Evidence, *evidentia*. This word in legall understanding (saith Coke I. Inst. 283) doth not only contain matters of record,...which are called evidences Instrumenta. But in a larger sense, it containeth also Testimonia, the Testimony of Witnesses, and other proofs, to be produced and given to a Jury for the finding of any Issue, joyned betweene the parties; And **it is called Evidence, because thereby the point in Issue is to be made evident** to the jury. *Probationes debent esse evidentes (id est) perspicuæ & facile intelligitur.* But let us now returne to *Littleton.* (Eure 1666: 137–38), Eure's roman emphasis given here as italic (the main text is in gothic), my boldface emphasis)

I have already discussed this text in the section on Coke, where it is worded only slightly differently.

Later in this chapter (or "Cap."), Eure says:

> But if a Feoffment be pleaded in fee, upon Issue non feoffavit modo et forma, a Feoffment upon Condition *is no Evidence, because it does not answer the Issue; and wheresoever Evidence is contrary to the Issue, and does not maintain it, the Evidence is not good.* 11 H. 3 Feoffments 41. (Eure 1666: 141, my emphasis)

This is on the page that Macnair cites, but is not exactly as Macnair quotes it from 1665 *Tryalls*; I do not mean the use of capital letters, which no doubt Macnair removed editorially. I mean the use of "H." for "Hen". Thus the 1666 version is not a mere reprint. I shall return to the term "contrary to the issue" when I come to Duncombe.

Eure says in the same chapter:

> Upon the general Issue, the Defendant may give any-
> thing in Evidence, which proves the Plaintiff hath no
> cause of Action, or which doth intitle the Defendant to
> the thing in question. (Eure 1666: 142)

This is a positive rule that relevant evidence is always admissible
on the general issue. Along these lines, Eure also says:

> Upon Issue, payment at the day [or] payment before or
> after the day [is] no Evidence. More 47. but upon Nil
> debet, *it is good Evidence, because it proves the Issue.*
> (Eure 1666: 148, my emphasis)

This too is clearly a relevance rule.
    Eure also says:

> Where the Evidence proves the effect and substance of
> the Issue, it is good. (Eure 1666: 140)

I call this the substance rule. In the section on Buller, I argue that it
is a rule that limits relevant evidence to the substantive merits of
the issue. In chapter 13 on verdicts, Eure goes so far as to say:

> If the matter and substance of the Issue be found, it is
> sufficient, though it be against the Letter of the Issue.
> (Eure 1666: 196)

In the margin to the left of the just-quoted text, Eure repeats:

> The Verdict may be against the Letter of the Issue, so
> [long as] the substance is found. (Eure 1666: 196, left
> margin)

The title page of 1666 *Tryals* says "By S. E. of the *Inner
Temple,...*" The Preface is initialed "S. E." as well.
    Macnair says that Duncombe (or Duncomb) was the second
editor of *Tryalls*. Duncombe says:

> The Plaintiff in Bar, that *W.* was seized in Fee of an
> House and Land, *&c.* whereunto he had in Common,...
> on 30th of *March,.....,* and the Jury found that *W.* made
> the Lease to Plaintiff on 25 *March*...; and held Plaintiff
> should recover, for tho' this not be the same Lease [with
> respect to its date], yet the **Substance of the Issue is,**
> whether Plaintiff has such a Lease as would entitle him
> to Common, and that he had, and the *Modo & forma* as
> to the rest **is not material.** *Hob.* 72. *Pope* v. *Skinner.*
> (Duncombe 1739: 363–64, Duncombe's italic emphasis,
> my boldface emphasis)

This looks like a substance rule. Duncombe says that in general:

> If the Matter and **Substance of the Issue** be found, it is sufficient, though it be against the Letter of the Issue....
> And generally where *modo & forma* are not of the **Substance of the Issue**, there it sufficeth, though the Verdict doth not find the precise Issue. (Duncombe 1739: 269–70, Duncombe's italic emphasis, my bold-face emphasis; see 262 and 271 for other statements of this rule)

This is basically the same as Eure.
Perhaps most important and difficult text for us is:

> ***Evidence which is contrary to that in Issue, or which is not agreeable to the Matter in Issue, is not good.***
> As appears by several cases which you may find in the Chapter of Evidence. **As upon the Issue**, Nothing passes by the Deed, **you cannot give in Evidence**, that it is not your Deed, for this is **contrary to the Issue**, and to that which is acknowledged in the Plea by Implication. 5 *H*. 4. f. 2.
> And so upon Not guilty in Assault and Battery, and Evidence that it was done in his own Defence, is not good.
> And so in Debt upon a Bail-Bond, you must plead, That there is not the name of Sheriff in it, & *issint nient son fait*, and **cannot give it in Evidence** upon *Non est factum*, **for it is contrariant**. 3 *E*. 4. 5.
> So upon issue of Common appendant, Common *pur Cause de vicinage* is **not agreeable to the Issue**, and **therefore cannot be given in Evidence**. 13 *H*. 7. 13.
> ***Where the Evidence proves the Effect and Substance of the Issue, it is good.***
> As to prove a Grant or Lease pleaded *simplement*, a Grant or Lease upon Condition, and the Condition executed, **is good; for this proves the Effect and Substance of the Issue**, 14 *H*. 8. 20. So a Promise to the Wife, and the Husband's Agreement proves a Promise to the Husband; and this you may see in many Cases in the Chapter of Evidence. (Duncombe 1739: 469–40, Duncombe's emphasis)

Is Duncombe saying that evidence against the plaintiff's claim is not good, and that only evidence that proves the plaintiff's claim is good? How then could a plaintiff ever lose? But I think that he is not saying this, for two reasons.

First, sheer charity in interpretation supposes that even back in the 1600s and 1700s, not only could there be good evidence against a plaintiff's claim, but a plaintiff could lose.

Second, plaintiffs are not even mentioned in the two rules which Duncombe italicizes. Only issues, or matters in issue, are.

Third and decisively, Duncombe equates being *contrary* to the issue with not being *agreeable* to the issue; and agreeing with the *issue* means not proving as opposed to disproving the issue, but only being relevant to the issue. Likewise, "the evidence is good" can only be read, "the evidence qua evidence is good," or in modern terms, "the evidence is admissible" because it is relevant, i.e., goes to the substance of the issue.

Therefore, I suggest that the first rule be read as saying: "Evidence which not agreeable *in content* to what it takes to prove or disprove the matter in issue, is not *admissible*."

Today's reader may still find it awkward to think it is not relevant that it is not your deed in the first place, where the question is whether anything is conveyed by the deed; or that you were only defending yourself, where you are charged with assault and battery. How could those defenses not be relevant? But let us chalk that up to the old case law, or to our misunderstanding of it. The main thing is that evidence must be "agreeable to," if not also "prove the effect and substance of," the issue in question.

We also find language of "Matter collateral" (Duncombe 1739: 206), "Matter of Surplusage" (Duncombe 1739: 474), and "the Variance" (Duncombe 1739: 472). This is implicitly negative or irrelevantist terminology best discussed later. The basic idea is that if proposed evidence is collateral to the issue, or is surplusage, or is a variance from the substance of the issue, then it is irrelevant. The terms "variance," "surplusage" and "collateral" matters do have different technical legal meanings. Phillipps explains "variance," and Greenleaf explains "surplusage" and "collateral facts," in different ways. But all of these terms concern relevance in one way or another. Phillipps discusses variance as a form of irrelevance, and Greenleaf discusses both surplusage and collateral facts in a chapter entitled "Of the Relevancy of Evidence." The differences among these terms should be duly noted. But for our purposes, the main point is that they all concern relevance in one way or another.

I omit more than I mention on relevance in Duncombe, but I doubt that readers will be interested on pleadings on the general issue or on special matters. Duncombe praises earlier writers such as Mascardus (*De Probationibus*), Fortescue (*De Laudibus*), and Faranacius (*De Testibus*) (Duncombe 1739: To the Practicers of the Law). I also omit the 1702 Gothic print edition of *Tryals Per Pais* (Duncombe 1702). On the title page, Duncombe is said to be "G.

D. of the *Inner-Temple*" (Duncombe 1702). By 1739, he is "Giles Duncombe late of the *Inner-Temple*" (Duncombe 1739).

Geoffrey Gilbert

We come next to Lord Chief Justice of England Geoffrey Gilbert (1674–1726). Many see Gilbert's book as the first English evidence law treatise. It may well have been written before Nelson's, but it was published posthumously some decades later. We may say it was the first major evidence law treatise, both in scope of presentation and in impact on the history of evidence law.

Gilbert was "Lord Chief Baron of the Court of Exchequer from 1722 until his death in 1726" (Twining 1994: 35). Montrose says, "The first substantial exposition of the [modern] law of [English] evidence was by Gilbert" (Montrose 1992 / 1954: 348 / 528). According to Montrose, Gilbert's 1756 *The Law of Evidence* is "largely a digest of case law" whose sole principle of evidence is the best evidence rule (Montrose 1992 / 1954: 348 / 528). Montrose says the 1756 published first edition "was written before 1726" (Montrose 1992 / 1954: 348 / 529 citing E. M. Morgan). Thus, according to Montrose, the theoretical interest of the work is that it attempts to subsume all evidence law under a single rule, the best evidence rule. And that is the received view today.

Gilbert states the best evidence rule as follows:

> The first therefore, and most signal Rule, in Relation to Evidence, is this, That a Man must have the utmost Evidence the Nature of the Fact is capable of; for the Design of the Law is to come to rigid Demonstration in Matters of Right, and there can be no Demonstration of a Fact without the *best evidence* that the Nature of the Thing is capable of. (Gilbert 1754: 4, my emphasis)

I do not think it follows from this text that for Gilbert, the best evidence rule subsumes all evidence law under a single rule. I think it follows at most only that he thinks, perhaps mistakenly, that the rule is the primary and most important rule of evidence law, or at least in his own exposition of evidence law. Even if he intends the rule to apply to all *evidence*, it does not follow that he thinks it subsumes all *rules* of evidence. For there logically might be other rules which, though perhaps less important, also apply to all evidence, and which are logically independent of the best evidence rule. We might then look for any such other rules in evidence law, or even in Gilbert's own exposition. But back to our story.

John H. Langbein quotes and agrees with Twining's view that "'Gilbert tried to subsume all the rules of evidence under a single principle, the "best evidence rule"""" (Langbein 1996: 1173 quoting Twining and citing Twining 1990: 178, 188; this is our Twining 1994). Langbein adds, "The later eighteenth-century writers on evidence, Bathurst and Buller, followed Gilbert's emphasis on the best evidence rule as the organizing principle of the law of evidence" (Langbein 1996: 1173). Langbein says the reason for this is simply that they were primarily concerned with documentary evidence, and primarily with the original document. The quest for evidence was, first and "foremost, a search for the determinative piece of written evidence" (Langbein 1996: 1173 n.21 quoting and citing Landsman 1990: 1149, 1154). Langbein adds, "The preference for written evidence extended back to the Middle Ages, and was particularly apparent in contract and [land] conveyancing" (Langbein 1996: 1183).

Thus it is curious that Langbein says, "The rest of Gilbert's book concerns the sufficiency of evidence" (Langbein 1996: 1174), which sounds like the sufficient weight or probative value, not to say sufficient relevancy, of evidence. Langbein specifies "Gilbert, Evidence [Dublin 1754] at 113–99" as what he means by "the rest of Gilbert's book" (Langbein 1996: 1174 n.25, 27; see 1172, 1172 n.16 for the Dublin 1754 original publication cite). Thus there may be some doubt whether Gilbert is really subsuming all evidence law under the best evidence rule, or whether he finds "sufficient evidence" to be a second basic topic.

Let us abstract for a moment from the law's historical concern with original documents as being the best. In every field, we always want the best *and* the most relevant evidence. And these are not the same, if we mean 'best in intrinsic quality' and 'most relevant to the point in issue'. Yet if we were to speak in ordinary language today of the "best" evidence, I think we would say that the best evidence is the most relevant evidence. If I am right, then I think that for us today, "If anything is evidence, then it is the best evidence if and only if it is the most relevant evidence" would be a synthetic *a priori* truth.

But as Langbein says, this is not at all what Gilbert means. He technically means evidence of the best quality, and he mainly has documents about property in mind. Thus he mainly means that we should admit an original document over a mere copy, or a good copy over a damaged copy. We today might think that there is nothing wrong with that, as far as it goes; but we would scarcely think that all evidence law could be subsumed under such a limited rule. Today, the best evidence rule is just one rule among many: Rule 1002 in the *Federal Rules of Evidence*. (To be fair, *FRE* article 10, entitled "Contents of Writings, Recordings, and Photographs," includes seven other rules as part of this.) The rule "largely withered away in the face of mechanical production"

(Macnair 1999: 23). This started with Gutenberg's printing press, and greatly accelerated with cameras, photocopiers, scanners, and emails.

Even on the technical understanding of the best evidence as the original document, or the closest to the original document that we can find, one might still argue for a connection between best evidence and relevant evidence. Namely, the original document is causally the most directly connected, and in that sense the most relevant, document to the matter at hand; and an excellent copy is more clearly, not to say more visibly, causally connected than a poor copy, or possibly even than a very badly damaged original. We may say that a good copy better or more intelligibly "preserves" the causal link of the original document to the matter at hand than a poor copy or a very badly damaged original. But this sort of causal "quality of preservation" relevance logically can be, and often is, overwhelmed by relevance per se. For millions of original documents around the world will be totally irrelevant to a certain local matter, and copies of copies of copies will be far more relevant. For example, the original Declaration of Independence in Philadelphia totally lacks the relevance of even a poor photocopy of my car title to the issue of whether I own the car in my driveway.

Thus the best evidence rule is dimly related at best to the concept of relevance. At most, it relates to relevance only within its own limited sphere of originals, copies, and records and testimonies about documents. We can only say that, *other things being equal*, an original document is causally more directly related to a matter in issue than a copy of that very same document. We can only say that the original, as such, is more relevant with respect to time and with respect to causal proximity.

Twining notes that Gilbert's philosophical hero is John Locke, and quotes Gilbert's quotation of Locke on the admission of degrees of probability which fall short of demonstration (Twining 1994: 36). Montrose, Twining, and Langbein may not know it, but Locke discusses the best evidence rule in his *Essay Concerning Human Understanding*. Locke says:

> ...I think, it may not be amiss to take notice of a rule observed in the law of England; which is, That though the attested copy of a record be good proof, yet the copy of a copy, ever so well attested and by ever so credible witnesses, will not be admitted as a proof in judicature. This is so generally approved as reasonable, and suited to the wisdom and caution to be used in our inquiry after material truths, that I never yet heard of any one that blamed it. This practice...carries this observation along with it, viz. *That any testimony, the further off it is from being the original truth, the less force and proof it has.*

> The being and existence of the thing itself, is what I call the original truth. A credible man vouching his knowledge of it is a good proof; but if another equally credible do witness it from his report, the testimony is weaker: and a third that attests the hearsay of an hearsay is yet less credible. So that in traditional truths, each remove weakens the force of the proof.... (Locke 1959 / 1690: vol. 2, 377–78, Locke's emphasis)

Locke generalizes the best evidence rule to include all testimony, as well as written records. But Locke does not even appear to reduce all rules of evidence to the best evidence rule. He simply calls it "a rule."

Keynes is well aware of Locke's endorsement of the best evidence rule, quotes Locke, and substantially agrees with Locke, though finding Locke's view "excessive." Keynes says:

> 20. One of the most ancient problems in probability is concerned with the gradual diminution of the probability of a past event, as the length of the tradition increases by which it is established....Locke raised the matter in chap. xvi. bk. iv. of the *Essay Concerning Human Understanding:* "Traditional testimonies the farther removed the less their proof....No probability can rise higher than its first original."...." This is certain," says Locke, "that what in one age was affirmed upon slight grounds, can never after come to be more valid in future ages, by being often repeated." In this connection he calls attention to "a rule observed in the law of England, which is, that though the attested copy of a record be good proof, yet the copy of a copy never so well attested, and by never so credible witnesses, will not be admitted in a proof in Judicature." If this is still a good rule of law, it seems to indicate an excessive subservience to the principle of the decay of evidence.
> But, although Locke affirms sound maxims, he gives no theory that can afford a basis for calculation. (Keynes 1962 / 1921: 184–85 quoting Locke 1959 / 1690: vol. 2, 377–79)

In his chapter 16 on "fundamental theorems," Keynes discusses Bayes' Theorem and the Principle of Inverse Probability in sections 11–14, and discusses the principle of the decay of evidence in section 20. There is no indication that he regards the principle of the decay of evidence as less fundamental than, much less as a special case of, the principle of inverse probability. And no wonder, since Bayes' Theorem is a same-time analysis, while decay is calculated as a rate over time. Keynes does not give a mathematical analysis of the principle of the decay of evidence, but he says that Arthur "Cayley's [algebraic solution] is correct" (Keynes 1962 / 1921: 185). No doubt, of course, he considers the two principles to be logically consistent. Thus there is no doubt that he can *apply* his analysis of irrelevance, as mathematically formalized in terms of probability, to any given moment in the decay of evidence over time. The mathematical principle of decay can be used to calculate the rate of decay. Strictly speaking, it can be used to calculate not the decay of the evidence itself, but of its probative value. Keynes' definitions of irrelevance can then identify the end point at which the probative value is so diminished that the evidence is no longer relevant, and is thus no longer evidence.

Both Locke and Keynes are well aware of the importance of the principle of the decay of evidence to religious traditions. Keynes dryly says, "'Craig', says Todhunter, 'concluded that faith in the Gospel so far as it depended on oral tradition expired about the year 880, and that so far as it depended on written tradition it would expire in the year 3150'...." (Keynes 1962 / 1921: 184).

For us, the most important thing is that Montrose, Twining, and Langbein claim that Gilbert subsumes or tries to subsume all evidence law under a single evidence rule, the best evidence rule. Gilbert does call the best evidence rule "[t]he first...and most signal rule." (Gilbert 1754: 4). But Macnair, Burke, and I hold that Gilbert also has a relevance rule, and that Gilbert does not even appear to subsume the relevance rule under the best evidence rule. Nor do I think that any such subsumption is conceptually possible.

In 1754, Gilbert says in the posthumous first edition of *The Law of Evidence*, concerning the admission of a prior verdict as evidence in another case:

> If a Verdict be had *on the same Point*, and between the same Parties, *it may be given in Evidence*, tho' the Trial was not had for the same Lands; for the Verdict in such Cases, is a very persuading Evidence, because what twelve Men have already thought of the Fact, may be supposed fit to direct the Determination of the present Jury.... (Gilbert 1754: 22, my emphasis)

Thus, in order to be admissible, evidence must be on point. Gilbert continues:

> But it is not necessary that the Verdict shou'd be in Relation to the same Land, for the Verdict is only set up **to prove the Point in Question,** and if the Verdict arise upon the same question, then 'tis, no Doubt, **a good Evidence**, for *every Matter is Evidence, that amounts to Proof of the Point in Question.* (Gilbert 1754: 23,

> Gilbert's italic emphasis, my boldface emphasis; see
> 1805: 25)

Here Gilbert italicizes his relevance rule. However, Gilbert says that the following sort of objection can be made:

> [W]hen a Verdict is produced in Evidence, it may be answer'd, that it *did not arise from the Merits of the Cause*, but from some formal Defect of the Proof, *and that makes it no Evidence, toward gaining the Point in Question*.... (Gilbert 1754: 24, my emphasis)

This is Gilbert's substance rule, or merits rule. It is a modification or clarification of his relevance rule. Note that the rule appears to be of the essence of evidence. For a verdict is "no Evidence" at all if it does not concern the "merits" of "the point in question."
Gilbert says more extensively:

> But a private Act of Parliament or any other private Record **may be brought in before the Jury if it relate to the Issue in Question,** tho' it be not pleaded, for **the Jury are to find the Truth of the Fact in Question, according to the Evidence brought before them**, and therefore **if** the private Act brought before them, **doth evince the Truth of the Matter in Question, it is as proper Evidence to the Purpose as any Record or Evidence whatsoever.**
> 　　[T]he Allegata to the Jury, says *Hobart*, is **every thing that may be offered in evidence so relating to the Issue....**
> 　　....for tho' this be a private Statute, yet **since it relates to the Issue, it may like all other Matters be given in Evidence**.... (Gilbert 1754: 32, Gilbert's italic emphasis, my boldface emphasis)

Here Gilbert states his relevance rule over and over again. It seems clear that his term for relevance is "relate" and its cognates.
Gilbert also says:

> [I]f the Wi[t]nesses prove Delivery at another Place than where it bears Date, it *doth not warrant the Issue;...and therefore no Proof of the Deed in question*....for the Place where the Deed was made *is no material Part of the Deed*. (Gilbert 1754: 114, my emphasis)

Once again, if the ostensible evidence does not "warrant the issue," then it is "no proof" at all. Once again, relevance is the essence of evidence.
Gilbert also says:

[W]here the *Issue* [of Infancy, i.e., of not being of legal age to make a contract] *relates to* a solemn Contract executed with the necessary Solemnities,...that is a *full Proof of the Issue* [of whether the contract is to be discharged, i.e., voided];.... (Gilbert 1754: 130, my emphasis)

Thus Montrose, Twining, and Langbein overlook six passages in the first edition of Gilbert in which Gilbert states a relevance rule in various ways. And I see nothing that even appears to suggest that Gilbert subsumes his relevance rule under his best evidence rule.

This relevance rule was published in the first major English evidence law treatise 150 years before the 1904 Keynes.

I proceed now to the 1791 edition of Gilbert. In volume 2, we actually see the word "relevant":

On an Action of *Slander*, the Defendant may either justify, or if he think proper, give in **Evidence, under the general Issue**, that the Words were spoken by him as Counsel, and are **relevant to the Cause**;.... (Gilbert 1791: 617, Gilbert's italic emphasis, my boldface emphasis)

Here we see the word "relevant" as relevance to the point in issue:

With regard to personal or private Libels, a Bill or Declaration in a legal suit is not to be considered as libellous, though it may import the severest Censure on the Character of the Party, if it be *relevant* **to the Point under judicial Inquiry**. (Gilbert 1791: 640, Gilbert's italic emphasis, my boldface emphasis)

See also:

....material to the Point in question. (Gilbert 1791: 640)

Here is the word "relevant" a third time:

The Perjury must be **in a point** *material*, that is, *relevant* **to the Point in issue**; it is by no means necessary it should be on a point sufficient to decide the Cause [of action]; if it is to any *circumstance* material, as the colour of a coat, in case of an highway robbery, the party thus wilfully swearing false is equally liable as if it were directly decisive on **the point in issue**. (Gilbert 1791: 660, Gilbert's italic emphasis, my boldface emphasis)

Here Gilbert cites Cicero:

> If the Words of the Defendant are false in the only sense
> in which they **relate to the subject in dispute**,* this is
> sufficient to convict him of Perjury, though in another
> sense, **foreign to the issue**, they might be true.
> * *Fraus enim adstringit, non dissolvit, Perjurium.*—Cic.
> de OFF. III. 32. (Gilbert 1791: 661, Gilbert's italic
> emphasis, my boldface emphasis)

Gilbert also cites Lord Mansfield:

> Lord Mansfield, in delivering the Opinion of the Court,
> recognized the Doctrine already stated, that Perjury must
> be a wilful false swearing on an Oath taken in a judicial
> Proceeding before a competent Jurisdiction, and **on a
> Point material** to the question depending. (Gilbert
> 1791: 662, Mansfield's italic emphasis, my boldface
> emphasis)

In these texts too, I see nothing that even appears to suggest that Gilbert subsumes his relevance rule under his best evidence rule. If Montrose, Twining, and Langbein do, they owe us an explanation. They provide no evidence for their claim that Gilbert even attempts to subsume all his evidence rules under his best evidence rule, where all his evidence rules include his relevance rule. In fact, I see nothing indicating that they even know he *has* a relevance rule.

The word "relevant" appears to be posthumously added to Gilbert. At least, I did not see it in the (also posthumous) 1754 edition. This is not much of a defense for Montrose, Twining, and Langbein, since there are plenty of other passages that do not use the word, but mean the same thing, and that presumably *are* from Gilbert, in the 1754 edition. But the word "relevant" in the 1791 edition is a major anticipation of Keynes. For the word occurs three times in an edition of the first major English evidence law treatise 113 years before the 1904 Keynes. Note the casual editorial equation of being relevant to / relating to / material to / the point in issue / the subject in dispute. This is typical of the times.

Consider now the 1805 edition of Gilbert. The "smoking gun" text where Gilbert states his relevance rule is in volume 1:

> [E]very matter is evidence, that amounts to the proof of
> the point in question. (Gilbert 1805: 25)

Also:

> And upon *non est factum*, if the witnesses prove delivery
> at another place than where it bears date, it does not
> **warrant the issue**; for this is a testimony contrary to the
> plain words of the deed, and therefore **no proof of the**

deed in question. (Gilbert 1805: 144, Gilbert's italic emphasis, my boldface emphasis; 1760: 162)

See also:

> ....that is a full *proof of the issue*.... (Gilbert 1805: 164, my emphasis; 1760: 186)

And:

> ....nothing can come in proof but the truth of the matter alleged. (Gilbert 1805: 244)

Mercifully, I will cut the quotations short.

The only possible way that I can see for there to be such a subsumption is to say that the best evidence is the most relevant. Then greatest relevance would be a consequence of best evidence. But this way is not open to us if "best evidence" simply means the original document or the closest thing we can get to the original document. For as we have seen, that is a *non sequitur*. For there are indefinitely many counterexamples in either direction. There are millions of original documents in the world that are irrelevant to any given point in issue, and there are millions of cases where there are far-from-original items of evidence that are far more relevant to the point in issue than most of the original documents in the world. Even worse, on this way out, the implication would be mutual. For the most relevant evidence would be the best. Thus we could equally well subsume the best evidence rule under the relevance rule. And then, if Gilbert really subsumes all his *other* evidence rules under his best evidence rule, then he would also be subsuming all his other rules, *including* his best evidence rule, under his relevance rule! He would be subsuming all evidence law under the relevance rule. And that would be the more rational and illuminating way to go. For what is the use or point in requiring the most original document if it is not the most relevant evidence? But here I depart from scholarship and enter into criticism, not of Gilbert, but of his main interpreters.

For a "smoking gun" citation to Gilbert's relevance rule, see the Burke section below. Macnair does not provide a cite, but is quite correct in saying Gilbert has a relevance rule.

.   Similarly for Best. Much the same scholars claim that Best, too, has only a best evidence rule. But there is a "smoking gun" text for a relevance rule in Best as well, as we shall see.

William Blackstone

Twining omits William Blackstone (1723–1780) from his review of modern English evidence law (Twining 1994: ch. 3, "The Rationalist Tradition of Evidence Scholarship"). Yet Blackstone's *Commentaries on the Laws of England* is widely considered to be the best book ever written on English law. It influenced American common law to remain basically English, and influenced attorneys from the first Chief Justice of the United States Supreme Court, John Marshall, down to the sixteenth President, Abraham Lincoln.

In the 1783 posthumous ninth edition of his *Commentaries*, "with the last corrections of the author," Blackstone says:

> The nature of my present design will not permit me to enter into the numberless niceties and distinctions of what is, or is not, legal *evidence* to a jury.[n] I shall only therefore select a few of the general heads and leading maxims, relative to this point, together with some observations on the manner of giving evidence.
> **AND, first, evidence signifies that which demonstrates, makes clear, or ascertains the truth of the very fact or point in issue, either on the one side or on the other; and no evidence ought to be admitted to any other point....**
> ...And the one general rule which runs through all the doctrine of trials is this, that the best evidence the nature of the case will admit of shall always be required, if possible to be had; but if not possible, then the best evidence that can be had shall be allowed. For if it be found that there is any better evidence existing than is produced, the very not producing it is a presumption that it would have detected some falsehood that at present is concealed.
> n[.] This is admirably well performed in lord chief baron Gilbert's excellent treatise of evidence: a work which it is impossible to abstract or abridge, without losing some beauty and destroying the chain of the whole.... (Blackstone 1783: 367–68, 367 note n, Blackstone's italic emphasis, my boldface emphasis)

Since Blackstone is discussing existing law, these rules clearly go back earlier than 1783.

In the boldface text, the terms "signifies" and "general rule" suggest that Blackstone is *defining* evidence as being (at least in part) that which is relevant to the point in issue. Thus it is once again *definitional* that evidence must be relevant. The text also suggests that he would find it a *non*definitional, though perhaps also a trivial, obvious, or even self-evident truth, that one ought always to require the best evidence that can be had. (Perhaps he might consider it synthetic *a priori*.) Thus the best evidence rule takes the back seat in Blackstone. This is why he discusses evidence as ascertainment of the point in issue *first* ("AND, first,") and the best evidence rule *second*. Note also that in effect he rejects evidence that does not (help) ascertain the point in issue as inadmissible.

Blackstone was a member of the Middle Temple.

Francis Buller

Francis Buller (1746–1800) says in the 1772 first edition of his *Introduction to the Law Relative to Trials at Nisi Prius*:

> The Ninth general Rule is, That if the Substance of the Issue be proved, it is sufficient. (Buller 1772: 294)

Buller repeats this rule in the corrected fourth edition of 1785 (Buller 1785: 299). The title page of each edition says that Buller is "of the Middle Temple."

This rule, which we may call the substance rule, is stated by many authors in many treatises. But is it a relevance rule? This also brings up a more general question: How do we recognize talk of relevance in the legal literature? Or at least, what is the usual terminology used? "Relating to the point in issue" may be easy enough. But these questions might be very controversial concerning the substance rule. However, the substance rule is typically used in conjunction with another rule that *is* clearly concerned with relevance. This other rule is that evidence is to be *confined* to the point in issue. We may call it the confinement rule. The substance rule modifies the confinement rule by saying that you do not have to establish the point in issue exactly and in every last detail, but only substantively. This does impact on relevance in the case. It means you do not have to provide relevant evidence, in the sense of evidence confined to the point in issue, for every detail of the point in issue. Thus it is a sort of scope-limiting rule. But its scope-limiting role is not enough to show that the substance rule itself is a relevance rule. I would say further that in fact the substance rule is not itself a relevance rule, but what we might call a "significant content" rule that concerns the content of the *point in issue* as opposed to the content of the *evidence for* the point in issue. The policy reason for the substance rule is to ensure that people will not lose important cases merely because they fail to provide sufficient evidence to establish some insignificant *part* of the point in issue, e.g., an unimportant mere formality in a contract. Thus the substance rule necessarily, but only indirectly, impacts on relevance as set forth in the confinement rule. The impact is that since you only have to show the substance of a point, you do not need to provide evidence for any insignificant minor aspects, i.e., evidence confined to establishing such minor aspects.

We may say that the substance rule is a relevance rule, but not a relevant *evidence* rule. For when the rule says that we need not provide evidence for insignificant, unimportant, or minor parts of the point in issue, it is really saying that insignificant *parts* of the point in issue are not relevant to the *substance* of the point in issue. Thus, the substance rule is a *sub-issue* or *sub-pleadings* relevance rule.

However, even if the substance rule is not itself a relevant evidence rule, and is only a relevant sub-pleadings rule, it is tightly connected to the confinement rule in the seventh edition.

Buller's posthumous seventh edition was edited by Richard Whalley Bridgman. The following note is now appended to the rule:

> The Ninth general Rule is, That if the Substance of the Issue be proved, it is sufficient. (*a*)
> (*a*) As the evidence must be applied to **the particular fact in dispute**, evidence which does not **relate** to the issue, or is [not] in some manner **connected** with it, **cannot be received**. Nor can character be called in question in a *civil* cause, unless **put in issue** by the very proceeding itself, for **every case is to be decided on its own circumstances**, and not to be prejudiced by any matter **foreign** to it. (Buller / Bridgman 1817: 298c; 298c n.(a), Buller / Bridgman's italic emphasis, my boldface emphasis)

I inserted the word "not" in square brackets, since otherwise the point opposite from the obviously intended point would be stated. The language in boldface seems very clearly about relevance. The key terms are "relate to," "connected with," and "foreign to." The language is negative or exclusionary. The note says that unrelated evidence cannot be "received" in the case or be used to "decide" the case. And "particular fact in dispute" is the same as "point in issue." Thus there seems no doubt that Bridgman's Buller not only admits a relevant evidence rule in this note, but takes it to be connected (literally, as a note) in some way to the substance rule.

The relevance rule itself is stated in positive terms: "Every case is to be decided on its own circumstances." As a philosopher, I for one find interesting overtones of relevance in the phrase "its own circumstances," e.g., its "proper" or "appropriate" circumstances. That is, relevant evidence is evidence that is proper or appropriate to the case.

Questions arise. First, why is this note appended to this rule? Is the relevant evidence rule intended to clarify or explain the substance rule as itself being a relevant evidence rule? Or does Bridgman's Buller merely take the relevant evidence rule to be a useful additional point worthy of being included as a note? But if the relevant evidence rule is a mere additional point, and if the substance rule is not to be understood as being itself a relevant evidence rule, then is the relevant evidence rule in the note at least intended to be *related* in some way to the substance rule? Is it, so to speak, intended to be *relevant* in some way to understanding the substance rule? And if so, then is this intent correct or mistaken? My best guess is that Bridgman's Buller merely wishes to remind us that even though it suffices merely to prove the substance of the issue, the evidence we provide must be *relevant* to the substance of the issue.

For our purposes, it does not really matter whether the substance rule is related to the relevance rule in this way. The main thing is the note, not the substance rule it is appended to. That is because it is the note that shows that Bridgman's Buller requires that evidence must be relevant. For it states his relevance rule.

William Murray Mansfield

William Murray Mansfield (1705–1793) was Lord Chief Justice of England and the first Earl of Mansfield. His Bristow v Wright was the leading English case on variances well into the nineteenth century. Mansfield, of course, was far more famous for other decisions, especially in Somersett's Case, where he freed any slave of any country who set foot on English soil. He also did much to make English law less medieval, and more rational and pragmatic.

In 1781, Mansfield says in *Bristow*:

> The distinction is that between that which may be rejected as *surplusage*, and what cannot. When the declaration contains *impertinent* matter, *foreign* to the cause, and which the master on a reference to him would strike out (*irrelevant* covenants for instance), that will be rejected by the court, and need not be proved. But if the very ground of the action is misstated, as where you undertake to recite that part of a deed on which the action is founded, that will be fatal. (Powell 1859: 188 quoting Mansfield in Bristow v. Wright, Dougl. 665, 1 Sm. L. C. 223, my emphasis)

Thus surplusage is matter that is impertinent, foreign, or irrelevant in the *pleadings*. More precisely, surplusage is matter irrelevant to the *intended* pleadings, but unfortunately written in the pleadings themselves. Thus it is a bad part of how the pleadings are written, as opposed to bad evidence for the truth or falsehood of the pleadings. Powell gives two examples of this. "If words which are [1] without meaning, or which [2] have been introduced by mistake, be inserted in pleadings, they will be struck out as surplusage at common law" (Powell 1859: 187). I especially wish to note the use of the term "irrelevant" by a Lord Chief Justice of England in 1781. Compare the section below on Powell on the substance rule.

John Morgan

In 1789, John Morgan, "of the Inner Temple, barrister at law," in his *Essays*, praises John Locke and William Paley for their views on the subject of human testimony:

> ....Lawyers are not the persons who have made observations upon human testimony....The subject hath not escaped the notice of Mr. *Locke*, Mr. *Paley*, and others. The observations of Mr. *Locke* are to the following purport: viz. that there are **several degrees from** perfect *certainty* and *demonstration*, down to *improbability* and *unlikeness,* **even to** the confines of *impossibility*; that there are several acts of the mind proportioned to these **degrees of evidence**, which may be called the degrees of *assent*, from full *assurance* and *confidence*, to *conjecture*, *doubt*, and *disbelief.*
>
> Human testimony, *i.e.* evidence given by one man to another, can [as such] never produce *certainty*....
>
> In the trial of causes, therefore, those to whom evidence is given, and who are to determine upon that evidence, must judge upon *probability*; *viz.* the highest **degree of probability** must govern their judgment; and it necessarily follows, that they ought to have before them *the best evidence of which the nature of the case will admit:* less is productive of *opinion* and *surmise* only, and does not give the mind entire satisfaction; for if, from the nature of the transaction, it appears that there is further [i.e. better] evidence, which hath not been produced, the non-production affords a presumption that it would have contradicted something which hath already appeared, and perhaps have varied the case essentially; therefore the mind does not acquiesce in less than the utmost evidence whereof the fact is capable.

> The preceding RULE must, consequently, be considered as *fundamental* in the law of evidence. (Morgan 1789: marginal p. 3, Morgan's italic and small caps emphasis, my boldface emphasis)

This text shows that Locke is the philosophical source for degrees of probability for Morgan as well as for Gilbert. Morgan expressly states that such talk, at least on the subject of testimony, did not come from lawyers. Morgan says that degrees of probability have *two* asymptotes: perfect certainty at the top, and impossibility at the bottom. Morgan then gives two arguments for the best evidence rule. First he argues that in court, "the highest degree of probability must govern their judgment;" therefore "it necessarily follows that they ought to" use "the best evidence" available. Second, he argues that if the best evidence is not produced, then we have a right to be suspicious why not. This second argument is the usual justification given during these times. However, it is stated on a very general level, and does not mention written documents in particular, though perhaps that is implied by the term "transaction," or is even simply assumed to be understood. Perhaps a transaction implies a contract, and a significant transaction would have a written contract.

Morgan says that the best evidence is "fundamental," but does not say that it is the *only* fundamental rule. (Compare logics or geometries which have several axioms.) This is very curious, since in his first argument he derives it from a more fundamental rule that courts are to be governed by the highest degree of probability. This more fundamental rule might be called an extreme relevance rule. That is in keeping with the times; courts across Europe often set the bar very high for evidence and proof.

Morgan says two pages later:

> According to Mr. J. *Blackstone, L.* III. *c.* 23. **evidence signifies** that which demonstrates, makes clear, or ascertains the truth of the **very act or point in issue**, either on the one side or the other, and **no evidence ought to be admitted to any other point**. (Morgan 1789: marginal p. 5, Morgan's italic emphasis, my boldface emphasis)

Morgan is referring to Mr. Justice William Blackstone, book ("L." means liber) 3, chapter 23 of the *Commentaries*, which I quoted above. Thus it seems that Morgan expressly follows Blackstone in making the relevancy of evidence definitional. The term "ascertain" might be taken to imply that the evidence must be of the highest probability. In any case, it seems that Morgan finds that evidence is relevant by definition, that it is axiomatic that courts must be governed by evidence of the highest degree of probability, and that it is merely a consequent theorem, derived from this axiom, that courts ought to admit the best evidence possible.

Edmund Burke

Edmund Burke (1729–1797) is famous for his political writings, especially his *Reflections on the Revolution in France*. It is less well-known that he also wrote about evidence law, and was "entered at the Middle Temple" (Mahoney 1955: viii). This is of interest because Keynes wrote "an unpublished hundred-page essay on 'The Political Doctrines of Edmund Burke' which was submitted for the University Members Prize for English Essay in November 1904, duly winning it" (Skidelsky 2005: 96). That is to say, we know that Keynes studied Burke in 1904, the same year that he read his first probability paper to the Apostles.

Twining quotes the 1794 Burke as saying that the rules of evidence law fit "'in so small a compass that a parrot... might...repeat them in five minutes'" (Twining 1994: 34 quoting Burke). Twining admits that we must make "due allowance for... rhetorical exaggeration" here, but does not tarry to describe Burke's views on evidence (Twining 1994: 34).

Edward Coke's Latin maxim is in the 1794 Burke. Burke's version of the maxim, posthumously published in 1852, is:

> *In re criminali*, said the rigourists, *probationes debent esse evidentes et luce meridianâ clariores*; and so undoubtedly it is in matters which admit such proof. (Burke 1852 / 1794: 81–82, Burke's emphasis)

This is in Burke's written "Report, made on the 30th April, 1794, from the Committee of the House of Commons, appointed to inspect the Lords' Journals, in relation to their proceeding on the trial of Warren Hastings, Esquire," under the section heading "Debates on Evidence" (Burke 1852 / 1794: 39; see 38).

The *probationes* maxim, as I noted earlier, might not imply relevance in any obvious way. But Burke has more to say about evidence. He even uses the word "relevant":

> Your committee conceives that the trial of a cause is not in the arguments or disputations of the prosecutors and the counsel, but in the *evidence*; and that **to refuse evidence is to refuse the cause**: nothing, therefore, but the most clear and weighty reasons, ought to preclude its production. Your committee conceives that, when evidence on the face of it **relevant, that is, connected with the party and the charge**, was denied to be

competent, *the burden lay upon those who opposed it*, to set for the authorities...wherein the courts have rejected evidence of that nature. (Burke 1852: 76–77, Burke's italic emphasis, my boldface emphasis)

Thus relevant evidence, or evidence "connected with the party and the charge," i.e., the pleadings or cause, is always to be admitted unless "the most clear and weighty reasons" prohibit it. He says:

Your committee....find that the term evidence, *evidentia*, from whence ours is taken, has a sense different in the Roman law, from what it is understood to bear in the English jurisprudence. The term most nearly answering to it in the Roman, being **probatio**, proof; which, like the term *evidence*, is a generic term, including **every thing by which a doubtful matter may be rendered more certain** to the judge; or, **as Gilbert expresses it, every matter is evidence which amounts to proof of the point in question**. (Burke 1853: 78–79 citing "Gilbert's Law of Evidence, p. 43," Burke's italic emphasis, my boldface emphasis)

This is not only relevantist, but close to Keynes. First, Burke says that the Roman legal term "most nearly answering to" the English term "evidence" is "probatio," which connotes probativeness. In the legal literature, that is just another term for relevance. Second, Burke anticipates Keynes, *Federal Rules of Evidence* Rule 401, and even Bayes' Theorem, when he says that proof, or evidence, includes everything that would make a claim more (or less) certain than it would otherwise be. This anticipation is so clear and so strong that I wonder if Keynes, who wrote a long paper on Burke in 1904, based his own probability theory on this very text, together with the earlier block-indented text where Burke uses the word "relevant."

Note that Burke attributes his relevance rule to Gilbert. This is in contrast to the scholars of our own time, who know Gilbert only as a champion of the best evidence rule.

Hadrian was one of the five so-called "good emperors" of the Roman Empire. Hadrian ruled that empire at its greatest extent, as marked in part by Hadrian's Wall in Britain. Burke quotes the Emperor Hadrian on the indefinability of the concept of evidence:

And there remains a rescript from the same prince ["his sacred majesty, Hadrian"] to Valerius Varus, on the bringing out the credit of witnesses. This appears to go more to the *general* principles of evidence. It is in these words: "what evidence, and in what **measure or degree**, shall amount to proof in each case, **can be defined in no**

> **manner whatsoever that is sufficiently certain**....In
> some cases, the number of the witnesses, in others their
> dignity and authority, is to be **weighed**; in others,
> concurring public fame [i.e. public opinion] tends to
> confirm the credit of the evidence in question. This alone
> I am able, and in a few words, to give you as my
> determination, that you ought not too readily to bind
> yourself to try the cause upon **any one description of
> evidence**; but you are to **estimate** by your own
> discretion what you ought to credit, or what appears to
> you not to be established by proof sufficient. (Burke
> 1852: 80 citing "Digest. 1. xxii. part 5, " Burke's italic
> emphasis, my boldface emphasis)

Hadrian and Burke anticipate Keynes' view that evidence is, in a certain basic sense, indefinable. They even anticipate Butchvarov's more radical argument in *The Concept of Knowledge* that we have no concept of evidence at all, not even an indefinable one, since there is no one thing which all the things we call evidence have in common (Butchvarov 1970: part 4). At least they anticipate the premiss of Butchvarov's argument; they do not draw Butchvarov's conclusion. Hadrian and Burke anticipate Keynes' view that there are degrees of evidence, and also Keynes' view that these degrees cannot always be assigned cardinal numbers, since they are to be "weighed," and we "are to estimate" their weight. Burke goes on to argue that the jurists of his own time have not been able to be more precise than Hadrian on the nature or definition of evidence (Burke 1852: 80ff.). I am tempted to recall Aristotle's view that it is a mark of lack of education to demand more precision than a subject matter allows. But per Russell, you never know when you might be able to provide a more precise definition or a further logical analysis in the future. See chapter 9 on whether logical analysis can be endless.

Might Keynes have read these texts when he was studying Burke? That Keynes does not discuss these topics in his Burke paper does not detract from this possibility.

Thomas Peake

Thomas Peake was a well regarded evidence law treatise writer of his time. In 1801, he says in the first edition of his *Compendium of the Law of Evidence*, chapter 1, "Of the General Rules of Evidence:

> Another rule is, that the evidence must be *applied to the particular fact in dispute*, and *therefore no evidence not*

relating to the issue, or in some manner connected with
it can be received.... (Peake 1801: 3, my emphasis)

Three pages later, he says, "The subject of proof being ascertained
by the preceding rules, the next thing which must be attended to is
that the best evidence that the nature of the case will admit of, be
produced...." (Peake 1801: 6–7). Thus the relevance rule is prior to
the best evidence rule. Not only that, but the relevance rule is one
of the rules that 'ascertain' 'the subject of proof'; and the best
evidence rule is not. This seems to imply that the relevance rule is
one of the rules that define what evidence is, and that the best
evidence rule is not.

In the 1804 "second edition, with considerable additions,"
Peake says:

> Another rule is, that the evidence must be applied to the
> particular fact in dispute, and therefore no evidence not
> *relating* to the issue, or *in some manner connected* with
> it can be received; (a) nor can the character of either
> party to a civil cause be called in question, unless put in
> issue by the very proceeding itself, for every cause is to
> be *decided by its own circumstances*, and not to be
> prejudiced by any matter *foreign* to it. (Peake 1804: 6,
> my emphasis)

This is in chapter 1, "Of the General Rules of Evidence." Here the
rule is only "Another rule" among others. Clearly the rule has an
exclusionary or gate-keeping function, as shown by the exclusion
of "any matter foreign to it." The title page says Peake is "of
Lincoln's-Inn."

Peake says in the 1824 edition:

> Another rule is that the evidence must be applied to the
> particular fact in dispute; and therefore no evidence not
> relating to the issue, or in some matter connected with it,
> can be received. (Peak 1824: 40)

This repeats the relevance rule of 1804 word for word. As before,
the terms "relating" and "connected with" connote relevancy.

Samuel March Phillipps

Samuel March Phillipps (1780–1862) was a major evidence law treatise writer of his time. He says in the 1816 edition of
his *Treatise on the Law of Evidence*, chapter 7, section 3:

> As the sole object and end of evidence is to ascertain the truth of the several disputed facts or points in issue on the one side or the other, no evidence ought to be admitted to any other point. (Phillipps 1820: 126)

He is saying in effect that evidence is to be confined to the point in issue. He seems to be saying it in a way that implies a relativity of evidence to points in issue, such that evidence for one point need not be evidence for another point. This certainly seems to be a relevance rule. The title page says that Phillipps is "of the Inner Temple."

Phillipps expressly says that evidence is to be confined to the points in issue in the 1820 edition of his *Treatise*. Chapter 7, section 3 is entitled, "Evidence is to be confined to the Points in Issue." There Phillipps says:

> As the sole object and end of evidence is to ascertain the truth of the several disputed facts or points in issue on the one side or on the other, no evidence ought to be admitted to any other point. (Phillipps 1820: 126, prior pagination *126)

Phillipps repeats the point a few pages later: "As evidence is to be confined to the points in issue,...." (Phillipps 1820: 138, prior pagination *139).

But the main thing of interest to us does not show on these pages. If we look at the table of contents, we see that there, and only there, section 3 has a subheading, "Relevancy of Evidence— Examples." (Phillipps 1820: xiv). This subheading is indicated for page 138, the page we were just quoting. The implication seems clear that for Phillipps, relevancy of evidence and confinement of evidence to the points in issue are one and the same thing. The terms "relevant to the point" and "confined to the point" would be logically equivalent and even synonymous for him. For according to the table of contents, he is placing his statement of the confinement rule under the already mentioned subheading, "Relevancy of Evidence."

In the 1822 edition of the *Treatise*, talk of "relevancy" now moves into the main text. Phillipps says:

> The sole object and evidence is, to ascertain the truth of the several disputed facts or points in issue on the one side or on the other; and no evidence ought to be admitted on any other point.
>
> Evidence must always be considered *with reference to* the subject-matter, to which it is applied....And it is material, therefore, to consider the view, with which particular evidence is offered, in order

to determine whether it *bears upon* the point in issue. Evidence may be admissible in one *point of view*, though not in another. A question, for instance, which would have been *irrelevant* and improper on the examination in chief, may be rendered necessary by the course of a cross-examination....

Such evidence alone ought to be admitted, as in some manner *bears upon* the *question at issue*. An inquiry into other transactions, besides those immediately contested, may in some cases be entirely *irrelevant*. The *relevancy* of evidence must depend upon the nature and circumstances of the particular case; for all evidence is to be considered *with reference to* the subject-matter, to which it is applied....

As evidence is to be *confined to the points in issue*, the character of either party cannot be inquired into, in a civil proceeding, unless it is put in issue by the nature of the proceeding itself....

The rule, that all manner of evidence ought to be rejected which is *foreign to the points in issue*, applies more strongly, if possible, to criminal prosecutions than to civil cases. This rule is to be founded in common justice; for no person can be expected to answer, unprepared and at once, for every action of his life. In treason, therefore, no evidence is to be admitted of any overt act that is not expressly laid in the indictment. (Phillipps 1822: 167–79, my emphasis)

He says this in chapter 7, "Of Certain General Rules of Evidence," section 3, "Evidence is to be Confined to the Points in Issue." If we look at the table of contents, we see that once again, section 3 has a subheading, "Relevancy of Proof" (Phillipps 1822: xii). This subheading is indicated for page 168, right in the middle of the pages we were just quoting. Thus Phillipps continues to equate relevance with confinement to the points in issue, and now in the main text.

The quotation above commingles materiality, admissibility, and relevancy—terms to which we assign different meanings today. But it clearly indicates that relevant evidence is relative to some things, in some sense or senses. It seems to be relative to (1) the subject matter, meaning the points in issue, (2) one's "point of view," which I gloss as one's theory of the case, and (3) possibly even to newly discovered material, such as might be uncovered "by the course of a cross-examination." If so, this would be yet another remarkable anticipation of *FRE* Rule 401 and of Keynes. We see the exclusionary function in terms like "irrelevant," "confined to the points in issue," and especially in the rule that "evidence ought to be rejected which is foreign to the points in issue."

The 1838 eighth edition of Phillipps' *Treatise on the Law of Evidence* was written with the assistance of Andrew Amos and with help from a Mr. Gale (Phillipps 1838: Advertisement to the Eighth Edition; see title page). Amos was Professor of Laws at Cambridge University, and Charles James Gale was a member of the Middle Temple. Several texts are of interest. Phillipps and Amos begin by saying, in part 1, chapter 1:

> The parties to a suit are not permitted to adduce every description of evidence which, according to their own notions, may be supposed to elucidate the matter in dispute; if such a latitude were permitted, evidence might often be brought forward, which would lead to error rather than to truth, the attention of the jury might be diverted by the introduction of *irrelevant or immaterial evidence,* and the investigation might be extended to a most inconvenient length. In order to guard against these evils, the law interferes, *in the first instance,* by limiting and regulating the admissibility of evidence.
>   It is the province of the Judge...to decide all questions on the admissibility of evidence...Upon this subject, it has been said by Mr. J[ustice] Buller, that whether there is any evidence is a question for the Judge, but whether the evidence is sufficient is a question for the jury. (Phillipps 1838: 2, my emphasis, cite omitted)

The term "according to their own notions" implies that relevance is an objective matter not to be decided by the parties' own personal notions of what is relevant. The term "in the first instance" seems to imply that, concerning the admissibility of evidence, relevance is the first thing to consider. The second paragraph distinguishes the admissibility of evidence from its weight. Admissibility concerns whether the evidence is relevant at all. Weight concerns the degree of relevance. The distinction is clearly stated, and is still used today.
    Phillipps presents the best evidence rule as an exclusionary rule which excludes anything less than the best evidence available (Phillipps 1813: 437). Phillipps says:

> The law excludes such evidence of facts as from the nature of the thing supposes still better evidence behind in the party's possession or power. The rule has been expressed in terms, that the best evidence must always be given. Other writers have stated it to be, that the law requires the best proof of which the nature of the thing is capable. But the precise import of the rule cannot, perhaps, be adequately comprehended without reference to it's [sic] application in various instances.
>   The [rule] is founded on the presumption, that there is something in the better evidence which is

withheld, which would make against the party resorting
to inferior evidence.... (Phillipps 1838: 437–38)

Thus the best evidence rule is there, and it is important. But it is not
the only rule, nor does it subsume or encompass the relevance rule
in any way that I can see. Quite the opposite. For Phillipps tellingly
says, "the rule in question relates only to the quality, and not to the
quantity or strength of the evidence" (Phillipps 1838: 440). We
may say that the best evidence rule pertains to the quality of the
evidence, and the relevance rule to its strength, and even to its
quantity, in the sense that if there is no relevant evidence, then
there is no evidence. If that is correct, then we may say that the best
evidence rule and the relevance rule are equally essential. For if our
evidence has no quality, then in this sense we have no evidence
worthy of the name; and if our evidence has no relevance, then in
that sense we have no evidence worthy of the name. In fact, the
idea that any thing must have both quantity and quality is very old,
and recalls Aristotle. If all this is correct, then neither the best
evidence rule nor the relevance rule can subsume the other.

Concerning the substance rule, Phillipps says:

SECTION 3.
The substance of the Issue to be proved.
With reference to the question, what will be **sufficient**
proof of an issue....it will be convenient to consider, in
the first place, what are the rules which determine
whether the allegations involved in the issue have been
properly **supported by** evidence, or whether there is
such a difference between the allegations and the
evidence as will constitute a **variance**,—and secondly,
what are the cases in which there is a **sufficient
approximation** of the evidence to the allegations, to
enable the judge to amend the statement in the pleadings,
so as to make it **conformable** with the evidence. In
treating of these subjects, **the term,** *variance***, is to be
understood to mean a fatal difference between the
evidence and the pleadings, unless the latter can be
amended**.
     A general rule, **governing the application of
evidence to the points in dispute** on any issue, is, that it
must be **sufficient to prove the substance** of the issue.
     It is a general principle of evidence, that all the
material facts in the declaration, which are **put in issue**,
must be established by legal proof. Another principle is,
that the nature and extent of the proof will depend upon
the manner in which the alleged facts are introduced....
Evidence, as Lord Mansfield used frequently to observe,
**is always to be taken with reference to the subject-
matter to which it is applied, and to the person**

against whom it is used. (Phillipps 1838: 845–46, Phillipps' italic emphasis, my boldface emphasis)

It seems from the boldface words that the substance rule, and also
the concept of variance, have *something* to do with the relevance or
relatedness of the evidence to the point in issue. We also see that
Phillipps adopts Lord Mansfield's version of the relevance rule.

The substance rule "governs" the relevance rule in the
sense that it requires that the relevant evidence "be sufficient to
prove the substance of the issue." Thus the substance rule goes, so
to speak, to the quantity or degree of relevant evidence needed, as
opposed to its quality.

The interesting thing about the concept of variance is that
if the evidence does not conform to the pleadings, then, at least to
some extent, the pleadings can be amended so as to make the
pleadings conform to the *evidence*, provided that the substance of
the pleadings remains. This basically seems to mean omitting
insignificant details from the pleadings. Thus relevance is a two-
way street. If our evidence is not relevant to the point in issue, we
would normally wish to find and present new evidence that is
relevant to the point in issue. But here it emerges that conversely,
we can amend the pleading, so that the existing evidence is now
relevant to the point in issue. The threshold requirement for doing
so is that the point in issue remain *substantially* the same. I suppose
that we could even take both approaches at once. That is, we could
both remove insignificant parts of the pleadings from the pleadings,
and find new evidence that is more relevant to the substance of the
pleadings. But I also suppose that the writers of the time may have
found there was no practical point in doing so, since they do not
discuss this dual possibility. I imagine that this is because if the
pleadings are changed so as to make the evidence suffice, then the
existing evidence need not be changed, since it has just been *made*
to suffice. And that seems a trivial, if not tautological, point.

My conclusion is that the substance rule is a sort of reverse
relevance rule. It reverses the approach of the relevance rule in that
it does not require our evidence to be relevant to the pleadings as
they are stated, but permits us to change our pleadings so as to
plead only the substance of the issue, so that if our existing
evidence is relevant to the substance of the issue, then we need not
seek further evidence to help establish the now-eliminated
irrelevant pleadings. That is, within the pleadings themselves, some
pleaded issues may be irrelevant to the substantive pleaded issues.

By parity of reason, talk of variance is a sort of reverse talk
of relevance, that is, a sort of talk of irrelevance. See also the index
on "RELEVANCY, of proof. See *Substance, variance*" (Phillipps

1838: 1050, Phillipps' emphasis). It seems that the substance rule may be also called the variance rule.

Phillipps also says:

> SECTION 2.
> *On the Relevancy of Presumptions.*
> With respect to presumptions which are too remote to admit of any reasonable direction to the jury in regard to the issue which they have to try, a very nice exercise of discretion often devolves upon the Judge. It is his duty to **confine the evidence to the points in issue**, lest the attention of juries be distracted, and the public time needlessly consumed.... (Phillipps 1838: 481, Phillipps' italic emphasis, my boldface emphasis)

Again, we see an express equation of relevancy with confinement to the point in issue. Phillipps seems to make it a judge's duty in general to confine evidence to the points in issue, and thereby to require relevance. This becomes even clearer when Phillipps later refers back to this text as follows:

> The power of cross-examination is generally acknowledged to afford one of the best securities against incomplete, garbled, or false evidence. Great latitude, therefore, is allowed in the mode of putting questions. The rule, however, is subject to certain limitations; the questions put must be *relevant* to the investigation, in which they are offered. The *relevancy* of a question, as directly bearing upon the *matter in issue*, has already been considered.(1)
> (1) *Ante*, p. 481. (Phillipps 1838: 907–8, 908 n.(1), my emphasis)

Here, to be relevant is to bear directly on the point in issue. But I am sure Phillipps would agree that this does not mean that every single item of evidence, taken by itself, must be relevant in the sense of bearing directly on the point. For it is generally understood that items of evidence must often work together in order for their relevance as a whole to be understood.

Phillipps does not limit the relevance rule to presumptions and cross-examination. On the next page, he writes generally of "The rules of evidence, excluding irrelevant matter" (Phillipps 1838: 909). I explained the main sorts of presumptions in chapter 6 (see the index of subjects).

An irrelevant issue may also be called a "collateral issue" (Phillipps 1838: 909–10). Phillipps says, "It is settled, that a witness cannot be cross-examined as to any fact,— which, if admitted, would be collateral, and wholly irrelevant to the matter in issue" (Phillipps 1838: 910).

In 1849, Phillipps says, in the sixth American edition from the ninth London edition of his *Treatise*:

> It is [the judge's] duty to *confine the evidence to the points in issue,* that the attention of jurors might not be distracted, nor the public time needlessly consumed....
> (Phillipps 1849: 460, my emphasis)

This is in chapter 9, section 2, "Of the Relevancy of Presumptive Proofs; and of the Rule which Confines Evidence to the Points in Issue," The section title makes it clear that Phillipps considers confinement to the point in issue to be the same as relevancy. The best evidence rule is independently discussed in chapter 8.

In 1859, Phillipps and Thomas James Arnold say, in the 10th English / 4th American edition of Phillipps' *Treatise*, chapter 10, section 3, "Of the Relevancy of Presumptive Proofs; and of the Rule which Confines Evidence to the Points in Issue":

> With respect to presumptions which are too remote to admit of any reasonable direction to a jury in regard to the issue which they have to try, a very nice exercise of discretion devolves upon the judge(1.) It is his duty to *confine the evidence to the points in issue,* that the attention of juries may not be distracted, nor the public time needlessly consumed....
> (1) NOTE 195.— The court always protect the jury from *irrelevant* testimony....
> If evidence be *irrelevant* at the time it is offered, it is not error to reject it because other evidence may be afterwards given, in connection with which it would become *relevant.* If it would be *relevant,* in conjunction with other facts, it should be proposed in connection with those facts, and an offer to follow the evidence proposed, with proof of those facts at a proper time. (Phillipps 1859: 732, my emphasis)

We see once again the equation of relevance with confinement to the points in issue, and once again that the relevance of a piece of evidence may be relative to the relevance of other items of evidence.

In 1868, Phillipps, now posthumous, and Arnold repeat this quotation word for word, under the same section 3 title, in the 10th English / 5th American edition (Phillipps: 614–15 / prior pagination *732). In both editions, we also see clearly how talk of variance is the logical contrapositive of talk of confinement to the issue. Phillipps says, in the very next note to the very same paragraph, "NOTE 196.—That proof must not vary from the issue, will be more clearly seen in the notes to the twelfth chapter" (Phillipps 1859: 733; Phillipps 1868: 615 / prior pagination *733). Clearly, "Proof must be confined to the issue" and "Proof must not vary from the issue" are logically equivalent to each other, and also to "Proof must relate to the issue." Recall that we are using the word "proof" not in the formal logical sense, but to mean sufficient probable evidence. The standard of sufficiency can vary depending on the type of case, from "beyond a reasonable doubt" in criminal law, through "clear and convincing" in some statutory law, to mere "preponderance of the evidence," meaning more likely than not, in civil law. All these standards are in effect rough degrees of probability.

Jeremy Bentham

Jeremy Bentham (1748–1822) was not just a great philosopher. He was also a bencher of Lincoln's Inn, and produced a huge amount of writing on evidence law and the philosophy of evidence. This writing was edited twice. First, there was a French edition that was soon translated back into English. Second, there was the monumental edition edited by John Stuart Mill, Russell's godfather. Bentham's influence was monumental in the nineteenth century. He was praised by some, criticized by others, and sometimes both at once.

In 1825, *A Treatise on Judicial Evidence*, the English translation of (Pierre) Étienne Louis Dumont's French edition of Bentham's writings, appeared. Dumont had met Bentham in person and was a great admirer. In book 7, "Of the Exclusion of Evidence," chapter 5, "Causes which Render Exclusion Always Proper," Bentham says:

[Even when] the witnesses ought not to be excluded, there are cases in which the testimony ought to be thrown out of doors;
1. When it is *pertinent*; 2. When it is **superfluous**.
To say that testimony is not **pertinent**, is to say that it is **foreign** to the case, has no **connection** with it, and does **not serve to prove the fact in question**; in a word, **it is to say, that it is not evidence**.
To say that testimony is **superfluous**, is to say, that, though it were admitted, it would **add nothing** to the effect of the other evidence, and would in no way **contribute** to the discovery of the truth.
Evidence, which is not **pertinent**, is more injurious than **superfluous** evidence. The latter occasions loss of time to the judge, and, to the parties, a

> proportional quantity of expense, delay, and vexation;
> but the former, in addition to these inconveniences,
> covers the case with clouds, creates incidental inquiries
> which only mislead, and infuses doubt and hesitation
> into the minds of the judges. This evil is still greater with
> a jury; because the men who compose it, having less
> experience than the judges, know not how to find their
> way out of the labyrinth. The case is in a proper
> condition to develope its true character, only after **all the
> evidence, which is not pertinent, has been set aside**.
> (Bentham 1825: 230, Bentham's italic emphasis, my
> boldface emphasis)

Pertinence would seem to be the same as relevance. It also seems that Bentham is *defining* evidence as that which is pertinent. Note the phrase, "in a word, it is to say, that it is not evidence." He is saying that pertinence is essential to evidence at the very least. For if it is not pertinent, then it is not evidence.

"Superfluous" is ordinarily taken to mean 'redundant'. But "superfluous" is defined differently here. Here, to be superfluous is to "add nothing to the effect of the other evidence," and to "in no way contribute to the discovery of the truth." That is, an item can be superfluous in either of two ways. First, it can be pertinent but redundant. Second, it can be nonpertinent. The first quoted phrase anticipates *FRE* Rule 401, or more precisely the exclusionary aspect of that rule. The second phrase implies that superfluity is the logical contrary, not to say contradictory, of use-relevance. This is due to the word "contribute." Indeed, I would say that for Bentham, the use or function of evidence is what defines evidence ("serve to prove"). Evidence is as evidence does. Compare deductive use-relevance in chapter 9 and in my (2012).

In 1827, *Rationale of Judicial Evidence*, John Stuart Mill's edition of Bentham, appeared. Mill was said to have edited it extensively. Indeed, the prose reads much like Mill's prose, at least to me. Mill's Bentham, says in volume 1:

> Evidence is a word of relation; it is of the number of
> those which, in their signification, involve, each of them,
> a necessary reference to the import expressed by some
> other; which other must be brought to view at the same
> time with it, or the import cannot be understood.
>   By the term evidence, considered according to
> the most extended application that is ever given to it,
> may be, and seems in general to be, understood,—any
> matter of fact, the effect, tendency, or design of which,
> when presented to the mind, is to produce a persuasion
> concerning the existence of some other matter of fact: a
> persuasion either affirmative or disaffirmative of its
> existence. (Bentham 1827: vol. 1: 17)

In the first paragraph, Bentham says that evidence is relational to other evidence. He is saying that the relevance of items of evidence (often) cannot be understood except in relation to other items of evidence. This anticipates the later Russell's holistic theory of empirical scientific knowledge and Quine's more radical holistic general theory of science. But it basically just reports the law as Phillipps describes it in the second paragraph of the last block-indented quotation in the previous section of this chapter. The law is the same today.

In the second paragraph just quoted from Bentham, he says that the scope of the term "evidence" includes anything which even merely *tends* to show us that something is or is not the case. This is just Keynes' view. Except for Keynes' formalizing the point, the only difference is verbal: Bentham uses "pertinent" where Keynes uses "relevant."

Concerning the second paragraph, and other Bentham texts like it, Montrose and Twining note that Bentham may be criticized for psychologizing relevance when he speaks of evidence as a tendency to produce a "'persuasion'" in "'the mind'" (Montrose 1992 / 1954: 358–59 / 538–39 quoting Bentham; Twining 1985: 29); but this need not detain us.

Montrose says that Bentham's evidence relation "has subsequently been called that of relevance" (Montrose 1992 / 1954: 349 / 529; see 358 / 538). Montrose says that Bentham:

> defines "facts" as "events or states of things," and classifies them as either "primary" or "evidentiary." Evidence is not conceived by Bentham as a concept employed only in courts of law: on the contrary, he considers that we rely on evidence in all human activities, scientific and non-scientific....Bentham's distinction between "primary fact" and "evidentiary fact" is more generally expressed as the distinction between *factum probandum* and *factum probans*. The relation between the two has subsequently been called that of **relevance**. (Montrose 1992 / 1954: 348–49 / 528–29, Montrose's italic emphasis, my boldface emphasis)

Twining concurs: "Although Bentham does not explicitly use the term in this context, the relation between the *factum probans* and *factum probandum* is normally referred to as 'relevance'" (Twining 1985: 29, Twining's emphasis). Montrose also correctly notes that Bentham is discussing evidence in general, and not just in evidence law.

Mill's Bentham says in volume 3:

[I]t is seldom that by any one such article, standing by itself, that a persuasion, strong enough to constitute a ground for action, is constituted in the mind of the judge.

By some greater number of such lots of circumstantial evidence, taken together, the fact may be said to be *proved.* Of the *probative force* of any one of them taken by itself, the utmost that can be said is, that by means of it the fact is *probabilized:*—rendered, in a greater or less degree, *probable.*

As there are facts—evidentiary facts—by the [probative] force of which of which a fact, considered in the character of a principal fact, is probabilized; so it will generally happen that there are others by which the same fact may be *disprobabilized:*— the existence of it rendered more or less improbable.

When a fact is thus probabilized, it is by the probative force of the evidentiary fact: by the strength of the inference by which, the existence of the evidentiary fact being affirmed, the existence of the principal fact is *inferred.* (Bentham 1827 vol. 3: 13, Bentham's emphasis)

Bentham also speaks of *"disprobative* force" as that which has "the opposite effect, *disprobabilization"* (Bentham 1827 vol. 3: 16 n.†, Bentham's emphasis). He says, "To probabilize any given fact will be the same as to disprobabilize its opposite" (Bentham 1827 vol. 3: 16 n.†).

Thus for an evidentiary fact to have probative force is for it to make a principal fact more probable than it would otherwise be. For an evidentiary fact to have disprobative force is for it to make an evidentiary fact less probable than it would otherwise be. (This is just like *FRE* Rule 401.) Thus it would appear that for Bentham, pertinence is relevance, and degree of probative force is degree of relevance. In any case, Dumont's Bentham's defining evidence as pertinence would be consistent with Mill's Bentham's admitting degrees of probative force. And we can and ought to understand both "pertinence" and "probative force" as meaning relevance.

Bentham says that "the degree of [probative] strength... would be capable of being expressed by numbers, in the same way as degrees of probability are expressed by mathematicians, viz. by the ratio of one number to another. But the nature of the case admits not of any such precision as that which would be given by employing different ratios (*i.e.* different pairs of numbers) as expressive of so many uniform degrees of probative force" (Bentham 1827 vol. 3: 220). Bentham says that "probative force....may be in any degree slight; and it may be strong in almost any degree short of conclusive" (Bentham 1827 vol. 3: 220). I take this to be basically the same as Keynes' view that degrees of probability cannot always be assigned determinate numbers, and basically the same as his view that certainty is an asymptote to which probability approaches.

In volume 4 of Mill's Bentham, book 9, "On Exclusion of Evidence," part 2, "View of the Cases in which Exclusion of Evidence is Proper," chapter 5, "Exclusion of Irrelevant Evidence Proper," Mill's Bentham says:

> EXCLUSION OF **IRRELEVANT** EVIDENCE [IS ALWAYS] PROPER
> Of the mischief liable to result from the admission of **irrelevant** evidence, no separate mention need be made: be what it may, it is resolvable *in toto* into the mischief producible by vexation, expense, and delay.
> The difference between the ground of exclusion in the present case, and in those others, consists in this:—in those three cases (*i.e.* in every case where the evidence is not **irrelevant**[, but produces vexation, expense, or delay]), there is an option to make, there is a quantity of mischief, a weight in each scale: there is something to lose by the proposed exclusion,—a chance in favour of justice; [but] there is [also] a disadvantage that must be incurred by the proposed exclusion,—a probability in favour of misdecision, or perhaps a certainty [of misdecision]. But, in this case, where the information proposed to be delivered is **irrelevant**, there is nothing that can be lost by the proposed exclusion: not the least danger of misdecision is incurred by it.
> In this case, then, the enquiry is much more simple than in any one of those three others: there, there are two quantities to weigh, two values to find: here, but one. Suppose the proposed evidence **irrelevant**, **exclusion** is the indisputable consequence.
> **Irrelevant** evidence is evidence that bears no efficient **relation** to **the fact which it is brought to prove**: evidence which **proves nothing**: as well might one say, **no evidence**. (Bentham 1827 vol. 4: 571–72, Bentham's italic emphasis, my boldface emphasis)

Here Bentham says that irrelevant evidence is always to be excluded. His argument is that if evidence is irrelevant, then by definition, there there *is* no relevance to weigh against such negative factors as vexation, expense, or delay. The final paragraph appears to define irrelevance in exactly the same way, and using almost exactly the same words, that Dumont's Bentham uses to define nonpertinence. Dumont's Bentham says of evidence that is not pertinent, "in a word, it is to say, that it is not evidence." Mill's Bentham says of evidence that is irrelevant, "as well might one say, no evidence." There is, of course, a difference between "it *is* to say" and "as well *might* one say." But these phrases are substantially, or if you please, functionally, the same. They might even be two renditions of the very same text in Bentham's original manuscript, the former being a translation from English to French and back, and the latter being edited by Mill. But I do not have access to the manuscript, nor do I regard this as very important to the main point, which is that Keynes could have easily learned from Bentham that evidence is relevant evidence, and that it makes the fact in issue more or less probable than it would otherwise be.

Keynes cites Bentham's *Rationale of Judicial Evidence* in his *Treatise on Probability*, Part 1, "Fundamental Ideas," chapter 2, "The Measurement of Probabilities" (Keynes 1962 / 1921: 20). Thus we know that Keynes did read Bentham on evidence, if only on the measurement of probabilities. Second, we saw that Keynes' theory was basically anticipated by Bentham. And third, Bentham expressly uses the terms "pertinent" and "irrelevant" as logical contradictories. Thus we have at least three reasons to believe that the heart of Keynes' theory may well have come from Bentham.

Thomas Starkie

Thomas Starkie (1782–1849) was a well-known evidence law writer of his time. He says in the 1839 edition of his *Practical Treatise on the Law of Evidence*:

> Sect. VII.—2dly, as to the *nature, quality*, and *quantity* of the evidence to be adduced by the parties (*l*).
> *In the first place, with respect to the *nature* of the evidence; as the business of trial is to ascertain the truth of the allegations put in issue, **no evidence is admissible which does not tend to prove or disprove the issue joined.** (Starkie 1830: 385, Starkie's italic emphasis, my boldface emphasis)

Directly to the right of this text, in the right side margin, is the header, "Evidence must be relevant" (Starkie 1830: 385). Thus Starkie appears to be equating the relevance of evidence with its tending to prove or disprove the point in issue. If there are degrees of tending to prove, as I think there must be, then this is Keynes' theory that relevance is degree of probability. Starkie is also saying that if proposed evidence does *not* tend to do this, then it is inadmissible. That all this concerns "the *nature* of the evidence" intimates that this is by definition of the term "evidence," unless "evidence" is indefinable. But whether "evidence" is definable or not, Starkie is saying that to be relevant to the point in issue, that is, to tend to prove or disprove the point in issue, is what it *is* to be evidence for the point in issue. That is Keynes' view, simply and beautifully stated 65 years before Keynes' Apostles paper on probability.

The title page says that Starkie is "of the Inner Temple." In fact, Starkie was "a lecturer in Common Law and Equity at the Inner Temple" (Twining 1994: 46). "He was a Senior Wrangler at Cambridge and [i]n 1823 he was elected to the Downing Chair at Cambridge;" but apparently he did not actually lecture very often either at the Inner Temple or at Cambridge (Twining 1994: 46).

In 1876, Starkie's posthumous *Practical Treatise* appeared in its "tenth American from the fourth London edition. By Dowdeswell and Malcolm." The title page says that all three are "of the Inner Temple," and that Starkie was "one of Her Majesty's counsel."

George Morley Dowdeswell (1809–1893) and John George Malcolm (*The Law Times* obit. April 13, 1872)'s Starkie says:

> In the first place, with respect to the nature of the evidence; as the business of trial is to ascertain the truth of the allegations put in issue, **no evidence is admissible which does not tend to prove or disprove the issue joined....[A]ll facts and circumstances are admissible in evidence which are in their nature capable of affording a reasonable presumption or inference as to the disputed fact.** (Starkie / Dowdeswell / Malcolm 1876: 616–17, my boldface emphasis)

This gives first the negative aspect and then the positive aspect of relevance. According to the table of contents, page 617 has the sub-heading, "Must be confined to the issue," but it does not appear on the page.

Henry Roscoe

Henry Roscoe (1800–1836) says in the 1831 second edition of his *Digest of the Law of Evidence*:

> OBJECT OF EVIDENCE
> The object of evidence is to *prove the point in issue* between the parties, and, in doing this, there are three rules to be observed: 1. *That the evidence be confined to the point in issue.* 2. That the substance of the issue only need be proved; and, 3. That the affirmative of the issue is to be proved....
> *EVIDENCE CONFINED TO THE ISSUE....*
>   In general, evidence of *collateral* facts is not admissible....

> Where the special damages sustained by the plaintiff is not stated in the declaration, it is not one of the *points in issue,* and evidence of it cannot be *received....*
>
> In general, evidence as to the character of either of the parties to a suit is *inadmissible,* it being *foreign to the point in issue.*
>
> Where the plaintiff has delivered a bill of the particulars of his demand, he will be *precluded* from giving any evidence of demands *not contained* in his particular. (Roscoe 1831: 35–38, my emphasis)

This is under the heading "Object of Evidence," first sub-heading, "Evidence confined to the Issue" (Roscoe 1831: v). However, Roscoe appears to be primarily a follower of the best evidence rule (Roscoe 1831: 1–2). In 1840, he says in his *Digest of the Law of Evidence in Criminal Cases*:

> It is the first and most signal rule of evidence, that the best evidence of which the case is capable shall be given, for if the best evidence be not produced, it affords a presumption that it would make against the party neglecting to produce it, Gilb. Ev. 3. Bull. N. P. 293 (1) (Roscoe 1840: 1)

As you can see, he cites Gilbert on this. But while the best evidence rule may be the "first and most signal rule" for him, it is far from being the only rule, and far from subsuming the other rules under it. Roscoe says:

> *EVIDENCE CONFINED TO THE ISSUE.
> *General Rule.*] It is a general rule, both in civil and criminal cases, that the evidence shall be confined to the point in issue. (Roscoe 1840: *73)

Nothing suggests that for Roscoe, this relevance rule is a version of, implied by, or somehow subsumed under the best evidence rule.

Roscoe says on the next page, "[W]here the evidence is referable to the point in issue, it will not be inadmissible, although it may incidentally apply to another person, or to another thing not included in the transaction in question, and with regard to whom, or to which, it is inadmissible" (Roscoe 1840: 74). This is the same sort of relativity of relevance to person in issue or to matter in issue that we have seen before.

The title page says that Roscoe is "of the Inner Temple."

Richard Newcombe Gresley

Richard Newcombe Gresley (1804–1837) is a less noted evidence law treatise writer. The second edition of his *Treatise on the Law of Evidence*, edited by Christopher Alderson Calvert, appeared posthumously in 1847. Calvert's Gresley says:

> Definition. *When evidence is said to be impertinent or irrelevant (which are almost synonymous terms)*, it is not intended to be understood that it does not bear upon the broad question of justice between the parties, or upon the matter in dispute, nor even that it does not support the case set forth in the pleadings, but that it does not apply to the *material* points which have been put *in issue* and which the court is prepared to decide.
>   Thus, *Impertinence* may be divided into several heads; First, *when the evidence relates to matters not in the pleadings;* Secondly, when it relates to matters that are *admitted* in the pleadings, and which are consequently *not in issue*; Thirdly, when it relates to issues which, although *in issue*, are *immaterial*, and therefore do not call for the decision of the Court. And to these ought perhaps be added; Fourthly, when it is needlessly prolix. (Gresley / Calvert 1847: 229 / 158, my emphasis)

This is in part 2, chapter 3, "Objections at the Hearing," section 1, "Evidence Impertinent." The header "Definition" occurs in the right margin. Calvert's Gresley adds, "In the old cases the principle of the Court seems to have been to sift the real merits in whatever way they could be discovered" (Gresley / Calvert 1847: 230 / 159). In effect, such a principle of practical utility is Benthamite. But on the whole, the book seems to emphasize the best evidence rule.

Calvert's Gresley says that impertinence and irrelevance are "almost synonymous." If so, then Bentham was speaking of impertinence as opposed to irrelevance; but impertinence would still be *almost* synonymous with irrelevance. Calvert's Gresley does not explain why he thinks these terms are not synonymous.

Simon Greenleaf

Simon Greenleaf (1783–1853) was the Royall Professor of Law in Harvard University, and taught there from 1833 to 1848. He wrote a three volume *A Treatise on the Law of Evidence*, which is considered a nineteenth century classic. He was a major influence on both sides of the Atlantic. The Simon Greenleaf School of Law in Anaheim, California is part of Trinity International University.

Greenleaf's 1842 *Treatise*, part 2, chapter 1 is entitled "Of the Relevancy of Evidence." There Greenleaf says:

> § 50....The production of evidence...is governed by certain principles....The *first* of these is, that the evidence must correspond with the allegations, and be confined to the point in issue.
>
> § 51....And it is an established rule, which we state as the FIRST RULE, governing in the production of evidence, that *the evidence offered must correspond with the allegations, and be confined to the point in issue.* This rule supposes the allegations to be *material* and necessary. *Surplusage*, therefore, need not be proved; and the proof, if offered, is to be rejected. The term, *surplusage*, comprehends whatever may be stricken from the record, without destroying the plaintiff's right of action....
>
> § 52. This rule excludes all evidence of *collateral facts*, or those, which are incapable of affording any reasonable presumption or inference, as to the *principal fact or matter in dispute*; and the reason is, that such evidence tends to draw away the minds of the jurors from the *point in issue*.... (Greenleaf 1997 / 1842: 58–59, Greenleaf's emphasis)

All this should be familiar by now. The chapter title shows that when Greenleaf requires that evidence "correspond with the allegations, and be confined to the point in issue," he is, in other words, requiring that evidence be relevant to the point in issue.

We see that the terms "surplusage" and "collateral fact" have different technical legal meanings for Greenleaf. We also see that he discusses both surplusage and collateral facts under the same chapter title, "Of...Relevancy...." And the meanings he gives them imply that he considers them both to be forms of irrelevancy.

The relevance rule excludes surplusage, that is, evidence that is not necessary to establish the point in issue. That falls under the heading of elegance, and is clearly analogous to elegance in the realm of deductive relevance as we discussed it in chapter 9, which now emerges as having a similar exclusionary nature.

The rule also excludes evidence of collateral facts, or as we may as well say, of facts having no rational bearing on the point in issue. This implies that relevant evidence is rationally related to, i.e., has a minimal reasonable connection to, the point in issue.

If we allow degrees of evidence to Greenleaf, as I think we must, then we basically have Keynes' theory in 1842. Indeed, when Greenleaf speaks of "the sufficiency and weight of the evidence" (Greenleaf 1997 / 1842: 57, § 49), he admits degrees of evidence.

In 1846, the third edition of his *Treatise* appeared. It was published in both Boston and London. The title page says that the London publisher was "in Lincoln's Inn." In the included "advertisement to the first edition" of 1842, Greenleaf praises "the excellent treatises of Mr. Starkie and Mr. Phillipps on Evidence" (Greenleaf 1846: vii). He says in part 1, chapter 1, "Preliminary Observations":

§ 1. The word EVIDENCE, in legal acceptation, includes all the means, by which any alleged matter of fact, the truth of which is submitted to investigation, is established or disproved.[1] This term, and the word *proof*, are often used indifferently, as synonymous with each other; but the latter is applied, by the most accurate logicians to the *effect* of evidence, and not to the *medium* by which truth is established.[2] None but mathematical truth is susceptible of that high degree of evidence, called *demonstration*, which excludes all possibility of error....Matters of fact are proved by *moral evidence* alone; by which is meant, not [p. 60] only that kind of evidence which is employed on subjects connected with moral conduct, but also all the evidence which is not obtained either from [intellectual] intuition, or from demonstration. In the ordinary affairs of life, we do not require demonstrative evidence, because it is not consistent with the nature of the subject, and to insist upon it would be unreasonable and absurd. The most that can be affirmed of such things is, that there is no reasonable doubt concerning them.[1] The *true question*, therefore, in trials of fact, is not whether it is possible that the testimony may be false, but whether there is *sufficient probability* of its truth; that is, whether the facts are shown by competent and satisfactory evidence. Things established by competent and satisfactory evidence are said to be *proved*.

§ 2. By **competent** evidence, is meant that by which the very nature of the thing to be proved requires, as the **fit and appropriate** proof in the particular case....By **satisfactory** evidence, which is sometimes called **sufficient** evidence, is intended that **amount** of proof, which ordinarily satisfies an unprejudiced mind, beyond reasonable doubt. The circumstances which will amount to this degree of proof can never be previously defined; the only legal test, of which they are susceptible, is their sufficiency to satisfy the mind and conscience of a common man....[p. 61] Questions, regarding the **competency and admissibility** of evidence, are entirely distinct from those, which respect its sufficiency or effect; **the former being exclusively within the**

province of the Court; the latter belonging exclusively
to the jury.
[p. 59] 1. See Wills on Circumstantial Evid. 2; 1 Stark.
Evid. 10; 1 Phil. Evid. 1.
[p. 59] 2. Whately's Logic, b. 4, ch. 3, § 1.
[p. 60] 1. See Gambier's Guide to the Study of Moral
Evidence, p. 121....
[p. 61] 1. 1 Stark. Evid. 514. (Greenleaf 1846: 59–60,
Greenleaf's italic and small caps emphases, my boldface
emphasis)

Here Greenleaf defines evidence, as understood in law, as any
means to establish or disprove matters of fact. He says that
evidence in law always concerns probability, as opposed to
intellectual intuition or demonstration in mathematics, and, we
might add, in deductive logic. Of course, Greenleaf might still be
the first to say that mathematical demonstration can play a role in a
legal case. For example, a business dispute can involve a question
whether certain expenses were added correctly.

The words in boldface seem to indicate talk of relevancy.
Notably, all competent evidence must be "fit and appropriate." The
term seems to be basically synonymous with "relevant." Also note
that Greenleaf ties competent evidence, or fit and appropriate
evidence, to admissible evidence. It seems that for Greenleaf,
evidence is admissible if and only if it is fit and appropriate, that is,
relevant. He assigns all questions of competency, i.e. of fitness and
appropriateness, and of admissibility, to the judge as opposed to the
jury. This is how relevance and admissibility are assigned in
Anglo-American jurisdictions today.

Part 2, chapter 1 is called "Of the Relevancy of Evidence."
Thus our current term is right in the chapter title. Greenleaf says:

§ 49....Whether there be any evidence, or not, is a
question for the Judge; whether it is sufficient evidence,
is a question for the Jury.... (Greenleaf 1846: 117)
§50. The production of evidence to the Jury is governed
by certain principles, which may be treated under four
general heads, or rules. The *first* of these is, that **the
evidence must correspond with the allegations, and
be confined to the point in issue.** The *second* is, that it
is sufficient, if the substance only of the issue be proved.
The *third* is, that the burden of proving a proposition, or
issue, lies on the party holding the affirmative. And the
fourth is, that the best evidence, of which the case, in its
nature, is susceptible, must always be produced....
(Greenleaf 1846: 119, Greenleaf's italic emphasis, my
boldface emphasis)
§51....And it is an established rule, which we state as the
FIRST RULE, governing in the production of evidence, that

> the evidence offered *must correspond with the allegations, and be confined to the point in issue.* This rule supposes the allegations to be **material** and necessary. **Surplusage,** therefore, need not be proved; and the proof, if offered, is to be rejected. The term, *surplusage,* comprehends whatever may be stricken from the record, without destroying the plaintiff's right of action.... (Greenleaf 1846: 120, Greenleaf's emphasis)
> §52. This rule excludes all evidence of *collateral facts,* or those, which are incapable of affording any reasonable presumption of inference, as to the **principal fact or matter in dispute;** and the reason is, that such evidence tends to draw away the minds of the Jurors from **the point in issue,** and to excite prejudice, and to mislead them; and moreover, the adverse party, having had no notice of such a course of evidence, is not prepared to rebut it.... (Greenleaf 1846: 120–21, Greenleaf's italic emphasis, my boldface emphasis)

Due to the chapter title, "Of the Relevancy of Evidence," it could scarcely be clearer that Greenleaf understands terms such as "must correspond with the allegations" and "be confined to the point in issue" as basically synonymous with the term "relevant."

We see again that the terms "surplusage" and "collateral fact" have different technical legal meanings for Greenleaf; but now he expressly discusses both surplusage and collateral facts under the same chapter title of "Relevancy." This confirms that he considers surplusage and collaterality to be different forms of irrelevancy.

Note that the best evidence rule is only the fourth and last of "four general heads." But as we shall see in a moment, "general head" is not necessarily the same as summum genus; and even if it were, Greenleaf would have not one but four summa genera.

Concerning the second general head, Greenleaf says in the next chapter:

> §56. A second rule, which governs in the production of evidence, is, that *it is sufficient, if the substance of the issue be proved....*Thus, if, in an action for malicious prosecution, the plaintiff alleges, that he was acquitted of the charge on a certain day; here the substance of the allegation is the acquittal, and it is sufficient, if this fact be proved on any day, the time not being **material** (Greenleaf 1846: 126, Greenleaf's italic emphasis, my boldface emphasis)

I think we may as well say "relevant" in place of "material." For the point is that if you have already been acquitted, then that is the only relevant point, and the exact day of the acquittal is irrelevant.

Thus there is an essential relevantist aspect to the substance rule. But here we are not finding that certain evidence is irrelevant to the point in issue and therefore inadmissible. We are finding that certain *language* in the *pleadings* is irrelevant to the point in issue, and striking out the language as superfluous, i.e., as "surplusage." Thus we may say that the substance rule is a sort of converse relevance rule. And in that sense, it is a relevance rule after all.

The four rules do not originate with Greenleaf. Thayer writes of "Greenleaf's *Treatise on Evidence,* where he follows, with a variation, an earlier writer [in admitting] four great, fundamental rules which are said to govern the production of testimony" (Thayer 1898: 484). Thayer is right that Greenleaf presents these rules only as governing the production of testimony. Greenleaf's part 2, from whence my quotations of Greenleaf come, is entitled "Of the Rules which Govern the Production of Testimony." But the rules themselves are stated as general rules of evidence, and make perfect sense that way.

William Mawdesley Best

William Mawdesley Best (1809–1869) accepts Bentham's general concept of evidence and calls it "natural evidence." This, as we saw, is basically relevant evidence. But Best also criticizes Bentham for giving evidence law short shrift, and argues that we also need a special concept of "judicial evidence." Best holds that courts need to be concerned with *both* sorts of evidence (Montrose 1992 / 1954: 349 / 529).

Montrose quotes Best as saying, "'Judicial evidence is, for the most part, nothing else more than natural evidence, restrained or modified by positive rules of law'" (Montrose 1992 / 1954: 349 / 529). Thus Best comes very close to reducing judicial evidence to rules of admissibility.

Montrose says:

> Best did not make the distinction between natural evidence and judicial evidence the basis of his treatment of the law of evidence. The distinction, though not completely ignored, is little stressed in his subsequent exposition. The principle which he uses as the framework for the exposition is the one to which Gilbert had already attached importance, *viz.*, the best evidence rule. It is in the later work of Stephen and Thayer that basic importance is attached to the distinction; in their writing it is discussed in the language of "relevance" and "admissibility." (Montrose 1992 / 1954: 350 /530)

Thus Montrose finds that Best does not really do much with the distinction between natural evidence and judicial evidence beyond merely stating it, and says that Best finds it more important to have a substantive rule for actually evaluating evidence. And what substantive rule is it? Montrose says that Best simply follows Gilbert in making the best evidence rule the basic rule of evidence law (Montrose 1992 / 1954: 350 / 530).

Montrose overlooks that Best also has a relevance rule, which Best says is "the most universal and most obvious" rule of evidence (Best 1854: 319). In 1854, Best's *Treatise on the Principles of Evidence and Practice as to Proofs in Courts of Common Law* appeared. There Best says:

> § 245. Of all rules of evidence, *the most universal and most obvious* is this—that the evidence adduced should be alike *directed and confined to the matters which are in dispute*. [This rule's] theoretical propriety can never be matter of doubt, whatever difficulties may arise in its application...; and, anything which is neither directly nor indirectly *relevant* to these matters, ought at once to be put aside...."Frustrà probatur quod probatum non relevat." (Best 1854: 319, my emphasis)

This is clearly a relevance rule, and Best states that "of all rules of evidence," it is "the most universal and most obvious." By its very nature, the rule clearly belongs to natural evidence as opposed to judicial evidence. For it is universal in scope, and logically does not apply only in courtrooms. This "most universal rule" may also explain why the distinction between natural evidence and judicial evidence is logically basic to Best's framework after all. For it is logically more basic than the best evidence rule. For it is universal in its scope of application, including outside of courtrooms, while the best evidence rule is basically limited to documents, and its policy exclusion of copies in favor of originals makes it more in the nature of a rule of judicial evidence, that is, of legal admissibility. Thus these two most basic rules in Best imply the distinction between natural evidence and judicial evidence. For the relevance rule is a rule of natural evidence and the best evidence rule is a rule of judicial evidence. And if I am right, this makes natural evidence more general and logically prior to judicial evidence, which is how one would think it should be. Of course, Montrose may still be right about the text, insofar as Best does not expressly develop these points the way I just did here. And Montrose is right that the later terms for the key concepts of what Best calls natural evidence and judicial evidence are respectively "relevance" and "admissibility."

420 Bertrand Russell on Modality and Logical Relevance

In the quoted text, "directed and confined to" the point in issue sounds just like relevance. Best even uses the term "relevant" later in the quote to repeat the rule. "Directed" sounds positive, and indicates an inclusionary rule that relevant evidence must always be admissible, absent policy exceptions ("applications"). "Confined" sounds negative, and indicates an exclusionary rule that irrelevant evidence must always be inadmissible. But this is only in contrast. If we "confine" a certain portion of water to a certain pitcher, we are not just negatively excluding it from being anywhere else. We are positively including or containing all of it in the pitcher. Thus confinement implies positive containment. If water is confined to a pitcher, then the pitcher positively contains the water. Likewise, if evidence is confined to the point in issue, then all of the evidence is positively relevant to the point in issue. (Compare whole-part deductively relevant containment inference in chapter 9.) Thus Best's view seems to be a biconditional ("if and only if") thesis, and both inclusionary and exclusionary. That is, it seems to be his view that absent policy exceptions, evidence is admissible if and only if it is relevant. And this implies that it is always to be excluded if it is irrelevant.

I see no attempt here by Best to reduce his relevance rule to, or to subsume it under, his best evidence rule. Since the best evidence rule is not about "best" in its ordinary general evaluative sense, but only about the most original documents available, I do not see how anyone could achieve such a reduction or subsumption. The biconditional that evidence is the most relevant if and only if it is the most original document available is absurd, and surely would not have been accepted by Best, nor even by Gilbert. I am not even invoking a principle of charity in interpretation. Granted, normally an original document is causally the most directly related one to the transaction in question. But is an original document that has nothing to do with a dispute more relevant than a copy of a document that the whole dispute is based on? Surely that is why Best presents his relevance rule as an independent basic rule that is logically unrelated to his best evidence rule, and likewise Gilbert.

The Latin maxim is often translated as, "It is useless to prove that which, when proved, is not relevant." Readers of chapter 9 will recognize this as a species of use-relevance.

Best was cited on relevancy by other writers of his time, as we shall see. Thus Montrose overlooks not only what Best says himself, but also how Best was understood by his contemporaries.

The title page says that Best is "of Gray's Inn."

John Pitt Taylor

John Pitt Taylor (1811–1888) was a major treatise writer. He is called John Pitt-Taylor in Edward Walford's obituary of him in the July 28, 1888 issue of *The Law Times*, and his son is called Frank Pitt-Taylor (Walford 1888: 236). But he is generally called John Pitt Taylor on the title pages of the editions of his treatise, and modern scholars such as Twining call him Taylor; so I shall follow that usage.

In 1848, the first edition of his *Treatise on the Law of Evidence, as Administered in England and Ireland* appeared. The title page says that Taylor is "of the Middle Temple."

In the Preface, Taylor expresses his great indebtedness to Greenleaf. He says his original intent was merely to produce a new edition of Greenleaf, but he eventually found that, in order to focus more on helping English and Irish lawyers with their law, it would be better to write his own treatise afresh.

The first two sentences of Taylor's preface to the first edition are, "The following Work is founded on 'Dr. Greenleaf's American Treatise on the Law of Evidence'. Indeed, when in July, 1843, my attention was first drawn to the subject of Evidence, with a view to publication, I undertook to discharge the duties of an editor only," and only later decided to write a treatise of his own. On the next page he says, "I have still, however, availed myself very largely of Dr. Greenleaf's labours, having adopted, with but few alterations, his excellent general arrangement,...and having borrowed many pages of his terse and luminous writing."

Taylor speaks of "Greenleaf's American Treatise," but in fact Greenleaf's *Treatise* was published in both Boston and London in 1842. Thus it was better known and more available in England than it might seem from Taylor.

Taylor says in volume 1, part 1, chapter 1, page 1:

> § 1. The word EVIDENCE, considered in relation to Law, includes all the legal means, which tend to prove or disprove any matter of fact, the truth of which is submitted to judicial investigation. (Taylor 1848: 1)

Thus he defines evidence as that which tends to prove or disprove the point in issue. We may as well say that he defines it in terms of probability. Later in the book, Taylor states what he takes to be the four general rules of evidence that govern the production of evidence:

> § 142. The production of evidence to the jury is governed by certain principles, which may be treated under four general rules. The *first* of these is, that the

> evidence must correspond with the allegations; but that it
> is sufficient if the substance only of the issues be proved.
> The *second* is, that the evidence must be confined to the
> points in issue. The *third* is, that the burden of proving a
> proposition at issue lies on the party holding the
> substantial affirmative. And the *fourth* is, that the best
> evidence, of which the case in its nature is susceptible,
> must always be produced. (Taylor 1848: 140)

It seems to me that Taylor presents these four rules as independent
of each other, though surely he is aware that 'correspondence with
the allegations' is a positive version of the more negative-sounding
'confinement to the points in issue'. But even if I am right that
those two terms are logically equivalent versions of each other, the
first two rules still differ in that the first permits that "the substance
only of the issues be proved." In any case, Taylor presents what I
have argued earlier to be two relevance rules first, and the best
evidence rule last. (The first relevance rule is the first conjunct of
the first stated rule: "the evidence must correspond with the
allegations.") Thus, even if his order of listing the rules implies no
ranking of fundamentality, it is at least clear that the best evidence
rule is just one of four different main rules (or five, if we split the
first rule into its two conjuncts; the "but" logically functions as an
"and").

In 1878, Taylor says, in the preface to the seventh edition
of his *Treatise on the Law of Evidence as Administered in England
and Ireland*, that he thinks it will be his last, and indicates that it
has been thirty years since the first edition appeared, meaning 1848
(Taylor 1878: v). He says in part 2, chapter 2, "Confining Evidence
to Points in Issue":

> §298. The *second general rule*, which governs the
> production of testimony, is, that *the evidence must be
> confined to the points in issue.* (Taylor 1878: 283,
> Taylor's emphasis)

A few pages later, he says:

> §316. The rule **confining evidence to the points in
> issue**...excludes all evidence of *collateral facts*, which
> are incapable of providing any reasonable presumption
> as to the principle **matters in dispute**....The due
> application of this rule will occasionally tax to the
> utmost the firmness and discrimination of the judge; so
> that he shall reject, as too remote, every fact which
> merely furnishes a fanciful analogy or conjectural
> inference, he may admit as **relevant** the evidence of all
> those matters which shed a **real**, though perhaps an

indirect and feeble, light on the **questions in issue**.
(Taylor 1878: 296, Taylor's italic emphasis, my boldface
emphasis)

According to the index at the end of volume 2, pages 296 and 297
are under the sub-heading "IRRELEVANT FACTS, not evidence"
(Taylor 1878: 1659).

The posthumous 1897 American edition of the ninth
English edition of Taylor's *Treatise* was "in part re-written by G.
Pitt-Lewis" per the title page. The American editor, Charles
Frederic Chamberlayne, says in the preface, "The ninth English
edition embodies many extensive and painstaking improvements by
G. Pitt-Lewis" (Chamberlayne 1897: iii).

Chamberlayne's Taylor distinguishes logical relevance
from legal relevance:

> RELEVANCY.—**This logical relation of one fact to
> another, is termed "relevancy."** Of this the law
> furnishes no test. The test is furnished by the ordinary
> principles of logic **or a conscious perception of the
> relation**. A legal definition of relevancy was indeed
> courageously attempted by Sir James Fitz-James Stephen
> in the first edition of the "Digest of the Law of
> Evidence," based largely on the relation of causation.
> This definition was abandoned. The amended definition
> seems free from objection[:] Two facts are **relevant** to
> each other when so **related** "that, according to the
> common course of events, one, either taken by itself or
> in connection with other facts, proves or renders
> **probable** the past, present, or future existence or non-
> existence of the other" (Dig. Law of Evid. Art. 1.)
> The Rule Further Examined.—Such being the
> fundamental rule of evidence, that all evidence **logically
> probative** is admissible, the further law of evidence
> consists of excluding certain facts of the evidence
> otherwise admissible under this fundamental general rule
> [for policy reasons]....
> (1) LEGAL RELEVANCY.—The search for
> abstract truth, scientific or otherwise, is not usually
> limited in time. No fact at all is too remotely **relevant** to
> deserve consideration. No pressing necessity usually
> exists that the precise fact should be ascertained this year
> or next year, or, indeed, within the next century. Under
> such conditions, logic is given its unimpeded course. All
> facts **logically relevant** demand and receive
> consideration.
> But the course of trials in Courts of law by no
> means admits of such extended search into the minutiae
> of proof. The tribunal sits for a limited time....The
> proceedings are expensive....There is a recognized

necessity that matters should be as speedily disposed of as the interests of justice will admit....

(2) FEAR OF THE JURY.—....The average jury is composed of men selected by chance from the general community, brought together for a short time and for a limited object, with minds usually entirely untrained in the difficult art of justly balancing the weight of conflicting statements. Jurymen, almost of necessity, are seldom given to reasoning with logical exactness....

EXCLUSIONS.—For these and similar reasons, the law of evidence excludes much evidence **logically relevant**, either (1) By applying a higher standard of relevancy than mere logic by requiring a certain high grade of probative effect, which may be called legal relevancy; and (2) By absolutely excluding certain facts both **logically** and legally **relevant**. What facts are so highly probative as to comply with the standard of legal relevancy cannot be reduced to a definite rule. (Taylor 1897: 2^6–2^8, my boldface emphasis)

We will discuss Chamberlayne and Stephen in their own sections later, and we will discuss legal relevance later. The important thing is that we see Keynes' term, "logically relevant." The 1897 edition was published in Boston and London. Keynes could have read it while he was at Cambridge University studying legal cases for his own treatise on probability. Taylor's "according to the common course of events" suggests the frequency theory of probability common at the time, which Keynes rejects. But at the same time, Taylor makes relevancy a "logical relation" known by "conscious perception." And that is just Keynes' view on the nature of the relation. The only substantive difference between Taylor and Keynes is that Taylor makes the relata of the evidence relation *facts*, instead of the propositions that *describe* the facts. This is actually better than Keynes insofar as facts, not propositions, are evidence for the obtainment of other facts, or for the truth of propositions about other facts. It is more direct, more elegant, more realistic, and more plausible. Thus here, Keynes' theory emerges as a retrograde step.

While Taylor's admission of basic elements of both the frequency theory and Keynes' sort of theory may seem confused, I find it consistent enough. The frequency theory itself is a form of logical theory of probability, insofar as "many" and "few" are notions of class theory. More than that, I find it common sense. For there would be something very wrong with Keynes' theory if in the end it did not basically find what is usually the case more probable than not. In fact, if any of the three main theories of probability were not as good at assessing probabilities as the other two, then it would be unworthier than they.

Taylor's phrases "a higher standard of relevancy" and "a certain high grade of probative effect" imply that his distinction between logical relevance and legal relevance is one of degree, not one of kind. Thus for him at bottom, there are not really two kinds of relevance, one logical and one legal. Thus the distinction is open to criticism for being a slippery slope, and for committing the fallacies of composition and division. (These fallacies are strictly deductive fallacies, and this is strictly a deductive point *about* probability. For many scintillae of evidence logically can add up to a significant probability, and one scintilla logically can be the straw that breaks the camel's back of insignificant probability.) Such a distinction of degree is necessarily inexact. It is best described as "an appreciable, but indescribable distinction" (Powell 1859: 220).

Taylor was a member of the Middle Temple, which is right next to the Inner Temple in London. He wrote the preface to the first edition of his *Treatise* on February 10, 1848, at "2, Harcourt Buildings, Temple." The Middle and Inner Temples were named after the Knights Templar, who owned the land until their order was abolished in 1312. The three Harcourt Buildings were originally built in 1703. They are located just north of the Thames, and just south of where the Strand turns into Fleet Street (if you remember Fleta). The Honourable Society of the Inner Temple, also called the Inner Temple, is one of the four professional societies called Inns of Court for judges like Taylor, and also for barristers. A current connection to Cambridge University, where Russell and Keynes were students, is that Cambridge has a companion organization for its student would-be barristers, called the Cambridge University Inner Temple Society.

Keynes was a member of the Inner Temple, admitted in 1905. Thus Keynes might have known of Taylor through the Inner Temple, but I doubt he met him. According to *The Law Times*, July 28, 1888 obituary of Taylor at books. google.com, Taylor died on July 17, 1888. It says he "was one of the oldest and most respected members of the Legal Profession," was "entered...as a student of the Middle Temple" in 1833, and "was the author of 'A Treatise on the Law of Evidence'." The obituary says he was born December 30, 1811 and "was a contemporary of Mr. Gladstone" at Eton, "from which he passed to Christ Church, Oxford."

Morgan, Starkie, and Phillipps are all of the Inner Temple. John Dawson Mayne, whose treatise on the law of damages Keynes refers to in his *Treatise* (Keynes 1962 / 1921: 25), is of the Inner Temple as well. It is hard to see how Keynes could not have known that so many great evidence law writers of his own Inner Temple were writing of the relevance of evidence. In fact, perhaps the best explanation of why Keynes does not say he takes the term logical relevance from evidence law might be that he simply regarded its use as already commonplace among readers interested in the topic.

The Honourable Society of the Inner Temple online site does not describe Keynes as having any legal credentials himself, but only as being a member who was admitted in 1905, and as being an economist. And of course it is not conclusive evidence that Keynes finished a book draft on the logical relevance of evidence in 1914, and just happened to be admitted in 1905 as a member of an Inn of English law, many of whose members had published treatises on evidence and its logical relevance. But it strains credulity to think that just after joining a world-famous legal society in which "logically relevant" was the common term for the most basic concept of evidence, Keynes magically invented the very same term for the very same concept all by himself.

Jacob R. Halsted

We have seen that Best's contemporaries were well aware that Best has a relevance rule, even though our scholars today are not. Here, Best is the very first source cited for the relevance rule.

In 1859, Jacob R. Halsted says in his *Digest of the Law of Evidence*:

> **RELEVANCY** OF EVIDENCE.
> The evidence offered in a cause must **correspond with** the allegations, and be **confined to** the point in issue. **Best's Ev. §§ 229, 248.**
> The evidence need not bear directly on the issue; it is admissible if it *tends* **to prove the issue**, or constitutes a link in the chain of proof. *Jones* v. *Van Zadt*, 2 McLean, 596....
> Evidence, having **no relation** to the allegations in the pleadings, will not be received. *May* v *Ransom*, 5 An. 424....
> *Relevancy of Evidence....*
> 42. **Irrelevant** matter may be properly excluded from the jury. *State* v. *Roper*, 3 Eng. 491.
> 52. Testimony cannot be excluded as **irrelevant** which would have a **tendency, however remote, to establish the probability or improbability of the fact in controversy.** *Trull* v. *True*, 33 Maine, (3 Red.) 367.
> 58....And it is a sufficient answer to an exception for the rejection of evidence, that it was **irrelevant.** *The State* v. *Arnold*, 13 Ired. 184.
> 67. It is error to permit testimony, not **relevant to the issue**, to go to the jury. *Maslin* v. *Thomas*, 8 Gill, 18.

85. The rule which requires the evidence to be **strictly confined to the point at issue**, is not violated by evidence of facts which happened before and after the principal transaction, yet which have a **direct relation** to the main subject in controversy. *Horton* v. *Reynolds*, 8 Texas, 284.

134. Evidence that is **pertinent**, and **applicable to the issue**, should be admitted.... *Lazare* v *Peytavin*, 9 M. 567

135. An instrument, **relevant** to the matter at issue and duly proved, must be admitted without inquiry into its effect.... *Livermore* v. *Morgan*, 6 N. S. 136; *Dick* v *Chew*, Ib. 396; *Gayle* v. *Gray*, Ib. 694.

137. Evidence having **no relation** to the allegations in the pleadings will not be received. *Colsson* v. *Consolidated Bank*, 12 Lon. 105; *May* v *Ransom*, 5 An. 424. (Halsted 1859: 95–118, Halsted's italic emphasis, my boldface emphasis)

The most striking cite is ruling #52, Trull v True. It is an astonishing anticipation of *FRE* Rule 401. *Trull* states, albeit in a negative way, that to be relevant is to have a tendency, however slight, to make the point in issue either more probable or less probable than it would be otherwise. Perhaps the negative aspect makes *Trull* even closer to Keynes' definitions of irrelevancy than it is to *FRE* Rule 401.

Halsted's citations of legal cases suggest that it is not just a few treatise writers, but also hundreds of judges making rulings in a wide variety of legal jurisdictions, who are speaking about relevance by the middle of the nineteenth century. Halsted cites 222 court rulings under his italicized sub-heading "*Relevancy of Evidence*," though not every ruling uses the *word* "relevant." Thus it seems that to view treatise writers as the origin of the concept of relevance is to put the cart before the horse.

Halsted's language sounds quite modern, even though the American Civil War would not start for another two years.

Halsted praises "the invaluable treatises of Phillips [sic] and Greenleaf" in the Preface (Halsted 1859: iv).

Edmund Powell

In 1859, Edmund Powell (1826?–1864), in his *Principles and Practice of the Laws of Evidence*, upholds the best evidence rule for the usual reason, namely "the presumption that [an offer of] inferior evidence...arises either from fraud, or from gross negligence, which is tantamount to fraud" (Powell 1859: 41).

Concerning the substance rule, Powell says:

Chapter 19.
ON THE SUBSTANCE OF THE ISSUE.
It is enough if only the *substance* of the issue be proved.
In other words, a party will have proved *sufficiently* his
case if he establish *substantially* his allegations; and he
will not be prejudiced by failing to prove matter which is
unnecessary to support his claim, and which may
therefore be disregarded as *surplusage*. But it is not
every *unnecessary* allegation which may be treated as
surplusage; for *irrelevant* matter may be so connected
and incorporated with essential matter, as to render them
legally inseparable; and where this is so the *irrelevant*
matter must be proved. (Powell 1859: 187, my
emphasis)

Thus Powell firmly connects the substance rule with the concept of
surplusage, and ties the concept of surplusage with the concept of
irrelevance. His equation of irrelevant matter with unnecessary
matter suggests that relevance is use-relevance. Compare deductive
use-relevance in chapter 9.

As we saw in the Mansfield section, earlier, Powell quotes
Mansfield's *Bristow* case of 1781:

The distinction is that between that which may be
rejected as *surplusage*, and what cannot. When the
declaration contains *impertinent* matter, *foreign* to the
cause, and which the master on a reference to him would
strike out (*irrelevant* covenants for instance), that will be
rejected by the court, and need not be proved.... (Powell
1859: 188 quoting Mansfield in Bristow v. Wright,
Dougl. 665, 1 Sm. L. C. 223, my emphasis)

For Mansfield, surplusage is matter that is impertinent, foreign, or
irrelevant in the *pleadings*. See the Mansfield section above for a
fuller quotation.

In chapter 21, Powell equates relevancy with confinement
to the points in issue:

Chapter 21.
ON THE RELEVANCY OF EVIDENCE.
As it is the object of pleading to reduce the case of each
litigating party to one or more *substantial* issues which
involve the *merits* of the question; and as for this
purpose none but *material* allegations which tend to the
raising of such issues are admissible; so it is the object of
evidence to provide that, when such allegations have
been made, and such issues selected, they shall be
supported by *strictly relevant* proof. It is impossible to
define the distinction between *relevant* and *irrelevant*

evidence, and even the cases illustrate the difference unsatisfactorily. In the case of direct evidence, there is little difficulty in drawing the line; but, since a large proportion of evidence is of a presumptive or circumstantial character, it requires the keenest perspicacity to distinguish between *legitimate* presumption and *irrelevant* hypothesis; and it is in observing this appreciable, but indescribable distinction, that the sense and wariness of an able judge appear. The rule is that—

The evidence must *correspond with* the allegations, and be *confined to the points in issue.*[1]
1. Greenl. 58; Tayl. 194. (Powell 1859: 220, citing Greenleaf and Taylor, my emphasis)

This is yet another equation of relevancy with correspondence to the allegations, and with confinement to the point in issue. There are also relevantist shades of *substantial* issues, *merits* of the question, *material* allegations, and *legitimate* presumptions.

Powell sums up at the end of the chapter:

The principles according to which the *relevancy* and *irrelevancy* of evidence are distinguished have been now explained. They are *co-extensive and identical with* the principles of presumptive evidence; and, in fact, *embrace the whole subject of legal evidence.* It is equally a condition of direct evidence as of presumptive [or circumstantial] evidence, that it should be *relevant to the issue*; and it is pre-eminently the duty of a judge to admit no evidence which he does not consider to be *relevant*, either as direct proof, or as the ground of legitimate inference. In many cases, as in the principal issues in civil cases, the *relevancy* of evidence has been *defined* by the *amount of proof* which is usually given and required to support them. In criminal cases, where practically there is no issue but the general issue, the line of demarcation has been drawn less distinctly; and the discretion of the judge requires, therefore, to be exercised with proportionable vigilance. (Powell 1859: 22, my emphasis)

Here, Powell comes close to defining evidence as what is relevant, and then defining relevance in turn as degree of "proof," not to say probability. But he does not actually leap over those narrow ditches into Keynesian theory. Possibly this is because he is concerned to report the outlines of the law, and is not a philosophical theorist at heart. Still, this looks like another striking anticipation of Keynes.

The title page says that Powell is "of the Inner Temple."

The 1904 posthumous Powell is even simpler and clearer:

Chapter 21.
THE RELEVANCY OF EVIDENCE.
[I]t is the object of evidence to provide that [allegations and issues] shall be supported by *strictly relevant* proof. The rule is that—

> The evidence must *correspond with* the allegations, and be *confined to the points in issue.*

Or as it is sometimes stated that—
The evidence must be relevant to the issue— (Powell 1904: 441)

The synonymity of "relevant" with "corresponding with the allegations and confined to the points in issue" is too expressly stated and too obvious to need comment.

William Gillespie Dickson

In 1864, William Gillespie Dickson (1823–1876) says in his *Treatise on the Law of Evidence in Scotland*:

> § 17. The proper object in every trial being to lead the jury to a correct verdict upon the issue, it is the practice to *exclude* evidence which cannot afford an inference on some point in *favour* of either party....(*a*)....(*b*)....
> (*a*)....Wherever facts have been found *irrelevant*, they will not be allowed to be proved; M'Laren *v.* Buik, 1829, 7 S., 780.
> (*b*) This is also the English practice; 2 Starkie Ev., 313—1 Starkie Ev., 603—Haigh *v.* Belcher, 1838, 7 C. and P., 389. (W. Dickson 1864: 18, 18 n.(*a*), 18 n.(*b*), my emphasis)

Thus Dickson equates being unable to make any point 'favorable' with being inadmissible, and with being "irrelevant." This is in part 1, "General Rules Applicable to All Kinds of Evidence," title 2, "Of the Rule that the Evidence Must Be Relevant." The best evidence rule appears two titles later, in title 4, "Of the Rule Which Requires the Best Evidence." The relevance rule and the best evidence rule appear to be completely independent of each other.

In the quotation above, Dickson pushes the case law on relevance back to 1829. In the quotation below, Dickson finds a judicial ruling as early as 1810 that links the receiving of proof to:

> tending to shew the probabilities...(*x*)....
> (*x*) As in Murray *v.* Tod, 1817, 1 Mur., 225—Buchanan *v.* Buchanan, 1810, Buch. Rep., 89. *This is the constant practice in such cases.* (W. Dickson 1864: 22, 22 n.(*x*), my emphasis)

Thus, much like Halsted, Dickson shows that relevance was not just a theoretical concept found in treatises, but was "constantly" being ruled on by judges in courts.

The important thing for us is that Dickson ties relevance to probability in both directions. First, he equates evidence that does not make any point or its denial (more) probable with irrelevant evidence. Second, he equates receivability of proof with "tending to show the probabilities." And the heading at the top of the page is, "RELEVANCY OF EVIDENCE." Thus it seems that for Dickson, to be relevant, and to be receivable as evidence, is to tend to show the probabilities concerning a point in question

In the preface to the first edition, dated July 19, 1855, Dickson cites "the comprehensive and philosophical work of Professor Greenleaf" (W. Dickson 1864: vii).

John Dawson Mayne

John Dawson Mayne (1828–1917) wrote primarily on the law of damages resulting from tort (personal injury) cases. This may seem irrelevant to our topic. But it is worth looking into, since Keynes cites *Mayne on Damages*. In fact, there is much in Mayne on relevance. We will see the usual terms, such as "relevant" and "point in issue." But we will need to learn some new concepts in order to understand the full depth of Mayne on relevance: proximate cause, reasonably foreseeable cause, and remote cause.

A tort is a civil, as opposed to criminal, action for injury in some sense. Basically, a tort has four elements that must be proved. First, there must be some legal, as opposed to privately agreed upon, duty. Second, there must be some violation of the duty by a person who owed the duty to someone. Third, there must be some sort of damage or injury that results from the violation to the person to whom the duty was owed. Fourth, the injury must have been either intended or negligent. If the damage was intended, then it is an intentional tort. If the damage was unintended, but was proximately caused or at least reasonably foreseeable, then it is a negligence tort.

Historically speaking, the two main tests of negligence have been proximate causation and reasonable foreseeability. The first of these is often taken to be less clear than the second; and therefore it has often been replaced by the second.

Proximate cause and reasonable foreseeability are the two concepts of greatest interest to us here. Reasonable foreseeability implies probabilistic relevance. Proximate causation implies causal necessity. For a proximate cause is a cause. But whether an act is a proximate cause of a damage, or of anything else, may be unclear, if the concept itself is unclear.

Sometimes proximate cause is defined away as, or is understood as being or as replaced by, reasonable foreseeability. But traditionally this has not been so. "Proximate cause" is traditionally understood as direct or immediate as opposed to remote or mediated cause. But it is often taken to *imply* reasonable foreseeability. For otherwise there would not be much point in blaming anyone for the damage. So, it is often understood as immediate *and obvious* cause. Of course, "obvious," in its ordinary connotation, implies far more than just reasonably foreseeable. Being obvious would seem to equate to being clear and convincing, if not to beyond a reasonable doubt. But we could legally *define* "obvious" as meaning reasonably obvious, that is, as reasonably foreseeable. But such a definition must not be confused with the *standard of proof*. The standard of proof of a cause's being immediate and obvious may well be *less* than that of obviousness in the ordinary sense of "obvious." Typically, in a civil case such as a tort case, the standard of proof is merely preponderance of the evidence, meaning more likely than not. We may say that an event is reasonably foreseeable just in case it is more likely than not to happen, and that the standard of proof of reasonable foreseeability in a tort case is *also* preponderance of the evidence, meaning more likely than not. For example, a jury may find it more likely than not that *Smith* found or ought objectively to have found it more likely than not that his act would cause the damage. Or a jury may find it more likely than not that Smith found or ought to have found that it was *immediate and obvious* that his act would cause the damage, and find (say) for *gross* negligence.

We may say that in a negligence tort, there are four broad kinds of predictability of the damage. For the action to lie, meaning for the tort to be found, the damage must be either (1) the proximate (immediate and obvious) effect, or at least (2) the reasonably foreseeable effect. But the damage cannot be (3) a remote (not immediate and not obvious) effect, nor can it be an effect that was not reasonably foreseeable. Again, (1) and (2) have not always been distinguished, but they typically are, and certainly should be. Please note in this regard that a remote effect in one case can be more reasonably foreseeable than an immediate effect in another case, unless we define "remote" as meaning not only distant in the chain of events and not obvious, but also not reasonably foreseeable.

These four broad kinds of predictability are also four broad kinds of probabilistic relevance. Kinds (1) and (3) are also kinds of causal relevance. Kinds (3) and (4) can diminish to nullity.

In kind (2), we may further distinguish between general and specific reasonable foreseeability. For example, if you handle explosives on a railway platform filled with people, it might be *generally* reasonably foreseeable that if you handle them carelessly, they might explode and cause *some* sort of damage to *someone* there. But it might not be *specifically* reasonably foreseeable who in particular would be injured or what the particular injury would be. There might even be a *specific* chain of events no one could have possibly predicted, such that no one could have ever imagined that a certain specific person would be injured, or that she would receive the specific injury she did. Lawyers will know that I am tacitly referring to Palsgraf v Long Island Railroad Co., 248 N.Y. 339, 162 N.E. 99 (N.Y. 1928). *Palsgraf* is the leading American case on point, and is studied in every or almost every American first year torts class. But we need not be detained by *Palsgraf* here.

Black's Law Dictionary defines "proximately" as meaning

> [a] Directly or immediately. [b] Pertaining to that which in an ordinary natural sequence produces a specific result, no independent disturbing agency intervening. (H. Black 1991: 853)

Definitions (a) and (b) are not logically equivalent, insofar as (b) implies reasonable foreseeability and (a) does not. Concerning (a), directness or immediacy of cause does not imply foreseeability at all. We may be completely surprised by the effect. But in (b), the term "ordinary" seems to imply, and seems intended to imply, reasonable foreseeability. The term also seems to take into account ordinary background causal factors, at least in the negative sense of ruling out intervening causal factors. Science has long abandoned the simplistic model of bang-bang, one-one cause-effect in favor of systems of interacting variables. Strictly speaking, there is no such thing as direct or immediate causation by a single causal event. We can only say there often is one "foreground" or "triggering" event that draws our attention more than the many background factors. Thus (b) is also scientifically better than (a). Note that immediacy does not mean temporal immediacy, but only that there is no mediation by other causal factors. If all causes were temporally immediate, the universe would not last longer than an instant, even if the series of causes were infinitely many. This includes "sustaining" causes of the duration of a thing, operating immediately across temporal instants.

Black's Law Dictionary defines "proximate cause" as alternatively but somewhat repetitively meaning:

> [1] That which, in a natural and continuous sequence, unbroken by any efficient intervening cause, produces

injury, and without which the result would not have occurred. [2] That which is nearest in the order of responsible cause. [3] That which stands next in causation to the effect, not necessarily in time or space but in causal relation. [4] The proximate cause of an injury is the primary or moving cause, or that which, in a natural and continuous sequence, unbroken by any efficient intervening cause, produces the injury and without which the accident could not have happened, *if* the injury be one which might be *reasonably anticipated or foreseen* as a natural consequence of the wrongful act. [5] An injury of damage is proximately cause by an act, or a failure to act, whenever it appears from the evidence in the case, that the act or omission played a substantial part in bringing about or actually causing the injury or damage; *and* that the injury or damage was either a direct result *or* a *reasonably probable cause* of the act or omission. (H. Black 1991: 852–53, my emphasis)

Definitions (4) and (5) include reasonable foreseeability, and definitions (1)–(3) do not. Thus definitions (1)–(3) seem practically worthless, since if an injury were not reasonably foreseeable by the actor at the time, then the actor could not be reasonably blamed. In definition (4), the word "if" makes reasonable foreseeability a logically necessary condition of proximate cause, as I think it must be, if actors are to be reasonably blamed. But in definition (5), the word "or" makes reasonable foreseeability only one disjunct of two, the other disjunct being directness of result. Compare the problem I find with Stephen's disjunctive definition of relevance in the section below on Stephen. In sum, in definition (5), reasonable foreseeability is not a logically necessary condition of proximate cause, and the definition is just as worthless as the first three. I should remark that in these definitions, I do not take the terms "natural" or "order of responsible cause" to imply, and certainly not *clearly* to imply, reasonable foreseeability. For these terms appear to refer *only* to the physical order of nature, which may or may not be reasonably foreseeable to us in light of our experience and understanding. I take "order of responsible cause" to mean 'order of physical cause which results in the damage in question'. Surely a physical cause is not morally responsible for the damage. If anything, it is the actor who chooses to initiate the sequence of physical events who is morally responsible.

Definitions (4) and (5) do not even require proximate cause to be direct or immediate, and this goes against the ordinary meaning of "proximate." But we can offer technical definitions as we please, and I think that the omission of this requirement is a good thing. For as we noted a few paragraphs ago, strictly speaking there is no such thing as direct or immediate causation, but a mix of interacting variables. But even if there were such a thing, and in the ordinary sense in which we often say there is, the directness or immediacy of a result does not imply the result's foreseeability. For some sequence of several events can be more foreseeable to us in our circumstances than some direct or immediate cause. I shall not make the obvious criticism of vagueness. Yes, we can have trouble distinguishing 'immediate' cause from 'mediated' cause, depending on how we logically parse events. But "proximate cause" is a term of legal art; and as Aristotle would say, it is a mark of lack of education to expect logical precision where the nature of the subject does not allow it.

We may say that in torts, the concepts of proximate cause, immediate cause, obvious cause, and remote cause *ought* to be logically related to the concept of relevant cause, i.e., to the concept of logical relevance, in the sense of reasonable foreseeability. And this is on pain of the defendant's otherwise not being reasonably blameworthy.

In 1872, Mayne's *Treatise on the Law of Damages*, "by John D. Mayne, of the Inner Temple....THE SECOND EDITION by Lumley Smith, of the Inner Temple....," was published. Mayne and Smith say:

> In many cases of torts, no measure of damage can be stated at all.... (Mayne 1872: viii; 1894: viii)

This is the point Keynes cites Mayne for. But Mayne and Smith also have much to say that concerns logical relevance. They say more fully:

> In many cases of torts, no measure of damage can be stated at all; and the only way of approximating to such a measure, is by ascertaining what evidence could be adduced *in support of the issue*. All this has made many parts of the present work resemble a treatise on the law of Nisi Prius [i.e. of evidentiary trial by jury], rather than one exclusively appropriated to Damages (Mayne 1872: viii, ; 1984: viii, my emphasis)

They say:

> We may now proceed to the more important inquiry, as to the general rules which determine the amount of substantial damages. It will be convenient to examine in order,
> I. The principles upon which damages are given in actions of contract and tort.
> II. What damages are *inadmissible on grounds of remoteness*.

III. The period of time in reference to which damages may be assessed.

IV. The cases in which evidence may be given to reduce damages. (Mayne 1872: 7, my emphasis)

And:

The plaintiff was held entitled to recover the loss...as being the *direct, immediate, and necessary consequence* of the defendant's breach. (Mayne 1872: 15, my emphasis)

And:

Damage is said to be *remote*, when although arising out of the cause of action, it does not so *immediately and necessarily* flow from it, as that the offending party can be made *responsible* for it. (Mayne 1872: 26, my emphasis; see 217, 296–97, 309 for similar language)

And:

Erle, C. J.,...says that damage will be too *remote* unless it *immediately and according to the common course of events* follows from the defendant's wrong, and the two are *known by common experience* to be *usually in sequence*. (Mayne 1872: 27 n.(*n*), my emphasis)

And:

Pollock, C. B., expressed a strong doubt whether a man is responsible for all the consequences that may under any circumstances arise in respect of mischief, which by *no possibility* could he have *foreseen*, and which *no reasonable person* could be called on to have *anticipated*. He intimated that the rule was that a man is expected to guard against all *reasonable* consequences. (Mayne 1872: 37, my emphasis)

And:

[C]ould any judge leave to the jury, as *relevant* evidence, facts going to show the *collateral* liability of other parties?....

Two cases which are frequently cited seem to be reducible to the same rule as to the *inadmissibility*, in reduction of damages, of *extrinsic* matter arising subsequent to the cause of action. (Mayne 1872: 68; 1894: 112, my emphasis)

Here we see them use the term "relevant" evidentially in the 1872 edition of the law treatise that Keynes cites in his 1921 *Treatise*.
      And:

> The true measure [of an insurance claim] is the amount of injury the plaintiff has sustained, not exceeding the entire sum insured; that is, the expense, and pain, and loss, it may be of a limb, connected with the *immediate* accident; but not the *remote* consequences that may follow.... (Mayne 1872: 251; 1894: 343, my emphasis)

And:

> In one instance,...Lord Kenyon allowed general evidence of the immodest character of a woman to go in bar of the action. He said, that in such a case character was the only *point in issue*, and that *was* public opinion, founded on the character of the party. He *therefore* considered that what that public thought was *evidence*. (Mayne 1872: 377; 1894: 486, my emphasis, cite omitted)

And:

> Whenever an agent violates his duties [to his principal, t]he loss or damage need not be **directly or immediately** caused by the act....It will be sufficient if it be fairly attributable to it, as a **natural result**, or a just consequence. But it will not be sufficient if it be merely a **remote consequence**, or an **accidental** mischief; for in such a case, as in many others, the maxim applies, *Causa proxima, non remota, spectatur.* [The nearest (or immediate) cause, not the remote, is to be looked at (considered).] Mayne 1872: 411, Mayne's italic emphasis, my boldface emphasis)

And:

> The damages must also be the *proximate and natural* result of the neglect. [But the agent] is not responsible for *remote* consequences that may accrue....Speculative damages...ought never to be given; but *positive and direct loss*, arising *plainly and immediately* from the breach of orders, may be taken into the estimate. (Mayne 1872: 415, my emphasis)

The term "plainly" goes to foreseeability. It implies very clear and obvious foreseeability. How can that not be evidentially relevant?
      And:

The law upon this point was laid down in an old case as follows: "Where the matter omitted to be inquired into by the principal jury was such as goes to *the very point of the issue,* and upon which, if found by the jury, an attaint will lie against them by the party, if they have given a false verdict, there such matter cannot be supplied by a writ of inquiry, because thereby the plaintiff may lose his action of attaint....But where the matters omitted to be inquired into by the jury did not go to *the point in issue,* or *necessary* consequences thereof, but were things *merely collateral,*...such may be inquired of by a subsequent writ of inquiry. (Mayne 1872: 441, my emphasis, cite omitted; compare 1894: 574–75)

And:

Many of the principles upon this point are quite *unconnected* with the topics discussed in this treatise. There is one, however, *directly relevant....* (Mayne 1894: 577, my emphasis)

And:

Lord Kenyon said, the injury was too *remote,* and *impossible to be connected* with the cause assigned to is....Such special damage is not the *natural or necessary* consequence of the [libelous] words. (Mayne 1872: 372; 1894: 478, my emphasis)

And:

But such libels must be shown to *relate* to the *subject-matter* of those published by the defendant....
      Such evidence must, in any case, be *confined to the particular trait which is attacked in the libel....* (Mayne 1872: 373–74; 1894: 480, my emphasis)

And:

Evidence of a *mere collateral fact*...cannot be given in mitigation of damages. (Mayne 1872: 374, my emphasis; see 1894: 481)

And:

...[I]t was held to be no ground for a new trial, as it did not amount to a misdirection, not being wrong information on a matter which was *directly in issue,* or which was *substantially connected* with the finding *on the issue*. (Mayne 1872: 454–55; 1894: 582)

In 1894, the fifth edition of *Mayne's Treatise on Damages*, "by John D. Mayne, of the Inner Temple....and Lumley Smith, of the Inner Temple....," was published. Here they add Lord Bacon's vicious infinite regress argument for the requirement of proximate cause:

> Every cause leads to an infinite sequence of effects. But the author of the initial cause cannot be made responsible for all the effects in the series. In the case where a passenger, who had been set down with his wife at a wrong station, sought to recover from the railway company damages for a cold which his wife had caught by walking in the rain at night, Cockburn, C.J., said: "You must have something **immediately** flowing out of the breach of contract complained of, something **immediately** connected with it, and not merely connected with it through a series of causes **intervening** between the immediate consequence of the breach of contract and the damage or injury complained of (*k*)...."
> (*k*) See Lord Bacon's maxim:—"It were infinite for the law to judge the cause of causes, and their impulsions one of another; therefore, it contenteth itself with the **immediate** cause, and judgeth of acts by that, without looking to any further degree." Bac. Max. Reg. 1, cited by Blackburn, J., in stating the rule of our law to be that the **immediate** cause, the *causa proxima*, and not the **remote** cause, is to be looked at. (Mayne 1894: 48 quoting Chief Judge Cockburn and Lord Bacon, and citing Judge Blackburn, cites omitted, Mayne's italic emphasis, my boldface emphasis)

The regress argument seems a *non sequitur*. Surely more than the most direct and immediate effect is often reasonably foreseeable, and ought to be for the law to judge. And the argument's structure is very different from that of Thomas Aquinas' "first cause" regress argument. Where the present event is damage d and its immediate cause is neglect n, Aquinas argues that there must be some uncaused or self-caused "first cause" $n + m$, where n is cause number one going backwards in time, and m is a finite number greater than zero; since if causes went back to infinity, then d (and for that matter n) would not (be caused to) exist in the first place. And n itself cannot be such an uncaused or self-caused cause, since any such cause would have always existed; and an act of neglect is not that sort of cause. In sharp contrast, Bacon is not arguing, but merely claiming, that n is the only cause that can be judged in law to be a cause of d. Aquinas wants the earliest existing cause of d, namely $n + m$, while Bacon wants the most recent, namely n. Or if you please, Aquinas wants God, and Bacon, immediate blame.

Collectively, all the Mayne texts paint quite a relevantist picture. Thus Mayne is very much part of the relevantist legal tradition. He even uses the terms "relevant evidence" and "directly relevant" as early as 1872. But I am not suggesting that Keynes took his own term "relevant" from Mayne. Keynes only cites Mayne as a source for his view that probabilities are rarely measurable in real life. In fact, Keynes only cites "Mr Justice Jelf" as "[h]aving referred to 'Mayne on Damages' (8th ed., p. 70)," in his *Treatise on Probability* (Keynes 1962 / 1921: 24–25). Keynes does not indicate that he himself read "Mayne on Damages," and Mayne is not listed in the index. Again, this source is only part of his discussion of his view that not all degrees of probability can be exactly or numerically measured.

But it is a small world. The 1872 and 1894 title pages say that Mayne and Smith are "of the Inner Temple." Mayne died in 1917. Smith died in 1918 at the age of 85 (*The Annual Register* 1918: 181). And Arthur Richard Jelf (1837–1917) was a member of the Inner Temple too. Thus Keynes might have got his cites to *Mayne* and Jelf from Mayne, Smith, or Jelf *in person* at dinner in the Inner Temple in 1904. Like Keynes, Smith went to Trinity Hall, Cambridge, and was ninth Wrangler in 1857 (*The Annual Register* 1918: 181). Per the 1894 title page, Smith was "One of Her Majesty's Counsel, Judge of the Westminster County Court, Late Fellow of Trinity Hall, Cambridge." Later, Smith was "Judge of the City of London Court" (*The Annual Register* 1918: 181).

Alexander James Edmund Cockburn (1802–1880) of the Middle Temple "was Lord Chief Justice of England,...was educated at Trinity Hall, Cambridge, of which he was elected a fellow, and afterwards an honorary fellow[.] Lord John Russell[, Bertrand Russell's grandfather,] appointed him solicitor-general in 1850 and attorney-general in 1851" (Fact-Index.com 2015). Lord Justice Colin Blackburn (1813–1896) went to Trinity Hall, Cambridge too, and was of the Inner Temple. This too goes to the small world, even if Keynes could not have dined with them in 1904.

James Fitzjames Stephen

James Fitzjames Stephen (1829–1894) wrote the Indian Evidence Act "almost entirely on his own" (Twining 1994: 53); it is still the evidence law of India today (Twining 1994: 54). In England, he was quite famous for this. Later he served as a judge. "Stephen was called to the Bar by the Inner Temple on 26 January 1854" Hostettler 2013: 148).

Twining says that like Gilbert, Stephen tried to subsume all evidence law under a single principle; but Gilbert "unhelpful[ly]" chose the best evidence rule, while Stephen chose the relevance rule, which was deeper and more plausible, and was a "fruitful failure" in stimulating further work on the concept of relevance (Twining 1994: 56–57). We saw that earlier that Twining is wrong about Gilbert; we are about to see he is wrong about Stephen too. For just as Best has a relevance rule which Best does not subsume under the best evidence rule, so Stephen has a best evidence rule which Stephen does not subsume under the relevance rule, though Stephen certainly regards the best evidence rule as less important.

It might be objected that it all depends on what we mean by "subsume under." But if we mean 'show to be a version or aspect of', 'logically derive from', 'explain in terms of', or even just 'find to be intellectually illuminated by', I find no subsumption of either of these two rules under the other in Gilbert or Stephen, or in any other law treatise writer that I discuss in this chapter. If we mean 'classify under' in a species-genus relation, then we need to be able to state what the genus is and what the difference is according to the law treatise writer in question. And beyond that, I am not sure what else we might reasonably mean by "subsume under." Even 'find to be intellectually illuminated by' is not enough in my opinion. For analogies often illuminate but fail to suffice for classification, much less explanation, derivation, aspecthood, or versionhood. And really the burden is on the authors who use the word "subsume" to explain what precisely *they* mean by it. I can only suggest the only plausible meanings that *I* can think of.

Murphy says, "The concept of relevance was developed in the nineteenth century, and refined principally by Sir James Fitzjames Stephen" (Murphy 2008: 9). Murphy finds that Stephen's work was eventually superseded (Murphy 2008: 9).

Stephen makes Best's distinction between natural and judicial evidence basic to evidence law, which Montrose says Best himself did not do (Montrose 1992 / 1954: 350 / 550). Stephen deems Best's natural evidence, which was Bentham's evidence in general, to be *(logically) relevant* evidence, and he deems Best's judicial evidence to be *legally relevant* evidence. Thus Stephen admits a basic dualism in relevance: there is logical relevance, and there is legal relevance. Legal relevance is generally narrower than logical relevance, and functions to exclude some logically relevant evidence as legally irrelevant. No doubt Chamberlayne's Taylor gets his distinction between logical relevance and legal relevance from Stephen (Taylor 1897: 2[6]–2[8]).

In fact, Stephen was going in the right direction, deeming the legal rules of evidence to be basically exclusionary (Twining 1994: 54). What he failed to see was that they were not *evidentiary* in nature at all, since they are not *relevant* to the point in issue at all. Instead, they are rules that exclude natural evidence (which *is* evidentiary and *is* relevant) as *legally inadmissible* for various general *policy* reasons which may or may not have anything to do with evidentiary concerns. The rule against admitting hearsay is largely based on the evidentiary unreliability of hearsay in general. But the rule against self-incrimination is largely a protection against forced confession regardless of the evidentiary reliability of torture or other coercion.

In 1872, the year Russell was born, Sir James Fitzjames Stephen wrote in the Preface to *The Indian Evidence Act* that "On the 5th March, 1872, in moving that the 'Indian Evidence Act' should be taken into consideration by the Legislative Council, I said" (Stephen 1872: v):

> "The subject is one which reaches far beyond law. The law of evidence is nothing unless it is founded upon a rational conception of the manner in which truth as to all matters of fact ought to be investigated." (Stephen 1872: v, quoting his own speech to the Legislative Council on March 5, 1872)

This is natural evidence. In the Introduction, under the heading "Fundamental Rules of English Law of Evidence," Stephen says:

> That part of the English law of evidence which professes to be founded upon anything in the nature of a theory may be reduced to the following rules:—
>
> (1) Evidence must be *confined to the matters in issue.*
>
> (2) Hearsay evidence is not to be admitted.
>
> (3) In all cases the best evidence must be given....
>
> Each of these rules is very loosely expressed. The word 'evidence', which is the leading term of each, is undefined and ambiguous.
>
> It sometimes *means* the words uttered and things exhibited by witnesses before a court of justice.
>
> At other times, it *means* the facts proved to exist by these things....
>
> Again, it is sometimes used as *meaning* to assert that a particular fact is *relevant* to the matter under inquiry. (Stephen 1872: 3, my emphasis)

We see that Stephen places the relevance rule first, the hearsay rule second, and the best evidence rule third, and that he does not reduce any of these rules to any of the others. Instead, he says that any part of English evidence law that is capable of theoretical treatment "may be reduced to" those three rules, which he treats as equally logically fundamental, *pace* Twining. Stephen does not explain exactly what he means by 'reduce', but surely it must be a logical relation of *some* sort, in the broad sense of intellectual or conceptual relation.

We also see that Stephen makes relevance one of the three *meanings* that can be expressed by the word "evidence." When the word "evidence" is used with that meaning, this of course makes the thesis that evidence is relevant into a tautology, as opposed to an informative logical analysis. Thus it makes rule (1) tautological, insofar as to be relevant is to be confined to the matters in issue.

Stephen regards the relevance rule as the most important one. He says, "[T]he question, 'what facts are relevant',...is the most important of all the questions that can be asked about the law of evidence" (Stephen 1872: 4).

Stephen discusses relevancy further on pages 9–11. He distinguishes facts in issue from relevant facts. He says:

> (1) [Facts such that] the existence of the disputed right or liability would be a legal inference from them....may be called facts in issue...." (Stephen 1872: 9)

Then he says:

> (2) Facts, which are not themselves in issue in the sense above explained, may *affect the probability* of the existence of facts in issue, and be used as the foundations of inferences respecting them; such facts are described in the Evidence Act as *relevant* facts.
> All the facts with which it can in any event be necessary for courts of justice to concern themselves, are included in these two classes.
> The first great question, therefore, which the law of evidence should decide is, what facts are *relevant*. (Stephen 1872: 9–10, my emphasis)

All the foregoing is from the introductory chapter 1. The discussion is very logical and very modern. Note that in provision (2), he defines (or essentially describes) relevance in terms of probability. The definition is basically the same as American *FRE* Rule 401.

Chapter 2, "Induction and Deduction," occupies pages 13–51. The final header is "Degrees of Probability" (Stephen 1872: 51).

Chapter 3, "The Theory of Relevancy, with Illustration[s]," occupies pages 52–128. After some argumentation, he concludes:

> The rule, therefore, that facts may be regarded as relevant which can be shown to stand either in the

> relation of cause or in the relation of effect to the fact
> which they are said to be relevant, may be accepted as
> true, *subject to* the caution that, when an inference is to
> be founded upon the existence of such a connection,
> every step by which the connection is made out must be
> proved, or be so probable under the circumstances of the
> case that it may be presumed without proof. (Stephen
> 1872: 53–54, my emphasis)

Here he wisely requires not only that there be a causal relation, but also that it be provable or at least probable. That is to say, he is requiring that the causal relation be evidentially relevant. My only criticism is that we should be going by probability alone, since in some cases we may not be able to make any *specific* causal relation probable. For example, suppose three people conspire to murder a fourth. They load three physically identical guns, one with bullets and two with blanks. They pick up the guns at random and shoot at the victim at the same time in a firing squad in front of hundreds of witnesses and video cameras. They then destroy the guns in a vat of molten steel. Supposing that this describes all the evidence, no one shooter is the probable *specific* agential cause of the murder, since there is only a one third chance any one of them shot the victim. Even they have no idea who did it. But that there *was* a murder, not to mention a conspiracy to murder, would seem very probable indeed. No doubt there are indefinitely many cases where one person puts another in harm's way, and the harm is inevitable in one way or another, but the specific cause of the harm is unknowable. For example, one could lock another in a room with ten bombs hidden in locations where the prisoner would inevitably go, and in such a way that any bomb would destroy all the evidence.

Whether we accept Stephen's definition or not, we may still agree with him that:

> These sections [on relevancy] are by far the most
> important, as they are the most original part of the
> Evidence Act, as they affirm positively what facts may
> be proved, whereas the English law assumes this to be
> known, and merely declares negatively that certain facts
> shall not be proved. (Stephen 1872: 55)

But I am not sure I agree with the "whereas." Looking to what we have reviewed so far, I think he might be a bit harsh on English law as discussed by his predecessors.

In 1876, Stephen's summary *Digest of the Law of Evidence* appeared. He says in the Introduction:

> The arrangement of the book is the same as that of the
> Indian Evidence Act, and is based on the distinction
> between relevancy and proof....The neglect of this
> distinction, which is concealed by the ambiguity of the
> word evidence (a word which sometimes means
> testimony and at other times relevancy) has thrown the
> whole subject into confusion, and has made what was
> really plain enough appear almost incomprehensible....
>   The facts which may be proved are facts in
> issue, or facts relevant to the issue.
>   Facts in issue are those facts upon the existence
> of which the right or liability to be ascertained in the
> proceeding depends.
>   Facts relevant to the issue are facts from the
> existence of which inference as to the existence of the
> facts in issue may be drawn.
>   A fact is relevant to another fact when the
> existence of the one can be shown to be the cause or one
> of the causes, or the effect or one of the effects, of the
> existence of the other, *or* when the existence of the one,
> either alone or together with other facts, renders the
> existence of the other highly probable, or improbable,
> according to the common course of events. (Stephen
> 1876: viii–x, my emphasis)

The disjunctive "or" definition of relevance in the last paragraph is
very different from the conditional "subject to" definition in the
Act. I have three criticisms of this new disjunctive definition.

First, if it suffices for relevance that a fact make a fact in
issue highly probable, or even merely more probable than it would
be otherwise, then the alternative disjunct, making a causal relation
a sufficient condition of relevance, is needless. And if the causation
was improbable, then it is irrelevant. Of course, if a fact is shown
to be either a cause or an effect of a fact in issue, then we have a
causal proof. I mean by "causal proof" that if a fact F is proved to
exist, and is proved to be either the cause or an effect of fact G,
then the existence of fact G is proved. But the question is whether
we can give such a causal proof in the situation at hand. Fact F may
indeed *be* the cause or an effect of fact G. But fact F is *relevant
evidence* for fact G only if we can *show* that it is the cause or an
effect of G.

Second, not every cause or effect of a fact is relevant to a
matter in issue. My shooting a person may cause someone else to
be sad, but the sadness is evidentially irrelevant to whether I shot
the person. Of course, one can validly argue that (1) the sadness
exists and (2) the sadness was caused by my shooting the person,
therefore (3) I shot the person. That would be a valid causal proof.
But premiss (2), that the sadness was caused by my shooting the

person, begs the question on whether I shot the person. Thus, considered by itself, a sadness that is later in time is not evidence. We might not even be able to infer that *any* act in particular made the person sad, much less that it was my act. It might have been just a wave of sadness caused by the brain. This is not to mention remote causes or remote effects, or more to the point, unlikely causes or effects.

Third, the very same cause or effect may be relevant or irrelevant depending on how it is described. As we saw in chapter 6, causation is referentially opaque (Føllesdal 1971: 53–54). "I shot the hooded man" does not imply "I shot my brother." Thus if evidential relevance is causal, then it is referentially opaque.

These three criticisms also apply to the disjunctive definition (5) of proximate cause in *Black's Law Dictionary* which I criticized in the section on Mayne. Of course, *Black's* is correct as a mere report of Stephen's usage.

One might object to the third criticism that evidence is referentially opaque in any case. For one and the same body of evidence can always be described in different ways. For example, "Witnesses saw that I shot the hooded man" makes it less probable that I shot my brother than does "Witnesses saw that I shot my brother." My reply is that all evidence as such is already under a description. For evidence is always relative to cognitive beings and to their points of view. That is, evidence is *our* evidence, and our evidence is always our evidence *as we understand it.* If there were no conscious beings, then there would be no evidence either. Not so for causation, which is there in the world independently of how we think of or describe the world. But because our understanding of the evidence *is* essential to what the evidence is, evidence cannot be described in *essentially* different ways and remain the evidence it is. (Of course, it can be described in *accidentally* different ways, such as "the evidence that I collected last night.") What is evidence for me might not be evidence for you, or for some super-scientist. To sum up, evidence is *essentially not* referentially opaque. It belongs to the world of seeming as opposed to the world of being. Specifically, it is rational or relevant seeming. In contrast, facts in issue belong to the world of being. And we try to use our rational seemings to prove what happened in the world of being. This is not at all to say that seemings are subjective. Rational seemings are objective to the extent that they are rational. Also, seemings can be shared, or public. Then they are relative to the public understanding of the world.

One might further reply that what evidentially seems to be the case is what is given, and what is given is preconceptual, predescriptive "pure" experience. Therefore evidence is essentially preconceptual and predescriptive, and thus cannot be referentially opaque, since it cannot be described at all, much less in different ways. My reply is that the premiss may be true, but the implied conclusion does not follow, that *evidence* is pure experience. Perhaps evidence includes or ultimately involves pure experience, but evidence for something is not pure experience. It is a concept, and a highly abstract concept at that. Evidence is ultimately perception as opposed to pure experience, and as such it is often describable. Thus the way out is to distinguish essential description from accidental description of evidence. Evidential seemings are perceptions as opposed to pure experience, and often describable. In contrast, pure experience is nameable by logically proper names; this includes naming simple sense-qualities. Even in a scientific study of what colors we saw, which might be evidence for what chemical was used to murder someone, the colors must be perceptually established as factually the case. I shall return to this point shortly.

Russell gives two arguments that there must be a pure datum of sense if there is to be any perception at all, and an argument that can be rewritten as a vicious regress argument for the same conclusion. These arguments were given in chapter 4 as:

(Psychological) Argument #3. Perception cannot be pure interpretation, that is, interpretation that is *of* nothing. Therefore there must be something perceived which is not nothing (IMT 124–25).

(Epistemological) Argument #4. There must be a pure datum. For data cannot be conceptualization alone. Conceptualization must be *of* something (HK 167–70).

(Epistemological) Argument #5. Each datum has its own evidential weight which is not nothing. Otherwise knowledge will be impossible due to a vicious epistemic regress (IMT 124–25; see HK 157, 189–90). This weight is intrinsic, hence preconceptual.

I accept arguments #3 and #4 as clear and convincing, though not as absolutely certain, partly because I am not absolutely certain what absolute certainty is.

I take argument #5 as rewritable for a different conclusion as follows. If, every sensation were a conceptualized percept, then it would have a conceptual component and a sensation component. But then the sensation component would be a percept in turn, and would have its own conceptual component and sensation component. And so on to infinity. But the regress is vicious, since if there were no sensation, there could be no perception. Thus there must be a "first" sensation which is purely sensational. We may call this argument #5a. The first thing to note is that Russell goes not give it. But I think he might be very sympathetic to it, since he gives the *similar* #5, and since he gives #4 for the same *conclusion* as that of #5a. The second thing to note is that #4 arguably states the basis of #5a. I mean that #5a argues that the regress must stop because percepts must include sensations; and that it is intuitively plausible to say that the deeper *reason* it must stop, besides the mere definitional fact that percepts must include sensations, is that conceptualization must be *of* something; and in a percept, the conceptualization could only be of a sensation.

One might object that an infinite series of sensation components guarantees not just one, but infinitely many sensations, albeit conceptualized ones. My reply is that this is contrary to the phenomenology of perception. We are simply not presented with any such series in perception. When we are presented with a perceptual object, we are presented with just one such object, and it is presented through sensation. That we may *focus* on, say, the redness of an apple, and then ask ourselves about its conceptual component and its sensation component, does not detract from this point. Quite the opposite. That we have to change our focus to single out another percept, the apple's redness as opposed to the red apple, is actually further proof of the point.

Still, I favor arguments #3 and #4 as better than #5a, partly because of the difficulty of evaluating regress arguments, and partly because #3 and #4 are simpler, clearer, deeper, and more direct.

The large literature on the "given" is beyond the scope of this book. Briefly, it is plausible to analyze an ordinary perceptual object into a sensation component and a conceptual component; and it seems from arguments #3 and #4 that this is what the 1940–48 Russell does. In 1912 *Problems*, the perception of an ordinary thing involves sense-data given in acquaintance, and a description that goes beyond that immediate experience. The description involves a universal, and "a universal of which we are aware" is a concept (PP 52). Thus there is a pure sensation and a conceptual component in *Problems* as well.

Of course, for the 1912 Russell, *physical* evidence can only be known by description. This is consistent with the 1912 Russell's views that *sense-data* are self-evident (PP 114), and that we cannot have physical evidence *without* sense-data; they are a necessary condition.

The deepest rejoinder to my reply, that all evidence as such is already under an essential description, would be that this is simply not true. We often have good evidence based on our experience that we are simply unable to describe. I agree with a point very much like this one in note 4 to this chapter. There I hold that we cannot always describe our reasons for our views; and that is pretty much the same thing. For our evidence is our reason to believe. My reply is to distinguish description from conceptualization. That is, perceptual evidence is essentially *conceptualized,* but we may not always be able to *describe* it, that is, to state our reasons for believing some view. Thus I amend my reply so as to say that all evidence as such is already under an essential *conceptualization* (but not necessarily under any *description*). And that is enough to make all evidence as such already *conceptually opaque*, as opposed to causation that is out there in the world. I need not add that conceptualizations, as such, are not linguistic like descriptions.

A final objection to my view is that if all evidence is conceptualized, then pure sensations are not evidence. My reply is that this is generally true. There may be exceptions where we are doing a frequency prediction of occurrences of pure sensations, or predicting a pure sensation such as a phenomenal after-image, or the like. But in ordinary life, typical science, and typical courts of law, our evidence is never or almost never pure, uninterpreted sensation. Courts want witnesses to report only the facts and not add their own opinions; but these facts are already conceptualized ordinary things. Again, even in a scientific study of what colors we saw, which might be evidence for what chemical was used to murder someone, the colors must be perceptually established as factually the case.

Murphy has noticed that Stephen closely anticipates *FRE* Rule 401. Murphy says:

In *DPP* v *Kilbourne* [1973] AC 729 at 756 Lord Simon of Glaisdale said:

> Evidence is *relevant* if it is *logically probative or disprobative* of some matter which requires proof. It is sufficient to say, even at the risk of etymological tautology, that *relevant* (*i.e., logically probative or disprobative*) evidence is evidence which makes the matter which requires proof *more or less probable.*

This is, perhaps, a simpler and more satisfactory, if less comprehensive definition of relevance, than the classic formulation in Stephen's *Digest*, according to which the word signified that:[22]

> any two facts to which it is applied are so *related* to each other that according to the common course of events, one either taken by itself or in connection with other facts *proves or renders probable* the past, present or future

> *existence or non-existence* of the other.
>
> Neither attains the appealing simplicity of the American Federal Rule of Evidence 401, whereby the term "relevant evidence"
>
>> means evidence having any tendency to make the existence of any fact that is of consequence to the determination of the action *more probable or less probable than it would be without the evidence.*
>
> Thus, relevant evidence is evidence which has probative value in assisting the court or jury to determine the facts in issue. *Relevance is not a legal concept, but a logical one, which describes the relationship between a piece of evidence and a fact in issue....If the evidence contributes in a logical sense, to any extent, either to the proof or the disproof of the fact in issue, then the evidence is relevant to the fact in issue. If not, it is irrelevant.* It is a fundamental rule of the law of evidence that...evidence must be relevant in order to be admissible. The converse, however, is not true, because much relevant evidence is inadmissible under the specific rules of evidence affecting admissibility.
> 22. *Digest of the Law of Evidence*, 12th ed., art. 1. The definition was somewhat different in earlier editions, but this seems to be the author's mature view. (Murphy 2008: 29, my emphasis, except for case and book titles)

I take it that the following is a definitional logical equivalence for Stephen, Lord Simon, Murphy, and *FRE* Rule 401 alike: Evidence is relevant if and only if that evidence, "taken by itself or in connection with other facts," makes the fact in issue more or less probable "than it would be without the evidence." Here, relevant evidence logically can, but need not be, intrinsically relevant.

By updating our account to the 1936 twelfth edition of the *Digest* (Murphy 2008: 29 n.22; Stephen 1936), Murphy shows us that the posthumous Stephen avoids the problems I raised with his 1876 disjunctive definition of "relevant."

It seems that for Stephen, probabilistic relevance is implicitly grounded in the modality of epistemic necessity. Stephen says:

ARTICLE 8.
FACTS *NECESSARY* TO EXPLAIN OR INTRODUCE *RELEVANT* FACTS.

> Facts *necessary* to be known to explain or introduce a
> fact in issue or *relevant* fact, or which support or rebut
> an inference suggested by a fact in issue or *relevant* fact,
> or which establish the identity of any thing or person
> whose identity is at issue or relevant to the issue, or
> which fix the time and place at which any fact in issue or
> relevant fact happened, or which show that any
> document produced is genuine or otherwise, or which
> show the relation of the parties by whom any such fact
> was transacted, or which afforded an opportunity for its
> occurrence or transaction, or which are *necessary* to be
> known in order to show the relevancy of other facts, are
> *relevant in so far as they are necessary* for those
> purposes respectively. (Stephen 1876: 11, my emphasis)

The key phrase is "relevant in so far as they are necessary for those
purposes." This implies that for the purposes mentioned, evidence
is relevant if and only if it is necessary. The twice-used phrase
"necessary to be known" bases relevance on *epistemic* necessity.
But it seems trivial that to provide evidence, it is also *logically* and
essentially necessary to provide relevant facts, since evidence is
essentially relevant. Correspondingly, in deductive logic, that a
premiss is necessary to prove a conclusion is a strict sense of what
Anderson and Belnap and others call use-relevance. A looser sense
would be that the premiss is necessary to *some* proof, which cannot
succeed without it, but there are or may be alternative proofs which
do not need to use it, in order to succeed. One would think there is
a corresponding looser sense for probabilistic evidence as well.

    Might Keynes have known of Stephen on evidence law
simply because Stephen was famous? John Hostettler says:

> In the early 19th-century vast areas of India were
> controlled by the East India Company...It is difficult to
> overestimate Stephen's impact on the English political
> scene following his Indian experiences. For years he had
> used his pen in England to write numerous articles in
> popular journals and engage in controversy with the
> most important people of the day. His name was
> everywhere. Disraeli was later to write Lord Lytton in
> 1881, "It is a thousand pities that J F Stephen is a Judge;
> he might have done anything and everything as a leader
> of the future Conservative party." (Hostettler 2013: 151)

The young Keynes actually worked in the India Office, the office in
Great Britain that controlled all Indian affairs, while working on his
theory of probability. How could he not have known one of the
most famous names of British India?

Keynes and Russell might at least have heard of Stephen as a major conservative critic of John Stuart Mill, Russell's godfather. Stephen's major critique of Mill, *Liberty, Equality, and Fraternity*, was published in 1873, the year after Russell was born (Hostettler 2013: 152). But Stephen also greatly praises Mill for updating logic. The days of Locke's being the main philosophical inspiration for legal writers on evidence are now gone (Twining 1994: 52). This is not mention the inspiration of Bentham, especially in Mill's edition.

James Bradley Thayer

James Bradley Thayer (1831–1902) was Royall Professor of Law at Harvard, and later Weld Professor. He gave us the view we accept today, but not at first. This is not well known. Montrose and Twining omit Thayer's early view.

The 1880–81 "early" Thayer accepts both logical relevance and legal relevance. He says in an essay called "Bedingfeld's Case—Declarations as a Part of the Res Gesta":

> Whatsoever is irrelevant may, of course, be rejected; whatsoever, also, though in strictness relevant, is, as the case stands, clearly inadequate, and so immaterial; whatsoever, though relevant and not quite immaterial, yet, having regard to the bearing of it in other parts of the case or the use that is likely to be made of it, is really colorable. No doubt the exercise of these functions is a delicate matter; but the right to exercise them points to a difference between parts of the *res gestae*, which are **legally admissible**, and other parts. We are to consider, then, that just as **there is a relevancy which is logical but not legal,**—so that when we talk in a **legal** discussion, we mean **legal relevancy,**—so in a **legal** discussion about evidence the expression, "a part of the *res gestae*," means such a part of it as is **admissible in evidence**, having regard to all the rules. (Thayer 1880–81: 285, Thayer's italic emphasis, my boldface emphasis)

Thus Thayer admits both "a relevancy which is logical but not legal" and "legal relevancy"—and equates legal relevancy with the legal admissibility of evidence. But the distinction appears to be one of degree, with the degrees ranging from "immaterial" to "not quite immaterial" and beyond. Compare Chamberlayne's Taylor.

Material relevance is indeed relevance to the point in issue, but it is conceptual and legal as opposed to evidentiary and empirical in nature. It does not prove anything or make anything probable.

The popular Perry Mason phrase "incompetent, irrelevant, and immaterial" is confused. Nothing can be all three. *Witnesses* are competent if they are qualified to *testify*. *Evidence*, including the testimony of witnesses, is relevant if it helps establish some *fact*. A *fact* is material if it conceptually relates to some legal issue, i.e., if it *would* help establish the legal issue if there *were* evidence for the fact. The popular phrase is best left to television shows.

The 1898–1900 "later" or "mature" Thayer admits logically relevant evidence, but sees that what is called legal relevance is not evidentiary in nature at all, but is merely a grab bag of unrelated policy restrictions on the *admissibility* of logically relevant evidence. "It was Thayer who demonstrated most fully the basic distinction between" logical relevance and admissibility" (Montrose 1992 / 1954: 351 / 531). Wigmore follows Thayer, and so does the world of Anglo-American evidence law today.

In one of the most influential passages on evidence law, Thayer says in his 1898 (the book says "copyright 1896, 1898" on the title page, but was first published in 1898) *Preliminary Treatise on Evidence*:

> There is a principle—not so much a rule of evidence as a presupposition involved in the very conception of a rational system of evidence, as contrasted with the old formal and mechanical systems—which forbids receiving anything *irrelevant, not logically probative.* How are we to know what these forbidden things are? Not by any rule of law. The law furnishes no test of relevancy. For this it tacitly refers to logic and general experience....
> There is another precept which should be laid down as preliminary...namely, that *unless excluded by some principle or law, all that is logically probative is admissible.* This general admissibility, however, is not, like the former principle, a necessary presupposition in a rational system of evidence; there are many exceptions to it....These rules of exclusion [and] their exceptions [are] the chief part of the law of evidence. (Thayer 1898: 264–66, my emphasis)

We see two principles here. First is the negative principle that what is irrelevant is inadmissible. Second is the positive precept that what is relevant is admissible unless it is excluded by some rule of exclusion. Thus, in order for evidence to be admissible, it must pass a two prong test. First, it must be logically relevant. Second, it must not be excluded by any of the exclusionary policy rules (Thayer 1898: 266). As Thayer says later in the book:

In all cases, upon offering evidence, two questions may arise: one of its *logical relevancy*, and another of its admissibility, under the excluding rules of evidence. [These respectively involve] the *logical principle of relevancy*, and the excluding operation of the general rules of evidence.... (Thayer 1898: 468–69, my emphasis; see 514–15)

Thayer says, "This excluding function is the characteristic one in our law of evidence" (Thayer 1898: 264).

Thus Thayer no longer admits two types of relevance, logical and legal. He admits only logical relevance. He finds it confusing to consider the grab bag of exclusionary rules to amount to legal relevance, or even to an evidentiary concept at all. He says:

[I]t is a question of where lies the balance of practical advantage. To discuss such questions...even if we introduced *the poor notion of legal relevancy, as contrasted with logical relevancy*—tends to obscure the nature of the inquiry. There is in truth no rule of law to apply [consistently to the huge and confusing mass of court opinions on when to exclude relevant evidence]. Thayer 1898: 517, my emphasis)

Thayer dislikes the best evidence rule. In his first sub-title in chapter 11 on the best evidence rule, Thayer calls it "A large and vague thing" (Thayer 1898: xii). The whole chapter is a sustained critique of the best evidence rule which I will not describe here.

Thayer sums up his views in chapter 12, "The Present and Future of the Law of Evidence." Four sub-titles are: "Its principles few, but its rules many and perplexed.—Much of it is really a mistaken expression of doctrines of the substantive law.—Excluding rules.—Relevancy" (Thayer 1898:xii).

Thayer finds the concept of legal relevance confused for two reasons. First, where probability is concerned, any concept of relevance makes sense only as an evidentiary concept. But the so-called concept of legal relevance is not an evidentiary concept at all. It really concerns policy reasons for *not* admitting evidence that *is* relevant. Thus it is really the concept of admissibility. Second, there is one thing that logical relevance is. Namely, it is the general relation of being objective, rational evidence for something. And as such, it belongs to logic, not to law. But there is no one thing that so-called "legal relevance" can be. For the term refers to a grab bag of unrelated policy reasons for excluding evidence. Some such reasons do indeed have an evidentiary aspect, such as excluding hearsay; but even here the policy reason is not merely that hearsay is unreliable, but also that it can be misleading or even prejudicial.

In his brief 1900 paper, "Law and Logic," Thayer replies to a critic of his 1898 *Preliminary Treatise*. Thayer says the thesis of his book is that:

> [O]ur law of evidence is a *rational* system[;] that in admitting evidence in our law, it is always assumed to be logically probative, i.e., probative in its own nature.—according to the rules that govern the process of reasoning; that the considerations determining this logical quality are not fixed by the law, and that, so far as legal determinations do proceed merely on such considerations, they do not belong to the domain of law; that the law of evidence, however, *excludes* much which is logically good, that is to say, good according to the tests of reason and general experience; and that the rules of exclusion make up the main part of the law of evidence. The reasons for these views...are indicated in the book....
> **Now this book uses the word "relevancy" merely as importing a logical relation, that is to say, a relation determined by the reasoning faculty. The word "admissibility" is the term which it applies to the determinations of the law of evidence.** (Thayer 1900: 307–8, Thayer's italic emphasis, my boldface emphasis)

This is another deeply influential passage from Thayer. Except for Thayer's not admitting logical relevance as a timeless Platonic entity in metaphysics, the first boldface sentence is Keynes exactly. The second boldface sentence sounds the death knell of legal relevancy.

Today everyone or almost everyone rejects the confusing distinction between logical relevance and legal relevance, which makes it sound as if there were two kinds of evidentiary relevance: one being the general rational kind, and the other being a specific kind peculiar to law. Today we find it correct to distinguish between logical relevance and legal *admissibility* of evidence, which is what talk of "legal relevance" was really about. Admissibility is not a kind of relevance, but is a laundry list of *curbs on* relevant evidence due to various policy reasons. Compare the very modern Murphy (2008: 29–33). See also *Federal Rules of Evidence*: Article 4, "Relevancy and Its Limits," encompassing Rules 401–415, on many topics; Article 8, "Hearsay," encompassing Rules 801–806, on the admissibility of hearsay; Rule 105 on limited admissibility, and so on. Finally, I am honored to cite the treatise of my University of Michigan School of Law professor, Rick Lempert, *A Modern Approach to Evidence* (2011: ch. 3, "Relevance," ch. 4, "Relevant But Inadmissible," and elsewhere). I took his course in 1995 and helped correct the treatise draft (Lempert 2000: vi).

Concerning logical relevance, Taylor and Thayer agree that mere or bare logical relevance is not enough, and basically for the same reason:

> The law of evidence undoubtedly requires that evidence to a jury shall be clearly relevant, and not merely slightly so; it must not barely afford a basis for conjecture, but for real belief; it must not merely be remotely relevant, but proximately so. (Thayer 1898: 516)

That is, evidence must be not only logically relevant but clearly relevant, weighty enough to be a basis for real belief, and proximately (foreseeably) relevant as opposed to remotely relevant. That would be a departure from philosophical theory of relevance. In fact, it is technically an exclusion of relevant evidence, and is thus a kind of inadmissibility. Arguably, it also falls under *FRE* Rule 403's "exclusion of relevant evidence...by considerations of undue delay, waste of time, or needless presentation of cumulative evidence." But the important point is that logical relevance is the proper *locus* for this sort of difference in degree ("slightly so," "barely afford"). That is in the sharpest terminological difference from calling a higher degree of logical relevance "legal relevance," as if it were different in kind.

Shapiro appears to disagree with me on Thayer. She says:

> Although most early and mid-nineteenth century treatises emphasize the similarity between legal reasoning and evidence and ordinary reasoning and evidence, it must be admitted that James Thayer's influential *Preliminary Treatise on Evidence at the Common Law* represents a departure from this position....Thayer appears to be of several minds whether, or to what degree, legal evidence and reasoning differ from evidence and reasoning in other fields of inquiry. At one point he differentiates between legal evidence and historical and religious evidence and insists that legal evidence is concerned with what is admissible, not what is logically probative. Yet he also admits that the rules of legal argument are "mainly an affair of logic and general experience, not legal precept," and they do not call "into play any different faculties or involve any new principles or methods."....Thayer thus represents something of a departure from previous thinkers. On the one hand he differentiates legal from mathematical reasoning on the traditional ground that the law does not deal with demonstration. On the other hand, unlike most of his predecessors, he distinguishes legal reasoning from other

types of evidence that deal with probabilities. (Shapiro 1991: 38–39)

Granted, Thayer is of two minds, "early" and "later." And the early Thayer is confused and needs correcting, certainly according to the later Thayer. But Shapiro gives no indication that she is aware of the early Thayer. And her statement is a misdescription of the later Thayer from start to finish. The sentence beginning "At one point" misdescribes Thayer's view that the so-called legal "evidence rules" for excluding evidence concern admissibility. The sentence beginning "Yet he also" misdescribes his view that all reasoning from evidence is based on general principles of logic and general experience in every field, and that there is no special rational faculty or special rational method for law, or for that matter, for any field. The sentence beginning "On the one hand" misdescribes his view that mathematics is a deductive science while law concerns inductive logic. And the sentence beginning "On the other hand" misdescribes the fact that he chiefly differs from his predecessors in that he holds that the so-called legal evidence rules are not rules for assessing the specific evidentiary value of specific evidence, but for excluding evidence for various policy reasons that have nothing in common with each other, and that range from excluding hearsay as unreliable in general to protecting the rights of the accused.

Thayer is the culminating flower of the assimilative tradition of making evidence in law just like any other evidence. He is the fulfiller of Bentham's general concept of evidence, which Best calls natural evidence. He says that general or natural evidence is the only kind of evidence there is, in law or elsewhere. He denies that general evidence is a genus with a legal species. He finds that general evidence is not a genus at all, since it has no species. He says that the so-called "evidence rules" in law are really admissibility rules.

Though Thayer was an American legal scholar, Keynes could have easily read him, not to mention hearing about him or his ideas, as far as dating is concerned. Thayer was writing of logical relevance in a way that involves degrees of logical relevance at least six years before Keynes read Moore's book in 1904. Taylor was even earlier, and lived and worked as a judge in London. Keynes could have read even the posthumous Taylor quite easily, and have taken from him his concept of logical relevance, which would have been the only one of interest to Keynes. There is no reason why Keynes would have been interested in legal relevance as opposed to logical relevance. And Keynes could have learned all this at lunch in the Inner Temple from lawyers who read Thayer, and who knew Taylor personally for many years.

Charles Frederic Chamberlayne

Charles Frederic Chamberlayne (1855–1913) studied under Thayer at Harvard Law School, and "was recommended by Thayer to be the American editor of Best's *Principles*[. He wrote the] American notes for three editions of that work, which was commended by Thayer 'as the most authoritative and reliable treatise on the subject of evidence in the English language'" (Twining 1994: 61 quoting Thayer). And as we saw earlier, Chamberlayne also wrote the notes to the 1897 edition of Taylor. The first volume of Chamberlayne's own treatise appeared in 1911.

Chamberlayne knew Thayer and his work well. No doubt he knew Thayer wrote of logical relevancy as early as 1880/81.

In 1883, Chamberlayne uses the terms "logical relevancy" and "logically relevant" in a note in his 1883 American edition of posthumous Best. Chamberlayne says in his note 1 to Best's § 251:

> §251. **Of all rules of evidence, the most universal and the most obvious is this,**—that the evidence adduced should be alike **directed and confined to the matters which are in dispute**, or which form the subject of the investigation.[1]
> 1. *Facts in Issue.* —The "facts in issue" in any action are those so constituted by the pleadings or the nature of the investigation. Facts which **logically** and obviously tend to determine the existence, extent, or nature of the right, liability, or disability asserted or denies in any such action, are facts **relevant** to the issue....Conf. Steph. Dig. Law. Eviden., 3d ed., Art. 1;....
> *Relevancy.*—Mr. Justice Stephen in his third edition **defines relevancy** in an unexceptionable manner. Two facts are said to be **relevant** to each other when so related "that, according to the common course of events, one, either taken by itself or in connection with other facts, **proves or renders probable** the past, present, or future existence or non-existence of the other." (Dig. Law Evid., Art. 1) **This is relevancy,—in a logical sense.** Legal relevancy, which is essential to admissible evidence, requires a higher standard of evidentiary force. It includes **logical relevancy**; and for reasons of practical convenience, demands a close connection between the fact to be proved and the fact offered to prove it. **All evidence must be logically relevant,**—that is absolutely essential. The fact, however, that it is **logically relevant**, does not insure admissibility; it must also be **legally relevant**. A fact which "in connection with other facts renders probable the existence" of a fact in issue, may still be rejected, if in the opinion of the judge and under the circumstances of the case it be

considered essentially misleading or too remote. U.S. *v.* Ross, 92. U.S. 281, 284, per Strong, J.; Morrissey *v.* Ingham, 111 Mass. 63; Jones *v.* State, 26 Miss. 247. See § 90, *supra.*...

Relevancy not Sole Test of Admissibility.— **Logical relevancy** is assumed by Mr. Justice Stephen throughout the Digest of Evidence to be the **sole rational test of admissibility**; that the two, relevancy and admissibility, are or ought to be coextensive and interchangeable terms. This is certainly a mistake. Public policy considerations of fairness, the practical necessity for reaching speedy decisions, these and similar reasons cause constantly the necessary rejection of much evidence entirely relevant, and they must continue to do so. All admissible evidence. as has been said supra, is relevant; but all relevant evidence is not therefore admissible. A communication to a legal adviser, or a criminal confession improperly obtained, may, undoubtedly, be relevant to a high degree. They are none the less inadmissible. Conf. § 33, n. 1, *supra.* (Best 1883: 257 main text; Chamberlayne 1883: 257–58 n.1 note to main text, Chamberlayne's italic emphasis, my boldface emphasis)

Mr. Justice Stephen is James Fitzjames Stephen, and the *Digest* is the third edition of Stephen's *Digest.*

I cannot say this is the first use of the terms "logical relevancy" and "logically relevant" in a major evidence law treatise. But it does show that those terms were used in a major evidence law treatise in 1883, over twenty years before Keynes read Moore's book. Of course, we saw that the 1880–81 Thayer was basically already using them:

[T]here is *a relevancy which is logical* but not legal....
[W]hen we talk in a legal discussion, we mean legal relevancy,... (Thayer 1880–81: 285, my emphasis)

The text is remarkable for other reasons too. Chamberlayne starts by distinguishing logical relevancy from legal relevancy. He not only considers *both* kinds of relevancy to be evidentiary in nature, but says, "Legal relevancy...requires a *higher* standard of evidentiary force" (my emphasis). Thus, as with Chamberlayne's Taylor and the early Thayer, the difference is really one of degree. But by the end of the quoted text, he has replaced "logically relevant" with "relevant," and has replaced "legally relevant" with "admissible" with respect to "public policy considerations." These replacements are, in effect, the later Thayer's critique of the theory that there are two kinds of relevancy, logical and legal, in a nutshell. But here Chamberlayne slides from the one pair of terms to the other pair as if it made no difference.

The policy reasons why logically relevant evidence may be inadmissible include violations of attorney-client confidentiality, and improperly obtained confessions. This is quite modern.

Unlike some recent commentators who believe that Best chiefly subscribes to the best evidence rule, Chamberlayne knows that Best says that "the most universal and the most obvious" rule of evidence is that evidence "should be alike directed and confined to the matters in dispute." Chamberlayne immediately identifies being "directed and confined" with being "logically relevant." "Directed" sounds positive and "confined" sounds negative, but I argued earlier that confinement implies positive containment. If water is confined to a pitcher, then the pitcher positively contains the water. Likewise, if evidence is confined to the point in issue, then all of the evidence is positively relevant to the point in issue.

Chamberlayne says that in his editing, he consulted the treatises of Greenleaf and of Francis Wharton (1820–1889), and Stephen's "eminently useful Digest" (Chamberlayne 1883: iv). He says, "Especially is the editor under a sense of deep obligation to Professor James B. Thayer of the Harvard Law School, without whose kindly encouragement the present work would certainly not have been undertaken, and to whose exact scholarship, patient research, and well-known devotion to the Law of Evidence, such value as it may be found upon examination to possess should perhaps be more justly ascribed" (Chamberlayne 1883: iv–v). This too suggests that in writing his notes on Best, Chamberlayne was basically following Thayer's views—by which I mean the early or 1880–81 Thayer's views. In particular, it seems to me that when Chamberlayne distinguishes between logical and legal relevance, he is following the early Thayer, since that is the early Thayer's view. And the same can be said of Chamberlayne's 1897 edition of Taylor, but with the irony that Thayer had changed his view by 1896. The mature or 1896–1900 Thayer rejects legal relevance as practically a contradiction in terms, since relevance is evidentiary and legal relevance is not. Thus while Chamberlayne's editing of Best was timely, his editing of Taylor was outdated, at least insofar as the editings were intended to reflect Thayer's views.

The seventh English edition of Best crossed the Atlantic quickly. Chamberlayne wrote the preface to the American edition of it in Cambridge, Massachusetts on June 1, 1883. J. M. Lely had written the preface to the seventh English edition at The Temple in December, 1882, just half a year earlier. For his part, Lely "most thankfully acknowledges his obligations to the exhaustive work of Mr. Pitt-Taylor and the well-known Digest of Mr. Justice Stephen"

(Lely 1883: viii). Thus this edition of Best was well-known in legal circles on both sides of the Atlantic by 1883.

I omit Chamberlayne's own treatise (1911) as published too late to have influenced the 1906 Keynes. An anonymous reviewer says in *Oklahoma Law Journal*, "[T]his work is the production of a Specialist on this most important branch of the law," and "the work of a master in the whole field of the law," who "has stood for years as an authority...." (Anon. 1911: 468). Chamberlayne was a judge for some years, and a member of the Boston bar.

Frank Sumner Rice

In 1892, Frank Sumner Rice's (1850–1898) *General Principles of the Law of Evidence* appeared. Chapter 12, "Relevancy," occupies pages 488–524. The chapter starts with a survey of definitions of relevancy. One is from the Trull v True case that was cited by Halsted (Rice 1892: 489). Rice discusses Stephen the most, and praises some of Stephen's formulations (Rice 1892: 490–81, 492–93). Rice quotes Chamberlayne's commentary on Best's *Principles of the Law of Evidence* as using, in a criticism of Stephen, the term "'Logical relevancy'" (Rice 1892: 492 quoting Chamberlayne). Rice says:

> § 252. **Relevancy not the Sole Test of Admissibility.**
> a. **Dissenting View.**—Mr. Chamberlayne, in his commentary upon Best's Principles of the Law of Evidence, vigorously dissents from some conclusions reached by Sir James Stephen. His assault upon the English jurist...has...had the effect of emphasizing a distinction it is highly proper to observe, and but too frequently overlooked. The learned commentator said: "Logical relevancy is assumed by *Mr. Justice* Stephen throughout the Digest of Evidence to be the sole rational test of admissibility; that the two, relevancy and admissibility, are or ought to be co-extensive and interchangeable terms. This is certainly a mistake. Public policy, considerations of fairness, the practical necessity for reaching speedy decisions, these and similar reasons cause constantly the necessary rejection of much evidence entirely relevant, and they must continue to do so. All admissible evidence, as has been said, *supra*, is relevant; but not all evidence is therefore admissible. A communication to a legal adviser, or a criminal confession improperly obtained, may, undoubtedly, be relevant, in a high degree. They are none the less inadmissible." Best, Ev. 251, *note*, Chamberlayne's ed.

(Rice 1892: 492, Rice's emphasis; see ch. 7, "Relevancy")

This is pure Thayer. What is more, Rice says that *Stephen* assumes that "logical relevancy" is "the sole rational test of admissibility" "throughout the *Digest of Evidence*." I think that is quite correct. Thus Rice not only uses the term "logical relevancy" in 1892, but he finds that logical relevancy is basic to the 1876 Stephen, and to the 1872 Stephen by implication, since the *Digest* is precisely a digest of Stephen's views in *The Indian Evidence Act*.

In the next section of the same chapter, Rice says that the United States Supreme Court has "greatly simplified" the question of what relevancy is:

> § 252. **Relevancy not the Sole Test of Admissibility.**
> a. **Dissenting View.**—Mr. Chamberlayne....
> b. **Views of United States Supreme Court.**—The entire question has been greatly simplified by an unmistakable formula from the United States Supreme Court. It is impossible to misconstrue such language as the following: "It is well settled that if the evidence offered conduces in any reasonable degree to establish the probability or improbability of the fact in controversy, it should go to the jury....*Hart* v. Newland, 3 Hawkes, 122...." *Home Ins. Co.* v *Weide*, 78 U.S. 11 Wall. 438, 20 L. ed. 197. (Rice 1892: 492–93, Rice's emphasis)

He means "it should go to the jury" because it is relevant. I omit the usual exclusionary exceptions to the general relevance rule.

Rice praises Best, Phillipps, Taylor, and Starkie, but says they are now out of date, and agrees with Greenleaf that their writing is too massively detailed to study easily (Rice 1892: iii–iv).

Rice was admitted to the bar in 1877 in Saratoga Springs, New York. Keynes is not very likely to have read him. But Rice helps to show that the term and concept of logical relevance were the cutting edge of Anglo-American evidence law over twenty years before Keynes read his 1904 paper on probability to the Apostles.

John Henry Gillett

In 1897, John Henry Gillett (1860–1920) sees Stephen and Best as consistent with each other insofar as that they both admit both a relevance rule and a best evidence rule (Gillett 1897: § 51). I myself see Stephen and Best as inconsistent with each other at most in their claims as to which rule is primary. Let us pretend that

Stephen seeks to reduce all evidence law to the sole principle that all evidence must be relevant in some sense, while Best seeks to reduce it to the sole principle that all evidence must be the best evidence in some sense. If so, there is no logical conflict in the sense that either reduction can be used, if indeed both are logically possible. Compare reducing the operators of propositional logic to the Sheffer stroke as the sole primitive operator, or to the Sheffer dagger. The statement, "All the operators of propositional logic can be reduced to either the stroke or the dagger," is logically consistent. In fact, it is far more than logically consistent. It is true. We can also either define conjunction in terms of negation and disjunction, or disjunction in terms of negation and conjunction. In Frege's logic, we can define either (1) functions in terms of objects and thoughts, (2) objects in terms of thoughts and functions, or (3) thoughts in terms of objects and functions. All these examples are technical and trivial. It would be more interesting to ask if "the best evidence" and "the most relevant evidence" are interdefinable, or if we can define any one of the following terms using the other two: "relevant fact," "probable," and "fact in issue."

Augustus Straker

In 1899, S. Augustus Straker says in his *Compendium of Evidence*, chapter 1, "Definition and Division":

> Definitions. Evidence is...."That which tends to render evident or to generate proof." *Best on Ev.*, p. 10. (Straker 1899: 22, my emphasis)
> Primary evidence is the *best* evidence which goes to prove the true [state] of fact to which it *relates*. In saying the best evidence, we mean the highest quality of evidence attainable. (Straker 1899: 23, my emphasis)

Thus Straker says Best *defines* ("Definitions") evidence in general as relevant evidence. Thus it appears that for Best, that evidence is relevant is definitional, while the best evidence rule that evidence ought to be the best is not. Straker in effect defines *primary* evidence as having two elements. It is the best evidence, and it also "relates" to the fact in issue. It is only *primary* evidence that is the best. Thus for Straker, if not also for Best, relevant evidence is the genus, and best evidence is the primary species.

Straker appears to find the terms "relevant evidence" and "competent evidence" logically equivalent, if not synonymous:

> Competent evidence is that which by the general rules of evidence is properly to be admitted in proof of the facts

alleged. This distinction is adopted, to prevent the admission of testimony *not properly relating* to the subject matter to be investigated. It is akin to *relevant* evidence, and the difference is so small as to make it a *distinction without a difference.*

It is important in trials to restrict the testimony to its competency, so as to prevent that which does not elucidate the fact and make single the issue as well as to hinder confusion in the minds of the Jury and lead them off into strange paths. (Straker 1899: 25, my emphasis)

This is about competent evidence, not competent witnesses.

John Henry Wigmore

In 1899, the sixteenth edition of Greenleaf's *Treatise on the Law of Evidence* appeared. Its editor was to become perhaps the greatest treatise writer on evidence law, John Henry Wigmore (1863–1943). The first edition of Wigmore's four-volume *Treatise on the System of Evidence in Trials at Common Law* was published in 1904, the year Keynes met Russell, read Moore's *Principia Ethica*, wrote his first paper on probability as a response to Moore, and read it to the Apostles (see Skidelsky 1986: 152–53, 183–84). Wigmore adopts Thayer's views on relevance, but goes far beyond Thayer by writing a comprehensive study of all aspects of evidence law, which Thayer never did. Wigmore's *Treatise* is arguably still the best Anglo-American work on evidence law today.

I shall discuss Wigmore's edition of Greenleaf first, and then Wigmore's own treatise.

Wigmore notes that Greenleaf "died on October 6, 1853, and that "fifteen editions of the first volume [were published in] 1842, 1844, 1846, 1848, 1850, 1852, 1854, 1856, 1858, 1860, 1863, 1866, 1876, 1883, and 1892" (Wigmore 1899: v). Wigmore says that Greenleaf wrote the first seven editions, and that the next eight were posthumous (Wigmore 1899: vi). Wigmore says:

In none of these posthumous editions was there any attempt to deal with the text, except in a few instances, chiefly by the insertion of brief references to statutory changes. But for the present edition a different treatment seemed to have become necessary. The broad statutory changes in the past two generations, the detailed development of many doctrines, the numerous novel applications of established principles, required not only many additions which could not be conveniently relegated to cumbrous notes, but also the omission of some portions of the text rendered obsolete by statutory abolitions. Moreover, in the expositions of principles, account could not fail to be taken of the new epoch in the understanding of the rules of evidence, due to the historical studies of Professor James Bradley Thayer, the great master of the law of evidence. No book purporting to represent the present state of our knowledge could omit to recognize and make use of his results, in the exposition of the principles of evidence. (Wigmore 1899: vi)

Here Wigmore testifies that the torch has passed from Greenleaf to Thayer, "the great master" who has introduced "the new epoch" in evidence law. But Wigmore also has high praise for Greenleaf:

On the other hand, it was necessary to leave the original text still available in its classical integrity. The profession has long been accustomed to rely on this work. In the opinions of every Court for the last fifty years there occur references to its sections; and, even of the errors that are to be found in its pages, it may often be said that they have become law in many jurisdictions because they were put forth in these pages (Wigmore 1899: vi)

Wigmore's Greenleaf says in chapter 1:

§ 1. **Definitions**. The word EVIDENCE, in legal acceptation, includes all the means by which any alleged matter of fact, the truth of which is submitted to investigation, is established or disproved.[1] This term, and the word *proof*, are often used indifferently, as synonymous with each other; but the latter is applied by the most accurate logicians to the effect of evidence, and not to the medium by which truth is established.[2] None but mathematical truth is susceptible of that high degree of evidence, called *demonstration*, which excludes all possibility of error....Matters of fact are proved by moral evidence alone; by which is meant not only that kind of evidence which is employed on subjects connected with moral conduct, but also all the evidence which is not obtained either from intuition, or from demonstration. In the ordinary affairs of life, we do not require demonstrative evidence, because it is not consistent with the nature of the subject, and to insist upon it would be unreasonable and absurd. The most that can be affirmed of such things is, that there is no reasonable doubt concerning them.[3] The true question, therefore, in trials of fact, is not whether it is possible that the testimony may be false, but whether there is sufficient probability of its truth....

1. See Wills on Circumstantial Evid. 2; 1 Stark. Evid. 10; 1 Phil. Evid. 1; [compare Thayer, Preliminary Treatise on Evidence, ch. 6]
2. Whately's Logic, b. 4, ch. 3, § 1.
3. See Gambier's Guide to the Study of Moral Evidence, p. 121. (Greenleaf 1899: 3–4, Greenleaf's emphases, Wigmore's square brackets for his addition of material to Greenleaf)

The general picture is much the same as in Locke. Here, evidence, as understood in law, is defined as any means to establish or disprove matters of fact. Evidence in this sense is very clearly said to concern probability, as distinguished from intuition or demonstration in mathematics, and, one might add, deductive logic. Of course I am sure Wigmore would be the first to say that demonstration can sometimes play a role in a legal case. A business dispute could involve a question whether certain expenses were added correctly. But that would only be arithmetic, not evidence in the sense with which Wigmore is concerned. Of course, Wigmore's definition of evidence makes evidence essentially relevant to the matter alleged.

Chapter 5 is entitled "Relevancy; Circumstantial Evidence." Wigmore's Greenleaf says:

> It is not the law which furnishes the test of relevancy, but logic. Probative value, or capability of supporting an inference, is a matter of reasoning, and the modes of reasoning must be the same in a court-room as in a laboratory; it is only the subject-matter which differs. Whatever rulings upon relevancy are found in our precedents are mere applications of logic by the Court....In other words, there is a law of relevancy,[3] consisting of those rulings which declare when one fact may be received in a court as the basis of inference to another....Thus a marked feature of our [Anglo-American] system of evidence, distinguishing it radically from the Continental system, and historically due to the separation of function between judge and jury, is the distinction between admissibility and proof. Our law of evidence leaves it usually to the jury to say what constitutes proof or demonstration [in the probabilistic sense]; and the rules of relevancy aim only to determine whether a given fact is of sufficient probative value to be admissible at all....
> 3. Professor Thayer, in 3 Harv. L. Rev. 143, 145, seems to take a contrary view. Yet, at any rate, the fact remains that such decisions exist, and whether they be termed logical or legal rulings, trials will be conducted according to them, and the profession must take note of

them. See Cushing, C[hief] J[ustice], in State *v.* Lapage, 57 N. H. 288. (Greenleaf 1899: 36, Greenleaf's emphasis, my square bracket additions of material)

Wigmore's Greenleaf is very Thayerian here, *pace* note 3, which concerns only the banner under which the work is done ("whether they be termed"). Wigmore's Greenleaf goes on to say:

> The degree of strength..., *i.e.* the test of probative value for purposes of admissibility, can hardly be stated except in terms so general as to be practically of little use. It us usually said that the fact [must indicate the fact to be proved] with a fair or reasonable degree of probability. Only rarely can anything more precise be attempted in the way of a general formula.... (Greenleaf 1899: 36, Greenleaf's emphasis, cite omitted)

In the context of the chapter, this is a frank equation of degree of relevance with degree of probability. Wigmore expressly identifies relevance with probative value on the next page. Wigmore says, "[A fact may have probative value or relevancy, and still be excluded for collateral reasons, *i.e.* reasons independent of its probative value...." (Greenleaf 1899: 37, Wigmore's beginning square bracket for his addition of new material to Greenleaf, Wigmore's emphasis). The vagueness of degree of probability in the block indented quotation is, of course, completely Keynesian as well, and antedates Keynes on probability by five years.

    I proceed to discuss Wigmore's own *Treatise*. The *Treatise* was published in Boston and is dedicated to the memory of two Americans, Charles Doe and James Bradley Thayer. It had a great impact on all major later Anglo-American legal theories of evidence, and shows a thorough knowledge of American, English, and Canadian law.

    Wigmore discusses Thayer and Stephen on relevance, and is also well versed on Greenleaf and Starkie. Wigmore says:

> Its one master, now passed away, James Bradley Thayer, set the example and marked the lines for all subsequent research....It was part of the aim in this work to fill out the missing places, accepting the results already reached by him. Portions of this remaining history, as here set forth, had been seen and accepted by him; [but the rest] lost the good fortune of his friendly perusal and possible concurrence. (Wigmore 1904: xii)

Wigmore identifies "Relevance" with "Probative Value" (Wigmore 1904: § 12 / p. 38). He considers Thayer and Stephen to be "two of the most original thinkers in the law of evidence" (Wigmore 1904:

§ 27 / p. 88). He sides with Thayer against Stephen by distinguishing logical relevance from admissibility and holding that there is no such thing as legal relevance, unless it be "a mere difference of phraseology" or "nomenclature only" from admissibility (Wigmore 1904: § 12 / pp. 38–39). Logical relevance is not a legal concept, and concerns the nature of all evidence. Wigmore says the concept of "*rational probative value* [applies regardless of] whether [the evidence is] practical or scientific, coarse and ready[,] or refined and systematic" (Wigmore 1904: § 9 / p. 31, Wigmore's emphasis; see § 27 / p. 88). Wigmore expressly admits degrees of probative value, and requires that evidence presented to a jury be of more than minimum probative value.

Wigmore says:

> [Courts] require a generally higher **degree of probative value** than would be asked in ordinary reasoning. The judge, in his efforts to prevent the jury from being satisfied by matters of slight value, capable of being exaggerated by prejudice and hasty reasoning, has constantly seen fit to exclude matter which does not rise to a clearly sufficient **degree of [probative] value**. In other words, legal relevancy [i.e. **logical relevancy as admissible in law**] denotes, first of all, something more than a minimum of probative value. **Each single piece of evidence must have a plus value.**[1]
> 1. **The degree of admissible probative value** is more particularly considered, for circumstantial evidence, post, § 38, and for testimonial evidence, post, §§ 475–478. (Wigmore 1904: § 28 / p. 91, Wigmore's italic emphasis, my boldface emphasis)

This is the heart of Keynes and of *FRE* Rule 401. But the sentence, "Each single piece of evidence must have a plus value," implies that every item of evidence, considered entirely by itself, must make a significant difference to what the evidence would otherwise be. This is liable to the criticism of slippery slope, and commits the fallacies of composition and division. There is no conceptual room for the accumulation of "mere scintillae" of evidence, or for one scintilla to be the straw that breaks the camel's back. This is also called the problem of the heap in the logical literature. (By extension, this is a problem with Rule 401 as well, if that rule is so interpreted. But it is clear to me that Rule 401 is *not* best so interpreted, since it speaks of "*any* tendency" to make the point in issue "more probable or less probable than it would be" otherwise. At least Wigmore makes it clear that for him, "legal relevancy" is really just a high degree of "logical relevancy," so that for him, the difference in degree is really within its proper *locus*, logical relevance.

Wigmore says on the next page:

> [The function of judges], in determining Relevancy, is not that of final arbiters, but merely of preliminary testers, *i.e.* that the evidentiary fact offered does not need to have strong, full, superlative, probative value,...but merely to be worth consideration by the jury. It is for the jury to give it the appropriate weight in effecting persuasion. The rule of law which the judge employs is concerned merely with admitting the fact through the evidentiary portal. The judge thus warns the opponent of the evidence that he is not entitled to complain of its lack of demonstrative power; **a mere capacity to help is enough for its admission**. (Wigmore 1904: § 29 / p, 92, Wigmore's italic emphasis, my boldface emphasis)

But evidently, an item's "capacity to help" is its "plus value."

Wigmore's *Treatise* was published in Boston in 1904, the same year Keynes wrote his first paper on probability, but two years before Keynes' more serious work on probability.

Courtenay Peregrine Ilbert

In 1902, the tenth edition of the *Encyclopaedia Britannica* appeared. It consisted of the ninth edition plus some new volumes. Volume 28, the fourth of the new volumes, included an article on "Evidence, Law of" by Courtenay Peregrine Ilbert (1841–1924), who became Clerk of the House of Commons the same year. The article is perhaps the best brief general summary of the history of English evidence law up to 1900 ever written. And it was written by a specialist at the end of that period. Thus the present section will be something of a brief review of the period.

Ilbert says of early English law, "Early Teutonic procedure knew nothing of evidence in the modern sense....The court had no desire to hear or weigh conflicting testimony. To do so would have been to exercise critical faculties, which the court did not possess, and the exercise of which would have been foreign to the whole spirit of the age" (Ilbert 1902: 331).

In Europe, interest in evidence began with Pope Innocent III and the Inquisition. But the standard of "full proof" was so high that almost nothing was ever fully proved. Thus there came to be a premium on confession, and thereby a premium on torture. "'Every safeguard of innocence was abolished or disregarded; torture was freely used. Everything seems to have been done to secure a conviction'" (Ilbert 1902: 331 quoting without citing the author). Nonetheless, there were rules of evidence, however poor and unused they may have been. "The rules of evidence attempted to graduate the weight to be attached to different types of testimony and almost to estimate that weight in numerical terms" (Ilbert 1902: 331).

Ilbert says:

> The first systematic treatise on the English law of evidence appears to have been written by Chief Baron Gilbert, who died in 1726, but whose Law of Evidence was not published until 1761. In writing it he is said to have been much influenced by Locke. It was highly praised by Blackstone [but severely criticized by Bentham]. (Ilbert 1902: 331–32, citation to Locke omitted)

Ilbert says:

> Bentham wrote his *Rationale of Judicial Evidence, Specially Applied to English Practice*, at various times between the years 1802 and 1812. By this time he had lost the nervous and simple style of his youth, and required an editor to make him readable....The manuscript...was edited for English reading, and to a great extent rewritten, by J. S. Mill, and was published in five volumes in 1827. [So edited, the book was] always shrewd and often profound. Bentham examined the practice of the courts by the light of practical utility. Starting from the principle that the object of judicial evidence is the discovery of truth, he condemned the rules which excluded some of the best sources of evidence. The most characteristic feature of the common-law rules of evidence, was, as Bentham pointed out, and, indeed, still is, their exclusionary character. They excluded and prohibited the use of certain kinds of evidence which would be used in ordinary inquiries. (Ilbert 1902: 332)

Ilbert beautifully states his criticism of Stephen's work:

> Its most original feature, but unfortunately also its weakest point, is its theory of relevancy. Pondering the multitude of "exclusionary" rules which had been laid down by the English courts, Stephen thought he had discovered the general principle on which those rules reposed, and could devise a formula by which the principle could be expressed. "My study of the subject," he says, "both practically and in books has convinced me that the doctrine that all facts in issue and relevant to the issue, and no others, may be proved, is the unexpressed principle which forms the centre of and gives utility to all the express negative rules which form the great mass

of this law." The result was the chapter on the Relevancy of Facts in the Indian Evidence Act, and the definition of relevancy in s. 7 of that Act. This definition was based on the view that a distinction could be drawn between things which were and things which were not causally connected with each other, and that relevancy depended on causal connexion. Subsequent criticism convinced Stephen that his definition was in some respects too narrow and in others too wide, and eventually he adopted a definition out of which all reference to causality was dropped. But even in their amended form the provisions about relevancy are open to serious criticism. The doctrine of relevancy, *i.e.* of the probative effect of facts, is a branch of logic, not of law, and is out of place both in an enactment of the Legislature and in a compendium of legal rules. The necessity under which Stephen found himself of extending the range of relevant facts by making it include facts "deemed to be relevant," and then narrowing it by enabling the judge to exclude evidence of facts which are relevant, illustrates the difference between the rules of logic and the rules of law. Relevancy is one thing; admissibility is another; and the confusion between them, which is much older than Stephen, is to be regretted. Rightly or wrongly English judges have, on practical grounds, declared [as] inadmissible evidence of facts, which are relevant in the ordinary sense of the term, and which are so treated in non-judicial inquiries. Under these circumstances the attempt so to define relevancy as to make it conterminous with admissibility is misleading, and most readers of Stephen's Act and Digest would find them more intelligible and more useful if "admissible" were substituted for "relevant" throughout. Indeed it is hardly too much to say that Stephen's doctrine of relevancy is theoretically unsound and practically useless. (Ilbert 1902: 333)

This criticism is basically the same as Thayer's. Ilbert agrees with Thayer that relevance belongs to logic as opposed to the law, and is not to be confused with legal admissibility. Ilbert agrees with Thayer that there is only logical relevance, that there is no such thing as legal relevance, and that talk of legal relevance ought to be replaced with talk about admissibility.

    Ilbert mentions Thayer three times elsewhere in the article (Ilbert 1902: 331, 334, 342). Ilbert says that "among modern text-writers,...the late Professor Thayer, of Harvard, was perhaps the most independent, instructive, and suggestive" (Ilbert 1902: 334). At the end of the article, Ilbert cites Thayer's *Preliminary Treatise on Evidence at the Common law* as a principal source on "the history of the English law of evidence" (Ilbert 1902: 342). Thus

Thayer was well-known in the English evidence law literature as early as 1902, and was even in the 1902 *Encyclopedia Britannica*, where any educated person with access to the *Encyclopedia* could read Ilbert's brief and clear advocacy of the theory that relevance belongs to "the rules of logic" and not to "the rules of law."

Despite agreeing with Thayer that Stephen overreaches on the concept of relevance, Ilbert accepts the same four basic rules of evidence law that Stephen does:

> The rules will be found, as might be expected, to be vague, to overlap each other, to require much explanation, and to be subject to many exceptions. They may be stated as follows:—(1) Facts not relevant to the issue cannot be admitted as evidence. (2) The evidence produced must be the best obtainable under the circumstances. (3) Hearsay is not evidence. (4) Opinion is not evidence. Ilbert 1902: 336)

Ilbert finds the first rule, the relevance rule, to have been "laid down [in England] by Baron Parke in 1837 (Wright v. Doe and Tatham, 7 A. and E. 384), when he described 'one great principle' in the law of evidence as being that 'all facts which are relevant to the issue may be proved'" (Ilbert 1902: 336 quoting Parke). This takes not only the rule, but even the term "relevant," back to 1837 in England. Baron James Parke (1782–1868) was a member of the Inner Temple, and went to Trinity College, Cambridge.

Ilbert continues:

> Stated in different forms, the rule has been made by FitzJames Stephen the central point of his theory of evidence. But relevancy, in the proper and natural sense, as we have said, is a matter not of law, but of logic. If Baron Parke's dictum relates to relevancy in its natural sense it is not true; if it relates to relevancy in a narrow and artificial sense, as equivalent to admissible, it is tautological. (Ilbert 1902: 336)

Ilbert holds that *not* "'all facts which are relevant to the issue may be proved'," due to the many policy rules that exclude much relevant evidence from being admissible, Ilbert says:

> Such practical importance as the rule of relevancy possesses consists, not in what it includes, but in what it excludes, and for that reason it seems better to state the rule in a negative or exclusive form. (Ilbert 1902: 336)

And as we saw, Ilbert does just that. His first rule is that whatever is irrelevant is to be excluded. But the contrapositive of this is that whatever is to be included as evidence is relevant, which seems awkward and unhelpful. Do we not also want a positive rule that, in the absence of issues of admissibility, whatever is relevant is to be included?

Ilbert now comes very close to Keynes indeed:

> But whether the rule is stated in a positive way or in a negative form its vagueness is apparent. No precise line can be drawn between "relevant" and "irrelevant" facts. The two classes shade into each other by imperceptible degrees. (Ilbert 1902: 336)

Is it possible that Keynes took his theory of degrees of probability as often unmeasurable from the *Encyclopedia Britannica*?

Ilbert says that the best evidence rule, which is the second of his own four foundational rules of evidence law, and which first came into prominence in the pronouncements of "Chief Justice Holt about the beginning of the 18th century," and in Lord Chief Baron Gilbert's book soon after, "does not seem to be more than a useful guiding principle which underlies, or may be used in support of, several rules" (Ilbert 1902: 337).

Ilbert and Stephen knew each other well. Ilbert succeeded Stephen as Law Member of the Council of the Governor-General of India / East India Company, in which capacity Stephen prepared the India Evidence Act. The Charter Act of 1833 created a Law Member for the Council of the East India Company (Hostettler 2013: 149). Thomas Babington Macaulay was the first Law Member. Stephen was the second, being appointed in July 1869 (Hostettler 2013: 150). "Sir Courtenay Ilbert...succeeded Stephen as Law Member," praising Stephen's work for its "strong will," if not always agreeing with Stephen (Hostettler 2013: 151). Ilbert was a member of Lincoln's Inn.

Elliott and Elliott

Byron Kosciusko Elliott (1835–1913) was a judge on the Indiana Supreme Court for twelve years; William Frederick Elliott (1859–1927) was his son, law partner, and co-author (Graydon 1927: 142–43). I discuss the Elliotts not because Keynes was likely to have read them, but because they deepen and illuminate the intellectual history of logical relevance in evidence law.

Almost every legal writer today understands Thayer's view and accepts it. But at the time Thayer wrote, not everyone agreed with him. The Elliotts argue for a concept of legal relevance in addition to the concept of logical relevance, even in the face of the later Thayer. Like the early Thayer, Chamberlayne's Taylor,

Chamberlayne, and Wigmore, they make legal relevance a higher degree of logical relevance, i.e., different only in degree. But that is not all they do.

In 1904, the Elliotts argue in their *Treatise on the Law of Evidence* that there is still room for a concept of legal relevance, as a sort of halfway-house between logical relevance on the one hand and legal admissibility on the other. They begin by agreeing with me that there is more to Best than the rule of best evidence:

> § 143. Generally—Views of older text writers.—The older text writers treated the rule requiring evidence to be relevant as one of the four great rules of evidence, and as, perhaps, the most important of all. Thus, Best says: "of all the rules of evidence the most universal and the most obvious is this—that the evidence adduced should be alike directed and confined to the matters which are in dispute, or which form the subject of investigation."[1] So, Greenleaf says: "We state as the first rule governing in the production of evidence, that the evidence must correspond with the allegations, and be confined to the point in issue."[2] Frustra probatur, quod probatum non relevat. Stephen goes even further and makes the admissibility of evidence depend almost entirely upon the question of relevancy, using the term "relevant" so as to be practically synonymous with "admissible."
>
> 1. 1 Best Ev. (Morgan's Ed.) § 251.
> 2. 1 Greenleaf Ev. § 51. See, also, Ferguson, &c. Co. v Manhattan Trust Co. 118 Fed. 791, 795; Edd v. Union, &c. Co. 25 Utah, 293, 71 Pac. 215. (Elliott 1904: 198)

All these authors identify the term "confined to" the point in issue as another way of saying that something is relevant to the point in issue. I translated the Latin earlier.

The Elliotts say in chapter 8, "Relevancy," under their boldfaced heading, "**Meaning of the term**":

> [F]acts relevant to the issue are facts from the existence of which inferences as to the truth of existence of the facts in issue may be justly drawn. As a general proposition, therefore, it may be said that *any* evidence that tends in *any reasonable* degree to establish the probability or improbability of a fact in issue, *no matter how slight* its weight may be, is relevant.[4]
> 4.....Indeed, it is said that "it is relevant to put in evidence any circumstance which tends to make the proposition at issue either more or less probable." 1 Wharton's Ev. § 21.... (Elliott 1904: 199, my emphasis)

This is very much like *FRE* Rule 401 and Keynes Perhaps the word "justly" is too legal, though it may simply mean "fairly." The main connection is that of relevance to probability. The Elliotts also say on the same page, "As a general rule,...there must be a *logical relation* between the evidentiary fact and a fact in issue" (Elliott 1904: 199, my emphasis). Like many writers before them, they allow that often a fact is relevant to a point in issue only in combination with other facts, as "a link in the chain of evidence tending to prove the issue by reasonable inference" (Elliott 1904: 199). Thus we see here a fourfold equation of (1) relevance, (2) confinement to the point in issue, (3) making the point in issue more or less probable (than it would be otherwise), and (4) there being a (nondeductive) logical (in the broad sense of rational) relation between the evidentiary fact and the point in issue.

The Elliotts say that so far, they have been basically discussing logical relevancy. They say, "If there is such a thing as legal relevancy distinct from logical relevancy it is at least based upon logical relevancy, for evidence cannot well be relevant in any sense unless it is logically relevant," since "no evidence is admissible unless it is logically relevant" (Elliott 1904: 200). After a preliminary discussion of the issues, they present Thayer's view, and then argue for legal relevancy. I think it is worth presenting their argument at length:

> **§ 147. Theoretical Objections.**—Professor Thayer says that the law furnishes no test of relevancy, but tacitly refers to logic and general experience for the test....He denies that there is any law or rule of legal relevancy[. He holds that] there are no rules of evidence that fix the limits and determine what is relevant....It is true that the law furnishes no very definite general rule for determining the relevancy of evidence in all cases, and that the admissibility of evidence is determined, in the main, by logic or modes of reasoning which are peculiar only in respect to the subject matter to which they are applied....But, in applying such reasoning and rules of logic to concrete cases, the courts have laid down rules or established precedents that may well be considered as constituting a law of relevancy, and we are not left wholly without a guide....
> **§ 148. Legal relevancy.**—Some of the authorities deny that there is any such thing as legal relevancy, and Professor Thayer calls it a "poor notion." Others draw a distinction between logical relevancy and legal relevancy, and consider that the term legal relevancy applies only to such matters as are not only logically relevant, but are not rendered inadmissible by any of the excluding rules of evidence. It seems to us that *a third view may be taken* which is more helpful and more

nearly correct than either of the others. We have already intimated that, in our opinion, there is such a thing as legal relevancy or a law of relevancy, although few attempts have been made to define it, and it is probably incapable of exact definition. In one case it is said: "Legal relevancy includes logical relevancy and requires *a higher standard* of evidentiary force. A fact logically relevant may be rejected, if in the opinion of the judge and under the circumstances of the case, it is considered essentially misleading or too remote." *It is, perhaps, not strictly accurate to say that legal relevancy requires "a higher standard of evidentiary force," but the statement quoted indicates the distinction we would draw.* If there were no rules of evidence and no established system, everything bearing in the *slightest* degree upon the controversy might well be admitted as logically relevant. But owning doubtless to our jury system, and the separation of functions of judge and jury, and also in part to reasons of convenience, it is for the court to say whether a matter is of *sufficient probative value* to be admissible or is too remote and conjectural to furnish any aid to the jury consistent with the practical administration of justice under our system; and it is for the jury to determine its weight or effect as proof where admitted. We think it may be said, therefore, that [for] evidence to be legally relevant, [it] must, in general, *reasonably* tend to establish the probability or improbability of a fact in issue....

§ **149. Legal relevancy—rules of exclusion**. As intimated in the last preceding section, it seems to us to be of little practical use, if not indeed misleading, to say that nothing is legally relevant if it comes within any rule of exclusion. If this view is taken[,] the term legal relevancy would seem to mean nothing more nor less than admissibility. Is it true that many matters are excluded that are logically relevant, but are they excluded because they are not legally relevant? Hearsay is excluded, but certainly not because it has no probative value....In these and other cases, evidence that would probably be of high probative value or effect if admitted, is excluded by some rule of exclusion based on convenience, policy, or some other consideration that may have nothing to do with the question as to whether it has any *reasonable* probative value or not. It seems to us a misuse of terms to say that evidence which is proximately connected with a fact in issue, and is of sufficient probative value as tending to prove it, is not relevant. If it is logically relevant, not too remote to furnish assistance in getting at the truth of the matter in controversy, and, except for some rule of exclusion based on other grounds, would be received by the courts

> in accordance with established rules, it is legally relevant, no matter whether it is inadmissible upon some other ground or not....To be legally relevant it must, we think, as a general rule at least, *reasonably* tend to render a fact in issue more or less probable or improbable [than it would otherwise be]. (Elliott 1904: 201–4, the Elliotts' boldface emphasis, my italic emphasis, cites omitted)

To sum up, the Elliotts may be said to define evidence as legally relevant just in case the evidence: (1) is logically relevant, (2) is of sufficiently high probative value to aid the jury; (3) reasonably tends to make a point in issue more or less probable than it would be otherwise; and (4) is not excluded as inadmissible by any of the exclusionary policy rules.

Conjunct (1) is in effect the genus, and conjuncts (2)–(4) are in effect three conjoined differences (differentiae). In contrast, the early Thayer, Chamberlayne's Taylor, Chamberlayne, and Wigmore make conjunct (2) the sole difference (differentia). No doubt there are indefinitely many ways to make such a dialectical move by adding new differences (new limiting conjuncts) to the genus, but I shall discuss only the conjuncts the Elliotts themselves add.

I have already argued earlier against conjunct (2) that it is a slippery slope (is a version of the problem of the heap), and commits the fallacies of composition and division.

Conjunct (3) contains the Elliotts' beautifully chosen key term, "reasonable." No better general term could be chosen. No other term could better express the essential vagueness which is needed here. As Aristotle says, it is a mark of lack of education to expect precision in a subject whose nature does not allow it. Yet the term only postpones the problems I have detected with conjunct (1). For conjuncts (1) and (2) are logically equivalent, and the reason they are is that for the Elliotts, the term "reasonable" means or mutually implies "sufficiently high probative value." For they are not going to apply either term unless they apply the other. Thus all the problems with conjunct (1) are also problems with conjunct (2).

I turn now to conjunct (3). For the Elliotts, legal relevance is a species of logical relevance. And not violating the exclusionary rules could be a differentia. But since these policy rules are not evidentiary in nature, they are really admissibility rules as opposed to evidentiary rules, just as the later Thayer says.

For the Elliotts to succeed, they need to use *evidentiary* rules in their definition of legal relevance. For if legal relevance is not essentially *evidentiary*, then legal relevance is *not* a species of evidentiary relevance. But on their own account of the exclusionary rules, all they are entitled to speak of is *policy* rules.

One might object that for the Elliotts, legal relevance is evidentiary because its genus is evidentiary, not to mention conjuncts (2) and (3). My reply is that this is correct, but legal relevance is really a hybrid concept, since conjunct (4) concerns the concept of policy admissibility, while the rest concerns the concept of evidence. And perhaps that is not so bad, if we waive the problems with conjuncts (1) and (2). Perhaps such a concept of legal relevance may even be useful. But it is a hybrid concept for all that. To that extent we have left the realm of evidence behind. Conjunct (4) is properly a mere scope restriction, not a difference of a genus. It would be like saying that brown is a difference of the genus cat. Yes, "brown cat" excludes nonbrown cats from its scope. But brown is nothing like a difference. For brown cat is nothing like a species of cat. "Brown cat" fails to state the essence of a species of cat. Brown cat is not what any species of cat is. The color of a cat is accidental.

The Elliotts are right to note that the exclusionary rules of evidence law always or almost function *as a matter of fact* to raise the bar of relevance, that is, to raise the degree of relevance, or at least the degree of clarity of relevance. But that is an accidental as opposed to essential function of theirs. It is not their essential reason for being. It is not their essential purpose. It is not why we have them. They are not rules or guidelines of inductive logic. They are not axioms or theorems of probability theory. They are not scientific theories or even guidelines. They are not essential to evaluating the evidence qua evidence. They do not function to evaluate the evidence as such at all. Strictly speaking, such rules have no impact on the specific evidentiary situation, and only a logically accidental impact on the level or quality of evidence admitted in a court. The reasons we have them are *simply not evidentiary reasons* for judges' deciding what evidence the jury may or may not consider.

Let us use the Elliott's own example. Why do we generally exclude hearsay? Is it because hearsay is not probative? No. To quote the Elliotts themselves again, "Hearsay is excluded, but certainly not because it has no probative value" (Elliott 1904: 203). And they explain why it *is* excluded: "In these and other cases, evidence that would probably be of high probative value or effect if admitted, is excluded by some rule of exclusion based on convenience, policy, or some other consideration that may have nothing to do with the question as to whether it has any reasonable probative value or not" (Elliott 1904: 203).

Assume now that the hearsay rule prohibits all hearsay in general for the reason that hearsay in general is not very *reliable evidence*. This would make the rule essentially concerned with evidentiary relevance on a *general* level. But the rule would still not function to weigh the *specific* probative value of each particular item of hearsay evidence. And if the rule *were* essentially concerned with weighing probative value, then that is what it *would* do in individual cases of hearsay. That is, it would function to evaluate cases of hearsay on whether or not they are members of the hearsay species of logically relevant evidence.

To sum up, if hearsay is excluded by policy, then hearsay evidence is much like brown cat. There is a general scope restriction. But when hearsay is excluded by policy, it is being excluded from being a *species* of evidence, or more precisely a difference. It is really a species (or difference) of the genus of inadmissible items. And policy exclusions do not, as such, state either what evidence is or what it is not. Policy is not what evidence is. Policy is not even part of what evidence is. Logically relevant is what evidence is. The genus of inadmissible items includes both logically irrelevant items and policy-excluded logically relevant items. Cases of hearsay can belong to either of those two types of inadmissible items, so it is a cross-classification relative to those two sub-categories.

The Elliotts recognize the relativity of both relevance and admissibility, and even what may be called their multiple relativity:

> [Evidence] may be relevant to one issue or fact in issue. although not to another....Evidence may be relevant and admissible upon one issue or for one purpose or as against one party, although it would be irrelevant or inadmissible for some other reason upon another issue in the case or for another purpose or against another party. (Elliott 1904: 204)

Evidence can be relevant not only to certain issues, but to certain parties, and to certain purposes. Other things being equal, a bloody knife with Smith's name on it is more relevant to a stabbing than to a theft, more relevant to Smith than to Jones, and more relevant to showing who owned the knife than showing who used it. And the relativity of relevance may be more multiple than that. Keynes, we know, holds that the probability of an event is always relative to the body of evidence we have.

This concludes my review of Anglo-American evidence law on the topic of relevance. The following two charts of the history of Anglo-American evidence law show the main trends:

History Chart of Relevance Rules

Evidence must (be):
Today: logically relevant, that is, tend to make more or less probable (Am.; Eng.)
1985 Cross: logically relevant (Eng.)
1958 Cross: relevant (Eng.)
1941 James: logically relevant (Am.)
1921 Keynes: logically relevant (Eng. philosopher-economist)
1906 Keynes: relevant (Eng. philosopher-economist)
1904 Elliott and Elliott: logically and legally relevant (Am.)
1900 Thayer: logically relevant; there is no legal relevance (Am.)
1899 Straker: ascertain the fact or point in issue, for or against (Am. citing Eng.)
1898 Thayer: logically relevant; there is no legal relevance (Am.)
1897 Chamberlayne's Taylor: logically and legally relevant (Am.)
1894 Mayne: relevant
1883: Chamberlayne's notes in Best: logically and legally relevant (Am.)
1880–81 Thayer: logically and legally relevant (Am.)
1876 Stephen: relevant (Eng.)
1876 Starkie: tend to prove or disprove the point in issue (Eng.)
1872 Mayne: relevant
1868 Phillipps: relevant; confined to points in issue (Eng.; Am. ed.)
1864 Dickson: not be irrelevant (Scot.)
1859 Phillipps: relevant; confined to points in issue (Eng.; Am. ed.)
1859 Halsted: relevant and pertinent; tend to prove the issue; confined to the issue (Am.)
1859 Powell: relevant; confined to the points in issue; correspond with the allegations (Eng.)
1854 Best: directed and confined to the matters in dispute; directly or indirectly relevant (Eng.)
1852 Burke: relevant (Eng. philosopher)
1847 Calvert's Gresley: relevant and pertinent to the issue (Eng.)
1842 Greenleaf: relevant; confined to the point in issue; correspond with the allegations (Am.)
1842 Taylor: confined to the points in issue; tend to prove or disprove the matter of fact under investigation (Eng.)
1839 Starkie: tend to prove or disprove the issue (Eng.)
1838 Phillipps: approximate to the allegations (Eng.)
1837 Parke: "all facts which are relevant to the issue may be proved" (Eng.)
1831 Roscoe: confined to the issue (Eng.)
1830 Starkie: tend to prove or disprove the point in issue; ascertain the truth of the allegations (Eng.; Am. ed.)

1827 Bentham: pertinent; add / contribute to discovery of the truth; tend to produce a persuasion for or against (Eng.)
1824 Peake: relate or connect to issue in dispute (Eng.; Am. ed.)
1822 Phillipps: bear upon / confined to the point in issue (Eng.)
1820 Phillipps: relate / refer to / ascertain the facts in issue (Eng.; Am. ed.)
1817 Buller: relate or connect to the issue; prove no more than the substance of the issue (Eng.)
1816 Phillipps: confined to facts or points in issue (Eng.; Am. ed.)
1791 Gilbert: relevant to the cause of action; relevant to the point under judicial inquiry; relevant to the point in issue; relate to the subject in dispute
1789 Morgan: ascertain the very point in issue (Irish pub.)
1785 Buller: prove no more than substance of point in issue (Eng.)
1772 Buller: prove no more than substance of issue (Eng.)
1768 Blackstone: ascertain the very point in issue (Eng.)
1739 Duncombe: agreeable to the issue; not collateral, surplusage, or a variance (Eng.)
1726 Gilbert: admit degrees of proof (Eng.)
1717 Nelson: answer the issue / maintain the issue (Eng.)
1717 Blount citing Coke: make the point at issue evident (Eng.)
1690 Locke: admit degrees of probability (Eng. philosopher)
1666 Eure: answer the issue / prove the issue / make the point in issue evident to the jury (Eng.)
1628 Coke: make the point in issue evident to the jury (Eng.)
1256 Bracton: (medieval, no relevance rule) (Eng.)

I omit some court opinions. I also omit the relevance rules that are special to tort law. A chart of broad time periods follows:

History Chart of Common Terms for Relevance

Evidence must (be):
1880–81–today: logically relevant
1791–today: relevant
1830–today: conform with / ascertain the allegations
1772–today: be confined to / prove no more than (the substance of) what is in issue
1690–today: admit of degrees of probability / proof / certainty
1628–today: (help) ascertain / make evident the point in issue

I omit the common terms that are special to tort law.
     Keynes appears to belong to all five of these general phases of the Anglo–American legal tradition, expressly or implicitly.

Here is a third chart of special interest on Keynes and the origins of his theory that probability is degree of logical relevance:

Relevantist Members of the Inner Temple

John Maynard Keynes (1883–1946)
Arthur Richard Jelf (1837–1917)
Lumley Smith (1833?–1918)
John Dawson Mayne (1828–1917)
James Fitzjames Stephen (1829–1894)
John George Malcolm (obit. 1872)
Edmund Powell (1826?–1864)
Colin Blackburn (1813–1896)
George Morley Dowdeswell (1809–1893)
Henry Roscoe (1800–1836)
James Parke (1782–1868)
Thomas Starkie (1782–1849)
Samuel March Phillipps (1780–1862)
John Morgan (fl. 1789)
William Nelson (fl. 1717)
Giles Duncombe (fl. 1702)
Thomas Blount (1618–1679)
Samson Eure (d. 1659)
Edward Coke (1552–1634)
Thomas Littleton (ca. 1415–1481)

Anglo-American Relevance Law Today

Today logical relevance is the heart of Anglo-American evidence law, as any good English or American law school course on evidence law will teach, and as any good English or American treatise on evidence law will explain (Lempert 2011; Cross 1985). The rule that only logically relevant evidence is admissible applies in courts having jurisdiction over hundreds of millions of people.

Thayer's arguments for logical relevance and against legal relevance are the basis of American state and federal evidence law today. Thayer is praised in the Advisory Committee's Note to *Federal Rules of Evidence* Rule 402, and in George F. James' 1941 article, "Relevancy, Probability, and the Law" (James 1992 / 1941: 389–90 / 701–5), which the Advisory Committee's Note to Rule 401 cites.

Federal Rules does not expressly speak either of "logical" relevance or of "legal" relevance. But *Federal Rules* certainly does not speak as if there were two kinds of relevance; and Rule 401 clearly has logical relevance in mind. It basically defines "relevant evidence" as Thayer and Keynes understand it. Rule 401 says:

Rule 401. Definition of "Relevant Evidence"
"Relevant evidence" means any evidence having any tendency to make the existence of any fact that is of consequence to the determination of the action more or less probable than it would be without the evidence. (West 1995: Rule 401)

Granted, Rule 401 reverses Keynes and defines relevance in terms of probability instead of the other way around. But the basic implication of either definition is that the two terms are logically equivalent. Then in modern classical logic, either term can be formally used to define the other. For Frege or Russell, there would be nothing *formally* wrong either with Keynes or with Rule 401, even though the definitions go in opposite directions. Formally speaking, the choice of definition would be logically arbitrary. It would be no different from defining equilateral as equiangular or vice versa. Either way, we eliminate a term and logically guarantee truth-preservation. But I suggest that in philosophy, we want more than that. We want theoretical definitions that state what a thing is, if at all possible. We want to illuminate what things are. And my own logical intuition is that it is intellectually more illuminating to use the (intuitively) *relatively* clearer notion of relevance to explain the relatively more obscure notion of probability.

I grant that the whole history of logical relevance, both in deductive and in inductive logic, shows that the notion of relevance is problematic. But the problems with relevance are basically technical issues in logic, as we have seen in chapter 9. No one doubts that relevance exists in the sense that *some* evidence is relevant to a given issue and other evidence is not. We may say that ordinary probabilistic relevance, in some sense or senses, *exists*. Of course, one may object that there is no one concept of relevance, if there is no one thing that is appropriately called relevance. But the situation is different for probability. There the problem is precisely whether there is *any* such thing, that is, whether we can develop a plausible theory of probability such that *anything* is probable, even if the word "probability" is taken to be both ordinary and univocal. That is Hume's problem of skepticism.

One might well object that if Hume denies probability, then he would deny probabilistic relevance as well. He would only admit patterns of impressions. And conversely, if Keynes admits synthetic *a posteriori* logical relevance, then he would admit probability as well. My reply is that this only shows that the two concepts stand or fall together. And that only shows that they are interdefinable after all. Thus we come back to my original intuition, which is only that if the two concepts are logically equivalent, which is all the objector is pointing out, then it is more illuminating to define probability in terms of relevance than the other way around. And even if there is a battle of conflicting intuitions on the point, I am not clearly wrong.

Let us assume for the sake of the argument that I am right that in philosophy, it is best to define probability as relevance, and not the other way around, so as to illuminate the true nature of things. From that, it does not follow in the least that *outside* of philosophy, there logically cannot be good reasons for going in the opposite direction and defining relevance as probability. Now, the Advisory Committee's Note to Rule 401 suggests two *practical* reasons for defining relevance in terms of probability in the field of evidence law. The Note says:

> Compare Uniform Rule 1(2) which states the crux of relevancy as "a tendency in reason," thus [1] perhaps emphasizing unduly the logical process and ignoring the need to draw upon experience or science to validate the general principle upon which relevancy in a particular situation depends....
>
> Dealing with probability in the language of the rule has the added virtue of [2] avoiding confusion between questions of admissibility and questions of the sufficiency of the evidence. (Advisory Committee's Note to Rule 401, my square bracket numbering of the reasons)

Clearly, any such practical reasons would not apply to a theoretical definition in philosophy. As to practical reason (1), Keynes makes relevance a purely logical relationship between propositions, yet can very easily and correctly note that experience and scientific findings are precisely what we ordinarily assert in our evidentiary premises. Thus for Keynes, there is no undue emphasis of logic over experience in our understanding of probability. As to practical reason (2), Keynes' theory does not even appear to confuse either the concept of probability or the concept of evidentiary relevance with the concept of legal admissibility. For that matter, neither do the frequency theory or Ramsey's theory. Philosophical theories of probability, as such, have nothing to do with the legal admissibility of evidence.

Yet these two practical reasons may be very useful indeed for attorneys. The very fact the Advisory Committee saw fit to state them practically tells us what many attorneys are prone to do.

The Advisory Committee in effect agrees with Keynes that "Relevancy is not an inherent characteristic of any item of evidence but exists only as a relation between an item of evidence and....the fact to be proved" (Advisory Committee's Note to Rule 401). The Committee also agrees with Thayer that, in the rationalist tradition of evidence theory, to which Keynes belongs:

> The provisions that all relevant evidence is admissible, with certain exceptions, and that evidence which is not relevant is not admissible are "a presupposition involved in the very conception of a rational system of evidence" Thayer, Preliminary Treatise on Evidence 264 (1898). (Advisory Committee's Note to Rule 402)

These similarities between Keynes and the Advisory Committee are structurally deeper than the issue whether logical relevance is best defined in terms of probability or vice versa. See Twining (1994: ch. 3, "The Rationalist Tradition of Evidence Scholarship"; 1986: ch. 1, "The Rationalist Tradition of Evidence Scholarship".

For a more detailed discussion of various rival definitions of legal relevance than I can offer here, see Hunt (2012).

Continental Evidence Law

What is Continental European evidence law like? Mirjan R. Damaška finds that in "legal systems outside the [Anglo-American] common law world, we find that relevance so understood plays hardly any role in legal discourse. In the Continental tradition[,] the probative value of information is seldom discussed apart from the credibility of its carrier" (Damaška 1997: 55). Damaška asks, "Why is a conceptual tool so central in Anglo-American procedure without importance in other systems?" (Damaška 1997: 55). He answers that the Anglo-American system bifurcates the court into judge and jury, where the judge is the gate-keeper of admissibility and the jury weighs degree of relevance or probative value. But in Continental unitary courts, judges handle everything, so to them "the need to express these two aspects of evidence processing by two separate conceptual categories appears as a barren theoretical impulse" (Damaška 1997: 56). My reply is that this only shows that the concept of relevance does not matter in *practice* in Continental law. It matters in *theory* to everyone. For theory is general. And it advances the theoretical analysis to distinguish relevance from admissibility. Anglo-American logical niceties, such as the distinction between direct and indirect relevance, and relatedly, among levels of (interim, penultimate, and ultimate) probanda (T. Anderson 2005: ch. 2–3), advance the analysis even further, but need not detain us here. Within the theory of Anglo-American evidence law, our mission is a simple one. We need only point out that Damaška, and Continental evidence law in general, overlook the obvious. Namely, Bentham's general concept of evidence, its survival in Best's concept of natural evidence, and its development in Stephen as relevance and in Thayer as logical relevance, is precisely a concept of *evidence in general*, which both intends to and succeeds in going beyond not only Anglo-American law in particular, but all law in general. Thus to say there is no "Anglo-American" concept of relevance on the Continent is to say that there is no *general* concept of evidence on the Continent. The only sense in which the concept of logical relevance is Anglo-American is the historical sense in which it was developed by Anglo-American thinkers. And ironically, even in this historical sense, the logical theory of probability was originally Continental. As we saw near the beginning of this chapter, Leibniz and a host of other early modern Continental thinkers developed this theory. And perhaps Continental jurists do not think they need a general logical concept of evidence. But on the theoretical level, that is their loss. Was it not traditional Continental philosophy of education that professionals in every field should have at least some understanding of the philosophical foundations of their subject?

Panayot Butchvarov argues that there is no general concept of evidence because there is nothing all the things we deem to be evidence have in common (Butchvarov 1970: 283–87). And even if the general concept of evidence is that of logical relevance, I think Butchvarov might well reply in turn that there is no one thing that all the things we deem to be *logically relevant* have in common. My reply is that on my own theory, there is something they all have in common, something phenomenological: objectively seeming to be the case. See note 4 to the present chapter

Langbein says:

> The great chasm that separates the modern Continental legal systems from the Anglo-American systems is largely about the conduct of fact-finding. On the Continent, professional judges take the main responsibility for investigating....Prototypically, our trial judge sits with a jury....
>
> Sit in one of our trial courtrooms, civil or criminal, and you hear counsel interrupting incessantly to raise objections founded upon the rules of evidence. These incantations are so familiar that they have passed into the popular culture. Close your eyes and you can hear Perry Mason or the protagonists of "L.A. Law" or similar television fare bound to their feet, objecting fiercely: "Immaterial!" "Hearsay!" "Opinion!" "Leading question!"
>
> Cross the Channel, enter a French or an Italian or a Swedish courtroom, and you hear none of this. Over the past two decades I have had frequent occasion to

observe German civil and criminal proceedings. I have heard much hearsay testimony, but never a hearsay objection. No one complains of leading questions, and opinion evidence pours in without objection. (Langbein 1996: 1168–69)

Langbein duly cites Damaška, but quotes "a famous dictum in the *Berkeley Peerage Case* in 1816" to show that English judges have long been aware that Continental judges felt free to admit hearsay because they considered themselves objective professionals and trusted their judgment, while in England this could not be done. In England, an exclusionary rule was found by experience to be needed because the jury decides what the facts are, and they are ordinary laypersons unpredictably swayed by hearsay (Langbein 1996: 1169). Hearsay, of course, is just one example of a policy objection to admitting relevant evidence.

Langbein is right that Damaška's view, that evidence law as Anglo-American lawyers know it does not exist in Continental law due to the absence of the jury system, is far from new. The major writers agree with the *Berkeley* dictum. Thayer says in 1898:

> It seems, then, that our law of evidence, while it is, emphatically, a rational system, is yet a peculiar one. In the shape it has taken, it is not at all a necessary development of the rational method of proof; so that, where people did not have the jury, or, having once had it, did not keep it, as on the continent of Europe, although they, no less than we, worked out a rational system, they developed under the head of evidence, no separate and systematized branch of the law. (Thayer 1898: 270)

Wigmore's Greenleaf says in 1899:

> Thus a marked feature of our [Anglo-American] system of evidence, distinguishing it radically from the Continental system, and historically due to the separation of function between judge and jury, is the distinction between admissibility and proof. Our law of evidence leaves it usually to the jury to say what constitutes proof or demonstration [in the probabilistic sense]; and the rules of relevancy aim only to determine whether a given fact is of sufficient probative value to be admissible at all.... (Greenleaf 1899: 36)

Ilbert says in 1902:

> It was by reference to trial by jury that the English rules of evidence were originally framed; it is by the

> peculiarities of this form of trial that many of them are to be explained; it is to this form of trial alone that some of the most important of them are exclusively applicable. The negative, exclusive, or exclusionary rules which form the characteristic features of the English law of evidence, are [precisely] the rules in accordance with which the judge guides the jury....These rules of exclusion are peculiar to English law and to systems derived from English law. (Ilbert 1902: 333)

And the Elliotts say in 1904:

> But, owing doubtless to our jury system, and the separation of the functions of judge and jury, and also in part to reasons of convenience, it is for the court to say whether a matter is of sufficient probative value to be admissible...consistent with the practical administration of justice under our system.... (Elliott 1904: 202)

No doubt there are earlier statements.

Why is there no real Continental jury system? It is because Continental evidence law is basically inquisitorial and descends from the papal Inquisition. Ilbert says:

> Modern Continental procedure, as embodied in the most recent codes, has removed the worst features of inquisitorial procedure....[But] the French Code of Criminal Procedure...still retains some of the features of the unreformed procedure which was condemned in the 18th century by Voltaire and the *philosophes*. Military procedure is in the rear of civil procedure, and the trial of Dreyfus at Rennes presented some interesting archaisms. Among these were the weight attached to the rank and position of witnesses as opposed to the intrinsic character or their evidence, and the extraordinary importance attributed to confession even when made under suspicious circumstances and supported by flimsy evidence. (Ilbert 1902: 331, Ilbert's emphasis)

Again, the inquisitorial standard of proof was so high, it rarely could be met. The result was that torture to gain confessions was used well into the nineteenth century, until Cesare Beccaria (1738–1794) awakened the conscience of Europe with his *On Crimes and Punishents* (Beccaria 1963 / 1764). But even with torture abolished and other improvements, the Continent remained inquisitorial and never adopted the jury system as a safeguard of human rights. Of course, the Continental democracies have many other safeguards of human rights, and are very democratic on the whole. In some ways, they may be more democratic than Anglo-American nations.

The Modern Logic Background

In everyday use, legal use, and Keynes' use alike, "logical" means much the same thing as 'rational' or 'reasonable'; and "relevant to" means much the same as 'significant for' or 'related to'. Thus "logically relevant to" simply means 'rationally related to as evidence'. This meaning is so general that either deductive logic, inductive logic, or both might well be meant. But while Keynes and some lawyers today use "logically relevant" in this broad way, some nineteenth century legal writers discuss evidence in a specific way that casts inductive logic in the garb of deductive logic.

To explain what many nineteenth century legal theorists have in mind, I will use an example. Where a lawyer might offer a simple probability argument from two particular facts to a third:

(A)   1. In bloody murder #1, DNA identified people on scene.
        2. In bloody murder #2, DNA identified people on scene.
        3. Therefore probably, in bloody murder #3, DNA will identify people on scene.

Stephen, Taylor, and Thayer would first generalize to a universal statement:

(B)   1. In bloody murder #1, DNA identified people on scene.
        2. In bloody murder #2, DNA identified people on scene.
        3. Therefore probably, in all bloody murders DNA will identify people on scene.

They would then use universal statement (B3) as the major premiss of this *formally valid deductive* argument:

(C)   1. Probably, in all bloody murders DNA will identify people on scene. (inductive general principle as major premiss)
        2. Bloody murder #3 takes place (evidence as minor premiss).
        3. Therefore probably, in bloody murder #3 DNA will identify people on scene (material fact to be proved).

While argument (C) is a deductive argument in form, that is just window dressing, since our only evidence for (C)'s major premiss (1) is described in the premises of inductive argument (B). (B) and (C) taken together are a way of saying what argument (A) says, but with (C) in deductively valid syllogistic form. The benefit is that we are forced to articulate a universal statement which will be both the conclusion (3) of (B) and the major premiss (1) of (C). Often there is no one best way of doing that, since there are different generalizations we might make about the earlier bloody murders. Thus we are forced to articulate exactly which probable universal statement we are basing our conclusion on, and that may affect how good our argument is. This is what I meant when I spoke of the analytically helpful but superficially deductive, frankly syllogistic format of such arguments earlier in this chapter.

Probabilistic syllogisms were studied in the eighteenth century by Johann Heinrich Lambert. Lambert argued in 1764 that "three quarters of the A's are B's; C is an A, therefore with probability 3/4, C is a B" (Hailperin 1988: 144); compare Wigmore (1904: § 30). For a recent discussion, see Murphy (2008: 5–6).

The probabilistic syllogism is due to Aristotle. Richard Sorabji says of Aristotle's *Posterior Analytics*:

> [Aristotle recognizes] that in natural science it is not always possible to obtain exceptionless generalisations. Often a predicate will attach to members of the kind only for the most part. In An. Post., he is not confident that broadness of leaf, or coagulation of sap, will have its effect of making the leaves fall in every instance. Twice, therefore, he discusses degenerate scientific syllogisms in which the predicates attach only for the most part to their subjects (An. Post. I 30, 87*b*19–27; II 12, 96*a*8–19). In these syllogisms, the thing to be explained will be a truth that holds for the most part, and the explanatory premisses will be neither necessary nor universal, but again true only for the most part. (Sorabji 1980: 50)

I omit the subtleties of Sorabji's discussion (Sorabji 1980: 50–51).

Paul Slomkowski points out that in Aristotle's *Topics*, topoi of the greater, lesser, or like degree include syllogisms about greater, lesser, or similar probabilities or likelihoods (Slomkowski 1997: 147 quoting Aristotle, *Topics* 115a6–8; Aristotle 1960: 373).

I myself could point out that Aristotle says in the *Rhetoric*:

> Again, conclusions that state what is merely usual or possible must be drawn from premises that do the same, just as 'necessary' conclusions must be drawn from 'necessary' premises; this too is clear to us from the *Analytics*.[13]
> 13. *An. Pr.* 1. 8, 12–14, 27. (*Rhetoric* 1357a25–30 / Aristotle 1968c: 1332, note 13 by the editor)

Thus Leibniz was unfair to disparage Aristotle for lacking any logic of probability (Leibniz 1966 / 1765 / 1704: 466).

Again, Anglo-American evidence law did not develop a logical interpretation of probability so much as a logical framework for analyzing probability arguments. Legal scholars came to see that inductive arguments can always be rewritten as deductive arguments, and that while that could not alter the strength of an argument, it could articulate more precisely what the induction was. The deductive arguments were conceived as Aristotelian syllogisms whose major premisses describe general principles arrived at inductively, whose minor premisses describe items of evidence, and whose conclusions describe the probability that certain material facts obtain or fail to obtain. In this way, evidence law maintained a connection between formal deductive relevance and probabilistic relevance, though merely as a matter of format.

As Shapiro documents so well, the early modern tradition of evidence law sought to assimilate evidence law to logic at virtually every turn (Shapiro 1991: 30). In the eighteenth century, lawyers often cited the 1724 Isaac Watts, *Logick, or the Right Use of Reason in the Inquiry after Truth* (Shapiro 1991: 31). In the nineteenth century, they often cited the 1807 Richard Kirwan, *Logick, or an Essay on the Elements, Principles, and Different Modes of Reasoning*. Kirwan recommends that logic be carefully studied in all countries using the jury system, and often cites legal matters. Shapiro says:

> Indeed Kirwan appeared to have considered lawyers and prospective jurors as his primary audience....
>   It is thus not surprising that David Hoffman should recommend Kirwan's *Logick* and [Thomas] Reid's *Essays* to students of law or that other writers on legal evidence should recommend logical or epistemological oriented treatises such as those of Locke, Hartley, Reid, Abercrombie, Kirwan, and others.... [L]ater writers favored Kirwan, [Whately], and John Stuart Mill over earlier works. (Shapiro 1991: 32)

James Glassford, Daniel McKinnon, and William Wills treated evidence law as based on, if not literally part of, logic. This view became quite common by the nineteenth century. Indeed, most eighteenth and nineteenth century scholars saw nothing special about legal reasoning (Shapiro 1991: 34, 228, 232–33). As Murphy says in his *Murphy on Evidence*, sect. 1.3, "Philosophical Basis for Use of Evidence":

> Twining draws attention to the fact that, despite a wide divergence of opinion as to the detail of both the science and the law of evidence, every writer on the subject since it began to be the subject of methodical study in

> the eighteenth century has agreed, either explicitly or implicitly, on a philosophical basis for evidence....The basic tenet...is that the drawing of rational inferences from evidence is capable of leading to correct knowledge of past events, and is the only, or the only known, method of arriving at correct knowledge of past events. (Murphy 2008: 3–4, cites omitted)

In contrast, early modern legal scholars were generally against applying the mathematical probability calculus of Laplace, partly because criminal convictions required the beyond a reasonable doubt standard, but chiefly because outside of actuarial situations, early attempts to apply the calculus were unworkable. Numbers simply could not be assigned to the contractual risks and evidentiary likelihoods that triers of fact had to weigh (Shapiro 1991: 253–55; Franklin 1991: 123–44). And that is just what Mayne and Keynes say. Keynes resolves the problem by holding that not all degrees of probability, i.e., degrees of logical relevance, can be assigned numbers. In this way, Keynes crowns the assimilative tradition by assimilating evidence law and the probability calculus alike to Russell's logic in *Principles*. But he is far from original on whether probabilities can always be assigned numerical values.

When Did Keynes First Write of Relevance?

So far, I have mainly discussed only whether Keynes might have learned of relevance from Burke, Bentham, or Mayne. These are all plausible sources of his view. I shall shortly discuss what I think the main possibilities are. But first we must briefly discuss *when* Keynes first acquired the concept of logical relevance, so as to set an upper time limit to our time line of possible origins.

Again, 1904 is the year Keynes read Moore, wrote his first paper on probability, and read it to the Apostles. There is no doubt that Keynes read Moore's book carefully. Skidelsky says, "The inside covers of Keynes' own copy of *Principia Ethica* are covered with pencilled notes" (Skidelsky 1986: 146).

In 1906, Keynes wrote the first version of his fellowship dissertation on probability; it was deemed unready for submission. In 1907, he wrote the second and final version, which he submitted. Vincent Barnett says:

> In the autumn of 1905, [Keynes] sketched out a draft outline for a project called a "Scheme for an Essay on the Principles of Probability." In December 1907, he submitted as a fellowship dissertation to King's College

a work entitled "The Principles of Probability." Thus, between the end of 1905 and the end of 1907, he had continued working on [probability.] (Barnett 2013: 24)

Barnett says a few pages later:

Chapter 16 of Keynes's 1907 dissertation on "The Principles of Probability" was entitled "The relation of Probability to Ethics, and the Doctrine of Mathematical Expectation." This was directly connectable to the chapter in Moore's book entitled "Ethics in Relation to Conduct." [Thus] his early interest in probability was linked to his early interest in ethics. (Barnett 2013: 32)

Of course, ethics and probability were linked for Moore as well.

Keynes writes in chapter 1 of his second or revised dissertation on probability, which he submitted on December 12, 1907:

In the ordinary course of thought and argument we are constantly asserting that the truth of one statement, while not [deductively] *proving* another, is nonetheless *some ground* for believing the second. We assert that, with the evidence at our command, we *ought* to hold such and such a belief. We expressly say we have *rational* grounds for assertions which are, in the usual logical sense, unproved. We allow, in fact, that statements may be unproved, without for that reason being unfounded. Nor does reflexion show that it is information of purely psychological import which we wish to convey when we use such expressions as these....We are in fact claiming to **cognize** correctly a **logical connexion** between one set of propositions which we call our evidence and which we take to be true, and another set which we call our conclusions and to which we attach more or less weight according to the grounds supplied by the first. We recognise that *objectively* evidence can be *real* evidence and yet not *conclusive* evidence....I do not think I am straining the use of words in speaking of this as the **probability** relation or the relation of **probability**. (Skidelsky 1983: 183 quoting Keynes 1907: ch. 1, Keynes' italic emphasis, my boldface emphasis)

Thus Keynes states a logicist theory of probability as early as 1907. Keynes' dismissal of "psychological import" is much like Frege's and Husserl's anti-psychologism. Keynes continues:

The idea of a premisses's having *some* weight to establish a conclusion, of its lying *somewhere* between cogency and [total] *irrelevancy*, is altogether foreign to a logic in which the premiss must either prove or not prove the alleged conclusion. This opinion is, from the nature of the case, incapable of positive proof. The notion presents itself to the mind, I feel, as something independent and unique....

Yet that 'probability' is, *in the strict sense* indefinable, need not trouble us much; it is a characteristic which it shares with many of our most necessary and fundamental ideas.... (Skidelsky 1983: 184 quoting Keynes 1907: ch. 1, my emphasis)

This text includes most of his basic ideas in just a few words. All that is missing is the relativity of probability to one's body of evidence. Most importantly for our purposes, Keynes uses the term "irrelevancy" as a term applicable in logic, though not in formal deductive logic. That is, for him the *locus* of relevance is in logic. Of course, his Platonic theory of logic as timelessly real, and its attendant theory of cognition of abstract logical entities, goes beyond evidence law and comes from Russell, if not also from Moore. For a premiss to be *totally* irrelevant to a conclusion is for it to have to have *no* logical connection with that conclusion at all. Evidently it is only later that he understands there to be degrees of logical relevance which are degrees of probability. But the texts do imply that there is a theoretical continuum between deductive logic and inductive logic, with deductive logic at the extremes and inductive logic covering everything in between. Deductive implication and total irrelevancy are opposite extremes, with what he calls "partial relevancy" years later in the *Treatise* covering everything in between.

The only improvement I would make to Keynes here would be to say that not just "many," but by definition of "fundamental," *all* of our logically fundamental ideas are indefinable. But he does not appear to be using the word "fundamental" in this way, since he writes of "our *most* fundamental ideas," thus allowing for *degrees* of fundamentality, while my more usual definition of "fundamental" as meaning 'logically indefinable' would not. He also qualifies his talk of "indefinable" by saying "*in the strict sense* indefinable," just as he does in the *Treatise*. Thus he appears wisely to allow that a term can be indefinable in one sense and definable in another sense. This is just what allows him to offer a theoretical definition of probability as degree of logical relevance. This is his logically informative analysis of one term as logically equivalent to a clearer term. Such analyses are basic to modern classical logic. Beyond than that, probability, or logical relevance, is a logically primitive logical relation which either we intuit or we do not.

To sum up, it seems that we have a window of three years at most, from 1904 to December 12, 1907, in which Keynes first starts to use the term "relevance," or more precisely, one of its negative grammatical forms, "irrelevancy," to describe his theory of probability as belonging to logic. For he uses the term in this way on December 12, 1907. Of course, he may have used the term earlier than that.

Stephen and Ilbert as Possible "India Connections"

Keynes was working in the India Office while working on his theory of probability. Might Keynes have personally known or at least heard of Stephen or Ilbert through an "India connection"?

Stephen and Ilbert do not seem to have had any personal communication with Keynes. They are not named in the indexes to the three volumes of Skidelsky's *John Maynard Keynes* (Skidelsky 1986; 1994; 2001), nor in the index to Harrod (1951), nor in the index to Moggridge (1992). Nor is it likely that Keynes met them. Stephen died in 1894. And while Ilbert was in London as Clerk of the House of Commons starting in 1902, Keynes was merely one of ten junior clerks over in the India Office. Keynes worked first in the Military Department starting on October 16, 1906, and then in the Revenue, Statistics and Commerce Department, ending with his resignation on June 5, 1908, or if you prefer, with his final day of work on July 20, 1908. (Skidelsky 1983: 175, 177, 186). These particular departments would scarcely be old stamping grounds for Ilbert, a lawyer who worked on evidence law and legal statutes. And for all I know, Ilbert might never have visited the India Office after 1902 at all.

But we cannot completely rule out the possibility that Keynes somehow learned of relevance in the India Office, and learned of it as it was discussed by Stephen, Ilbert, or both. The head of the Military Department was Sir Thomas Holderness. The Secretary of State, who was in charge of the India Office, meaning he was in charge of India, was John Morley. And the Permanent Under-Secretary was Sir Arthur Godley (Skidelsky 1983: 176). Keynes knew all three; they knew him; and on the whole they were indulgent on his working on probability theory in his spare time, which was most of his time at work. "Keynes seems to have had the utmost sympathy and understanding of his superiors" (Skidelsky 1983: 177). Any one of these three superiors might have known of Stephen and Ilbert, and might have mentioned their legal work on relevance to Keynes. And it is precisely during this period in the India Office that he seems to have been writing of probability as relevance (Skidelsky 1983: 184). Skidelsky agrees with Elizabeth

Johnson that Keynes "expanded" his relationship with the India Office in the years after he left it (Skidelsky 1983: 186); but we are looking for 1907 or earlier origins of Keynes' talk of probability as logical relevance.

In any case, Keynes might well have learned of Stephen, Ilbert, or both through his job at the India Office, and thereby learned of their major contributions on relevance in evidence law. It might have been one of the first things his superiors told him, once they learned that he was interested in probability theory.

There might be an indirect India connection of Keynes to Stephen through Mayne. We know Keynes knew of Mayne, since Keynes mentions Mayne in his *Treatise on Probability*. Mayne's Wikipedia article says "he is remembered as the author of *Mayne's Hindu Law*[,] regarded as the most authoritative book on the Indian Penal Code." Stephen knew the Indian Penal Code well. He praised it highly, and even worked on it a little. Leslie Stephen says of his brother Fitzjames, "In regard to the famous Penal Code, of which he always speaks with enthusiasm, his action was confined to filling up a few omissions" (L. Stephen 1895: 266). Macaulay, Stephen's predecessor as Law Member of the Council, had been in charge of the Indian Penal Code; Stephen apparently did some final editing. It is possible that Mayne and Stephen knew or knew of each other through an India Penal Code connection. In any case, both did years of legal work in India. But it is unlikely that they had a significant personal connection with each other, since Mayne is not mentioned in Leslie's biography of Fitzjames.

Lytton Strachey and Thoby Stephen
as Possible Indirect "India Connections"

If I were looking for a possible indirect "India connection" between Keynes and Stephen on relevance in evidence law, I would look to Keynes' early friendship with (Giles) Lytton Strachey, who was later the author of *Eminent Victorians*, and to Keynes' early friendship with Stephen's nephew, (Julian) Thoby Stephen.

Keynes biographers Harrod, Skidelsky, and Moggridge all discuss the Strachey family in their biographies of Keynes. Harrod says, "Among the undergraduates who arrived at Trinity in the year 1899, five soon became intimate friends. When Maynard went up five years later, he found them there, a close circle, and was adopted by them. These men [included] Thoby Stephen, Clive Bell,...Leonard Woolf and Lytton Strachey" (Harrod 1851: 81–82). Thus Keynes was "adopted" by both Lytton and Thoby in 1904. I shall discuss Lytton first, and then Thoby.

Barbara Caine's *Bombay to Bloomsbury: A Biography of the Strachey Family* explores the deep roots of the Strachey family in India during the British Raj. Lytton's parents were Richard and Jane, and his uncle was John Strachey. Richard was a military officer. John was chairman of the East India Railway; he "retired and returned to England in the 1870s" (Caine 2005: 33). Richard and John spent many years in India. Jane and Lytton did not, though Jane did visit. "Like other Raj families, the Stracheys took it for granted that school-age children should remain in England" (Caine 2005: 38).

Lytton was anti-imperialist and wanted nothing to do with the Raj of his father's generation. "Lytton...absolutely rejected the idea of Indian or any other form of imperial service" (Caine 2005: 4). But the question here is how much Lytton *knew* about India from his family, and in particular, if Lytton had heard about Stephen's evidence code and its relevance rule connecting relevance with probability, and if Lytton might have passed this on to Keynes.

My evidence is only circumstantial. Caine says the Strachey family discussed all sorts of things in great detail, and says the Raj was central to the family history (see Caine 2005: Introduction and chs. 1–3 generally). Caine says:

> At least a decade before the controversy over the Ilbert Bill, a measure that would have given Indian magistrates the capacity to preside over cases involving British men and women, John Strachey was in no doubt of the impossibility of giving Indian magistrates any form of authority over British settlers and clearly his sympathies lay with his own countrymen. Both he and Richard ultimately adhered closely to the views of *John's great friend, Fitzjames Stephen* concerning the need to ensure that all positions of authority in India were held by Europeans. Caine 2005: 48, cite omitted, my emphasis)

This is a "smoking gun" text. James Fitzjames Stephen, the famous evidence law writer, was Lytton's Uncle "John's great friend."

In addition, John, Richard, and Jane Strachey all had a close friend in Lord Lytton. Caine says:

> John's very close relationship with Lord Lytton was also important. The friendship between them was intense: Lytton once told Richard Strachey that of all the men he know, John Strachey was the one he would most like as a brother. (Caine 2005: 30)

Caine adds:

> Although Jane engaged in amateur theatricals with Lord
> Elgin in the early 1860s, the viceregal family to whom
> she became closest were the Lyttons. She was not the
> only member of the Strachey family for whom this was
> the case. Lytton had worked closely with John Strachey
> from the time he (Lytton] arrived in India as viceroy in
> 1875 and the two men became very close friends. Lytton
> courted Richard Strachey when he went out to purchase
> the land for the East India Railway in 1877 and when
> Jane went out a year later to join her husband, she and
> the viceroy became very close friends. (Caine 2005: 37)

Thus John, Richard, and Jane Strachey were all close friends with
Lord Lytton—who was a supporter of James Fitzjames Stephen.
Again, Stephen's *Indian Evidence Act* was enacted in 1872, and his
Digest of the Law of Evidence came out in 1876. Could it be
possible that Lytton Strachey's parents were unaware of Stephen
and his theory that evidence is what is relevant? And if they *were*
aware, how likely would it be that Lytton Strachey knew of that
theory too, and passed it on to Keynes? I can only say the Strachey
family was famous for its prodigious intellectual discussions. And
ironically, in light of his anti-imperialism, I suspect that Lytton
Strachey was named after Lord Lytton. That might speak volumes
about an India connection between Keynes and Stephen through
the two Lyttons: Lytton Strachey and his namesake, Lord Lytton,
with this possible "Lytton connection" mediated in turn by Richard
and Jane Strachey, if not also by Uncle John.

The very possible "Thoby connection" between Keynes
and Stephen would be even more direct.

Thoby was the "son of Leslie Stephen" (Harrod 1951: 82).
And Leslie Stephen (1832–1904) was James Fitzjames Stephen's
brother. Leslie wrote a biography of Fitzjames, as he calls him,
including some brief words on Fitzjames' theory of evidence law,
which I shall quote shortly. Leslie thanks "Sir John Strachey" for
providing "information as to the Indian career" of Fitzjames (L.
Stephen 1895: vii–viii). Leslie says that Fitzjames "made some
valued friends in India; chief among whom, I think, was Sir John
Strachey, of whom he always speaks in the warmest terms, and
whose friendship he especially valued in later years" (L. Stephen
1895: 245). This proves beyond doubt that John Strachey knew and
was a good friend of Thoby's uncle, James Fitzjames Stephen, the
evidence law writer.

As a sort of preface to the quote to come, I would like to
note the general picture of the human connections involved. Leslie
Stephen says that James Mill, John Stuart Mill's father and the
"foremost" "disciple" of Jeremy Bentham, "upon whom Bentham's
mantle had fallen, held a leading position at the India House, and

his evidence before a parliamentary committee had an important influence in determining the outlines of the new system" for managing India (L. Stephen 1895: 246–47). Bentham was against the common law as a judge-made morass, and favored the utility of law codes that were relatively simple and easy to use. Following Bentham, James Mill favored codification as well (L. Stephen 1895: 246, 247). The first such law code for India, the penal code of 1834, "was an accomplishment of Benthamite aspirations" (L. Stephen 1895: 247). Leslie says the penal code "served as a model for all the later Indian codes" (L. Stephen 1895: 248). Fitzjames' evidence code was also Benthamite in this sense. It was a great simplification of the morass of common law on evidence. But while Bentham wanted to abolish all legal rules for evidence, and simply rely on science and common experience, Fitzjames felt that the gist of the historical common law development of rules (or, we may say, of the common law experience) was worth preserving in a simplified form as a law code (see L. Stephen 1895: 272–73, not mentioning Bentham). Thus we see at least an indirect connection between Stephen's evidence code and evidence law philosopher Bentham, a connection reported by Stephen's brother Leslie.

    Now we come to the text which shows that Leslie Stephen basically understood his brother Fitzjames' work on relevance in evidence law, and thus could have easily explained it to his son Thoby, who could have just as easily explained it in turn to his friend Keynes. Leslie Stephen says:

> The English system, although the product of special historical developments, had resulted in laying down substantially sound and useful rules. They do in fact *keep inquiries within reasonable limits*, which, in courts not guarded by such rules, are apt to ramble step by step into *remoter* and *less relevant topics*, and often end by accumulating masses of useless and irritating scandals. Moreover, they would protect and guide the judges, who, unless you prohibited all rules whatever, would infallibly [I think he means inevitably] be guided by the practices of English courts. To abolish the rules of evidence would be simply to leave everything 'to mere personal discretion'. Moreover, the rules have a 'real though a *negative*' value as providing tests of solid truth. The best shoes will not enable a man to walk nor the best glasses to see; and the best rules of evidence will not enable a man to reason any better upon the facts before him. It is a partial perception of this which has caused the common [and the Benthamite] distrust of them. But they do supply *'negative' tests*, warranted by long experience, upon two great points. The first is that *when you have to make an inference from facts, the facts should be closely*

> connected in specified ways with the fact to be decided.
> The second is, that whatever fact has to be proved,
> should be proved by the best evidence, by the actual
> document alleged, or by the man who has seen with his
> own eyes or heard with his own ears the things or the
> words asserted to have occurred.
>
> If, however, these rules are substantially the
> expression of sound common sense, worked out by
> practical sagacity, it is equally true that 'no body of rules
> upon an important subject were ever expressed so
> loosely, in such an intricate manner, or at such
> intolerable length'. (L. Stephen 1895: 272–73, presum-
> ably quoting James Fitzjames Stephen, my emphasis)

We see at the start the rejection of Bentham's rejection of "judge-
made law." We see at the end the endorsement of Bentham's
complaint that common law was a hopeless morass, which was the
reason for Bentham's rejection of judge-made law—a sort of
cleansing of the Augean stables, if you will. In the middle, we see
the positive relevance rule itself, and also its negative gate-keeping
function. The term "closely connected" expresses the concept of
relevance, though perhaps not as clearly as we might like. Of
course, the concept of relevance is by its nature not perfectly
determinate. And this is a work intended to be a popular biography
written by a legal amateur. For the sort of book he is writing, I
think Leslie is doing well on the topic of relevance.

The term "specified ways" indicates a general requirement
that it must be specified (and therefore must be specifiable), for
each piece of evidence, just what its close connection is to the point
in issue. I suggest that the implicit principle here is that if there is
no specifiable connection, then there is no relevant connection. If
so, then my criticism is that evidentiary connections are not always
specifiable in the sense of being describable in language. Of
course, my criticism concerns evidence in general, not evidence in
law.

Leslie Stephen is also well aware of Ilbert, and of Ilbert's
comments on Fitzjames' work. (L. Stephen 1895: 246n., 279, 280,
378, 379, 461). Thus Leslie could have discussed Ilbert with Thoby
as well.

It is hard for me to believe that Keynes would not have
known of Thoby's father Leslie, or would not have known about
Leslie's biography of Fitzjames, by the end of 1904. In fact,
Keynes might possibly have met Leslie, who died on February 22,
1904 (Harrod 1951: 172). Harrod says that Leslie had been a tutor
at Trinity Hall in Cambridge, and that "Thoby had already been
bringing his friends to Hyde Park Gate," Leslie Stephen's home
until he died (Harrod 1951: 172–33). However, Keynes may have

come on the scene after Leslie's death. Also, "Towards the end [Leslie] Stephen became very deaf, and in his last two years was ill with cancer" (Harrod 1951: 173). Thus even if Keynes met Leslie, Leslie might not have communicated very much to him. Thoby died from typhoid fever in 1906 (Skidelsky 1994: 16); but he is still in the window for Keynes' having learned of relevance by December 12, 1907.

There is a more general and indirect "Bloomsbury Group" connection between Fitzjames Stephen and Keynes. Thoby and his sisters Vanessa and Virginia were children of Leslie's second marriage. Vanessa married "one of Thoby's best friends at Trinity, Mr. Clive Bell" (Harrod 1951: 173). Virginia married Leonard Woolf, another of Thoby's best friends. Vanessa Bell and Virginia Woolf were "part of the central core" of the Bloomsbury Group (Harrod 1951: 175). Moore's philosophy of ethics fit well with the agnosticism of Leslie Stephen and the later free thinking of the Bloomsbury group (see Harrod 1951: 180). Regardless of whether everyone liked each other (Skidelsky 1994: 15), it was a small intellectual world, and it intellectually included both Keynes and three of Leslie Stephen's children. Skidelsky says, "Intellectual life in Victorian Cambridge was shaped by the crisis and eventual decline in religious belief. The 1860s were the decade when Cambridge men lost their religious belief, [including] Leslie Stephen, Henry Sidgwick, [and the economist] Alfred Marshall.... The decade opened with the consequences of Darwin's *Origin of Species*, published in 1859" (Skidelsky 1986: 26). This was the climate for the later Bloomsbury Group, and was the climate in which Moore wrote his ethics book.

Certainly Keynes was reading Leslie Stephen by 1924. On November 6, 1924, Keynes gave the Sidney Ball lecture at Oxford, "The End of *Laissez-Faire*" (Skidelsky 1994: 225). An "essay version" "was published in 1926;" "An important source was Leslie Stephen's *English Thought in the Eighteenth Century*" (Skidelsky 1994: 225).

It was an even smaller world than that. On April 26, 1902, the Council of the Senate of Cambridge University "received a memorial from 126 members of the Senate" (Moggridge 1992: 91). "A Syndicate, including...Neville Keynes..., was appointed" to expand economics "and associated branches of Political Science" (Moggridge 1992: 91). "Neville Keynes did not sign the Memorial," but "Bertrand Russell,...Leslie Stephen,...John Venn and James Ward" signed it; and so did the great historian of early English law, "F. W. Maitland" (Moggridge 1992: 91n.). Thus it seems likely that Keynes' father Neville and Fitzjames Stephen's brother Leslie knew or knew of each other.

As a smaller world yet, Fitzjames Stephen was an Apostle, or member of the Cambridge Conversazione Society, and so was his son Thoby—and so were Keynes, Russell, and Moore. Leslie Stephen says:

> In October 1847 my brother [Fitzjames] went into residence at Trinity College, Cambridge....
> My brother became intimate with several very able men of his own age, and formed friendships which lasted for life. He met them especially in two societies, which influenced him as they influenced many men destined to achieve eminence. The first was the 'Union'....
> The other society was one which has included a very remarkable number of eminent men. In my undergraduate days we used to speak with bated breath of the 'Apostles'—the accepted nickname for what was officially called the Cambridge Conversazione Society. It was founded about 1820....
> [Fitzjames was elected] at an unusually early part of his career....
> [Henry Summer] Maine brought Fitzjames into the apostles in his first term.[2]
> [Fitzjames] visited Cambridge in later years and was my guest, and long afterwards the guest of his friend Maine, at certain Christmas festivities in Trinity Hall. He speaks in warmest terms of his appreciation of the place, 'old and dignified, yet fresh and vigorous.' Nearly his last visit was in the autumn of 1885, when he gave a dinner to the apostles, of whom his son James was then a member.
> 2. He was proposed by Maine on October 30, and elected November 13, 1847. (L. Stephen: 1895: 91, 98, 99–100, 101, 102, 102 n.2, 110)

Thus not only was Fitzjames' nephew Thoby an Apostle, but so was Fitzjames' own son James, as well as Fitzjames himself. Could there be *three* Stephen family members who were Apostles, Fitzjames, James, and Keynes' dear friend Thoby, with Thoby being a member at the very same time Keynes was, and Keynes not learn that Fitzjames characterized probable evidence as relevant evidence? We see that Fitzjames gave a dinner to the then-current Apostles in 1885, almost forty years after he became a member. In doing so, he seems to have been keeping up something which was already a tradition when he became a member himself. Leslie says that when Fitzjames joined the Apostles, "Old members... occasionally attended meetings" (L. Stephen 1895: 102). And the 1885 visit was not his last, though it was "Nearly his last visit."

It was a smaller world yet. Leslie Stephen says, "In January 1876, Lord Lytton was appointed Governor-General of India. In February, Fitzjames dined in his company at Lord Arthur Russell's" (L. Stephen 1895: 386). Lord Arthur Russell (1825–1892) was a nephew of Lord John Russell (1792–1828); both served in Parliament. Lord John, Bertrand Russell's grandfather, was the one who appointed Lord Lytton to be Viceroy and Governor-General of India. At that time, Lord John was Prime Minister of the United Kingdom for the second time. (Lord Lytton arrived in India in 1876. One of his first official acts was to proclaim that Queen Victoria was Empress of India. The vast ceremony took place on January 1, 1877 in Delhi with all or nearly all the princes of India in attendance.) Lord John had been elevated to the peerage as the first Earl Russell and as Viscount Amberley in 1861. Some fourteen years earlier, in 1847, Queen Victoria had given Pembroke Lodge to Lord John and his second wife, Lady John, née Lady Francis Anna-Maria Elliott-Murray-Kynynmound, as a place to live. That was during the first time Lord John was Prime Minister, while he was still only Lord John. Lord and Lady John were living in retirement at Pembroke Lodge when Russell was sent there by court order to live with them at the age of three (see Russell 1987: 12). Lord John died on May 26, 1878, when Russell was six. Russell briefly recalls his grandfather in his *Autobiography* (Russell 1987: 15). Thus it appears that Arthur Russell, nephew of Bertrand Russell's grandfather John, not only knew Fitzjames Stephen, but invited him to dinner. Of course, this is not a Keynes connection but a Russell connection. I cannot take it seriously, but it is dimly possible that Russell himself somehow knew about Fitzjames Stephen on relevance and told Keynes. But if anything, it would be more likely that Russell somehow learned of it from Leslie.

I am not expecting there to be a thread on logical relevance going specifically from Fitzjames Stephen through Lord Arthur or Lord Lytton to Lord John, and then somehow to Bertrand Russell and / or Keynes. Russell was only six when his grandfather died, and Keynes' interest in probability started in 1904, some twenty-six years later. I am noting only that it was a small world. I mean to show only that if Keynes' terminology of relevance originated somehow from Fitzjames Stephen, then there could have been any number of ways that could have happened through a small group of people who socially knew each other very well. Fitzjames Stephen dined with Lord Arthur, the nephew of Russell's grandfather Lord John. And as public figures, all three of them must have known many hundreds of people who would have known Stephen's view, in the then-famous Indian Evidence Act, that evidence must be relevant. And many of those people might have been able to tell

Keynes about that, either at Cambridge while Keynes was a student there, or in the India Office while Keynes was a junior clerk there. Once Keynes mentioned that he was making a major study of probability, it would have been a very natural thing to tell him. The Stephen family and the Strachey family are only the more obvious possibilities.

The Economists Edgeworth and Marshall

Of course, there might have been a personal connection on logical relevance in evidence law between Keynes and someone other than the people I have just described. For example, it might have been Francis Ysidro Edgeworth. Though Edgeworth did not practice law, he was admitted to the bar in the Inner Temple in 1877. Lluís Barbé says that Edgeworth said "he had 'studied Law' at the Inner Temple of London, just like his grandfather, and had been called to 'the English Bar' in 1877" (Barbé 2010: 65 quoting Edgeworth, "Report to the Council of King's College, submitted in June of 1988").

Barbé says that Edgeworth "was called to the Bar by the Inner Temple. This meant he had successfully completed his studies in law at the professional level. However, by then he had decided not to pursue a legal career" (Barbé 2010: 85). Charles R. McCann, Jr. says of Edgeworth, "Called to the Bar in 1887 (while never having practised law, he described himself in his early writings as Barrister-at-Law)" (McCann 1996 / 1922: xii). Stephen M. Stigler says that Edgeworth "undertook the study of commercial law....[H]e was called to the bar in 1877, but well before 1877 he must have realized that a career as a barrister could not satisfy either his intellectual curiosity or his ambition for recognition as a scholar" (Stigler 1986: 305).

Edgeworth and Keynes' father Neville knew each other well. Alfred Marshall wrote to John Neville Keynes that he (Neville) was preferred by "'*Everyone*'" to be the first editor of *The Economic Journal* (Harrod 1951: 10 quoting Marshall's letter to Neville Keynes dated February 8, 1889, Marshall's emphasis). Neville Keynes rejected the offer, and the first editor was Edgeworth (Harrod 1951: 158; Moggridge 1992: 208).

Maynard Keynes knew Edgeworth well and cites him often in the *Treatise*. Edgeworth was the first editor of the *Economic Journal* from 1891 to 1912; Keynes was his immediate successor as the second editor from 1912 to 1944. From 1919 to 1926, Keynes and Edgeworth were joint editors of *The Economic Journal* because Keynes was so involved in the post-war "peace-making" process (Harrod 1951: 151 n.1). Edgeworth reviewed Keynes'

Treatise in 1922, and Keynes wrote Edgeworth's obituary in *The Economic Journal* in 1926. Keynes published two letters in the *Journal of the Royal Statistical Society* in 1910 and 1911; Edgeworth was president of that society in 1912–14.

Keynes was reading Edgeworth on economics as early as 1905 (Moggridge 1992: 95). Edgeworth, as one of Keynes' examiners, criticized an essay Keynes wrote on index numbers in 1909. Keynes felt Edgeworth's criticisms to be *"hopeless"* and to show a *"closed* mind" (Harrod 1951: 148 quoting Keynes' letter of May 10, 1909 to Duncan Grant, Keynes' emphasis). But Harrod adds:

> On 13th February [1926,] F. Y. Edgeworth, Keynes' collaborator in editorship of the *Economic Journal,* died, and Keynes wrote one of his charming obituary notices. Despite his early rage at Edgeworth's obtuseness on the subject of index numbers, he had come to appreciate the qualities of that great man. The appreciation was reciprocal. Edgeworth could not say too much in praise of Keynes. (Harrod 1951: 373)

In any case, the timing was right for Edgeworth to have influenced Keynes' theory of probability at any time from 1905 to 1921.

Edgeworth wrote on probability years before Keynes read Moore. Edgeworth begins promisingly in his article, "Probability and Calculus of Probabilities," in R. H. Inglis Palgrave's *The Dictionary of Political Economy.* His first sentence is, "Probability means a greater or less degree of credibility" (Edgeworth 2003 / 1899: 495). This sounds just like Keynes. But his second sentence is, "The probability of an event is measured by the frequency with which it has occurred in past experience" (Edgeworth 2003 / 1899: 495), and he cites "Venn, *Logic of Chance"* as the source of his view. Thus Edgeworth is just a Venn frequentist. Still, the first sentence does sound like the view Keynes adopted years later.

In his review of Keynes' *Treatise,* Edgeworth declines to discuss Keynes' philosophical theory of probability. He seems uninterested in philosophical theories of probability in general, and in Keynes' logical theory of probability in particular, throughout his lifetime of publications. Edgeworth says in the review:

> We cannot now follow him to the speculative heights.... This is not the place to enquire...in what sense there is a degree of belief which is "rational,": the conclusion standing in an "objective" relation to the premisses.... (Edgeworth 1996 / 1922: vol. 1, 152)

This is consistent with Stigler's careful summation of Edgeworth's contributions, in which no philosophical theory of probability is even mentioned by Stigler (Stigler 1986: ch. 9).

I found no philosophical theory of probability in the three volumes of Edgeworth's *Writings in Probability, Statistics, and Economics*, certainly not a developed one (Edgeworth 1996/ 1922). However, as we saw, Edgeworth briefly indicates that he is a Venn frequentist in his 1899 article on probability.

Keynes does not cite Edgeworth on relevance. Edgeworth might not have studied evidence law at all, since he specialized in business law. But evidence law is the sort of thing which every good lawyer needs to know something about. Even in business cases, how could Edgeworth have expected to present evidence for anything without knowing the basics of evidence law?

There seems to be no Edgeworth-Russell connection, Russell does not mention Edgeworth in his *Autobiography*, and Russell is not mentioned in Barbé's biography, *Francis Ysidro Edgeworth: A Portrait with Family and Friends*.

No doubt like most economists, Edgeworth's colleague Alfred Marshall too "was basically uninterested in what he called 'philosophical economics'" (Moggridge 1992: 17 possibly quoting Marshall). D. E. Moggridge adds that Marshall "was unhappy with [Keynes' father] Neville Keynes' sharp distinctions and attempts at classification, and tried to blur them wherever possible" (Moggridge 1992: 17). Thus Marshall seems even less likely than Edgeworth to have told Keyne about relevance in evidence law. Of course, both Edgeworth and Marshall were primarily economists.

Keynes Dines at the Inner Temple

The best and most direct link of Keynes to evidence law might be through Arthur Spokes. Phyllis Deane says that after John Maynard Keynes received his undergraduate degree on June 20, 1904:

> he could take his time weighing up and choosing between different career options. Always risk-averse, Neville instantly introduced an outside possibility by arranging for them (Maynard and Neville] to lunch with Arthur Spokes—his [Neville's] University College contemporary, now a well-established barrister—who could sponsor Maynard's entry to the Inner Temple. However unenthusiastic the latter may have felt about the examination-ridden route to the Bar, he embarked cheerfully on the traditional programme of "eating dinners" with members of the legal fraternity. Within a

week of his graduation, the Diary reported with satisfaction that he had "now eaten two dinners at the Inner Temple." Deane 2001: 272–73 quoting Neville Keynes' diary)

Thus Keynes dined *at least* twice in the Inner Temple in 1904, since he dined there twice in a single week. Neville Keynes had known Arthur Spokes at least since 1872 (Deane 2001: 13). Spokes was close enough to be one of the "only two of Neville's friends [who first] knew of his engagement" to Florence (Deane 2001: 107 n.39). And if Spokes was a "well-established barrister," how could he have failed to know the basics of evidence law? Mayne and Jelf were also members at the time. Keynes may have met them too.

Another real possibility is that Keynes could have simply browsed the Inner Temple Library, possibly with someone pointing him in the right direction. The Inner Temple Library Catalogue lists the following works as held as of September 2013: John Pitt Taylor, *A Treatise on the Law of Evidence as Administered in England and Ireland, with Illustrations from Scotch, Indian, American and other Legal Systems*, 9th ed. (1895); James Bradley Thayer, *A Preliminary Treatise on Evidence at the Common Law* (1895); Simon Greenleaf, *A Treatise on the Law of Evidence*, 15th ed. (1892); 7th ed., vol. 1 (1854); 6th ed., vol. 2 (1856); and 3rd ed., vol. 3 (1856); Thomas Starkie, *A Practical Treatise of the Law of Evidence and Digest of Proofs, in Criminal and Civil Proceedings* 4th ed. (1853); Thomas Peake, *A Compendium of the Law of Evidence*, 2nd ed. (1804); and Sir William Blackstone, *Commentaries on the Laws of England in Four Books*, 23rd ed. (1854) (Inner Temple 2013). But we cannot tell from these holdings in 1913 what was available to Keynes in 1904. That is because, as the online site of the Inner Temple Library says:

The accommodation for the Library has had a chequered history. The old building used by Coke and Selden was burned down in the Great Fire of 1666, and its replacement was blown up in 1678 in an endeavour to stop the spread of another fire. There was another rebuilding, this time in gothic style, in 1835. The Victorian building (1870), designed by Smirke in the same perpendicular style as the hall, was remarkable for its distinctive clock-tower surmounted by a pegasus weather-vane. That building was destroyed in 1941, with the loss of about 40,000 volumes, though the manuscripts and rarest books had been removed to the country and saved. (Inner Temple 2013a)

James Conway Davies says, "In 1941 [the] Library ceased to be.... The records of the Library itself up to 1940 had been burnt" (Davies 1972: 11). Thus whether its original holdings included any of the treatises I listed, no one can say. There I will leave the matter for other researchers. Even if we had, say, a 1904 card catalog showing that Keynes signed out every treatise I listed, it would still be only circumstantial evidence that he took the terminology of logical relevance from one of them. Likewise for learning it from one of his fellow Inner Temple members at dinner.

I shall not explore the possibility that Keynes learned of logical relevance in evidence law from an attorney, friend, library, or encyclopedia any further. That is a question for the Keynes biographers. I discuss Edgeworth and Spokes only as examples of the *sort* of personal connection one *ought* to be looking for. Keynes could have just as easily learned of logical relevance from a book, article, or court opinion. Certainly it would be very hard to prove that his term "logical relevance" did *not* come from evidence law. Where else could it have come from?

Conclusion: Keynes Likely Knew of Relevance Law

This concludes my examination of the topic of relevance in modern evidence law, so as to document that it is by far the most probable historical origin of Keynes' theory of probability as degree of logical relevance. My conclusion is that it is far more likely than not that Keynes did not invent the concept and terminology of logical relevance himself, but took them from evidence law, and then formalized and Platonized the relevance relation in the manner of the early Russell.

Evidence law required evidence to be "relevant" as early as the 1791 Gilbert. Thayer enthroned "logical relevancy" as the most basic requirement of evidence law as early as 1880–81.[5] And we do not find talk of probable evidence as relevant evidence in any other field. At least, I have not. Legal terms that are equivalent to "relevant" go back at least to 1628. I believe that further research can only strengthen my case with additional material.

Keynes developed his basic theory of probability some six years before Russell's *Problems of Philosophy*. Based on Russell's acknowledgment of Keynes in that work, it seems far more likely than not that the 1912 Russell knew of and adopted Keynes' theory of probability, if not the term "relevant," and not the thesis that every item of evidence must make a difference. These things are not in *Problems*. But they are in Russell's review of Keynes (Russell 1922: 153), and also in Russell's discussion of Keynes in

Human Knowledge (HK 374–75). No doubt Russell learned of them by 1914, when he read the proofs of Keynes' book.

Three Objections

There are three main problems with my argument that legal scholars are the origin of Keynes' theory of probability as degree of logical relevance.

(1) All my evidence is purely circumstantial. I found no direct evidence that Keynes was aware of legal talk of logical relevance. In his *Treatise*, Keynes refers only to four legal cases and one legal treatise (Keynes 1962 / 1921: 24–27). These are: Sapwell v. Bass, 2 K.B. 486 (1910); Chaplin v. Hicks, 2 K.B. 786 (1911); Watson v. Ambergate, Nottingham, and Boston Railway Company, 15 Jur. 448 (1851; "Ambergate" is misspelled as "Ambergah" in my copy of Keynes); Simpson v. London and North Western Railway Company, 1 Q.B.D. 274 (1876); and *Mayne's Treatise on Damages* None of the legal cases mentions logical relevance, or even relevance at all. But Mayne uses the terms "relevant evidence" and "directly relevant" as early as 1872 (Mayne 1872: 112, 577). Keynes does not cite Mayne for any of the cases; but Mayne (1894) lists both *Ambergate* and *Simpson* in the Table of Cases. (*Sapwell* and *Chaplin* were decided 1910–11.) Keynes' five legal citations only show that he was studying English law on on the question whether there are degrees of probability which cannot be numerically measured. And Skidelsky says:

> On 16 July [1905] Neville had written in his diary, "We have not yet decided whether Maynard shall take Part II of the Moral Sciences Tripos or the Economics Tripos." Fearing the worst, he had also kept open the legal option, making his son a member of the Inner Temple in London. (Skidelsky 1986: 162)

Thus it seems that Neville Keynes had his son enrolled as a student member merely as an emergency backup career option which was never exercised.

(2) When legal scholars say that relevance is a logical relation, their understanding is not the same as Keynes', in that their understanding is not metaphysical. The American legal scholar, James, says, "Relevancy is [a] formal relation between two propositions" (James 1992 / 1941: 384 n.15 / 696 n.15). James observes that in an evidentiary argument at law, the premiss is an evidentiary proposition describing the item of evidence, and the conclusion is a material proposition describing the material fact

(James 1992 / 1941: 384 n.15 / 696 n.15). This much is the same in Keynes. But Keynes understands his degrees of logical relevance as intellectually intuited, Platonically real logical relations of premisses to conclusions. Again, I doubt that Anglo-American law is committed to such an extreme metaphysical realism.

(3) Skidelsky gives a far simpler and more elegant account which may be regarded as the principal account today. He holds that Keynes simply developed his theory that probability is degree of logical relevance on his own, then added the early Russell's formal approach and metaphysical Platonism.

Replies to the Objections

I admit all three problems as genuine, and reply as follows.

(1) Yes, my evidence is only circumstantial. But it is still a fantastic coincidence that so many English and American evidence law treatises discussed logical relevance some years before Keynes started working on probability in 1904, that Keynes studied English legal cases discussing degrees of probability which cannot be numerically measured, and that Keynes eventually advanced the theory that degrees of probability are degrees of logical relevance, even if they cannot be numerically measured, not even ordinally.

I have not found the term "logical relevance," or "logically relevant," used as referring to probable evidence, in any of the other main fields the early Keynes studied, including mathematics, economics, and philosophy. Among philosophers and logicians, I do not find the term or its grammatical variants so used, or used at all, in Kirwan (1807), Venn (1994 / 1889; 1973 / 1907), John Stuart Mill, Neville Keynes, Jevons, or the pre-Keynes William Johnson. It is only in evidence law that I find the term and its grammatical variants so used, and used abundantly, in the decades before Keynes wrote on probability.

(2) Yes, the legal scholars of and before Keynes' time were not particularly metaphysical in their legal studies of evidence. But I never said that Keynes' Platonic realism came from the legal scholars. I agree with Skidelsky's mainstream account that this aspect of Keynes came from Russell and Moore. That said, we saw that several legal scholars expressly say that relevance is a "logical relation": Chamberlayne's Taylor (1897: 2[6]); Thayer (1900: 308); Elliott 1904: 199). (George F. James, who also says that relevance is a logical relation, comes later.) This is not to mention grammatical variants, including "logically relevant to" and "logical relevancy to."

(3) On the mainstream account, Keynes developed his theory that probability is logical relevance out of his own head, like

a deus ex machina, or Athena springing out of the head of Zeus, or even creation ex nihilo, including even his specific term "logical relevance." On my account, we have a very specific explanation of where Keynes' theory came from, and his specific term. Namely, it came from evidence law. Probably, it came from a fellow member of the Inner Temple. Of course, even on my account, I cannot be perfectly specific by naming one single person or text as the origin.

This concludes the main argument of this chapter, which may be stated as a syllogism: (1) The circumstantial evidence is overwhelming that Anglo-American evidence law is the origin of Keynes' theory of probability as degree of logical relevance. (2) Keynes influenced the 1912 Russell into accepting Keynes' logical theory, and into making the principle of induction a logical principle, though weaker than deductive logic. Again, Russell thanks Keynes in the preface to *Problems*. And what would he be thanking him for, if not his theory of probability as *a priori* and as admitting logical degrees of strength? Therefore (3) the case is very strong indeed that evidence law is the origin of the 1912 Russell's logical theory of probability, indirectly through Keynes.

Other Possible Influences on Keynes

If I am wrong, then Skidelsky's theory that Keynes arrived at his theory of probability independently while criticizing Moore's probability arguments concerning ethics would be the best theory. Moore had no theory of probability in *Principia Ethica*, and it is quite a leap from *Principia Ethica* to the concept of probability as logical relevance. Thus Keynes scarcely found it in Moore's book, nor for that matter in Moore's *Ethics* (Moore 1912: ch. 5). But we cannot rest here with Skidelsky's view that Keynes simply made up his theory himself, if there are other possible origins of Keynes' theory yet to be explored.

If neither Skidelsky nor I am right, then the next best candidate for chief influence on Keynes' theory of probability as logical relevance might be Keynes' father's best friend, William Ernest Johnson. Howard E. Smokler says:

> Johnson was committed to an analysis of probability as a logical relation between propositions which is not in all cases numerically determinable or even quantitatively comparable. This analysis was, in fact, very close to the one that Keynes provided. (Smokler 1967: 293)

Keynes praises Johnson first and possibly foremost, even before he praises Moore and Russell, on the first page of the Preface to his *Treatise* (Keynes 1962 / 1921: 3). Keynes says later in the book:

> A further occasion of diffidence and apology in introducing this Part of my Treatise arises out of the extent of my debt to Mr. W. E. Johnson. I worked out the first scheme in complete independence of his work....But there was an intermediate stage, at which I submitted what I had done for his criticism....The result is that in its final form it is difficult to indicate the exact extent of my indebtedness to him. (Keynes 1962 / 1921: 116)

But there are two points to make about this eulogy. First, Keynes says he developed his "first scheme in complete independence of [Johnson's] work." Second, Keynes places this praise of Johnson at the beginning not of Part 1 of the *Treatise*, "Fundamental Ideas," but of Part 2, "Fundamental Theorems." Also, Johnson does not discuss probability in his major pre-Keynes published contribution to logic, a series of three papers in *Mind* (Johnson 1892)

After Johnson, the next best candidate for chief influence on Keynes might be MacColl. MacColl makes degree of probability part of logic, and makes logic basically propositional. And Keynes cites several works by MacColl in the bibliography of his *Treatise*, including MacColl's 1906 book, *Symbolic Logic*, as well as several papers before 1904. But Keynes says that he arrived at his theory independently before he read MacColl:

> The conception of probability as a relation between propositions underlies [MacColl's] symbolism, as it does mine.[1]
> 1. I did not come across [MacColl's writings] until my own method was considerably developed. Mr. M[a]cColl has been the first to use the fundamental symbol of Probability. (Keynes 1962 / 1921: 155, 155 n.1)

After MacColl, the next best candidate for chief influence on Keynes might be Bolzano. But Hailperin says:

> For Bolzano probability was a part of logic....Almost a century before Keynes (whose *1921* makes no mention of him), Bolzano takes probability to be a relation between propositions but, unlike Keynes for whom it was an undefined, informally described, primitive notion, Bolzano provides a definition. (Hailperin 1988: 148; Bolzano 1972: 238–45)

Thus Hailperin finds two problems with the thesis that Keynes' theory of probability originates from Bolzano. First, Bolzano defines probability, while Keynes says "'probability' is in the strict sense indefinable" (Skidelsky 1983: 184 quoting Keynes 1907: ch. 1). (I do not entirely agree that this problem exists, since I hold both that Keynes holds that probability is degree of logical relevance, and that this qualifies as a theoretical definition.) Second, Bolzano is not mentioned in Keynes' *Treatise*. Here I might add that as we saw in chapter 8, Russell apparently did not read Bolzano's *Theory of Science*, so that there is no indirect link of Bolzano to Keynes via Russell.

Beyond that, there were plenty of early modern writers in the logical tradition of probability theory, such as Bernoulli and Leibniz, as we saw earlier.

I omit Dorothy Wrinch and Harold Jeffreys. Braithwaite says that "Keynes had not seen" "an article by Dorothy Wrinch and Harold Jeffreys in 1919" (Braithwaite 1973: xvi). The article also appeared twelve years after Keynes had basically developed his theory in his 1907 dissertation.

I also omit Thomas Bayes. Bayes' Theorem is provable from the axioms of the uninterpreted probability calculus, of which frequency theory, Keynes' theory, and Ramsey's theory are all rival interpretations. Thus Keynes is *interpreting* Bayes, not taking his interpretation or theory *from* Bayes. Keynes briefly discusses Bayes' Theorem, finding it "of great importance" (Keynes 1962 / 1921: 174ff., 379ff.) Of course, Keynes' theory must conform to Bayes' Theorem. But then Keynes' theory must conform to *every* axiom and *every* theorem of the probability calculus, and so must every other theory or interpretation of that calculus.

The Keynes-Russell Type of Probability Theory as a Philosophical Foundation for Evidence Law

I have argued it is more likely than not that Keynes takes both his conception and his terminology of logical relevance from modern evidence law. If I am right, then it seems clear that modern evidence law indirectly influenced Russell as well. And if all of that is right, then it is only natural to note that, in effect, Keynes and Russell can return the favor by providing their theories as a philosophical analysis, and thereby philosophical foundation, of the evidence law community's own most considered views. In fact, whether I am right or not about the legal origins of Keynes' theory of probability, Keynes' and Russell's being open to both mathematical and non-mathematical probabilities might be the best theoretical framework for resolving conflicts among legal theorists on whether and when mathematical probabilities ought to be allowed in judicial proceedings. By admitting three sorts of probability—cardinal, ordinal, and incommensurable—the Keynes-Russell framework provides an accommodating synthesis which can find a reasonable place for all the rival legal views. (Russell at least reports this threefold distinction as Keynes' in Russell 1922: 153; HK 373; MPD 143. But I am sure this is Russell's view as well; compare *Principles* on sorts of magnitudes.) The legal views range from the thesis that mathematical probabilities can be useful and ought to be admissible as legal evidence, to the antithesis that they ought never to be so used. The antithesis may seem extreme, but Lawrence Tribe has an important point when he says that someone should not, say, be ordered to pay restitution based on a purely mathematical argument that it is exactly 51% likely that she owes the money (the example is mine). For that is too much like justice by spinning a roulette wheel. For brief summaries of these conflicts, see Terence Anderson (2005: 250 discussing Michael Finkelstein and William Fairley, Tribe, Lempert); and Twining (1994: 119ff. citing and sometimes discussing Finkelstein and Fairley, Tribe, John Kaplan, Richard Eggleston and Glanville Williams, Alan Cullison, and Jonathan Cohen). Although Lempert does not focus on any of the great philosophers on probability, such as Keynes or Russell, he suggests a sophisticated, conciliatory approach for which Keynes or Russell could easily provide the philosophical foundation. Terence Anderson, David Schum, and William Twining say:

> An influential paper by Richard Lempert on relevance (1977) considers how the weight of evidence should be graded in probabilistic terms. In this work Lempert advised other legal scholars and practitioners not to ignore research on probabilistic reading regardless of what Professor Tribe said about the evils of [the use of] mathematics [in making legal decisions, as in "Trial by Mathematics"]. Lempert's essential argument was that probabilistic analyses of evidential issues could be very informative to jurors in a variety of ways. Lempert's work was very influential in arousing interest in probabilistic issues on the part of other evidence scholars in law. (T. Anderson 2005: 250 citing Lempert 1977)

My compliments to Lempert on his judicious view.

Probability in Russell's *Theory of Knowledge*

This chapter has been on Keynes as the origin of Russell's theory of probability in *The Problems of Philosophy*. But Russell had much more to say about probability in his later works from 1913 to 1959, and I would like to say at least a little about them, to sketch a complete picture of Keynes' influence on Russell on probability.

Problems was published in 1912. The next year, Russell wrote a much more technical book-length work called *Theory of Knowledge*. Elizabeth Ramsden Eames says "*The Problems of Philosophy* was a first sketch" of the 1913 work (Eames 1993: xxi). Perhaps the work is most noted for Russell's abandoning it due to Wittgenstein's brief criticism of its theory of judgment. Wittgenstein wrote in a June 1913 letter to Russell:

> I can now express my objection to your theory of judgment exactly: I believe it is obvious that, from the prop[osition] "A judges that (say) a is in the Rel[ation] R to b", if correctly analysed, the prop[osition] [Rab ∨ ¬Rab] must follow directly *without the use of any other premiss*. This condition is not fulfilled by your theory. (Eames 1993: xxvii quoting Wittgenstein)

But the condition *is* fulfilled by Russell's theory. It is fulfilled by *any* theory, true *or* false, since *Rab* ∨ ¬*Rab* is a logical truth, and *any* true or false statement (a theory is a conjunctive statement) strictly implies any logical truth. And the "following from" *is* direct, on Wittgenstein's own theory of truth-tables in the *Tractatus*. It is direct in virtue of the direct truth-ground containment shown by the truth-table. Thus Wittgenstein's criticism is surprisingly poor. Of course, it is pre-Tractarian.

The last chapter of *Theory of Knowledge* is "Degrees of Certainty." Oddly, from the present perspective, Russell does not discuss Keynes, but mainly Meinong. For at about this time, Russell was "going through the proofs of Keynes' *Treatise on Probability* and discussing it with...Keynes" (Eames 1993: xxxvii n.79). Another oddity is that Russell distinguishes degrees of (objective) certainty from degrees of (objective) probability. (Russell 1993 / 1913: 168). No doubt the concepts differ, but the distinction is without a substantive difference. For the degrees can scarcely vary inversely, or in any way but exactly together. The main thing is that the 1913 Russell's theory is basically the same as in *Problems*, and therefore remains basically the same as Keynes'. However, one major difference is that Russell finds the sole difference between full certainty and degrees of certainty to be cognitive vagueness in the latter (Russell 1993 / 1913: 174–76). This is nothing like partial entailment as in Keynes (1962: 52) or Wittgenstein (T 5.15), though it arguably might be a logically sufficient basis of Keynes' degrees of probability in indefinitely many cases. Instead, Russell's theory that degrees of certainty equate to degrees of cognitive vagueness seems much more like Aristotelian intellection, which I discuss at the end of this chapter.

Probability in Russell's *Outline*

Bas C. van Fraassen, in a paper called "Russell's Philosophical Account of Probability," finds "two main episodes in Russell's thought about probability and inductive inference," the first being around 1930, and the second beginning in 1944 (Fraassen 1979: 384). The first phase begins with the 1927 book *Philosophy*, later reprinted as *An Outline of Philosophy*. The second phase flowers into *Human Knowledge: Its Scope and Limits* (Fraassen 1979: 384–85). Thus Fraassen overlooks Russell's 1912 *Problems*, his 1913 *Theory of Knowledge*, and basically everything discussed so far in this chapter. I cannot discuss *Outline* or *Human Knowledge* in detail here, but I shall make brief remarks about each.

Fraassen thinks that in *Outline*, Russell takes a harsh view of Keynes. He says that "Russell explicitly notes his dissatisfaction" with Keynes' answers to several questions raised by Keynes' theory, and that "Russell is not satisfied with Keynes' interpretation of probability as a logical relation" (Fraassen 1979: 386). While this is strictly correct, I think Fraassen misreports the tone of Russell's discussion. Russell himself cautiously concludes:

> [T]he frequency theory, if it could be maintained, would be preferable to Mr. Keynes's, because [i] it would get rid of the necessity for treating probability as indefinable, and [ii] would bring probability into much closer touch with what actually occurs....Nevertheless, the difficulties of the frequency theory [many of which were raised by Keynes] are so considerable that I cannot venture to advocate it definitely. (OP 286)

Thus Russell basically leaves the Keynes-versus-frequency theory dispute undecided in *Outline*. Keynes himself states advantages (i) and (ii) of frequency theory (Keynes 1962 / 1921: 94–95). Thus Russell may well have taken them from Keynes.

Probability in Russell's *Human Knowledge*

In 1948 in *Human Knowledge*, Russell resolves the tension between frequency theory and Keynes' theory by adopting them both in what may be called a mixed theory of probability in which Keynes' theory plays the major role and frequency theory plays a minor role. Russell says that in his "examination of probability[,] the conclusion reached is, in the main, that advocated by Keynes" (HK xv). Thus Russell was basically a Keynesian in the end (1948 HK), just as he was in the beginning (1912 PP), despite some wavering in the middle (1927 OP).

Russell admits objectively rational intuited "degrees of credibility" in *Human Knowledge* (HK 342–44, 380–99). This is basically just Keynes' theory, since as we saw earlier, all Keynes means by "degree of logical relevance" is simply degree of intuited objective rational probability (Keynes 1962 / 1921: 4, 98).

Part 5 of *Human Knowledge* is entitled "Probability." In the introduction to part 5, Russell distinguishes "mathematical probability" from "degrees of credibility" and finds the two "quite different" (HK 335–37). He distinguishes the latter from Keynes' theory on the ground that "data and inferential premises may be uncertain" (HK 337), but it is hard for me to think that Keynes would not agree with this. If probabilities are incommensurable, how can they fail to be uncertain?

In part 5, chapter 1, Russell finds that mathematical probability, considered as pure mathematics, is unproblematic, and says that "the simplest course" is to hold that "any concept which satisfies [the] axioms [of probability theory] has an equal right, from the mathematician's point of view, to be called 'probability'" (HK 339). For example, we can interpret mathematical probability as the ratio or proportion of any two classes of occurrences. This sort of probability works for arbitrarily defined classes (HK 339–41). Mathematical probability applies to artificial situations such as coin tossing or drawing black or white balls out of a bag (HK 348–49). But it is useless in real life situations because:

> the proportion will vary according to our choice of class B; we shall thus obtain different probabilities, all equally valid from the mathematical standpoint. If probability is to be a guide in practice, we must have some way of selecting one probability as *the* probability. If we cannot do this, all the different probabilities will remain equally valid, and we shall be left without guidance. (HK 341, Russell's emphasis).

And we cannot even always choose classes whose memberships are definite and known (HK 341–42).
   Russell says:

> But there is another sort [of probability], which I call "degree of credibility." This sort applies to single propositions, and takes account always of all *relevant* evidence....It is this sort, and not mathematical probability, that is *relevant* when it is said that all our knowledge is only probable, and that probability is the guide of life. (HK 343–44, my emphasis)

Here Russell uses the term "relevant" twice in the manner of Keynes and the evidence law tradition. Degree of credibility: (a) "applies to single propositions" (HK 344), (b) "is relative...to all data" (HK 342) as opposed to selected arbitrary classes, and (c) "applies even in certain cases where there is no known evidence" (HK 344). But there are also cases where (d) degree of credibility concerns "what may be called 'intrinsic doubtfulness'" (HK 342). This improves on Keynes, since no prior body of evidence is required.
   Degree of credibility can only sometimes be analyzed into mathematical probability. Nonetheless, "it is not...purely subject-I've" (HK 342–43). There is a "subjective" sort of "degree of" merely psychological "conviction," but that is not what Russell has in mind (HK 343). There is also an objective sort of "degree of conviction" which "is objective in the sense that it is the degree of credence that a rational man will give;" and this is what Russell has in mind (HK 343). It is rational because here an increase in conviction "goes with an increase of evidence" (HK 343), and I assume similarly for a decrease. This seems somewhat circular to me. Russell is explaining degree of objective conviction or credibility in terms of degree of objective evidence. Grice and Strawson might call it a "family circle" of interdefinable terms (Grice 1956). Yet I think Russell's it is intrinsically a very plausible and natural explanation, and much the same as Keynes'. For both Russell and Keyne's explanations go in the right direction. It is better to define objective credibility (relevance) in terms of objective evidence (probability) than the other way around. Note that this implies that objective evidence must make a difference to objective credibility.
   Russell says that these two concepts of probability, the mathematical concept and the degree of credibility concept, "have an equal claim to be called 'probability'," and both merit study; but only the latter is "the guide of life" in Butler's sense (HK 343).

This is Russell's mixed theory of probability, with the Keynesian concept clearly predominating as the guide of life.

In *Human Knowledge*, part 5, chapter 2, Russell discusses mathematical probability. He says, "Following Johnson and Keynes, we will denote by 'p/h' the undefined notion, 'The probability of p given h'" (HK 345). He says the notion *is* defined by the axioms of mathematical probability theory, but only in the sense that Peano's axioms define the natural numbers, namely, that any interpretation that satisfies the axioms is as valid as any other (HK 345). And for Russell, this is a very limited sense. For Russell rejects Peano's definition of the natural numbers, since on it they cannot even be used to count things (HK 345; see my 2005–2007 paper on Peano, Russell, and Quine).

I shall omit *Human Knowledge*, part 5, chapters 3 and 4 as basically irrelevant to the topic of relevance. In chapter 3, Russell discusses what he calls the "finite-frequency" theory of probability, where at least one of two classes is finite, and we simply ask the probability that any randomly chosen member of the other class is also a member of the first class. In chapter 4, Russell discusses the Mises-Reichenbach frequency theory.

In part 5, chapter 5, Russell discusses Keynes' theory of probability. Among other things, he discusses Keynes' conception of irrelevance. He says, "Roughly speaking, an added premise is 'irrelevant' if it does not change the [existing] probability" (HK 374). This is just Keynes' conception.

Russell considers a typical empiricist objection to Keynes' theory. Namely, only "tautologies" can be known independently of experience, and Keynes' basic probability relations are not (even claimed by Keynes to be) tautologous; so how can they be known (HK 375)? Russell is sympathetic to the objection, but he does not find it "decisive," since on this sort of "strict" empiricism, "science is impossible" (HK 376). Indeed, the objection is even more general than Russell indicates. For it applies not just to science, but to any attempt to justify probable knowledge, including Russell's own principle of induction as a weak synthetic *a priori* principle in his 1912 *Problems*, and Russell's own five postulates of nondeductive inference in *Human Knowledge*. All of these are non-tautologous, and the five postulates are not even *a priori*.

The objection overlooks that synthetic *a priori* principles can be known independently of experience, and arguably can justify probable knowledge. This includes the 1912 Russell's principle of induction, at least on his own view, as well as my own neo-Chisholmian, neo-Carneadean synthetic *a priori* principle that if something *seems* to us to be the case, then we have reason to believe it. Indeed, the most natural line of defense for Keynes is to say that his theory that probability is degree of logical relevance, and that the probability relations we intuit between our statements of what the evidence is and our statements about what the evidence is for, are all synthetic *a priori*. Indeed, I do not see how else he could justify them, since he says they are rationally intuited, yet they are not analytic.

Appealing to synthetic *a priori* intuitions or principles is arguably the best way to justify the later Russell's five postulates of nondeductive inference as well. This cannot be done directly, since the postulates themselves are not even *a priori*. Perhaps it can be done on a higher or meta-level. For insofar as they objectively *seem* to be correct, *my* synthetic *a priori* principle of seeming entails that we have objective reason to believe them. That is, if, based on all our experience, Russell's five postulates objectively *seem* more likely than not to be true, my principle would justify them as rational. Likewise, the 1912 Russell's principle of induction might be used to justify them, if it is indeed *a priori*. Indeed, taking all our experience as our body of evidence, even Keynes might rationally intuit that Russell's five postulates have some probability of being true. This is ironic, since Russell is trying to rescue Keynes by means of these postulates, and it should be the other way around.

A deeper question arises. Assume I am right that either (1) my *a priori* principle of seeming, (2) the 1912 Russell's allegedly *a priori* principle of induction, or (3) Keynes' seemingly *a priori* intuitive judgments of probability can be used to justify the 1948 Russell's five non-*a priori* postulates of nondeductive inference as having some minimal objective reason for their acceptance, based on our experience. Then what about using any of (1), (2) or (3) to justify the other two in an *a priori* way? Or more simply, which of (1), (2), or (3), if any, is or ought to be the most basic within the *a priori* foundations of our epistemology?

I shall argue that my principle is a better candidate than the others for being taken as the most basic. The principle of induction does not seem to be *a priori* in the first place. Certainly Hume did not think so. Hume's problem of induction would not even exist if the principle were *a priori*. I am tempted to suggest that Russell is the only philosopher, or almost the only philosopher, who thought that it is *a priori*. If I and the vast majority of thinkers are right that it is not, then (1) can justify (2), but (2) cannot justify (1). I turn now to Keynes. My principle simply and directly applies to anything that seems to be the case, from single statements considered on their intrinsic merits to complex bodies of evidence. But Keynes' theory has a more complex structure. It involves a two-step approach. First, we intuit a basic probability relation between one set of propositions and another proposition, i.e., between the premises and conclusion of our probability argument. Second, we intuitively judge the (not necessarily exact or numerical) probability of the other proposition (the conclusion) on the basis of the probability relation we intuited in the first step. But my principle eliminates the first step as needless baggage. Thus it is simpler and more elegant. In fact, it is a deep objection to Keynes that we often cannot describe our evidence.

It might be objected that precisely because Keynes' theory involves two steps, it is deeper because it is more analytic. It finds two components where I find only one. One reply might be that in a sense, my principle has two steps too. First, we find that something seems to us to be correct. Second, we infer that we have reason to believe it. But these steps are different in kind from Keynes' steps. My steps do not require a probability relation among propositions, or even a plurality of propositions at all. I can consider a single proposition by itself, find that it intrinsically seems to me to be true, and infer from this that there is reason to believe that it is true. But Keynes cannot do that. On his theory, he can only find a proposition to be likely in relation to some set of other propositions. And even where we do appeal to a body of evidence, my theory does not need that body of evidence to be describable in a set of propositions.

The deeper reply to the objection is simply that my theory is simpler and more elegant. This is not a matter of Ockham's razor. It is a matter of best logical analysis of our justification of probability.

We can see the relationality of Keynes' theory in the very word "relevance." The relevance is always of a set of propositions to some other proposition. (If the propositions were the same, then we would have deductive containment relevance.) But the only relationality involved in my principle is a proposition's seeming true *to me*, and in *my* having reason to believe it. This is a different kind of relationality entirely. For as a general rule, I myself am not evidence for the proposition that I have reason to believe. The only exceptions would be arguments like "I exist as a private mind and cause my behavior to be purposive, therefore probably other minds animate the other human bodies around me which appear to be acting purposively." It is in the sense of not requiring any prior evidential premisses, any already existing body of evidence, that my principle is simple and Keynes' is complex. My principle requires only a proposition being considered and a considerer.

Next in *Human Knowledge*, Russell discusses two objections to Keynes. He takes the second to be "more vital" than the first (HK 377).

The first objection is that one and the same proposition would have different probabilities at the same time for the same person if we consider different subsets of propositions already known to that person, so that we should make the proposition's probability relative to the totality of propositions already known to that person (HK 376–77). But Russell then says, "All this, however, Keynes no doubt would admit. The objection is, in fact, only to a certain looseness of statement, not to anything essential to the theory" (HK 377). As we saw earlier, the frequency theory has much the same problem. What is usually the case can vary relative to the class of cases we consider. Thus we should state the frequency theory with a qualification: "Relative to the totality of already known propositions, what is probable is what is usual." Recall that Russell does admit 'frequent' as one of the two main valid *senses* of "probable," and admits frequency theory as a valid but comparatively unimportant part of his own mixed theory.

Russell's second and "more vital" (HK 377) objection is based on a more complex argument. He starts by saying that he is "merely inquiring how we *can*" know Keynes' basic propositional relations of probability (HK 377, Russell's emphasis). So far, the objection is a very plausible and natural one, and not very different from Ramsey's. As we noted earlier, it was Ramsey who criticized Keynes for relying on logical intuitions which nobody could intuit. Ramsey could not discover such intuitions in himself, and found that other people's supposed intuitions of probabilities conflict with each other (Ramsey 1931: 161–63). But after that first sentence, Russell suddenly veers off into a rather different line of objection for the rest of the paragraph and beyond. He notes that all our logically clear systems have primitive terms and unproved axioms. He notes further that a primitive term cannot occur in a theorem proved from the axioms unless it already occurs in at least one of the axioms used in the proof. In short, every primitive term must occur in some axiom if it is to occur in any theorem at all. (Ironically, this is very close to the basic intuition of Anderson and Belnap on variable sharing, and very far from Russell's own modern classical logic, in which we can prove theorem "*p* or *q*" from axiom "*p*".) In contrast, no *defined* term needs to occur in any axiom *or* theorem, since it can be replaced by the primitive terms that define it. Russell then poses the problem: if probability "cannot be defined, [then] there must, if we are to know anything about it, be propositions [about it] which we know without extraneous evidence" (HK 377). He then goes on to ask what Keynes thinks we "directly know" as axioms "in our knowledge of probability" (HK 377). He then argues in some detail that "what the principle of indifference really asserts is that probability is a relation between propositional functions, not between propositions" (HK 379). The principle of indifference is that "The probabilities of *a* and *b* relative to given evidence are equal if there is no *relevant* evidence relating to *a* without corresponding evidence relating to *b*; that is to say, the probabilities of *a* and *b* relative to the evidence are equal, if the evidence is symmetrical with respect to *a* and *b*" (HK 375, my emphasis). The term "relevant evidence" here is to be understood in terms of the basic definition that "an added premise is '*irrelevant*' if it does not change the probability" (HK 374, my emphasis). He says, "My conclusion is that the chief *formal* defect in Keynes' theory of probability consists in his regarding probability as a relation between propositions rather than between propositional functions" (HK 380, Russell's emphasis). The details of Russell's argument need not detain us because three of my comments concern the nature of his conclusion, and the fourth concerns how he sets up the objection in the first place.

My four comments follow.

First, Russell himself admits that his criticism is merely one of "*formal* defect" (HK 380, Russell's emphasis). This leaves it open that there is no substantive problem with Keynes, and what is more, leaves it open that there is no substantive difference between Russell and Keynes on degree of probability (or credibility). And on Russell's own view, there will be no difference between Russell and Keynes, if we apply Russell's theory of propositional functions so as to remove the formal defect Russell purports to find in Keynes, as least as far as this "more vital" objection is concerned.

Second, the specific formal defect Russell finds in Keynes is that Keynes conflates propositions and propositional functions. But the 1927 Russell abolishes the distinction between real variables and apparent variables, and finds that the propositional function "'*Fx*' is always true" is logically equivalent to and rewritable as the proposition "(*x*)(*Fx*)". Thus we can rewrite Keynes to avoid the objection—or rewrite Russell himself to face it. For, to repeat part of my earlier quotation of Ducasse again, it is:

> perfectly arbitrary which one of such a pair of sentences we chose to describe as a "disguise" of the other, and which one therefore to describe as what the other "really" is.... (Ducasse 1941: 94–95)

Thus, just as we saw earlier that Russell and MacColl sink or swim together, so Russell and Keynes sink or swim together. And since Russell abolishes the distinction in his introduction to the 1927 second edition of *Principia*, Russell in effect destroys his 1948 criticism of Keynes twenty-one years before he makes it.

Just as with his objection to MacColl's theory of modality, Russell's objection of formal defect in Keynes loses all credibility in light of Russell's abolition of the distinction between real variables and apparent variables. This is not just an ad hominem or tu quoque against Russell. The distinction between real variables and apparent variables can be intelligibly stated as a formal distinction, and is easily understood and applied even by first-year logic students. Basically, all we need to know is the distinction between propositions and propositional functions. But it is really quite pointless, as Russell came to see. For, as Russell in effect admits when he abolishes the distinction between these two sorts of variables, "always true" and "not always true" are nothing more than crude early syntactical versions of his later universal and existential quantifiers. I say crude because they cannot distinguish multiple, not to say nested, variables. This is as opposed to "(x)", which we know right away concerns variable x and not variables y or z. To eliminate the crudity, we would have to use cumbersome expressions such as "is always true with respect to x", or "is not always false with respect to y". Whether or not Russell greatly changes his semantic *theory* of variables and quantification from *Principles* to *Principia* does not detract from this syntactical point. For a discussion of whether he changed his theory, and in particular, of whether his variables still range over all entities or now only over particulars, see Landini (2007: ch. 1–4).

That Russell's objections to MacColl and Keynes should be the same, and should lose all credibility for the same reason, is not surprising. For MacColl and Keynes are as one in regarding a universal statement as stating a probability of 100%, or a certainty, and in that sense a necessity. In that respect, their views coalesce.

Third, when we look for a substantive difference between Keynes and Russell, there seems to be none. The difference between degree of "probability" (Keynes) and degree of objective rational "credibility" (Russell) seems merely terminological. And it seems to me that Russell uses the very same family circle of terms to describe credibility that Keynes uses to describe probability: "rational," "objective," and "(rational objective) evidence." In this way, and indeed I think that in any event, credibility is exactly as definable (or indefinable) for Russell as probability is for Keynes.

Fourth, Russell sets up the problem as the question whether "probability" is definable, since if it is not, then it must occur in at least one axiom we must know directly, if we are to know what probability is at all. This was Russell's second and "more vital" (HK 377) objection to Keynes. But here he has forgotten his own philosophy of analysis. As we saw in chapter 9, he argues in several works that it is unimportant whether we can define everything at the present time, since there is no reason to expect either that analysis will end in simples or that analysis can go on forever because there are no simples (PLA 202; IMP 3–4; HK 252; MPD 164 quoting PLA 202; MPD 165 quoting HK 252). Now, this applies universally to all topics, including probability. This is not just an internal conflict in Russell's views. The issue of whether logical analysis involves a vicious infinite regress of analyses of analyses is a substantive issue that directly bears on Russell's second and "more vital" objection to Keynes. Russell does not even see the problem, much less discuss it. The problem is just that if analysis goes on forever, then everything can be defined on indefinitely many levels of analysis, including probability. If so, then the term "probability" is not primitive, and need not occur in a directly known axiom if we are to know what probability is. Or, if definitions require an undefined term as an ultimate starting point, on pain of vicious infinite regress of definitions of defining terms, then we cannot define what anything is, if all series of definitions are in fact endless.

In the rest of the book, Russell presents his own theory of probability. He offers various technical criticisms of Keynes, but they are more in the nature of improvements to, than rejections of, Keynes' theory (HK 386–87, 408–10, 435–38, 439–43). They are all in the nature of pointing out correctable "formal defects" which Russell proceeds to correct. And Russell's concept of degrees of objective rational credibility is basically the same as Keynes' concept of degrees of probability. Russell also agrees with Keynes that induction is not axiomatic but derivative (HK part 6 ch. 2; MPD 144, 148, 149). Russell says that his own postulates of nondeductive inference "are designed only to confer that antecedent probability which Keynes needs to validate his inductions" (MPD 149). Thus the whole point of Russell's own postulates of nondeductive inference is to "validate" Keynes. (As we saw earlier, the validation ought to be the other way around.)

The deepest and most general similarity between Russell and Keynes is that for Russell, a mathematical probability is "the ratio of the numbers of two finite classes," i.e., a frequency relation between two propositional functions, while epistemic probability concerns individual propositions, i.e., the objective rational credibility of a proposition in light of "all *relevant* evidence" (HK 381, my emphasis; see 384–91). Thus in Russell's *Human Knowledge*, the two thinkers agree on Keynes' most basic view, with Russell using Keynes' own term "relevant evidence."

The major distinction I see between Russell and Keynes on probability is one I have already mentioned. Namely, Keynes has a complex two-step process for assigning probabilities to individual statements, while Russell accepts directly intuited likelihoods that some individual statements are true, which likelihoods are not based on the known truth or likelihood of any other statements, in major works from *Problems* to *Human Knowledge* (PP 135–40; IMT ch. 9–11; HK 381–84; 391–92). He calls such statements "self-evident truths" (PP 109, 114), "basic propositions" (IMT ch.

10), or "data" (HK 392). In the extreme case, for the early Russell, we have "knowledge by acquaintance" of their truth. But even the early Russell seems to find no datum absolutely certain, not even in logic (PM 12–13, 59–60).

The greatest difference between Russell and Keynes on probability is that Russell can and does admit epistemologically foundational data, including sense-data and the principle of induction itself, while Keynes, with his two-step process, cannot. One might even suspect Keynes' theory of implying a vicious epistemological regress for this reason: how does he come by his initial probabilities for his initial relational statements? My reply is that the difference between Russell and Keynes is not that great. For Keynes, we directly intuit the evidentiary *relations* among propositions, so that *these* are his self-evident or basic data. But I think there may be a vicious regress in Keynes after all, concerning not these intuited relations among propositions, but the first *relatum* of each such relation. I am referring to his bodies of evidence, i.e., his antecedent or background assessments of probability that such bodies of evidence are themselves veridical, or at least more likely veridical than not. These are what is really "initial" for Keynes. The dilemma is that either his two-step process applies to the statements describing his bodies of evidence or it does not. If it does, then we have a vicious regress of applications of the two-step process. If it does not, then the two-step process is a false analysis of probability. For there will always be a probability it never applies to, namely, the probability that the body of evidence is veridical. If I am right, then Russell and Keynes are very different indeed. For Russell prevents any such regress by admitting self-evident statements and statements about self-evident data. This is just the same as my earlier point that my principle of seeming is simpler and more basic than Keynes' theory. Some seemings are self-evident; and in a certain sense they all are, as when it just seems to me that a certain complex argument is sound.

Russell argues that vagueness is in many ways the basis of degrees of credibility (HK part 5, ch, 6, sect. c). I find this circular, since vagueness is by definition the absence of the very sort of determinacy that allows mathematical probability, as opposed to degrees of credibility, to apply. This is certainly so on Russell's definition of "vagueness" in his 1923 paper entitled "Vagueness." There Russell first defines precision as a one-one correspondence of terms and the relations among terms in a representing structure and a represented structure (Russell 1923: 89). Then he says:

> *Per contra*, a representation is *vague* when the relation
> of the representing system to the represented system is

not one-one, but one-many. For example, a photograph
which is so smudged that it might equally represent
Brown or Jones is vague. (Russell 1923: 89)

Thus for Russell, vagueness is by definition a necessary condition
of the applicability of the concept of degrees of epistemic
credibility as opposed to the concept of mathematical probability.
But it is not a sufficient condition, since for the 1923 Russell
vagueness also occurs in logic and mathematics, and in general
whenever we cannot prove or disprove a universal statement. For
example, Goldbach's conjecture is the claim that every even
number is the sum of two primes. Since we cannot prove or
disprove it, we do not know if there is a one-one correspondence
between even numbers and sums of two primes. Thus it is vague in
Russell's sense, at least until we prove or disprove it. Yet the
concept of degrees of credibility seems inapplicable to it, or
minimally applicable at best, since the even numbers are infinitely
many, and we only know finitely many of them to be sums of two
primes. This is unlike rough or estimated arithmetic, where we
round the numbers or otherwise simplify the calculation so as to
approximate the correct result. In rough arithmetic, degree of
credibility does apply, and corresponds to degree of roughness.
One might object that the more even numbers we find to be sums of
two primes, the closer we approximate the conjecture as the result.
But that is only if the conjecture is *true*. In contrast, in rough
arithmetic we are approximating a result we *know* we can prove. In
fact, if we could not prove the actual determinate result, we would
not know if we were approximating it at all. Thus we cannot even
approximate Goldbach's conjecture by a tally of the even numbers
we have confirmed as sums of two primes so far. And perhaps that
is the best argument why the concept of degrees of credibility does
not apply to Goldbach's conjecture, and in general why vagueness
is not a sufficient condition of the applicability of that concept.
This is just an illustration of the general fact that many
philosophical issues have a way of becoming clearer in philosophy
of mathematics. This is also like my criticism of Ramsey that if we
do not already know an objective probability, then we cannot know
if our learning curve of bets approximates to it.

Probability in *My Philosophical Development*

In 1959 in *My Philosophical Development*, Russell briefly
summarizes his theory of knowledge in *Human Knowledge* as
follows. "There are two kinds of probability," (1) statistical and (2)
"degrees of credibility" (MPD 142–43). This is his mixed theory

again. Now, the frequency theory is that the *only* kind of probability is statistical (MPD 142). Thus for Russell, the frequency theory is strictly false, since it has only a limited scope of application. Considered as pure mathematics, the statistical theory of probability is perfectly acceptable, but it applies only to a narrow range of cases in the empirical world, namely, clear and definite cases, such as drawing cards out of a deck (MPD 142). Thus "wherever probability is definite, the frequency theory is applicable" (MPD 143). Russell says that Keynes holds a theory of kind (2) in his *Treatise on Probability*. For Keynes, the probability relation obtains between two propositions, "is indefinable[,] and capable of varying degrees" including truth, falsehood, and every degree in between (MPD 142–43). For Keynes, not all degrees of probability "are measurable or reducible, even in theory, to frequencies" (MPD 143). Russell's own theory of degrees of credibility is a "conception...to which something more like Keynes's theory is applicable" (MPD 143). Thus Russell holds a mixed theory that includes both kinds (1) and (2). He holds that (1) applies to a narrow range of definite cases, and he holds that (2) applies to everything else. He says that probability in the sense of degrees of credibility is "much more important" than probability in the sense of frequency of occurrence (MPD 143).

For Russell, probability can be justified only by principles which are "not logically demonstrative" (MPD 143). Based on his own study of non-demonstrative inference, he admits induction, but not as one of the basic or primitive principles (MPD 144). This is very different from his view in 1912. But one view remains the same: in modern science, causation is not a matter of simple laws of the form "If *A*, then *B*," but of complex laws that are multi-variable and often statistical (MPD 146–47).

Russell then briefly reiterates his five basic "postulates" of non-demonstrative inference. He says that they are neither *a priori* nor even necessary conditions of probable inference, but are sufficient to justify the ordinary and scientific probable inferences we normally accept. For us, the most important thing he says is that his five postulates "are designed *only* to confer that antecedent probability *which Keynes needs to validate his inductions*" (MPD 149, my emphasis). This shows that Russell intends his own theory not to destroy Keynes' theory, but to fulfill it.

On the whole, I think Russell gives a very fair summary of *Human Knowledge* in *My Philosophical Development*.

Induction and Intellection

Supposedly, Aristotle sharply separates deduction from induction. Supposedly, Aristotle takes an exclusively frequency approach to probability. But at bottom, Aristotle basically justifies probability just as Keynes and Russell do, namely, as an objective, rational, direct evidential presentation, either of a degree of logical relevance (Keynes), a degree of objective credibility (Russell), or a degree of intellectual intuition (Aristotle). The great Aristotle scholar W. D. Ross says, "Essentially, induction for [Aristotle] is a process not of reasoning but of direct insight, mediated psychologically by a review of particular instances" (Ross 1960: 44). Ross says:

> The root nature of induction seems to be, for [Aristotle], that it is the "leading on" of one person by another from particular knowledge to universal. Whether one instance or a few or many or all are needed depends on the relative *intelligibility* of the subject-matter....Where the form is easily separated in thought from the matter, as in mathematics, the mind passes from the perception of the truth in a single instance to grasping its applicability to all instances of a kind; where the form is less easily dissevered from the matter, an induction from several instances is necessary. But *in both cases the same activity of "intellection" is involved.* (Ross 1960: 43, my emphasis)

I see no real difference between Aristotle on degree of intelligibility and Russell on degree of vagueness. In fact, the two appear to be mirror inversions of each other. Ross concludes, "The passage from particulars to the universals implicit in them is described as induction; the grasping of the universals which become the first premises of science must, we are told, be the work of a faculty higher than science, and this can only be intuitive reason" (Ross 1960: 58, 168, 211; see *Posterior Analytics (An. Post.)* 88*a*12–17, 100*a*5–*b*15 / Aristotle 1968a: 154–55, 185–86). For Aristotle, "'imperfect induction'...reaches a merely probable conclusion" (Ross 1960: 211). Clearly, this is not only consistent with Aristotle's frequency theory of probability, but can underwrite that theory as justified by intellectual intuition as probably true. Perhaps then the ultimate origin of Keynes' and Russell's theory, through the medium of millennia of inductive logic, is Aristotle.

While Keynes is well aware of Aristotelian induction, he does not base Aristotle's frequency sense of induction on Aristotle's abstractive intellective sense, and keeps Aristotle's two senses "quite distinct" (Keynes 1962 / 1921: 274). The honor of justifying the principle of induction as probably true based on a weak but direct *a priori* intellectual intuition may be due to Russell in *Problems*.

Thus it appears that both Russell and Aristotle hold a mixed theory of probability on which frequency theory and induction alike are justified by a deeper, more general theory of objectively intuited probability. This sophisticated and complex theory is very hard to argue for or against, I think the best argument in its favor is that it is hard to find a more plausible account. This may sound like an appeal to ignorance, but appeal to ignorance is a fallacy only in deductive logic. I prefer to think of it as more like a deductively valid proof by cases, since there are only a few major rival theories of probability. What major rival to this mixed theory are there, besides pure frequency theory, pure logical theory, and pure subjectivist theory? As in ontology (my 2003), the pace in epistemology is glacial.

The most serious problem facing Russell's extension of logical relevance to inductive logic is explaining partial containment of the conclusion in the premises. While probabilistic *syllogisms* are deductive, their deductive form is mere window dressing, as we saw. The problem is that neither the principle of induction, nor specific cases of induction, seems to involve, nor even seems able to involve, any such partial containment.

Perhaps we may appeal to Wittgenstein's logical theory of probability in the *Tractatus*. The theory extends his conception of extensional truth-ground containment to inductive logic (T 4.464, 5.15–5.156). If a conclusion is true on every row on which all the premises are true, we have a deductively valid, i.e., tautologous inference, which we may call 100% logical probability. If a conclusion is true on no row, we have a logically false inference, which we may call 0% logical probability. But in many truth-tables, a conclusion is true on some *proper subset* of the rows on which all the premises are true. We may call this "partial truth-ground containment." For example, $P \supset Q$ has a logical probability of 75%, since it is true on exactly three of the four rows of its truth-table. Now, this sort of logical probability applies to truth-tables for any finite number n of atomic statements, approaching infinity.

Georg Henrik von Wright notes that "equal possibilities," often called indifference, exchangeability, or equiprobability in the literature, are logically guaranteed in Wittgenstein's theory. Wright says:

A purified and generalized form of the possibility view was suggested by Bolzano in his *Wissenschaftslehre* of the year 1837, and renewed by Wittgenstein in the *Tractatus Logico-Philosophicus* (1921–22). The Bolzano-Wittgenstein definition does not mention equal possibilities. Yet it can be shown that this definition is a sufficient basis for the deduction of the branch of mathematics known as the ("classical") Calculus of Probability. " (Wright 1960: 168)

But this is not enough for probability as a guide to life, which rarely offers equal possibilities outside the gaming halls.

I propose the following further extension of Wittgenstein's extension. By applying the methods of the infinitesimal calculus to Wittgenstein's purely logical theory of probability, we can come infinitesimally close to tautology without reaching it. The notion of an infinitesimal can be analyzed using Karl Weierstrass's theory of limits, as Russell himself does. Or it can be logically defined as in Robinson arithmetic (A. Robinson 1996; 1979; 1979a / 1961). (This is Abraham Robinson's arithmetic, not to be confused with Richard Robinson's arithmetic.) Thus this application of the calculus can be interpreted as consistent with the logicist program of analyzing mathematics in terms of logic. For example, Robinson uses Skolem sets with infinite members. But I wonder why Frege could not have just as easily logically defined an infinitesimal, or one simple sort of infinitesimal, as the number one divided by Cantor's number aleph null. Frege defines aleph null as the number of positive integers; and the set of positive integers has infinitely many members. Since sets with infinitely many members are called nonstandard, Robinson arithmetic is called nonstandard, and so is the resulting calculus. Robinson's nonstandard arithmetic is not the only one today (they differ in logical foundations, but give the same mathematics), but it was the first. But a Fregean / Cantorian infinitesimal, e.g., 1/aleph null, would be in effect nonstandard too.

My proposed extension of Wittgenstein's logical theory of probability to truth-tables for any finite number of atomic statements approaching infinity gives us infinitely many infinitesimal gradations of degree of purely logical probability. However, it fails to give us indeterminate or incommensurable degrees of probability. And it is impracticable. There are only so many atomic statements we can write in a lifetime, or discover to be relevant to the statement with whose probability we are concerned, unless we use mathematical induction over atomic statements. I conclude that my proposed extension is too theoretical and too artificial to ground probability as a guide to life either, though it does give a better approximation in its way. In fact, it is not so much an extension of Wittgenstein's theory as it is a mere recognition that his truth-tables can have any finite number of rows and columns.

Wittgenstein's theory of logically relevant probability is a modern link between deductive and inductive logical relevance very different from the ancient link I find in Aristotle's conception of induction as a main kind of intellection. For Aristotelian intellection is intensional, while Wittgenstein's theory of probability is extensional, and might well be called logical bean-counting, since it is truth-table row counting. Thus ironically, Wittgensteinian logical probability is a special kind of frequency theory. But this purely extensional theory of probability is surely only the genus of which the sorts of probability we are interested in are species. If so, then this even more ironically makes frequency theory the genus of probability theory, and Keynes-Russell degrees of relevance or credibility merely a differentia. This may seem an unusual result for those of us who think of frequency theory as mainly useful only for large and definite populations of study, i.e., for epidemiology. But Wittgenstein's theory is a very special kind of frequency theory. It is very different from the ordinary sort of mathematical probability that is used by game players and other epidemiologists. The existence of this ordinary sort of mathematical probability is why I, too, hold a mixed theory of probability. Perhaps the best statement of my theory is my (2012a: 60–65), but my most recent statement is in note 4 to the present chapter.

Summary of Main Argument of the Chapter

Again, the main argument of this chapter may be stated as a syllogism. (1) From 1912 *Problems of Philosophy* on, Russell's theory of probability originates from Keynes and is fundamentally that of Keynes. This is both accepted in the literature (Skidelsky 2005: 286; Monteiro 2001: 66) and fairly obvious from a "smoking gun" acknowledgment by Russell in the book's preface (PP vi), not to mention from the nature and later time of Russell's theory. (2) The circumstantial case is overwhelming that Keynes' theory of probability originates in turn from Anglo-American evidence law and is fundamentally that of Anglo-American evidence law. It took 132 pages (368–500) to show this. This is except for Keynes' Platonic realism, which originates from and is basically the same as that in Russell's *Principles*. (3) Therefore, the circumstantial case is basically overwhelming that except for its Platonic realism, Russell's theory of probability as logical relevance indirectly originates from Anglo-American evidence law through Keynes, and is fundamentally that of Anglo-American evidence law. Premiss (2) and conclusion (3) are what is new to the study of Russell on probability, and bring it to a new level of depth and understanding.

But I have no evidence that Russell was ever aware of this indirect legal origin of his theory. In fact, I have no evidence that Keynes was aware of the full extent of the legal origin of his own theory, or was even aware of it to the limited but substantial extent to which I have described it. I am arguing only that Keynes was very likely aware *that* his theory that probability is degree of logical relevance *did* originate in evidence law, concerning premiss (2) of my argument. He may well have simply taken that theory as common knowledge, at least among legal scholars.

Summary of Main Aim of the Book

I hope to have presented the most comprehensive portrait of Russell on modality and logical relevance ever written. I hope even more to shake off people's preconceptions of Russell as being a modern classical logician who found no place for modality or logical relevance, or better, to shake off people's preconceptions of modern classical logic as a logic which has no place for modality or logical relevance. I hope most of all to have created two new fields of Russell studies, and to throw Russell, modality, and logical relevance into a new light for further study.

Thus this book is written toward the reunion of modern classical logicians with *other* modal logicians and relevantists. On the reunion of modern classical logicians with other relevantists, please see also *The Concept of Relevance and the Logic Diagram Tradition* (my 2012).

I may have created a new field of legal study as well. For my 132 page history of logical relevance in evidence law is a small book in itself, and I know of no other. There are many articles on the *concept* of logical relevance in evidence law, but only with brief descriptions of its *history*. I may have presented the most comprehensive history of the concept ever written, or at any rate philosophically the deepest; but it is merely introductory. I can only hope to have thrown the concept into a new historical light for further study.

Notes

Chapter 1: Introduction

1. Gustav Bergmann notes in effect a second problem with FG–MDL. Evidently, some fully general truths are not true in virtue of their logical form, but instead true in virtue of the fact that in an ideal language, any attempt to deny them would be ill-formed. This is Bergmann's distinction between what is impossible$_1$ (ill-formed), impossible$_2$ (analytically false), and impossible$_3$ (synthetic *a priori* false) (Bergmann 1967: 23–24). Assuming that modern classical logic is an ideal language, meaning that its logical structure mirrors the metaphysical (categorial) structure of the world, it is "possible$_1$ for several ordinary things to have exactly the same properties" (Bergman 1967: 23), since "$(\exists x)(\exists y)(F)[(x \neq y) \,\&\, (Fx \equiv Fy)]$" is well-formed in modern classical logic. On the same assumption, it is also possible$_1$ for some particulars to have no properties, e.g., possible$_1$ that Bergmann's bare particulars exist, since "$(\exists x)(F)\neg Fx$" is well-formed in modern classical logic. But, still on the same assumption, it is necessary$_1$ that particulars are not properties of particulars, since "ab" is ill-formed in modern classical logic.

Insofar as the syntax of a logic mirrors the metaphysical categories of the world, its necessity is necessity$_1$ as well as logical. The concept of necessity$_1$ is related to the saying-showing distinction in Wittgenstein's *Tractatus*, and to Frege's thesis that we cannot refer to the (metaphysically incomplete) concept *horse* by means of the (grammatically complete) singular definite description "the concept *horse*" (TW 46). We may say that necessary$_1$ truths are true in virtue of logical form in the negative sense that their denial is ill-formed. In contrast, the denial of an analytic truth or a synthetic *a priori* truth is always well-formed.

2. I offer eight arguments for the veridical interpretation of *Principia*'s individual quantifier in Dejnožka (2003: 169–79), *pace* Quine, Douglas Lackey, and Landini.

Wayne Patterson attempts to rescue the standard existential interpretation in his very kind review of my first book. He notes that Russell admits existence-facts and general facts in a way that parallels his individual and universal quantifiers, and finds this hard to reconcile with my view (W. Patterson 1997: 544). I find existence-facts easy to reconcile with my view. For all of Russell's existence-facts concern logical fictions (hippopotami, sheep, people). And that ordinary individuals are logical fictions supports my interpretation of the individual quantifier as merely veridical and lacking ontological commitment (PLA 213–14, 234–35).

Quine, Lackey, Landini, and Patterson might suggest that Russell casually or carelessly uses bad examples from ordinary thought or language, since strictly speaking hippopotami and sheep are not entities for Russell, but are logically constructed out of sensibilia. My reply is that my interpretation makes Russell's examples apt instead of foolish. For they are absurd only on the existential interpretation of the individual quantifier, and make all the sense in the world on the veridical interpretation.

What is at stake is the issue of whether Russell's logic was intended to be useful for ordinary thinking in ordinary language at all. If the ordinary existence assertions we make about hippopotami, sheep, and people cannot be directly rendered by means of the individual quantifier veridically interpreted, then we are committed to using that quantifier (if we use it at all) to quantify over indefinitely many sensed and unsensed sensibilia, just to say "There is no hippopotamus in this room." Such a paraphrase is unworkable; we could never complete it. In fact, this is one of my eight arguments for the veridical interpretation, though I speak generally of body B, not specifically of hippopotami (Dejnožka 2003: 175–78). Even worse, on the existential interpretation, we could quantify only over simple entities, if everything complex is a logical fiction. And if analysis is endless, then there are no simple entities, and there would be nothing that we could quantify over at all.

One might argue that these two interpretations of *Principia* can be reconciled through the concept of degrees of ontological commitment. Namely, the simpler the sort of entity we quantify over, the higher the degree of ontological commitment we may find in our existential quantifier. Russell says in 1959:

> If a waiter in a restaurant tells me, "We have some very nice fresh asparagus," I shall be justly incensed if he explains that his remark was purely linguistic and bore no reference to any actual asparagus [due to logical analysis]. This degree of ontological commitment is involved in all ordinary speech. (MPD 173)

We might say that the existential interpretation involves only "this degree of ontological commitment" to ordinary things. But while it seems plausible to apply this view retrospectively to *Principia*, my eight arguments for the veridical interpretation of *Principia* at the time it was written are unaffected. The retrospection is 49 years, from 1959 back to 1910. There does not even appear to be a theory of degrees of ontological commitment in *Principia*, nor in the theory of stages of logical analysis in the 1927 *The Analysis of Matter*.

3. Etchemendy is discussing Bolzano's theory of satisfiability and analytic propositions (Bolzano 1972 / 1837: 193–99). Bolzano's theory of necessity and possibility is different (Bolzano 1972 / 1837: 255–59).

Chapter 2: Propositional Functions and Possible Worlds

1. Values of variables, as opposed to values of propositional functions, can be all sorts of things (PM 4). As late as 1959, Russell still distinguishes between "values of the function" and "values of the variable" in a similar way (MPD 92). Values of propositional functions seem to be sentences, and values of variables seem to be things. Concerning the latter, Russell seems to equate "all possible values of variable *x*" with "everything in the universe" (MPD 52), but no doubt restricts "everything" to everything of the proper logical type (MPD 53; see 62–63 on totalities). Russell's (nonsubstitutional) equation of assigning a value to a variable *x* with substituting "a proper name for '*x*'" (MPD 92) shows how the second way out of the howlers can come into play if ordinary names, as well as logically proper names, are meant.

2. I repeat the list given in chapter 1: review of Hugh MacColl's *Symbolic Logic and Its Applications* (Russell 1906: 257); "'If' and 'Imply', A Reply to Mr. MacColl" (Russell 1908: 301); "Mathematical Logic as Based on the Theory of Types" (LK 66n); "On the Notion of Cause" (ONC 176); "The Philosophy of Logical Atomism" (PLA 231, 232, 233, 240, 242, 254–55); *Introduction to Mathematical Philosophy* (IMP 165); *The Analysis of Matter*, (AMA 170); and *Inquiry* (IMT 37). The respective dates of publication are 1906, 1908, 1908, 1913 (essay), 1918, 1919, 1927, and 1940.

3. I repeat the list given in chapter 1: "The Study of Mathematics" (MAL 65); *The Problems of Philosophy* (PP 78); *Our Knowledge of the External World* (KEW 145); "The Philosophy of Logical Atomism" (PLA 240); *Introduction to Mathematical Philosophy* (IMP 141, 192–93, 203–4); *The Analysis of Mind* (AMI 268); *The Analysis of Matter* (AMA 200); *The Principles of Mathematics*, 2d ed. (POM viii); and *Human Knowledge* (HK 157). The respective dates of publication are 1907 (essay), 1912, 1914, 1918, 1919, 1921, 1927, 1938, and 1948.

4. The respective dates of publication are 1918 (twice), 1919, and 1927.

Chapter 3: Russell's Three Levels of Modality

    1. Anthony Manser also anticipates me (Manser 1985: 276). Compare Marge Reimer, "Russell's Anticipation of Donnellan's Distinction" (Reimer 1991).
    2. Kripke says "something [is] a [weak] *rigid designator* if in every possible world it designated the same object....Of course we don't require that the objects exist in all possible worlds" (Kripke 1980: 48, Kripke's emphasis).
    I am puzzled why Kripke ignores Russell's logically proper names, and establishes only that Russell's *descriptions* are not rigid designators, which few would dispute. Kripke does not notice that Russell's logically proper names rigidly designate sensed particulars, much less that descriptions rigidly designate *attributes*, i.e., the universals that are their determinate constituents (compare Burge 1983: 80). Nor does Kripke acknowledge that Russell surely views "this = this," and presumably also "this = that," as necessarily true if true at all. See Kripke (1980: 310; 27 n.4). See PLA 201 on "this," and PLA 245–47 on "Scott = Scott" as tautologous if it is true and if "Scott" is a logically proper name. Even "Cicero = Tully" would be tautologous if true, and if "Cicero" and "Tully" were logically proper names, since in that case the same sense-datum would be the meaning, as well as the denotation, of both names.
    Kripke does credit Russell with "some notion of ostension, of primitive reference" (Kripke 1980: 97 n.44). He says, "Russell did think that [when you name your own sense-datum with several logically proper names,] "there should never be any empirical question whether two names have the same reference[;] "you can tell without empirical investigation that you're naming the same thing twice" (Kripke 1980. He says that "Russell does seem to have held...for 'logically proper names'" "a doctrine of the universal substitutivity of proper names[, which] can be taken as saying [of logically proper names that name the same thing that they are intersubstitutable *salva analycitate*, or even] equivalent for all semantic purposes" (Kripke 1980: 20). Kripke even says that he (Kripke) "never intended to go so far" in his own theory (Kripke 1980: 20). Here Kripke is right on target both on Russell and on himself. But this is not at all the same as saying that a logically proper name is a rigid designator, which means that one and the same name designates the same object in every possible world in which it exists. Equivalence for all semantic purposes does not even appear to imply rigid designation. For expressions that designate different things in different worlds, or that do not designate anything, or that cannot designate anything in any possi-

ble world, can be equivalent for all semantic purposes, but cannot be rigid designators.

The distinction between being a rigid designator and being intersubstitutable *salva analycitate* with other names of the same sort which all designate the same object is exceptionally clear in the case of Russell's ordinary proper names, which for Russell are covertly definite descriptions. Take "the equilateral datum I now sense" and "the equiangular datum I now sense." In any possible world, they logically must denote the same object. But they can denote different objects in different worlds, since they are really definite descriptions. I might now sense a large blue triangle in one world, and a small green triangle in another. But Russell's logically proper names cannot denote different things in different worlds.

There is nothing descriptive about Russell's logically proper names. Two logically proper names naming the same sense-datum of mine are not at all two logically equivalent definite descriptions, such as "the equilateral datum I now sense" and "the equiangular datum I now sense." Two logically proper names, or even one such name, cannot possibly designate anything but the sense-datum it actually does.

Why Kripke never comes out and expressly says that Russell's logically proper names are rigid designators escapes me. Perhaps the reason is simply that Kripke's project in *Naming and Necessity* is to develop his own theory, not to expound Russell. But I still wonder why he could not have added just one simple extra statement to make it clear that Russell's logically proper names are rigid designators. Does he think it is too obvious to be worth stating? Or if he does *not* think they are rigid designators, then why does he not say so and explain why he thinks so? Does he credit Russell *only* with "some notion of ostension, of primitive reference" (Kripke 1980: 97 n.44)? It would only enhance Kripke's book to address this issue and make it clear just how close to or far from rigid designators he thinks Russell's logically proper names are. For he takes Russell's theory of names as the main alternative to his own, and as the paradigm he is working to overcome. I find it surprising that in a book about naming and necessity, and that takes Russell as its chief rival, Kripke will not even tell us whether Russell's logically proper names, which are the most obvious, not to say the only, candidates for being rigid designators in Russell's theory, are or are not rigid designators, and why. At least to this Russell scholar, it looks like he is ducking the most important question. Now, we might think we may charitably suppose that when Kripke says that he (Kripke) "never intended to go so far" as "a doctrine of the universal substitutivity of proper names," which "Russell does seem to have held...for 'logically proper names'" (Kripke 1980: 20), he implies not only that Russell's logically proper names *are* rigid designators, but that they are *more* than rigid designators, since they have the additional feature of being intersubstitutable *salva analycitate*. But perhaps Kripke intends no such implication. Perhaps he intends only to say that Russell seems to hold a certain doctrine about Russell's own logically proper names which he (Kripke) would never go so far as to hold concerning his (Kripke's) own names. which are rigid designators, unlike Russell's logically proper names. That would be a stricter reading of Kripke's text. But it may be best simply to say the text is not clear enough to allow us to decide which of these two alternative readings of it is correct.

Two rigid designators which designate the same object in every possible world in which they have a designation can fail to be intersubstitutable *salva analycitate*. "The equilateral plane triangle" and "the equiangular plane triangle" are a case in point. But the converse is not true. Because those two terms are intersubstitutable *salva analycitate*, they must designate the same object in every possible world in which they have a designation. This is not the same thing as referential opacity. Smith might not believe that a certain equilateral triangle is equiangular.

Keith Donnellan says, "I think Russell...may have thought of acquaintance as a sufficient condition for genuine nam[e]ability" (Donnellan 1990: 105). I agree. Acquaintance is also a necessary condition for Russell, due to his famous principle of acquaintance. Russell says, "Every proposition which we can understand must be composed wholly of constituents with which we are acquainted" (PP 58, Russell's emphasis removed). This includes understanding every name in every proposition. Russell says, "[Y]ou cannot name anything you are not acquainted with" (PLA 201).

Two other authors, R. M. Sainsbury and Bernard Linsky, come close to my views on Russell on modality. "Sainsbury finds a surprising resemblance between Russell's theory of communication and recent theories of rigid designation" (Irvine 1993: x). Bernard Linsky reports that David Kaplan uses Russellian Propositions to explain direct reference, which is circuitously connected to possible worlds construed as "circumstances of evaluation" (B. Linsky 1993: 193; see D. Kaplan 1987: 239–41). They might be interested in my more direct arguments that Russell's logically proper names *are* rigid designators (ch. 3; ch. 3 n.4; Dejnožka 2003: 203; 1990: 395). I see no need to drag in "theories of communication" or "circumstances of evaluation." In fact, Russell says that a logically perfect language, in which every name is a logically proper name, would be "very largely private to one speaker. That is to say, all the names that it would use would be private to that speaker and could not enter into the language of another speaker" (PLA 198; see 195–96). In this regard, the "theory of communication" would be that there can be no communication. And the only "circumstance of evaluation" needed or even possible would be acquaintance with one's own sense-data. However, I am glad for these independent confirmations of my general view that Russell is more like Kripke than Kripke seems to think.

Kripke is perhaps the most famous critic of Russell who seems unaware that Russell holds a causal theory of reference somewhat like Kripke's own (Kripke 1980). Reference theorists in general focus on the 1905–18 Russell, and thus are unaware that the 1921–48 Russell offers a sophisticated causal theory of names involving social use, habits, training, reflexes, and laws of association in *The Analysis of Mind*, chapter 10, *An Outline of Philosophy*, part 1, chapter 4, and *Human Knowledge*, part 2, chapters 1–3. Obviously the later Russell wants a much fuller theory of how ordinary names denote than his old descriptivist theory of 1905–18. The seeds of this pivotal change may be seen in Russell's 1919 paper, "On Propositions: What They Are and How They Mean" (Russell 1971c). The change is basically complete in his 1921 *The Analysis of Mind*. There Russell says:

> The community that speaks a language has learnt it, and modified it by processes almost all of which are not deliberate, but the results of causes operating according to more or less ascertainable laws. (AMI 190)

No doubt this includes names and descriptions.

Kripke is just following the crowd. For another example, Leonard Linsky expounds Russell without a clue as to *either* Russell's cluster of descriptions theory for ordinary names (HK 79; MAL 209–10) *or* his causal reference theory, and even suggests Russell would be much improved by adding aspects of both of those theories! (L. Linsky 1977: 93–111). On cluster or family of descriptions theory, Kripke cites Wittgenstein's *Investigations* (PI #79) and, as "a *locus classicus*," John R. Searle (Kripke 1980: 31). Why does Kripke not cite his supposed chief opponent, Russell?

Hilary Putnam's suggestion that names refer to whatever a community of experts would refer to by them, and the suggestion that names refer to whatever the 'linguistic community' at large refers to by them, are anticipated by Russell's encyclopedia and geography book examples (HK 79, 102). Putnam says in praise of Michael Devitt's *Designation*,

> In recent years a new 'causal' theory of reference and meaning, based on the works of Saul Kripke, Hilary Putnam, and Keith Donnellan, has taken a position of prominence in the philosophy of language. The first serious effort to work out...the details of the new theory,

> Michael Devitt's book provides a theory of...
> 'designation'—and shows the bearing of this relationship
> on the meanings of various simple and complex express-
> ions. (Putnam 1981)

Putnam is treating Russell as if he died in 1918. Putnam's praise
for providing a causal theory of reference better describes *Human
Knowledge* (1948), the *Inquiry* (1940), which appeared over forty
years before Devitt's book, or *The Analysis of Matter* (1927),
which already connected Jones by multiple causal lines to users of
"Jones" (AMA 154, 203, 217, 314), or even *The Analysis of Mind*
(1921), written sixty years before Devitt's book.

    Any discussion of Russell's causal theory or theories of
reference is beyond the scope of this book.

    That Russell has a Humean analysis of causation does not
detract from anything I have said in this note.

    I see nothing in Gérard Bornet's paper, "Has Kripke
Refuted Russell?" (Bornet 1982–83: 31–40), that goes against my
views in this note.

    See note 4 for more on rigid designation.

    3. Kaplan defines "haecceitism" as "the view that it
[makes] sense to ask—without reference to common attributes and
behavior—whether this is the same individual in another possible
world." (D. Kaplan 1975: 722–23). Kaplan rightly deems Russell a
haecceitist in *Principles* and in *Principia* (Kaplan 1975: 725; see
1987: 239–41). Kaplan's definition applies to the 1918 Russell's
logically proper names of sense-data. The 1903 Russell is an
extreme haecceitist, since every possible term has an immediate
identity of its own prior to its possessing any properties (POM
451–52), and "no change can be conceived in it which would not
destroy its identity and make it another term" (POM 44).

    4. Saul A. Kripke, in *Naming and Necessity*, uses his two
main "terms quasi-technically" (Kripke 1980: 48):

> Let's call something a [weak] *rigid designator* if in every
> possible world it designated the same object, a *nonrigid*
> or *accidental designator* if that is not the case. Of course
> we don't require that the objects exist in all possible
> worlds. Certainly Nixon might not have existed [and we
> rigidly designate Nixon when we say that]....A rigid
> designator of a necessary existent can be called *strongly
> rigid*. (Kripke 1980: 48, Kripke's emphasis)

In light of Kripke's discussion of Keith Donnellan's distinction
between referential (singling out) and attributive (discussing the
object that has a certain attribute, whatever object that might be), it
seems we could equally well call rigid designators *referential*, and

nonrigid designators attributive (Kripke 1980: 25, 25n.). Kripke explains that he is discussing names in the sense of ordinary proper names, as opposed to both definite descriptions (Kripke 1980: 24) and Russell's logically proper names, which he declines to discuss (Kripke 1980: 27 n.). His main thesis is that (ordinary) names are rigid designators (Kripke 1980: 48–49). He explains that for him, merely possible worlds do not exist, but are only ways the actual world might have been (Kripke 1980: 18), and that he is not discussing names used by merely possible people in merely possible worlds, but only actual names used by actual people in the actual world (Kripke 1980: 77). He gives a causal chain theory of the reference of names. He says Russell "did not consider modal questions[,] and the rigidity issue was not mentioned" by him (Kripke 1980: 14). Kripke says much more, but this will be enough for us. Five comments follow.

First, while Russell does not use Kripke's *term* "rigid," Russell's logically proper names *are* rigid designators. There are four arguments for thinking so. (a) Their meaning is their denotation. Therefore to change their meaning is to change their denotation, and to change their denotation is to change their meaning. (b) We are acquainted with the sense-data they denote, and acquaintance is direct cognition of a thing exactly as it appears to be. (c) They refer. They do not describe. Thus they can scarcely be attributive. That Russell's term is "denote" does not detract from this. We must look not to his term "denote," but to how he uses it in the case of logically proper names, as opposed to the case of descriptions. I give arguments (a)–(c) in the main body of this chapter. Charles Pigden adds an elliptical fourth argument (d):

> [A] Russellian logically proper name must be rigid.... No bearer, no logically proper name; hence if there is a logically proper name there must be a bearer. (Pigden 1998)

The hidden premiss is that the bearer cannot vary across worlds; and that is true for logically proper names.

Pigden's point is that, as we saw earlier, for Russell the use of expressions as names has an implication much like that intended by the ontological argument. That is, a name must be a name of something (IMT 32). And if I may use possible worlds talk, if a sense-datum is not in a certain possible world, then there can be no logically proper name for that sense-datum in that world either. For it would lack meaning and denotation. This primary level modal feature (iii) of particulars, or transcendental Parmenideanism. The existence of a particular is transcendentally necessary with respect to thought and language. That is, it is logically necessary, in order for us to be acquainted with or to be able to name a particular, that it exist in the primary, Parmenidean sense of not being nothing. An acquaintance must be an acquaintance *with* something, and a genuine name must be a name *of* something. Thus transcendental Parmenideanism implies rigid designation. And for the 1914–1918 Russell, the implication is mutual.

My second comment is that any causal theory of reference must preclude rigid designation. For causal theories of reference can only be attributive. For on any such theory, the name denotes the cause of our use of it, *whatever that cause might be*. Thus on causal theories of reference, there is never a referentially used designator. Thus there never is rigid designation either. This argument may be posed as a vicious regress of causal references, since we never single anything out referentially in the Donnellanian sense; but that does not really add anything to the argument.

Referentially singling an object out, in the Donnellanian sense, is always singling out *this* object. It is essentially cognitive and intentional, as opposed to causal. Russell's logically proper names are essentially cognitive and intentional names of sense-data we are given in acquaintance. Russell's ordinary proper names are always attributive, since for him they are always covert definite descriptions. More precisely, they are not names at all, since his theory of definite descriptions is an eliminative analysis of ordinary names qua names; according to the theory, ordinary names are covert definite descriptions. But ordinary proper names certainly can be cognitive and intentional in a very ordinary sense, if I am speaking about an object my audience and I can see at the time, and arguably even if we have singled out the object in the past and remember it. Arguably, all of that is phenomenologically given to us as the case. But no one alive has singled out Aristotle perceptually. Perhaps we can arguably single him out as an object of thought. But if I single out Aristotle *only* qua object of thought, I am not literally singling *him* out, since he is (or was) not really or essentially a mere object of thought. In short, I must single out perceptible objects *in* perception, or must *have* singled them out in perception, in order for me to single them out referentially. Otherwise they are behind the curtain of my present and memorial sense-experience, and can only be attributively described by me. This point is neutral concerning which theory of perception is correct. For Russell, sense-data are the barrier between us and any external world that may exist. For me, ordinary objects of perception or thought (which are Continental-style phenomena, and not objects in themselves) are the barrier.

To sum up the second comment, causal reference theory is not a kind of rigid designation theory.

Third, causation has a background role in references to ordinary objects, meaning there are background causal conditions; but that is all it can have.

Fourth, any causal theory of reference precludes strongly rigid designation of necessary existents unless necessary existents are capable of causation. Perhaps God can cause me to think of him, single him out, and strongly rigidly designate him. For God is an agent, in fact the most powerful agent conceivable. But the usual suspects, such as numbers, classes, logical forms, and universals *ante rem*, are generally considered acausal. In contrast, a cognitive and intentional theory of reference is the natural sort of theory for referring to any such abstract acausal entities.

The above four criticisms of causal theory of reference apply to the later Russell's causal theory of reference as well. The later Russell admits a probably real scientific world, but would use descriptions for anything we cannot single out beyond the curtain of perception. The later Russell admits at least generic universals, and surely admits awareness of them of some sort.

Fifth, intentionality and intensionality are tied. Certainly they are in Frege. Kripke criticizes Frege's senses for being merely attributive (Kripke 1980: 27). Yet a Fregean sense contains a mode of cognitive presentation, a way an entity can be singled out. I have discussed this elsewhere and do not wish to belabor the scholarly point here (Dejnožka 2010a: 120–21, 21n.2; 2007: 72, 105 n.15). But even aside from Frege, who was primarily concerned with logical and mathematical entities, all of which have infinitely many necessarily unique properties and relationships to each other (FA ii, 15), it seems splitting hairs to distinguish singling out the number two from describing it as, say, the only even prime number. How else *can* we single out a number or any other abstract object, when we single it out *only* in thought (as opposed, say, to seeing three cats), except in terms of a uniquely necessary property? What is the cash value of the distinction here? What does it amount to? Surely it is otiose to say "the only even prime number, whatever number that might be." As if it could be anything but the number two! My point applies only to people who have already learned the identity of the only even prime number, or similar identities. It does not apply to logical or mathematical identities which have yet to be proved, and which are, so to speak, behind the curtain of proof. But the point remains that intentionality and intensionality are essentially tied for abstract objects in a way that blends or blurs the distinction between reference and attribution. Either that, or we will have to abandon strongly rigid designators for them, since there is no other way to single them out purely in thought. Note that this point is not necessarily limited to small numbers or to numbers we know well. To think so is to confuse abstract cognition with perception or with imaging. The whole point of Frege's examples of large collections of things whose images we cannot distinguish (FA 10–11), or for that matter René Descartes' chiliagon (1,000 sided figure) and 1,001 sided figure, is that we can often intellectually think of logically necessary differences among large numbers quite clearly, even though we cannot image their differences clearly at all (Descartes 1969 / 1642: 185–86). For example, 1,000 is clearly divisible by 2, 4, 5, 100, 250, and 500, while 1,001 is clearly not, yet we cannot image or perceive the difference between a 1,000 sided figure and a 1,001 sided figure.

There is a second tie. Even attributive descriptions make "reference...to attributes" (Burge 1983: 80). Certainly they do for Russell due to his principle of acquaintance, since every description has a universal for its determinate constituent, and we must be acquainted with the universal in order to understand the description.

Here is a third tie: Merrill B. Hintikka and Jaakko Hintikka suggest replacing "Husserl's conception of 'intentionality as directedness' by a deeper conception of intentionality as an intrinsically modal ideal ('intentionality as intensionality'), i.e., as involving always a range of alternative possibilities" (M. Hintikka 1986: 150). Here we might seek to understand either intentionality in terms of intensionality, or the reverse, or perhaps in both ways. If the two terms are logically equivalent, we may define either as the other, and the question devolves to which term better illuminates the other. I hold that intentionality is primary, since we must intend universals in order to have them as our concepts *á la* Russell. See my argument that singling out is prior to reference, and reference is prior to truth-conditions (my 2003: 286–87).

The early Russell makes a fourth tie. Since for him the meaning of a logically proper name is the object it denotes, acquaintance with that object is both intensional (meaning) and intentional (denotation).

5. Sense-particulars do have what I have called primary level modal features (i)–(iii) in chapter 3. Does Russell then "hold that among the contents of the actual world there are modal or intensional entities," or even entities "that have a modal property or characteristic" (Loux 1979: 49)? Thanks to the eliminative nature of transcendental Parmenideanism and of MDL, I think not. The 1911–27 Russell also admits what we would ordinarily regard as *de re* predications of universals of their instances, e.g., red of an instance of red. And he also admits in effect *de re* predications of type 2 order 0 universals of type 1 order 0 universals. This is in the sense that three conditions obtain: (1) he predicates type 2 order 0 propositional functions of type 1 order 0 propositional functions; (2) type 2 order 0 universals are "determinate constituents" (MAL

220–21) of type 2 order 0 propositional functions; and (3) type 1 order 0 universals are determinate constituents of type 1 order 0 propositional functions. Now, we would not ordinarily regard many of those predications as *de re*, since they are logically contingent. For instance, suppose that all individuals were red. We would not ordinarily say that universality, or in MDL, necessity, is predicable *de re* of red. This predication of 'always true' would be *de re*, since it relates two nonlinguistic universals into a nonlinguistic general fact. And it would be necessary in the MDL or Parmenidean sense that for Russell, the only possible red individuals are actual red individuals; there are no merely possible red individuals for him. What is more, Russell's principal of acquaintance demands no less. The principle of acquaintance is, "Every proposition which we can understand must be composed wholly of constituents with which we are acquainted" (PP 58, italic emphasis deleted; see OD 56 for its earliest published statement in 1905). Thus not only must the universals *universality* and *red* be constituents of the proposition that all individuals are red, but we also must be acquainted with both of them in order to be able to understand the proposition. Yet if all individuals were red, that would be logically contingent. Here we seem to return to the howlers of MDL, but my resolutions are still available, including the Parmenidean resolution just noted.

Concerning the objects of Wittgenstein's *Tractatus*, Merrill B. Hintikka and Jaakko Hintikka suggest replacing "Husserl's conception of 'intentionality as directedness' by a deeper conception of intentionality as an intrinsically modal ideal ('intentionality as intensionality'), i.e., as involving always a range of alternative possibilities" (M. Hintikka 1986: 150). Jaakko Hintikka is cited as a reference (J. Hintikka 1973: title essay). But replacement is one thing and scholarship is another. And a *replacement* cannot even be suggested for Russell's conception of acquaintance. That is because for Russell, the meaning of a logically proper name *is* the object it denotes. Thus acquaintance with that object *already is* both intensional (meaning) and intentional (denotation).

6. Diodorus Cronus and his student Philo of Megara appear to be the first temporal modal logicians.

If we were to look for an implicit temporal modal logic in the great philosophers, we would look to Aristotle, Aquinas, Spinoza, and Leibniz.

Aquinas says, in his third way to prove that God exists:

> The third way is based on what need not be and on what must be, and runs as follows. Some of the things we come across can be but need not be, for we find them springing up and dying away, thus sometimes in being

> and sometimes not. Now everything cannot be like this, for a thing that need not be, once was not; and if everything need not be, once upon a time there was nothing. But if that were true there would be nothing even now, because something that does not exist can only be brought into being by something already existing. So that if nothing was in being nothing could be brought into being, and nothing would be in being now, which contradicts observation. Not everything therefore is the sort of thing that need not be; there has got to be something that must be. (Aquinas 1969: 69)

The key premiss is that if a thing is non-necessary, then it cannot have always existed in time. If so, then it follows by contraposition that something that has always existed is a necessary thing. If logical necessity is meant, then both the argument and its contrapositive are plainly *non sequitur*. A stock counterexample to both is that candles are logically contingent things, yet it is logically possible that a certain candle has always existed and always will. The detail of the argument has some superficial plausibility. How could a thing have always existed unless it were a necessary thing? But this fails to distinguish merely happening to have always existed from being a logically necessary being, and thus begs the question against the possibility of there being logically contingent beings that merely happen to have always existed. The further claim that if everything need not be, then there must have been a time when nothing was, only compounds the *non sequitur* with a fallacy of composition. For it is logically possible that an infinite temporal series of temporally overlapping candles go back infinitely in time, so that at every past time, at least one candle existed. And to assume that there is some special temporal sense of possibility that validates the argument only begs the question.

    Thomas Gilby cites these precursors of Aquinas' third way:

> Plato reasons that were nothing deathless nothing now would be alive [*Phædo* 72; *Phædrus* 245–47]; Plotinus and Augustine pick up the same theme [*Enneads* IV, 7; *Confessions* XI, 4]....St Thomas owes more to the Arabic philosophers than to [Aristotle], or to Boethius and the *Liber de Causis*. His wording echoes Maimonides, who took the proof from Avicenna. Everything that is exists either as a 'bound to be' or as a 'possible'....
>   [Aristotle] tries to show that something which always existed and will exist is something that must exist [*De Cælo* I, 11–12 / 281*a*–283*b*26]. (Aquinas 1969: 281, 284, cites omitted or placed in square brackets)

Gilby recommends simply dropping the temporal aspect of Aquinas' argument and retaining only an argument that contingent beings must ultimately depend on there being a necessary being (Aquinas 1969: 284). But this does not remove the problem. For it is logically possible that logically contingent beings always have caused each other to exist. At least, an infinite regress of logically contingent causes would seem benign on its face. And perhaps it is ultimately a primitive logical intuition whether such regresses are benign or vicious. But I offer arguments by analogy in "Zeno's Paradoxes and the Cosmological Argument" (Dejnožka 1989).

On the thesis that all things in time are necessary beings, see Spinoza's *Ethic*, propositions 16, 23, 29, 33, and 35, and the attendant discussions (Spinoza 1958: 113, 115, 122–23, 125, 129).

There is nothing like any of this in Russell. Indeed, Russell says of Leibniz, "If every proposition ascribes a predicate to some existent, then we cannot maintain, as an ultimate truth, that the non-existent is possible....Thus Leibniz falls...into a Spinozistic necessity: only the actual is possible, the non-existent is impossible, and the ground for contingency has disappeared" (PL 183).

Chapter 4: Their Ontological Foundation

1. Both (i) "the class of classes not members of themselves" (POM 101–7) and (ii) "the null class" (POM 75) must be nondenoting. Russell says (iii) the phrase "is 30. per cent. healthier" is nondenoting (POM 176). (iv) The phrase "the particularized relation" (i.e., 'the relation which is a particular') is nondenoting (POM 211); compare Frege on the problem of the concept *horse* (TW 46). (v) Russell rejects Frege's view that certain function- expressions denote functions (POM 508–10). (vi) All motions are fictions (POM 473). Thus expressions for motions are nondenoting. (vii) A component vector of a motion "is doubly a fiction," not even being a motion (POM 474). Thus motion vector expressions are nondenoting. (viii) Infinitesimal rational or real numbers are rejected as impossible (POM 335). Thus expressions for such numbers are nondenoting. (ix) Infinitesimal magnitudes as orders of functions are rejected as impossible (POM 336–37). Thus expressions for such magnitudes are nondenoting.

Russell says in the preface that it was an "error" for him to reject the null class in the main text (POM xvi). Surely he means that it was an intellectual error, not an editing error. In *Principia*. the null class is the only class lacking class existence, where class existence is defined as meaning having at least one member. But in *Principia*, "class existence" is existence in name only. *No* classes have ontological status in *Principia*. All classes are ontologically nothing. Thus all classes are rejected in *Principia*, not just the null class. Thus the null class is now the ontological equal of all other classes. Ontologically, all classes are equally rejected in *Principia*. In this sense, the *Principles* "error" is now gone.

2. Actually, "object" is wider, including terms and classes as many (POM 55n).

3. Russell allows that there may be entities simpler than those which we have regarded as simple in our language, thought, and acquaintance so far. But he says only sometimes that there must be simples if there are complexes (LK 337). Elsewhere he says he *believes* there are simples but admits that analysis *may* have no end (PLA 202; compare AMA 276). Although unpresented simples could not be assigned logically proper names, they would belong to modal level (1*). Their three modal features would be: (i*) Their existence is absolutely contingent, at least if they belong to the natural world. (ii*) There are no *merely possible* unpresented (alien) simples. (iii*) Unpresented simples can only be described. But if, *per impossibile*, they *could* be named with logically proper names, then they *would* be transcendentally necessary.

4. *Inquiry* and *Human Knowledge* distinguish between the perceptual object and its sensational core. The texts I cite reflect a different issue: Russell's abandonment of the act-object distinction.

Chapter 5: Rescher's Case Against Russell

1. As C. I. Lewis and C. H. Langford put it: "[L]ogic and deductive systems are never concerned with existence except in a hypothetical sense....Thus 'existence' has to do with the possibility of intellectual construction, or of definite conception which is free from inconsistency" (C. Lewis 1932: 182 n.10). One might even compare Descartes or Hume on necessary truths as timelessly obtaining relations of ideas.

2. Russell's usage reflects the fact that since in the primary senses of "actual" and "possible," the only possible things are actual things, something true of all actual things is true of all possible things in MDL {1}. That the primary aim of the usage concerns theory of types does not detract from my point. See page 156.

Ivor Grattan-Guinness (1977: 113n) gives a list of studies of Russell's notion of implication. On Diodorus Cronus, see William Kneale and Martha Kneale (Kneale 1964: 117ff.).

Chapter 6: *Russell's Eight Implicit Modal Logics*

1. For convenience, I am using Raymond Bradley (1983: 205–8), which takes "some liberties" with C. I. Lewis's S-systems, both simplificational and terminological. Compare C. Lewis (1932: 492–502; 1918: chapter 5), A. N. Prior (1955: 305), and G. E. Hughes and M. J. Cresswell (Hughes 1968: chapters 12–13).

2. Where "*Fx*" is a *Principia* schema representing elementary propositions (PM 129), Landini notes that *Principia* includes a rule of universal generalization, $Fx \supset (x)Fx$, which resembles what Hughes and Cresswell call the rule of necessitation N: $\vdash P \to \vdash \Box P$ (Landini 1993). In MDL, "$(x)Fx$" means by definition that *Fx* is necessary with respect to *x*. N is the metalinguistic rule that if "*P*" is a thesis (i.e. valid axiom or theorem), then (it is derivable that) "$\Box P$" is a thesis. N is not a rule of S1, S2, or S3, but is a rule of S4 and S5 (Hughes 1972: 236). But Hughes and Cresswell allow a restricted version, N(S1), which restricts N to theses containing no modal operators. N(S1) is a metalinguistic rule of S1, and therefore of S1–S5 (Hughes 1972: 225). N and N(S1) are not to be confused with the object-language "invalid wff" N*: $P \supset \Box P$, which is not a thesis in any of S1–S5 (Hughes 1972: 31). N* asserts that whatever is true is necessary, or if you like, that whatever is actual is necessary. Thus N* is Parmenidean, and is closest to the primary level of Russell's theory of modality, which is reflected in MDL. That is, N resembles Russell's express definition of "is necessary" as meaning "is always true" in MDL. Landini is absolutely right about that. But the analogy limps badly with respect to whether MDL could be a modal logic, since of course MDL cannot be a modal logic. For a modal logic prefixes modal operators to statements. Now, N and N* are true or false statements whose consequents prefix or involve the prefixing of modal operators to statements. But "is always true," or if you please, "is necessary with respect to *x*," is an incomplete modal expression predicated of lower level incomplete expressions.

3. Wright and others would disagree with me (Wright 1951: 41, 57; but see 41n).

4. Quine says:

> Russell's theory of descriptions, in its original formulation, involved distinctions of so-called 'scope'. Change in the scope of a description was indifferent to the truth value of any statement, however, unless the description failed to name....On the other hand, Smullyan allows differences of scope to affect truth value even in cases where the description concerned succeeds in naming. (FLPV 154n)

As Quine knows, for Russell no description is a name. Therefore all descriptions fail to name merely in virtue of being descriptions, not names. I therefore charitably take it that by "failed to name," Quine means "failed to denote." Now, the "original formulation" of Russell's theory of descriptions is in "On Denoting." There Russell gives an example, "the present King of France." This definite description fails to denote, since there is no present King of France. But Russell's other example of a definite description in "On Denoting" involves no such failure to denote. There Russell says:

> I have heard a touchy yacht owner to whom a guest, on first seeing it, remarked, 'I thought your yacht was larger than it is'; and the owner replied, 'No, my yacht is not larger than it is'. What the guest meant was, 'The size I thought your yacht was is greater than the size your yacht is'; the meaning attributed to him is, 'I thought the size of your yacht was greater than the size of your yacht'. (OD 52)

Here the two occurrences of "the size of your yacht" successfully denote the size of the yacht, but "The size I thought your yacht was" does not. The scope change makes a big difference to the truth-value of the guest's statement. Therefore Quine is wrong, if I have interpreted him correctly. The change of truth-value has nothing to do with failure to denote (unlike "the present King of France"), and everything to do with what Russell calls propositional attitude and Quine calls referential opacity. But the better interpretation of Quine is that he simply means that there is no reference in contexts of referential opacity. That is, when he says "failed to name," he really means "failed to refer to the *normal* or *intended* referent." Compare Frege on sense and reference.

Smullyan says Russell and Whitehead "inadvertently assert" scope indifference in *Principia*, at least in the sense that the proposition with larger scope "always implies" the proposition with smaller scope (Smullyan 1971: 38; PM 186). It is inadvertent because they admit non-truth-functional functions in *Principia* (PM 8), while scope indifference obtains only in truth-functional logic (Smullyan 1971: 37). Smullyan is strictly correct. But it takes little charity to assume that Russell and Whitehead are asserting scope indifference only in the context of pursuing their basic project of logicizing mathematics. That project is entirely truth-functional.

5. Per my seminar notes for 1973–74. I cannot find an endorsement of mental cause-mental-effect in Bergmann's published writings. But it would be consistent with his Humean "constant conjunction" theory of causation. Herbert Hochberg says:

There is no fundamental difference between cases of causal connection, where the cause and effect are both physical and where one is physical and the other mental, on a Humean style view....For we do not deal with "essential necessary connections" but with general facts [or] generalities—constant correlations, if you will (Hochberg 2001: 316)

Likewise, on a Humean view, where the cause and effect are both mental. "Any time I think of the death of my friend, I feel sad" is, if true, not *logically* true. But we should not expect to find many such simple constant conjunctions in the mental world, and should look for complex systems of interacting variables, just as we do in the physical world. Bergmann would be the first to tell us that.

Chapter 7: Does Russell Have an Implicit Possible Worlds Logic?

1. As for iteration, compare Carnap (1967a: 174) with Carnap (1963: 62) on interpreting modalities as properties of propositions. I see no reason why Russell could not interpret Carnap's iterative operator "N" as Russell's "is analytic." And Russell easily could use my sentence S near the beginning of chapter 2. Here I omit Russell's doubts about defining Carnap's analyticity in 1938 (POM ix; see xii), and Russell's abandonment of any clear criteria of analyticity in 1948 (HK 76–81, 138–41, 237–42).

Nicholas Griffin rightly sees that there is no iteration in MDL (Griffin 1980: 126). But he raises the question only because he wrongly thinks MDL is Russell's (implicit) modal logic. MDL is only a trio of definitions of incomplete expressions. It is only the basic building block of FG–MDL and FG–MDL*. Griffin appears to be mixing up MDL with FG–MDL in particular (Griffin 1980: 132). Both FG–MDL and FG–MDL* clearly allow iteration.

Griffin criticizes MDL on the basis of his interpretation of *Principles of Mathematics*, even though, as Griffin knows, MDL is not in *Principles*, and is in fact Russell's replacement of *Principles*' Moorean theory of degrees of implicative necessity (Griffin 1980: 121–28). Griffin's criticism does not even seem to get *Principles* right. He begins by quoting *Principles* as using p and q to stand for propositions (Griffin 1980: 122), but soon construes p and q as variables (Griffin 1980: 123), and draws the wildest consequences for MDL. Again, MDL is not even in *Principles* in the first place.

Variables in MDL do not and cannot take propositions as values. In "'x is red' is necessary," which means by definition "'x is red' is always true", *x* ranges over individuals, not propositions. For Russell, propositions cannot *be* "always true", much less "not always true". They are and can only be true or false. That "'*x* is a proposition' is always true" is well-formed does not detract from this point. Where *x* ranges over individuals, "*x* is a proposition" is always false for categorial reasons.

2. Gustav Bergmann thought of this years before I did. See Hochberg (1994: 10). It is strictly incorrect to say that bareness would be an essential property of bare particulars. The term "bare" grammatically functions not to ascribe an ontological property of bareness, but to deny the ascription of ontological properties. None the less, a thing truly said to be bare of properties is also truly said to be essentially bare, since the bareness is for categorial reasons. We may call essential bareness "veridical essentialism" as opposed to ontological essentialism, since bareness is not a property, and to say a thing is bare (of properties) is simply to say that the thing has no properties.

3. Like me, Peter Simons holds that Tractarian objects are in all possible worlds (Simons 1992: 343). Simons follows Georg Henrik von Wright in finding an implicit S5 modal logic in the *Tractatus* (Simons 1992: 342). This puts Wittgenstein in the Leibniz-Russell camp.

Chapter 8: Motives and Origins of Russell's Theory of Modality

1. Quine's very kind note to me continues, "But our colleagues in modal logic will not settle for anything so innocent" (Quine: 1990). Compare Quine, "Reply to Dagfinn Føllesdal" (PQ 114); "Reply to David Kaplan" (PQ 292); (PT 30, 73); (FLPV 4).

2. Russell's admission of "unreals" (merely possible entities) in *Principles* has been questioned by Nicholas Griffin. Following Nino Cocchiarella and "to some extent also [Peter] Hylton" (Griffin 1996: 47), Griffin argues that *Principles* is not a neo-Meinongian work. Griffin seems to mean by this only that *definite descriptions* such as "the Homeric god of war" do not ontologically commit the 1903 Russell to admitting nonexistent entities such as the Homeric gods. But one of the texts Griffin quotes as attributing neo-Meinongianism to the 1903 Russell, namely, J. O. Urmson's text, makes no such claim about definite descriptions in *Principles* (Griffin 1996: 26–27). Urmson says only that the 1903 Russell *admits* nonexistent entities—a position which Griffin is careful not to deny, or at least does not deny. Griffin never explains exactly what he means by neo-Meinongianism. Griffin does say that his view of *Principles* leads to a major reinterpretation of "On Denoting," since it cannot be the main

purpose of "On Denoting" to shave away Russell's own neo-Meinongian jungle if Russell never had one in the first place. And this suggests that Griffin finds no nonexistent entities in *Principles* after all.

Griffin indicates definite descriptions by quotation marks, e.g., "the present King of France," and denoting concepts by slash marks, e.g., /the present King of France/. Griffin claims that "the present King of France" stands for a denoting concept, /the present King of France/, and this denoting concept does not, or at least need not, *denote* the entity, the nonexistent King of France, even if Russell *admits* the nonexistent King of France as an entity in his ontology. Thus Griffin admits that Russell can admit nonexistents, even if denoting concepts need not denote them.

Griffin's interpretation of *Principles* raises some questions. If Russell *does* admit nonexistent entities, then why would his definite descriptions and his denoting concepts *not* denote them? Indeed, how could they *fail* to denote them? Could he talk about them only by using names as opposed to descriptions?

Griffin's argument seems to be that denoting concepts need not denote entities, therefore Russell need not admit nonexistent entities. The premiss is true. Griffin cites a good example, /the null class/, since Russell requires classes to have members. The chief example is, of course, the famous /the class of all classes not members of themselves/, since Russell clearly holds there is no such class. But such examples show only that denoting concepts do not and cannot denote *impossible* entities, since there are and can be no such entities there to be denoted. But this leaves all the room in the world for denoting concepts to be able to denote, and even to be required to denote, merely *possible* entities For there are and can be merely possible entities for Russell in *Principles*. Thus Griffin makes a hasty generalization. For it may well be, and it seems very plausible to suppose, that Russell requires his denoting concepts to denote terms even if the terms are merely *possible* terms, precisely because he admits such entities. Why else would he call his denoting concepts "*denoting* concepts"? What other job would such concepts have, what else would they do, if the entities are there to be denoted?

Griffin proceeds to three subtler arguments. (1) Even though Russell has analyzed numbers away by defining them as classes, Russell would still have to admit the number two as the denotation of /the number two/, if all denoting concepts must denote. That is, he would have to admit an entity he analyzed away (Griffin 1996: 50). (2) Existence proofs are not needed in mathematics if every denoting concept already denotes (Griffin 1996: 51, attributed to Hylton). (3) At least one basic law of logic will be falsified, since /the round square/ would denote the round square, which term would violate the law of noncontradiction (Griffin 1996: 51–52). These arguments are aimed only at the thesis that every denoting concept denotes, not at the thesis that there are nonexistent objects. (Objects include both terms, i.e. entities, which are one, and classes, which are many.) And each argument has a fatal weakness.

Argument (1) fails to distinguish showing that two has a merely logical nature from showing that two is not an object at all. That is the whole difference between reductive and eliminative definition. The 1903 Russell is a reductivist. For the 1903 Russell, /the number two/ *does* denote the number two. For when the number two is defined, it is not *eliminated*, but is merely reduced to a *logical* object, namely, the class of pairs. It remains just as much an entity as ever. It loses only its special mathematical character. The 1905 Russell becomes an eliminativist in "on Denoting."

Argument (2) overlooks Russell's careful distinction among mathematical existence, empirical existence, and being. Mathematical existence proofs prove only mathematical existence, which for Russell reduces to logical existence. But nonexistents are objects which do not exist *either* mathematically *or* empirically. Nonexistent objects have *neither* kind of *existence*. They have only *being*. The only connection is the negative one that mathematical proofs of *non*existence, e.g. of the nonexistence of the greatest prime number, are also proofs that there is and can be no such entity or *being*. Positive existence proofs are still needed for numbers like two. They show mathematical existence, and thereby being.

Argument (3) concerns only *impossible* objects, which Russell rejects. All logically possible objects, including all merely possible objects, do conform to the law of noncontradiction.

The chief text favoring Griffin's view is Russell's saying that propositions like "chimaeras are animals" and "even primes other than two are numbers" "appear to be true, and it would seem that they are not concerned with the denoting concepts, but with what these concepts denote; yet that is impossible, for the concepts in question do not denote anything" (POM 73). Unlike even primes other than two, surely chimaeras are possible entities. They are simply animals consisting of animal parts of different species. But Russell is discussing not whether there is a class of nonexistent chimaeras, but whether there is a null class to be denoted here. Russell goes on to allow the null class as a device to logicians due to its utility. But he says that "the class of interpretations considered in the present chapter, which are dependent upon actual classes, fail where we are concerned with null class-concepts, on the ground there is no actual null-class" (POM 74–75). Thus Russell rejects "chimaeras are animals" as false, "while retaining as true the various other propositions that would be equivalent to it if there were chimaeras;" this includes "any chimaera is an animal" (POM 74), which, because it is true, *does* denote some one nonexistent chimaera (POM 59).

The chief text favoring Griffin seems anomalous. But it is not even an anomaly. For the proposition "centaurs are animals" simply fails to include a denoting phrase in the first place, since none of the six magic words ("any," "all," "a," etc.), nor any synonym for "some one of them," occurs in it (POM 56). I doubt that *Principles* on the whole is best understood as restricting classes to classes of existents, despite chapter 6's use of expressions such as "classes in existence" and "actual classes" (POM 68, 75), and despite the book's apparent lack of any examples of classes of nonexistents. Indeed, Russell's specifying "classes in existence" and "actual classes" suggests the opposite. Surely it is *because* he admits classes of nonexistents that he sometimes needs to specify that he is discussing *actual* classes or classes *of existents*. And are not chimaeras and the Homeric gods precisely Russell's examples of classes of nonexistents?

Griffin says, "There seems no ground for thinking it was Russell's view that chimaeras were countable" (Griffin 1996: 54–55). But it *was* Russell's view. Russell says "every term is *one*," including "a chimaera" (POM 43). Russell expressly says "a chimaera and a four-dimensional space, are certainly two" (POM 71). Thus, just as with Leibniz and Frege, Russell's arithmetic is supremely general and applies to everything there is. (For Frege, of course, chimaeras are not.) Thus Russell *must* admit the class of chimaeras, if his mathematics is to be truly universal (see POM xvii–xviii). For his numbers are classes of classes. Note that if there is any exegetical problem here, it is about admitting classes of chimaeras, not admitting chimaeras. For I just quoted two texts in which Russell expressly admits chimaeras.

Griffin believes that the toughest texts for his view to explain are Russell's official lists of terms, which include chimaeras, the Homeric gods, and the pseudo-existents of a novel. Griffin's solution is to say that these are not really lists of terms, but lists of denoting concepts. This is quite wrong. Russell says, "A man, a moment,...a chimaera,...is sure to be a term" (POM 43; compare POM 71). Strictly speaking, Griffin is right that these are denoting phrases, thanks to the word "a." But surely Russell is using the word "a" casually here. For he does not say "is sure to be a denoting concept." He says, "is sure to be a term." And looking at the context of the quoted sentence, the whole paragraph is a discussion of terms. Griffin is stumbling over the tree of Russell's casual use of the word "a." He misses the forest that the paragraph is all about terms. Besides the "a," what else could be the reason for his view?

In fact the toughest texts for Griffin to explain are those in which Russell: (1) distinguishes existence from being, allowing for and evidently admitting nonexistent beings (POM 71, 449); (2) says that anything thinkable is an entity, evidently finding many nonexistent beings eminently thinkable (POM 43, 449); and (3) gives a private language argument which establishes an extreme realism on which any object of thought which people can publicly discuss is real (POM 450–51); the argument plainly applies to nonexistents. It is these deep, substantive texts which best explain how to understand Russell's lists of nonexistent terms, notwithstanding his casual use of the word "a." Griffin does not attempt to explain many of these texts. Griffin does not even notice that Russell's main mission in "On Denoting" is to eliminate nonexistent objects, not only in Meinong, but also in his own book, *Principles*. Russell makes this clear in the second edition (POM x). And if Russell was rejecting nonexistent objects in *Principles*, surely he would have said so in that book. Surely he would have made that clear so. Or at least he would not have written "On Denoting" to make it sound as if he was rejecting nonexistents for the first time.

Griffin does argue that Russell's objects of thought are denoting concepts. But in his private language argument, Russell speaks of "numbers, relations, and many other objects of thought" (POM 450–51). There are no magic words such as "a" or "the" in the list. And Russell says, "Whatever may be an object of thought...I call a *term*" (POM 43; see 449). Here, by the way, it is obvious that we *must* discount the "an" as casual talk, or even as what Frege would call "an awkwardness of language" (TW 46). Again, possible objects of thought are what can be counted (POM 71 and 449, clarifying 43). Russell says "every term is *one*," including "a chimaera" (POM 43). Russell expressly says "a chimaera and a four-dimensional space, are certainly two" (POM 71). How can they be counted unless they are entities? Certainly the null class and the class of all classes not members of themselves are two in some sense as well, even though they are *not* entities; and that may seem to support Griffin. (Griffin does not make this point.) But *those* classes are *impossible*. It seems obvious that when Russell speaks of counting "a chimaera and a four-dimensional space" as "two," he is speaking of entities. In contrast, all the expressions in *Principles* for impossible items would denote *impossibilia* if they denoted anything; but they are all nondenoting. Therefore there are no *impossibilia* in *Principles*. See chapter 4, note 1 for a list of nine nondenoting expressions in *Principles*.

My conclusion is that all denoting concepts are possible objects of thought, but not all possible objects of thought are denoting concepts. They include all of Russell's entities, all of which are thinkable, since he rejects impossible entities. This note includes material from but supersedes Dejnožka (1997).

3. Not everyone agrees that Aristotle's modal logic is S5. Richard Patterson denies that Aristotle's modal logic is S5 or even S4. Patterson says, "The point is simply that we would like, as far as possible, to express the relevant insights and proofs in the way Aristotle did. There was no formal model available to him, let alone one as powerful as quantified S4 or S5" (R. Patterson 1995: 179). And

> there is the additional problem that...quantified S4 or S5...would be much stronger" than Aristotle's system, in that it would contain not only the syllogisms he regarded as valid but also some he deliberately did not include. To begin with, these systems are built on modern first-order predicate calculus, which already extends far beyond Aristotle's assertoric syllogisms. An analogous point would hold for modal portions of the system. This might not seem particularly disturbing. After all, one could regard Aristotle's system as a fragment, interesting from certain historical or philosophical points of view, of a more powerful modern logic. Indeed, this would make possible an interesting comparison of the strength of Aristotle's system with contemporary modal logics....
> As worthwhile as that may be—again, overlooking for a moment problems with carrying out the required translations—the drawback is that it obscures the manner in which Aristotle actually built up his system. (R. Patterson 1995: 227)

I do not wish to deny Patterson's points. I only wish to reiterate my simple point, *mutatis mutandis*, for Aristotle's modal logic, and also for his general syllogistic. Let us rewrite every syllogistic form as a conditional formal statements. Obviously, the statements will be true in virtue of their logical form for Aristotle if and only if the corresponding syllogistic forms are valid for Aristotle. But they will also be necessarily possible if they are possible, again in virtue of their form. And that is the distinguishing axiom of S5. Further, if it is possible that they are possible, then they are possible. And that is the distinguishing axiom of S4. Here I am in the business of providing logically equivalent rewrites. Aristotle did not consider his general syllogistic to be a modal logic. Nonetheless, it is beyond a reasonable doubt that if we *were* to prefix the conditional statements that *correspond* to his 256 syllogisms with appropriate modal operators, the result *would* be S5. That his syllogistic is a limited part of modern classical logic (since modern classical logic can paraphrase it simply by adding existential import through the inclusion of existential quantifiers) only confirms this point. There can be indefinitely many systems which are S5, but which are not proper sub-parts of modern classical logic. But the fact that syllogistic is a valid part of modern classical logic only confirms my point that syllogistic is S5, since modern classical logic is S5.

Chapter 9: Russell's Implicit Relevance Logic

1. Mares says the Routley-Meyer semantics described in Anderson (1992) makes it "abundantly clear" that Anderson-Belnap relevance is not "any sort of containment relation" (Mares 1997). But it is obvious that Anderson and Belnap themselves think of both primitive entailment and tautological entailment as containment relations. They state that their approach honors Kant's "principle of 'containment'," and they use the word "contained" to describe primitive entailment (Anderson 1975: 155). And their use easily carries over to tautological entailment. For just as they say, the containment is of atomic statement letters in certain patterns in the premises and conclusion.

Containment is said in many ways. Here are the twelve most relevant ways: (1) It can mean literal physical containment of one thing inside another, as a hat in a box. (2) it can mean literally being a part of a whole, as a cog in a watch or a heart in an animal. (3) It can mean the containment of a conclusion in the premises as visibly shown in logic diagrams. (4) It can mean the containment of truth-grounds; (4) can be an interpretation of (3). (5) It can mean the containment of truth-conditions; (5) can be an interpretation of (3). The truth-condition or truth-maker of "Snow is white" is that snow is white; the truth-ground of "Snow is white" is its truth. (6) It can mean being a member of a class or set; (6) can be an interpretation of (3). (7) It can mean being a sub-class or subset of a class or set, which can be an interpretation of (3). (8) It can mean that contradictions contain all statements and tautologies contain no statements. (9) It can mean that a universal contains or exhausts the nature of its instances. (10) It can mean that P strictly implies Q just in case all possible worlds in which P is true are worlds in which Q is true. We may call this possible worlds containment. (11) It can mean that a subject contains a predicate *á la* Kant. (12) It can mean some sort of variable sharing. Thus, just like the word "relevance," the word "containment" is said in many ways. And they are often said in parallel ways, but not always. Sense (1) is a case in point. At least, I see no relevance of the hat to the box, except that it is small enough to fit inside. Thus, far from cornering the market on the use of such terms, Anderson and Belnap use them in a rather limited sense, specifically, in sense (12). The list is not intended to be exhaustive. No doubt there are indefinitely many ways that containment can be said, and likewise for relevance. I give a list of fifteen criteria of entailment near the end of chapter 9.

Mares notes a close relation between my containment criterion of logical relevance and David Lewis's definition of four relations of logical relevance, respectively in terms of identity, inclusion, overlap, and connection of "least subject matters" (Mares 1997; D. Lewis 1988: 168). Lewis describes mereological partitions of possible worlds to show that truth-preservation is relevant in a containment sense, and to provide clear senses in which necessary truths are about nothing and impossible falsehoods are vacuously about everything (D. Lewis 1988: 161, 165). Lewis takes an ahistorical approach, citing nothing before 1972. Venn diagrams show that truth-preservation is containment-relevant more elegantly than Lewis by not assuming possible worlds and not even using talk of possible worlds. Of course, we can interpret Venn diagrams in terms of possible worlds if we wish, though it is more usual to interpret them in terms of classes, or even directly in terms of truth-grounds. Indeed, one might better interpret possible worlds talk in terms of truth-grounds than the other way around. After all, which is clearer and more innocent than which?

What could be more relevant to logical relevance in deductive logic than containment of the conclusion in the premises? What more could be wanted? I believe Anderson and Belnap would agree with me on this very general level. Venn diagrams visibly show the truth-ground containment relevance of disjunctive syllogism and modus ponens in a way that merely verbal notation does not. If Anderson and Belnap think that Venn diagrams do not show relevance, they owe us an explanation of why not. It will not do merely to insist on their own views. They must explain away the very plain appearance that Venn diagrams show containment relevance. This includes syllogism Barbara, which is rewritable as hypothetical syllogism, which Anderson and Belnap reject. And unlike two-dimensional Venn diagrams, three-dimensional "Vennis balls" can handle any finite number of terms (Edwards 2004).

2. The synthetic *a priori* yellow-red and good-bad exclusionary inferences belong to deductive logic, but not to formal deductive logic. They are intuitively valid, but not formally valid. Russell calls them "derivable" instead of "deducible."

3. In American law, there are four main ways the word "presumption" is used in law. In descending order of strength, they are: conclusive (irrebuttable), burden of proof, burden of produc-

tion of evidence, and permissible inferences. Properly speaking, only the two kinds of burden are presumptions. Irrebuttable presumptions are really substantive rules of law; and permissible inferences are not grantings of any presumptive status (see Lempert 1983: 803–5; 2011: 1352ff.). In legal terms, Russell's presumption would be a burden of proof or production.

4. Relevance in the broad sense should not be defined as deducibility, *pace* Wright, since even vague talk of deducibility in general as opposed to in some particular system would still be far too specific. But deducibility remains a vague logically sufficient criterion of entailment. Don Paul Snyder says, "The minimal requirement for the entailment of a statement 'q' by another 'p' is that 'p' be relevant to 'q' in some appropriate [logical] sense" (Snyder 1971: 214). As a definition of entailment, this is not only vague but circular. At least Wright avoids such circularity.

5. Focusing on questions of the ontological dependence of some objects upon others, Peter Simons finds that a mereological interpretation of the *Tractatus* is partly, but not completely, correct (Simons 1992: 339–52; see 1987: 3, 253–323 on mereology and modality generally). This is a different issue from Copi's.

Concerning the diagram criterion, it may be worth noting that there is a close affinity between mereology and Boolean algebra. In fact, there is only one difference (Jordan 1967: 384). The key difference is that membership is transitive for mereological sets but not for distributive sets (Woleński 1989: 155). Stanisław Leśniewski's mereology is an extra-logical theory of sets in their collective (or mereological) sense. The only primitive term in mereology is "part of." On the mereological interpretation of set theory, a set is a whole, a collection or aggregate containing parts. On this view, a set with one member is identical with that member. Also, there will be no empty set. Leśniewski limits the objects to physical objects, such as the set of inhabitants of Poland. Mereological sets are opposed to distributive sets (classes), whose members are defined as whatever satisfies some condition. Of course, distributive sets, too, have whole-part relationships to each other and to their members, if any. Venn diagrams can be used to represent either sort of set.

The 1903 Russell has an objection to defining whole and part in terms of logical priority. Namely, the whole-part relation is simple, but the relation of logical priority is complex. A is logically prior to B just in case (1) A follows from B and (2) B does not follow from A (POM 137–38). The objection might apply to defining whole and part in terms of deducibility as well, since deducibility too is a complex relation. But while deducibility is definable in terms of ten principles of deduction for the 1903 Russell, and is in that sense logically complex, still it is not a conjunction of two relations (one relation plus the negation of its converse) in the way logical priority is, since in some cases *A* and *B* are deducible from each other, and in those cases there is no logical priority of either over the other. Thus a very different sort of complexity is involved. Nor would we try to define whole and part in terms of deducibility unless we were defining whole-part deductive containment, which *is* complex, since it consists of the truth-grounds of the premisses' containing the truth-grounds of the conclusion; and since the truth-tables for that are always complex.

I am not trying to define deducibility in terms of whole and part or to define whole and part in terms of deducibility. I offer diagrammability only as a logically sufficient test of entailment. And since modern classical validity can be diagrammed to show the premisses contain the conclusion, it passes the test and thus is a form of entailment, *pace* Anderson and Belnap.

6. Griffin thinks Russell may have anticipated relevantist variable sharing in 1903 *Principles*, chapter 1, sentence 1. Russell says:

> Pure mathematics is the class of all propositions of the form "p implies q," where p and q are propositions containing one or more variables, the same in the two propositions, and neither p nor q contains any constants except logical constants. (POM 3)

Call this text #1, and call its requirement "Russell's requirement." In effect, it is a fourfold requirement to: (a) admit only conditional statements (b) of fully general logic, (c) pull all the quantifiers to the left (thanks to Torkel Frántzen 2001 for noting this), and (d) ensure that the variable each quantifier governs occurs in both the antecedent and the consequent. These may be called Russell's subrequirements (a)–(d). Griffin is evidently asking if this text might anticipate Anderson and Belnap, since theirs is the only type of relevance logic he admits.

Two further texts quickly follow in *Principles* and appear to clarify the first. Text #2 is:

> We assert always in mathematics that if a certain assertion p is true of some entity x, or of any set of entities x, y, z,..., then some other assertion q is true of those entities. We assert a relation between the assertions p and q, which I shall call formal implication. (POM 5)

Text #3 is:

> The typical proposition of mathematics is of the form
> 'F(x, y, z...) implies G(x, y, z...), whatever values x, y,
> z...may have'.... (POM 6)

I have ten comments.

First, Russell's requirement is not a sufficient condition of modern classical validity, so it can scarcely be a sufficient condition of any narrower form of relevant entailment. For example, "$(Fx \lor Gx) \supset (Fx \mathbin{\&} Gx)$" (alternation materially implies conjunction) is not even true, much less logically true. Or more simply, consider "$Fx \supset \neg Fx$" (a statement materially implies its denial). Thus Russell's requirement is a requirement neither of validity nor of relevance, but at most of the correct general logical form for all statements in pure mathematics, regardless of whether they are true or false.

Second, Russell is concerned in all three texts only to characterize pure mathematics, not pure logic. And while Russell aims to reduce mathematics to logic, that would show only that all mathematics is logic, not that all logic is mathematics. In fact, much of logic is not mathematics at all, including the two examples of false statements of pure logic given in the previous paragraph. Thus these two examples also show that Russell's requirement is too broad to cover mathematics alone, since it covers all formal implications that can be written in logic, including all those which do not paraphrase any mathematical statements.

Third, all three texts concern quantificational logic. Thus Russell evidently thinks that all mathematics belongs to quantificational logic. In contrast, modus ponens and disjunctive syllogism belong to propositional logic.

Fourth, however, as we saw earlier, statements of propositional logic are always rewritable in quantificational logic. And we can write quantificational versions of modus ponens and disjunctive syllogism which meet Russell's requirement. "$P \mathbin{\&} (P \supset Q)) \supset Q$" becomes "$(F(x, y, z...) \mathbin{\&} (F(x, y, z...) \supset G(x, y, z,...))) \supset G(x, y, z...)$". And "$P \mathbin{\&} (\neg P \lor Q)) \supset Q$" becomes "$(F(x, y, z...) \mathbin{\&} (\neg F(x, y, z...) \lor G(x, y, z,...))) \supset G(x, y, z...)$". The rewrites meet Russell's requirement, including subrequirement (d) that all variables x, y, z... occur in both antecedent and consequent. Thus Russell's requirement does not rule out the validity of these forms, much less rule out their having correct logical form for inference. This is the first thing Griffin should have checked, if he really thought Russell's requirement anticipates Anderson and Belnap's variable sharing requirement. Likewise for hypothetical syllogism and other staples of modern classical logic, such as "$(P \mathbin{\&} \neg P) \supset Q$" and "$P \supset (Q \supset P)$", which the reader can easily rewrite in the manner of my rewrites above.

Fifth, Russell does not indicate whether subrequirement (d) that all variables occur in both antecedent and consequent includes predicate variables as well as individual variables. Must all predicates be quantified over too, so that there will be predicate variables? If so, then all predicate variables would have to occur in both antecedent and consequent as well. And our quantificational rewrites of modus ponens and disjunctive syllogism would then fail to meet subrequirement (d).

But if we take Russell's three texts as logically equivalent, and take texts #2 and #3 as clarifying text #1, then quantification over the predicate letters does *not* seem required. Russell's own example of assertions p and q in texts #1 and #2 seems to make that clear, not to mention his example of predicates F and G in text #3. In fact, in his choice of different letters p and q and different letters F and G *in all three texts*, Russell seems to be insisting on the opposite. Therefore predicate variables do not seem required to occur in both the antecedent and the consequent. Thus our rewrites seem safe.

Sixth, however, even if Russell (or we, acting on our own) *did* extend subrequirement (d) to predicate variables, thus killing our rewrites of modus ponens and disjunctive syllogism, we can *still* cook up versions of those argument forms which meet subrequirement (d), but which no relevance logician would accept. For example, "$(x)(F)(G)(((Fx \lor Gx) \,\&\, \neg Fx) \supset Gx)$" fails to include "$F$" in the consequent. But we can simply add "$\neg Fx$" to the consequent, so that now we have "$(x)(F)(G)(((Fx \lor Gx) \,\&\, \neg Fx) \supset (\neg Fx \,\&\, Gx))$." This satisfies subrequirement (d) even if we extend (d) to predicate variables. Yet it is basically just disjunctive syllogism in conditional form, with "$\neg Fx$" innocuously added to the consequent. The addition is so innocent that "$(x)(F)(G)(((Fx \lor Gx) \,\&\, \neg Fx) \supset \neg Fx)$", considered by itself, is merely a quantified version of the rule of simplification, "$(A \,\&\, B) \supset B$".

Seventh, in traditional whole-part containment terms, Russell's sub-requirement that all variables occurring in the antecedent also occur in the consequent seems puzzling and unnecessary. For relevant containment in arguments means only that the *conclusion* is contained in the *premisses*, and not also that the premisses are contained in the conclusion. By parity of reason, we should require only that all variables occurring in the *consequent* also occur in the *antecedent*, and not that all variables occurring in the antecedent also occur in the consequent. We should require mutual variable containment only in cases of mutual implication, in effect, in cases of logically true biconditional statements. Russell seems to want to ensure that the subject-matter of antecedent and consequent is identical, that antecedent and consequent are about the same entities. But then we need to distinguish identity of subject matter from relevant containment. Perhaps the simplest example distinguishing the two is "(*A* & *B*) ⊃ *A*". The relevant containment of the consequent in the antecedent could scarcely be more obvious, yet it is equally obvious that the consequent does not contain "*B*". Of course, all mathematical equations equate to logically true biconditionals, but Russell does not limit mathematical statements to equations. Far from it. All three texts show that he characterizes mathematics in terms of formal implication in general. In fact, all of his examples in texts #1–3 are of one-way implications. I think that is because mathematical proofs need not have a biconditional (or equational) premiss and conclusion, but must move at least one-way from premiss to conclusion, once mathematics is rewritten as quantified logic. All the proofs in *Principles* and *Principia* conform to this requirement, insofar as they have premisses and a conclusion.

Ninth, we have seen that Russell's requirement is consistent with modern classical logic. And what is more, looking to *Principles* as a whole, charity demands that we interpret Russell's requirement to be clearly *intended* by Russell to be consistent with modern classical logic. For there is no doubt that *Principles* is a major work of modern classical logic. Russell accepts modus ponens (POM 14), accepts hypothetical syllogism as one of his ten deductive principles (POM 16, principle #6), accepts Barbara in two forms (POM 31), accepts ex falso quodlibet (POM 17), and evidently accepts disjunctive syllogism (POM 57–58).

Tenth, I conclude from all this that when Griffin says, "Russell tries to pick up on [relevant logic's (weaker) variable sharing condition on entailment] through his notion of formal implication" (Griffin 2001: 293), Griffin is ascribing to Russell an ahistorical intention that is simply not there. For the obvious and in fact the only thing to check is whether Russell's requirement excludes the argument forms which the relevantists reject. Clearly, it does not. For clearly, it is consistent with modern classical logic. Thus, if anything, Russell's requirement is clearly intended *not* to exclude modus ponens and disjunctive syllogism. Thus Russell is clearly trying "to pick up on" *modern classical* variable sharing. In this regard, we must remember that Russell's relevance relation here is not formal implication, but *always true* formal implication.

As we saw in chapter 10, there is also a very relevant text in *Human Knowledge*. There Russell notes that all our logically clear systems have primitive terms and unproved axioms. He notes further that a primitive term cannot occur in a theorem proved from the axioms unless it already occurs in at least one of the axioms used in the proof. In short, every primitive term must occur in some axiom if it is to occur in any theorem at all. In contrast, no defined term needs to occur in any axiom or theorem, since it can be replaced by the primitive terms that define it. (HK 377). This may seem close to the basic intuition of Anderson and Belnap, but really it is not. For if we replace primitive terms with atomic statements, and require only that an atomic statement must occur in at least one of the premisses of an argument if it is to occur in the conclusion, then modus ponens, disjunctive syllogism, and hypothetical syllogism clearly satisfy the requirement. But ex contradictione, as the formal inference "P and not-P, therefore Q," just as clearly does not.

7. Surprisingly, in light of this extended history, Eric Hammer and Sun-Joo Shin say "it seems clear that Euler was the first to extend the use of closed curves to represent categorical sentences systematically" (Hammer 1998: 3). But see Bocheński (1961: inset facing 260) for a photo of Leibniz's circular diagrams. And Peirce deems Vives the original diagrammer of logic (Peirce 1960: 93). Evidently even Aristotle uses logic diagrams of some sort (Ross 1960: 36–37; Gardner 1968: 32–33; Englebretsen 1998: 7–8; Greaves 2002: 116–17). The specific use of closed curves (circles) is of no logical importance.

8. Jan Łukasiewicz and Kurt Gödel also have mathematical interpretations of logic. Łukasiewicz was first intrigued by the algebraicization of logic as described to him by Kazimierz Twardowski (Kotarbiński 1967: 11). In 1922 Łukasiewicz offered an interpretation of *Principia Mathematica* using the real numbers between 0 and 1 as the domain. It was in effect a multi-valued interpretation on which 0 is falsehood, 1 is truth, and all the numbers in between are various possibilities or probabilities (Łukasiewicz 1970). Gödel's arithmeticization of language (Jordan 1967: 366 n.2) is famous. He assigns numbers to sentences in his famous diagonal proof of the incompleteness of quantificational logic. Tarski's metalogical mathematical constructions are famous too (Jordan 1967 373). These are mathematical interpretations of logic (Jordan 1967: 374). "Tarski [even] gave a topological interpretation of intuitionistic logic" (Woleński 1989: 136).

Such metalogical procedures might seem to be problematic for logicists such as Russell or Frege. They may seem to be nonrigorous or even circular, if one aims to reduce mathematics to logic in order to provide it with rigor. One answer might be that logic and mathematics are distinct in reason, so that either can be rewritten as the other. My reply would be while that may be true, it does not follow that one can interpret, define, or explain each in terms of the other without circularity. The question then devolves to explanatory priority, where explanatory priority becomes the criterion of logical priority (Dejnožka 2003: 10–12). Logic is more basic than arithmetic. Therefore, arithmetic should be explained in terms of logic, and this very fact indicates that logic is logically prior to arithmetic in a crucial explanatory sense, even though they are interdefinable in the technical sense of logical equivalence. But there is no problem of circularity for logicists. For when they reduce mathematics to logic, they validate mathematics as essentially logical, and can then use *logicized* mathematics, i.e., *logic*, or the part of logic that was used to rewrite mathematics, in metalanguages to prove things about logic.

There may be a limit here to the logicist program. We can represent points along the axes of Cartesian analytic geometry by numbers, and, through logicization, we can rewrite numbers as classes of classes. But that does not alter or remove the essential geometrical character of the axes themselves. By parity of reason, logicizing arithmetic does not alter or remove the essential arithmetical character of the numbers themselves. The easiest answer is that this is our old friend, the paradox of analysis. And here we might follow the scholastic adage that when faced with a paradox, i.e., apparent contradiction, draw a distinction. Namely, numbers and classes are *intensionally* different, but *extensionally* the same. But there is a second distinction as well. For example, Russell in *Principles*, with his distinction between formal geometry and empirical geometry, sees no problem for logicism. He is only logicizing *formal* geometry, not *empirical* geometry. Russell makes the distinction as early as 1897 in his philosophy of geometry book, but was not then a logicist (Russell 1956). The two distinctions are quite different. For the logicist intensional-extensional distinction applies only to formal geometry and its logicization.

9. The history of logic is not clear on what disjunction is or on how it might be diagrammed. Lambert denies that mutually exclusive disjunction of the form "All A are either B or C (but not both)" can be diagrammed. Nonetheless, Lambert diagrams it, and Venn and Kant diagram it as well (Venn 1971: 124–25, 522–25; Bocheński 1961: 119–21), *pace* Shin, who reports that Venn "almost seems to conclude that diagrams are not equipped to handle...disjunctive information" (Shin 1994: 178). But this does not matter for our purposes. We are concerned with inclusive disjunctions of the form "*p* or *q* (or both)." Any representative diagram will do. Indeed, I just described one, inspired by Copi. This refutes Shin's argument that "disjunctive information" can only be shown, not said, by means of diagrams (Shin 1994: 179–84). As the early Wittgenstein's saying-showing distinction is generally understood, what is represented is said not shown. Yet Shin admits that Peirce "introduced a syntactic device" to diagram disjunction (Shin 1994: 179). Shin's complaint is that such devices are "purely conventional" and "lose...visual power" (Shin 1994: 180–81). But Shin admits that Peirce's "device is a line" (Shin 1994: 179). Does not a line have visual power? Peirce could have

used a purely nongeometrical device lacking any visual illumination, such as the letter "d" for disjunction, but he does not do so. Intuitively, the line represents a truth channel or conduit. As to the famous device "x" representing negation, that is not the *letter* "x", but a visual crossing or slashing out. We *say* we use the letter "x" to cross out things, but this use is not of the letter *as* a letter. Thus this is *not* a purely conventional use, but an emphatic, primarily visual blocking or mutilation which allows us to see what is being rejected. We must not confuse the concept of a *syntactical letter* with the concept of a purely conventional or arbitrary *visual symbol*, especially when the symbols in question have helpful visual aspects. This is not to deny that the cross mark has a definable logical function in what we might call the "logical grammar" of the diagram, and in that sense belongs to logical syntax. For the circles of a Venn diagram belong to logical syntax in that sense too, and in that sense, *nothing* in the diagram has visual power. Conversely, there is an element of convention even in the use of circles. More importantly, how the line and the cross mark are *placed* within a geometrical diagram is how they are used to make statements, and their placement is both conventional and geometrical. Circles are literally geometrical, crossouts are physical blockouts, and both belong to logical syntax as well, precisely due to (and through) their *physical* placement according to the *logical* formation rules for the diagrams. This is not so different from any other formal language, as Shin well knows. Most deeply, Shin has shown that diagram logics can be defined just as formally as verbal logics (Shin 1994). And then what difference does Shin's distinction between logical syntax and visual symbol make?

10. Frege would not have known of Whately's distinction between information and instruction. But about a dozen years after criticizing logic diagrams as applicable only to uninformatively valid arguments, Frege himself distinguishes sense from reference, i.e. intension from extension, so that indefinitely many arguments whose validity can be shown by diagrams have conclusions expressing thoughts (propositional senses) not expressed in the premisses, and are therefore to that extent informative. Frege might still object that diagrams bring in geometric intuition. One reply might be that this does not matter if we take diagrammability only as a *sufficient condition* of relevance, as *showing* relevance. A better reply is that logic diagrams do *not* bring in geometric intuition, or at least *need* not. For Sun-Joo Shin has shown that diagram logics can be defined just as formally as verbal logics (Shin 1994). In general, any notation that formally shows truth-ground containment shows formal deducibility and formal entailment by that very fact. Indeed, Frege's own notation is semi-diagrammatic, yet leaves no room for intuition, except perhaps for

his underlying intuitive assumption that every concept determines a class, which leads to Russell's paradox. But that could be formally remedied by going beyond Frege's own simple theory of types.

11. Wittgenstein's defense of disjunctive syllogism as a valid argument-pattern easily parries Stephen Read's fancy footwork (Read 1988: 136–48). Read's distinction between extensional and intensional disjunctive syllogism not only seems similar to Anderson's and Belnap's own distinction between extensional and intensional disjunction, but is used to attempt much the same rescue of "official" relevance logic from the threat of disjunctive syllogism (Anderson 1975: 165–66; Meyer 1975: 296–300). Like Anderson and Belnap, Read finds disjunctive syllogism perfectly fine if "or" is taken intensionally. Again, if the test of intensional "or" is that its use implies subjunctive conditional statements, then modern classical logic's truth-functional "or" passes the test. For example, take the modern classical truth-table for disjunctive statements. If "*P* or *Q*" *were* true, then at least one of "*P*" and "*Q*" *would* be true too. For another example using the same truth-table, if "*P* or *Q*" *were* true, and if "*P*" *were* false, then "*Q*" *would* be true. And that subjunctive conditional is just the one implied by disjunctive syllogism. Indeed, a subjunctive conditional of the form, "If the premises *were* true, then the conclusion *would* be true," is implied by *every* modern classical valid argument form, including modus ponens, hypothetical syllogism, and even, in a *per impossibile* sense, ex contradictione, in modern classical logic. And that is precisely the truth-preserving function of modern classical logic. The relevantists might now take a different tack and claim that their own test of intensionality is really a phony one, since anyone who considers a given inference—even a purely extensional inference—from *P* to *Q* to be valid will consider the corresponding subjunctive conditional, "If *P* were the case, then *Q* would be the case," to be true simply in virtue of that validity. Or they might say that "this kind" of implication of a subjunctive conditional is not the "kind" that shows intensionality. But then they need to distinguish the supposed two kinds of implication of a subjunctive conditional in a non-question begging way, that is, without saying "This is the kind that shows intensionality, and that is the kind that even extensional inferences can have." That is, they really must find another test that shows that their "or" is intensional and modern classical logic's "or" is not. For my part, I find their test to define one plausible kind of intensionality: the subjunctive-conditional-implying kind. And using perfectly ordinary "were-would" talk, modern classical "or" easily passes the test. I also find "intensional" to be said in many ways, including at least three ways in *Principia*, as described earlier in this book (see page 14).

12. In *Relevant Logics and Their Rivals*, Richard Routley, Val Plumwood, Robert K. Meyer, and Ross T. Brady seem aware that Russell explains deducibility much as Wright explains entailment, namely, that one can know $A \supset B$ without knowing whether A is false or B true (Routley 1982: 74). Their chief criticism is the difficulty of formalizing that explanation. Apparently they would reject Russell's view, as I argue for it here, that deducibility *is* an adequate formalization of entailment, where deducibility is truth-ground containment shown by truth-tables. Their general view that relevance should not be approached directly, but "is a by-product of any good implication relation" (Routley 1982: x), is virtually the same as my view that there are many, perhaps indefinitely many (compare their "any"), kinds of entailment. But apparently they do not consider truth-ground containment, as visibly shown in truth-tables and other logic diagrams, to *be* a good implication relation. They view Russell's universal conditional as an attempt to formalize what is merely the generic determinable of all determinate entailment relations, namely implication in general (Routley 1982: 138 and 138n). That is consistent with my view that for Russell, *always true* formal implication *is* a determinate relevance relation, since it is a form of truth-ground containment, though expressed in a primitive notation for quantification. More deeply, their view is consistent with my view that, quite aside from Russell, truth-ground containment is the summum genus of entailment. For to preserve truth by truth-ground containment is to entail, precisely in virtue of the containment; and no inference that fails to preserve truth in that manner can be any form of entailment.

    Routley and company find disjunctive syllogism relevant, and say that the Anderson and Belnap "case against Disjunctive Syllogism...does not stand up to much examination" (Routley 1982: 358). They say Anderson and Belnap's "main criticism is that [disjunctive syllogism] 'commits a fallacy of relevance'—when $\lor$ is construed extensionally" (Routley 1982: 359). They say, "It is apparent however that Disjunctive Syllogism does not commit a fallacy of relevance in any obvious way, since B is relevant to, and shares variables with, A & ($\neg$A $\lor$ B); for B is a component of A & ($\neg$A $\lor$ B)" (Routley 1982: 359 citing Anderson 1975: 17 as "ABE, p. 17;" my negation sign). I believe they are quite right in their analysis showing that disjunctive syllogism is relevant, and quite right to note that this does not even appear to satisfy the Anderson-Belnap variable sharing requirement. Thus they appear to be rejecting the Anderson-Belnap requirement by implication, but without saying so at this point. They then distinguish "*principle* or *implicational* relevance" from "systemic relevance," and find that disjunctive syllogism "prima facie exhibits" the former, and "cannot be accused of" the latter, since disjunctive syllogism is not a systemic logic but only a single argument form; and if we *consider* it to be an entire system of logic by itself, then it is relevant in the *first* sense (Routley 1982: 359, their emphasis). Routley and company conclude:

> Since Disjunctive Syllogism appears to lead to neither sort of irrelevance, we are obliged to reject Anderson and Belnap's main criticism: while it is a good criticism of [modern] classical and strict [implication] systems it is no criticism of Disjunctive Syllogism or a cogent reason for singling it out for special criticism. There are things seriously wrong with Disjunctive Syllogism (see e.g. 2.9), but such irrelevance on its own is not one of them. (Routley 1982: 359)

Routley and company then criticize disjunctive syllogism on other grounds. Their main criticism is that there are non-trivial inconsistent "deductive situations" in which disjunctive syllogism can be used to prove incorrectly that everything is true, given the resident inconsistency (Routley 1982: 53, 155–56). That is, they are criticizing it in ex contradictione situations. Their examples are philosophical, mathematical, and scientific theories or systems in which the theorist asserts inconsistent things but does not assert or (intend to) imply every truth under the sun (Routley 1982: 53, 156). They say that semantically, such "situations" amount to being restricted impossible worlds, while classical disjunctive syllogism depends for its plausibility on using a narrow semantics of possible worlds (Routley 1982: 155). My reply is that from the modern classical point of view, they give us verbally contrived implications based on verbally contrived impossible worlds. This is so even though for Russell, even *possible* worlds are verbally contrived, if they are not the actual world. For possible worlds are at least self-consistent. Here I must leave the matter. I discuss Russell's anti-Meinongianism elsewhere (Dejnožka 2003: ch. 4). In the present book, see the first page of chapter 3 for the basic idea.

Routley and company "do not dispute the truism that classical logic is correct in classical contexts, i.e. in those contexts where it is correct" (Routley 1982: 50–51). The question then devolves to cases, and in my opinion, to the concept of relevance.

13. Russell says that even though self-evidence is an epistemic concept, it sheds light on the nature of logic. He explains that *a priori* knowability "is a characteristic, not of logical propositions in themselves, but of the way in which we know them. It has, however, a bearing upon the question what their nature may be, since there are some kinds of propositions which it would be

very difficult to suppose we could know without experience" (IMP 204). Russell also cautions that "since people have tried to prove propositions, they have found that many of them [that had been deemed self-evident] are false. Self-evidence is often a mere will-o'-the wisp, which is sure to lead us astray if we take it as our guide" (MAL 73).

Chapter 10: Probability as Degree of Logical Relevance

1. Arthur N. Prior credits John Neville Keynes with anticipating C. I. Lewis on the paradoxes of strict implication (Prior 1967: 551). Routley, Plumwood, Meyer, and Brady say "Lewis...rediscovered in 1913 the modal definition of strict implication known to modal logicians" (Routley 1982: 358). And as we saw earlier, Prior also credits Diodorus Cronus with discussing much the same paradoxes of strict implication that Lewis does (Prior 1955: 193–94).
    William Ernest Johnson is the only person John Maynard Keynes cites in *A Treatise on Probability* regarding ("favourable") relevance (Keynes 1962 / 1921: 68). The context does not suggest that the notion of logical relevance is actually due to Johnson.
2. Lempert and Saltzburg principally mention Thayer, whom I shall discuss later (Lempert 2011: 224; 1983: 153).
    It does not appear that Keynes was conversely an influence on legal discussions of logical relevance. One looks in vain for mention of Keynes in legal scholarship. In the Westlaw databases for American state and federal cases up to 1999, there are only thirteen cases which mention Keynes, and they do so only in connection with his economic or political views. When they mention his views on probability at all, they mention only his using risk analysis in economics. In the Westlaw database for combined legal journals and law reviews, Keynes' book *A Treatise on Probability* is cited in only four articles. Of the four, only one discusses his views on relevance in probability theory, but not in connection with Rule 401 or any similar rule of evidence (Kaye 1986). Nor does the official comment to Rule 401 mention or cite Keynes (West 1995).
3. The very term "relevant" suggests Keynes. But as we shall see, the term flourishes in the history of evidence law, and that is the origin of its use in Rule 401.
4. I myself advocate a mixed theory of probability. The idea of a mixed theory is not new (Braithwaite 1975: 239–40). For mass repetitive events, I adopt frequency theory. For unusual or nonrecurrent particular events, I reject both Keynes and Ramsey, and offer a rationalist cognitive interpretation of my own. This two-level or "mixed" theory is much like Russell's in *Human*

Knowledge, but substitutes Continental-style phenomenological objects for his British empiricist sense-data or his (later) noticed events (see especially HK 392). For unique or nonrecurrent events, I interpret degrees of probability as being what cognitively seems more or less strongly to be the case. Simplifying Roderick M. Chisholm's fine work, which is based in turn on that of Carneades, I admit a principle which I call the principle of seeming. The principle is that if it objectively seems to subject *S* that proposition *P* is true, then, regardless of whether *S* actually believes *P*, *S* has (some minimal objective) reason to believe that *P*. An even simpler statement of the principle would be: If it seems to *S* that *P*, then it is reasonable to *S* that *P*. See Chisholm (1966: 44–55); compare Snyder (1971: 204–5; see 208 for Snyder's list of epistemic theorems).

The principle has a phenomenological antecedent and an epistemic consequent, and I therefore consider it to be synthetic *a priori*. It is what equates, in my theory, to Keynes' implicit principle that if we intuit a degree of logical relevance of body of evidence *e* to hypothesis *h*, then *h* is to that extent probable given *e*. I consider that principle to be intended to be synthetic *a priori*, not just because it follows from his theoretical definition that probability is degree of logical relevance, but also because of what its own nature would be if it were true. I simply replace Keynes' intellectual intuition of a logical relation between *e* and *h* with my relation that, based on *e*, it objectively seems to subject *S* that *h* is true. If *e* is itself simply the seeming that *h* seems to be true, then *e* itself seems to be *h*. For example, if we simply seem to see an apple, then the seeming apple seems itself to be the apple. Or if my principle simply seems to be true, or intrinsically plausible, or self-evident, then the seemingly true principle itself seems to be the true principle. In both cases, the relation is that the seeming seems to be *F*. Thus, where Keynes' theory is that probability is degree of logical relevance, my theory is that probability is degree of stronger or weaker reason for *S* to believe *P*, which is in turn degree of stronger or weaker objective seeming to *S* that *P*. Thus on my theory, degree of objective seeming grounds degree of rational strength for belief (though not *of* belief, since actual belief is not required); and degree of rational strength for belief grounds degree of probability in turn, all to subject *S*. By "ground" I mean explain or account for in virtue of being the metaphysical basis of, so as to result in an intuitive mutual entailment, or at least in an explanatory logical equivalence. Degree of rational strength in my theory equates to degree of logical relevance in Keynes; and as Keynes tells us, that is all he *means* by "logical relevance." Thus, as with Keynes, I ground probability as degree of logical relevance. But for me, degree of logical relevance is not directly intuited, and is not the ultimate explanation, but is instead grounded in turn as degree of objective seeming. Thus I ground probability more deeply as degree of objectively seeming to be the case. And *that* is our direct "intuition." Thus I see Keynes not so much as wrong, but shallow.

As with Keynes, the degrees of probability in my theory of seeming can be cardinal, ordinal, or incommensurable. Certainly they objectively seem that way! And in my opinion, the fact that degrees of probability are often a matter of one's best intuitive and experienced judgment is far better and more naturally explained in terms of objective phenomenological seemings, which come and go and change in this world, than in terms of intellectual intuitions of timelessly real relations among timelessly real propositions in a Platonic realm of changeless being. It is not only more elegant in not needing to postulate such a Platonic realm of being, but more natural in that its ontological *locus* is in the natural world of change. Of course, our logical seemings may well include logical seemings of logical intuitions of logical entities and their logical relationships to logician *L*. And there may well be reason to believe that such logical intuitions and logical entities exist. But our logical seemings belong to the world of change, just as the logicians who have them do.

All the main starting points (data) in epistemology, such as the data of common sense, or of science, ordinary language, or the intellectual light of reason, are grounded in what seems to be the case, but the reverse is not so. If these other starting points did not even seem to be the case, or better, if it did not even seem to be the case that they were good starting points, or that they were evidence or evidentiary data for anything, then we would not rely on them. But conversely, if the data of common sense, science, and so on do seem to be the case, then (and only then) would we, or could we rationally or justifiably, start from them.

The principle of seeming is grounded even more deeply than just in objective seemings. For in my theory of qualified objects, I ground objective seemings in turn as qualified objects. And if they are veridical or illusory (not: delusory) objective seemings, I ground that which they seem to be as unqualified objects, i.e., objects in themselves. A qualified object is an object which is an objectual way an object in itself can be (rightly or wrongly) conceived or regarded. If there is an object in itself, then the qualified object "is" the object in itself, in a certain special sense of the term "is." If there is no object in itself, then the qualified object is an objectual way an object in itself *would* or *could* be conceived or regarded, if there *were* an object in itself. The first disjunct covers both veridical ("true") and illusory ("false") perception. The second disjunct covers delusory ("there is no object in itself") perception. For example, the Morning Star and

Evening Star are basically veridical qualified objects both of which "are," in a special sense of "are," the planet Venus, which is an object in itself.

The notion of a qualified substance or qualified thing may be traced from Aristotle through antiquity, the middle ages and beyond. But as far as I know, I am the only one who allows illusory or delusory qualified objects. That is because I have redefined the notion so as to allow it to play a basic role in explaining informative existence and informative identity statements on the level of generality of Frege's senses and Russell's descriptions. The *traditional* notion explains informative identity statements only for *veridical* situations, as in "Coriscus in the Lyceum is the musical person," and explain informative existence statements not at all. And my qualified objects are more natural and ordinary than Frege's obscure, abstract senses, and are not limited to linguistic situations the way Russell's descriptions are. Further, my qualified objects can be and often are epistemological seemings. They can be and often are what objects in themselves seem to be. But no ordinary object in itself can seem to be a sense or a description.

Qualified objects may be defined as objects that (1) essentially involve how an object in itself can be conceived or regarded, but such that (2) there may or may not be an object in itself, and such that (3) if there is an object in itself, the qualified object may or may not conceive or regard it veridically. So defined, they are logically prior to the dispute whether epistemological data are private ("first person" or Cartesian) or social ("third person" or scientific / holistic). We conceive or regard some things as private mental entities, and others as public or social; and we can conceive or regard some things either way, as when Berkeley regards a house as a bundle of mental ideas across persons.

As noted in chapter 1, my theory of qualified objects is based on and is very much like Panayot Butchvarov's theory of objects. But I use publicly available ordinary "qualified objects" in place of Butchvarov's private, momentary objects, which cannot be singled out twice even by the same person. And I use (sometimes merely probable) real entities which are "out there" in place of Butchvarov's entities, which are mere conceptual constructions of his objects. Again, just as Butchvarov eliminatively replaces the subjunctive conditional notion of existence as identifiability indefinitely many times (i.e. we *would* single it out if we *were* there now) "with the idea that a thing exists if *there is* [indicative tense] an indefinite number of objects[,] each identical with it, whether or not we have encountered any of them" (Butchvarov 1994: 44), so I can do the same thing using an indefinite number of my qualified objects. And my qualified objects are ordinary (qualified) public things, while Butchvarov's objects, like Russell's sense-data, are creatures of analysis we are almost never presented with as such in ordinary life. Russell gives the game away when he says that to become acquainted with sense-data, we must learn to see things as the painter sees: "the painter has to unlearn the habit of thinking that things seem to have the colour which common sense says they 'really' have, and to learn the habit of seeing things as they appear" (PP 9). These are difficult topics I cannot discuss here (see Dejnožka 2003: xxvi, 47, 61, 73, 123–35; Butchvarov 1979: 122–53, 212–38). Thus I am describing this deeper level of my theory only to set it aside; and I shall discuss only objective seemings and the principle of seeming in the present book.

Again, the principle of seeming does not require a realm of timeless being the way Keynes' theory does. But by no means does my theory *preclude* admitting such a realm, and one might have *other* reasons, having nothing to do with probability theory or with theory of knowledge, for admitting such a realm. For example, one might find it best to ground the timeless truths of logic and mathematics in a timeless realm of abstract entities in the manner of Frege and the early Russell; and that would include the uninterpreted probability calculus as a branch of mathematics. In fact, my principle of seeming allows us to admit both intellectual seemings of abstract entities and perceptual seemings of ordinary physical objects; and both would be kinds of objective seemings. For example, we can admit logical seemings (I mean objective seemings *about* logic) as *phenomenological* intellectual intuitions of logical entities in our phenomenology of logic. Logical seemings would be a species of the genus intellectual seemings, within the summum genus of objective seemings. And we would not be liable to Ramsey's criticisms, since our logical seemings are merely the objective seemings we obviously do have in this world. They are not obscure, occult Platonic intuitions, but are simply how logic seems to us. Some things certainly seem to us to be the case in logic. And surely what is true in logic objectively seems different to different people.

I do not claim that the frequency side of my mixed theory resolves David Hume's famous problem of induction. Indeed, I agree with Mises that frequency theory presupposes induction (Mises 1961: ix). At least it does insofar as we cannot observe a total empirical frequency across the whole of space and time. But it seems to me that my principle of seeming is our best hope of justifying *both* the frequency-inductive side of my theory *and* the nonrepetitive or unique event side. Namely, if it objectively seems to us that the frequency theory of probability is true for mass repetitive events, and that the principle of induction on which it is based is true, then we have reason to believe that they are true, even if we cannot describe the reason.

I believe that my principle, that if it objectively seems to *S* that *P*, then S has reason to believe that *P*, is *a priori*. I also believe that if it objectively seems to *S* that the principle of induction is true, then *S* has reason to believe that the principle of induction is true. But I believe that my principle does not and cannot explain or justify the principle of induction as being *itself* a weak synthetic *a priori* truth, as Russell claims. I believe with Hume against Russell that the principle of induction is not and cannot be *a priori*. More than that, I believe that the principle does not even *seem* to be *a priori*. The same point applies to the frequency theory of repetitive events. That theory is not itself *a priori*, nor does it even seem to be. Now, if the total frequency of events across space and time could be perceptually presented to an omnipresent observer, then for such an observer, the theory *might as well* be *a priori*, for all practical intents and purposes. But the empirical frequency of all events in space and time themselves would still be *a posteriori*, could not be otherwise, and would not even seem to be otherwise, even to such an omnipresent observer. The principle of induction would be *known to be true or false* by such an observer, but that would not make it *a priori*. Even an omniscient observer could only know the principle of induction to be true by empirical experience. And all my principle implies is that if it objectively seems to us that the principle of induction is true, then we have reason to believe that it is true, even if we agree with Hume that the principle is not *a priori*, and even if we agree with him that we are unable to state a noncircular argument for the principle, and are thus unable to describe the reason it seems to be true.

We need not be able to explain *why* it objectively seems to us that *P*, that is, describe the *reason* we have to believe that *P*. (Again, this is regardless of whether we *actually* believe that *P*.) That is not required by my principle about seeming. I believe, as many do, that we can have reason to believe something even if, for whatever reason, we cannot describe the reason or reasons we have, or cannot describe them well. Lord William Murray Mansfield goes even further than that. He notes that there are people who make good decisions based on their common sense or long experience, but who can only describe, perhaps because they can only find, *bad* reasons for their decisions. Such people are good intuitive judges of things, i.e., of what seems to be the case, but bad at describing the reasons for their judgments. Nor are they just lucky guessers. To the contrary, such people are often known to be both intuitively skilled and very experienced at weighing what seems to be the case in various practical matters, but to be very bad at verbally describing why they weigh, or should weigh, things the way they do. In fact, all or most of us are like this to some degree. But allow me to give Mansfield's extreme and thereby very clear example.

A general was appointed Governor of a West Indies island, and would therefore now also have to be a judge for the first time. Having no legal background, he asked his old friend Mansfield for advice. Mansfield famously replied, "[C]onsider what you think justice requires, and then decide accordingly. But never give your reasons;—your judgment will probably be right, but your reasons will certainly be wrong" (Campbell 1878: 481, quoting Mansfield). John Campbell says that things went very well for the new judge— until he came to have so high an opinion of himself as a jurist that he actually described his reasons for a decision, and they turned out to be very bad reasons indeed (Campbell 1878: 481). My principle about seeming is very much like that. Mansfield knew this particular friend of his well. But we all know, or ought to know, how hard it is to state good reasons for us to believe in, say, the existence of an external world, even though it objectively seems to us to exist. Of course, sometimes we *can* state the reasons we have, or at least state them to some degree; and we should state our reasons if we can. But that might be easier in practical life than in fundamental philosophy.

There is a major qualification to what I just said. Namely, we can in general *always* describe our reason to believe as follows: The minimal objective reason for S to believe that P is simply and precisely that it objectively seems to S that P. The qualification is that *other than* that always describable and always correct *general* reason, we need not be able to describe any more *specific* reason for S to believe that P, in order for the principle of seeming to be true.

I also must distinguish within phenomenology between a mere presentation as such, and an objective seeming. An objective seeming is a presentation that objectively seems to be veridical. I think the distinction was well-established by Plato in the form of his thesis that mere sensation is not knowledge or, for that matter, even evidence. We have many presentations that do not objectively seem to be the case, from mirages in the desert to optical illusions.

Again, my theory avoids Ramsey's criticism of Keynes that we simply do not have the Platonic "logical intuition[s]" (Keynes 1962 / 1921: 18) Keynes' theory is based on (Ramsey 1931: 161). For I have replaced logical intuitions with seemings. The existence of seemings is not in doubt. Certainly, and in a perfectly ordinary sense, it objectively seems to us that many things are the case. And even objective seemings about logic and mathematics are themselves neither timeless nor *a priori*. Their existence is always *a posteriori* and relative to at least a possible thinker. When it seems to me that two plus two equals four, the seeming is always at a certain time. Public seemings can occur across times and people.

My theory also avoids Ramsey's other main criticism, that any logical intuitions of probability would be unreliable, since we disagree so often on how probable a thing is. For my theory is relative to subject S to begin with. If it seems that P to *S1*, and if it seems that *not-P* to *S2*, then on my theory, *S1* has reason to believe that P, and *S2* has reason to believe that *not-P*. There is nothing self-contradictory about that. In fact, it happens all the time. I think the 1948 Russell avoids these criticisms too. My only advantage is that I have a more natural, ordinary, and plausible phenomenology. In fact, Ramsey's second criticism does not even apply well to Keynes. I see nothing wrong with conflicts among weak logical intuitions about degrees of logical relevance. Such conflicts are only to be expected. We are not ideal logicians with perfect logical intuitions. Still, on Keynes' theory, if people disagree in their intellectual intuitions about what is the case in the Platonic world, at most one of them can be right, the rest must be wrong, and we simply cannot tell who is right or wrong. There is nothing like that in my theory. Yes, if there are conflicting objective seemings, at most one can be veridical, the rest must be illusory or delusory, and we cannot tell what is really the case behind the veil of seemings. I mean that on my theory, there is more to it than just that. There are all sorts of degrees of objective seeming, and degrees of reason to believe, for us to weigh and assess as best we can. This is not at all the bang-bang, yes-no, right-wrong, binary, polarized sort of logical-intuition-or-no-logical-intuition theory Keynes has, or at least that Ramsey believes Keynes has.

To be sure, I may be unable to estimate a probability even roughly due to complicated conflicts in my own evidence, i.e., in what objectively seems to me to be the case. But my theory admits and explains that fact in terms of phenomenologically presented incommensurabilities among conflicting seemings, and does not even attempt to resolve what no theory of probability can resolve.

On a deeper and more general level, my theory *is* much like Keynes'. I do reject his view that logical intuitions play a role in probability theory. But both my theory of objective seemings and his theory of logical intuitions are species of his more general theory that degrees of probability are "degrees of rational belief" (Keynes 1962 / 1921: 20, Keynes' emphasis omitted). We disagree only on what rationality *consists of* in probability judgments. For Keynes, it consists of timeless Platonic logical intuitions of degrees of reason to believe. For me, that rationality consists of phenomenological objective seemings, including seemings about logic, in the world of change.

I shall now discuss six objections to my principle of seeming. The first three concern seeming counterexamples.

First, it might be objected that it may objectively seem to S that P, where P is *not* reasonable to S. I have two replies . First, this is not a reason to reject my principle, but a mere, flat, bald denial of its truth. Second, I wholly grant that it is both categorially possible and analytically possible that my principle is false. For its denial is neither ill-formed nor self-contradictory. But my principle is still a necessary truth, since it is a synthetic *a priori* truth.

Second, it might be objected that it may be reasonable to S that P, even though it objectively seems to S that *not-P*. I have two replies. First, my principle says only that if it objectively seems to S that P, then it is reasonable to S that P. It does not say or imply the converse. That is, it does not say or imply that if it is reasonable to S that P, then it objectively seems to S that P. That is not part of my principle. My principle is not a biconditional, i.e., not an "if and only if" statement. I come now to a fine point. Insofar as I hold that there is no way to have reason to believe other than by an objective seeming, I am committed to the converse of my principle, even if my principle itself does not imply its converse. That is, insofar as that is what I hold, then I am committed to two different principles, my principle of seeming and its converse. And the objection would apply to the converse principle. But it begs the question against the converse principle. It is a mere, flat, bald denial that the converse principle is true. And both my principle of seeming and its converse objectively seem to be synthetic *a priori* truths, at least to me. And if I am right, then there are not going to be any counterexamples of this sort. My second reply is that if this type of situation is possible, then it can only be a misjudged conflict in our evidence. We often choose among reasonable alternative beliefs in subtle, complex situations. Obviously, if it objectively seems to us that P, then we know that it seems to us that P, since even an objective seeming is a presented seeming; and as Descartes says, at least we know what seems to us to be the case. And on my theory, we would *have* reason to believe that P. But we may not know what would be *most* reasonable for us to believe, since we may not have done the *best* reasoning about the situation. Here I think we can and must distinguish between the best reason we actually have, or even could have actually come up with under the circumstances, and the best reason we could have found under ideal circumstances, or perhaps in retrospect. This reply also addresses cases where it seems that it is more reasonable to S that P than not, but objectively seems to S that *not-P* more than not.

A third objection to my principle of seeming is this. It may the case that: (1) it seems to S that P, (2) P is reasonable to S, and (3) P is more reasonable to S than not-P, yet (4) S may (and logically can) believe not-P, even though not-P is *absurd* to S, perhaps out of pure and simple faith. Tertullian says he believes that God exists *because* it is absurd, perhaps meaning that he must believe in God by faith alone, since reason goes against it. In my discussion, I shall flip *P* and not-*P* around for convenience in writing. One reply is that if *S* truly finds *P* absurd, or sufficiently absurd, then it does *not* seem to *S* that *P*, and *S* does not and cannot believe *P*. Of course, this begs the question against the possibility of belief through faith. A second reply is that *P* might be reasonable *enough* to *S* for *S* to believe *P*, even though *S* *also* finds absurd *aspects* to *P*. This would be just a case of conflict in one's own evidence. The second reply subsumes the first insofar as *S* finds believing out of pure and simple faith to be reasonable enough. The problem with this reply is that the specified counterexample does not logically require or entail any such conflict of evidence. A third reply is that when we believe on faith, we usually have some minimal reason to believe, such as apostolic or other testimonial evidence. The problem with this reply is that the counterexample logically allows pure and simple nonrational belief based on pure and simple nonrational faith. And it is quite true that there is nothing in my principle of seeming which logically prohibits belief for no reason, or even for a bad reason. It implies only that *if* it objectively seems to *S* that *P*, and *if S* believes that *P*, *then S* has reason for *S*'s belief that *P*. But the fourth and best reply is that the principle of seeming has nothing to do with actual belief in the first place. The principle concerns not the mere fact of belief as such, but the rationality of any belief there may be.

The principle of seeming has nothing to say on the question whether people can choose their beliefs. We often say that people believe what they want, or even what they choose. But we also admit that if several ordinary people are looking at an apple in a basket under ordinary conditions, then they have no choice but to believe there is an apple in the basket. The only thing my principle implies is that *if* it objectively seems to us that we have a (or no) choice to believe that *P*, then we have *reason* to believe that we have a (or no) choice to believe that *P*. And I think that if there is no objective seeming that there is any evidence at all, then we cannot *rationally* believe, much less *rationally* choose to believe. This includes not only metaphysical statements about what is in the real world behind the curtain of seemings, but also statements known to be randomly selected. I myself hold that we *do* have objective seemings giving us minimal reason to believe that there is at least a real physical world, but that we have no objective seemings giving us even minimal reason to believe statements known to be randomly selected, or even statements deterministically selected by a computer algorithm known to have nothing to do with any relevant evidence.

The principle of seeming has nothing to do with irrational, subjective, or merely psychological beliefs. Not all beliefs are rational. Far from it. The principle may be spelled out more fully as, "If it *objectively* seems to S that P, then S has *objective* reason to believe *objectively* that P." So spelled out, the principle is not even indirectly about merely psychological beliefs, or what might be called subjective seemings. And degree of psychological strength of belief is not the same as degree of objective likelihood of belief. That it might be hard or sometimes even impossible to tell in practice whether our belief is objective or subjective, the difference in the concepts is clear enough. This is shown by the fact that it is quite intelligible that we can and often do later judge a belief as either more subjective or more objective than we had thought at first. Compare Kant's view that in practice we cannot always tell whether our motives are moral or selfish, though the distinction is clear in theory.

Next, I consider two dialectical objections to my principle.

Fourth, the contrapositive of my principle is that if we have no reason to believe that P, then P does not seem to us to be the case to us to be the case. And this implies that if we have no reason to believe either P or not P, then neither P nor not-P seems to us to be the case. And trivially, if we have no reason to believe either P or not-P, then we cannot rationally believe anything about whether P is true. We may call this the "doxastic equivalent," or perhaps better, the doxastic instance, of the problem of Buridan's ass. Jean Buridan questions the principle of sufficient reason, i.e., the principle that everything has a reason, or more fully stated, that if anything exists, then there is *some* kind of reason or explanation that suffices to explain why it exists. (For an Aristotelian, any one of Aristotle's four kinds of cause would do.) Buridan asks us to consider an ass standing equidistant from two equally good piles of hay. The ass would starve to death if the principle of sufficient reason were true, since there is no reason for it to choose one pile over the other. Likewise, one might urge, for the principle of doxastic sufficient reason, i.e., the principle that every belief has a reason. Suppose we humans are rationally equidistant from all the indefinitely many logically possible metaphysically real worlds that could exist hidden behind the curtain of empirical appearances. Then we could never believe anything about the real world, if the principle of doxastic reason were true. For, setting up the issues in this way, we could have no more reason to believe that God, physical objects, and other minds exist than to believe they do not. But people do have in fact all kinds of beliefs about the real world, therefore my principle is false by contraposition. Here I am waiving nonrational causes of beliefs.

My reply would be to note that the principle of doxastic sufficient reason is an instance of the far more general principle of sufficient reason. For if everything has a reason, then all our beliefs have reasons. Therefore, any *solution* of a problem with the general principle also applies to the doxastic principle by instantiation. (Again, I am waiving the distinction between reasons for believing and other sorts of causes of why our beliefs exist, such as efficient causes.) Now, the problem of Buridan's ass is commonly held to be solved by admitting higher level reasons. Namely, the ass will choose a pile at random precisely to avoid starving to death; and that is a higher level reason. In similar situations, we often toss a coin, simply to make an arbitrary choice. We may even say the ass does a mental equivalent of tossing a coin. Pascal's Wager is arguably a higher level reason for believing in God, if not a spiritually very admirable one. Inference to the best explanation, and Quinean considerations of simplicity and conservatism, are arguably higher level reasons for believing in, say, physical objects. Compare my (2006) on Quine's view that simplicity and conservatism of theory are literally kinds of scientific evidence. Quine admits a robust realism of physical objects behind the curtain of observations; and simplicity and conservatism are his reasons for doing so. Thus Quine conforms to the principle of sufficient reason by having higher level reasons; and this is arguably so even if he is wrong to think that simplicity and conservatism are literally kinds of evidence. By parity of reason, or by instantiation, the first dialectical objection to the principle of doxastic sufficient reason can be resolved by using higher level reasons as well. In fact, Quine's beliefs are a case in point. And if Quine, then why not us?

The fifth (and second dialectical) objection to my principle is this. It may be very well for Keynes, Russell, and Broad to hold that our empirical evidence for the principle of induction is always getting stronger, since as time goes on, we are always continuing to see further examples of the future's resembling the past. But when Frege says that "once given the possibility [that other people exist], the probability [based on my perceptual evidence] is very great, so great that it cannot be distinguished from certainty" (Frege 1968: 530), this is totally different. For, at least waiving our "higher reason" resolution of the first dialectical objection, no confirmation of *any* sort is possible even in principle of what, if anything, lies behind the curtain of appearances. This leads to a philosophical standoff. On the one hand, if my principle is right, then it allows us to go behind the curtain, in the sense of having reason to believe that there is an external world, since it objectively seems to us that there is, even if we cannot describe what the reason is, beyond merely saying that it objectively seems to us to be the case. On the other hand, if the problem of whether there is an external world behind the curtain of appearances is an instance of the problem of Buridan's ass, then my principle must be false. As in so many other topics, one philosopher's modus ponens is another philosopher's modus tollens. My solution is, of course, that my principle is the very sort of higher level reason that can resolve Buridan's problem. But that is only because it does objectively seem to us that there is an external physical world. The solution would not help the ass, if the piles of hay objectively seem equally good to it. The ass needs to choose on the basis of a very different sort of higher level reason, if it rationally chooses at all.

Russell describes several versions of Buridan's ass for the real world behind the curtain of appearances. Famously, he asks us to disprove that "the world sprang into existence five minutes ago, exactly as it then was, with a population that 'remembered' a wholly unreal past" (AMI 159; see 160), and "complete with fossils" (OP 7 indirectly citing Gosse 1857). But he also says more fully:

> The hypothesis that the heavenly bodies are permanent "things" is not logically necessary....This may be called the hypothesis of "complete realism." At the other end is the hypothesis of "complete phenomenalism," according to which bright [heavenly phenomenal] dots exist [only] when observed. Between these two are an infinite number of other hypotheses, e.g., that Venus is "real" but Mars is not, or that Venus is "real" on Mondays, Wednesdays, and Fridays, but not on Tuesdays, Thursdays, and Saturdays. Both extremes and all intermediate hypotheses are consistent with the observed facts; if we choose between them, our choice cannot have any basis in observation alone. (HK 481)

Here, observed facts are the curtain of appearances, and theories like Keynes', Russell's, and mine try to provide a rational basis for belief in a real world that goes beyond empirical observation alone. Again, my solution is simply an application of my principle of seeming. It objectively seems to us that Venus exists every day of the week; therefore we have reason to believe that it does.

The sixth and final objection is this. A few paragraphs ago, I waived the difference between a reason for believing a statement and a reason for the mere existence of the belief, such as an efficient cause. The concepts are different. Of course, my reason for believing may *happen* to be the reason for the existence of the belief. I may even happen *never* to believe without reason. But it would seem logically possible that I might sometimes believe without having any reason to do so, and that the cause of my belief be nonrational, or even irrational, or in a word, a *mere* efficient cause.

My reply echoes my reply to the third objection. Namely, the principle of seeming is not even about belief in the first place. I mean it does not say that if it objectively seems to S that P, then S *believes* that P. The principle says only that if it objectively seems to S that P, then S has *reason* to believe that P, regardless of whether S actually believes that P or not. And the principle of seeming does not imply that all beliefs are rational. That is the very different principle, "If B is a belief, then B is rational." We may also state it as, "If S believes that P, then S has reason to believe that P." We may call that the principle of belief. The principle of belief seems obviously false to me. However, it can be restated to make it true: "If B is an objective belief held by S, then B is rational to S."

My second reply is this. For our purposes here, we need not even try to answer such questions. To defeat radical skepticism about the external world, and to justify the principle of induction, it is enough if my principle of seeming is true, and if we have the objective seemings in question. We need not have a principle of belief and objective beliefs as well.

My concluding discussion is mostly but not entirely review.

The principle of seeming is best understood in light of Hume's skepticism about induction, which in turn is best seen as skepticism about probability in general. Hume argues that there is no reason whatsoever to believe that the principle of induction is true, that the future will resemble the past, or that the sun will rise tomorrow. In sharp contrast, I am arguing that if it objectively seems to us that the sun will rise tomorrow, then we have some minimal objective reason to believe that it will, even if we cannot describe the reason other than to say that it objectively seems to us to be the case, and even if the reason might not be sufficient reason to justify our belief, if any, even as more likely than not. Likewise for the principle of induction itself, the thesis that the future will resemble the past. the thesis that every physical event has a cause, and for the principle of sufficient reason, which is that there is a reason for every thing. On the principle of seeming, we have reason to believe that all of those principles are true, if they objectively seem to us to be true. This is so regardless of whether they are *a priori*. On my principle of seeming, if they seem to be *a priori*, then we have reason to believe that they are *a priori*. But they do not even seem to be *a priori*. The only principle that seems *a priori* is the principle of seeming itself. It seems synthetic *a priori*.

My principle of seeming may be understood as a case of containment entailment as follows. If something objectively seems to us to be the case, then we have some minimal objective reason to believe it; and this minimal objective reason is simply and precisely that it objectively seems to us to be the case. However, although that *is* what the reason is, the concepts of seeming and of reason are clearly different. Seeming belongs to phenomenology, and reason belongs to logic. Thus the principle of seeming is not analytic, and it is not a tautological containment entailment. Rather, it is a synthetic *a priori* entailment. It is a containment entailment much like that in "If anything is red, then it has color." Just as red contains color, so objective seeming includes objective reason to believe. And this explains why people cannot ever have irrational objective seemings. We cannot have irrational objective seemings for the same reason that there cannot be colorless red apples.

As is often noted, we would accept the explanation that the weather near the Great Lakes is unpredictable because its causes are complex and poorly understood; but we would never accept the explanation that it is unpredictable because it has no cause. And that might be taken as evidence that, or even as showing that, the principle of sufficient reason is true *a priori*. But I think it shows nothing of the kind. For the point is not about the weather, but about what we would accept as an explanation. Thus the point is about us, not the weather. It would be about the weather only on a Kantian theory that we impose causation on our experience. Thus the point is not evidence that the principle that every physical event has a cause is *a priori*, nor even that it is true, and likewise for the principle of sufficient reason. Thus, such principles stand in need of justification themselves, much as Hume would say. My principle of seeming will justify them, but only if they objectively seem to be true or likely to be true. If it objectively seems to S that P, and does not objectively seem to S that not-P, then S has some minimal reason to believe that P, and no reason to believe that not-P, and it follows further that to S, it is more likely than not that P.

The principle of seeming is consistent with, and can help us understand, conflicts in our evidence. Cases of conflicting evidence are cases of conflicting objective seemings. It may objectively seem to me that I just saw Smith shoot Brown in a dark alley. But because the alley was dark, I may not be sure of this. If it seems to me, upon reflection, that the alley was really too dark for me to identify the shooter, then it will no longer even seem to me that I saw Smith. It will then seem only that I had thought I saw Smith.

The principle of seeming is that if it objectively seems to subject S that proposition P is true, then S has objective reason to believe that P. The principle does not say or imply that if it objectively seems to S that P, then S *does* believe P, or that S has *sufficient* reason to believe that P, or even that S *ought* to believe P.

The principle implies only that if it objectively seems to *S* that *P*, then *if* S *does* believe that *P*, then *S* has reason to believe that *P*.

The principle of doxastic sufficient reason is that if subject *S* believes that *P*, then there is a reason of *some* kind that suffices to explain why *S* believes that *P*. (Again, this principle is an instance of the principle of sufficient reason.) The reason may be rational, i.e., evidentiary, or it may be a mere efficient cause that is not rationally related to the belief. I never said or implied that we have rational or evidentiary reason to believe every belief we have. The principle of seeming implies only that *if* we have a belief, then *if* what we believe objectively seems to us to be the case, then we have some minimal objective reason for our belief. This implies further that *if* we have a belief, then if we have *no* reason for our belief, then our belief does *not* objectively seem to us to be true. This simply contraposits the conditional consequent of the first conditional statement.

Let us call the following principle the principle of belief: "If subject *S* believes proposition *P*, then it objectively seems to *S* that *P*." Some philosophers seem to think that this principle is true, and true *a priori*. But I think that it is quite false. And I think the reason is a familiar one. Namely, people have nonrational and even irrational beliefs all the time. As Keynes says, "the actual beliefs of particular individuals...may or may not be rational" (Keynes 1962 / 1921: 4). Thus the principle of belief is not true synthetic *a priori*. If it were true, it would be a logically contingent truth. But as Keynes points out in effect, the principle of belief is simply false. In contrast, the principle of seeming is true synthetic *a priori*. That is because for conceptual reasons, there simply cannot be nonrational or irrational objective seemings.

Thus I disagree with Chisholm, who advances principles that base having reason to believe on believing (Chisholm 1966: 45 principle B, 47 principle C). In my opinion, Chisholm would have done better to stick to Carneades' phenomenological principle. To be fair, Chisholm does require the beliefs to be about perceived states. But this by itself does not entail that the beliefs are rational. In this connection, there is a well-known ambiguity in the word "perceive." In normal circumstances, "I perceive a rat" implies that there is a real rat there to be perceived. But "Last night in a dream, I perceived a rat" implies no such thing. I am not saying that this ambiguity applies to Chisholm's principles. But I am saying that his talk of perception in his principles cannot be taken to imply that the beliefs are veridical, or even to give any reason to believe that the beliefs are veridical, without begging the question of the truth of his principles. Believing and objective seeming are not the same. But an objective seeming is rational in virtue of its very objectivity.

We might rescue Chisholm by distinguishing objective beliefs from subjective beliefs, and placing objective beliefs on a par with objective seemings. And if we mean by "objective," rational, this begs the question for either seemings or beliefs. But the fundamental thing is the seeming that gives rise to the belief. Also, an objective seeming can give some minimal reason to believe without our actually being led to believe. Thus my theory is on the proper level of generality, but Chisholm's theory is too narrow. For we do not always actually believe when we have some minimal reason to believe based on an objective seeming. Far from it. Thus I think that my theory, which is far more like that of Carneades than like that of Chisholm, is better than Chisholm's.

There can be higher levels of objective seemings. If I objectively seem to see a pink rat, then I have reason to believe there is one. But what if it occurs to me that I am drunk? Or what if I find out later that someone gave me a drug? This invites talk of higher levels of objective seeming, based on taking in more epistemically relevant context. I think that our epistemic thinking often does have this sort of subtle complexity. There may be no easy answer to such questions. But my principle of seeming was never intended to remove every difficulty or vagueness about objective seemings, much less remove every difficulty or vagueness in phenomenology or epistemology.

The deeper questions are, What are objective seemings? Do we ever have them? How can we know that a seeming is objective? Can we define them by genus and difference as seemings that are objective? But how helpful is that? Is that not circular? This may be rock bottom. There may be no deeper or more illuminating answers to be had, and either we accept that the principle of seeming is true and that we have objective seemings, or we do not. To *define* objectivity in terms of rationality would be for my principle of seeming to become analytic, which might seem better; but such a definition would only beg the question. Or we can try to explicate objectivity in negative terms, such as 'not influenced by our thoughts, beliefs, feelings, and so on'. But we should not understand a term negatively unless the term is a negative one. And it is not clear that "objective" is essentially a negative term. On the face of it, it seems positive. And the "and so on" seems lame. But the positive analogy, "Objective seeming implies reason to believe as red implies color," seems to apply straightforwardly. And this analogy seems enough for my principle to be noncircularly understood. After all, if a thing is red, it must have color; but its being red is normally not taken to be a begging of the question as to its having color.

Finally, we now have four ontological *loci* for probability, depending on which theory we accept. On frequency theory, the *locus* of a natural (empirical) probability is in the natural world, or in classes of things in the natural world. On Keynes' theory, the *locus* is his Platonic realm of timeless relations among what can only be timeless propositions. On Ramsey's theory, the *locus* is in ourselves: our disposition (willingness) to bet, and our learning curve as created by rewards of winning and punishments of losing. On my theory, the locus is phenomenological seemings, or more deeply, qualified objects which are mind-independent, but whose logical possibility depends on the logical possibility of minds.

5. Dov M. Gabbay and John Woods write as if today there are still "two notions of relevance. One is probabilistic (or what legal theorists call logical) relevance. The other is called legal (i.e. worth-hearing or practical) relevance. It is a useful distinction" (Gabbay 2010: 242). They cite Thayer as "[w]riting to the same effect" (Gabbay 2010: 243), as if Thayer embraced the very distinction he rejects. Their own quote of Thayer, and their own highlighting of that quote, suggest the opposite: "To discuss such questions...even if we introduced *the poor notion of legal relevancy, as contrasted with logical relevancy*—tends to obscure the nature of the inquiry" (Gabbay 2010: 243 quoting Thayer 1927 / 1898: 5108, Gabbay's and Woods' emphasis).

The legal theorist George F. James had it right when he said in his famous essay, "Relevancy, Probability, and the Law" that by replacing the concept of legal relevance with a set of exclusionary rules which operate to restrict logically relevant evidence for a wide variety of largely unrelated policy reasons, "[t]he largely unrelated principles making up the concept of 'legal relevancy' [might] be disentangled, and that ambiguous phrase returned to the grave wherein the great Professor Thayer laid it almost fifty years ago" (James 1992 / 1941: 392 / 705).

Gabbay and Woods even think that *I* accept the concept of legal relevance. They say:

> Some legal writers make the point that historically the gap between a logician's and a lawyer's appreciation is not all that wide, as witness (Dejnoska [sic], 2004):

> > My conclusion is that it is both possible and likely that [the logician] Keynes was inspired by English law. English law required evidence to be "relevant" as early as 1783, and *articulated relevance as "logical relevance"* as early as 1897.... [Gabbay's and Woods' square brackets in their quote of me]

> *In fact, however*, it is easy to show that there is a considerable *difficulty* in associating *legal* probability with the concept analyzed by the probability calculus (Gabbay 2010: 250 quoting my 2004 /1996, my emphasis)

Just as with Thayer, their own quotation of me shows the opposite. As I hope my italicized emphases make clear, I was writing about logical relevance, not legal relevance. The paper of mine that they cite does not even mention legal relevance. Besides logical relevance, the only types of relevance I mention are relevance in analogical arguments, and causal-statistical-scientific-explanatory relevance; and I mention them only to set them aside.

I follow Thayer, James, and almost every legal writer in the Anglo-American tradition today in accepting only logical relevance, and in replacing the confused concept of legal relevance with a set of exclusionary rules. The concept of an exclusionary rule is not the concept of a kind of relevance at all. It is the concept of a rule for excluding evidence that *is* relevant for policy reasons. Thayer's point is that there is no such thing as legal relevance, no such concept, but only a grab bag of policy rules for excluding logically relevant evidence.

Douglas Walton is another logician who makes this mistake. Walton says, "Rule 403 shows most dramatically the distinction between logical relevance and legal relevance, as defined by the FRE" (Walton 2004: 21). Rule 403 shows no such thing. There is no such distinction anywhere in the *Federal Rules*. The *Federal Rules* do not even mention legal relevance, much less admit a distinction between legal relevance and logical relevance. The *Federal Rules* follow Thayer in abolishing the concept of legal relevance and replacing it with the concept of admissibility. As far the *Federal Rules* are concerned, Thayer consigned legal relevance to the dust bin of history.

Rule 403 says:

> **Rule 403. Exclusion of Relevant Evidence on Grounds of Prejudice, Confusion, or Waste of Time.**
> Although relevant, evidence may be excluded if its probative value is substantially outweighed by the danger of unfair prejudice, confusion of the issues, or misleading the jury, or by considerations of undue delay, waste of time, or needless presentation of cumulative evidence. (West 1995: Rule 403)

The term "relevant" occurs only once, and it is used in the sense of logical relevance. Note that implicitly, the rule would permit even a scintilla of evidence to be admissible, if its probative value is not substantially outweighed by the dangers and considerations listed, including *needless* presentation of cumulative evidence. As I noted concerning Rule 401 and elsewhere in chapter 10, items of evidence often must work together, since often the true probative weight (or even relevance at all) of each item is apparent only in the context of the group or collection taken as a whole. This includes *needful* presentations of cumulative evidence as having *collective* weight, and to think otherwise is to commit the fallacies of composition and division. I classify Rule 403 as a meta-rule of admissibility which weighs probative value against certain policy reasons for excluding relevant evidence as inadmissible.

References

These are abbreviations for selected works. Citations are below.

Frege:
TW   *Translations from the Philosophical Writings of Gottlob Frege* (various dates)

Russell:

AMA	*The Analysis of Matter* (1927)
AMI	*The Analysis of Mind* (1921)
HK	*Human Knowledge: Its Scope and Limits* (1948)
HS	*Human Society in Ethics and Politics* (1954)
HWP	*A History of Western Philosophy* (1945)
IMP	*Introduction to Mathematical Philosophy* (1919)
IMT	*An Inquiry Into Meaning and Truth* (1940)
KEW	*Our Knowledge of the External World* (1914, rev. 1929)
LK	*Logic and Knowledge* (1971)
MAL	*Mysticism and Logic* (1918)
MPD	*My Philosophical Development* (1959)
OD	"On Denoting" (1905)
ONA	"On The Nature of Acquaintance" (1914)
ONC	"On the Notion of Cause" (1913)
OP	*An Outline of Philosophy* (1927)
PE	*Philosophical Essays* (1910)
PL	*A Critical Exposition of the Philosophy of Leibniz* (1900)
PLA	"The Philosophy of Logical Atomism" (1918)
PM	*Principia Mathematica*, vol. 1 (1910, 2d ed. 1927)
PM2	*Principia Mathematica*, vol. 2 (1912, 2d ed. 1927)
POM	*The Principles of Mathematics* (1903, 2d ed. 1938)
PP	*The Problems of Philosophy* (1912)
RUP	"On the Relations of Universals and Particulars" (1911)

Wittgenstein:

PI	*Philosophical Investigations* (completed 1945–49)
RFM	*Remarks on the Foundations of Mathematics* (1937–44)
T	*Tractatus Logico-Philosophicus* (German 1921)

Quine:

FLPV	*From a Logical Point of View* (1953)
PQ	Replies in *The Philosophy of W. V. Quine* (1987)
PT	*Pursuit of Truth* (rev. ed. 1992)

Abeles, Francine F. 1990. "Lewis Carroll's Method of Trees: Its Origin in Studies in Logic." *Modern Logic* 1/1.

Adams, Robert Merrihew. 1982. "Leibniz's Theories of Contingency." In Hooker, ed., *Leibniz: Critical and InterpretI've Essays*.

Allaire, Edwin B. 1970. "Another Look at Bare Particulars." In Loux (1970).

———. 1970a. "Bare Particulars." In Loux (1970).

Almog, Joseph. 1989. "Logic and the World." In (1989a).

———, Perry, John, and Howard Wettstein, eds. 1989a. *Themes from Kaplan*. New York: Oxford University Press.

Anderson, Alan Ross, Nuel D. Belnap, Jr., and Jon Michael Dunn. 1992. *Entailment: The Logic of Relevance and Necessity*. vol. 2. Princeton, N.J.: Princeton University Press.

———, and Belnap, Jr., Nuel D. 1975. *Entailment: The Logic of Relevance and Necessity*. vol. 1. Princeton, N.J.: Princeton University Press.

Anderson, Terence, David Schum, and William Twining. 2005. *Analysis of Evidence*. 2d ed. Cambridge, England: Cambridge University Press.

Anellis, Irving. 1990. "From Semantic Tableaux to Smullyan Trees: A History of the Development of the Falsifiability Tree Method." *Modern Logic* 1/1.

Anonymous. 1911. Review of Chamberlayne (1911). *Oklahoma Law Journal*. 9 Okla. L. J. 468.

Anscombe, G. E. M. 1971. *An Introduction to Wittgenstein's Tractatus*. Philadelphia: University of Pennsylvania Press.

Aquinas, Thomas. 1969. *Summa Theologiae*. Vol. 1, part 1, questions 1–13. General ed. Thomas Gilby. Garden City N.Y.: Doubleday. Image Books.

Aristotle. 1987. *A New Aristotle Reader*. Ed. by J. L. Ackrill. Princeton, N.J.: Princeton University Press.

———. 1968. *The Basic Works of Aristotle*. Ed. by Richard McKeon. New York: Random House.

———. 1968a. *Posterior Analytics*. Trans. by G. R. G. Mure. In (1968).

———. 1968b. *Prior Analytics*. Trans. by A. J. Jenkinson. In (1968).

———. 1968c. *Rhetoric*. Trans. by W. Rhys Roberts. In (1968).

———. 1960. *Topica*. Trans. by E. S. Forster. In *Posterior Analytics / Topica*. Cambridge, Mass.: Harvard University Press. The Loeb Classical Library.

Ayer, Alfred Jules. 1971. *Russell and Moore*. Cambridge, Mass.: Harvard University Press.

Barbé, Lluís. 2010. *Francis Ysidro Edgeworth: A Portrait with Family and Friends*. Trans. by Mary C. Black. Cheltenham, England: Edward Elgar Publishing Limited. Substantially revised from the Catalan 1st ed., 2006.

Barnes, Jonathan. 1975. "Aristotle's Theory of Demonstration." In Barnes, Malcolm Schofield, and Richard Sorabji, eds., *Articles on Aristotle*. London: Duckworth. Vol. 1: Science.

Barnett, Vincent. 2013. *John Maynard Keynes*. London: Routledge. Routledge Historical Biographies Series.

Bartley, William Warren III. 1972. "Lewis Carroll's Lost Book on Logic." *Scientific American* 227/1.

Bateman, Bradley W., and John B. Davis, eds. 1991. Introduction to (1991a).

———, and John B. Davis, eds. 1991a. *Keynes and Philosophy: Essays on the Origins of Keynes's Thought*. Aldershot, England: Edward Elgar Publishing Limited.

Bayes, Thomas. 1963. *Facsimiles of Two Papers by Bayes*. New York: Harper.

Beccaria, Cesare. 1963. *On Crimes and Punishments*. Trans. by Henry Paolucci. Indianapolis, Ind.: Bobbs-Merrill. The Library of Liberal Arts. 1764 Italian.

Benardete, José A. 1958. "The Analytic 'A Posteriori' and the Foundations of Metaphysics." *Journal of Philosophy* 55.

Bentham, Jeremy. 1827. *Rationale of Judicial Evidence, Specially Applied to English Practice*. "From the Manuscripts of Jeremy Bentham, Esq.[,] Bencher of Lincoln's Inn." vols. 1, 3, 4. London: Hunt and Clarke.

———. 1825. *A Treatise on Judicial Evidence*. Extracted from the manuscripts of Jeremy Bentham by M. Dumont. Trans. into English from Dumont's French translation. London: Messrs. Baldwin, Cradock, and Joy.

Berbeira Gardón, José Luis. 1998. "Relevance and Modality." *Revista Alicantina de Estudios Ingleses* 11.

Berg, Jan. 1962. *Bolzano's Logic*. Stockholm: Almqvist & Wiksell.

Bergmann, Gustav. 1971. "Russell on Particulars." In Klemke (1971).

———. 1967. *Realism: A Critique of Brentano and Meinong*. Madison: University of Wisconsin Press.

Berkowitz, David S., and Samuel E. Thorne, Selectors. 1979. *Classics of English History in the Modern Era*. New York: Garland Publishing. Inc. A Garland Series.

Best, William Mawdesley. 1883. *The Principles of the Law of Evidence with Elementary Rules for Conducting the Examination and Cross-Examination of Witnesses*. American ed. from 7th English ed. Ed. by Charles F. Chamberlayne. Boston: Soule and Bugbee.

——. 1854. *A Treatise on the Principles of Evidence and Practice as to Proofs in Courts of Common Law*. 2d ed. London: S. Sweet.

Black, Henry Campbell, Joseph R. Nolan, and Jacqueline M. Nolan-Haley. 1991. *Black's Law Dictionary*. Abridged 6th ed. Centennial Edition (1891–1991). St. Paul, Minn.: West Publishing Co.

Black, Max. 1970. *A Companion to Wittgenstein's Tractatus*. Ithaca, N.Y.: Cornell University Press.

Blackstone, William. 1854. *Commentaries on the Laws of England*. 21st ed., collated with the edition of 1783, together with notes adapting the work to the American Student by John L. Wendell. New York: Harper and Brothers.

——. 1768. *Commentaries on the Laws of England*. Book 3. Oxford: Clarendon Press. Facsimile of the first edition. Special Edition privately printed for the members of the Legal Classics Library. New York: The Legal Classics Library, 1983.

Blount, Thomas. 1717. *Law-Dictionary and Glossary, Interpreting such Difficult and Obscure Words and Terms, as are found either in Our Common or Statute, Ancient or Modern, Laws*. 3d ed. London: Browne, Walthoe, Nicholson, Tooke, Midwinter, Cowse, Wellington, Gosling, Mears, Browne, Hooke, Clay, and Nutt.

Blumenfeld, David. 1982. "Superessentialism, Counterparts, and Freedom." In Hooker (1982).

Bocheński, Innocentius Marie. 1961. *A History of Formal Logic*. Trans. by Ivo Thomas. Notre Dame, Ind.: University of Notre Dame Press.

Bolzano, Bernard. 1972. *Theory of Science: Attempt at a Detailed and in the main Novel Exposition of Logic with Constant Attention to Earlier Authors*. Trans. and ed. by Rolf George. Berkeley: University of California Press. 1837 German.

——. 1950. *Paradoxes of the Infinite*. Trans. by Donald A. Steele from the German ed. by F. Přihonský. New Haven, Conn.: Yale University Press. 1851 German.

Bornet, Gérard. 1982–83. "Has Kripke Refuted Russell?" *Russell* n.s. 2/2.

Borst, C. V., ed. 1970. *The Mind-Brain Identity Theory*. New York: St. Martin's Press.

de Bracton, Henry. 1968. *Bracton on the Laws and Customs of England*. Ed. by George E. Woodbine, trans. and rev. by Samuel E. Thorne. Cambridge, Mass.: Belknap Press of Harvard University Press. Completed in 1256 A.D.

Bradley, Raymond. 1992. *The Nature of All Being.* New York: Oxford University Press.

——, and Norman Swartz. 1983. *Possible Worlds: An Introduction to Logic and Its Philosophy.* Indianapolis, Ind.: Hackett.

Braithwaite, Richard B. 1975. "Keynes as a Philosopher." In M. Keynes (1975).

——. 1973. Editorial Foreword to John Maynard Keynes, *A Treatise on Probability.* New York: St. Martin's Press for the Royal Economic Society. *The Collected Writings of John Maynard Keynes*, vol. 8.

Broad, C. D. 1968. Critical notice of *A Treatise on Probability.* In *Induction, Probability, and Causation: Selected Papers by C. D. Broad.* Ed. by Donald Davidson, Jaakko Hintikka, Gabriël Nuchelmans, and Wesley C. Salmon. Dordrecht: D. Reidel.

——. 1922. Critical notice of *A Treatise on Probability. Mind* n.s. 31/121. Reprinted in Broad (1968).

Brouwer, Luitzen Egbertus Jan. 1977. "On the Significance of the Principle of Excluded Middle in Mathematics, Especially in Function Theory." In Heijenoort (1977). Trans. by Stefan Bauer-Mengelberg and Jean van Heijenoort. German 1923.

——. 1975. "The Unreliability of the Logical Principles." In *Collected Works*, vol. 1, *Philosophy and Foundations of Mathematics.* Ed. and trans. by Arend Heyting. Amsterdam: North-Holland. Dutch 1908.

Brunner, Heinrich. 1887. *Deutsche Rechtgeschichte.* vol. 1. Leipzig: Verlag von Dunckler & Humblot.

Buller, Francis. 1817. *An Introduction to the Law Relative to Trials at Nisi Prius.* 7th ed. Ed. by Richard Whalley Bridgman. London: R. Pheney and S. Sweet.

——. 1785. *An Introduction to the Law Relative to Trials at Nisi Prius.* 4th ed. London: W. Straham and W. Woodfall.

——. 1772. *An Introduction to the Law Relative to Trials at Nisi Prius.* 1st ed. London: W. Straham and W. Woodfall.

Burge, Tyler. 1983. "Russell's Problem and Intentional Identity." In James K. Tomberlin, ed., *Agent, Language, and the Structure of the World.* Indianapolis, Ind.: Hackett.

Burke, Edmund. 1955. *Reflections on the Revolution in France.* Ed. by Thomas H. D. Mahoney. Indianapolis, Ind.: Bobbs-Merrill. The Library of Liberal Arts. 1790.

——. 1852."Report, made on the 30th April, 1794, from the Committee of the House of Commons, Appointed to Inspect the Lords' Journals, in Relation to their Proceeding on the Trial of Warren Hastings, Esquire." In *The Works*

and Correspondence of the Right Honourable Edmund
Burke. New ed. vol. 8. London: Francis & John Rivington.
1794.

Burkhardt, Hans. 1988. "Modalities in Language, Thought and
Reality in Leibniz, Descartes and Crusius." *Synthese* 75/2.

Butchvarov, Panayot. 1994. "The Truth and the Untruth of Skepticism." *Proceedings and Addresses of the American Philosophical Association* 67/4.

———. 1989. *Skepticism in Ethics*. Bloomington: Indiana University
Press.

———. 1979. *Being Qua Being: A Theory of Identity, Existence, and
Predication*. Bloomington: Indiana University Press.

———. 1974. "The Limits of Ontological Analysis." In Moltke S.
Gram and Elmer D. Klemke, eds., *The Ontological Turn:
Studies in the Philosophy of Gustav Bergmann*. Iowa City:
University of Iowa Press.

———. 1970. *The Concept of Knowledge*. Evanston, Ill.: Northwestern University Press.

———. 1966. *Resemblance and Identity*. Bloomington: Indiana University Press.

Caine, Barbara. 2005. *Bombay to Bloomsbury: A Biography of the
Strachey Family*. Oxford: Oxford University Press.

Campbell, Baron John Campbell, and Sir Joseph Arnould. 1878.
The Lives of the Chief Justices of England. 7th ed. vol. 3.
New York: Cockcroft & Company.

Candlish, Stewart. 1996. "The Unity of the Proposition and
Russell's Theories of Judgement." In Monk (1996).

Carabelli, Anna. 1992. "Organic Interdependence and Keynes's
Choice of Units in the *General Theory*." In Gerrard (1992).

———. 1991. "The Methodology of the Critique of the Classical
Theory: Keynes on Organic Interdependence." In Bateman
(1991a).

Carnap, Rudolf. 1967. *Meaning and Necessity: A Study in Semantics and Modal Logic*. Phoenix Edition. Chicago:
University of Chicago Press.

———. 1963. "Intellectual Autobiography." In Schilpp (1963).

Carroll, Lewis. 1977. *Symbolic Logic*. Ed. by William Warren Bartley III. New York: Clarkson N. Potter. Part I, Elementary,
5th ed., 1896. Part 2, Advanced, never previously
published. Part 2, Book 7 "The Method of Trees" galley
proof mailed November 6, 1896.

Casullo, Albert. 1996. Abstract of "Fallible A Priori Knowledge."
*Proceedings and Addresses of the American Philosophical
Association* 69/3.

Chamberlayne, Charles Frederic. 1911. *A Treatise on the Modern Law of Evidence*. Albany, N.Y.: M. Bender. London: Sweet & Maxwell.

———. Preface to Taylor (1897).

———. Preface and notes to Best (1883).

Chisholm, Roderick M. 1966. *Theory of Knowledge*. Englewood Cliffs, N.J.: Prentice-Hall.

Clark, Robert. 1998. "Re: 1 million 1's in PI?" Email posted to Mathforum.org on August 2, 1998, 7:55 AM. Mathforum .org/ kb/message.jspa?messageID=136779.

Cocchiarella, Nino. 1991. "Quantification, Time, and Necessity." In Lambert (1991).

———. 1987. *Logical Studies in Early Analytic Philosophy*. Columbus: Ohio State University Press.

———. 1984. "Philosophical Perspectives on Quantification in Tense and Modal Logic." In Gabbay (1984).

———. 1980. "The Development of the Theory of Logical Types and the Notion of a Logical Subject in Russell's Early Philosophy." *Synthese* 45.

———. 1975. "On the Primary and Secondary Semantics of Logical Necessity." *Journal of Philosophical Logic* 4.

Coke, Edward. 1823. *The First Part of the Institutes of the Laws of England; Or, a Commentary Upon Littleton*. 18th ed., revised and corrected by Francis Hargrave and Charles Butler. vol 2. London: J. & W. T. Clarke; R. Pheney; and S. Brooke.

Copi, Irving M. 1978. *Introduction to Logic*. 5th ed. New York: Macmillan.

———. 1970. *Symbolic Logic*. 3d ed. New York: Macmillan.

Cross, Rupert, and Colin Tapper. 1985. *Cross on Evidence*. 6th ed. London: Butterworths.

Dalen, Dirk. 2013. *L. E. J. Brouwer — Topologist, Intuitionist, Philosopher: How Mathematics is Rooted in Life*. London: Springer.

Damaška, Mirjan R. 1997. *Evidence Law Adrift*. New Haven: Yale University Press.

Davies, James Conway. 1972. Introduction to ed., *Catalogue of Manuscripts in the Library of the Honourable Society of the Inner Temple*. vol. 1. Oxford: Oxford University Press.

Davis, John B. 1991. "Keynes's View of Economics as a Moral Science." In Bateman (1991a).

Deane, Phyllis. 2001. *The Life and Times of J. Neville Keynes*. Cheltenham, England: Edward Elgar Publishing, Inc.

Dejnožka, Jan. 2012. *The Concept of Relevance and the Logic Diagram Tradition*. Ann Arbor, MI: CreateSpace.

———. 2012a. *The Growth of a Thinker: A Chapbook of Poems*. Ann Arbor, MI: CreateSpace.

———. 2010. "The Concept of Relevance and the Logic Diagram Tradition." *Logica Universalis* 4/1.

———. 2010a. "Dummett's Forward Road to Frege and to Intuitionism." *Diametros* 25.

———. 2007. "Dummett's Backward Road to Frege and to Intuitionism." In Randall E. Auxier, ed., *The Philosophy of Michael Dummett*. Chicago, Ill.: Open Court. Library of Living Philosophers, vol. 31.

———. 2006. "Observational Ecumenicism, Holist Sectarianism: The Quine-Carnap Conflict on Metaphysical Realism." *Philo* 9/2.

———. 2005–2007. "Are the Natural Numbers Just Any Progression? Peano, Russell, and Quine." *The Review of Modern Logic* vol. 10, nos. 3–4 (issue 32).

———. 2004. "Logical Relevance." http://www.members.tripod.com/~Jan_Dejnozka/logical relevance.pdf. Edited for the Web. Written for Richard D. Friedman's advanced evidence course at the University of Michigan School of Law, Ann Arbor, in 1996. First draft of ch. 10 of the present book.

———. 2003. *The Ontology of the Analytic Tradition and Its Origins: Realism and Identity in Frege, Russell, Wittgenstein, and Quine*. Lanham, MD: Littlefield Adams. Reprinted with further corrections, 2003. Reprinted with corrections, 2002. Original printing, 1996.

———. 2001. "Origin of Russell's Early Theory of Logical Truth as Purely General Truth: Bolzano, Peirce, Frege, Venn, or MacColl?" *Modern Logic* 8/3–4.

———. 2001a. "Russell and MacColl: A Reply to Grattan-Guinness, Woleński, and Read." *Nordic Journal of Philosophical Logic* 6/1.

———. 1997. Essay review of Ray Monk and Anthony Palmer, eds., *Bertrand Russell and the Origins of Analytical Philosophy*. *History and Philosophy of Logic* 18.

———. 1991. "Russell's Seventeen Private-Language Arguments." *Russell* 11/1.

———. 1990. "The Ontological Foundation of Russell's Theory of Modality." *Erkenntnis* 32.

———. 1989. "Zeno's Paradoxes and the Cosmological Argument." *International Journal for Philosophy of Religion* 25.

———. 1988. "Russell's Robust Sense of Reality: A Reply to Butchvarov." *Grazer Philosophische Studien* 32.

Descartes, René. 1969. *Meditations on First Philosophy*. Trans. by Elizabeth S. Haldane from the 2d Latin ed. In *The Philosophical Works of Descartes*, trans. by Elizabeth S. Haldane and G. R. T. Ross. vol. 1. Med. 6. Cambridge, England: Cambridge University Press. Latin 1642.

Dickson, Mark W. 1998. Electronic mail to Jan Dejnožka dated January 1 and July 23.

Dickson, William Gillespie. 1864. *A Treatise on the Law of Evidence in Scotland*. 2d ed. Ed. by John Skelton. Edinburgh: Bell & Bradfute.

van Ditmarsch, Hans, Wiebe van der Hoek, and Barteld Kooi. 2006. *Dynamic Epistemic Logic*. Berlin: Springer.

Donnellan, Keith. 1990. "Genuine Names and Knowledge by Acquaintance." *Dialectica* 44.

———. 1972. "Reference and Definite Descriptions." In Herbert Feigl, Wilfrid Sellars, and Keith Lehrer, eds., *New Readings in Philosophical Analysis*. New York: Appleton-Century-Crofts.

Došen, Kosta. 1985. "Sequent-Systems for Modal logic." *The Journal of Symbolic Logic* 50/1.

Ducasse, Curt John. 1941. *Philosophy as a Science, Its Matter and Its Method*. New York: Oskar-Piest.

Dummett, Michael. 1995. "The Context Principle: Centre of Frege's Philosophy." In Max (1995).

———. 1981. *Frege: Philosophy of Language*. 2d ed. Cambridge, Mass.: Harvard University Press.

Duncombe, Giles. 1739. *Trials per Pais: Or, The Law of England Concerning Juries by Nisi Prius, &c...With a Compleat Treatise of The Law of Evidence....* 7th ed. "with large additions." "[B]y Giles Duncombe late of the *Inner-Temple*." London: E. and R. Nutt and R. Gosling.

———. 1702. *Tryals Per Pais: Or, The Law of England Concerning Juries by Nisi Prius, &c.,...To which is now Added, a farther Treatise of Evidence*. 4th ed. "with Large Additions." "By G. D. of the *Inner-Temple*." London: Printed by the Assigns of Richard and Edward Atkins for John Walthoe in the Middle-Temple Cloysters.

Dunn, Jon Michael. 2015. "The Relevance of Relevance to Relevance Logic." *Lecture Notes in Computer Science*.

———. 1990. "Relevant Predication 3: Essential Properties." In (1990a).

———, and Anil Gupta, eds. 1990a. *Truth or Consequences: Essays in Honor of Nuel Belnap*. Dordrecht: Kluwer.

Eames, Elizabeth Ramsden. 1993. Introduction to Russell (1993).

Edgeworth, Francis Ysidro. 2003. "Probability and Calculus of Probabilities." In *Mathematical Psychics and Further*

Papers on Political Economy, ed. by Peter Newman. Oxford: Oxford University Press. Originally in Palgrave's *The Dictionary of Political Economy*, vol. 3, 1899.

———. 1996. *F. Y. Edgeworth: Writings in Probability, Statistics, and Economics*. Ed. by Charles Robert McCann, Jr. vols. 1–3. Cheltenham, England: Edward Elgar Publishing Limited. 1922.

Edwards, Anthony W. F. 2004. *Cogwheels of the Mind: The Story of Venn Diagrams*. Baltimore, Md.: The Johns Hopkins University Press.

Edwards, Paul, Editor in Chief. 1967. *The Encyclopedia of Philosophy*. New York: Macmillan and The Free Press.

Elliott, Byron K. and William F. Elliott. 1904. *A Treatise on the Law of Evidence*. vol. 1. Indianapolis, Ind.: Bobbs-Merrill.

Engel, Pascal. 1988. "Plenitude and Contingency: Modal Concepts in Nineteenth Century France." In Knuuttila (1988).

Englebretsen, George. 1998. *Line Diagrams for Logic: Drawing Conclusions*. Lewiston, N.Y.: Edwin Mellen. Problems in Contemporary Philosophy, vol. 40.

Etchemendy, John. 1990. *The Concept of Logical Consequence*. Cambridge, Mass.: Harvard University Press.

Eure, Samson. 1666. *Tryals per Pais, or the Law, Concerning Juries by Nisi Prius, &c. Methodically Composed for the Publick Good, in the 16th Year of the Reign of our Soveraign Lord CHARLES the Second, King of England, Scotland, France and Ireland, &c.* London: Printed for George Dawes over against Lincoln's-Lane Gate in Chancery Lane. Reproduction of the original in the Lincoln's Inn Library in London, England. Early English Books Online (EEBO). ProQuest. Print digitization undated.

Everdell, William R. 1997. *The First Moderns: Profiles in the Origins of Twentieth-Century Thought*. Chicago: University of Chicago Press.

Fact-Index.com. 2015. "Alexander Cockburn (Lord Chief Justice)." http://www.fact-index.com/a/al/alexander_cockburn_lord_chief_justice.html.

Fagin, Ronald, Joseph Y. Halpern, Yoram Moses, and Moshe Y. Vardi. 1995. *Reasoning about Knowledge*. Cambridge, Mass: The M.I.T. Press.

Fitzgibbons, Athol. 1991. "The Significance of Keynes's Idealism." In Bateman (1991a).

Føllesdal, Dagfinn. 1971. "Quantification into Causal Contexts." In L. Linsky (1971a).

Forrester, James W. 1996. *Being Good and Being Logical: Philosophical Groundwork for a New Deontic Logic.* Armonk, N.Y.: M. E. Sharpe.

Franklin, James. 1991. "The Ancient Legal Sources of Seventeenth-Century Probability." In Gaukroger (1991).

van Fraassen, Bas C. 1979. "Russell's Philosophical Account of Probability." In G. Roberts (1979).

Frege, Friedrich Ludwig Gottlob. 1980. *Philosophical and Mathematical Correspondence.* Ed. by Gottfried Gabriel, Hans Hermes, Friedrich Kambartel, Christian Thiel, and Albert Veraart. Chicago: University of Chicago Press.

———. 1979. *Posthumous Writings.* Trans. by Peter Long and Roger White. Ed. by Hans Hermes, Friedrich Kambartel, and Friedrich Kaulbach. Chicago: University of Chicago Press.

———. 1977. *Begriffsschrift, a Formula Language, Modeled Upon That of Arithmetic, for Pure Thought.* Trans. by Stefan Bauer-Mengelberg. In Heijenoort (1977). German 1879.

———. 1974. *The Foundations of Arithmetic.* 2d rev. ed. Trans. by J. L. Austin. Evanston, Ill.: Northwestern University Press. German 1884.

———. 1972. *Conceptual Notation and Related Articles.* Trans. and ed. by Terrell Ward Bynum. Oxford: Clarendon.

———. 1970. *Translations from the Philosophical Writings of Gottlob Frege.* Various translators. Ed. by Peter Geach and Max Black. 2d ed. Oxford: Basil Blackwell.

———. 1968. "The Thought." In Klemke (1968). Trans. by A. M. and Marcelle Quinton. German 1918.

Friedman, Richard D. 1991. *The Elements of Evidence.* St. Paul, Minn.: West Publishing Company.

Gabbay, Dov M. and John Woods. 2010. "Relevance and the Law." Ch. 12 in Dov M. Gabbay, Patrice Canivez, Shahid Rahman, and Alexandre Thiercelin, eds., *Approaches to Legal Rationality.* Dordrecht: Springer. Logic, Epistemology, and the Unity of Science Series, vol. 20.

Gabbay, Dov M. and F. Guenthner, eds. 1984. *Extensions of Classical Logic.* Dordrecht: D. Reidel. *Handbook of Philosophical Logic,* vol. 2.

Gardner, Martin. 1968. *Logic Machines, Diagrams and Boolean Algebra.* Dover ed. New York: Dover.

Gaukroger, Stephen, ed. 1991. *The Uses of Antiquity: The Scientific Revolution and the Classical Tradition.* Dordrecht: Kluwer.

———. 1989. *Cartesian Logic: An Essay on Descartes's Conception of Inference.* Oxford: Oxford University Press.

Geach, Peter T. 1977. Review of Anderson (1975). *Philosophy* 52.

——. 1972. *Logic Matters*. Berkeley: University of California Press.

George, Rolf. 1972. Editor's Introduction to Bolzano (1972 / 1837).

Gerrard, Bill and John Hillard, eds. 1992. *The Philosophy and Economics of J. M. Keynes*. Aldershot, England: Edward Elgar Publishing Limited.

Giaquinto, M. 1993. "Visualizing in Arithmetic." *Philosophy and Phenomenological Research* 53/2.

Gilbert, Lord Chief Baron Geoffrey. 1754. *The Law of Evidence: With all the Original References, Carefully Compared, To which is Added, A Great Number of New References, from the Best Authorities*. "And now first publish'd from an Exact Copy taken from the Original Manuscript." 1st ed. Dublin: Printed for Sarah Cotter under Dick's Coffee-House in Skinner-Row. Facsimile reprint in Berkowitz (1979).

——. 1805. *The Law of Evidence*. 7th ed. vol. 1. Philadelphia: Joseph Crukshank.

——. 1791. *The Law of Evidence*. Considerably enlarged by Capel Lofft. No ed. number. vol. 2. London: A. Straham and W. Woodfall.

——. 1760. *The Law of Evidence by a Late Learned Judge*. 2d ed. vol. 2. London: W. Owen.

Gillett, John Henry. 1897. *A Treatise on the Law of Indirect and Collateral Evidence*. Indianapolis. Ind.: The Bowen-Merrill Company.

Gillies, Donald. 2003. "Probability and Uncertainty in Keynes's *The General Theory*." In Jochen Runde and Sohei Mizuhara, eds., *The Philosophy of Keynes's Economics: Probability, Uncertainty, and Convention*. London: Routledge.

Gosse, Philip Henry. 1857. *Omphalos: An Attempt to Untie the Geological Knot*. London: John van Voorst.

Grattan-Guinness, Ivor. 1985–86. "Russell's Logicism versus Oxbridge Logics, 1890–1925." *Russell* 5/2.

——. 1977. *Dear Russell-Dear Jourdain: A Commentary on Russell's Logic, Based on his Correspondence with Philip Jourdain*. New York: Columbia University Press.

Graydon, Katharine Merrill, ed. 1927. *The Butler Alumnal Quarterly* 16/2. Greenfield, Ind.: The Butler University Alumni Association. Digitized by Internet Archive.

Greaves, Mark. 2002. *The Philosophical Status of Diagrams*. Stanford, Calif.: Center for the Study of Language and Information (CSLI).

Greenleaf, Simon. 1997. *A Treatise on the Law of Evidence.* Holmes Beach, Florida: Gaunt, Inc. Reprint of Boston: Charles C. Little & James Brown, and London: A. Maxwell. 1842.

———. 1899. *A Treatise on the Law of Evidence.* 16th ed. vol. 1. Ed. by John Henry Wigmore. Boston: Little, Brown, and Company.

———. 1846. *A Treatise on the Law of Evidence.* 3rd ed. vol. 1. Boston: Charles C. Little and James Brown. London: A. Maxwell & Son.

Gresley, Richard Newcombe. 1847. *A Treatise on the Law of Evidence in the Courts of Equity.* 2d ed. Ed. by Christopher Alderson Calvert. London: William Benning & Co.

Grice, H. Paul. 1989. *Studies in the Way of Words.* Cambridge, Mass.: Harvard University Press.

———, and Peter F. Strawson. 1996. "In Defense of a Dogma." *The Philosophical Review* 65/2.

Griffin, Nicholas. 2001. Review of my (1999). *Studia Logica* 68/2, 289–94.

———. 1996. "Denoting Concepts in *The Principles of Mathematics.*" In Monk (1996).

———. 1980. "Russell on the Nature of Logic (1903–1913)." *Synthese* 45.

Grossmann, Reinhardt. 1968. "Frege's Ontology." In Klemke (1968).

Haaparanta, Leila. 1985. *Frege's Notion of Being.* Helsinki: Acta Philosophica Fennica, vol. 39.

Hacking, Ian. 1978. *The Emergence of Probability: A Philosophical Study of Early Ideas about Probability, Induction and Statistical Inference.* London: Cambridge University Press.

Hahn, Lewis Edwin, and Paul Arthur Schilpp, eds. 1987. *The Philosophy of W. V. Quine.* La Salle, Ill.: Open Court.

Hailperin, Theodore. 1988. "The Development of Probability Logic from Leibniz to MacColl." *History and Philosophy of Logic* 9.

Hald, Anders. 2003. *History of Probability and Statistics and Their Applications before 1750.* Hoboken, N.J.: John Wiley & Sons, Inc. Wiley Series in Probability and Statistics.

Hammer, Eric and Sun-Joo Shin. 1998. "Euler's Visual Logic." *History and Philosophy of Logic* 19.

Hanfling, Oswald. 1981. *Logical Positivism.* New York: Columbia University Press.

Hare, Richard Mervyn. 2001. *The Language of Morals.* Oxford: Clarendon Press. 1952.

Harrod, Roy F. 1951. *The Life of John Maynard Keynes*. London: Macmillan.

Halsted, Jacob R. 1859. *Halsted's Digest of the Law of Evidence, Embracing the Rules Established by Writers of Acknowledged Authority, and Affirmed by the Decisions of the Federal Courts, and the Courts of All the States, Down to the Present Time, with Copious References to English Adjudications*. 2d ed. vol. 1. New York: John S. Voorhies.

van Heijenoort, Jean, ed. 1977. *From Frege to Gödel: A Source Book in Mathematical Logic, 1879–1931*. Cambridge, Mass.: Harvard University Press.

Hendricks, Vincent and John Symons. 2009. "Epistemic Logic." In Edward N. Zalta, ed., *The Stanford Encyclopedia of Philosophy*. Spring 2009 Edition. http://plato.stanford.edu-archives /spr2009/entries/logic-epistemic/.

Hintikka, Jaakko. 1973. *The Intentions of Intentionality and Other New Models for Modalities*. Dordrecht: D. Reidel.

———. 1962. *Knowledge and Belief: An Introduction to the Logic of the Two Notions*. Ithaca, N.Y.: Cornell University Press.

Hintikka, Merrill B. and Jaakko Hintikka. 1986. *Investigating Wittgenstein*. Oxford: Basil Blackwell.

Hochberg, Herbert. 2001. *The Positivist and the Ontologist: Bergmann, Carnap and Logical Realism*. Amsterdam: Rodopi.

———. 1994. "From Carnap's Vienna to Meinong's Graz: Gustav Bergmann's Ontological Odyssey." *Grazer Philosophische Studien* 48.

———. 1978. *Thought, Fact, and Reference: The Origins and Ontology of Logical Atomism*. Minneapolis: University of Minnesota Press.

van der Hoek, Wiebe. 1996. "Systems for Knowledge and Belief." *Journal of Logic and Computation* 3.

Hooker, Michael, ed. 1982. *Leibniz: Critical and Interpretive Essays*. Minneapolis: University of Minnesota Press.

Hostettler, John. 2013. *Twenty Famous Lawyers*. Sherfield on Lodden: Waterside Press.

Howell, Robert. 1974. "The Logical Structure of Pictorial Representation." *Theoria* 40.

Hughes, G. E., and M. J. Cresswell. 1972. *An Introduction to Modal Logic*. 2d ed. London: Methuen.

———, and M. J. Cresswell. 1968. *An Introduction to Modal Logic*. London: Methuen.

Hunt, Ted Robert. 2012. "Reconstructing Relevance in Missouri Evidence Law." *Journal of the Missouri Bar* 68.

Huntingdon, Edward V. 1935. "The Mathematical Structure of Lewis's Theory of Strict Implication." *Fundamenta Mathematicae* 25.

References 607

Ilbert, Courtenay Peregrine. 1902. "Evidence, Law of." In *The New Volumes of the Encyclopaedia Britannica, Constituting[,] in Combination with the Existing Volumes of the Ninth Edition[,] the Tenth Edition of that Work*. vol. 28 (the fourth new vol.). Ed. by Sir Donald MacKenzie Wallace, Arthur T. Hadley, and Hugh Chisholm. Edinburgh & London: Adam and Charles Black.
Inner Temple Library. 2013. http://www.innertemple-library.org/.
———. 2013a. http://www.innertemplelibrary.org.uk/templehistory/-inner-temple-history-the-library.htm.
Irvine, A. D., and G. A. Wedeking. 1993. *Russell and Analytic Philosophy*. Toronto: University of Toronto Press.
James, George F. 1941. "Relevancy, Probability and the Law." *California Law Review* 29/689–705. Reprinted in Twining (1992).
Jeffrey, Richard C. 1967. *Formal Logic: Its Scope and Limits*. New York: McGraw-Hill.
Jevons, William Stanley. 1965. *Elementary Lessons in Logic: Deductive and Inductive, with Copious Questions and Examples and a Vocabulary of Logical Terms*. London: Macmillan & Co Ltd. 1870.
———. 1958. *The Principles of Science: A Treatise on Logic and Scientific Method*. 2d ed. New York: Dover. 1st ed. 1873; 2d ed. 1877.
Johnson, William Ernest. 1921. *Logic*. Part 1. Cambridge, England: Cambridge University Press.
———. 1892. "The Logical Calculus." Published in three parts. "The Logical Calculus. I. General Principles." *Mind* n.s. 1/1. "The Logical Calculus. II." *Mind* n.s. 1/2. "The Logical Calculus. (III.)." *Mind* n.s. 1/3.
Jordan, Zbigniew. 1967. "The Development of Mathematical Logic in Poland between the Two Wars." In McCall (1967a).
Kahn, Charles H. 1986. "Retrospect on the Verb 'To Be' and the Concept of Being." In Knuuttila (1986).
Kant, Immanuel. 1988. *Logic ("Jäsche Logik")*. Ed. by Gottlob Benjamin Jäsche. Trans. by Robert S. Hartman and Wolfgang Schwarz. New York: Dover. German 1800.
———. 1965. *Critique of Pure Reason*. Unabridged ed. of Kant's 2d ed. Trans. by Norman Kemp Smith. New York: St. Martin's Press. German 2d ed. 1787. German 1st ed. 1781.
———. 1950. *Prolegomena to Any Future Metaphysics*. Ed. by Lewis White Beck. Based on English trans. by Carus, Mahaffy, and Bax. Indianapolis, Ind.: Bobbs-Merrill. The Library of Liberal Arts. German 1783.
Kaplan, David. 1987. "Opacity." In Hahn (1987).

——. 1975. "How to Russell a Frege-Church." *The Journal of Philosophy* 72.

Kaye, David H. 1986. "Symposium: Probability and Inference in the Law of Evidence." 6 *Boston University Law Review* 657.

Keynes, John Maynard. 1962. *A Treatise on Probability*. New York: Harper and Row. Also published as vol. 8, *The Collected Writings of John Maynard Keynes*, New York: St. Martin's Press for the Royal Economic Society, in 1973. 1921.

——. 1908. *The Principles of Probability*. Keynes Papers, King's College Library. Revision of 1907 paper of the same name.

——. 1904. "Ethics in Relation to Conduct." Keynes Papers, King's College Library.

Keynes, John Neville. 1887. *Studies and Exercises in Logic, Including a General Application of Logical Processes in their Application to Complex Inferences*. 2d ed. revised and enlarged. London: Macmillan and Co.

Keynes, Milo, ed. 1975. *Essays on John Maynard Keynes*. London: Cambridge University Press.

Kim, Jaegwon. 1993. *Supervenience and Mind*. Cambridge, England: Cambridge University Press.

Kirwan, Christopher. 1807. *Logick.; Or, An Essay on the Elements, Principles, and Different Modes of Reasoning*. London: Payne and MacKinley.

Klemke, Elmer D., ed. 1971. *Essays on Bertrand Russell*. Urbana: University of Illinois Press.

——. 1971a. "Logic and Ontology in Russell's Philosophy." In (1971).

——, ed. 1968. *Essays on Frege*. Urbana: University of Illinois Press.

Kluge, Eike-Henner W. 1980. *The Metaphysics of Gottlob Frege: An Essay in Ontological Reconstruction*. The Hague: Martinus Nijhoff.

Kneale, William, and Martha Kneale. 1964. *The Development of Logic*. Oxford: Clarendon Press.

Knuuttila, Simo. 1988. Introduction to (1988a).

——, ed. 1988a. *Modern Modalities: Studies of the History of Modal Theories from Medieval Nominalism to Logical Positivism*. Dordrecht: Kluwer.

——, and Hintikka, Jaakko, eds. 1986. *The Logic of Being: Historical Studies*. Dordrecht: D. Reidel.

——. 1981. Introduction to (1981a).

——, ed. 1981a. *Reforging the Great Chain of Being: Studies of the History of Modal Theories*. Dordrecht: D. Reidel.

Kosko, Bart. 1993. *Fuzzy Thinking: The New Science of Logic.* New York: Hyperion.

Kotarbiński, Tadeusz. 1967. "Introduction: Notes on the Formal Development of Logic in Poland in the years 1900–39." In McCall (1967a).

Kreisel, G. 1972. "Bertrand Russell's Logic." In Pears (1972).

Kripke, Saul A. 1982. *Wittgenstein on Rules and Private Language.* Cambridge, Mass.: Harvard University Press.

———. 1980. *Naming and Necessity.* Cambridge, Mass.: Harvard University Press.

von Kutschera, F. 1976. *Einführung in die Intensional Semantik.* Berlin: Walter de Gruyter.

Kyburg, Jr., Harry E., and Howard E. Smokler, eds. 1964. *Studies in Subjective Probability.* New York: John Wiley & Sons.

Lambert, Karel, ed. 1991. *Philosophical Applications of Free Logic.* New York: Oxford University Press.

Landsman, Stephan. 1990. "From Gilbert to Bentham: The Reconceptualization of Evidence Theory." *Wayne Law Review,* vol. 36.

Landini, Gregory. 2007. *Wittgenstein's Apprenticeship with Russell.* Cambridge, England: Cambridge University Press.

———. 1998. *Russell's Hidden Substitutional Theory.* Oxford: Oxford University Press.

———. 1996. "Will the Real *Principia Mathematica* Please Stand Up? Reflections on the Formal Logic of the *Principia.*" In Monk (1996).

———. 1993. "Notes on Dejnožka's Manuscript."

———. 1993a. "Reconciling *PM*'s Ramified Type Theory with the Doctrine of the Unrestricted Variable of the *Principles.*" In Irvine (1993).

Langbein, John H. 1996. "The Historical Foundations of the Law of Evidence: A View from the Ryder Sources." Yale Law School Legal Scholarship Repository. Faculty Scholarship Series. Paper 551. http://digitalcommons.law.yale.edu/fss_papers/551.

von Leibniz, Gottfried Wilhelm. 1966. *New Essays on Human Understanding.* Trans. and ed. by Peter Remnant and Jonathan Bennett. Cambridge, England: Cambridge University Press. Cambridge Texts in the History of Philosophy. First published 1765. First draft 1704.

Lempert, Richard O., Samuel R. Gross, James S. Liebman, John H. Blume, Stephan Landsman, and Fredric I. Lederer, eds. 2011. *A Modern Approach to Evidence: Text, Problems, Transcripts and Cases.* 4th ed. St. Paul, Minn.: West Publishing Company. American Casebook Series.

——, Samuel R. Gross, and James S. Liebman. 2000. *A Modern Approach to Evidence: Text, Problems, Transcripts and Cases*. 3rd ed. St. Paul, Minn.: West Publishing Company. American Casebook Series.

——, and Stephen A. Saltzburg. 1983. *A Modern Approach to Evidence: Text, Problems, Transcripts and Cases*. 2d ed. St. Paul, Minn.: West Publishing Company. American Casebook Series.

——. 1977. "Modeling Relevance." 75 *Michigan Law Review* 1021 –1057.

Lenzen, Wolfgang. 1984. "Leibniz und die Boolesche Algebra." *Studia Leibnitiana* 16/2.

——. 1978. "Recent Work in Epistemic Logic." *Acta Philosophica Fennica* 30.

Lewis, Clarence Irving, and Cooper H. Langford. 1932. *Symbolic Logic*. New York: The Century Co.

——. 1918. *A Survey of Symbolic Logic*. Berkeley: University of California Press.

Lewis, David. 1988. "Relevant Implication." *Theoria* 54.

Linsky, Bernard. 1993. "Why Russell Abandoned Russellian Propositions." In Irvine (1993).

Linsky, Leonard. 1977. *Names and Descriptions*. Chicago: University of Chicago Press.

——. 1971. "Reference, Essentialism, and Modality." In (1971a).

——, ed. 1971a. *Reference and Modality*. London: Oxford University Press.

Locke, John. 1959. *An Essay Concerning Human Understanding*. Collation of 1st ed. of 1690 by Alexander Campbell Fraser in 1894. New York: Dover.

Loux, Michael J., ed. 1979. *The Possible and the Actual: Readings in the Metaphysics of Modality*. Ithaca, N.Y.: Cornell University Press.

——, ed. 1970. *Universals and Particulars: Readings in Ontology*. Doubleday: Garden City, N.Y.

Lovejoy, Arthur O. 1974. *The Great Chain of Being*. Cambridge, Mass.: Harvard University Press.

Lucas, Th., and R. Lavendhomme. 1990. "Varying Modal Theories." *Notre Dame Journal of Formal Logic* 31/3.

Łukasiewicz, Jan. 1970. *Selected Works*. Ed. by L. Borkowski. Amsterdam: North-Holland Publishing Company.

MacColl, Hugh. 1906. *Symbolic Logic and Its Applications*. London: Longmans, Green, and Co.

——. 1905. "The Existential Import of Propositions." *Mind* n.s. 14.

——. 1905a. "Symbolic Reasoning (6)." *Mind* n.s. 14.

——. 1905b. "Symbolic Reasoning (7)." *Mind* n.s. 14.

——. 1903. "Symbolic Reasoning (5)." *Mind* n.s. 12.

——. 1902. "Symbolic Reasoning (4)." *Mind* n.s. 11.

——. 1900. "Symbolic Reasoning (3)." *Mind* n.s. 9.

——. 1897. "Symbolic Reasoning (2)." *Mind* n.s. 6.

——. 1880. "Symbolic Reasoning (1)." *Mind* n.s. 5.

Macnair, Michael Richard Trench. 1999. *The Law of Proof in Early Modern Equity*. Berlin: Duncker and Humblot.

Mahoney, Thomas H. D. 1955. Introduction to Burke (1955).

Manser, Anthony. 1985. "Russell's Criticism of Frege." *Philosophical Investigations* 8/4.

Mares, Edwin. 1997. Electronic correspondence to Jan Dejnožka dated June 12, 13, 18 (six messages), 22, and 23.

Mayne, John Dawson. 1909. *Mayne's Treatise on Damages*. Ed. by Lumley Smith. 8th ed. London: Stevens and Haynes.

——, and Lumley Smith. 1894. *Mayne's Treatise on Damages*. 5th ed. London: Stevens and Haynes.

——. 1872. *A Treatise on the Law of Damages: Comprising Their Measure, The Mode in Which They are Assessed and Reviewed, the Practice of Granting New Trials, and the Law of Set-Off*. 2d ed. by Lumley Smith. London: Stevens and Haynes.

Max, Ingolf, and Werner Stelzner. 1995. *Logik und Mathematik: Frege-Kolloquium Jena 1993*. Berlin: Walter de Gruyter.

McCall, Storrs. 1967. "MacColl." In "Logic, History of," in Edwards (1967), vol. 4.

——. ed. 1967a. *Polish Logic 1920–1939*. Oxford: Clarendon Press.

McCann, Charles R. Jr. 1996. "Introduction: Edgeworth's Contributions to Probability and Statistics." In Edgeworth (1996 / 1922), vol. 1.

McDonough, Richard M. 1986. *The Argument of the Tractatus: Its Relevance to Contemporary Theories of Logic, Language, Mind, and Philosophical Truth*. Albany: SUNY Press.

McKay, Thomas J. 1975. "Essentialism in Quantified Modal Logic." *Journal of Philosophical Logic* 4.

McKinsey, J. C. C. 1945. "On the Syntactical Construction of Systems of Modal Logic." *Journal of Symbolic Logic* 10.

——. 1941. "A Solution of the Decision Problem for the Lewis Systems S2 and S4, with an Application to Topology." *Journal of Symbolic Logic* 6.

Meyer, Robert K. 1985. "A Farewell to Entailment." In Georg Dorn and Paul Weingartner, eds., 1985, *Foundations of Logic and Linguistics: Problems and Their Solutions*. New York: Plenum Press. Selected papers from the Seventh International Congress of Logic, Methodology, and

Philosophy of Science, July 11–16, 1983, in Salzburg, Austria.

———. 1975. "Relevance is not reducible to modality." In Anderson (1975).

Mill, John Stuart. 1872. *A System of Logic: Ratiocinative and Inductive, Being a Connected View of the Principles of Evidence and the Methods of Scientific Investigation*. 8th ed. London: Longmans, Green, Reader, and Dyer. 1st ed. 1843.

Mini, Piero V. 1994. *John Maynard Keynes: A Study in the Psychology of Original Work*. New York: St. Martin's Press.

Moggridge, D. E. 1992. *Maynard Keynes: An Economist's Biography*. London: Routledge.

Monk, Ray, and Anthony Palmer, eds. 1996. *Bertrand Russell and the Origins of Analytical Philosophy*. Bristol, U.K.: Thoemmes Press.

Monteiro, João Paulo. 2001. "Russell and Humean Inferences." *Principia* 51/2.

Montrose, James Louis. 1954. "Basic Concepts of the Law of Evidence." *The Law Quarterly Review* 70/527–55. Reprinted in Twining (1992).

Moore, George Edward. 1966. "Is Existence a Predicate?" In (1988a).

———. 1966a. *Philosophical Papers*. New York: Collier.

———. 1951. "External and Internal Relations." In (1951a).

———. 1951a. *Philosophical Studies*. New York: The Humanities Press.

———. 1912. *Ethics*. London: Williams & Norgate.

———. 1903. *Principia Ethica*. Cambridge, England: Cambridge University Press.

———. 1900. "Necessity." *Mind* n.s. 9.

Morgan, John. 1789. *Essays Upon 1. The Law of Evidence. 2. New Trials. 3. Special Verdicts. 4. Trials at Bar. and 5. Repleaders*. vol. 1. Dublin: Messrs. E. Lynch, H. Chamberlaine, L. White, P. Byrne, A. Gruebier, C. Lewis, J. Jones, and J. Moore.

Nelson, E. J. 1930. "Intensional Relations." *Mind* n.s. 39.

Nissan, Ephraim. 2012. *Computer Applications for Handling Legal Evidence, Police Investigation and Case Argumentation*. vol. 1. Dordrecht: Springer. Law, Governance and Technology Series 5.

Murphy, Peter. 2008. *Murphy on Evidence*. 10th ed. Oxford: Oxford University Press.

Niiniluuto, Ilkka. 1988. "From Possibility to Probability: British Discussions on Modality in the Nineteenth Century." In Knuuttila (1988a).

Nute, Donald, ed. 1997. "Apparent Obligation." In (1997a).

———, ed. 1997a. *Defeasible Deontic Logic.* Dordrecht: Kluwer.

Pap, Arthur. 1958. *Semantics and Necessary Truth.* New Haven, Conn.: Yale University Press.

Parsons, Terence. 1971. "Essentialism and Quantified Modal Logic." In Linsky, ed., *Reference and Modality.*

Passmore, John. 1985. *Recent Philosophers.* La Salle, Ill.: Open Court.

Patterson, Richard. 1995. *Aristotle's Modal Logic.* Cambridge, England: Cambridge University Press.

Patterson, Wayne. 1997. Book review of Jan Dejnožka, *The Ontology of the Analytic Tradition and Its Origins. Australasian Journal of Philosophy* 75/4.

Peacocke, Christopher. 1975. "Proper Names, Reference, and Rigid Designation." In Simon Blackburn, ed., *Meaning, Reference and Necessity: New Studies in Semantics.* Cambridge, England: Cambridge University Press.

Peake, Thomas. 1824. *A Compendium of the Law of Evidence.* The American edition from the London 5th ed. Philadelphia, Penn.: Abraham Small.

———. 1804. *A Compendium of the Law of Evidence.* 2d ed. London: Brooke and Clarke.

———. 1801. *A Compendium of the Law of Evidence.* 1st ed. London: E. & R. Brooke & J. Rider. Facsimile reprint in Berkowitz (1979).

Peloubet, S. S. 1880. *A Collection of Legal Maxims in Law and Equity, with English Translations.* New York: George S. Diossy.

Pears, David F. 1989. "Russell's 1913 *Theory of Knowledge* Manuscript." In C. Wade Savage and C. Anthony Anderson, eds., *Rereading Russell: Essays in Bertrand Russell's Metaphysics and Epistemology.* Minneapolis: University of Minnesota Press. Minnesota Studies in the Philosophy of Science, vol. 22.

———, ed. 1972. *Bertrand Russell: A Collection of Critical Essays.* Garden City, N.Y.: Doubleday.

———. 1972a. "Russell's Logical Atomism." In (1972).

Peirce, Charles Sanders. 1993. *Writings of Charles S. Peirce: A Chronological Edition.* Vol. 5, 1884–1886. Ed. by Christian J. W. Kloesel. Bloomington: Indiana University Press.

——. 1960. "Modality." James Mark Baldwin, ed., *Dictionary of Philosophy and Psychology*. New ed. with corrections. vol. 2. Gloucester, Mass.: Peter Smith. 1901.

——. 1933. *Collected Papers of Charles Sanders Peirce*. vol. 4. Ed. by Charles Hartshorne and Paul Weiss. Cambridge, Mass.: Harvard University Press.

——. 1886. "Qualitative Logic." In (1993).

Phillipps, Samuel March, and Thomas James Arnold. 1868. *A Treatise on the Law of Evidence*. 10th English ed., 5th American ed. vol. 1. New York: Banks & Brothers.

——, and Thomas James Arnold. 1859. *A Treatise on the Law of Evidence*. 10th English ed., 4th American ed. vol. 1. New York: Banks & Brothers. The title pages of Phillipps (1868) and (1859) both say "Tenth English Edition," but (1868) says "Fifth American Edition," while (1859) says "Fourth American Edition."

——. 1849. *A Treatise on the Law of Evidence*. "Sixth American, from the ninth London edition." Lower on the same title page: "Vol. I. Third Edition." New York: Banks, Gould, & Co.

——, and Andrew Amos. 1838. *A Treatise on the Law of Evidence*. 8th ed. "with considerable additions." London: Saunders and Benning.

——. 1822. *A Treatise on the Law of Evidence*. 5th ed. vol. 1. London: Joseph Butterworth and Son.

——. 1820. *A Treatise on the Law of Evidence*. 2d American ed. from the 3rd London ed. vol. 1. New York: Gould and Banks.

——. 1816. *A Treatise on the Law of Evidence*. 1st American ed., from 2d London ed. vol. 1. Albany, N.Y.: Gould, Banks, & Gould.

Pigden, Charles. 1998. Electronic mail to Jan Dejnožka dated January 19 and 22.

Pitcher, George. 1964. *The Philosophy of Wittgenstein*. Englewood Cliffs, N.J.: Prentice-Hall.

Place, Ullin T. 1970. "Is Consciousness a Brain Process?" In Borst (1970).

Plato. 1937. *The Dialogues of Plato*. Trans. by Benjamin Jowett. New York: Random House.

——. 1937a. *Sophist*. In (1937).

——. 1937b. *Meno*. In (1937).

——. 1937c. *Theaetetus*. In (1937).

Pollock, Sir Frederick, and Frederic William Maitland. 2010. *The History of English Law Before the Time of Edward I*. 2d ed. Indianapolis, Ind.: Liberty Fund. 2d ed. 1898. 1st ed. 1895.

Popper, Karl. 2007. *Conjectures and Refutations: The Growth of Scientific Knowledge*. London: Routledge. 1963.

——. 1979. *Objective Knowledge: An Evolutionary Approach*. rev. ed. Oxford: Clarendon Press. 1972.

Powell, Edmund. 1904. *The Principles and Practice of the Laws of Evidence*. 8th ed. Ed. by John Cutler and Charles F. Cagney. London: Butterworth & Co.

——. 1859. *The Principles and Practice of the Laws of Evidence*. 2d ed. London: Butterworths.

Prior, Arthur N., and Kit Fine. 1977. *Worlds, Times, and Selves*. London: Duckworth.

——. 1967. "Keynes[, John Neville]." In "Logic, History of," in Edwards (1967), vol. 4.

——. 1967a. "Modal Logic." In Edwards (1967), vol. 5.

——. 1967b. "Peirce." In "Logic, History of," in Edwards (1967), vol. 4.

——. 1955. *Formal Logic*. London: Clarendon Press.

Putnam, Hilary. 1981. Blurb on dust jacket of Hanfling (1981).

Quine, Willard Van Orman. 1992. *Pursuit of Truth*. rev. ed. Cambridge, Mass.: Harvard University Press.

——. 1990. Note to Dejnožka dated 23 October.

——. 1987. "Reply to Dagfinn Føllesdal." In Hahn (1987).

——. 1987a. "Reply to David Kaplan." In Hahn (1987).

——. 1976. "Three Grades of Modal Involvement." In (1976a).

——. 1976a. *The Ways of Paradox and Other Essays*. rev. ed. Cambridge, Mass.: Harvard University Press.

——. 1975. *Word and Object*. Cambridge, Mass.: The M.I.T. Press. 1960.

——. 1971. *From a Logical Point of View*. 2d rev. ed. Cambridge, Mass.: Harvard University Press.

——. 1971a. "Russell's Ontological Development." In Klemke (1971).

——. 1959. *Methods of Logic*. rev. ed. New York: Holt, Rinehart and Winston.

——. 1951. "Two Dogmas of Empiricism." *Philosophical Review* 60.

Quinton, Anthony. 1972. "Russell's Philosophy of Mind." In Pears (1972).

Rahman, Shahid. 2002. Review of my (1999). *History and Philosophy of Logic* 22.

Ramsey, Frank Plumpton. 1931. *The Foundations of Mathematics and Other Logical Essays*. Ed. by R. B. Braithwaite. London: Kegan Paul, Trench, Trubner & Co.

Read, Stephen. 1988. *Relevant Logic: A Philosophical Examination of Inference*. Oxford: Basil Blackwell.

Recanati, François. 1993. *Direct Reference: From Language to Thought*. Oxford: Blackwell.

Rescher, Nicholas. 1988. Letter to Dejnožka dated 30 July.

——. 1979. "The Ontology of the Possible." In Loux (1979).

——. 1979a. "Russell and Modal Logic." In G. Roberts (1979).

Restall, Greg: 1996. "Information Flow and Relevant Logics." In Seligman (1996).

Rice, Frank Sumner. 1892. *The General Principles of the Law of Evidence*. Rochester, N.Y.: The Lawyers' Co-Operative Publishing Co.

Roberts, Don D. 1973. *The Existential Graphs of Charles S. Peirce*. The Hague: Mouton.

Roberts, George W., ed. 1979. *Bertrand Russell Memorial Volume*. London: George Allen and Unwin.

Robinson, Abraham. 1996. *Non-Standard Analysis*. Rev. ed. Princeton, N.J.: Princeton University Press. 1st ed. 1974.

——. 1979. "Formalism." In (1979b).

——. 1979a. Non-Standard Analysis." In 1979b. First published in 1961 in *Koninklijke Nederlandse Akademie van Wetenschappen* Proceedings, ser. A, Mathematical Sciences, vol. 64.

——. 1979b. *Selected Papers of Abraham Robinson*. vol. 2, *Non-Standard Analysis and Philosophy*. Ed. by W. Luxemburg and S. Körner. New Haven: Yale University Press.

Rodríguez-Consuegra, Francisco. 1991. *The Mathematical Philosophy of Bertrand Russell: Origins and Development*. Basel, Switzerland: Birkhäuser Verlag.

Roscoe, Henry. 1840. *A Digest of the Law of Evidence in Criminal Cases*. 2d ed. "with considerable additions...by T. C. Granger." Philadelphia: T. & J. W. Johnson.

——. 1831. *Digest of the Law of Evidence on the Trial of Actions at Nisi Prius*. 2d ed. London: Saunders & Benning.

Ross, William David. 1960. *Aristotle*. 5th ed. New York: Meridian.

Routley, Richard, with Val Plumwood, Robert K. Meyer, and Ross T. Brady. 1982. *Relevant Logics and Their Rivals: Part 1. The Basic Philosophical and Semantical Theory*. Atascadero, Calif.: Ridgewood.

——, and Robert K. Meyer. 1973. "The Semantics of Entailment." In Hughes Leblanc, ed., *Truth, Syntax and Modality: Proceedings of the Temple University Conference on Alternative Semantics*. Amsterdam: North-Holland Publishing Company.

Russell, Bertrand. 1994. *Foundations of Logic 1903–05*. Ed. by Alasdair Urquhart. Routledge. *The Collected Papers of Bertrand Russell*, vol. 4.

——. 1994a. "Necessity and Possibility." In (1994). The original Ms. is (ca. 1903–05).

——. 1993. *Theory of Knowledge: The 1913 Manuscript*. Ed. by Elizabeth Ramsden Eames in collaboration with Kenneth Blackwell. London: George Allen & Unwin. *The Collected Papers of Bertrand Russell*, vol. 7. 1984.

——. 1992. *Logical and Philosophical Papers 1909—13*. Ed. by John G. Slater. London: Routledge. *The Collected Papers of Bertrand Russell*, vol. 6.

——. 1992a. "On the Axioms of the Infinite and of the Transfinite." In (1992).

——. 1989. "Reply to Criticisms." In Schilpp (1989). 1944.

——. 1987. *Autobiography*. One volume edition. London: Unwin. vol. 1, 1967; vol. 2, 1968; vol. 3, 1969.

——. 1985. *An Inquiry into Meaning and Truth*. London: Unwin. 1940.

——. 1985a. *My Philosophical Development*. London: Unwin. 1959.

——. 1976. *Human Knowledge: Its Scope and Limits*. New York: Simon and Schuster. 1948.

——. 1974. *An Outline of Philosophy*. New York: Meridian. 1927.

——. 1974a. *The Problems of Philosophy*. London: Oxford University Press. 1912.

——. 1973. "The Axiom of Infinity." In (1973a).

——. 1973a. *Essays in Analysis*. Ed. by Douglas Lackey. London: George Allen & Unwin.

——. 1973b. "On 'Insolubilia' and their Solution by Symbolic Logic." In (1973). First published in 1906 as "Les Paradoxes de la Logique."

——. 1973c. "On The Substitutional Theory of Classes and Relations." In (1973).

——. 1973d. "On Some Difficulties in the Theory of Transfinite Numbers and Order Types." In (1973).

——. 1973e. "The Philosophical Implications of Mathematical Logic." In (1973).

——. 1971. *Logic and Knowledge*. Ed. by Robert. C. Marsh. New York: Capricorn Books.

——. 1971a. "Mathematical Logic as Based on the Theory of Types." In (1971); Heijenoort (1977). 1908.

——. 1971b. "On Denoting." In (1971). 1905.

——. 1971c. "On Propositions: What They Are and How They Mean." In (1971). 1919.

——. 1971d. "On the Nature of Acquaintance." In (1971). 1914.

——. 1971e. "On the Relations of Universals and Particulars." In (1971). 1911.

——. 1971f. "The Philosophy of Logical Atomism." In (1971) 1918.

——. 1969. Letter to Dr. Angel dated May 10, 1958. In Barry Feinberg and Ronald Kasrils, eds., *Dear Bertrand Russell: A Selection of His Correspondence with the General Public, 1950–1968*. London: George Allen and Unwin.

——. 1966. *Philosophical Essays*. New York: Simon and Schuster.

——. 1964. *Principles of Mathematics*. 2d ed. New York: W. W. Norton. 2d ed. 1938; 1st ed. 1903.

——. 1962. *Human Society in Ethics and Politics*. New York: Mentor. 1954.

——. 1960. *Our Knowledge of the External World as a Field for Scientific Method in Philosophy*. 2d ed. New York: Mentor. 2d ed. 1929; 1st ed. 1914.

——. 1957. "Knowledge By Acquaintance and Knowledge by Description." In (1957b).

——. 1957a. "Mysticism and Logic." In (1957b).

——. 1957b. *Mysticism and Logic*. Garden City, N.Y.: Doubleday Anchor Books.

——. 1957c. "On the Notion of a Cause." In (1957b).

——. 1957d. "The Study of Mathematics." In (1957b).

——. 1956. *An Essay on the Foundations of Geometry*. New York: Dover. 1897.

——. 1954. *The Analysis of Matter*. New York: Dover. 1927.

——, and Alfred North Whitehead. 1950. *Principia Mathematica*. See Whitehead.

——. 1945. *A History of Western Philosophy*. 16th pbk. reprint. New York: Simon and Schuster. A Clarion Book.

——. 1937. *A Critical Exposition of the Philosophy of Leibniz*. 2d ed. London: George Allen & Unwin Ltd. 1st ed. 1900.

——. 1933. *The Analysis of Mind*. London: George Allen and Unwin.

——. 1923. "Vagueness." *Australasian Journal of Philosophy* 1.

——. 1922. Review of *A Treatise on Probability*. *The Mathematical Gazette* 32/300.

——. 1919. *Introduction to Mathematical Philosophy*. London: Allen and Unwin.

——. 1908. "'If' and 'Imply', A Reply to Mr. MacColl." *Mind* n.s. 17.

———. 1906. Review of Hugh MacColl's *Symbolic Logic and Its Applications. Mind* n.s. 15.

———. 1905. "The Existential Import of Propositions." *Mind* n.s. 14.

———. ca. 1903–05. "Necessity and Possibility." Ms. #220.010860. Hamilton, Canada: The Bertrand Russell Archives. Page cites are to (1994a).

———. 1896. *German Social Democracy*. London: Longman, Green & Company. *Studies in Economics and Political Science*, vol. 7.

Sainsbury, R. M. 1993. "Russell on Names and Communication." In Irvine (1993).

———. 1979. *Russell*. London: Routledge and Kegan Paul.

Salmon, Nathan U. 1986. *Frege's Puzzle*. Cambridge, Mass.: The M.I.T. Press.

———. 1981. *Reference and Essence*. Princeton, N.J.: Princeton University Press.

Schilpp, Paul A., ed. 1989. *The Philosophy of Bertrand Russell*. 5th ed. La Salle, Ill.: Open Court. 1944.

———. 1963. *The Philosophy of Rudolf Carnap*. La Salle, Ill.: Open Court.

Searle, John R. 1967. "Determinables and Determinates." In Edwards (1967), vol. 2.

Sedlár, Igor. 2014. Review of my (2012). *Organon F* 21.

Seligman, Jerry, and Dag Westerståhl. 1996. *Logic, Language and Computation*. vol. 1. Stanford, Calif.: Center for the Study of Language and Information Publications (CSLI).

Shapiro, Barbara J. 1991. *"Beyond Reasonable Doubt" and "Probable Cause": Historical Perspectives on the Anglo-American Law of Evidence*. Berkeley: University of California Press.

———. 1983. *Probability and Certainty in Seventeenth-Century England: A Study of the Relationships between Natural Science, Religion, History, Law, and Literature*. Princeton, N.J.: Princeton University Press.

Shimojima, Atsushi. 1996. "Reasoning with Diagrams and Geometrical Constraints." In Seligman (1996).

Shin, Sun-Joo. 1994. *The Logical Status of Diagrams*. Cambridge, England: Cambridge University Press.

Simons, Peter. 1992. *Philosophy and Logic in Central Europe from Bolzano to Tarski: Selected Essays*. Dordrecht: Kluwer.

———. 1987. *Parts: A Study in Ontology*, Oxford: Clarendon Press.

Skidelsky, Robert. 2005. *John Maynard Keynes 1883–1946: Economist, Philosopher, Statesman*. London: Macmillan. Rev. and abridged combined ed. of (2001), (1994), and (1986).

———. 2001. *John Maynard Keynes: Volume Three: Fighting for Freedom, 1937–1947.* 1st American ed. New York: Viking Penguin. 2000.

———. 1996. *Keynes.* Oxford: Oxford University Press.

———. 1994. *John Maynard Keynes: Volume Two: The Economist as Savior, 1920–1937.* 1st American ed. New York: Viking Penguin. 1992.

———. 1986. *John Maynard Keynes: Volume One: Hopes Betrayed, 1883–1920.* 1st American ed. New York: Viking Penguin. 1983.

Slater, B. H. 1998. "Peirce's Graphs Amended." *History and Philosophy of Logic* 19.

Slater, John G. 1997. Introduction to Bertrand Russell, *A Critical Exposition of the Philosophy of Leibniz.* London: Routledge.

Slomkowski, Paul. 1997. *Aristotle's Topics.* Leiden: Brill.

Sorabji, Richard. 1980. *Necessity, Cause, and Blame: Perspectives on Aristotle's Theory.* Ithaca, N.Y.: Cornell University Press.

Smart, J. J. C. 1970. "Sensations and Brain Processes." In Borst (1970).

———. 1967. "Utilitarianism." In Edwards (1967), vol. 8.

Smokler, Howard E. 1967. "Johnson, William Ernest." In Edwards (1967), vol. 4.

Smullyan, Arthur. 1971. "Modality and Description." In L. Linsky (1971).

Snyder, D. Paul. 1971. *Modal Logic and its Applications.* New York: Van Nostrand Reinhold.

Solomon, Graham. 1999. Electronic mail to Jan Dejnožka dated February 9.

Sorabji, Richard. 1980. *Necessity, Cause, and Blame: Perspectives on Aristotle's Theory.* Ithaca, N.Y.: Cornell University Press.

Sperber, Dan, and Deirdre Wilson. 1986. *Relevance: Communication and Cognition.* Oxford: Basil Blackwell.

Sprigge, Timothy. 1979. "Russell and Bradley on Relations." In G. Roberts (1979).

Spinoza, Benedict (Baruch). 1958. *Ethic.* In *Spinoza Selections.* Ed. by John Wild. New York: Charles Scribner's Sons. 1930.

Starkie, Thomas. 1876. *A Practical Treatise of the Law of Evidence.* 10th American ed. from the 4th London ed. Philadelphia, Penn.: T. & J. W. Johnson & Co.

———. 1830. *A Practical Treatise on the Law of Evidence, and Digest of Proofs, in Civil and Criminal Proceedings.* 3d

American ed. Philadelphia, Penn.: P. H. Nicklin & T. Johnson.

Steele, Donald A. 1950. Historical Introduction to Kant (1950 / 1783).

Stephen, James Fitzjames, with Harry Lushington Stephen and Lewis Frederick Sturge. 1936. *A Digest of the Law of Evidence*. 12th ed. London: Macmillan.

——. 1903. *A Digest of the Law of Evidence*. From the 5th ed. of 1899, with American notes. Hartford, Conn.: Dissell.

——. 1876. *A Digest of the Law of Evidence*. 2d ed. London: Macmillan and Co.

——. 1872. *The Indian Evidence Act (I of 1872), with an Introduction on the Principles of Judicial Evidence*. London: Macmillan & Co.

Stephen, Leslie. 1895. *The Life of Sir James Fitzjames Stephen: BART., K.C.S.I.: A Judge of the High Court of Justice*. London: Smith, Elder, & Co.

Stigler, Stephen M. 1986. *The History of Statistics: The Measurement of Uncertainty before 1900*. Cambridge, Mass.: The Belknap Press of Harvard University Press.

Strachey, Giles Lytton. 1918. *Eminent Victorians*. New York: Random House. The Modern Library.

Straker, D. Augustus. 1899. *A Compendium of Evidence*. Detroit, Mich.: The Richmond and Backus Co.

Strawson, Peter F. 1985. *Introduction to Logical Theory*. London: Methuen. 1952.

Sumner, L. W., and John Woods, eds. 1969: *Necessary Truth: A Book of Readings*. New York: Random House.

Swinburne, Richard, ed. 2002. *Bayes's Theorem*. Oxford: Oxford University Press. Proceedings of the British Academy 113.

Sylvan, Richard. 2000. *Sociative Logics and their Applications: Essays by the Late Richard Sylvan*. Ed. by Dominic Hyde and Graham Priest. Aldershot, England: Ashgate.

Tang, Tsao-Chen. 1938. "Algebraic Postulates and a Geometric Interpretation for the Lewis Calculus of Strict Implication." *Bulletin of the American Mathematical Society* 44.

Tarski, Alfred. 1983. *Logic, Science, Metamathematics*. 2d ed. Trans. by J. H. Woodger. Ed. by John Corcoran. Indianapolis, Ind.: Hackett. 1st ed. 1956.

Taylor, John Pitt. 1897. *A Treatise on the Law of Evidence as administered in England and Ireland*. Ed. by Charles Frederic Chamberlayne. American ed. of the 9th English ed. vol. 1. "In part re-written by G. Pitt-Lewis....With notes as to American law by Charles F. Chamberlayne." Boston: The Boston Book Company. London: Sweet and Maxwell.

——. 1878. *A Treatise on the Law of Evidence as Administered in England and Ireland*. 7th ed. vols. 1, 2. London: William Maxwell & Son.

——. 1848. *A Treatise of the Law of Evidence, as Administered in England and Ireland*. 1st ed. vol. 1. London: A. Maxwell & Son.

Thayer, James Bradley. 1908. *Legal Essays*. Ed. by his son, Ezra Ripley Thayer. Boston: The Boston Book Company.

——. 1900. "Law and Logic." In Thayer (1908). First published in the *Harvard Law Review*: 14 Harv. Law Rev. 139.

——. 1898. *A Preliminary Treatise on Evidence at the Common Law*. Boston, Mass.: Little, Brown, and Company.

——. 1880–81. "Bedingfield's Case—Declarations as a Part of the Res Gesta." In Thayer (1908). First published in *The American Law Review* in three parts: 14 Am. Law Rev. 817; 15 Am. Law Rev. 1, 71.

The Annual Register. 1918. Ed. by Edmund Burke. vol. 160. June obituary section. London: Longmans, Green, and Co.

Twining, William. 1994. *Rethinking Evidence: Exploratory Essays*. Evanston, Ill.: Northwestern University Press. 1990.

——, and Alex Stein, eds. 1992. *Evidence and Proof*. New York: New York University Press.

——. 1985. *Theories of Evidence: Bentham and Wigmore*. London: Weidenfeld and Nicolson.

Urquhart, Alasdair. 1994. Note prefacing Russell, "Necessity and Possibility." In Russell (1994).

——. 1992. "§ 65." In Anderson (1992).

Ushenko, Andrew Paul. 1989. "Russell's Critique of Empiricism." In Schilpp (1989).

Venn, John. 1994. *The Principles of Empirical or Inductive Logic*. 1st ed. Bristol: Thoemmes Press. Reprint of 1st ed. of 1889. 2d ed. 1907.

——. 1973. *The Principles of Inductive Logic*. 2d ed. New York: Chelsea Publishing Company. 2d ed. 1907. 1st ed. 1889.

——. 1971. *Symbolic Logic*. 2d ed. New York: Chelsea Publishing Company. 1st ed. 1881; 2d ed. 1894.

——. 1964. "The Subjective Side of Probability." In Kyburg (1964). Reprinted from *The Logic of Chance*, 3d ed. 1888.

——. 1879. "The Difficulties of Material Logic." *Mind* n.s. 4.

Walford, Edward. 1888. "Legal Obituary." In *The Law Times: The Journal and Record of the Law and the Lawyers*. From May to October 1988. vol. 85. July 28 issue. London: The Office of the Law Times.

Wallenmeier, Thomas E. 1967. *The Broad-Keynes-Russell Theory for the Explanation and Justification of Induction*. In Marquette University: *Master's Theses 1922–2009.* Paper 139. Milwaukee, Wisc.: Marquette University.

Walton, Douglas. 2005. *Argumentation Methods for Artificial Intelligence in Law.* Berlin: Springer.

——. 2004. *Relevance in Argumentation.* Mahwah, N.J.: Lawrence Erlbaum Associates.

Wang, Hao. 1986. *Beyond Analytic Philosophy: Doing Justice to What We Know.* Cambridge, Mass.: The M.I.T. Press.

West Publishing Company: 1995, *Evidence Rules: Federal Rules of Evidence and California Evidence Code.* St. Paul, Minn.: West Publishing Company.

Whately, Richard. 1851. *Elements of Logic.* 9th ed. Boston, Mass.: James Munroe and Company.

Whitehead, Alfred North, and Bertrand Russell. 1950. *Principia Mathematica.* 2d ed. London: Cambridge University Press. *Principia Mathematica to *56* (London: Cambridge University Press, 1978) is the same as vol. 1, pp. 1–326. Reprint of 2d ed., 1927. 1st ed., 1910.

Wiggins, David. 1970. "The Individuation of Things and Places." In Loux (1970).

Wigmore. 1904–1905. *A Treatise on the System of Evidence in Trials at Common Law: Including the Statutes and Judicial Decisions of all Jurisdictions of the United States.* 4 vols. Boston: Little, Brown, and Co. The title soon changed, and eventually the work included ten volumes. My former law school advanced evidence professor, Richard D. Friedman, has been general editor of *The New Wigmore.*

——. 1899. Preface to Greenleaf (1899).

Wittgenstein, Ludwig. 1972. *Remarks on the Foundations of Mathematics.* Trans. by G. E. M. Anscombe. Cambridge, Mass.: The M.I.T. Press.

——. 1968. *Philosophical Investigations.* 3d ed. Trans. by G. E. M. Anscombe. New York: Macmillan.

——. 1961. *Tractatus Logico-Philosophicus.* Trans. by D. F. Pears and B. F. McGuinness. London: Routledge and Kegan Paul. English 1922; German 1921.

Woleński, Jan. 1989. *Logic and Philosophy in the Lvov-Warsaw School.* Dordrecht: Kluwer.

von Wright, Georg Henrik. 1960. *A Treatise on Induction and Probability.* Paterson, N.J.: Littlefield, Adams, & Co. The International Library of Psychology, Philosophy and Scientific Method. 1951.

——. 1957. *Logical Studies.* New York: The Humanities Press.

——. 1951. *An Essay in Modal Logic.* Amsterdam: North-Holland Publishing Company.

Zabell, S. L. 2005. *Symmetry and its Discontents: Essays on the History of Inductive Probability.* Cambridge, England: Cambridge University Press.

Index of Names

Abeles, Francine, 302
Abercrombie, John, 491
Ackermann, Wilhelm, 227, 323
Ackrill, J. L., 284–85
Adams, Robert Merrihew, 207
Alexander of Aphrodisias, 281, 289
Allaire, Edwin B., 180
Allen, Layman, xv, 309
Almog, Joseph, 27
Alsted(ius), Johann H., 280, 283
Anellis, Irving, 302
Amos, Andrew, 399–400
Anderson, Alan Ross, 31, 224–33, 235–37, 240–41, 250, 254, 272–73, 277, 279, 280–81, 285, 289–90, 299–300, 302, 304–15, 317, 323–25, 451, 522, 560–561, 563–64, 567, 570–72
Anderson, Terence, 487, 515
Aquinas, St. Thomas, 239, 257, 439–40, 547–49
Aristotle, 31, 62, 77, 89, 135–36, 145–46, 149–50, 152, 200, 208–10, 224–25, 230, 233, 239, 258, 268, 279, 280–81, 284–86, 289, 302, 308, 316, 323, 329, 334, 344, 347–48, 350, 352, 354, 363, 364, 369, 396, 401, 435, 477, 490–91, 516, 529–30, 532, 544, 547–48, 559, 567, 576, 583
Austin, J. L., 325
Avicenna, 548
Ayer, Alfred Jules, 3, 44

Bacon, Francis, Lord Chancellor of England, 439–40
Bain, Alexander, 288
Barbé, Lluís, 504, 506
Barnes, Jonathan, 285
Barnett, Vincent, 355, 492–93

Bartley, William Warren III, 302
Barwise, Jon, 282
Bateman, Bradley W., 341, 356
Bayes, Thomas, 343, 348, 350–53, 382, 395, 513
Beccaria, Cesare, 488
Bell, Clive, 496, 501
Bell, Vanessa, née Stephen, 501
Belnap, Nuel D., 31, 224–37, 240–41, 250, 254, 272–73, 277, 279–80, 285, 289, 299–300, 302, 304–15, 317, 323–25, 351, 522, 560–61, 563–64, 567, 570–72
Benardete, José A., 180, 314
Bentham, Jeremy, 356, 368, 405–10, 413, 418, 441, 452, 457, 470, 481, 486, 492, 498–500
Berbeira Gardón, José Luis, 317
Berg, Jan, 202
Bergmann, Gustav, 137, 148–49, 178, 179–80, 535, 552–53, 554
Berkeley, George, 53, 186, 576
Bernoulli, Jakob / James, 333, 353, 354–55, 513
Best, William Mawdesley, 365, 368, 387, 418–20, 426, 441, 457, 458–63, 474, 480, 486
Beth, Evert Willem, 27, 165, 283, 301
Binkley, R. W., 238, 307
Black, Henry Campbell, 433–34
Black, Max, 85, 182, 183, 219–20, 333–34
Blackburn, Colin, Lord Justice, 439–40, 482
Blackstone, William, Justice of King's Bench, and of Common Pleas, 368, 388–89, 393, 470, 481, 507

630   Bertrand Russell on Modality and Logical Relevance

Index of Subjects

a priori, 19, 49, 104–5, 115, 131, 132, 136, 143, 152, 175, 188, 193, 195, 228, 238, 247, 251, 268, 286, 297, 307, 314, 322, 323, 329–31, 333, 334, 511, 519–20, 528, 572, 578–79, 586–88; analytic, 133, 195, 202, 238, 297, 322, 346; contingent, 314; degrees of / weak / fallible / inductive, 31–32, 239, 314, 315, 330–31, 341, 511, 519–20, 530, 578; synthetic, 20, 28–29, 31, 79, 81, 99, 104–5, 125, 128, 131, 133, 137–38, 175, 189, 191, 202, 235, 238, 239, 247, 253, 266, 292, 297, 315, 322, 323, 331, 345–46, 380, 389, 519–20, 535, 561, 574, 581, 586–88

a posteriori, 578–79; analytic, 314; necessary, 314; synthetic, 46, 105–6, 115, 132, 483

abduction, 339

abstract entities, 143, 494, 577; numbers, 143, 545; relations (universal), 358; senses (Frege), 576; the universal of goodness, 132, 153; universals in general, 19, 23, 121–22, 132, 136–37, 143, 153, 178, 337

abstraction, 121–22, 125, 136, 137, 153, 178–79; linguistic, 74; temporal, 316

accident, 97, 135, 143

accident in tort law, 437

accidental descriptions, 446–47

accidental designators, 542

accidental features, 29–30, 143, 145, 478

accidental generalities, 44, 81, 106, 109, 110, 115, 133

acquaintance, 19, 20, 21, 23, 27, 29, 38, 54, 56–60, 63, 69, 71, 78, 109, 122, 125, 137, 138, 143, 153–54, 156, 166–70, 172, 179, 180, 183, 326, 330–31, 448, 526, 540–41, 543–44, 546–47, 550, 577; knowledge by, 122, 526

the actual world / real world; the actual, 23–24, 48–49, 51, 66, 84, 116–17, 119–21, 128, 148, 153, 163–65, 167, 171–72, 181–83, 205, 216, 217, 310, 331, 339, 543, 546, 572; the actual as all that is possible, 17, 115, 116, 206, 214, 217, 549; as the Frege-Russell implicit intended semantic model, 119, 165, 310; the real, 5, 146, 234, 582–83, 585

admissibility of evidence in law, 349–50, 367, 376, 378, 383, 399–400, 410–12, 415–16, 418–20, 423, 426, 428, 430, 435–36, 442, 450, 452–62, 466–68, 471–79, 482, 484–85, 487–88, 514, 591–92

algebraic models of logic, 290, 293, 567; of intuitionistic logic, 290; of modal logic, 290; of relevance logic, 290

alien objects, 51–52, 81, 166, 171, 181–82, 220

analysis, eliminative, 2, 6–7, 9, 95, 195, 483, 556; of bodies, 43, 54, 261; of causation, 77, 106, 107, 109, 110; of classes, 12–14, 23; of de re quantification, 135; of definite descriptions, 54, 142, 157; of the entailment relation, 316; of existence, 2–3, 196, 576; of functions, 23; of geometry, 43; of intuition, 20, 294; of logical forms, 162; of logically necessary inference,

universals, 19–24, 27, 38, 47, 58–59, 65–68, 71, 75, 78, 104–5, 115, 133, 136–38, 143, 145, 154, 167–70, 172, 175–80, 213, 238–39, 259, 262, 329–31, 448, 529, 538, 546–47, 560; abstraction of, 121–22, 125, 137, 153, 178–79; alien, 167–68; ante rem, 19–20, 23, 58, 68, 167, 183, 545; categorial; 180; conception of (Russell), 38, 143, 169, 448, 546; de re, 38, 137, 546; empirical, 5; epistemic, 115; ethical / value-, 118, 121–23, 125, 130–31, 132, 133, 238; generic, 56, 138, 167, 177, 180, 239, 545; in re, 23; intellection of (Aristotle), 529–30, 532; logical, 19, 21–22, 23, 25, 41, 89, 105, 170, 337; logical forms as, 8, 104, 121, 123, 146, 170; probability, 130; specific / sensible / quality-, 16, 29, 65, 136–37, 143, 167, 176–78, 180, 239; simple, 27, 56
use vs. mention, 249
use-relevance, see relevance

vagueness, 85, 90, 182, 191, 205, 216, 227, 233–34, 248, 325, 435, 467, 472, 473, 477, 516, 526–27, 529, 562, 589; Russell's three levels of, 234
values in Russell's logic, what are, 44–45
variable sharing, 224–25, 229, 280, 302, 311, 522, 560, 563–64, 566, 571, see atomic (or variable sharing) requirement
variables, apparent (bound) vs. real (free), 204, 206, 214, 244, 523–24
variances (law), 378, 391, 401–4, 481

Venn diagrams, 241, 271–72, 278–89, 290–91, 301, 308, 343, 561–62, 569
Vennis balls, 561

whole-part containment theory of deductive inference, xii, 30, 31, 81, 137, 180–81, 202, 209, 214, 224, 239, 241, 251, 271, 273–74, 275–76, 277, 282, 287, 290, 294, 295–98, 302, 307, 308, 309, 314, 420, 565
world, the actual / real, see actual / real world, the
worlds, possible, see possible worlds

Zeno's paradoxes, 106, 549
zetetic possibility, see possibility, zetetic

Glossary

Term	Meaning
P	Any statement
$P =\text{Df } Q$	P is defined as Q
$\neg P$	Not-P
$P \mathbin{\&} Q$	P and Q (following Russell, Quine uses $P \cdot Q$)
$P \lor Q$	P or Q or both P and Q (inclusive disjunction)
$P \supset Q$	If P then Q (material implication)
$P \equiv Q$	P if and only if Q (material biconditional)
$P \mid Q$	Not-$(P \mathbin{\&} Q)$ (Sheffer stroke)
$P = Q$	P is identical with Q
$\Diamond P$	Possibly, P (a modal operator on statement P)
$\Box P$	Necessarily, P (a modal operator on statement P)
$\Box(P \supset Q)$	Necessarily, if P then Q (strict implication)
$P \to Q$	Necessarily, if P then Q (strict implication). We may say that $P \to Q =\text{Df } \Box(P \supset Q)$. But Anderson and Belnap use the arrow symbol very differently to mean P entails Q (entailment)
$P \leftrightarrow Q$	Necessarily, P if and only if Q (strict biconditional)
Fa	Individual a has property F
Rab	Individual a stands in relation R to individual b
$(x)Fx$	Propositional function Fx is always true with respect to variable x
$(\exists x)Fx$	Fx is not always false with respect to variable x
$(\Box x)Fx$	Propositional function Fx is necessary with respect to variable x
$(\Diamond x)Fx$	Propositional function Fx is possible with respect to variable x
$\vdash P$	P is a thesis, i.e., axiom or theorem

Formalizations

Formal definition of MDL, paraphrased with bound variables:

1. $(\Box x)Fx$ =Df $(x)Fx$
2. $(\Diamond x)Fx$ =Df $(\exists x)Fx$
3. $\neg(\Diamond x)Fx$ =Df $\neg(\exists x)Fx$
MDL* is MDL constrained to truth in virtue of logical form.

Formal axiomatization of all eight implicit modal logics as S5:

1. $P \to \Diamond P$. That is, if P, then it is possible that P.
2. $\Diamond(P \& Q) \to \Diamond P$. That is, if it is possible that (P and Q), then it is possible that P.
3. $(P \to Q) \to (\Diamond P \to \Diamond Q)$. That is, if P implies Q, then the possibility of P implies the possibility of Q.
4. $\Diamond\Diamond P \to \Diamond P$. That is, if it is possible that P is possible, then P is possible.
5. $\Diamond P \to \Box\Diamond P$. That is, if P is possible, then it is necessary that P is possible.

Paraphrases of Russell into implicit formal modal logics:

1. FG–MDL. $\Box P$ =Df P is true and fully general (contains only variables and logical expressions).
2. FG–MDL*. $\Box P$ =Df P is true, fully general, and true in virtue of its logical form.
3. FG–MDL+syn. $\Box P$ =Df P is true *a priori* (true in FG–MDL or true synthetic *a priori*).
3. FG–MDL*+syn. $\Box P$ =Df P is true *a priori* (true in FG–MDL* or true synthetic *a priori*).
4. MDL–C. $\Box P$ =Df P is a true universal conditional statement, but is not fully general, *a priori*, or true in virtue of its logical form.
5. MDL–D. $\Box P$ =Df P is the objectively right act, i.e. "will probably produce the best results" in intrinsic goodness (PE 59).
6. MDL–D*. $\Box P$ =Df P is the objectively right act, i.e. will probably produce the best results in felt human happiness (HS 41, 95; see 93).
7. MDL–E. $\Diamond P$ =Df "We do not know if [P]; '[P]' is a value of the propositional function, 'Px'; and that propositional function is not always false" (PLA 254–55).

All of these paraphrases of Russell's texts into formal modal logics are so plain and direct, they seem beyond any reasonable doubt. Since the four modal operators are interdefinable, we only need to paraphrase Russell into one modal operator for each implicit logic.

51589953R00365

Made in the USA
Charleston, SC
24 January 2016